London
for Children

timeout.com

Time Out Guides Ltd
Universal House
251 Tottenham Court Road
London W1T 7AB
United Kingdom
Tel: +44 (0)20 7813 3000
Fax: +44 (0)20 7813 6001
Email: guides@timeout.com
www.timeout.com

Published by Time Out Guides Ltd, a wholly owned subsidiary of Time Out Group Ltd.
Time Out and the Time Out logo are trademarks of Time Out Group Ltd.

© **Time Out Group Ltd 2011**
Previous editions 2001, 2002, 2003, 2004, 2005, 2006, 2007, 2008, 2009, 2010

10 9 8 7 6 5 4 3 2 1

London 2012 emblems © The London Organising Committee of the Olympic Games and Paralympic Games Ltd
(LOCOG) 2007. London 2012 mascots © LOCOG 2009-2010. London 2012 Pictograms © LOCOG 2009.
All rights reserved.

This edition first published in Great Britain in 2011 by Ebury Publishing.
A Random House Group Company
20 Vauxhall Bridge Road, London SW1V 2SA

Random House Australia Pty Ltd 20 Alfred Street, Milsons Point, Sydney, New South Wales 2061, Australia

Random House New Zealand Ltd 18 Poland Road, Glenfield, Auckland 10, New Zealand

Random House South Africa (Pty) Ltd Isle of Houghton, Corner Boundary Road & Carse O'Gowrie,
Houghton 2198, South Africa

Random House UK Limited Reg. No. 954009

Distributed in the US and Latin America by Publishers Group West (1-510-809-3700)
Distributed in Canada by Publishers Group Canada (1-800-747-8147)

For further distribution details, see www.timeout.com.

ISBN 978-1-84670-237-2

A CIP catalogue record for this book is available from the British Library.

Printed and bound by Firmengruppe APPL, aprinta druck, Wemding, Germany.

The Random House Group Limited supports The Forest Stewardship Council (FSC), the leading international
forest certification organisation. All our titles that are printed on Greenpeace approved FSC certified paper
carry the FSC logo. Our paper procurement policy can be found at www.randomhouse.co.uk/environment.

Time Out carbon-offsets its flights with Trees for Cities (www.treesforcities.org).

MIX
Paper from
responsible sources
FSC
www.fsc.org FSC™ C004592

Published by
Time Out Guides Limited
Universal House
251 Tottenham Court Road
London W1T 7AB
Tel +44 (0)20 7813 3000
Fax +44 (0)20 7813 6001
email guides@timeout.com
www.timeout.com

Sections in this guide were written by
Air Today, Gone Tomorrow Emma Perry. **Den of Equity** Emma Perry. **Trips & Tours** Elizabeth Winding. **Festivals & Events** William Crow. **Everyone's a Winner** Emma Perry. **Explore** Simon Coppock, Hugh Graham. **Attractions** Ronnie Haydon, Emma Perry, Tom Howard (*Neighbourhood Watch: South Bank, Westminster, Covent Garden* Dominic Earle; *View from the Crypt* Emma Perry; *All Hands on Deck* Dominic Earle; *Ride the River* Dominic Earle; *My Sport: Cricket* Emma Perry). **Museums & Galleries** Ronnie Haydon, Emma Perry, Meryl O'Rourke, Peter Watts, Elizabeth Winding, Simon Coppock (*Neighbourhood Watch: Bloomsbury, Docklands, South Kensington* Dominic Earle; *Night at the Museum* Dominic Earle; *Culture Shop* Sara O'Reilly; *My Sport: Paralympic Athletics, Kung Fu, Diving, Sailing* Emma Perry; *My London 2012* Emma Perry). **Parks & Gardens** Emma Perry (*Neighbourhood Watch: Chelsea, Greenwich, Camden* Dominic Earle; *Queen Elizabeth Olympic Park* Emma Perry; *Up the Creek* Elizabeth Winding; *My Sport: Judo* Emma Perry; *My London 2012* Emma Perry). **Meet the Animals** Emma Perry (*Neighbourhood Watch: Marylebone* Dominic Earle; *Interactive Fun* Emma Perry *My Sport: Tennis, Boxing* Emma Perry; *My London 2012* Emma Perry). **Sport & Activities** Dominic Earle, Emma Perry (*Swimming Tips* Rebecca Adlington Emma Perry; *Capital Growth* William Crow; *Horse Play* Kate Miller; *My Sport: Wheelchair Rugby, Swimming, Football, Gymnastics* Emma Perry; *My London 2012* Emma Perry). **Arts & Entertainment** Elizabeth Winding, Emma Perry, Dominic Earle (*On the Waterfront* Dominic Earle; *My Sport: Ballet, Capoeira* Emma Perry). **Parties** Meryl O'Rourke, Emma Perry (*Sport Parties* Emma Perry; *My Sport: Hockey* Emma Perry; *My London 2012* Emma Perry). **Eating** Contributors to Time Out's *London's Best Restaurants* (*The Big Breakfast* Emma Perry and contributors to Time Out's *London's Best Restaurants*; *Chain Reaction* Emma Perry and contributors to Time Out's *London's Best Restaurants*; *Anyone for Tea?* Emma Perry; *Bouled Over* William Crow). **Shopping** Emma Perry, Dominic Earle, Elizabeth Winding (*Kids Corner: Hampstead, Northcote Road, Stoke Newington, Crouch End, East Dulwich, Notting Hill; London 2012 Souvenirs* Simon Coppock; *Get Fitted for London 2012* Emma Perry; *Added Extras* Emma Perry; *Clothes & Toys on the Web* Emma Perry).

Maps john@jsgraphics.co.uk

Front cover photography Ben Rowe

Back cover photography Christina Theisen, Jonathan Perugia, Heloise Bergman

Contents

Introduction

TIME OUT LONDON FOR CHILDREN GUIDE

This is the 11th edition of the Time Out *London for Children Guide*, produced by the people behind the successful listings magazines and travel guide series. It is written by resident experts to provide you with all the information you'll need to explore the city, whether you're a local or a first-time visitor.

THE LOWDOWN ON THE LISTINGS

Addresses, phone numbers, websites, transport information, opening times, admission prices and credit card details are included in the listings. Details of facilities, services and events were all checked and correct as we went to press.

Before you go out of your way, however, we'd advise you to phone and check opening times, ticket prices and other particulars. While every effort has been made to ensure the accuracy of the information contained in this guide, the publishers cannot accept any responsibility for any errors that it may contain.

FAMILY-FRIENDLY INFORMATION

Having visited all the places with our children, we've added essential information for families. Where we think it's important, we've stated whether a building can accommodate buggies, or if there's a place to change a nappy. We've also listed the nearest picnic place.

Attractions are required to provide reasonable facilities for disabled visitors, although it's best to check accessibility before setting out.

PRICES AND PAYMENT

We have noted where venues accept the following credit cards: American Express (AmEx), MasterCard (MC) and Visa (V).

THE LIE OF THE LAND

Map references are included for each venue that falls within the area covered by our London street maps, starting on page 326. We would recommend that you also use a standard A-Z map of the city.

PHONE NUMBERS

The area code for London is 020. All phone numbers given in this guide take this code unless otherwise stated, so add 020 if you're calling from outside London; otherwise, simply dial the number as written. The international dialling code for the UK is 44.

LET US KNOW WHAT YOU THINK

We hope that you enjoy this book and we'd like to know what you think of it. Email us at guides@timeout.com.

ADVERTISERS

We would like to stress that no establishment has been included in this guide because it has advertised in any of our publications and no payment of any kind has influenced any review. The opinions given in this book are those of Time Out writers and editors and are entirely independent.

Out & About

Air Today, Gone Tomorrow

The new atmosphere gallery at the Science Museum explores the past, present and future of climate change science.

The floor of the Science Museum's futuristic new atmosphere gallery represents the land and water masses on Earth, while the installation hanging from the ceiling plays the part of the atmosphere. The blue-hued design isn't purely decorative, though, and both floor and ceiling form a giant board for Interconnected Earth, an interactive game hub introducing the subject of climate change to visitors. Interactivity is key inside this visually striking gallery aimed at children aged eight and above (and, of course, adults), who will be able to make the most of the exhibits and written material.

The gallery is split into five zones. Zones A-D look at the history and development of climate change science, while Zone E asks what scientists are doing to combat the unprecedented changes in temperature and CO_2 levels.

Although it's not immediately obvious where to start, head for the left hand side as you go in, and progress in a clockwise direction. Otherwise, it's all too tempting to be drawn straight to the arresting hydrogen-powered urban car on the right hand side (part of Zone E).

Starting at the beginning, Zone A asks how scientists know what the Earth's climate was like in the past. Exhibits include an interpretation of data provided by tree rings, sediment samples and stalagmite slices, as well as a time-travelling game.

Zone B looks at some of the pioneering scientists

involved in the development of climate change – from Joseph Fourier (1768-1830), who suggested the atmosphere could regulate the Earth's surface temperature, to Guy Callendar (1898-1964), who established the link between fossil fuel energy and rising carbon dioxide levels in the atmosphere.

Zone C has the most exciting exhibit of all. A metre-long ice core from Antarctica (the only one on display in the UK) that can tell us exactly what the air was like in the year 1410, thanks to the bubbles trapped inside the ice. Quite apart from its scientific usefulness, it's a beautiful sculptural object.

Zone D asks how scientists know that the Earth's climate is changing and explores the many instruments used across the globe to collect data. From radiosondes to argo floats and satellite altimeters, this part of the gallery will appeal to budding inventors and gadget freaks of all ages. Once you've checked out the hardware, there's a chance to have a go at Modelling the Future, an interactive display that brings home the drastic effects of emission changes and temperature rises around the globe.

The atmosphere gallery isn't all doom and gloom, though. Yes, it provokes some serious thought about the sort of energy we use in our cars and homes, but it also offers news of some radical and exciting developments in combating climate change. For optimism and a dose of childish wonder, move forward to Zone E. Here you'll find artificial trees that collect CO_2, paving slabs that generate energy as people walk across them, domestic energy monitors that encourage individual families to cut their energy use, solar reflection devices that deflect heat from the Earth's surface, and the aforementioned hydrogen-powered car.

Also look out for the series of contemporary art commissions created for the atmosphere gallery. The first is by David Shrigley and uses the metaphor of a house of cards to represent the fragility of the Earth's environmental balance. Children will also enjoy the four Tell stations, which allow them to ask further questions online, read updated news reports and email articles to themselves for further study.

Out & About

Den of Equity

A monster supplies shop has recently opened up in Shoreditch,
but what lies behind the secret door?

At 159 Hoxton Street, the sign hanging
on the shop door says: 'Official notice: the
proprietor is hereby licensed to sell items
including, but not limited to, malodorous
gases, children's ears, gore, fear (tinned
only), pencils, and other items as specified
in the monster retailer's act of 1827,
clause 14, subsection 5, revision (b).'

It's not kidding, either. Through
the door is a new shop full of freshly
extracted nails, zombie mints, thickest
human snot, fang floss, neck bolt
tighteners, tins of fear, unease and panic,
an invisible cat, a monster hotline and

a door beyond which no one can go
without a magic password.

The Hoxton Street Monster Supplies
shop was set up by Co-Directors Lucy
Macnab, who used to work in the
Southbank's Learning and Participation
Department, and theatre writer and
director Ben Payne, with help from
Nick Hornby. The model was based
on a project run by Dave Eggers in the
US that offered underprivileged inner-city
children a chance to explore their literary
creativity – behind that secret door lies
the Ministry of Stories, a writing centre

OLDE FASHIONED
BRAIN JAM

for local kids, many of whom have no quiet space at home to call their own.

'A lot of people in London had heard about Dave Eggers' 826 Valencia project in San Francisco,' says Macnab. 'I was doing a course with Ben and we started talking about it over lunch. We applied for some funding and found a graphic designer, but it wasn't until Dave Eggers came to town and did a shout out for volunteers after a reading that it became concrete. It took us a long time to find the right premises in a suitable location. There were loads of empty shops but not many landlords who were keen on what we were doing. Everything has been made by volunteer architects and designers, and most things, including the carpet, were donated for free.'

The Ministry of Stories offers a project room and a quiet study room for budding local writers aged eight to 18. It aims to act as a drop-in centre for children after school and on Saturdays. Kids can bring in their own project and get one-to-one help

THICKEST
HUMAN SNOT

from volunteer mentors, or be guided, using the Ministry's prompts, exercises and workshops, to find inspiration.

'We consulted local children at the planning stage,' says Macnab, 'and what they said they wanted was exciting things to write with, to be able to write on the walls, and to have a space to call their own. Children of all ages responded really well to the idea of it being a secret place behind a shop.'

The Ministry's volunteers include writers, artists, designers, editors, teachers and locals who want to help out. 'The important thing for the children is to get individual help from an adult mentor, even if it's just someone who says: "Wow that's a great idea, what happened next?" But it has also proved to be a great experience and community for the volunteers,' says Macnab.

Check the website for news of upcoming events open to all or explore the shop. For full listings details, *see p297.*

Out & About

Trips & Tours

London's landmarks by bus, boat, bicycle or black cab.

Trafalgar Square.

Getting around

If speed is of the essence, it's generally best to hop on the tube (*see p336*), but taking the bus is far more scenic. Good routes for city sightseeing are the 7, 8, 11 and 12 (all double-deckers) and, along the South Bank, the single-decker RV1. A couple of old-style Routemaster buses – numbers 9 and 15 – now run as Heritage Routes: the 9 runs from Aldwych via the Strand, Trafalgar Square and Piccadilly Circus to the Royal Albert Hall; and the 15 from Trafalgar Square to Tower Hill. Normal fares apply.

Tourist information

To get the most from the capital, a tourist information office is an essential port of call. **Visit London** (7234 5800, www.visitlondon.com) is the official tourist information service, with its main office in Lower Regent Street. There are also outposts in Greenwich, Leicester Square and just by St Paul's Cathedral.

If your programme takes in some of the pricier sights, a London Pass (01664 485020, www.londonpass.com) gives you pre-paid access to over 50 attractions.

In our listings, the initials 'EH' mean that English Heritage members, and their kids, get in free. 'NT' means National Trust members get free admission.

Britain & London Visitor Centre *1 Lower Regent Street, SW1Y 4XT (7808 3800, www.visitbritain.com). Piccadilly Circus tube.* **Open** *Summer* 9.30am-6.30pm Mon; 9am-6.30pm Tue-Fri; 9am-5pm Sat; 10am-4pm Sun. *Winter* 9.30am-6pm Mon; 9am-6pm Tue-Fri; 10am-4pm Sat, Sun.

London Information Centre *Leicester Square, WC2H 7BP (7292 2333, www.londontown.com). Leicester Square tube.* **Open** *Phone enquiries* 8am-10pm Mon-Fri; 10am-8pm Sat, Sun. *In person* 10am-6pm Mon-Fri; noon-6pm Sat, Sun.

Out & About (rotated sidebar text)

Out & About

Moving experiences

On the river

City Cruises *7740 0400, www.citycruises. com*. **Departures** check website for details. **Tickets** vary. **Credit** MC, V.
City Cruises' handy Rail River Rover ticket (£14.50; £7.25 5-16s, reductions; free under-5s) combines hop-on, hop-off travel on any of its regular cruises (pick-up points: Westminster, Waterloo, Tower and Greenwich piers) with unlimited travel on the DLR.

London Duck Tours *7928 3132, www. londonducktours.co.uk*. **Tours** daily; phone for details. *Pick-up* Chicheley Street, behind the London Eye. **Fares** £20; £16 reductions; £14 1-12s; £58 family (2+2). **Credit** MC, V.
Climb aboard one of these yellow amphibious vehicles for a thrilling road and river trip, lasting 75 minutes. Starts at the London Eye and plunges into the Thames at Vauxhall.

London RIB Voyages *7928 8933, www.londonribvoyages.com*. **Departures** check website for details. **Tickets** £32.50-£45; £19.50-£28 under-16s. **Credit** MC, V.
RIB's speedboat trips power passengers from the London Eye to Canary Wharf (50mins) or the Thames Barrier (80mins). Book in advance.

London Waterbus Company *7482 2660, www.londonwaterbus.com*. **Departures** check website. **Fares** *Single* £6.70; £5.50 3-15s, reductions. *Return* £9.70; £7.70 3-15s, reductions. Free under-3s. **Credit** MC, V.
Navigate Regent's Canal in a narrowboat. Trips run between Camden Lock and Little Venice, stopping off at London Zoo.

Thames Clippers *0870 781 5049, www.thamesclippers.com*. **Departures** 6am-midnight Mon-Fri; 8.30am-midnight Sat, Sun. **Tickets** vary. **Credit** MC, V.
Equipped with a River Roamer ticket (£12; £6 5-15s; free under-5s) you can hop on and off along the Thames between Millbank Pier and Royal Arsenal Woolwich pier, with stops at Waterloo, Embankment, London Bridge, Tower, Canary Wharf, Greenwich and the O2. The Family Roamer costs £25 (2+3).

On the buses

Big Bus Company *0800 169 1365, 7233 9533, www.bigbustours.com*. **Departures** every 10-20mins. *Summer* 8.30am-6pm daily. *Winter* 8.30am-4.30pm daily. *Pick-up* Green Park (near the Ritz); Marble Arch (Speakers' Corner); Victoria (outside Thistle Victoria Hotel, 48 Buckingham Palace Road, SW1W 0RN). **Fares** £26; £10 5-15s; free under-5s.

Tickets valid for 24hrs, interchangeable between routes. **Credit** AmEx, MC, V.
These open-top buses, with commentary, stop at the major tourist sights, where customers can hop on and off at will.

Original London Sightseeing Tour
8877 1722, www.theoriginaltour.com. **Departures** *Summer* every 10-15mins, 8.30am-8pm daily. *Winter* every 15-20mins, 8.30am-5.30pm daily. *Pick-up* Grosvenor Gardens; Marble Arch (Speakers' Corner); Haymarket (Piccadilly Circus); Trafalgar Square. **Fares** £25; £12 5-15s; free under-5s. **Credit** AmEx, MC, V.
Another open-top bus operation, taking a circuit of the sights. The Kids' Club tours include a special activity pack.

Pedal power

London Bicycle Tour Company *1A Gabriel's Wharf, 56 Upper Ground, SE1 9PP (7928 6838, www.londonbicycle.com)*. *Waterloo tube/rail*. **Open** 10am-6pm daily. **Hire** £3.50/hr; £20/1st day, £10/day thereafter. **Credit** AmEx, MC, V.
Bike and tandem hire; children's bike seats are free with an adult bike. There are guided tours covering major sights beginning at 10.30am.

London Pedicabs *01737 812268, www.londonpedicabs.com*. **Fares** from £3 per person per mile. **No credit cards**.
Hard-working cycle rickshaws, based in Covent Garden and Soho.

Take a hike

Guided walking tours are also offered by **And Did Those Feet** (8806 4325, www.chr.org.uk), **Performing London** (01234 404774, www.performinglondon. co.uk) and **Silver Cane Tours** (07720 715295, www.silvercanetours.com).

Original London Walks *7624 3978, www.walks.com*. **Tours** £8; £6 reductions; 1 free under-15 per adult. **No credit cards**.
These themed walks criss-cross the capital. Plenty appeal to kids, not least the Harry Potter walk (6.30pm Mon, adults only; 2pm Sat, Sun) and Ghosts of the Old City (7.30pm Tue, Sat).

'Taxi!'

Black Taxi Tours of London *7935 9363, www.blacktaxitours.co.uk*. **Cost** £100-£115. **No credit cards**.
This company runs two-hour tours by taxi for up to five people.

Festivals & Events

Big fun for little people.

London always has something to celebrate, whether it's the thoroughly traditional delights of Trooping the Colour (*see below*) or the eccentric pleasures of Chap & Hendrick's Olympiad (*see p17*). There's something to suit all ages and tastes all year round: what's more, most of it won't cost you a penny.

While we've included the regular events and festivals that keep the city in a giddy social whirl, there's always more going on: check *Time Out* magazine for the latest one-off celebrations and cultural happenings. We've given exact dates for events where possible; phone or check websites nearer the time for unconfirmed timings.

SUMMER

Coin Street Festival
Bernie Spain Gardens, next to Oxo Tower Wharf, SE1 9PH (7021 1686, www.coin street.org). Southwark tube or Waterloo tube/rail. **Date** June-July 2011. **Map** p334 N7.
This welcoming, family-friendly summer shindig brings a series of culturally themed weekday and weekend events that celebrate different communities in the capital. Festivities take place in the open spaces around Bernie Spain Gardens, Gabriel's Wharf and the South Bank and include music, dance and performances, as well as craft and refreshment stalls and workshops. Check the website for more information nearer the time.

Beating Retreat
Horse Guards Parade, Whitehall, SW1A 2AX (booking 0844 847 2435). Westminster tube or Charing Cross tube/rail. **Date** June. **Map** p333 K8.
Held on two June evenings, this spirited, stirring ceremony kicks off at 9pm, with the 'Retreat' beaten on drums by the Mounted Bands of the Household Cavalry and the Massed Bands of the Guards Division.

Trooping the Colour
Horse Guards Parade, Whitehall, SW1A 2AX (7414 2479). Westminster tube or Charing Cross tube/rail. **Date** 2nd Sat June. **Map** p333 K8.
The Queen was actually born on 21 April, but this is her official birthday celebration, for practical reasons. At 10.45am, Her Majesty makes the journey from Buckingham Palace to Horse Guards Parade, then scoots home to watch a Royal Air Force flypast and receive a formal gun salute from Green Park.

Open Garden Squares Weekend
Various venues (www.opensquares.org). **Date** 2nd weekend June.
For one weekend a year, the London Parks & Gardens Trust opens locked and gated green spaces to one and all. Tickets allow entry to all participating gardens, which range from secret 'children-only' play areas to allotments and exclusive garden squares. Many are wheelchair-accessible and host activities and plant sales; if you're lucky, there might be home-made cakes to munch on as you admire the greenery. Check online for the full list.

City of London Festival
Venues across the City, EC2-EC4 (7583 3585, www.colf.org). St Paul's tube or Bank tube/DLR or Cannon Street, Farringdon or Moorgate tube/rail or Blackfriars rail. **Date** 26 June-16 July 2011.
Founded in 1962, with the aim of revitalising the City's cultural life, this summer festival stages indoor ticketed concerts and free outdoor events in and around some of the Square Mile's finest historic buildings. Outdoor events, including walks, street theatre, jazz concerts and dance performances, run until early August.

Wimbledon Lawn Tennis Championships
All England Lawn Tennis Club, PO Box 98, Church Road, SW19 5AE (8944 1066, 8946

Out & About

Watch This Space.

2244 info, www.wimbledon.org).
Southfields tube, Wimbledon tube/rail.
Date 20 June-3 July 2011.
To nab tickets for this prestigious tennis tournament, you'll need to plan ahead. For Centre Court and Court Number One seats, request an application form from the All England Lawn Tennis Club between August and mid December the year before; you'll then be entered into the public ticket ballot. Queuing on the day should gain you entry to the outside courts. In the afternoon, returned show-court tickets are available from the booth opposite Court One, so it may be worth hanging about to see the stars slicing, serving and mopping their perspiring brows on one of the world's most famous courts.

Greenwich & Docklands International Festival
Various venues (8305 1818, www.festival. org). **Date** 23 June-3 July 2011.
With its vibrant mixture of theatre, music and spectacle, this free festival has been bringing spectacle and colour to the varied backdrops of Maritime Greenwich, the Isle of Dogs, Canary Wharf and Woolwich since 2007. The 2010 theme was Earth (drawing on Greenwich's Prime Meridian fame), and the 2011 and 2012 editions will focus on Fire and Air respectively.

Henley Royal Regatta
Henley Reach, Henley-on-Thames, Oxon RG9 2LY (01491 572153, www.hrr.co.uk). Henley-on-Thames rail. **Date** 29 June-3 July 2011.
First held in 1839, and under royal patronage since 1851, Henley is still going strong; it's now a five-day affair. Boat races range from open events for men and women through club and student crews to the Princess Elizabeth race for juniors (boys under the age of 19). Straw boaters and blazers are de rigueur, as is bringing a picnic.

Watch This Space
Theatre Square, outside the National Theatre, South Bank, SE1 9PX (7452 3400, www.nationaltheatre.org.uk/wts). Waterloo tube/rail. **Date** July-Sept 2011. **Map** p334 M7.
This superb free festival brings all manner of entertainment to an artificial lawn laid out on the South Bank. Lounge in the sunshine and catch the best street theatre, circus, cinema, music, art and dance from all over the world.

London Youth Games
Various venues (7717 1570, www. londonyouthgames.org). **Date** (finals) 2-3 July 2011.
In 2010 this mini-Olympics attracted more than 50,000 sporting hopefuls, all of them under 17, representing their London borough in 30 different sports – including archery, fencing, canoeing, cycling, rugby and athletics. The finals weekend takes place at Crystal Palace Sports Ground, while other competitions are held at venues around the capital throughout the summer. Extra entertainment includes dance performances, DJs, street sport demonstrations and graffiti art.

Underage
Victoria Park, Old Ford Road, E3 (0844 477 1000 tickets, www.underagefestivals.com). Mile End tube or Cambridge Heath or Hackney Wick rail or bus 8, 26, 30, 55. **Date** 5 July 2011. **Tickets** from £25.
Strictly for 14- to 18-year-olds, Underage attracts an enviable line-up of alternative, rock and electro bands. In 2010, hipper-than-thou acts included the Horrors, Santigold, Little Boots and Ladyhawke. The ban on alcohol (and adults) is firmly enforced.

Chap & Hendrick's Olympiad
Bedford Square Gardens, WC1 (www.hendricksgin.com). Tottenham Court Road tube. **Date** 16 July 2011. **Map** p331 K5.
Expect a surreally splendid afternoon out at this terribly silly, terribly English event, where children can watch adults engage in all manner of tomfoolery. Events kick off with the lighting of the Olympic Pipe, with 'sports' including umbrella jousting, freestyle trouser gymnastics and synchronised hat doffing.

BBC Sir Henry Wood Promenade Concerts
Royal Albert Hall, Kensington Gore, SW7 2AP (7589 8212 box office, www.bbc.co.uk/ proms). Knightsbridge or South Kensington tube or bus 9, 10, 52. **Date** 15 July-10 Sept 2011. **Map** p329 D9.
While plenty of the concerts are broadcast on the radio or TV, there's nothing like seeing them in person. Choose carefully and you should find something in the main programme that will appeal to children; there are also special family events, and a young composers' competition. Under-16s get half-price tickets to every prom, bar the legendary Last Night.

Lambeth Country Show

Brockwell Park, SE24 0NG (7926 7085, www.lambeth.gov.uk). Brixton tube/rail, then bus 2, 3, 196 or Herne Hill rail. **Date** 16-17 July 2011.

Hankering for the countryside, and an escape from the urban grind and grime? No need to leave town; instead, head down to Brockwell Park's free country show. Aside from meeting and greeting assorted farmyard beasts, children can cheer on horse and dog shows, watch sheep-shearing and birds of prey demonstrations, and have fun on numerous bouncy castles and fairground rides. An international array of food stalls keep the masses well fed (don't miss the jerk chicken), while the strains of brass bands fill the air.

Carnaval del Pueblo

Finsbury Park, N4 (7928 4277, www.carnavaldelpueblo.co.uk). Finsbury Park or Manor House tube. **Date** 24-25 July 2011.

The UK's largest Latin American festival attracts up to 60,000 people and includes over 100 food and crafts stalls, a children's zone and four stages; the live Brazilian samba, Latin hip hop, Mexican mariachi and Colombian salsa soon gets everyone dancing. The festival is scheduled to move venue from Burgess Park to Finsbury Park in 2011.

Sundae on the Common

Clapham Common, SW4 (www.benjerry. co.uk/sundae). Clapham Common tube. **Date** late July 2011.

A family-friendly mix of fairground activities and live music, last year's Sundae featured banana jousting (Fairtrade, of course) and toe wrestling – not to mention free ice cream all day. You can pet farm animals, make cookies, scoot down the helter-skelter, pelt the coconut shy and have your fortune told by Mystic Moo. See the website for the latest musical line-up; in previous years, headline acts have included the the likes of Doves and Idlewild. Tickets go on sale in June.

Kidsweek

Various venues (0844 248 5151, www.kidsweek.co.uk). **Date** Aug 2011.

It's called Kidsweek, but this festival actually runs over a fortnight as part of the West End Festival. The idea is to encourage families to get to London's great theatre shows, and with this in mind, they offer one under-16 ticket free, and up to two additional children's tickets at half price, when you buy a full-price adult ticket. There are accompanying workshops, Q&As and other activities.

Notting Hill Carnival

Notting Hill, W10 & W11 (7727 0072, www.thenottinghillcarnival.com). Ladbroke Grove, Notting Hill Gate or Westbourne Park tube. **Date** 28-29 Aug 2011.

Held over the August bank holiday weekend, the annual Notting Hill Carnival is as loud, colourful and chaotic as they come – and the Sunday is traditionally decreed to be children's day. Masquerades, steel bands, decorative floats and ground-shaking sound systems take over the streets of Notting Hill, and there's curried goat, roti and fried plantain to sample. Its reputation for bringing short, sharp spikes to the annual crime rate continues to court controversy, but increasing commercialism and a strong police presence have made the carnival safer than ever.

AUTUMN

Mayor of London's Skyride

www.goskyride.com. **Date** early Sept 2011.

Each year since 2007, this cycling festival has encouraged around 50,000 people to don branded flourescent vests and ride a traffic-free route from Buckingham Palace to the Tower of London, as well as any number of subsidiary routes. Enjoy music, car-less roads and the chance to meet sports stars along the way.

Great River Race

River Thames, from Docklands, E14 to Ham House, Richmond, Surrey (8398 9057, www.greatriverrace.co.uk). **Date** 17 Sept 2011.

Vessels of every shape and size compete over a 22-mile (35km) course in this traditional boat championship, from Viking longboats to Hawaiian war canoes. The race begins at 11am and reaches the finish at around 3.30pm. The best viewing points are at Richmond Bridge, along the South Bank or on the Millennium and Hungerford Bridges.

Regent Street Festival

Regent Street, W1 (7038 3715, www.regent streetonline.com). Oxford Circus or Piccadilly Circus tube. **Date** 25 Sept 2011. **Map** p332 J7.

All traffic is banned from Regent Street for this annual event; in its place, fairground rides, storytellers, street entertainers and musicians

Discover Dogs. *See p22.*

take over the tarmac for a day of fun. There's usually plenty of input from Regent Street's resident toy emporium, Hamleys.

Mayor's Thames Festival
Between Westminster & Tower Bridges (7983 4100, www.thamesfestival.org). London Bridge or Waterloo tube/rail or Blackfriars rail. **Date** 10-11 Sept 2011.
This jolly celebration of the Thames brings a weekend of riverside stalls, performers, sand sculptures, environmental activities and creative workshops. A lantern procession and dramatic fireworks display bring proceedings to a close on Sunday evening.

Spitalfields Show & Green Fair
Allen Gardens & Spitalfields City Farm, Buxton Street, E1 (7375 0441, www.alternativearts.co.uk). Whitechapel tube. **Date** 11 Sept 2011. **Map** p335 S5.
Oodles of own-made produce, handicrafts, Fairtrade goods and healing therapies are on offer at this east London horticultural show, along with plenty of advice on growing your own, composting, and other ways to go green.

City Harvest Festival
Capel Manor Gardens, Bullsmoor Lane, Enfield, Middx EN1 4RQ (0845 612 2122, www.capel.ac.uk). Turkey Street rail (closed Sun) or bus 217. **Date** 17 Sept 2011.
Every year, London's city farms and community gardens gather in the grounds of Capel Manor College to hold a harvest festival. Events and activities include an animal show, milking and shearing demonstrations, vegetable and plant sales, crafts displays and food stalls.

Horseman's Sunday
Church of St John's Hyde Park, Hyde Park Crescent, W2 2QD (7262 1732, www.stjohns-hydepark.com). Edgware Road or Lancaster Gate tube or Paddington tube/rail. **Date** 18 Sept 2011. **Map** p329 E6.
The first Horseman's Sunday was held in 1967, when local stables, threatened with closure, held an outdoor service to protest. Since then, it's become an equine institution: at noon, after morning service, the vicar of St John's rides out to bless and present rosettes to a procession of horses and riders, then delivers a short service. There are children's activities and games.

Chinese New Year Festival. *See p23*.

Story of London

Various venues (7983 4000, www.london. gov.uk/storyoflondon). **Date** Oct 2011.

Story of London is a month-long festival of events and activities, celebrating the city's past, present and future. Involving a collaboration of institutions from all over the capital, led by the Mayor's office, the ambitious programme incorporates music, history, film, walks and architecture. Check online for the full list of events.

Big Draw

Venues across London & nationwide (www. thebigdraw.org.uk). **Date** 1-31 Oct 2011.

Pencils at the ready – this brilliant annual event aims to bring out the inner artist in everyone, with imaginative free events running in libraries, community centres, shopping centres, gardens and cultural institutions across the country. London's big museums and galleries always come up with some excellent offerings.

Punch & Judy Festival

Covent Garden Piazza, WC2 (0870 780 5001, www.coventgardenlondonuk.com). Covent Garden tube. **Date** early Oct 2011. **Map** p331 L6.

That's the way to do it! Slapstick humour and violent altercations between Punch and his missus hold kids enthralled, with performances taking place around the market building. Call nearer the time to confirm this year's date.

Children's Book Week

8516 2977, www.booktrust.org.uk. **Date** 3-9 Oct 2011.

This festival aims to encourage children of primary school age to get reading – and enjoy it. Hands-on activities and author visits take place across the country, and there's always plenty going on in London's schools and libraries. National Poetry Day (www.national poetryday.co.uk) takes place during the festival.

Pearly Kings & Queens Harvest Festival

St Paul's Church, Bedford Street, WC2E 9ED (8778 8670, www.pearlysociety.co.uk). Covent Garden tube. **Date** 9 Oct 2011. **Map** p333 L7.

Pearly kings and queens – so named because of the shiny white pearl buttons sewn in elaborate designs on their dark suits – have their origins in the 'aristocracy' of London's early Victorian costermongers, who elected their own royalty to look after their interests.

Now charity representatives, today's pearly monarchs gather in their resplendent garb an hour before the 11am thanksgiving service.

The Baby Show

Earl's Court Exhibition Centre, SW5 9TA (0870 122 1313 booking, www.thebaby show.co.uk). Earl's Court tube. **Date** 28-30 Oct 2011. **Map** p328 A11.

Earl's Court overflows with all manner of baby-related paraphernalia, with a mind-boggling array of pregnancy gear, nursery equipment and stimulating toys. Consult the website to search for your area of interest.

Trafalgar Day Parade

Trafalgar Square, WC2 (7928 8978, www.ms-sc.org). Charing Cross tube/rail. **Date** 23 Oct 2011. **Map** p333 K7.

Over 500 sea cadets parade with marching bands and musical performances, in celebration of the British victory at Trafalgar. Events culminate in a wreath laying ceremony at the foot of Nelson's Column, in honour of the mortally wounded admiral.

London to Brighton Veteran Car Run

Start at Serpentine Road, Hyde Park, W2 (01327 856024, www.lbvcr.com). Hyde Park Corner tube. **Date** 6 Nov 2011. **Map** p327 F8.

There's no time for lie-ins if you want to see this parade of gleaming vintage motors leaving London, or join the crowds lining the route. The buffed-up fleet sets off from Hyde Park at 7am, with the first cars reaching Brighton around 10am. The rest arrive by 4pm; bear in mind that the average speed is a stately 32kph (20mph). The vehicles are on display in Regent Street the day before (11am-3pm, Saturday 5 October).

Bonfire Night

Date 5 Nov.

The weekend nearest to 5 November sees numerous public pyrotechnic displays commemorating Guy Fawkes and his ill-fated Gunpowder Plot. Those at Battersea Park, Alexandra Palace and Crystal Palace are among London's best; for an overview, book a late ride on the London Eye (*see p46*).

Lord Mayor's Show

The City, EC2-EC4 (7332 3456, www.lord mayorsshow.org). Mansion House, St Paul's or Temple tube or Bank tube/DLR or Blackfriars rail. **Date** 12 Nov 2011.

Out & About

This is the day when, under the conditions of the Magna Carta, the newly elected Lord Mayor is presented for approval to the monarch, or his or her justices. Amid a procession of around 140 floats, the Lord Mayor leaves Mansion House at 11am and travels through the City to the Royal Courts of Justice on the Strand, then receives a blessing at St Paul's Cathedral before returning to Mansion House. The procession takes around 75 minutes to pass by. At around 5pm, fireworks are set off from a barge moored on the Thames between Waterloo and Blackfriars Bridges.

Discover Dogs
Earl's Court 2 Exhibition Centre, entrance on Lillie Road, SW5 9TA (7518 1012, www. discoverdogs.org.uk). West Brompton tube/ rail. **Date** 12-13 Nov 2011. **Map** p328 A11.
They say every dog has its day – and this is a chance for mutts that don't quite fit Crufts' criteria to take centre stage. Visitors can meet around 190 pedigree pooches and their breeders, watch Heelwork to Music displays and see husky team and police dog agility demonstrations. Competition categories might include 'dog that looks most like a celebrity' or Scruffts (family crossbreed dog of the year).

Children's Film Festival
Main venue: Barbican Centre, Silk Street, EC2Y 8DS (7638 8891 Barbican box office, www.londonchildrenfilm.org.uk). Barbican tube. **Date** Oct & Nov 2011. **Map** p334 P5.
This annual festival proves that kids are interested in more sophisticated film fare than big blockbusters. The line-up features foreign language films, documentaries and animations; seven- to 12-year-olds are invited to join a jury and become film critics. Check online for workshops and events, many of which are free.

State Opening of Parliament
House of Lords, Palace of Westminster, SW1A 0PW (7219 4272, www.parliament. uk). Westminster tube. **Date** Nov 2011. **Map** p333 L9.
In a ceremony that has changed little since the 16th century, the Queen reopens Parliament after its summer recess. Watch Her Majesty arrive and depart in her Irish or Australian State Coach, attended by the Household Cavalry.

Christmas Lights & Tree
Covent Garden (0870 780 5001, www.covent gardenlondon.com); Oxford Street (7462 0680, www.newwestend.com); Regent Street

(7038 3715, www.regentstreetonline.com); Bond Street (www.bondstreetassociation. com); Trafalgar Square (7983 4234, www.london.gov.uk). **Date** Nov-Dec 2011.
The glittering lights on St Christopher's Place, Marylebone High Street, Bond Street and Kensington High Street add a magical touch to grey winter days. The giant fir tree that stands in pride of place in Trafalgar Square is an annual gift from the Norwegian people, in gratitude for Britain's role in liberating their country from the Nazis during World War II.

WINTER

London International Horse Show
Olympia Exhibition Centre, Hammersmith Road, W14 8UX (01753 847900, www.olympiahorseshow.com). Kensington (Olympia) tube/rail. **Date** Dec 2011.
Enthusiasts of all things equestrian can enjoy dressage, show-jumping, dog agility contests and a Shetland Pony Grand National. The grand finale features Father Christmas (with a sledge pulled by horses), and there are over 200 trade stands, so you can also do some seasonal shopping.

Peter Pan Swimming Race
The Serpentine, Hyde Park, W2 (7298 2000, www.royalparks.gov.uk). Hyde Park Corner tube. **Date** 25 Dec. **Map** p327 E8.
Established in 1864 by *Peter Pan* author JM Barrie, this chilly 100-yard race draws intrepid swimmers (Serpentine Swimming Club members only) and spectators every Christmas morning, competing for the Peter Pan cup. However mild the weather is, the Serpentine always looks less than inviting.

New Year's Eve Celebrations
Date 31 Dec.
London's New Year revelry has traditionally been concentrated around Trafalgar Square; the fireworks on the South Bank are a more recent draw. Both attract huge crowds, and can be nightmarish with younger children in tow.

London International Mime Festival
Various venues (7637 5661, www.mimefest.co.uk). **Date** 14-29 Jan 2012.
An international array of companies and artists perform visual theatre of every genre: circus skills, mask, mime, clown and visual theatre shows appeal to audiences of all ages.

Out & About

Chinese New Year Festival

Around Gerrard Street, Chinatown, W1, Leicester Square, WC2 & Trafalgar Square, WC2 (7851 6686, www.londonchinatown.org). Leicester Square or Piccadilly Circus tube. **Date** 23 Jan 2012. **Map** p333 K7.

Riotous celebrations to mark Chinese New Year begin at 11am with a children's parade that weaves its way from Leicester Square Gardens to Trafalgar Square, where lion and dragon dance teams entertain the masses.

National Storytelling Week

Theatres, museums, bookshops, arts centres, schools, libraries & pubs (8866 4232 Del Reid, www.sfs.org.uk). **Date** 27 Jan-4 Feb 2012.

This annual celebration of storytelling, which has been around for over a decade now, sees theatres, bookshops, community centres and schools across the country hosting events for tellers and listeners.

Imagine Children's Festival

Southbank Centre, Belvedere Road, SE1 8XX (0844 875 0073, www.southbankcentre.co.uk). Embankment tube/Waterloo tube/rail. **Date** mid Feb 2012. **Map** p333 M8.

The Southbank Centre's inspirational kids' festival brings together two weeks of family-friendly activities on the banks of the Thames,

with everything from readings and film screenings to stand-up comedy and rock concerts for tots, along with free exhibitions and a children's poetry lounge.

Great Spitalfields Pancake Day Race

Dray Walk, Old Truman Brewery, 91 Brick Lane, E1 6QL (7375 0441, www.alternative arts.co.uk). Aldgate East tube or Liverpool Street tube/rail. **Date** 21 Feb 2012. **Map** p335 S5.

Relay teams of four toss pancakes as they race along Dray Walk, with heats starting at 12.30pm; all proceeds go to the London Air Ambulance charity. Register in advance if you fancy taking part and bring your own frying pan (pancakes are provided); everyone races together, so it isn't suitable for younger children. It's fun to go along as a spectator though, as fancy dress-clad teams get flipping and pancakes hit the pavement.

SPRING

National Science & Engineering Week

Various venues (0870 770 7101, www.britishscienceassociation.org). **Date** mid Mar 2012.

Great Spitalfields Pancake Day Race.

Out & About

A week of scientific shenanigans, hosted by the British Association for the Advancement of Science. From hands-on shows, workshops and guided nature walks for youngsters to a series of in-depth discussions for adults, each event celebrates different aspects of science, engineering and technology. Check the website for more details.

St Patrick's Day Parade & Festival

Trafalgar Square, Leicester Square & Covent Garden (7983 4000, www. london.gov.uk). **Date** 17 Mar. **Map** p333 K7.

This good-natured, raucous parade departs from Hyde Park Corner at noon and continues to romp through the streets until 6pm. Expect lively performances of traditional Irish music in Trafalgar Square, a Covent Garden food market, ceilidh dancers in Leicester Square and lots of other activities for all ages.

Kempton Park Family Fun Days

Kempton Park, Sunbury-on-Thames, Middx TW16 5AQ (01932 782292, www.kempton.co.uk). Kempton Park rail. **Date** Apr & May 2012.

Take the train from Waterloo for a day at the races. Free entertainment (simulator rides, crafts, soft play area, face painting, balloon modelling) is laid on and previous years have seen lavish concerts to keep the youngsters happy while you blow their university fees on the gee-gees.

Shakespeare's Birthday

Various venues around South Bank & Bankside (7902 1400, www.shakespeares-globe.com). **Date** 23 Apr 2012.

Celebrations of the Bard's birth date centre around Shakespeare's Globe and Southwark Cathedral, with all sorts of performances, music, readings and walks marking his contribution to literature.

London Marathon

Greenwich Park to the Mall via the Isle of Dogs, Victoria Embankment & St James's Park (7902 0200, www.virginlondon marathon.com). **Date** 22 Apr 2012.

Completing this 26.2 mile (42km) marathon course is no mean feat, so the runners need all the support they can get. Energetic 11- to 17-year-olds can compete in the three-mile Mini London Marathon – check online for details of time trials.

Canalway Cavalcade

Little Venice, W9 (01494 783453, www.waterways.org.uk). Warwick Avenue tube or Paddington tube/rail. **Date** 5-7 May 2012.

Decked out in bunting and flowers, more than 150 colourful narrowboats assemble in the pool of Little Venice to celebrate this three-day Bank Holiday boat bash. Stalls line the area, and events include a teddy bears' picnic, Punch and Judy shows, music and (of course) boat trips. The beautiful lantern-lit boat procession on Sunday evening is a must-see and will enchant youngsters.

May Fayre & Puppet Festival

St Paul's Church Garden, Bedford Street, WC2E 9ED (7375 0441, www. alternativearts.co.uk). Covent Garden tube. **Date** early May 2012. **Map** p333 L7.

Marking the first recorded sighting of Mr Punch in England (by Pepys, in 1662), this free event offers puppetry galore from 10.30am to 5.30pm. A brass band procession around Covent Garden is followed by a service at 11.30am in St Paul's Church, with Mr Punch in the pulpit. Then there are puppet shows, booths and stalls, plus workshops for puppet-making and dressing-up. Folk music and maypole dancing, clowns and jugglers add to the mayhem.

Museums at Night

Various venues (www.culture24.org.uk/museumsatnight). **Date** mid May 2012.

Since 2009, there has been an annual awakening of museums around the country at night. More than 50 London venues take part in the celebrations and offer all sorts of fantastic events across the capital. For more details of planned events, visit the website. *See also p95* **Night at the Museum**.

Kew Summer Festival

Royal Botanic Gardens, Kew, Richmond, Surrey TW9 3AB (8332 5655, www.kew. org). Kew Gardens tube/rail or Kew Bridge rail. **Date** May-Sept 2012.

Each season at Kew Gardens brings a new and varied programme of events and family activities. Last year saw the temporary Plantastic Play area, where children could explore the inner workings of a plant by tunnelling through gigantic roots and up through the stem and flower parts of a plant – learning all about photosynthesis and pollination along the way.

Out & About

London 2012

Everyone's a Winner

The London 2012 Festival will open up the arts to all.

This year, *London for Children* celebrates a whole spectrum of youthful sporting endeavour in the run-up to the London 2012 Olympic and Paralympic Games. But the main event isn't just about sport. The London 2012 Festival will run from 21 June 2012 until the last day of the Paralympic Games on 9 September 2012, and will feature leading arts figures in an exciting programme of music, dance, theatre, film and art events across the UK.

Events in the capital include an outdoor music event in east London hosted by BBC Radio 1; Big Dance 2012; a new work by Damon Albarn, Rufus Norris and Jamie Hewlett; *Gross und Klein*, a new theatre production at the Barbican from the Sydney Theatre Company starring Cate Blanchett; *Metamorphosis: Titian 2012*, a collaboration between the National Gallery and the Royal Opera House responding to works by Renaissance master Titian; and the Southbank Centre's Poetry Parnassus with Simon Armitage. On the eve of the Olympic Games Opening Ceremony in July 2012, Rivers of Music will feature free music events at various key sites along the Thames for 500,000 spectators.

High-profile art exhibitions will include David Hockney at the Royal Academy, Lucian Freud at the National Portrait Gallery, Damien Hirst at Tate Modern and Rachel Whiteread at the Whitechapel Gallery.

The Festival website goes live in summer 2011, giving away a million free tickets. The remainder of the tickets for over 1,000 Festival events will go on sale in October 2011. Keep up to date at www.london2012.com/festival.

You don't have to wait until 2012 to join in. There are opportunities for kids of all ages to contribute creatively right now through the Cultural Olympiad.

Make a short film

Fourteen- to 25-year-olds are invited to make a short film celebrating the values of the Olympic and Paralympic Games and exploring the theme of 'Truce'. The winning films will be screened at venues during London 2012. *www.filmnation.org.uk.*

Sing for the Games

Youth Music Voices is a new project gathering 14-to 19-year-old singers to perform during the Cultural Olympiad. *www.youthmusic.org.uk/voices.*

Create a community project

The Inspire Programme was created to encourage everyone to feel part of London 2012. Non-commercial cultural, sporting and education projects and events can receive the official London 2012 Inspire mark. *www.london2012.com/beinspired.*

Become a curator

Stories of the World encourages 14- to 24-year-olds to explore their local museums. In London, 23 museums are involved, offering film-making, pottery and more. *www.mla.gov.uk.*

Join in with Open Weekend

Open Weekend 2011 (22-24 July) will celebrate one year to go to the Games. As in 2010, it will encourage people to try something new – from the arts to sport. *www.london2012.com/openweekend.*

London 2012

Open Weekend.

Stories of the World.

Open Weekend.

Explore

What's where for the London 2012 Games.

An extraordinary transformation has been made to the mostly derelict, former industrial land around Stratford and the River Lea. In just a few years, a cluster of remarkable venues have sprung up – all due for completion in summer 2011 and all impressive in scale and design.

Unless you're lucky enough to get a place on a guided tour of the site, there's no access to the **Olympic Park** (*see p32*) until the London 2012 Olympic and Paralympic Games are under way, but its riverside location makes for a fascinating day out on foot or by bicycle.

You can, of course, already visit the several historic venues that are also to be used in the 2012 Games. **Horse Guards Parade** (*see p36*), **Hyde Park** (*see p36*) and **Greenwich Park** (*see p37*), **Wimbledon** (*see p39*), **Lord's Cricket Ground** (*see p36*) and **Wembley Stadium** (*see p39*) are among them.

The lie of the land

The London 2012 Games are divided into three principal areas – the Olympic Park, the Central Zone and the River Zone – with a number of satellite venues around them.

The **Olympic Park** (*see pp32-35*) is quite staggering – as an architectural, environmental and logistical achievement, for sure, but also in its sheer scale as you walk or cycle beside it. More than half the bridges were complete by summer 2010, and planting in the parklands was well under way – the 'golden meadow', carefully planted to flower in July and August 2012, first bloomed in summer 2010. In this chapter, we list the sporting venues and the events they will host in 2012, but there are many other significant structures in the Park. The innovative, eco-friendly Energy Centre is now operational, while the 'brown roof' of the Main Press Centre is being made out of wood and seeds recycled from the developing parkland habitat around it. In Stratford City, to the east of the Olympic Park, Phase I of the development of the vast Westfield shopping mall should be complete in 2011, while the apartment blocks that will house some 17,000 athletes and officials during the Games have taken shape in the Athletes' Village. It is a rare boon for competitors that they'll be staying within walking distance of the major competition venues for London 2012. Everything will be connected to central London by the new Javelin® shuttle service, promising journey times of just seven minutes to St Pancras International come the Games.

The **Central Zone** (*see pp35-36*) brings events for the 2012 Games into the heart of 'tourist London': **Horse Guards Parade** is just down the road from Buckingham Palace (*see p57*), while **Hyde Park** is handy for the posh shops of Mayfair. People interested in getting a flavour of London 2012 venues prior to the events themselves are able to explore all of these and more – given good weather, a day spent watching a

London 2012

Olympic Stadium. *See p32.*

Indicative map of the Olympic Park at Games time

Waltham
Forest

Athletes'
Village

Stratford
International
station

Loop Road

BMX
Track

Basketball
Arena

Eton Manor

Velodrome

North-East Concourse

River Lea

Temporary Northern
Spectator
Transport Mall

Entrance

Hockey

North-Wes

Hockey
warm-up
area

Handball
Arena

International Broadcast Centre/
Main Press Centre

Energy
Centre

Hackney

Entrance point

Trees

Competition venues
Non-competition venues
Back of house
Spectator services
Entrance area
Loop road
Transport malls

Metres

0   200   400   N

Stratford station

Newham

Stratford City

Stratford
High Street

Temporary Southern
Spectator
Transport Mall

West Ham station

Entrance

Sponsors'
Hospitality
Zone

Aquatics
Centre

Water Polo

Entrance

Central Concourse

The Orbit

Concourse

Olympic
Stadium

Warm-up
area

The Greenway

Loop Road

Tower Hamlets

cricket match at **Lord's Cricket Ground**, for example, is a great treat for young sports fans.

The Olympic Park has transformed a vast, once-decrepit area of east London, but the **River Zone** (*see pp36-37*) may prove to have a subtle long-term influence on how Londoners understand their city. Locals generally conceive of London as divided by the River Thames into south and north, but infrastructure improvements linking south bank venues such as **Greenwich Park** and the **North Greenwich Arena** (*see p37*) to **ExCeL** (*see p36*) on the north bank may encourage people to consider the Thames as less of an absolute barrier, especially when the proposed cross-river cable car (*see p71*) cranks into action. Whatever your level of interest in the Games, the UNESCO World Heritage Site of Maritime Greenwich (*see pp132-133*), is a must-see sight.

Beyond these three major zones, the 2012 Games will visit two further historic London venues – **Wembley Stadium and Wimbledon** (*see pp37-39*), respectively the heart of English football and the centre of world tennis – along with a number of improved or purpose-built sites **outside London** (*see pp39-40*).

For succinct advice about planning your trip, *see p43* **Visit**. For details on general transport around London, *see p302* **Getting Around**.

OLYMPIC PARK

Stratford tube/DLR/rail or West Ham tube/rail. **Map** pp30-31.

The centre of the Games is the combination of permanent stadiums and temporary venues that make up the **Olympic Park** in east London. This has already become a major destination for both locals and tourists. A self-guided tour is the best way to enjoy the last stages of the Park's development. The raised Greenway foot- and cyclepath, and towpaths north and south along the River Lea, make casual viewing from outside the perimeter fence a pleasure, with the **View Tube** (*see p245*) near Pudding Mill Lane DLR supplying fine vistas over the Park and good-quality café food.

Olympic Stadium

On Stadium Island, in the south section of the Park, across the Central Concourse from the Aquatics Centre.

The focal venue in the Olympic Park – host to the Opening and Closing Ceremonies, as well as both the Olympic and Paralympic Games Athletics – looks like a kind of giant

.quatics Centre.

Basketball Arena. *See p35.*

mechanical lotus flower, especially when you see its 14 stanchions of floodlights, open like 60m-long petals, reflected in the junction of the Lea Navigation and Hertford Union Canal. It sits on an island between three rivers, crossed by a total of five bridges. When the stadium is complete, its top layer will be covered by material stretched over a cable-net roof to provide perfect conditions for the competitors and shelter for two-thirds of the 80,000 seats.

Within the Stadium, there are 700 rooms (medical facilities, changing rooms, toilets) and a 60m warm-up track, but most of the normal stadium functions have been moved outside: refreshments, merchandising and information desks are to be stationed in a 'village' around the perimeter, giving the Park a festival feel.

This – and the division of seating into 25,000 permanent seats below temporary stands for a further 55,000 – has allowed the weight of materials to be kept low, reducing the carbon footprint created by their manufacture and transport.

🏃 *Athletics*
♿ *Paralympic Athletics*

Aquatics Centre & Water Polo Arena

In the south-east of the Park, between the Olympic Stadium and Stratford City.

Another of the Olympic Park's iconic buildings, the Aquatics Centre will be the first building many spectators see – it's on the approach from Stratford station, with visitors crossing a vast bridge that conceals the training pool, a river and a railway line. The Aquatics Centre was designed by Iraqi-born architect Zaha Hadid in typically uncompromising style. Its talking point is the huge, wave-shaped roof – steel and glass on the outside, treated timber within – that is flanked by 42m-high temporary stands on either side. These will accommodate the majority of spectators, with a smaller number seated on permanent concrete terracing. Inside, there are a 50m competition pool, 25m competition diving pool and a 50m warm-up pool. The first of 180,000 pool tiles was laid by world record-holding swimmer Mark Foster on 23 September 2010; the venue as a whole will use more than 800,000 ceramic tiles.

Located next door to the Aquatics Centre, the 5,000-capacity Water Polo Arena is to be one of several temporary structures in the Olympic Park. Work on it began in spring 2011.

🤿 *Aquatics – Diving*
🏊 *Aquatics – Swimming*
🤽 *Aquatics – Synchronised Swimming*
🤽 *Aquatics – Water Polo*
🏊 *Modern Pentathlon – Swimming*
🏊 *Paralympic Swimming*

Velodrome & BMX Track

At the northern end of the North-East Concourse, between the Basketball Arena and Eton Manor.

Until the Olympic Park opens to ticket-holders, the Velodrome will remain the least accessible of the three key venues to curious onlookers: the Stadium (*see p32*) and Aquatics Centre (*see left*) can be admired from the riverbank, but the Velodrome is set back from the river beside a major arterial road. It's a shame, because this 6,000 capacity venue, shaped like a Pringle crisp, is a stunner. Sir Chris Hoy – four career golds and a major part of the UK's cycling

London 2012

London 2012 venues: Greater London area

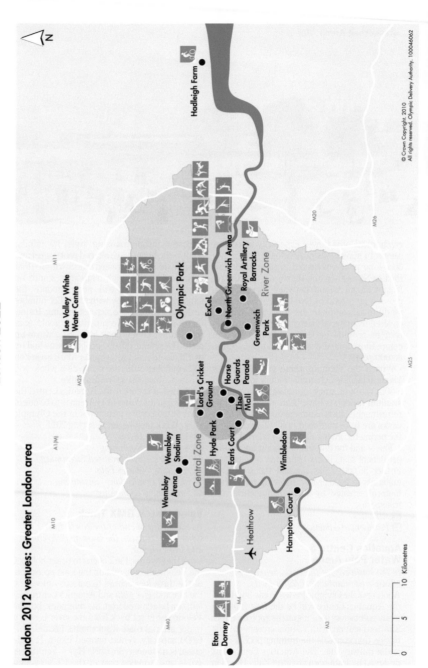

triumph at Beijing 2008 – helped to select the winning design team for the Velodrome. Inside, the slope of the track and the best temperature have been carefully worked out to produce the optimal conditions for fast rides. The track is made of sustainable Siberian pine wood and the whole structure built from lightweight materials (including another cable-net roof) to keep transport and manufacture emissions low. Great pains have been taken to use daylight, rather than artificial lighting, and natural ventilation. The Velodrome even catches rainwater for recycling. Unimpressed by the engineering? Aesthetes will get great views of east London via a glass wall between upper and lower seating.

Work started on the BMX Track, right next door, in spring 2011. There will be temporary seating during the Games, and afterwards the track is to be relocated to form part of the VeloPark.

Cycling – BMX
Cycling – Track
Paralympic Cycling – Track

Basketball Arena

In the north-east of the Park, between the Velodrome and the Athletes' Village, on the North-East Concourse.

It will have a capacity of 12,000 , making it the Olympic Park's third-largest venue, and is going to be one of the busiest parts of the Park, with events happening daily throughout the Games, but the Basketball Arena is only temporary. In fact, it's one of the largest impermanent structures built for any Games. Erected in only three months, it is covered with a stretched white material that will be used for light projections during London 2012, in a style perhaps reminiscent of the Beijing 2008 Water Cube.

Basketball (preliminary rounds; women's quarter-finals)
Handball (men's quarter-finals; men's & women's semi-finals, finals)
Wheelchair Basketball
Wheelchair Rugby

Eton Manor

In the most northerly section of the Olympic Park.

Perhaps the lowest profile of the Park's new, permanent constructions, this venue is on the site of the early 20th-century Eton Manor Sports Club, which had fallen into disuse by 2001. For the Games themselves, it will contain three 50m training pools for the Swimming

and smaller pools for the other Aquatics disciplines, as well as a 5,000-capacity show court set aside for the Wheelchair Tennis. Memorials to sportsmen from the original club who died in World War I and II, moved off-site during construction, will return once the work is complete – and remain here after the Games, when Eton Manor will become a sports centre with facilities for Tennis, Hockey and 5-a-side Football.

Wheelchair Tennis

Handball Arena

On the west side of the Park, just off the North-West Concourse, between the Olympic Stadium and the Hockey Centre.

The Handball Arena is a sleek, boxy modernist structure, but its appearance is designed to change over time: the exterior is adorned with around 3,000sq m of copper cladding that is intended to age and weather. Green initiatives include 88 pipes through the roof to let in natural light and reduce the need for artificial lighting, and rainwater pipes for recycling water. The athletes might be more excited about the sprung wood floor in the competition area. After the Games, a combination of permanent and retractable seating will enable the venue to be converted into a flexible indoor sports centre.

Handball (preliminary rounds; women's quarter-finals)
Modern Pentathlon – Fencing
Goalball

Hockey Centre

At the north end of the North-West Concourse, west of the Velodrome.

The Hockey Centre will have two pitches: the main one will have a capacity of 16,000, while the smaller will be principally intended for warming up. It is hoped that, after the Games, both pitches will be moved north to Eton Manor (*see left*).

Hockey
Paralympic 5-a-side & 7-a-side Football

CENTRAL ZONE

Taking the 2012 Games right into the very heart of tourist London, the Central Zone mixes sightseeing (**Horse Guards Parade**, **Hyde Park**) and sporting history (**Lord's Cricket Ground**, **Earls Court**).

London 2012

Olympic Park. *See p32.*

Earls Court

Warwick Road, SW5 9TA. Earl's Court or West Brompton tube. **Map** p34.

Usually associated with trade shows and concerts (this is where Pink Floyd built *The Wall*), the concrete Exhibition Centre has a strong Olympic past: it hosted the Boxing, Gymnastics and Wrestling for the 1948 Games. Built in 1937, the building has a certain retro flair: its architect also designed 1920s movie palaces. It will have a capacity of 15,000.
Volleyball

Horse Guards Parade

Horse Guards Road, SW1A 2BJ. Charing Cross tube/rail or Westminster tube. **Map** p34.

Best known for the Changing of the Guard and Trooping the Colour, this large parade ground is open along its eastern side to sleepy St James's Park (*see p144*). For London 2012, a temporary venue for Beach Volleyball will have a capacity of 15,000 – which might even manage to bring a smile to the lips of the legendarily deadpan Horse Guards.
Volleyball – Beach

Hyde Park

Hyde Park, W2 2UH. Hyde Park Corner, Lancaster Gate, Knightsbridge or Queensway tube. **Map** p34.

London's largest Royal Park (*see p143*) will provide one of the most scenic backdrops for London 2012. Triathletes will swim 1,500m in the Serpentine boating lake, cycle 40km over seven laps of the park's perimeter, taking in Constitution Hill and Buckingham Palace, and then run 10km around the lake in four equal laps. A 3,000-seat grandstand will have a clear view of the finish line. The Marathon Swimming 10km event will see athletes complete six laps of the Serpentine.
Aquatics – Swimming (Marathon Swimming)
Triathlon

Lord's Cricket Ground

St John's Wood Road, NW8 8QN. St John's Wood tube. **Map** p34.

Established in 1814, Lord's is the spiritual home of cricket (*see p163*). But, while much of the world remains immune to the charms of our summer sport, the 2012 Games will use this splendid setting instead to showcase a sport of far longer pedigree: Archery. The juxtaposition of the regal Victorian pavilion and the strikingly modern white pod of the media centre should be enjoyed by all spectators.
Archery

RIVER ZONE

This selection of venues is scattered north and south across the divide of the River Thames, with **Greenwich Park**, **North Greenwich Arena** and the **Royal Artillery Barracks** on the southern side, and **ExCeL** among the docks to the north.

ExCeL

1 Western Gateway, Royal Victoria Dock, E16 1XL. Custom House or Prince Regent DLR. **Map** p34.

Located between Canary Wharf and London City Airport, this convention centre is right on Royal Victoria Dock. For the London 2012 Games, ExCeL's 45,000sq m and two halls will be divided into five arenas accommodating 13 sports – it is to host the largest number of events of any venue outside the Olympic Park.

Boxing
Fencing
Judo
Table Tennis
Taekwondo
Weightlifting
Wrestling
Boccia
Paralympic Judo
Powerlifting
Paralympic Table Tennis
Volleyball – Sitting
Wheelchair Fencing

Greenwich Park

Greenwich Park, Greenwich, SE10 8XJ. Cutty Sark DLR or Greenwich DLR/rail. **Map** p34.

Greenwich Park (*see p143*) was, appropriately enough, a former royal hunting ground. Spectators will pack an arena set behind the National Maritime Museum (*see p119*) and the grand colonnades of the Old Royal Naval Hospital (*see p101*).

Equestrian – Dressage
Equestrian – Eventing
Equestrian – Jumping
Modern Pentathlon – Riding, Combined Event
Paralympic Equestrian

North Greenwich Arena

Millennium Way, North Greenwich, SE10 0PH. North Greenwich tube. **Map** p34.

Derided as an exorbitant New Labour vanity project when it opened in 2000, Lord Rogers' striking Millennium Dome has made a major comeback. As the North Greenwich Arena, it will play a major role in London 2012. A proposed cable car link with ExCeL (*see p71*) looks set to become reality.

Basketball (men's quarter-finals; men's & women's semi-finals, finals)
Gymnastics – Artistic
Gymnastics – Trampoline
Wheelchair Basketball

Royal Artillery Barracks

Greenwich, SE18 4BH. Woolwich Arsenal rail. **Map** p34.

Built in 1776, the Royal Artillery Barracks has the country's longest Georgian façade. To convert the area for Shooting and Paralympic Archery, a 62ft-high safety screen will be erected. Outdoor ranges are being built for Trap and Skeet; the Pistol and Rifle shooting will be held indoors. Grandstands, seating 7,500 spectators, will be built for each range.

Shooting
Paralympic Archery
Paralympic Shooting

WEMBLEY & WIMBLEDON

Providing a counterweight to the east London focus of the 2012 Games, these

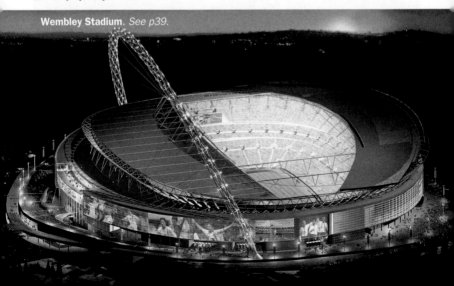

Wembley Stadium. *See p39.*

London 2012

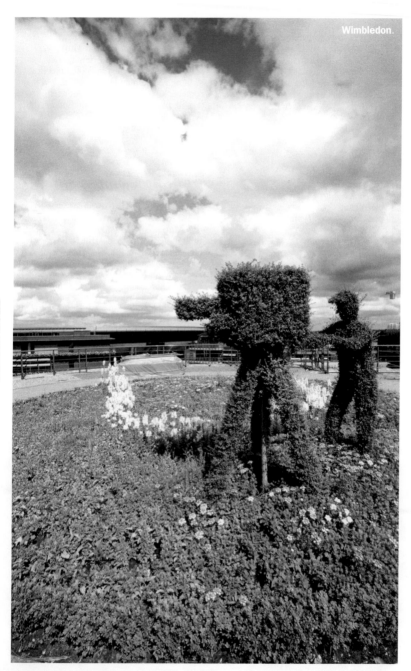

Wimbledon.

iconic venues are in the city's north-west (**Wembley**) and west (**Wimbledon**).

Wembley Stadium

Stadium Way, Wembley, Middx HA9 0WS. Wembley Park tube or Wembley Stadium rail. **Map** p34.

Lord Foster's reworked Wembley Stadium (*see p172*) will be a grand setting for several games during the London 2012 Football competition, including the finals. With a capacity of 90,000, it is Europe's second-largest stadium, and its 317m arch became an instant landmark when the new stadium opened back in 2007.

🔲 *Football*

Wembley Arena

Arena Square, Engineers Way, Wembley, Middx HA9 0DH. Wembley Park tube. **Map** p34.

Most Londoners know Wembley Arena as a music venue, but it was originally built in 1934 to host the Empire Games (forerunner of the Commonwealth Games). It has good Games credentials, having been the location for the Swimming in the 1948 Games. For London 2012, the Arena will have a capacity of 13,800.

🔲 *Badminton*
🔲 *Gymnastics – Rhythmic*

Wimbledon

All England Lawn Tennis Club, Church Road, Wimbledon, SW19 5AE. Southfields tube. **Map** p34.

There could only be one setting for the London 2012 Tennis competition: the world's only world-class grass-court venue, home of the game's most prestigious Grand Slam tournament (*see p15*). The revamped Centre Court, first used in 2009, seats 13,800 spectators.

🔲 *Tennis*

OUTSIDE LONDON

The following venues range from those on the fringes of London (**Hadleigh Farm**; **Eton Dorney**; **Lee Valley White Water Centre**) to the south coast, a hundred miles away (**Weymouth & Portland**). The Olympic Football competition might take you further yet: portions of the event will take place in Scotland (**Hampden Park**, Glasgow) and Wales (the **Millennium**

Factfile 2012

Some things you might not know.

The Games
10,500 Olympic athletes competing for 205 nations
4,200 Paralympic athletes competing for 162 nations
302 Olympic events over 19 days
503 Paralympic events over 11 days
34 venues, with five new permanent venues within the Olympic Park
70,000 volunteers
10.8 million tickets available for the Olympic and Paralympic Games, 75% of which are available to members of the public

The venues
More than 10,000 workers involved at the peak of construction on the Olympic Park and Athletes' Village
1mm – the accuracy to which the Olympic Stadium running track will be laid
723 inches – size of the two Panasonic TV screens inside the Olympic Stadium
More than 800,000 tiles used in the Aquatics Centre
26°C – the temperature (plus or minus 1°C) of the Aquatics Centre pools
28°C – the temperature at track level during races at the Velodrome

The equipment
510 adjustable hurdles
600 basketballs, **800** Water Polo balls and **2,400** footballs
270,000 clay targets (Shotgun)
1,630 metal discs (Weightlifting)
150 sets of Paralympic black-out goggles
200 gate poles for the Canoe Slalom

The Olympic parklands
250 different species in the London 2012 Garden
300,000 wetland plants and more than **30 bridges** to span the rivers and railways in the Olympic Park
100 hectares of open space
1.8m tonnes of material delivered to the Olympic Park by rail
98% of construction waste has been reused, recycled or recovered

The coverage
4 billion potential global audience
20,000 accredited media, to be served around **50,000 meals** a day

London 2012

Olympic Park. *See p32.*

Stadium, Cardiff), as well as the north of England (**Old Trafford**, Manchester; **St James' Park**, Newcastle) and the Midlands (**City of Coventry Stadium**).

Eton Dorney

Dorney Lake, off Court Lane, Dorney, Windsor, Berks SL4 6QP. Maidenhead, Slough or Windsor & Eton Riverside rail (approx 15-45mins from London Paddington station).

The 2012 Games should liven things up at Eton College, posh alma mater of Prime Minister David Cameron and London Mayor Boris Johnson. The lake, set in 400 acres of park, had a dry run for the Games when it hosted the 2006 Rowing World Championships, but subsequent improvements to the eight-lane, 2,200m course and the warm-up lanes were completed in summer 2010, along with a new cut-through and two bridges. The venue is expecting 30,000 visitors daily.

🛶 *Canoe Sprint*
🚣 *Rowing*
🚣 *Paralympic Rowing*

Hadleigh Farm

Castle Lane, Benfleet, Essex SS7 2AP. Leigh-on-Sea or Benfleet rail (approx 45-50mins from London Fenchurch Street station).

Hadleigh Farm is a mix of woodland, pasture, hay meadow and marsh, with glorious views of the Thames Estuary and a ruined 13th-century castle. The hilly terrain is ideal for hosting the

Mountain Bike competition and will have a temporary stadium for spectators.
🚵 *Cycling – Mountain Bike*

Lee Valley White Water Centre

Station Road, Waltham Cross, Herts EN9 1AB. Waltham Cross rail (approx 30mins from London Liverpool Street station).

The brand-new White Water Centre is located at the far northern end of Lee Valley Regional Park (*see p146*). The first new London 2012 venue to open to the public in spring 2011, it has two white-water courses. The 300m competition course and 160m training course are both fed from a starting lake filled with 25,000 cubic metres of water – enough to fill 5,000 Olympic-sized swimming pools. The lake pumps 15 cubic metres of water per second down the course, with parts of the course reaching 7mph.
🛶 *Canoe Slalom*

Weymouth & Portland

Weymouth & Portland National Sailing Academy, Osprey Road, Portland, Dorset DT5 1SA. Weymouth rail (approx 2hrs 40mins to 3hrs from London Waterloo station).

Improvements to the Weymouth & Portland National Sailing Academy were ready for competition by 2008 – making this the first London 2012 venue of any type to be finished. The new slipway, moorings and other facilities have already been used for several international events.
⛵ *Sailing*
⛵ *Paralympic Sailing*

London 2012 Olympic Games Schedule

SPORT	VENUE	W 25	Th 26	F 27	Sa 28	Su 29	M 30	Tu 31	W 1	Th 2	F 3	Sa 4	Su 5	M 6	Tu 7	W 8	Th 9	F 10	Sa 11	Su 12
		JULY							AUGUST											
Opening Ceremony	Olympic Stadium p32			•																
Closing Ceremony	Olympic Stadium p32																			•
Archery	Lord's Cricket Ground p36			•	•	•	•	•	•	•	•									
Athletics	Olympic Stadium p32										•	•	•	•	•	•	•	•	•	
Athletics – Marathon	The Mall												•							•
Athletics – Race Walk	The Mall											•						•		
Badminton	Wembley Arena p39				•	•	•	•	•	•	•	•								
Basketball	Basketball Arena p35				•	•	•	•	•	•	•	•	•	•	•					
	North Greenwich Arena p37															•	•	•	•	•
Beach Volleyball	Horse Guards Parade p36				•	•	•	•	•	•	•	•	•	•	•	•				
Boxing	ExCeL p36				•	•	•	•	•	•	•	•	•	•	•	•	•	•	•	•
Canoe Slalom	Lee Valley White Water Centre p40					•	•	•	•	•										
Canoe Sprint	Eton Dorney p40													•	•	•	•	•	•	
Cycling – BMX	BMX Circuit p33															•	•	•		
Cycling – Mountain Bike	Hadleigh Farm p40																		•	•
Cycling – Road	London				•	•			•											
Cycling – Track	Velodrome p33									•	•	•	•	•	•					
Diving	Aquatics Centre p33								•		•	•	•	•	•	•	•	•	•	
Equestrian – Dressage	Greenwich Park p37									•	•				•		•			
Equestrian – Eventing	Greenwich Park p37				•	•	•	•												
Equestrian – Jumping	Greenwich Park p37											•	•	•		•				
Fencing	ExCeL p36				•	•	•	•	•	•	•	•	•							
Football	City of Coventry Stadium, Coventry	•	•		•		•	•		•		•					•			
	Hampden Park, Glasgow	•	•		•				•		•									
	Millennium Stadium, Cardiff	•	•		•		•	•	•	•	•						•			
	Old Trafford, Manchester		•			•	•	•	•		•			•	•					
	St James' Park, Newcastle		•			•	•	•	•	•	•									
	Wembley Stadium p39					•	•	•	•	•	•			•	•		•		•	
Gymnastics – Artistic	North Greenwich Arena p37				•	•	•	•	•	•				•	•	•				
Gymnastics – Rhythmic	Wembley Arena p39																•	•	•	•
Gymnastics – Trampoline	North Greenwich Arena p37									•	•									
Handball	Handball Arena p35				•	•	•	•	•	•	•	•	•	•	•					
	Basketball Arena p35															•	•	•	•	•
Hockey	Hockey Centre p35				•	•	•	•	•	•	•	•	•	•	•	•	•	•	•	
Judo	ExCeL p36				•	•	•	•	•	•	•									
Modern Pentathlon	Handball Arena p35, Aquatics Centre p33 & Greenwich Park p37																		•	•
Rowing	Eton Dorney p40				•	•	•	•	•	•	•	•								
Sailing	Weymouth & Portland p40					•	•	•	•	•	•	•	•	•	•	•	•	•	•	
Shooting	Royal Artillery Barracks p37				•	•	•	•	•	•	•	•	•	•						
Swimming	Aquatics Centre p33				•	•	•	•	•	•	•	•								
Swimming – Marathon	Hyde Park p36																	•	•	
Synchronised Swimming	Aquatics Centre p33												•	•	•		•	•		
Table Tennis	ExCeL p36				•	•	•	•	•	•	•	•	•	•	•	•				
Taekwondo	ExCeL p36															•	•	•	•	
Tennis	Wimbledon p39				•	•	•	•	•	•	•	•	•							
Triathlon	Hyde Park p36														•		•			
Volleyball	Earls Court p36				•	•	•	•	•	•	•	•	•	•	•	•	•	•	•	•
Water Polo	Water Polo Arena p33					•	•	•	•	•	•	•	•	•	•	•	•	•	•	•
Weightlifting	ExCeL p36				•	•	•	•	•		•	•	•	•	•					
Wrestling – Freestyle	ExCeL p36																•	•	•	•
Wrestling – Greco-Roman	ExCeL p36													•	•	•				

NOTES

For more information, see www.london2012.com.

London 2012

Make it a great day out in London

With fun toys, gifts, books and accessories from The London 2012 Shop, located conveniently at St Pancras International, Paddington Station, Heathrow Terminal 5 and John Lewis Oxford Street.

london2012.com/shop

Visit

TICKETS

Regular ticketing updates about the London 2012 Olympic Games and Paralympic Games are available at www.tickets.london2012.com. There are special prices for young people and seniors across all 26 Olympic sports; tickets for the 20 sports of the Paralympic Games are priced to encourage families and groups to attend. Spectators with tickets for Games events in London will receive a Games Travelcard to use on public transport in London on the day of their event (see below).

GETTING AROUND

If you're planning your visit for 2012, you will need to think carefully about your travel arrangements. London is a big and busy city and lots will be going on during the Games, so you may need to travel differently to other visits to the capital. Follow these top tips when planning your travel:

● You will receive a one-day Games Travelcard with your event ticket for events in or around London. The Games Travelcard will entitle you to travel within zones 1-9 in London and by National Rail between London and the recommended stations for venues in London, and venues near London

(Eton Dorney, the Lee Valley White Water Centre and Hadleigh Farm). Games events include all ticketed sporting events and the Opening and Closing Ceremonies.

● Allow plenty of time to travel to and between venues, because London's transport system will be much busier than usual. Remember to allow for queuing times and walking within large venues, particularly with small children. When applying for tickets to events in London, make sure you allow two to three hours to travel between venues on the same day.

● Children aged ten and under travel for free within London. There are concession fares for 11- to 15-year-olds, 16- to 18-year-olds and students aged 18+. More information is available at www.tfl.gov.uk.

● Travelling by the 2012 Games coach service avoids passengers needing to interchange in central London, as coaches drop off and pick up at London 2012 venues. This may be a good option if you are travelling with younger children.

● Park-and-ride is a good, easy and reasonably priced way to attend events at the Olympic Park, ExCeL and venues on the outskirts of London, particularly if you're coming from outside London. Most park-and-ride sites are close to

venues and transfers by shuttle buses will be short. Park-and-ride services must be reserved in advance, so book early to make sure you get a parking space. However, do not drive to venues. There is no public parking available at, or near, any of the Olympic or Paralympic venues.

● Cycling to venues is much easier than you may think, and offers an easy and fun way of getting to your event. You could make a day of it by combining a cycle trip to visitor attractions on the way to or from your event. Cycle parking at each venue will be suitable for both adults' and children's bicycles.

● Visit www.london2012.com/travel for more information and advice on travelling to your event. London 2012 has produced travel tools and tips to make planning your travel easier.

ACCOMMODATION

New hotels are starting to appear near the Olympic Park – and there are plenty of business chains around Greenwich. If you are staying in central London, plan your journey carefully and allow plenty of time for travelling around the city. For more information on hotels, visit www.timeout.com/london.

London 2012

London 2012

My London 2012
Matt, 16

How will you be participating in the London 2012 Olympic and Paralympic Games?
As part of the London 2012 Young Leaders Programme, 100 young people from disadvantaged areas will have the opportunity to take a volunteering role during the Games. I'm hoping to be one of them.

How did you come to be involved?
The school thought I would benefit from being involved.

Tell us about what you have been working on as part of the Young Leaders Programme?
I've painted a mural for the London 2012 Games which I'm taking around local primary schools to inspire children to take part in sport and London 2012.

What do you hope your involvement in London 2012 will inspire you to achieve after the Games have finished?
I'd definitely like to work on another Olympic Games. Before taking part in the Young Leaders Programme, I wouldn't have dreamed of leading a project. But now my project management skills have improved immensely.

Which events would you like to see during London 2012?
Hockey – I used to play and now I coach hockey. I'd like to take my team to one of the events to see the sport at the highest level. I'd also love to see the Boxing.

London 2012

Sightseeing

Attractions

Take your pick from a cornucopia of capital treats.

Seeing the sights in London is a truly exciting prospect. Many of its buildings and attractions – from the very old to the very new – are world-famous, but there are lots of secret gems to be discovered too. From big-hitters like **Buckingham Palace** (*see p57*), the **Tower of London** (*see p60*) and **St Paul's Cathedral** (*see p51*) to the lesser known delights of **Dennis Severs' House** (*see p50*) and the **Centre of the Cell** (*see p60*), there is something for everyone in the capital.

Many of London's top tourist attractions charge high entry fees, so pick and choose carefully to make sure your child gets the most out of each experience. To help you along the way, we've looked at how they can be best enjoyed from a child's perspective, marking our recommended age ranges for each attraction in green.

ASTRONOMY

Royal Observatory & Planetarium

Greenwich Park, SE10 9NF (8312 6565, www.rog.nmm.ac.uk). Cutty Sark DLR or Greenwich DLR/rail. **Open** 10am-5pm daily (last entry 4.30pm). *Tours* phone for details. **Admission** free. *Space Safari* £6.50; £4.50 3-16s, reductions; free under-3s; £17.50 family (2+2). *Tours* free. **Credit** AmEx, MC, V. **3+ (5+ for shows)**

The start of each new day, and each new year, begins here. In the courtyard is the Greenwich Meridian Line, where visitors can stand with one foot in the Western Hemisphere and one in the Eastern, although from March 2011 it will cost £10 per person to do so. This imposing set of buildings is part of a World Heritage site and grouped in with the National Maritime Museum (*see p119*). The observatory, which was originally built for Charles II by Wren in 1675, underwent a £15m refurbishment in 2007. The Peter Harrison Planetarium is the impressive result. Inside, shows about the stars are presented by a Royal Observatory astronomer who tailors the material to the audience. A Space Safari lets under-sevens follow Ted the Teddy Bear into the galaxy; a Sky Tonight show lets over-fours explore the sky.

Neighbouring galleries chart timekeeping since the 14th century, and the observatory's dome houses the largest refracting telescope in the country. In the courtyard is a summerhouse, home to London's only public camera obscura.

The moving, real-time view of Greenwich and the Thames is best seen on a bright day. *See also p132* **Neighbourhood Watch**. *Buggy access (courtyard only). Café. Nappy-changing facilities. Nearest picnic place: Greenwich Park. Shop.*

BIRD'S EYE VIEWS

London Eye

Riverside Building (next to County Hall), Westminster Bridge Road, SE1 7PB (0870 990 8883, www.londoneye.com). Westminster tube or Waterloo tube/rail. **Open** *Sept-June* 10am-8.30pm daily. *July, Aug* 10am-9.30pm daily. **Admission** £18.60; £15 reductions (not offered at weekends, or July & Aug); £9.54 4-15s; free under-4s. Fast Track tickets £28.50. **Credit** AmEx, MC, V. **Map** p333 M8. **All ages**

The London Eye has become a firm favourite with Londoners and visitors alike. The majestic circle rising above the Thames can be glimpsed from all corners of the capital, from Tottenham Court Road to Parliament Hill. It's very near the top of every child's must-do list. Some kids, expecting a more white-knuckle affair, express disappointment that it turns so slowly, but there's no other view in London like it. Each ride (or flight, as the ticket office has it) is one complete revolution and takes half an hour – long enough to have a good look at the Queen's back garden and trace the snaking Thames.

The queues for tickets can be long, especially on clear days, but you can book a Fast Track ticket online which allows you to turn up just 15 minutes before the ride (there's a hefty tariff for the convenience). Night flights provide a twinkly experience, and the Eye gets festive with fairy lights at Christmas. You can also host a kids' party onboard with face painters, party hats and a birthday cake. Visit the website for special Eye and river cruise packages.

Buggy access. Café. Disabled access: toilet. Nappy-changing facilities. Nearest picnic place: Jubilee Gardens. Shop.

Monument

Monument Street, EC3R 8AH (7626 2717, www.themonument.info). Monument tube. **Open** 9.30am-5pm daily. **Admission** £3; £2 reductions; £1 5-15s; free under-5s. **No credit cards. Map** p335 Q7. **6+**

The tallest freestanding stone column in the world was designed by Christopher Wren and is a monument to the Great Fire of London of 1666. It is 61m (202ft) high, and located 61m (202ft) west of the exact location of the bakery in Pudding Lane where the fire broke out. The Monument won several architectural awards in 2010 for its recent refurbishment; the stone has been cleaned, the golden orb re-gilded and there's an improved viewing gallery at the top. Children who make it up the 311 steps can expect two treats: spectacular views and a commemorative certificate for the climb.

Nearest picnic place: riverside by London Bridge.

Tower Bridge Exhibition

Tower Bridge, SE1 2UP (7403 3761, www.towerbridge.org.uk). Tower Hill tube or Tower Gateway DLR. **Open** *Apr-Sept* 10am-6.30pm daily (last entry 5.30pm). *Oct-Mar* 9.30am-6pm daily (last entry 5pm). **Admission** £7; £5 reductions; £3 5-15s; free under-5s; £16 family (2+2). **Credit** AmEx, MC, V. **Map** p335 R8. **6+**

Tourists often refer to this bridge as London Bridge, but the two enormous towers offer some clue as to its proper identity. Its majestic structure (formed to support the bascules that raise when a ship needs to come through) is expecting 22,000 litres of blue paint to be aimed at it over the next four years in a programme of conservation. A lift takes you to the walkway foyer, 42m (138ft) above the Thames, where you watch a short film on the history of the bridge, then pass through both walkways to catch the stupendous views to the east and west. Large aerial photographs pinpoint famous landmarks (kids can take a playsheet and tick them off), and there are photo points where you can slide open the windows to get an unimpeded shot. Ring for details of children's events in the school holidays and for when the famous bascules will next be raised. From the walkways, it's a short stroll along to the south tower and the Victorian engine rooms, for a more thorough explanation of the hydraulics involved.

Buggy access. Disabled access: lift, toilet. Nappy-changing facilities. Nearest picnic place: Potters Field, Tower of London Gardens. Shop.

Sightseeing

London Eye.

Neighbourhood Watch
South Bank & Bankside

Skateboarders, street entertainers sky-high ferris wheels and sublime theatre, music and art combine to make the South Bank London's cultural capital par excellence. Add in the mighty Thames and the traffic-free views of a succession of city landmarks (Big Ben, St Paul's, the Tower of London) on the other side of the water, and you have all the ingredients for a brilliantly vibrant family day out. The wide, riverside promenade makes the ideal track for wheels of any sort (scooters, bikes or skates), while the concrete steps, slopes and drop-offs are a daredevil's dream – children of all ages will be impressed by the skate skills on display at the skateboarders' pit underneath the Hayward Gallery.

And if you fancy getting to know London's river a little better, there are countless boat trips from the London Eye pier, or grab a pair of walking boots and set off east or west on the long-distance **Thames Path**, which follows the river for 184 miles from its source in the Cotswolds, through the heart of London, to finish at the Thames Barrier in Greenwich.

The arts

The 2,900-seat **Royal Festival Hall** (*see p192*) is home to the prestigious London Philharmonic Orchestra, which organises three hugely popular FUNharmonics concerts each year – a wonderful introduction to classical music for youngsters, who also have the opportunity to try out some of the instruments before and after the concerts. Another surefire winner is the Southbank Centre's Imagine children's festival in February, featuring everything from dance to stand-up comedy. The RFH also hosts lots of free dance, music and poetry performances and events for families in the foyer or out on the terrace; check online for details. Since 2009, a large purple cow known as **Udderbelly** has squatted just the other

BFI IMAX.

side of Hungerford Bridge from the RFH during May, June and July, hosting a preview of Edinburgh Festival treats including comedy, music, circus and theatre, along with lots of children's shows and workshops.

The light, bright **Hayward Gallery** (*see p77*) is free for under-12s and exhibitions here often succeed in engaging both adults and children, such as Antony Gormley's Blind Light show a few years ago. Further east is the **BFI Southbank** (*see p195*); on Saturday mornings, junior film screenings bring a mix of current and classic hits. You can also book a viewing station in the mediathèque and choose from over 1,000 films and TV programmes from the BFI archive.

The **BFI IMAX** (*see p195*), with its 20-metre-high screen, is just around the corner. Kids enjoy wearing the special glasses, and the current fad for 3D films means the storylines no longer play second fiddle to the fantastic effects.

Strolling past the **National Theatre** – home to the free **Watch This Space Festival** (*see p17*) every summer – will take you to **Gabriel's Wharf**, where arts and crafts shops sit alongside cafés and restaurants. This area is always bustling, but never more so than during the **Coin Street Festival** (*see p15*), when it's overtaken by performers celebrating different communities in the capital.

All the events are free, taking place in and around the green spaces of Bernie Spain Gardens.

Head under Blackfriars Bridge, along Queen's Walk. Next stop for the arts is **Tate Modern** (*see p85*), once Bankside Power Station. Children absolutely love this vast gallery, which plans to expand dramatically by 2012 with a new Thameside construction that will soar above the original, increasing gallery space by some 65 per cent. For now, though, even the sloping entrance to the Turbine Hall is exciting to young eyes, and once inside, the sheer scale of the hall gives them pause for thought.

Further along Bankside is the distinctive **Shakespeare's Globe** (*see p213*), which offers guided tours of the building and seasonal performances of the bard's classics, interspersed with other works.

History writ large

At Southwark Bridge, one wall is covered with an etching depicting the frost fairs when the Thames was 'frozen o'er'. Walk as far as you can by the river until you are diverted past the Vinopolis wine museum, down Clink Street and straight to the **Clink Prison Museum** (*see p113*), where unsettling exhibitions reveal what life was like for the prisoners incarcerated here from 1247 to 1780.

Straight ahead, in Pickfords Wharf, is a replica of the **Golden Hinde** (*see p50*), the tiny vessel in which Sir Francis Drake circumnavigated the globe in the 16th century. Just around the corner is **Southwark Cathedral** (*see p53*); its gardens are great for a picnic. Turn left at the cathedral, taking the pavement studded with blue and green lights that

goes under London Bridge (Montague Close). Keep walking until you emerge on Tooley Street, not far from the **London Dungeon** (*see p70*), where London's great disasters and grisly murders are brought garishly to life. Those needing a pit stop and some 21st-century materialist diversions should follow the signs to **Hays Galleria**, a touristy enclave with shops and restaurants. It also houses a ship-like sculpture by David Kemp called *The Navigators*. A rather more substantial vessel looms up ahead, though. Rejoin the Thames footpath to see **HMS Belfast** (*see p117*), a floating wing of the Imperial War Museum that gives a fascinating insight into the cramped conditions on board a World War II warship. Carry on eastwards until you reach **City Hall**, the odd-shaped, glass-sided headquarters of Mayor Boris Johnson, the London Assembly and the Greater London Authority. This is part of a 13-acre development known as More London, which has some sculptural fountains that children love to play in. **Potters Fields Park** is next door, and a great place for a picnic with views of **Tower Bridge** (*see p47*) and the **Tower of London** (*see p60*), across the river.

Refreshments

Also in the area: Giraffe, Nando's, Pizza Express (four branches), Strada, Wagamama.
fish! *Cathedral Street, Borough Market, SE1 9AL (7407 3801, www.fishkitchen.com).* Posh fish and chips.
House of Crêpes *56 Upper Ground, SE1 9PP (7401 9816).* Flippin' lovely pancakes in sweet and savoury forms.
Riverside Terrace Café *Royal Festival Hall, Southbank Centre, SE1 8XX (0871 663 2501).* Arts centre café.
Table *83 Southwark Street, SE1 0HX (7401 2760, www.thetablecafe.com).* Superbly inventive salads, sarnies and hot meals.
Tate Modern Café 2 *2nd Floor, Tate Modern, SE1 9TG (7401 5014, www.tate.org.uk).* Highly recommended for children (*see p241*).

HMS Belfast.

Sightseeing

LIVING HISTORY

Dennis Severs' House

*18 Folgate Street, E1 6BX (7247 4013,
www.dennissevershouse.co.uk). Liverpool
Street tube/rail.* **Open** noon-2pm 1st & 3rd
Mon of mth; Mon evenings (times vary;
booking required); noon-4pm Sun.
Admission £8 Sun; £5 noon-2pm Mon;
£12 Mon evenings. No under-10s. **Credit**
MC, V. **Map** p335 R5. **10+**

This is history as art installation, with a side
order of atmospheric storytelling. Dennis
Severs (1948-1999) was the artist son of a
garage owner from California, who came to
Spitalfields and fell in love with the area and
this house. He restored the house to its original
splendour (living day-to-day sans bathroom,
electricity or modern cooking facilities), created
a fictional Huguenot silk-weaving family to live
in it and opened the doors to the public. Each
of the ten rooms is the scene of a drama, set
between 1724 and 1914. Visitors make their
way from the cellar to the kitchen, and on to the
grander entertaining rooms above, hearing
footsteps, whispers and doors closing, smelling
the scent of pomanders and seeing strewn
clothes and half-eaten meals. It's as if the
inhabitants deserted the rooms seconds before;
Severs called it a 'still life drama'. No museum
can provide an experience quite like it.
*Nearest picnic place: Broadgate Circus
(Liverpool Street Station), Elder Street
Gardens. Shop.*

Golden Hinde

*Pickfords Wharf, Clink Street, SE1 9DG
(7403 0123, www.goldenhinde.com).
Monument tube or London Bridge tube/rail.*
Open daily; times vary. Phone for details.
Tours phone for times. **Admission** £6; £4.50
reductions, 4-16s; free under-4s; £18 family
(2+3). **Credit** MC, V. **Map** p335 P8. **4+**

London's Tudor period is brought to life aboard
this seaworthy replica of Sir Francis Drake's
warship, the first ship to circumnavigate the
globe (in a voyage that began in 1577). It's
surprisingly small, and looks almost like an
expensive model toy. Take a self-guided tour or
join one of the costumed curators for a more
informative visit. Occasional Pirate Fun Days
offer storytelling, a treasure hunt and prizes for
the best pirate costume. Families can also
attend sleepovers, in which participants dress
in period clothes, eat Tudor food, learn ancient
seafaring skills and sleep next to the cannons.
These take place on Saturdays and cost £39.95

per person (minimum age for would-be recruits
is six years old). Costumes and entertainment
are provided; book ahead and bring a sleeping
bag. During the school holidays there are
storytelling sessions, craft activities and special
workshops every weekend. You can also have
a party here; ring or check online for details.
*Nearest picnic place: Southwark Cathedral
Gardens, riverside benches. Shop.*

Houses of Parliament

*Parliament Square, SW1A 0AA (7219
3000 Commons info, 7219 3107 Lords info,
7219 4206 tours, www.parliament.uk).
Westminster tube.* **Open** (when in session)
House of Commons Visitors' Gallery 2.30-
10.30pm Mon, Tue; 11.30am-7.30pm Wed;
10.30am-6.30pm Thur; 9.30am-3pm Fri.
Closed bank hols. *House of Lords Visitors'
Gallery* 2.30-10pm Mon, Tue; 3-10pm Wed;
11am-7.30pm Thur; 10am until close of
business Fri. Check website for debate times.
Tours summer recess only; phone for details
for other times. **Admission** *Visitors' Gallery*
free. *Tours* £15; £10 reductions; £6 5-15s;
free under-5s; £37 family (2+2). **Credit** MC,
V. **Map** p333 L9. **10+**

Built on the site of the Palace of Westminster,
the magnificent structure we see today, with its
1,100 rooms and three miles of corridors, was
rebuilt by Charles Barry and Augustus Pugin.
The coalition government in residence might
make a visit even more interesting for any
youngster learning about politics. Tours run all
year round for UK residents (overseas visitors
must wait until summer opening), when
Parliament is not sitting; visitors can also
attend debates and watch committees in
session. Children are usually satisfied by the
mere proximity of the big old bell known as Big
Ben, but only UK residents over 11 can climb
the Clock Tower to take a closer look. All visits
must be booked ahead through your MP.
*Buggy access. Disabled access: lift, toilet.
Nappy-changing facilities. Nearest picnic
place: Victoria Tower Gardens. Shop.*

Linley Sambourne House

*18 Stafford Terrace, W8 7BH (7602 3316
Mon-Fri, 7938 1295 Sat, Sun, www.rbkc.
gov.uk/linleysambournehouse). High Street
Kensington tube.* **Open** *Tours* (groups
only; max 12 people. Pre-booking essential)
11.15am, 2.15pm Wed; 11.15am, 1pm, 2.15pm,
3.30pm Sat, Sun; also by appointment.
Admission £6; £4 reductions; £1 under-18s.
Credit MC, V. **Map** p330 A9. **5+**

Golden Hinde.

As one of the best examples of a late Victorian middle class home still in existence, this 3D illustrated history lesson is great for children of all ages. Edward Linley Sambourne was a cartoonist and contributor to *Punch*, but it's his wife's diaries that form the basis for the eccentric and enjoyable costumed tours on Saturdays and Sundays offering glimpses into the upstairs-downstairs life of the Sambournes and their servants. There's also a visitors' centre, where children can take part in craftwork sessions relating to objects in the house. *Shop.*

St Paul's Cathedral

Ludgate Hill, EC4M 8AD (7236 4128, www.stpauls.co.uk). St Paul's tube. **Open** 8.30am-4pm Mon-Sat. *Galleries, crypt & ambulatory* 9.30am-4.15pm Mon-Sat. Closed for special services, sometimes at short notice. *Tours* 10.45am, 11.15am, 1.30pm, 2pm Mon-Sat. **Admission** *Cathedral, crypt & gallery* £14.50; £5 7-16s; £13.50 reductions; free under-7s; £34.50 family (2+2). *Tours* £3; £1 7-16s; £2.50 reductions; free under-7s. Audio guide £4; £3.50 reductions. **Credit** MC, V. **Map** p334 O6. **5+**

Despite the sophistication of modern building techniques, none of the high-rise upstarts jutting into the sky near St Paul's can hold a candle to the majesty of the cathedral's dome. You get some idea of the enormity of it from the cathedral's floor, but it's only when you climb the hundreds of winding steps to the top that the sheer scale of the place really hits you (that golden ball just beneath the cross on the dome is big enough to fit ten people inside). The present building is the fourth to sit on the site (on top of Ludgate Hill – the highest point in the City) and was designed by Sir Christopher Wren after the previous incumbent was burned down in the Great Fire of London. Wren had to campaign vociferously to get it built to his specifications – it was nearly vetoed on several occasions as being too ambitious and expensive. The cathedral was thoroughly cleaned for its 300th birthday in 2008, as part of a £40 million restoration project that also included a complete rebuild of the organ and the creation of a new set of ecclesiastical robes by Royal College of Art designer Marie Brisou.

The cathedral recently began offering a children's audioguide, which recounts quirky facts about everything from the organ pipes (some big enough to crawl through) to the unusual events held in the nave (including a cattle market). During Christmas and Easter holidays, there are trails that are rewarded at the end with a small prize; parents who need ideas for a self-guided tour can download the activity sheets for schools. Most fun of all is the Whispering Gallery, 259 steps up from the ground, whose acoustics simply have to be heard to be believed. From there, it's a few more steps up to the Stone Gallery for an amazing 360° view of London. If you're likely to have the energy to ascend further to the Golden Gallery, go early or you may find yourself jostled by boisterous teens on the cramped balcony.

Down in the crypt are the tombs of historical figures such as Nelson, Wellington and Wren; Lawrence of Arabia and Florence Nightingale are honoured with memorials. In 2010, new exhibition Oculus joined the list of underground entertainments (*see p61* **View from the Crypt**). At the back is the shop and Crypt Café. And if you want to experience the true spirit of St Paul's, come for evensong, held every day at 5pm.

Buggy access. Café. Disabled access: lift, ramp, toilet. Nappy-changing facilities. Nearest picnic space: garden. Restaurant. Shops.

Shakespeare's Globe

21 New Globe Walk, Bankside, SE1 9DT (7401 9919, 7902 1500 tour information, www.shakespeares-globe.org). Mansion House tube or London Bridge tube/rail. **Open** *Box office theatre bookings* 10am-6pm daily.

Sightseeing

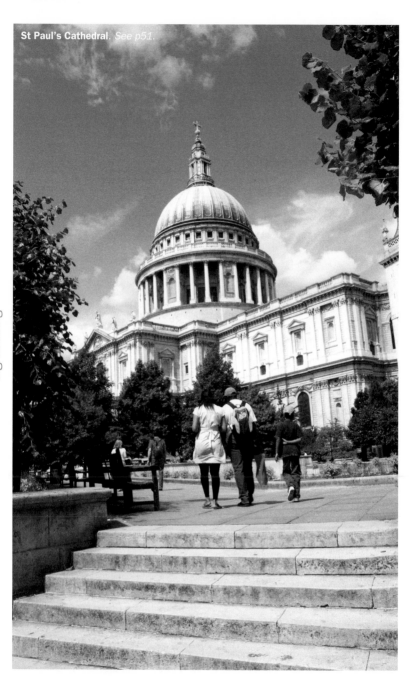

St Paul's Cathedral. *See p51.*

Sightseeing

Tours 9am-5pm daily. May-Sept afternoon tours only visit the Rose Theatre, not the Globe. **Tickets** £5-£33. *Tours* £11.50; £10 reductions; £7 5-15s; free under-5s; £32 family (2+3). **Credit** AmEx, MC, V. **Map** p334 P7. **8+**

Historically authentic performances of Shakespeare's plays make up the bulk of the programme at this riverside reconstruction of the Bard's own theatre, but new theatre also gets a showing. The season runs from late April to early October and in 2011 includes *Hamlet*, *All's Well That Ends Well* and *Much Ado About Nothing*, as well as a world premiere of Chris Hannan's *The God of Soho*. But there's more to visiting this theatre than watching a play. Tours take place all year, and include the UnderGlobe exhibition on the reconstruction, Elizabethan theatres and Shakespeare's London.

There's fun for all around the time of Shakespeare's birthday (23 April) and at the drama sessions for eight to 11s that accompany the theatre season; see the website or ring 7902 1433 for details. The remains of the Rose Theatre (www.rosetheatre.org.uk), where many of the Shakespeare's works were staged, are located around the corner in the basement of an office block.

Café. Disabled access: lift, toilet. Nappy-changing facilities. Nearest picnic place: South Bank benches. Restaurant. Shop.

Southwark Cathedral

London Bridge, SE1 9DA (7367 6700, 7367 6734 tours, www.dswark.org/cathedral). London Bridge tube/rail. **Open** 8am-6pm Mon-Fri; 8.30am-6pm Sat, Sun. *Restaurant* 9am-6pm Mon-Fri; 10am-6pm Sat, Sun. Closed 25 Dec, Good Friday, Easter Sunday. *Services* 8am, 8.15am, 12.30pm, 12.45pm, 5.30pm Mon-Fri; 9am, 9.15am, 4pm Sat; 8.45am, 9am, 11am, 3pm, 6.30pm Sun. **Admission** *Guided Tour* £5; £2.50 1-11s; £4 reductions. **Credit** MC, V. **Map** p335 P8. **5+**

Unusually for an English cathedral, it's hard to get a clear view of this 1,000 year-old place of worship, crammed as it is between the Thames, Borough Market and a major railway line coming out of London Bridge. Once inside, though, its simplistic beauty quickly makes an impression. The church fell into disrepair after the Reformation (one part was used as a bakery, another as a pigsty), but in 1905 it became a cathedral and now has a visitor's centre, a shop and a refectory. The only remaining medieval sections are the choir, lady chapel and north transept. The cathedral's popular, charismatic

and liberal Dean, Colin Slee, died in late 2010 and is replaced by the Rt Rev Christopher Chessun. His memorial will no doubt join existing tributes devoted to the 51 people who drowned in the 1989 Marchioness accident; Shakespeare (and Sam Wanamaker who persevered for over 20 years to get the Globe Theatre built nearby); John Gower; and John Harvard. The windows show images of Chaucer, who set off on a pilgrimage to Canterbury from a pub in Borough High Street, and John Bunyan, who preached locally. In the churchyard, hunt for the flattish, ribbed stone monument to Mahomet Weyomon, a Mohegan chief buried in the churchyard in 1735. He died of smallpox after travelling to London to state his case in the Mohegan Land Dispute.

The cathedral choir is one of the UK's best, and families cram inside to hear it at Christmas. You can also hear the choir sing evensong on Mondays and Thursdays (girls) and Tuesdays, Fridays and Sundays (boys). Joining the choir gives kids a fantastic musical education; phone for audition dates.

Buggy access. Disabled access: lift, ramp, toilet. Nappy-changing facilities. Nearest picnic place: gardens. Restaurant. Shop.

Westminster Abbey

20 Dean's Yard, SW1P 3PA (7222 5152, 7654 4900 tours, www.westminster-abbey.org). St James's Park or Westminster tube, or bus 11, 12, 24, 88, 159, 211. **Open** *Westminster Abbey* June-Sept 9.30am-3.30pm Mon, Tue, Thur, Fri; 9.30am-6pm Wed; 9.30am-3.30pm Sat. Oct-May 9.30am-3.30pm Mon, Tue, Thur, Fri; 9.30am-6pm Wed; 9.30am-1.30pm Sat. *Abbey Museum & Chapter House* 10.30am-4pm daily. *Cloisters* 8am-6pm daily. *College Garden* Apr-Sept 10am-6pm Tue-Thur. Oct-Mar 10am-4pm Tue-Thur (last entry 1hr before closing). *Tours* phone for details. **Admission** £16; £6 11-18s, reductions; free under-11s with adult; £32 family (2+1). *Chapter House* free. *Abbey Museum* free (audio guide free). *Tours* £3. **Credit** AmEx, MC, V. **Map** p333 K9. **5+**

Westminster Abbey is back in the limelight as the venue of choice for William and Kate's recent wedding. It has always had close links with royalty, not least because it has been the Coronation Church since 1066. It was also the scene of the Queen's wedding and Diana's funeral. The body of Edward the Confessor, who built the first church on the site, is entombed in the abbey, though no one knows exactly where: it was removed from its

Sightseeing

Neighbourhood Watch
Westminster

Westminster is London's epicentre of political power, home to the PM's Downing Street digs, the extravagant neo-Gothic Houses of Parliament, the Treasury, the Foreign Office and a hundred minor government sub-offices in between. It is also home to Buckingham Palace and Westminster Abbey, which has hosted every coronation since William the Conqueror. The iconic sights and sounds are endless, from the distinctive peal of Big Ben to the lions in Trafalgar Square, to the scarlet-clad Guards at Buckingham Palace.

National Gallery.

Nelson's patch

Although the official centre of London is just south of here (marked by a small plaque behind the equestrian statue of Charles I), tourist-thronged **Trafalgar Square** is the city's symbolic heart. Laid out in the 1820s by John Nash and once surrounded by busy roads, the square was improved markedly by the pedestrianisation in 2003 of the North Terrace, right in front of the National Gallery. Its delights are timeless: the great lions at the base of **Nelson's Column** are often overrun with children, who shelter between their massive paws or try to clamber astride their surprisingly high sun-warmed backs. Above the throng, Admiral Nelson gazes across the city from atop his 150-foot granite column.

There's plenty going on at his feet, with all manner of protests, performances and free festivals held here throughout the year. Dance a jig to lilting Irish fiddles in celebration of **St Patrick's Day** (*see p24*), see the famous fountains filled with floating lanterns for **Diwali**, or gawp at a fiery-mouthed dragon weaving its way through the revellers welcoming in **Chinese New Year** (*see p23*).

While George IV and two Victorian military heroes occupy three stone pedestals around the perimeter of the square, the fourth plinth showcases contemporary artworks. In 2012,

the plinth will host duo Elmgreen and Dragset's *Powerless Structures, Fig.101*, a bronze sculpture of a boy astride his rocking horse. Katharina Fritsch's *Hahn/Cock*, a giant cockerel in ultramarine blue, will follow in 2013.

Art for all

At the northern edge of Trafalgar Square, follow the broad flight of stairs up to the splendid **National Gallery** (*see p78*). You can pick up various audio tours and trails around the glorious artworks, or design and print out your own bespoke route in the Sainsbury Wing's ArtStart room. Sundays and school holidays are our favourite times to visit, with free art workshops for five to 11s and story sessions for under-fives; enquiring minded toddlers can squeeze on to the magic carpet to learn about a selected painting.

Alternatively, scoot up past the National Gallery and on to the **National Portrait Gallery** (*see p79*), where all sorts of famous faces peer down from the walls. Although the likes of Brunel and Darwin might not hold the kids' attention for long, the promise of David Beckham, Lily Allen and Roald Dahl should help. Afterwards, you can head to the rooftop Portrait Restaurant for a posh afternoon tea and some truly magnificent views.

For more down-to-earth grub and prices, take the kids to the excellent Café in the Crypt at nearby St-Martin-in-the-Fields – also home to the low-key but lovely **London Brass Rubbing Centre** (*see p218*).

All the queen's horses

Another option is to head down Whitehall, keeping your camera at the ready. Why? Well for a start, the dashing chaps of the **Household Cavalry** – and their trusty steeds – are headquartered here. At **Horse Guards Parade**, you can watch the mounted regiment change the Queen's Life Guard at 11am (10am on Sundays). With their shiny coats and well-polished hooves, the horses are every bit as dapper and professional as their riders; for a glimpse of them when they're off duty, visit the **Household Cavalry Museum** (*see p118*), which offers a sneaky peek into the stables. During the **London 2012 Olympic Games**, Horse Guards Parade will play host to an equally photogenic event – it is the venue for the Beach Volleyball competition.

Halfway down Whitehall, **Downing Street** is guarded by a phalanx of policemen. Though the road is closed to the public, you can peep through the heavy iron gates to see No.10. The road leads on to **Parliament Square**, **Westminster Abbey** (*see p53*), and the **Houses of Parliament** (*see p50*) – home, of course, to **Big Ben**.

A palatial park

The Abbey and the home of British politics are interesting for older children, but on a sunny day we'd be tempted to forgo its suits and seriousness in favour of a stroll and a nice ice-cream in **St James's Park** (*see p144*), and a quick peek at **Buckingham Palace** (*see p57*). The Changing of the Guard, as witnessed by Alice and Christopher Robin in AA Milne's famous ditty, takes place in the palace forecourt. The ceremony begins at 11.30am, and is held every day from May to July, then on alternate days for the rest of the year.

Crowds start to build behind the railings around half an hour before the start, and it can get very busy; if all you're really after is a spot of military marching and a gander at the famous bearskin hats, you might be better off mooching up to **St James's Palace** at elevenish. Here, you can get an unobstructed view of the Old Guard setting off along the Mall towards Buckingham Palace.

A no less august ceremony in these parts is the daily feeding of the pelicans at St James's Park. At 2.30pm, the hungry birds gather by the lake to feast on fresh fish; in 2006 one of them managed to swallow a live pigeon, but hasn't been seen to repeat the alarming feat since. They're friendly creatures (so long as you're not a tasty-looking pigeon); if you sit on one of the benches by the lake, you might find one alighting next to you. Afterwards, take the bridge across the lake for a fairytale view of Buckingham Palace, beautifully framed by the trees.

Refreshments

Also in the area: Pizza Express.

Café in the Crypt *St-Martin-in-the-Fields, Duncannon Street, WC2N 4JJ (7736 1158, www.smitf.org)*. Wholesome comfort food and nursery puds, with child-sized portions of main courses available on request.

Inn the Park *St James's Park, SW1A 2BJ (7451 9999, www.innthepark.com)*. Expensive but appealing back-to-British fare, in a sylvan setting; the self-service café area is cheaper than the proper restaurant (*see p250*).

Jom Makan *5-7 Pall Mall East, SW1Y 5BA (7925 2402, www.jommakan. co.uk)*. Noodles, curries and Malaysian street food for daring eaters, plus bite-sized side dishes and satay for cautious kids to try.

National Café East Wing *National Gallery, WC2N 4DN (7747 5942, www.thenationalcafe.com)*. Classic brasserie fare in smart but unstuffy surrounds, plus a simple kids' menu (*see p241*).

Thai Square *21-24 Cockspur Street, SW1Y 5BL (7839 4000, www.thai square.net)*. Hot and spicy fare, just off Trafalgar Square.

Sightseeing

Discover the best of Britain...

elaborate shrine and reburied in an unmarked spot during the Reformation. Henry III was responsible for the Gothic splendour of the current building, which was heavily influenced by the French architectural style of the period. Poets' Corner is the final resting place of Geoffrey Chaucer, and you can also see the graves of Dickens, Dryden, Johnson, Browning and Tennyson. Statues of several 20th-century martyrs (including Martin Luther King) occupy 15th-century niches above the west door.

It is a busy place at any time – during a typical year it can hold up to 1,500 services and worship sessions. You can escape the crowds in the 900-year-old College Garden, one of the oldest cultivated gardens in Britain. The Abbey Museum (Broad Sanctuary; free if you have a ticket to the Abbey, £1 otherwise) is in the vaulted area under the former monks' dormitory, in one of the oldest parts of the Abbey. Here you'll find a collection of effigies and waxworks of British monarchs such as Edward II and Henry VII, wearing the robes they donned in life; the Queen's Coronation robes are also on show. The Choir School is the only school in Britain exclusively for the education of boy choristers from eight to 13; voice trials are held twice a year. Its Christmas services are magnificent. Next door is St Margaret's Church, where the weddings of Samuel Pepys and Winston Churchill (in 1655 and 1908 respectively) took place; Sir Walter Raleigh is buried here.

Buggy access. Café. Disabled access: toilet. Nearest picnic place: College Garden (10am-6pm Tue-Thur), St James's Park. Shop.

PALACES & STRONGHOLDS

Buckingham Palace & Royal Mews

SW1A 1AA (7766 7300, www.royal collection.org.uk). Green Park or St James's Park tube, or Victoria tube/rail. **Open** *State Rooms* 1 Aug-25 Sept 9.45am-3.45pm. *Royal Mews* 3 Jan-25 Mar 11am-3.15pm Mon-Fri; 26 Mar-31 Oct 11am-4.15pm daily; 1 Nov-22 Dec 11am-3.15pm Mon-Sat. *Queen's Gallery* 10am-4.30pm (closes 5.30pm) daily. Closed during Ascot & state occasions. **Admission** *State Rooms* £17.50; £10 5-16s; £16 reductions; free under-5s; £46 family (2+3). *Royal Mews* £7.75; £5 5-16s; £7 reductions; free under-5s; £20.50 family (2+3). *Queen's Gallery* £8; £5 5-16s; £7.25 reductions; free under-5s; £21.25 family (2+3). *Joint ticket* (Royal Mews and Queen's

Gallery) £15.50; £8.75 5-16s; £14 reductions; £40 family (2+3). **Credit** AmEx, MC, V. **Map** p332 H9. **All ages (Royal Mews)**. **5+ (Queen's Gallery)**

While Buckingham Palace is not the world's most beautiful palace, it is probably the most famous, drawing millions of visitors every year. John Nash was originally employed to create a majestic frontage, but his designs were dismissed by Parliament as too expensive. Edward Blore, known at the time as 'Blore the Bore', was given the task of finishing the job after Queen Victoria moved in. She was the first monarch to make Buckingham Palace her home and it has remained the premier residence of the reigning monarch ever since. The famous Changing of the Guard takes place daily in the palace forecourt at 11.30am from May to July, and on alternate days the rest of the year.

The State Rooms were first opened to the public in 1993 (the fire at Windsor Castle the previous year meant the Queen had to raise some cash for reconstructions) and can be seen during August and September, while the Queen is at Balmoral. There are 19 rooms to see in all, including the White Drawing Room. Designed by John Nash and furnished in opulent luxury with treasures from the Royal Collection, this will set the children's imaginations spinning. The Queen's Gallery, open all year round, has changing exhibitions from the Royal Collection. 'Dutch Landscapes' runs until October 2011, and 'The Heart of the Great Alone: Scott, Shackleton and Antarctic Photography' runs from October 2011 to 15 April 2012.

In the gardens, there is a nature trail as well as a new café and family activity room, open during August and September. At the Royal Mews, children can watch the horses being groomed, fed and exercised, and examine the royal Rolls-Royces and the Gold State Coach, last used for the 2002 Golden Jubilee. *See also p54* **Neighbourhood Watch**.

Buggy access. Café. Disabled access: lift, toilet (Buckingham Palace). Nappy-changing facilities (Buckingham Palace). Nearest picnic place: Green Park. Shop.

Eltham Palace

Court Yard, SE9 5QE (8294 2548, www.elthampalace.org.uk). Eltham rail. **Open** *Apr-Oct* 10am-5pm Mon-Wed, Sun. *Feb, Mar, Nov, Dec,* 11am-4pm Mon-Wed, Sun. Closed week before Christmas-31 Jan. **Admission** *House & grounds* (incl audio tour) £9.30; £8.40 reductions; £5.60 5-15s; £24.20 family (2+3); free

Sightseeing

under-5s. *Gardens only* £5.80; £5.20 reductions; £3.50 5-15s; free under-5s.
Credit AmEx, MC, V. **5+**

Eltham Palace was a favourite with the royal family until Henry VIII decided he preferred nearby Greenwich. The palace went into rapid decline, and became a rather grand-looking tenanted farm. The remains of the Tudor palace include a bridge over the moat, as well as the impressive Great Hall. The biggest draw now, though, is the art deco beauty (one of London's architectural treasures) erected adjoining the Great Hall in 1936 by textiles heir Stephen Courtauld. Like his more famous brother Samuel (who founded the Courtauld Institute of Art in 1932), he was a collector of the arts. Stephen and his wife Virginia created a masterpiece, and the house was the scene of many a lavish party before World War II broke out and the building was commandeered by the War Office.

The furniture and fittings look like a film set – check out the pink leather chairs, ornate black and silver doors and moulded maple veneer in the dining room, or the onyx and gold-plated taps in Virginia's glamorous vaulted bathroom. The house was way ahead of its time when it came to mod cons, including underfloor heating, ensuite bathrooms and a quirky vacuum-cleaning system. Upstairs there's a chance to look at the Courtauld family's photos and artefacts, and enjoy a home movie of Stephen and Virginia with their pet lemur, Mahjong (who had his own, specially designed quarters).

The beautiful grounds are the setting for various summer events, like an art deco fair and Tudor trails for kids. The quaint tearoom and shop have a distinctly 1930s flavour.
Café. Disabled access: lift, toilet. Shop.

Fulham Palace & Museum

Bishop's Avenue, off Fulham Palace Road, SW6 6EA (7736 3233, www.fulhampalace. org). Hammersmith or Putney Bridge tube, or bus 220, 414, 430. **Open** 1-4pm Mon-Wed, Sat, Sun. *Tours* phone for details.
Admission *Museum* free; under-16s must be accompanied by an adult. *Tours* £5; free under-16s. **No credit cards. 3+**

This was once the largest moated site in England – the official residence of the Bishops of London from 704 until 1975. Somewhere with this much history doesn't give up its secrets readily, so a tour is a good way to get the most out of a visit. The main house – more manor than palace – is Tudor (try out the echo in the courtyard), with significant Georgian and Victorian additions. Refurbishment has left the East Quadrangle looking beautiful, and the café is a particularly pleasant place to sit. The museum has plenty of new interactive features, lots more room to display treasures dug up in

Tower of London. *See p60.*

the grounds (including a mummified rat found in the roof space of the Tudor courtyard), and a programme of theatre, exhibitions and activities for families: music workshops for nippers between two and five, for example, or craft sessions where over-fives turn out hobby horses or soldier skittles. All activities must be pre-booked; most cost £5-£10 per head. Leave time to admire the gorgeous gardens and make sure the children look out for the Holm Oak, which would have been visible to Elizabeth I when she visited, and the Bishop's Tree, a sculpture on one of the cedar of Lebanon trees on the North Lawn.

Buggy access. Café. Disabled access: toilet (in palace). Nearest picnic place: grounds. Shop.

Hampton Court Palace

East Molesey, Surrey KT8 9AU (0844 482 7777, www.hrp.org.uk). Hampton Court rail/riverboat from Westminster or Richmond to Hampton Court Pier (Apr-Oct). **Open** *Palace* Mar-Oct 10am-6pm daily. Nov-Feb 10am-4.30pm daily. Last entry 45mins before closing. *Park* dawn-dusk daily. **Admission** *Palace, courtyard, cloister & maze* £15.40; £12.65 reductions; £7.70 5-15s; free under-5s; £41.80 family (2+3). *Gardens only* £5.10; £4.40 reductions; free under-16s. *Maze only* £3.85; £2.75 5-15s; free under-5s; £11 family (2+3). **Credit** AmEx, MC, V. **6+**
Henry VIII is always a favourite monarch with children, who are fascinated by his large girth, eccentric ways and habit of having his wives executed. He had many homes, but this one positively oozes historical drama. Shakespeare performed here and Cromwell made it his home after the Civil War. The ghost of Henry's fifth wife, Catherine Howard, who was executed for adultery at the Tower of London, is said to shriek around in the Haunted Gallery.

But although Henry VIII has a reputation as a tyrant, Hampton Court was for the most part a pleasure palace. Archeologists recently found the remains of a wine fountain in the largest of the courtyards, and a lovingly crafted four-metre-tall reconstruction started serving wine from spring 2010. In Henry's time, there were tournaments and feasts, musical entertainment, plays, dances and more. The world famous gardens are truly wonderful, with the maze taking centre stage in any child's itinerary. It's the oldest in the country, having been planted between 1689 and 1694.

You can get to the palace by boat from Westminster, or by train (which is considerably quicker). It's worth the trek. The various Tudor and Baroque buildings sprawl across six acres, with costumed guides adding a lively dimension to the state apartments, courtyards and cloisters. Themed activities are plentiful during the school holidays, and on selected bank holidays and weekends Tudor cookery demonstrations take place in the huge kitchens, where children love the bubbling cauldrons and game bird carcasses (see the website for dates).

Buggy access. Café. Disabled access: lift, toilet. Nappy-changing facilities. Nearest picnic place: palace gardens/picnic area. Restaurant. Shops.

Kensington Palace

Kensington Gardens, W8 4PX (0844 482 7777, www.hrp.org.uk). Bayswater or High Street Kensington tube, or bus 9, 10, 49, 52, 70. **Open** *Mar-Oct* 10am-6pm daily. *Nov-Feb* 10am-5pm daily. Last entry 1hr before closing. **Admission** (incl audio guide) £12.50; £11 reductions; £6.25 5-15s; free under-5s; £34 family (2+3). **Credit** MC, V. **Map** p326 B8. **7+**
The original mansion was turned into a palace by Christopher Wren, as commissioned by William III and Mary II when they came to live here in 1689. Mary died of smallpox here in 1694, Queen Victoria was introduced to her beloved Albert here in 1836 and Princess Diana lived here before her death in 1997. Kensington Palace is undergoing a major refurbishment. When it's completed in 2012, this Jacobean mansion will have a new suite of rooms at the entrance that visitors can explore for free. The Gardens are also being reinterpreted to allow easier access from Kensington Gardens, and there will be a new café to take some of the pressure off the lovely Orangery (*see p255*). For now, though, the palace has an exciting exhibition to enjoy until January 2012. 'The Enchanted Palace' is a dazzling multimedia interpretation of the history of the palace and its inhabitants. At first the exhibition seems confusing – it's dark and hard to navigate – but you soon realise this is part of the thrill. Visitors are ushered up a back stairwell adorned with doodles and echoing with whispering voices. Taking on the quest of finding the hidden names of the palace's princesses is a brilliant way to keep older children occupied, although younger siblings will be equally diverted by the atmosphere, interactive throne and roaming theatre company Wildworks, who pop up in monk-like uniforms when you least expect it.

Buggy access. Disabled access: toilet. Nappy-changing facilities. Nearest picnic place: grounds. Restaurant. Shop.

Sightseeing

Tower of London

Tower Hill, EC3N 4AB (0844 482 7777, www.hrp.org.uk). Tower Hill tube or Tower Gateway DLR, or Fenchurch Street rail. **Open** *Mar-Oct* 10am-5.30pm Mon, Sun; 9am-5.30pm Tue-Sat (last entry 5pm). *Nov-Feb* 10am-4.30pm Mon, Sun; 9am-4.30pm Tue-Sat. *Tours* (outside only, weather permitting) every 30mins until 3.30pm (2.30pm in winter). **Admission** £18.70; £10.45 5-15s; £15.95 reductions; free under-5s; £51.70 family (2+3). Audio guide £4; £3 reductions. *Tours* free. **Credit** AmEx, MC, V. **Map** p335 R7. **5+**

This solid stone building is an iconic London landmark and a distinctive presence on the Thames. Since the early years of the 11th century, the Tower of London has made itself useful to King and country as a fortress, palace, prison, execution ground (two of Henry VIII's wives got the chop here) and tourist attraction. You can easily spend a whole day within its walls. The Medieval Palace, where kings and queens stayed until the reign of Elizabeth I, has recently been restored, and uses smells and sound effects to whisk you back in time. Interactive displays reveal the ordeals of life as a prisoner, while outside, Tower Green is the place where unfortunates such as Anne Boleyn and Lady Jane Grey were beheaded; a glass pillow sculpted by artist Brian Catling marks the spot. Battle nuts love the gleaming armoury on show in the White Tower; the presentation was reinterpreted in 2010 as the 'Fit for a King' exhibition.

The crown jewels are the Tower's biggest draw, with 23,578 gems on display. Highlights include a model of the uncut, fist-sized Cullinan I – the largest diamond in the world – and an illustrated description of how it was cut into nine smaller diamonds. You can't miss the two-metre-wide Grand Punch Bowl – it's big enough to bathe in. The beautiful vaulted chamber of the Bowyer Tower has been open to visitors since 2007. Legend has it that the Duke of Clarence met a grisly fate here in 1478, drowning in a barrel of malmsey wine. The most entertaining way to hear such stories is to join one of the free tours, led by a Yeoman Warder (Beefeater). The Warders, photogenic in their black and red finery, are genial hosts and a mine of information.

Children's trails and quizzes tackle different themes, including Knights and Princesses and the Peasants' Revolt. Check the website for details of daily special events and temporary exhibitions. A new exhibition opening in May 2011 looks at the exciting range of animals that have been housed in the Tower over the centuries as part of the royal menagerie, including elephants, leopards, tigers and grizzly bears.

Buggy access (Jewel House). Café. Nappy-changing facilities. Nearest picnic place: riverside benches, Trinity Square Memorial Gardens. Shops.

SCIENCE

Centre of the Cell

4 Newark Street, E1 2AT (7882 2562, www.centreofthecell.org). Whitechapel tube. **Open** *Sessions* 10-11.30am, noon-1.30pm, 2-3.30pm, 4-5.30pm, 6.30-8pm Mon-Wed, Fri; 10-11.30am, 11.30am-1pm, 3-4.30pm Sat. Session times may vary; phone to check. **Admission** free. **9+**

The RIBA award-winning Blizard Building, which opened late in 2009, is the home of an exciting educational resource for school-age children that might just get them excited about maths and science. Politicians and businessmen regularly complain that our school children aren't going into these subjects in sufficient numbers. Within the medical centre, a glass-walled walkway takes visitors over the labs and their 400 white-coated occupants to a large multimedia 'pod' (designed to take 40 people), which is where the fun takes place. A film introduces children to the amazing work going on around them, then a huge silver tube opens up to reveal more audio-visual magic and interactive jollies illustrating different aspects of biomedical science for key stages 2, 3 and 4. One game compares the size of a cell to a five-pence piece (a quarter of the size of one of the little dots around the coin edge), another charts the growth of an embryo. Other features show how to repair a damaged spinal cord, or grow real skin for grafts; there are even (oo-er!) real body organs. The pod is intended to be regularly updated in line with the discoveries of the boffins in the labs below.

The whole experience lasts around 90 minutes; thanks to the unique setting and the theatricality of the presentation, young 'uns will be entertained throughout – and hardly aware that they're learning things. School holidays see a variety of special events including Family Science Days and various workshops.

Buggy access. Disabled access: lift; toilet. Café. Nearest picnic place: Whitechapel hospital grounds. Shop.

View from the Crypt

Fancy a trip to the top of St Paul's Cathedral? It's now a virtual reality.

For those who can't make it up the 257 steps to the Whispering Gallery of St Paul's Cathedral – never mind the extra 119 steps to the Stone Gallery and the further 152 steps to the Golden Gallery – there is now a chance to see something of the infamous view from Christopher Wren's iconic dome from beneath the cathedral floor. Oculus is a new exhibition in a quiet room in the Crypt. A 270° film projection takes viewers on a virtual journey up the steps, through the Whispering Gallery and onwards up to the Golden Gallery to spit them out at the top to 'look' at the views. If you stand so that the projection takes up the whole of your vision, it's a giddy experience, producing actual queasiness. A neat trick, but the film doesn't stop at the top for long, plunging instead into a potted history of the

cathedral's many stages of evolution. This content is impressionistic and fleeting, so don't expect a thorough history lesson, but it would make a good springboard from which to explore the building's rich and varied cultural, architectural and political story.

STATELY HOMES

Chiswick House

Burlington Lane, W4 2RP (8995 0508, www.chgt.org.uk). Turnham Green tube, then bus E3, or Hammersmith tube, then bus 190, Chiswick rail. **Open** *Apr* 10am-5pm daily. *May-Oct* 10am-5pm Mon-Wed, Sun. Last entry 30mins before closing. Closed Nov-Mar. *Tours* by arrangement; phone for details. **Admission** *House* (EH) (incl audio guide) £5; £4.30 reductions; £2.50 5-16s; free under-5s; £12.50 family (2+3). *Gardens* free. **Credit** MC, V. **5+**

At a 'once in a lifetime' attic sale at Chatsworth in 2010, seven lots were bought by Chiswick House thanks to money from the Art Fund. From spring 2011, the earliest known design drawings for Chiswick House, one of the finest examples of neo-Palladian architecture in England, will be on display, along with the writing desk used by Georgiana, Duchess of Devonshire, a famous socialite and active campaigner on behalf of womens' rights.

The fifth Duke of Devonshire commissioned this grand manor to sit on the site of an old Jacobean mansion, and illustrious house guests have included Alexander Pope and Jonathan Swift (in more recent times, the Beatles filmed the video for *Paperback Writer* in its gardens). The house was built more as a private art gallery than a home, and exhibits aren't especially child-friendly – although eagle-eyed kids could look out for two sculptures of the Green Man and a lead Sphinx.

Children of all ages will love the grounds, which were renovated during 2009 and 2010. A walk through the gardens makes you feel as if you've stepped into a classical landscape painting – there are obelisks among the trees, an exquisitely domed temple, a lake and a cascading waterfall. The 96-metre-long conservatory has also been saved from dereliction and houses Chiswick House's collection of rare camelias, many of which have survived since they were planted in 1828 (they flower in March). The House Festival and kitchen garden activities for children take place during the summer months, and the café has reopened in a new contemporary building with fine views over the grounds.

Buggy access. Disabled access: stairlift, toilet. Nearest picnic place: Chiswick Park. Shop.

Fenton House

3 Hampstead Grove, NW3 6SP (7435 3471, 01494 755563 information, 0844 249 1895 box office, www.nationaltrust.org.uk).

Sightseeing

Hampstead tube or Hampstead Heath rail.
Open *Mar-Oct 11am-5pm* Wed-Sun, bank hols. *Tours* phone for times. **Admission** (NT) £6.50; £3 5-17s; free under-5s; £16 family (2+2). **Credit** MC, V. **5+**
When Hampstead was a small village in the countryside near the city of London in the 17th century, this was one of its earliest large houses. What's intriguing is how little the house changed during 300 years of continuous occupation. It's best known for the impressive Benton Fletcher collection of early keyboard instruments, including spinets, harpsichords, clavichords and virginals. Instruments were donated on the condition that professional musicians be allowed to play them; check the website for details of concerts.

There is also a collection of paintings and drawings by the Camden Town Group and many fine examples of English and Continental porcelain from George Salting (who donated his amazing Chinese pottery collection to the V&A). Children particularly enjoy the Meissen Harlequins and the 'curious grotesque teapot'. Outside, they can run around the carefully tended vegetable garden, herb garden, lawns and orchard, whose 30 varieties of old English apples can be sampled on Apple Day (24-25 Sept 2011). Occasional garden trails are available.
Buggy access. Disabled access: ramp. Nappy-changing facilities.

Guildhall

Corner of Gresham Street & Aldermanbury, EC2P 2UJ (7606 3030, 7606 3030 ext 1463 tours, www.corpoflondon.gov.uk). St Paul's tube or Bank tube/DLR, or Moorgate tube/rail. **Open** *May-Sept* 9.30am-5pm daily. *Oct-Apr* 9.30am-5pm Mon-Sat. Last entry 4.30pm. Closes for functions; phone ahead to check. *Tours* by arrangement; groups of 15 or more only. **Admission** free. **Map** p334 P6. **8+**
London can't compete with Rome for sheer depth of antiquity, but the Guildhall is one of the City of London's oldest intact buildings, thanks to the Great Fire of London. It was built between 1411 and 1440 and is now used as the seat of local government: the Court of Common Council meets at 1pm on selected Thursdays each month in the Great Hall (visitors are welcome; phone for dates). The Hall is also open when it's not being used for official business. The impressive space has a vaulted ceiling, marble monuments, and banners and shields of 100 livery companies on the walls; every Lord Mayor since 1189 is named on the windows. Two large wooden statues of Gog and Magog,

carved in 1953 to replace the pair destroyed in the Blitz, stand in the West Gallery. They represent the mythical conflict between Britons and Trojan invaders; the result of this struggle was the founding of Albion's capital city, New Troy, on whose site London is said to stand. On the north wall hangs a fascinating list of trials and grisly executions.

You can only nose round the Guildhall's enormous medieval crypt on a pre-booked group tour; tours last half an hour and are free. In the absence of an on-site café, packed lunches can be scoffed in the cloakroom area, which is equipped with a water cooler.
Buggy access. Disabled access: lift, ramp, toilet. Nappy-changing facilities. Nearest picnic place: grassy area by London Wall. Shop.

Ham House

Ham Street, Ham, Richmond, Surrey TW10 7RS (8940 1950, www.nationaltrust.org.uk). Richmond tube/rail, then bus 371. **Open** *House* Apr-Oct noon-4pm Mon-Thur, Sat, Sun. *Gardens* Jan-Early Feb, Nov-mid Dec 11am-4pm daily. Mid Feb-Oct 11am-5pm daily. Closed 1 Jan, 25, 26 Dec. *Tours* (pre-booking essential) phone for details. **Admission** (NT) *House & gardens* £9.10-£10.90; £4.85-£6.05 5-15s; free under-5s; £23.05-£27.90 family (2+2). *Gardens only* £1.85-£3.65; £1.25-£2.45 5-15s; free under-5s; £4.90-£9.75 family (2+2). **Credit** AmEx, MC, V. **5+ (house). All ages (gardens)**
Ham House sits on the River Thames in gorgeous landscaped grounds, which include the Cherry Garden, with its central statue of Bacchus and lavender parterres, and the maze-like Wilderness, as well as the oldest thorn bush and orangery in the country. Inside, very little has changed since it was built and furnished in the 17th century by William Murray (whipping boy to James I) and his descendants. Many of the original interiors have been lavishly restored, offering a rare chance to see the bold colour schemes of the day – strong, contrasting colours in damask, velvet and satin. Television drama *Elizabeth* was filmed here, and there are extensive collections of period furniture, art and textiles. Children tend to get more excited by Ham House's reputation as one of the most haunted buildings in Britain: ghostly visitors are said to include William's daughter, the Duchess of Lauderdale, and her pet dog. Regular family events include entertaining Ghost Tours, which are suitable for over-fives; a torch-lit adult version is also available.

Legoland. *See p69.*

Open-air theatre takes place in the garden in summer, and there are egg trails for Easter, art and craft days for the August bank holiday weekend, more spooky tours for Hallowe'en and all manner of carols, feasts and craft events for Christmas. A ferry crosses the river to Marble Hill House (*see below*) at weekends year round, and daily during the summer.
Café. Disabled access: lift, toilet.
Nappy-changing facilities. Shop.

Marble Hill House

Richmond Road, Middx TW1 2NL (8892 5115, www.english-heritage.org.uk). Richmond tube/rail or bus 33, 90, 290, H22, R70. **Open** *Apr-Oct* 10am-2pm Sat; 10am-5pm Sun. Closed Nov-Mar. **Admission** (EH) £5.30; £4.80 reductions; £3.20 5-15s; free under-5s; £13.80 family (2+2). Price includes tour. **Credit** MC, V. **5+**
Marble Hill House was built in the 1720s for Henrietta Howard, George II's mistress before he became King. In the days when Marble Hill House was constructed, Twickenham was a country retreat, fashionable for weekend salons. It's a superb Palladian villa packed to the brim with Georgian antiques and paintings, but the star of the show is the Honduran mahogany staircase, whose construction nearly sparked a war with Spain. Marble Hill House

hosts special events throughout the year, including Easter trails and open-air concerts; guided tours can be taken of the house and its surrounding parkland, and there's a ferry across the Thames to Ham House (*see above*).
Café. Disabled access: toilet. Nearest picnic place: Marble Hill Park. Shop.

19 Princelet Street

19 Princelet Street, E1 6QH (7247 5352, www.19princeletstreet.org.uk). Aldgate East tube or Liverpool Street tube/rail. **Open** check website or phone for occasional open days. *Tours* groups by appointment. **Admission** free; donations appreciated. **Map** p335 S5. **3+**
This 18th-century house, just around the corner from Brick Lane, looks ordinary enough from the outside. Inside, though, it's rather special. Shabby and beautiful, melancholic and atmospheric, the interior has changed little since it was built in 1719 and a family of refugee Huguenot weavers moved in. In 1869, Polish Jews built an Ashkenazi synagogue in the garden, and it's been housing London's newcomers ever since. It is now home to a museum devoted to immigration and cultural diversity and extensive restorations are planned – although until the £3 million funding is raised, it's quite difficult to visit the fragile

Neighbourhood Watch
Covent Garden

As you wander through the bustling streets around Covent Garden, doing your best to dodge the tourists snaking their way around the Piazza, it's hard to believe the area was nearly flattened in the 1970s to make way for a masterplan of modern hotels and conference centres. Thanks to determined locals, who campaigned to save the market that had served the area with fresh produce and flowers for over three centuries, Covent Garden retained its soul and is now a major attraction, day and night. Whether you fancy riding back in time at the excellent London Transport Museum, trawling round the boutiques, taking in some street theatre or coughing up for an evening of high culture in the hallowed surrounds of the Royal Opera House, this buzzing corner of WC2 has got it all.

The name is most likely drawn from the 'convent garden' that once surrounded the historic abbey of St Peter. The land that belonged to the Convent of St Peter at West Minster was handed over by the Crown to John Russell, the first Earl of Bedford, following Henry VIII's dissolution of the monasteries.

In the 1630s, the Earl commissioned master architect Inigo Jones to design a series of Palladian arcades. These wonderfully elegant terraces, opening on to a central courtyard, constituted the first public square in the country and proved popular with wealthy tenants, until the fruit and vegetable market expanded on to their exclusive patch.

These days, the stalls are full of gifts and souvenirs (Londoners have to travel to Vauxhall to find the original market), but the fruity theme lives on in the shape of a shiny new Apple store, which became the largest in the world when it opened in 2010.

Going underground

Weekdays in term time are best for exploring this area. Head straight down James Street from the tube exit, cut through the market, and start off at one of London's most fun museums, the **London Transport Museum** (*see p98*), which benefited hugely from an airy renovation a few years ago. Inside, children tend to steam past the historic timeline that puts London's travel achievements in context with other major cities, straight on to the interactive rooms. For the under-sixes, the All Aboard! Gallery has climb-on model vehicles and soft play. The Interchange Gallery is for older children (seven to 11s), who have train carriages and buses to explore (from the horse-drawn Shillibeer's model to a sliced-through modern bus), tricky computerised driving games to play, costumes to try on, mystery objects to guess at and – the ultimate excitement – the possibility of driving a bus. There's also a fantastic shop with imaginative themed gifts. With Boris about to launch the new 21st-century breed of red Routemasters on to the city's streets, this is a great place to indulge the kids in a bit of old-fashioned time travel.

Afterwards, you can nip upstairs to the friendly **Upper Deck café** (*see p254*), overlooking Covent Garden Piazza. In addition to the Upper Deck café, the museum also has a modest picnic area where visitors can tuck into their packed lunches.

The Piazza and beyond

Designed in the 19th century by architect Charles Fowler, the covered central market (0870 780 5001, www.coventgardenmarket.co.uk) is a mix of cool and quirky shops (toy shop Eric Snook, antiques seller Nauticalia) and upmarket chains (Hobbs, Crabtree & Evelyn and the like). The **Apple Market** in the North Hall is where you'll find antique stalls on Mondays, a general market Tuesday to Friday and hand-made crafts at weekends. **Jubilee Hall Market** is a bit tackier, flogging novelty T-shirts and other tat.

London Transport Museum.

Outside in the **Piazza**, usually in front of the portico of St Paul's Church, comedians, musicians and living statues perform for the amusement of tourists and families. It was under this portico that Samuel Pepys observed what is thought to have been Britain's first Punch and Judy show ('an Italian puppet play', as he described it) on 9 May 1662; fittingly, the **Punch & Judy Festival** (*see p21*) is held here on the first Sunday in October. You can also catch Punch and Judy's slapstick at the annual May Fair in St Paul's churchyard.

Every summer there are open-air operatics courtesy of the **Royal Opera House** (*see p197*). The Royal Opera House itself is a beautiful space, and has an upstairs café with wonderful views over the Piazza. Guided tours give

the curious a glimpse into working dressing rooms and rehearsal studios; if you have enough time to take in a performance, there are free lunchtime recitals on Mondays.

Out of the market, head towards the river and down to the Strand. In the 14th century, this was a swanky residential street that stood right on the riverbank. Gradually, the overflow of hoi polloi from Covent Garden threatened to overwhelm the narrow strip; by 1600 the wealthy folk had run away, and the Strand had a reputation for poverty and bawdiness. Sir Christopher Wren suggested the creation of a reclaimed embankment to ease congestion and house the main sewer, and by the mid 19th century the area's respectability was restored. Respectability further increased in late 2010 with the reopening of the iconic **Savoy Hotel** after a three-year, £220m refit. At the Strand's eastern end is the **Aldwych**, a grand crescent that dates to 1905 – although the name, 'ald wic' (old settlement), has its origins in the 14th century. On its south side stands the imposing bulk of **Somerset House** (*see p84*).

Refreshments

Also in the area: Pizza Express, Strada, Wagamama.
Café Pasta *2-4 Garrick Street, WC2E 9BH (7497 2779, www.cafe pasta.co.uk).* Straightforward pasta, pizza and grills.
Christopher's *18 Wellington Street, WC2E 7DD (7240 4222, www.christophersgrill.com).* A smart, upmarket restaurant with American cuisine and hearty brunches.
Upper Deck *London Transport Museum, WC2E 7BB (7379 6344, www.ltmuseum.co.uk).* Enjoyable museum café (*see p254*).
Wahaca *66 Chandos Place, WC2N 4HG (7240 1883, www.wahaca.co.uk).* Delicious Mexican street food at affordable prices.
World Food Café *1st Floor, 14 Neal's Yard, WC2H 9DP. (7379 0298, www.worldfoodcafe nealsyard.co.uk).* Homespun, tasty vegetarian platters.

Sightseeing

space. Still, it's worth making the effort to experience the haunting atmosphere and fascinating stories of its past inhabitants – Jewish scholar David Rodinsky simply disappeared one day from here (Iain Sinclair and Rachel Lichtenstein wrote *Rodinsky's Room* based on the story). Check website for open days.
Buggy access. Nearest picnic place: Christ Church grounds.

Osterley Park & House

Osterley Park, off Jersey Road, Isleworth, Middx TW7 4RB (8232 5050, www.national trust.org.uk). Osterley tube. **Open** *House* Mar-Oct noon-4.30pm Wed-Sun. Nov-mid Dec noon-3.30pm Sat, Sun. *Gardens* Mar-Oct 11am-5pm Wed-Sun. Nov noon-3.30pm Sat, Sun. *Park* Jan-Mar, Nov, Dec 8am-6pm daily. Apr-Oct 8am-7.30pm daily. *Tours* by arrangement; min 15 people. **Admission** (NT) *House & garden* £9.20; £4.60 5-18s; free under-5s; £23 family (2+3). *Garden only* £4; £2 5-18s; free under-5s. *Park* free. **Credit** MC, V. **3+**

Osterley House is a red-brick stately home whose Tudor beginnings were remodelled by Robert Adam for self-made banking magnate Sir Francis Child in the 18th century. No expense was spared during this transition and the house is incredibly grand. It was largely unchanged by Childs' descendants before being donated to the National Trust in 1949; the splendour of the state rooms alone makes the house worth a visit. Children will enjoy exploring 'below stairs' and discovering what life was like as a servant, before visiting the horses in the Tudor stables; there's also a resident spectre, said to lurk in the basement. Outside, Mrs Child's flower garden is still delightful, and the rest of the 357 acres are a pleasure to explore. Regular events include tours of the house, bluebell walks, outdoor performances and the annual (free) Osterley Day, full of arts and fun.
Buggy access (not when busy). Café. Disabled access: stair climber, toilet. Nappy-changing facilities. Nearest picnic place: front lawn, picnic benches in grounds. Shop.

PM Gallery & House

Walpole Park, Mattock Lane, W5 5EQ (8567 1227, www.ealing.gov.uk). Ealing Broadway tube/rail or bus 65. **Open** *May-Sept* 1-5pm Tue-Fri, Sun; 11am-5pm Sat. *Oct-Apr* 1-5pm Tue-Fri; 11am-5pm Sat. Closed bank hols. *Tours* by arrangement; phone for details. **Admission** free; audio guide £1.
Credit AmEx, MC, V. **5+**

Ealing isn't brimming with architectural gems, but this one is interesting. Anyone who has visited the Sir John Soane's Museum in Lincoln's Inn Fields (*see p94*) will know about the architect's wonderfully eccentric use of light and space. Soane built Pitzhanger Manor as his weekend country retreat and it is now, along with the PM Gallery, Ealing's flagship cultural centre.

Among the exhibits is the Hull Grundy Martinware pottery collection, and there's a workshop programme for all ages; special events for kids include half-term craft sessions and 'clay play'. Soane's ornamental gardens are now known as Walpole Park, Ealing Borough's rose-scented pride and joy, which hosts jazz and comedy in summer.
Buggy access. Disabled access: lift, ramp, toilet. Nappy-changing facilities. Nearest picnic place: Walpole Park.

Syon House

Syon Park, Brentford, Middx TW8 8JF (8560 0881, 8847 4730 Tropical Zoo, 8847 0946 Snakes & Ladders, www.syonpark.co.uk). Gunnersbury tube/rail, then bus 237, 267, or Kew Bridge rail. **Open** *House* mid Mar-Oct 11am-5pm Wed, Thur, Sun, bank hol Mon (last entry 4pm). *Gardens* Mar-Oct 10.30am-5pm daily. Nov-Feb 10.30am-4pm Sat, Sun. *Tours* by arrangement; phone for details. *Tropical Zoo* 10am-5.30pm daily. *Snakes & Ladders* 10am-6pm daily (last entry 5.15pm). **Admission** *House & gardens* £10; £8 reductions; £4 5-16s; free under-5s; £22 family (2+2). *Gardens only* £5; £3.50 5-16s; free under-4s; £11 family (2+2). *Tropical Zoo* £6.50; £5.50 3-15s; free under-3s; £22 family (2+3). *Snakes & Ladders* £5.30 under-2s; £6.30 under-5s; £7.30 over-5s; free over-16s. Reduced rate after 4pm. **Credit** MC, V. **5+**

Syon House is the last ducal residence complete with country estate in Greater London, the seat of the Duke of Northumberland for over 600 years. The magnificent turreted pile looks out over the Thames towards Kew. It was built on the site of a medieval abbey that was brutally dissolved by Henry VIII, and it was here that Henry's fifth wife Catherine Howard awaited her execution. Henry's coffin was later brought here in transit to Windsor Castle; as if by divine retribution, it mysteriously burst open during the night and the king's remains were found being licked by dogs. It was here, too, that the doomed Lady Jane Grey reluctantly accepted the crown and became queen for nine days. In short, it's bursting with history.

All Hands on Deck

The Cutty Sark will soon be ready for boarding again.

The Cutty Sark, which has seen several million little landlubbers climb aboard since it first pitched up at Greenwich Dry Dock in 1956, is set to reopen in spring 2012 following the devastating fire that ripped its heart out one night in May 2007. This famous tea clipper was built in 1869 in Dumbarton, Scotland, and launched in 1870 to tout for business on the vastly competitive tea trade run between China and London. Speed was of the essence, with huge bonuses for the ship arriving back with the first tea consignment of the year, and the Cutty Sark was one of the quickest on the circuit. Unfortunately for her, though, the Suez Canal opened the same year she was built, and before long steam rather than sail became the preferred mode of tea transport.

After a spell bringing wool back from Oz, she was sold to a Portuguese firm until eventually limping into dry dock retirement in the 1950s – where she has sat ever since as a star tourist attraction at the heart of the UNESCO World Heritage Site of Maritime Greenwich.

The fire which struck the ship in 2007, apparently caused by a vacuum cleaner overheating, was hugely devastating, but it could have been even worse – thankfully the ship was undergoing conservation work at the time, and about half of the fixtures and fittings had been removed, including the iconic figurehead, the masts and rigging, the coach house, and a significant amount of planking.

When the covers finally come off again, the restored vessel will be shipshape, 90 per cent original and, for the first time, raised ten feet above the ground, ready to receive the flood of new visitors expected to arrive on the shores of SE10 during summer 2012. For an update on the restoration and opening dates, visit www.cuttysark.org.uk.

Sightseeing

Madame Tussauds. *See p70.*

The rooms, designed by Robert Adam, are breathtaking (John Betjeman described Syon as 'the grand architectural walk'), from the grand Roman hallway in black and white marble to the Red Drawing Room, with its crimson silk walls and Roman statues. Its magnificently preserved grandeur has made it a popular filming location: *The Madness of King George* was filmed here, as were scenes from *Gosford Park* and Stephen Poliakoff's *The Lost Prince*. Outside, children will love the restored 19th-century Great Conservatory, with its huge iron and glass dome – and if the extensive Capability Brown-landscaped gardens aren't enough for a run around, there's also indoor adventure playground Snakes & Ladders (an extra charge applies). Then there's the London Tropical Zoo enclosure, full of endangered animals that live in or near water, such as piranhas, snakes, crocs and poison tree frogs.

A programme of family-friendly events includes demonstrations, re-enactments and after-dark walks in winter, when the woods are illuminated with dazzling light displays (check the website for details). In summer, movies are screened in the gardens (bring a picnic to consume on the lawns before the film begins) and local craft fairs are occasionally set out on the front lawn.
Café. Nappy-changing facilities. Nearest picnic place: Syon House Gardens, Syon Park. Shop.

THRILLS & CHILLS

Chessington World of Adventures
Leatherhead Road, Chessington, Surrey KT9 2NE (0871 663 4477, www.chessington.com). **Getting there** *By rail* Chessington South rail, then bus 71 or 10-min walk. *By car* J9 off M25. **Open** Check website for timetables. **Admission** (online advance price) £27.60; £20.40 3-15s; annual pass £70.20; £52.20 3-15s. Free under 1m tall. Check website for on-the-day prices & other annual passes. **Credit** AmEx, MC, V. **All ages**
Chessington Zoo was opened by animal enthusiast Reginald Goddard in 1931 – he had been looking for a site to show off his exotic animal collection for some time. It wasn't until 1987, long after Reginald's death, that the adventure park opened, with its list of exciting rides. The zoo is still keeping its end up and has ten Western Lowland gorillas, two Sumatran tigers, two Asiatic lions and a family of Persian leopards, as well as smaller animals. In the recently opened Wanyama Reserve, there are zebra, antelopes and oryxes. Chessington has taken a leaf out of London Zoo's book and introduced child-friendly animal antics presentations (2pm & 4pm). At the new Sea Life aquarium, a walk-through ocean tank offers a chance to get close to the sharks, while the Amazonian display includes piranhas.

Many of the adventure rides are geared towards families with young children, unlike the more extreme offerings at nearby stablemate Thorpe Park (*see p72*). There's lovable Beanoland with dodgems and foam ball firing, a large soft play area for younger tots, plus an extreme games area and more challenging white-knuckle rides for older kids, like the Vampire rollercoaster and Rameses Revenge water plunge. Guides dressed up as fun characters help families on their way round.

Buggy access. Café. Car park (free). Disabled access: toilet. Nappy-changing facilities. Restaurant. Shops.

Chislehurst Caves

Old Hill, Chislehurst, Kent BR7 5NB (8467 3264, www.chislehurstcaves.co.uk). **Getting there** *By rail* Chislehurst rail. **Open** 10am-4pm Wed-Sun. *Tours* phone for details. **Admission** £5; £3 5-15s, reductions; free under-5s. **Credit** MC, V. **8+**

These man-made caves lie 30 metres below the woodlands of Chislehurst. They were carved out of the chalk by Druids, Saxons and Romans, and since then the caves have been turned to all sorts of purposes, including an ammunition dump in World War I and a mushroom farm; during World War II, they acted as Britain's largest bomb shelter. Most of the underground scenes in the TV series *Merlin* were filmed here. The 45-minute lamplit tour covers a mile of the tunnels; children will enjoy locating the Druid Altar, the Caves Church and the Haunted Pool. *Restaurant. Shop.*

Legoland

Winkfield Road, Windsor, Berks SL4 4AY (0870 504 0404, www.legoland.co.uk). **Getting there** *By rail* Windsor & Eton Riverside or Windsor Central rail, then shuttlebus. *By car* J3 off M3 or J6 off M4. **Open** *Mid Mar-Oct* times may vary, check website for timetables. **Admission** *One-day ticket* £41.40; £31.20 3-15s, reductions; free under-3s. *Two-day ticket* £81.60; £61.20 3-15s; free under-3s. *Shuttlebus return* £4.20; £2.10 3-15s; free under-3s. **Credit** AmEx, MC, V. **All ages**

Fifty-five million Lego bricks have been used to create this themed adventure park, which gives you some idea of the sheer scale of the place. Visitors first glimpse what they're in for from the car park; the site cascades, ride after ride, down a steep hill with Berkshire's rolling countryside in the distance. Legoland remains an incredibly popular family day out – though

while it's suitable for all ages, even hard-to-please early teens, adults may occasionally struggle to see the appeal. That's largely because of the queues, which can be particularly testing for toddlers' tempers. The best advice is to come early and make a beeline for the rear of the site first, or rent a Q-Bot (£10-£40 per person). This small hand-held device allows you to reserve a virtual place in the queue for some of the most popular rides – not cheap, but well worth it on a busy weekend.

Queues aside, there are some brilliant attractions. Driving School puts six- to 13-year-olds behind the wheel of whizzy electric cars, amid roundabouts, traffic lights and much confusion; there's also a scaled-down version for tots. Other star turns include the twisting Dragon rollercoaster, Miniland's scaled-down London landmarks and the Imagination Theatre. Legoland is also 15 years old in 2011, so check the website for special events.

There's plenty to see while you wander from queue to queue, but those with preschool children should seize the chance to go in term time. It's also a good idea to take activities to keep the kids amused while they're waiting, and to draw up a hit list of the rides your children want to try; call the day before to check your chosen attractions will be running.

Buggy access. Cafés. Disabled access: toilet. Nappy-changing facilities. Nearest picnic place: grounds. Restaurants. Shops.

London Bridge Experience

2-4 Tooley Street, SE1 2SY (0844 847 2287, www.londonbridgeexperience.com). London Bridge tube/rail. **Open** 10am-5pm Mon-Fri; 10am-6pm Sat, Sun. **Admission** £23; £21 reductions; £17 under-16s; free under-5s; £74 family (2+2). **Credit** MC, V. **Map** p335 Q8. **All ages (Bridge Experience). 11+ (London Tombs)**

The experience is a split-level one. The first part is a fun-for-all-the-family history lesson that engages all five senses and serves the choicest cuts from the crossing's 2,000-year history. The second takes you underground to the 'London Tombs' – a former plague pit – and frightens the pants off you. We like the first bit best, where actors appear at every turn. In a cobwebbed replica of a Victorian study, we meet the ghostly portrait of Sir John Rennie, who designed the 1831 bridge and whose ravings are translated by a dusty butler; through heavy doors and along dank passages we're shown Boudicca's sacking of London, narrated by a bloodied Roman soldier amid

Sightseeing

disembowelled corpses. Next up is the Russell Crowe-like viking, who asks his guests to help pull down the bridge's wooden piers. After that, we're introduced to William Wallace's ghost and taken into a chamber of gore run by the chap in charge of heads on sticks, once proudly displayed on London Bridge. Each period involves interaction with the key players, who also include a garrulous lighterman's widow, the American who bought the bridge in 1970 (it's a myth that he thought he was buying Tower Bridge, he insists), and the Queen. It's all quite entertaining; the shocks and horrors come downstairs in the dark and threatening Tombs, where zombie actors show little mercy. *Buggy access. Café. Disabled access: lift; toilet. Nearest picnic place: South Bank. Shop.*

London Dungeon

28-34 Tooley Street, SE1 2SZ (7403 7221, www.thedungeons.com). London Bridge tube/rail. **Open** times vary, phone or check website for details. **Admission** £23.10; £21 reductions; £17.10 4-15s; £21 for registered disabled; free carers, under-4s. **Credit** AmEx, MC, V. **Map** p335 Q8. **10+**

Not many of London's attractions use smell as an integral part of their exhibits, but the London Dungeon thoroughly exploits the power of nasty aromas to disturb. Everything is set in thrillingly dark surrounds that leave visitors delightfully disengaged from their everyday life – all the better to be scared out of their wits. The London Dungeon concentrates on the more gruesome episodes of London's history. Costumed actors bring the city's characters and disasters to life, often pretending to be one of the waxwork models and frightening kids into delighted squeals by suddenly moving. There's a gruesome section devoted to Jack the Ripper, one for demonic 18th-century barber Sweeney Todd, and another for the operating room of Tooley Street's butcher surgeon. New in 2010 was 'Bloody Mary: Killer Queen' devoted to the deaths commissioned by Henry VIII's daughter.

Guaranteed to provoke even more high-pitched exclamation is 'Labyrinth of the Lost', the largest horror mirror maze in the world. If that's not enough depravity for you, there's the Traitor Boat Ride to Hell (visitors play the part of condemned prisoners, death sentence guaranteed), and Extremis: Drop Ride to Doom, which aims, charmingly, to recreate at least part of the experience of being hanged.

The Dungeon is clearly on to a winner, judging from the length of the weekend queues outside the Victorian railway arches that are its home. There are always plenty of small children standing in line, where gorily made-up Dungeon staff work the crowds, but we'd advise against taking anyone younger than ten. Tours last around 90 minutes; you can purchase fast-track tickets on the website. *Buggy access. Disabled access: toilet. Nappy-changing facilities. Nearest picnic place: Hay's Galleria. Shop.*

Madame Tussauds

Marylebone Road, NW1 5LR (0871 894 3000, www.madame-tussauds.co.uk). Baker Street tube or bus 13, 27, 74, 113, 159. **Open** 9am-6pm daily (last entry 5.30pm). Times vary during holiday periods. **Admission** £28.80; £24.60 4-15s; free under-4s. £99 family (2+2 or 1+3). **Credit** AmEx, MC, V. **Map** p330 G4. **3+**

Madame Tussaud first opened her exhibition near Baker Street in 1831. In many ways, it's incredible that nearly 200 years later, with advances in visual technology being what they are, a collection of static waxwork models is still such a popular tourist attraction. But the queues down Marylebone Road never dwindle. That's in part a testament to the efforts put in to ramp up the excitement. As you enter the Music Zone, you're dazzled by paparazzi flashbulbs; starry-eyed kids can then join in with Lady Gaga, Beyoncé, Amy Winehouse and Leona Lewis. New figures are constantly added – Russell Brand and Cheryl Cole have recently joined the throng – and old favourites updated: Kylie Minogue and the Queen have been recast no less than four times. There's a *Pirates of the Caribbean* diorama in the hull of the Black Pearl, staffed by Keira, Orlando and Johnny; the World Stage hall is an interactive room split into zones for sports, culture, politics, popular music, royals and history. Holographs and touch screens add pizzazz. Nobody prevents visitors hugging the stars (or pinching their bottoms, if so inclined).

Elsewhere, the kitsch Spirit of London ride takes you through 400 years of London life in a taxi pod. Children love this, and always want to ride again to spot the historic figures around them. Below stairs lurks Scream – the Chamber of Horrors, which isn't child-friendly at all. It surrounds you with corpses and eviscerated victims of torture, with a truly terrifying 'live' experience (actors dressed up as psycho killers jump out and stalk you; unsurprisingly, it's over-12s only). Such morbid thrills chime with the work of Marie Tussaud (1761-1850), who made death masks out of wax in the French

Sightseeing

Ride the River

A cross-Thames cable car looks set to make waves in 2012.

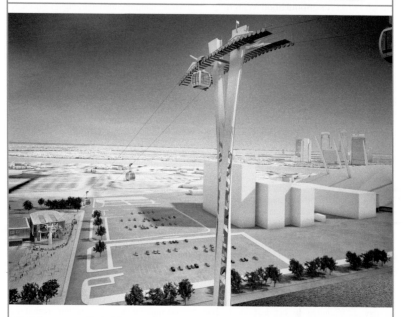

First there were Boris bikes and now it looks like there might be a Boris cable car strung up across the Thames to help Londoners on their daily commute and give them a more attractive view than the inside of the Greenwich Foot Tunnel along the way. This mayoral flight of fancy now looks set to become a riverside reality as the two councils at each end of the cable, Greenwich and Newham, both approved the scheme in January 2011.

The new project will provide a direct transport link between two major London 2012 venues – the North Greenwich Arena on the south side of the Thames and Royal Victoria Dock on the north bank, handy for ExCeL – as well as a cut-price theme park ride for young Londoners. Each of the 34 gondolas will be able to carry up to ten people at a time and will travel 50 metres above the murky depths on the five-minute crossing. It's an undeniably exciting

prospect, especially if you've got kids in tow, and in light of all the development at this end of the Thames over the last few years it's a much neeeded new pedestrian river crossing.

The height of the crossing means it won't interfere with shipping and it's also much cheaper and quicker to build than a bridge or tunnel, although projected costs have already risen from £25 million to £40 million. A fare structure has not been devised yet, but Transport for London plans to integrate the service into the Oyster system and is forecasting single fares at £2.50 for Oyster pay-as-you-go users and £3.50 for others. Whether the contraption actually sees the light of day remains to be seen, but Boris seems to have faith and is even rumoured to fancy a second route linking the North Greenwich Arena and Canary Wharf if this one is a soaring success. Perfect for big fish and small fry alike.

Revolution. Her cast of the mask of Marie-Jeanne du Barry, Louis XV's mistress, is the oldest work on display: it's now used as the face of the reclining, animatronic Sleeping Beauty. *See also p152* **Neighbourhood Watch**. *Café. Disabled access: lift, toilet. Nappy-changing facilities. Nearest picnic place: Regent's Park. Shop.*

Ripley's Believe It or Not!

1 Piccadilly Circus, London, W1J 0DA (3238 0022, www.ripleyslondon.com). Piccadilly Circus tube. **Open** 10am-10.30pm daily. **Admission** £23.25; £20.50 reductions; £17.95 4-15s; free under-4s. £73.60 family (2+2). **Credit** MC, V. **Map** p333 K7. **All ages** The five-floor London Ripley's has plenty of oddities to make your eyes pop; we particularly enjoyed the two-way gurning mirror, which has unsuspecting visitors trying out seemingly impossible facial contortions, unaware they're being watched by everyone else. The matchstick Tower Bridge fascinates children, as do the freak show exhibits, like two-headed calves and shrunken skulls.

A more dizzying delight is the Topsy Turvy Tunnel, which is like a bridge through a kaleidoscope that has you staggering drunkenly about while attempting to cross it. It's near the Mirror Maze, which engendered mutiny in the ranks when we learned you had to pay £4.95 extra to get lost in it. The admission price is high enough, without hidden extras. Still, Ripley would no doubt say that you have to go past a load of boring stuff in a regular museum before meeting things that make you say 'I don't believe it!' every time, which is what we said when we saw Leonardo da Vinci's *Last Supper* painted on a grain of rice. You'd better believe it.

Thorpe Park

Staines Road, Chertsey, Surrey KT16 8PN (0871 663 1673, www.thorpepark.com). **Getting there** *By rail* Staines rail, then 950 shuttlebus. *By car* J11 or J13 off M25. **Open** times vary, check website for timetables. Height restrictions vary, depending on rides. **Admission** £39.60; £26.40 under-12s; free under 1m tall; £105.60 family (2+2). Check the website or phone for advance bookings; allow 24hrs for processing. **Credit** MC, V. **5+** Thorpe Park is a perfect place for adolescents to wander free, bonding good-naturedly in the long, long queues (coming in wet weather and on school days is one way to avoid them). The

staff, for the most part, are young and extremely friendly, so the atmosphere in the park is surprisingly pleasant.

Many of the rides here are designed for teens and older children, and have height restrictions. That said, parents with young (or short) children will find plenty to do at Neptune's Beach (a big paddling and sunbathing spot), Octopus Garden (little, friendly rides) and the delightful Mr Monkey's Banana Ride, with its slightly sinister commentary.

Teenagers, meanwhile, will love the horrifyingly fast Stealth (standstill to 80mph in two seconds, plus a hideous vertical drop), the gore of horror-themed white-knuckler Saw, and the spiralling water drop raft ride Storm Surge (new for 2011). Saw is quite shockingly awful, but you're a wuss if you don't give it a go: this is, after all, Europe's most extreme G-force experience. Unless you make a beeline for it on entering the park at 10am, you'll have to be prepared to queue for up to two hours to experience the dark, blood-stained slasher movie build-up, the initial drops in pitch blackness, the climb to the top of the loop that has you looking at the sky dry-mouthed while you wait for the vertical downward rush. The screams are in earnest and the eyes are best kept tight shut; unsurprisingly, it's not recommended for under-12s (you have to be over 1.4 metres tall too). In 2010, the 'Saw Alive' horror maze (with six 'live action' rooms) was opened next door. *Buggy access. Café. Disabled access: toilet. Nappy-changing facilities. Restaurants. Shops.*

Trocadero

Coventry Street, W1D 7DH (7439 1791, www.londontrocadero.com). Piccadilly Circus tube. **Open** 10am-midnight Mon-Thur, Sun; 10am-1am Fri, Sat. **Admission** free; individual attractions vary. **Credit** varies. **Map** p333 K7. **5+** Inside Funland (some would beg to dispute this title), there is a vast arcade of coin-in-the-slot video games, simulator rides and dance machines. The noise and disorientating lights are a fast track to tantrums and headaches – and still they come to spend all their pocket money. There's a seven-screen cinema, dodgem track, ten-lane bowling alley, American pool lounge and various fast-food outlets. The sports bar is for grown-ups only. *Buggy access. Cafés. Disabled access: lift, toilet. Nappy-changing facilities. Nearest picnic place: Leicester Square, Trafalgar Square. Restaurants. Shops.*

Sightseeing

My Sport Cricket
Matthew, 12

What inspired you to take up cricket?
My dad is a coach at the club I go to.
He took me along and I liked it.

What do you like about cricket?
I just really like playing, and I've made
new friends there.

What level are you at?
I've played for my county before, but
then I broke my ankle. I've just had
my Essex trial to see if I can get back
in again and I think it went well. I play

on Tuesday and Wednesday evenings,
and on Saturday mornings, and I also
play indoor cricket on Friday evenings.

What's next for you in your sport?
I want to play for Essex again, then
keep going up to the next level.

**Which events would you like to see
at the London 2012 Olympic Games
and Paralympic Games?**
I'd like to see the Athletics, Basketball
and Tennis.

Sightseeing

Museums & Galleries

Lots of things to discover and do.

London has a lot to thank the Victorians for. Led by Queen Victoria and her influential consort Albert, the philanthropists and activists of the day fought for enlightenment and knowledge for all. The Victorian era gave us the great trio of museums on Exhibition Road – the **V&A** (*see p86*), the **Science Museum** (*see p112*) and the **Natural History Museum** (*see p104*) – as well as the underground trains on which to travel to them. These wonderful museums are constantly evolving, and there are lots of new openings to enjoy in 2011: the Darwin Centre at the Natural History Museum; the China and Medieval galleries at the Victoria & Albert Museum, and the revamped Wellcome Wing at the Science Museum.

You can see what life was like for Victorians in this great city at the new galleries at the **Museum of London** (*see p100*). The galleries took three years to complete, at a cost of £20 million, and the imaginative exhibits, touch screens, audio-visual installations and exhibitions set underneath glass flooring will appeal to children's sense of fun.

Greenwich also has a new attraction at the Old Royal Naval College. **Discover Greenwich** (*see p101*) is a visitor centre with a permanent gallery telling the story of Greenwich's illustrious 500-year history. Up in Camden, the **Jewish Museum** (*see p108*) has reopened its doors after expanding into the building next door and has put a lot of thought into making its exhibits child-friendly.

New openings aside, you'll find most of the capital's museums and galleries put considerable effort into making their exhibits accessible to children. The **British Museum** (*see p90*) may be more than 250 years old but the extraordinary collections aren't in the least bit stuffy, and the museum's trails really capture the attention of small minds.

There are all kinds of fantastic activities and workshops going on at venues listed in this chapter, but bear in mind that it's usually best to book ahead. Our top tip for a successful day out is to arrive early, pack lots of snacks and avoid trying to do too much in one day.

ART & DESIGN

Camden Arts Centre

Corner of Arkwright Road & Finchley Road, NW3 6DG (7472 5500, www. camdenartscentre.org). Finchley Road tube or Finchley Road & Frognal rail. **Open** 10am-6pm Tue, Thur-Sun; 10am-9pm Wed. **Admission** free. **Credit** MC, V. **5+ (parental advisory)**

Nowhere near Camden Town, but worth seeking out. This is a sleek contemporary arts centre hosting regular exhibitions in its three galleries, with a state-of-the-art ceramics studio attached. Half terms bring four-day courses in clay, mixed media, photography and sculpture for five to sevens and eight to 11s (£140; £70 reductions). The café is a gem, with a spacious terrace, daily specials, hearty sandwiches, great coffee and stripey marshmallow-topped hot chocolate.

Buggy access. Café. Disabled access: lift, toilet. Nappy-changing facilities. Nearest picnic place: gallery garden. Shop.

Design Museum

Shad Thames, SE1 2YD (7940 8790, www.designmuseum.org). Tower Hill tube or London Bridge tube/rail, or bus 47, 188. **Open** 10am-5.45pm daily. **Admission** £11; £7-£10 reductions; free under-12s. **Credit** MC, V. **Map** p335 S9. **5+**

This stylishly converted Thameside warehouse full of inspiring design is a surprisingly child-friendly sort of place: young visitors are given a Family Trail worksheet to doodle on, while acclaimed Get Creative! sessions usually run once a month. Here, creative five- to 11-year-olds can dabble in arty activities: the monthly-changing themes range from modern millinery to furniture design and architecture. The cost is £4.50 per child, though participants must be accompanied by a paying adult (£10); fees also cover admission to the museum's current crop of exhibitions.

Buggy access. Café. Disabled access: lift, toilet. Nappy-changing facilities. Nearest picnic place: Butler's Wharf riverside benches. Shop.

Dulwich Picture Gallery

Gallery Road, SE21 7AD (8693 5254, www.dulwichpicturegallery.org.uk). North Dulwich or West Dulwich rail. **Open** 10am-5pm Tue-Fri; 11am-5pm Sat, Sun, bank hol Mon. **Admission** £5; £4 reductions; free under-18s. **Credit** MC, V. **6+**

This tiny gallery, built by the eccentric, energetic Sir John Soane in 1811, punches well above its weight with its outstanding collection of 17th- and 18th-century old masters. They include paintings by the likes of Rembrandt, Tiepolo, Rubens, Van Dyck and Gainsborough, while temporary exhibitions romp across the centuries, including a Cy Twombly and Nicolas Poussin joint show in 2011 (until 25 Sept). It's also a community hub of arty activity. Tuesday's Evening Art School gives 15 to 18s the chance to develop their portfolios, Wednesday's quirkily themed after-school creative sessions are aimed at seven- to ten-year-olds, while there are six-week art courses on Thursday nights, devoted to different media (silk screen printing, paper cut-outs) for 11 to 14s; prices range from £50 and £60.

Holidays bring yet more activities, often involving making things along a seasonal theme; Art in the Garden gatherings are on Wednesdays in the summer hols and cost £2 per child. Artplay afternoons, which are held on the first and last Sunday of the month, invite parents and over-fours to partake in artist-led activities, from making sock puppets to designing African masks (£2; free with gallery ticket). Check online for details and fees of all courses and classes; booking is generally essential, although Art in the Garden and Artplay are drop-ins.

Buggy access. Café. Disabled access: toilet. Nappy-changing facilities. Nearest picnic place: gallery gardens. Shop.

Fashion & Textile Museum

83 Bermondsey Street, SE1 3XF (7407 8664, www.ftmlondon.org). London Bridge tube/rail. **Open** 11am-6pm Tue-Sat. Last entry 5.15pm. **Admission** £7; £4 reductions; free under-12s. **Credit** MC, V. **8+**

Founded by flamboyant British fashion designer Zandra Rhodes and now run by Newham College, this colourful museum showcases fashion, textiles and jewellery, with temporary exhibitions to supplement the permanent collection. We don't just mean colourful on the inside: there's no missing its bright orange premises (with flashes of take-no-prisoners pink and electric blue), which were designed by Mexican architect Ricardo

Geffrye Museum.
See p77.

Sightseeing

Sightseeing

National Gallery. *See p78.*

Legorreta. Inexpensive, inspiring children's workshops run in half term and the summer holidays, often led by industry professionals. Temporary exhibition From Catwalk to Cover runs from 18 November 2011 to 26 February 2012, perfect for fledgling fashionistas.
Buggy access. Café. Disabled access: lift, toilet. Nearest picnic place: Bermondsey Square.

Geffrye Museum

136 Kingsland Road, E2 8EA (7739 9893, www.geffrye-museum.org.uk). Hoxton rail. **Open** 10am-5pm Tue-Sat; noon-5pm Sun, bank hol Mon. **Admission** free; donations appreciated. *Almshouse* £2; £1 reductions; free under-16s. **Credit** AmEx, MC, V. **5+**
Set in one of the most urban sections of London, The Geffrye Museum is a strange oasis. The rooms within the attractive 18th-century almshouses recreate interiors from different periods, from the Elizabethan era to the present day. Visitors walk past in a roped-off corridor, admiring – or deploring – the tastes and styles of the past. It's like time-travelling without the Tardis. On the first Saturday of the month there are free quizzes and craft activities for five to 16s, while half terms bring hands-on workshops for all ages. In summer, there's an eclectic array of garden parties and family days; kids might learn bhangra dancing, make masks or listen to a Caribbean steel band. Events often spill into the glorious gardens, so bring a picnic to eat on the grass. In winter, the Christmas Past exhibition sees each room decorated for the festive season according to its period; the museum also holds an outdoor Twelfth Night ritual, with singing, holly- and ivy-burning and a taste of traditional Twelfth Night cake for the kids (and mulled wine for grown-ups). Temporary exhibitions are housed in the second, newer, half of the museum, along with the airy, inviting restaurant. At Home in Japan (until 29 Aug 2011) takes a peek behind the doors of modern urban homes in Japan.
Buggy access. Disabled access: lift, toilet. Nappy-changing facilities. Nearest picnic place: museum grounds. Restaurant. Shop.

Guildhall Art Gallery

Guildhall Yard, off Gresham Street, EC2V 5AE (7332 3700, www.guildhall-art-gallery.org.uk). Mansion House or St Paul's tube, or Bank tube/DLR, or Moorgate tube/rail, or bus 8, 25, 242. **Open** 10am-5pm Mon-Sat; noon-4pm Sun. **Admission** free. **Credit** (over £5) MC, V. **Map** p334 P6. **6+**

Perhaps the most exciting exhibit here for children is the Roman amphitheatre that lies under the courtyard. The remains are fairly scant and only the foundations of the walls and entrance survive – but the site does an excellent job of suggesting how the amphitheatre would have looked, with staggered seats printed on a screen, dynamic illustrations of gladiators and sound effects. Up in the Main Gallery is the vast *Defeat of the Floating Batteries at Gibraltar* by John Singleton Copley, the largest painting in Britain. The City of London's gallery has some gems, with works by Constable, Reynolds and the Pre-Raphaelites, and absorbing depictions of London through the ages. In October the gallery takes part in the annual Big Draw (*see p21*), and there are pre-bookable half-term workshops; every Friday, four free tours (hourly from 12.15pm, no booking needed) take in the highlights of the collection.
Buggy access. Disabled access: toilet. Nappy-changing facilities. Nearest picnic place: Finsbury Circus.

Hayward Gallery

Belvedere Road, SE1 8XX (7921 0813, www.southbankcentre.co.uk). Embankment tube or Waterloo tube/rail. **Open** 10am-6pm daily; call to check for late night openings **Admission** Prices vary; phone for details. **Credit** AmEx, MC, V. **Map** p334 M8. **7+ (parental advisory)**
The Hayward Gallery's position within the Southbank Centre makes it popular with families on a day out. The light, bright pavilion by Daniel Graham was added in 2003; children enjoy watching cartoons on the touch screens or just wandering around the visually confusing space created by curved, two-way mirrors. There are no permanent collections on display; instead, three or four major temporary exhibitions are staged through the year. Older children might enjoy 2011's major blockbuster retrospective, Tracey Emin: Love is What You Want (under-16s must be accompanied by an adult), which runs from 18 May to 29 August.
See also p48 **Neighbourhood Watch**.
Buggy access. Café. Disabled access: lift. Nappy-changing facilities. Nearest picnic place: Jubilee Gardens/riverside benches. Shop.

Kenwood House

Hampstead Lane, NW3 7JR (8348 1286, www.english-heritage.org.uk). Archway tube, then 210 bus. **Open** 11.30am-4pm daily. **Admission** free. **Credit** MC, V. **5+**

Sightseeing

Saatchi Gallery. *See p82.*

Sightseeing

English Heritage runs this majestic 17th-century mansion perched at the north end of Hampstead Heath. Your children are likely to ignore the house and instead go fizzy at the great rolling expanse of green in front that leads down to the lake, where there are a couple of excellent climbing trees to be found. They'll also like hide-and-seek in the rhododendrons, the posh ice-creams, lunch or (especially) breakfast in the Brew House (*see p244*), and the fact that the site provides a superb jumping-off point for all things Heathly. After letting off steam, they might be persuaded inside the house to see the paintings: Gainsborough, Vermeer, Reynolds, Van Dyck, Hals, Turner and a great Rembrandt self-portrait.
Buggy access. Café. Disabled access: toilets. Nappy-changing facilities. Nearest picnic place: House grounds, Hampstead Heath. Restaurant.

Museum of Brands, Packaging & Advertising

2 Colville Mews, Lonsdale Road, W11 2AR (7908 0880, www.museumofbrands.com). Ladbroke Grove or Notting Hill Gate tube or bus 23. **Open** 10am-6pm Tue-Sat; 11am-5pm Sun. Last entry 45mins before closing. **Admission** £6.50; £4 reductions; £2.25 7-16s; free under-7s; £15 family (2+2). **Credit** MC, V. **Map** p326 A6. **6+**
Spanning some 200 years of brands, the vast collections in this museum cover Victorian leisure pursuits, the advent of radio, the chirpy

thrift of wartime Britain and the liberal revolution of the swinging '60s. The displays, originally collected by consumer historian Robert Opie, who started his obsession at 16 when he decided to keep a Munchies wrapper rather than throw it in the bin, are geared towards nostalgic adults, but historically minded children may be amused by the antiquated toys, magazines and comics on show – not to mention old versions of all their favourite chocolate wrappers.
Buggy access. Café. Disabled access: toilet. Nappy-changing facilities. Nearest picnic place: Kensington Gardens. Shop.

National Gallery

Trafalgar Square, WC2N 5DN (7747 2885, www.nationalgallery.org.uk). Charing Cross tube/rail or bus 24, 29, 176. **Open** 10am-6pm Mon-Thur, Sat, Sun; 10am-9pm Fri. *Tours* 11.30am, 2.30pm daily. **Admission** free. *Temporary exhibitions* prices vary. *Tours* free. **Credit** MC, V. **Map** p333 K7. **5+**
There are 2,300 paintings to see here, all free of charge, which makes it a good idea to 'manage' a visit if accompanied by children, lest they get overwhelmed. The gallery is great at providing ways of doing this, and the latest innovation is the Artstart Interactive Guide, which can be found in the Sainsbury Wing and the East Wing's espresso bar. Choose a preselected tour, or design one of your own then print it out. Alternatively, children can guide their parents thanks to the Teach Your Grown-ups About

Art audio tour, which equips kids with a map and audio guide, then asks them to relay choice snippets to their elders. Other audio guides ask children to follow secret agents or hunt for kings and queens, learning about various paintings as they go. Printed trails – designed for specific age-groups and printable from the website – also help navigate the collections, which include many a masterpiece: Turner's *The Fighting Temeraire*, Botticelli's *Venus* and Jan Van Eyck's *Arnolfini Portrait* among them. Pick up a floorplan at the information desk before you set off. Major exhibitions for 2011 include the most complete display of Leonardo da Vinci's paintings ever held (9 Nov 2011-5 Feb 2012).

Family events include the magic carpet storytelling sessions for under-fives on Sunday mornings, plus two-hour art workshops for five to 11s (11am-1pm, 2-4pm); you can't book ahead, so turn up well in advance of start times (detailed on the website). The school holidays also bring a healthy spread of free activities, led by painters and sculptors.

Come lunchtime, Oliver Peyton's National Café (*see p241*) offers simple, sustaining fare to fuel the children's creativity: a boiled egg with soldiers, perhaps, or lovely creamy macaroni cheese. *See also p54* **Neighbourhood Watch**. *Buggy access. Café. Disabled access: lift, toilet. Nappy-changing facilities. Nearest picnic place: Trafalgar Square. Restaurant. Shop.*

National Portrait Gallery

2 St Martin's Place, WC2H 0HE (7306 0055, 7312 2483 tours, www.npg.org.uk). Leicester Square tube or Charing Cross tube/rail, or bus 24, 29, 176. **Open** *10am-5.50pm Mon-Wed, Sat, Sun; 10am-8.50pm Thur, Fri. Tours times vary, phone for details.* **Admission** *free. Temporary exhibitions prices vary. Video guide £3. Tours free.* **Credit** AmEx, MC, V.
Map p333 K7. **5+**
Likenesses of Britain's great and good make up the NPG's tremendous collection, from Tudor royalty to modern-day actors, writers, politicians and academics. Children will particularly enjoy the gory provenance of recent acquisition *Self* by Marc Quinn, a sculpture made out of the artist's own blood. The third Saturday of the month brings free storytelling for over-threes and crafts activities for over-fives, while school-holiday workshops might range from making clay portrait mugs to sketching oil-pastel portraits. *See also p54* **Neighbourhood Watch**.

Buggy access. Café. Disabled access (Orange Street entrance): lift, toilet. Nappy-changing facilities. Nearest picnic place: Leicester Square, Trafalgar Square. Restaurant. Shops.

Orleans House Gallery

Riverside, Twickenham, Middx TW1 3DJ (8831 6000, www.richmond.gov.uk/ orleans_house_gallery) St Margaret's, Richmond or Twickenham rail, or bus 33, 490, H22, R68, R70. **Open** *Apr-Sept 1-5.30pm Tue-Sat; 2-5.30pm Sun, bank hols. Oct-Mar 1-4.30pm Tue-Sat; 2-4.30pm Sun, bank hols.* **Admission** *free; donations appreciated.* **Credit** MC, V. **5+**
This elegant Thames-side gallery is on top form thanks to a recent Lottery cash injection, and was selected in 2010 to take part in museumaker. This is a project that teams craft makers with galleries to create new site-specific commissions. Upbeat children's workshops run year-round: the after-school Art Club caters for five- to ten-year-olds, while 10:15 entertains ten to 15s. All need to be booked in advance and are very popular (visit the website or phone the gallery). The Coach House education centre hosts holiday art workshops, using the gallery's exhibitions as a starting point. The team also co-ordinates the annual summer Larks in the Parks children's theatre festival, with performances in parks across the borough.
Buggy access. Café. Disabled access: toilet. Nappy-changing facilities. Nearest picnic place: Orleans House Gallery grounds, Marble Hill Park or riverside benches. Shop.

Queen's House

Romney Road, SE10 9NF (8312 6565, www.nmm.ac.uk). Cutty Sark DLR or Greenwich DLR/rail. **Open** *10am-5pm daily. Last entry 4.30pm. Tours times vary; call for details.* **Admission** *free; occasional charge for temporary exhibitions. Tours free.*
Credit *(over £5)* MC, V. **4+**
The first house to be built in Britain in a consciously Classical style was designed in 1616 by Inigo Jones and lived in by successive queens. It's now home to the National Maritime Museum's art collection, which includes all sorts of pictures of naval heroes, battles, uncharted lands and stormy seascapes. For a cherry-picked selection of its treasures, explore the second-floor Art for the Nation exhibition. An exhibition on the ground floor charts the house's former life as a naval boarding school (the timetable revolved around lessons in

Sightseeing

Neighbourhood Watch
Bloomsbury

Bloomsbury was one of London's first planned suburbs and its handsome squares still retain a refined air, despite its location just a short hop from the melee of Oxford Street. Blue plaques dotted around the area's grand squares attest to its popularity with literary and arty types (before a time when they could no longer afford to live here). WB Yeats lived at 5 Upper Woburn Place, Edgar Allan Poe at 83 Southampton Row and TS Eliot at 28 Bedford Place; 6 Store Street was the birthplace of Anthony Trollope; and Dickens lived at 48 Doughty Street, now the **Charles Dickens Museum** (see p93). It remains a pleasantly bookish, cultural sort of place, thanks to its fine clutch of museums – headed up, of course, by the mighty British Museum, officially the country's most popular tourist attraction – and specialist book and art supply shops.

Bloomsbury is also home to Lamb's Conduit Street, a Dickensian-looking thoroughfare that's become a bastion of independent traders. The bike shop, grocer's, bookshops and boutiques ooze character; happily, it's too compact to strike fear into shop-resistant children's souls. The perfect reward for good behaviour is just around the corner: the park, pets' corner and playground at Coram's Fields.

Welcome to the Ancient World

Step into the **British Museum** (see p90), and you're whisked into all sorts of weird and wonderful ancient civilisations. Star exhibits include the Rosetta Stone, the Parthenon (Elgin) Marbles and Lindow Man, so perfectly preserved in peat you can see his beard. Pick up activity backpacks and trails from the Paul Hamlyn Library or join a free eyeOpener tour. The tours, led by volunteers, are designed to introduce visitors to individual parts of the collection. There are 15 tours daily, lasting 30-40 minutes.

In one room, graceful Grecian youths strike nonchalant poses; in the Africa gallery on the floor below, you might find a defiantly bristling two-headed dog named Kozo (Room 23). On the upper floor, the Egyptian mummies in rooms 62 and 63 will send a delicious thrill down your spine, as the unseeing eyes of long-dead priests and pharoahs stare back at you; the first century AD mummified cat looks far friendlier.

Don't try to cram it all into one visit – and if the kids need a break from statues and sarcophagi, head to the vast glass-roofed Great Court, which surrounds the domed Reading Room. Below here, the Clore Education Centre and Ford Centre for Young Visitors host weekend and holiday activity sessions: mummy-making is an eternally popular offering.

For earnest Egyptologists, the **Petrie Museum of Egyptian Archaeology** (see p91) is also close by. The Petrie's recent reburbishment includes 3D image kiosks, which help to bring the treasures to life, but it's still a delightfully old-fashioned sort of establishment, run by enthusiastic staff; thrillingly, you can request a wind-up torch with which to explore the murkier recesses. Peek at the skeleton in a pot, write your name in hieroglyphs, and admire the eclectic array of beads, tools, pots and textiles, all displayed in rows of Victorian glass cabinets.

Have a field day

Seven acres of lawns, football pitches, sandpits, swings and slides await at **Coram's Fields** (see p134) – sheer heaven for space-starved city kids, who run rampant around the grass or splash around in the paddling pool. As a sign on the gate firmly states, unaccompanied adults are banned, giving parents extra peace of mind. Older kids can swoop along the flying fox or zoom down the helter-skelter while tinies potter around the ample sandpit or fearlessly ascend

Coram's Fields.

the climbing frame. Smell a certain fruity something in the air? That'll be the petting zoo – a whiffy but happy home to goats, geese, ducks, guinea pigs and other docile mini-beasts.

Bring a picnic to spread out on the grass, or eat at the on-site café. It's run by the Kipferl team, who also own a great little Austrian deli/café in Smithfield, so expect bretzels and sachertorte alongside open sarnies, hot dishes and soups.

By comparison to Coram's Fields, Bloomsbury's other squares are more sedate. Just north of Coram's, the tranquil, plane tree-shaded **St George's Gardens** (www.friendsofstgeorges gardens.org.uk) were a burial ground in the 18th and 19th centuries. Children can decipher the crumbling inscriptions on the tombs that dot the gardens, or hunt for the final resting-place of Oliver Cromwell's granddaughter, Anna Gibson; those who like their history dark and gory may be interested to learn that this was the site of the first recorded attempt at body-snatching, in 1777.

Past the uncompromising, concrete bulk of the Brunswick Centre (home to a massive Waitrose that's good for picnic provisions, along with various shops) lies **Russell Square** – a jewel among Bloomsbury's garden squares. It's a sun-dappled, quietly dignified expanse, with a water-jet fountain at the centre that cries out to be scampered through; at its northern end, the café

has a lovely terrace and does a fine trade in ice-cream cornets as well as more substantial sustenance.

Find out about the foundlings

In the 18th century, Coram's Fields was the site of the Foundling Hospital. A home for abandoned and destitute children, it was established by a kindly sea captain, Thomas Coram. Returning to England from America, Coram was appalled by the number of abandoned children he saw. Though the orphanage was demolished in the 1920s, its small inhabitants – and the adults who campaigned on their behalf – are remembered at the **Foundling Museum** (see p87) on Brunswick Square, overlooking Coram's Fields. The little love tokens left by the poverty-stricken mothers who abandoned their babies at the hospital would touch the hardest of hearts: a key; a button; a scrap of poetry; letters; a hazelnut shell. Look out for special family days, when activities might include making a family tree hanging mobile or a flower bouquet for Mother's Day.

Also in the area: ASK, Carluccio's Caffè, Giraffe, Hummus Bros, Pizza Express, Tas, Yo! Sushi, Wagamama.
Court Café British Museum, Great Russell Street, WC1B 3DG (7323 8990). A handy pit-stop for sarnies and cakes.
Fryer's Delight 19 Theobald's Road, WC1X 8SL (7405 4114). Glorious fish and chips (some say London's finest), served in kitsch surrounds.
Garden Café at Russell Square Russell Square Gardens, WC1B 5EH (7637 5093). Sun yourself on the patio while scoffing ice-creams.
Kipferl Coram's Fields 93 Guilford Street, WC1N 1DN (www.kipferl.co.uk). A summer-only joint offering superior light lunches and cakes, overlooking the playground; the café is closed on Mondays.
La Porchetta 33 Boswell Street, WC1N 3BP (7242 2434, www. laporchettapizzeria.co.uk). This busy pizzeria and pasta joint doesn't stint on portion sizes.

Sightseeing

seafaring and lashings of cocoa), while first floor galleries are devoted to the Tudors and early polar photography. On the Trail of the Stuarts is a 'detective notebook' that leads children around the building, while a trail for younger children tests out their observational skills; you can download them from the website before you go.

The Tulip Stairs was the first self-supporting spiral staircase to be built in the country: while adults admire its elegant lines and wrought iron fleurs-de-lys, children are advised to keep a watchful eye out for the resident ghost. It was supposedly captured on film by a couple of Canadian visitors in 1966 as it ascended the staircase, and it was spotted again in 2002 by a spooked gallery assistant, who saw it vanish through a wall. A colonnade connects the building to the National Maritime Museum (*see p119*).

Buggy access. Café. Disabled access: lift, toilet. Nappy-changing facilities. Nearest picnic place: picnic area on grounds, Greenwich Park. Shop.

Royal Academy of Arts

Burlington House, Piccadilly, W1J 0BD (7300 8000, www.royalacademy.org.uk). Green Park or Piccadilly Circus tube. **Open** *Temporary exhibitions* 10am-6pm Mon-Thur, Sat, Sun; 10am-10pm Fri. *John Madejski Fine Rooms* Tours only 1pm Tue; 1pm, 3pm Wed-Fri; 11.30am Sat. **Admission** *Fine Rooms* free. *Exhibitions* prices vary; free under-7s. **Credit** AmEx, DC, MC, V. **Map** p332 J7. **7+** George III established Britain's first art school in 1768. It moved to its present location at Burlington House a century later, and there's a real sense of occasion as you walk under the arches into its impressive courtyard. Works by British artists from the 18th century to the present day (Constable, Reynolds, Turner, Millais, Waterhouse, Hockney among them) are on permanent, free display in the John Madejski Fine Rooms – but the main focus is on the major temporary exhibitions. Who could forget Charles Saatchi's 1997 YBA show, Sensation? The annual Summer Exhibition, held from June to August, is incredibly popular; children will probably find the endless and unstructured rooms of work submitted by the general public overwhelming, although there are some interactive family workshops and gallery talks on offer. At other times, you can grab an activity sheet for 'art detectives' from reception. The fountains in the Burlington Courtyard (designed by the architects who brought us

similar watery pleasures at Somerset House) provide a welcome distraction on all but the frostiest of days.

Buggy access. Café. Disabled: lift, toilet. Nappy-changing facilities. Nearest picnic place: Green Park, St James's Square. Restaurant. Shop.

Saatchi Gallery

Duke Of York's HQ, Duke of York Square, King's Road, SW3 4SQ (7811 3085, www.saatchi-gallery.co.uk). Sloane Square tube. **Open** 10am-6pm daily (last admission 5.30pm). **Admission** free. **Map** p329 F11. **7+ (parental advisory)** After a stint in County Hall, the Saatchi Gallery moved to its current home off the King's Road in 2008, and immediately struck a resonant note with its inaugural exhibition: emerging young artists from China. The gallery's self-ascribed brief is to exhibit work by innovative, as-yet-unrecognised artists or by international artists with no real profile in this country, and this summer sees Shape of Things to Come: New Sculpture, which runs until 16 October 2011 and should help to fire the imagination. You'll need to do your 'suitability' homework before you go (best achieved through the Saatchi's extensive website as well as independent reviews). When you get there you'll find an open, airy, elegant set of conjoined spaces, which amount to just the right size for small legs to manage. An adventure in art – and best of all it's free. *See also p126* **Neighbourhood Watch**.

Buggy access. Disabled access: lift, toilets. Nappy-changing facilities. Nearest picnic place: Duke of York Square.

Serpentine Gallery

Kensington Gardens (near Albert Memorial), W2 3XA (7402 6075, www.serpentine gallery.org). Lancaster Gate or South Kensington tube. **Open** 10am-6pm daily. **Admission** free; donations appreciated. **Credit** AmEx, MC, V. **Map** p327 D8. **7+ (parental advisory)** Summer 2011 sees the 11th annual Serpentine Pavilion, a top-notch architectural commission; Jean Nouvel got the job last year. The permanent gallery may be housed in an unlikely looking 1930s park building, but it maintains a high profile in the art world with a rolling two-monthly line-up of exhibitions. The bonus of a family day trip here is the gallery's location in the middle of Kensington Gardens, which means that when the fidgets set in, families can

My Sport Paralympic Athletics
Nikki Emerson, 22

What inspired you to take up athletics?
I was always sporty and used to play lacrosse to a high standard, but then I had a car accident two years ago. While I was in hospital, I watched the Beijing 2008 Paralympics and I thought I'd like to get involved with sport again. I met Tanni Grey-Thompson (one of Britain's most successful Paralympians), and she was brilliant.

What do you like about your sport?
It involves lots of travel, which I love, and I get to meet really inspiring people.

What level are you at?
I spend 12 hours a week at athletics, and three to four hours cross training.

I'm taking part in the 2011 London Marathon and I came first in the Ladies Marathon Open in the Outeniqua Wheelchair Challenge, which was held in South Africa in February.

What's next for you in your sport?
I'm looking to qualify for the 400m, the 800m and the Marathon at the Paralympic Games in 2012.

Which events would you like to see at the London 2012 Olympic Games and Paralympic Games?
I'd love to watch Jessica Ennis in the Athletics events and some Gymnastics, as well as the Paralympic Rowing, Athletics and Cycling.

Sightseeing

Sightseeing

decamp straight on to the grass expanses outside the door. The events programme includes family days, artist-led drawing and painting courses, and trails relating to the current exhibitions; check the website for dates. A brand new gallery space, the Serpentine Sackler Gallery, should be up and running in 2012 on the north side of the Serpentine Bridge. *Buggy access. Disabled access: toilet. Nappy-changing facilities. Nearest picnic place: Hyde Park. Shop.*

Somerset House & Galleries

Strand, WC2R 1LA (7845 4600, www.somersethouse.org.uk). Embankment or Temple tube or Charing Cross tube/rail. **Open** *10am-6pm daily. Courtyard 7.30am-11pm daily. River terrace 8am-6pm daily (extended hours apply for restaurant). Embankment Galleries 10am-6pm Mon-Wed, Fri-Sun; 10am-9pm Thur. Courtauld Gallery 10am-6pm daily. Tours 1.15pm, 2.45pm Thur; 12.15pm, 1.15pm, 2.15pm, 3.15pm Sat.* **Admission** *Parts of South building, courtyard & river terrace free. Tours free. Temporary exhibitions prices vary; phone for details.* **Credit** MC, V. **Map** p333 M7. **8+ (galleries), 5+(courtyard)**

This one-time Tudor palace became a royal residence (Elizabeth I often stayed here before she was crowned) before it was remodelled into neo-classical splendour and used as offices by various public bodies (all gone, bar the Inland Revenue). These days it houses some of the UK's finest small galleries, although children will be equally enamoured of the enchanting courtyard with its ice-rink in winter and play fountains in summer; kids love running down the ever-shifting corridors of water as the jets dance up and down. The Courtauld Gallery has a huge collection of Impressionist and post-Impressionist paintings as well as older works, which are on permanent display. It also stages temporary exhibitions throughout the year. The Embankment Galleries, which opened in April 2008, focus on photography, design, fashion and architecture. London Fashion Week will return here in 2011.

There are imaginative free family workshops on Saturdays for six to 12s (2-3.30pm) and occasional Studio Days for 13- to 18-year-olds, themed around the art in the galleries; these must be booked ahead and cost £15. *Buggy access. Cafés. Disabled access: lift, toilet. Nappy-changing facilities. Nearest picnic place: courtyard. Restaurant. Shops.*

South London Gallery

65 Peckham Road, SE5 8UH (7703 6120, www.southlondongallery.org). Peckham Rye rail or bus 12, 36, 171, 345. **Open** *11am-6pm Tue, Thur-Sun; 11am-9pm Wed.* **Admission** free. **Credit** AmEx, MC, V. **5+ (parental advisory)**

A major extension of this Camberwell gallery opened in June 2010, incorporating the neighbouring Victorian house, which was converted into extra gallery space, a new café and a resident artist's flat. The gallery is known for its forward-thinking approach. In the 1990s, it was one of the main showcases for Young British Artists, giving shows to Marc Quinn, Gavin Turk and Tracey Emin; it was the first gallery to exhibit Emin's famous appliquéd tent. It remains one of the capital's foremost contemporary art galleries, with exhibitions that comprise installations, performance pieces and film, as well as paintings and sculpture. Inventive family workshops tie in with the current exhibitions: check online for details. *Buggy access. Disabled access: lift, toilet. Nappy-changing facilities. Nearest picnic place: gallery garden.*

Tate Britain

Millbank, SW1P 4RG (7887 8888, www.tate.org.uk). Pimlico tube, or bus 77A, 88, C10. **Open** *10am-6pm daily; late opening 6-10pm first Fri of mth. Tours 11am, noon, 2pm, 3pm Mon-Fri; noon, 3pm Sat, Sun.* **Admission** free. *Temporary exhibitions prices vary. Tours free.* **Credit** MC, V. **Map** p333 L7. **5+**

Downriver from its younger sister, Tate Britain possesses a princely collection of British fine art, sweeping from 1500 to the present day. It's an extraordinary spread, with something for everyone: from Constable's placid landscapes to Blake's apocalyptic visions; the Turner collection is magnificent. Every year, four shortlisted contenders for his namesake award (the Turner Prize) exhibit here, in a flurry of controversy and media hype. Tate Britain's temporary exhibitions are also a big draw, and children should enjoy Watercolour (until 21 Aug 2011), which presents a fresh assessment on the history and future of watercolour painting with rarely displayed works by artists ranging from JMW Turner and Thomas Girtin to Anish Kapoor and Tracey Emin.

A children's discovery trail, available from the information desks, explores the 'secret' Tate, and there's a cosy family reading area in the Rotunda outside Room 17 that offers tips on getting the most out of a visit. The venerable art trolley is wheeled out at weekends and during school holidays (10am-3pm), laden with activities. Check the website for more family and kids' goings-on. When you've finished here, you can cruise swiftly to Tate Modern for another art fix, on the Damien Hirst-decorated Tate to Tate boat.

Buggy access. Café. Disabled access: lift, toilet. Nappy-changing facilities. Nearest picnic place: lawns, Riverside Gardens. Restaurant. Shop.

Tate Modern

Bankside, SE1 9TG (7887 8000, www.tate. org.uk). St Paul's tube or Blackfriars rail. **Open** 10am-6pm Mon-Thur, Sun; 10am-10pm Fri, Sat. Last entry 45mins before closing. **Admission** free. *Temporary exhibitions* prices vary. **Credit** AmEx, MC, V. **Map** p334 O7. **5+**

Tate Modern isn't just a gallery, but a day out in its own right. Even getting here along the South Bank is an event. Then comes the excitement of reaching the doors of Turbine Hall via a wide dramatic slope. And once inside, the sheer scale of the gallery's major exhibition space is enough to give most children a sensory hit. This is where, each year, a large-scale, specially commissioned work is installed in the autumn and stays until April (Tacita Dean is the artist behind the 2011-12 installation). Another highlight for 2011 is the first major

Joan Miró retrospective (until 11 Sept) in the capital for nearly 50 years. The permanent collections are shown in four wings on Levels 3 and 5, guided by themes such as Cubism, Futurism and Vorticism, Surrealism, Abstract Expressionism and European Informal Art and Minimalism. Grand expansion plans are under way and due for completion in 2012, with a vast new exhibition and performance space inside the power station's old oil tanks, as well as a new structure on the south side of the gallery.

Early art appreciation is encouraged by the family activity packs available from Level 3. The Start team will help you choose which art materials, puzzles or architectural trails are suitable for your brood (available at weekends, noon-4pm, and in school hols). Family trails (free) and a kids' multimedia tour for the over fives (£3) are available anytime. On Level 5, the Bloomberg Learning Zone offers educational attractions for under-fives, including games, multimedia activities and a short film. *See also p48* **Neighbourhood Watch**.

Buggy access. Café. Disabled access: lift, toilet. Nappy-changing facilities. Nearest picnic place: grounds. Restaurant. Shops.

Vestry House Museum

Vestry Road, E17 9NH (8496 4391, www.walthamforest.gov.uk/rd/vestry-house). Walthamstow Central tube/rail. **Open** 10am-5pm Wed-Sun. *Tours* groups only, by prior arrangement. **Admission** free; donations appreciated. **No credit cards. 6+**

Ragged School Museum. *See p88.*

Sightseeing

Vestry House became a museum in 1932, but it was once a workhouse; look out for the stone plaque above the entrance, which decrees: 'if any would not work, neither should he eat' – one to remember when the kids won't tidy their rooms. It's an engaging little museum devoted to local history. One room displays vintage toys and games; another is done up as a Victorian parlour. On the ground floor you can see a reconstructed police cell (the building served a stint as a police station in the late 19th century), complete with amusing wax figures dressed as village bobby and drunkard. You can also walk through the workhouse garden, admire a reconstructed Bremer Car (London's first petrol-driven vehicle), and learn about the housewife's lot with a display of labour-intensive domestic paraphernalia (carpet beaters, flat irons, and other antiquated devices). Temporary exhibitions run for one to two months at a time and there are family workshops every third Sunday of the month and during school holidays.
Buggy access (ground floor). Disabled access: toilet (ground floor). Nappy-changing facilities. Nearest picnic place: museum garden. Shop.

Victoria & Albert Museum

Cromwell Road, SW7 2RL (7942 2000, www.vam.ac.uk). South Kensington tube. **Open** 10am-5.45pm Mon-Thur, Sat, Sun; 10am-10pm Fri. *Tours* hourly 10.30am-3.30pm daily. **Admission** free. *Temporary exhibitions* prices vary. **Credit** AmEx, MC, V. **Map** p329 E10. **5+**
The V&A's Future Plan has been a revelation. Much of its incredible collection of sculpture, ceramics, textiles, jewellery and decorative arts of every description is being displayed in dramatically fresh ways. The Medieval and Renaissance Galleries opened in December 2009 and show 1,800 objects in chronological order; the Gilbert Collection of silver, gold and gemmed ornaments has arrived from Somerset House; and the Ceramics Galleries have been renovated and supplemented with an eye-catching bridge.

Children will particularly like the pottery studio, where they can sometimes watch demonstrations. The British Galleries are good for hands-on exhibits: kids can squeeze into a corset and crinoline, try on an armoured gauntlet or construct the Crystal Palace; other interactive displays are marked on the museum's floorplan with a special symbol. Family trails (designed for seven to 12s) can

V&A Museum of Childhood. *See p88.*

also be picked up from the information desk. On Saturdays and school holidays, over-fives can take their pick of various activity backpacks, then delve in to find puzzles, games and challenges linked to the displays.

There's also lots going on in the art studios and media labs at the museum's Sackler Centre. Sunday's Drop-in Design events bring all sorts of arts and crafts, from making extravagant accessories to designing crazy cups for the Mad Hatter's tea party, and there are also some brilliant holiday sessions on offer. The café (*see p254*) offers high chairs, and under-tens can order half-price portions of adult main courses. Give the children a run around in the grassy courtyard (they can even paddle in summer) then check out the Theatre and Performance galleries – a visual feast of costume, puppets and stage sets, which might inspire the kids to stage a show of their own back at home. *See also p120* **Neighbourhood Watch**.
Buggy access. Café. Disabled access: lift, toilet. Nappy-changing facilities. Nearest picnic place: basement picnic room (weekends & school holidays), museum garden, Pirelli Gardens. Restaurant. Shop.

Sightseeing

Wallace Collection

Hertford House, Manchester Square,
W1U 3BN (7563 9500, www.wallace
collection.org). Bond Street tube or bus
2, 10, 12, 30, 74, 113. **Open** 10am-5pm
daily. **Admission** free. **Credit** MC, V.
Map p330 G5. **6+**

An important collection of 18th- and 19th-
century art lies in this London townhouse, once
the city residence of the Marquesses of
Hertford, the Wallaces. There are paintings by
great masters like Titian, Rembrandt and
Velázquez as well as a series of grand,
irresistibly opulent rooms showcasing Sèvres
porcelain, Louis XIV and XV furnishings and
other fabulously costly trinkets. The biggest
draw for most youngsters, though, is the
magnificent armoury; regular events invite kids
to handle some of the collection's treasures,
while would-be gallant champions can stagger
under the weight of a replica suit of armour in
the Conservation Gallery. The house oozes
grandeur – but stately demeanour belies the
gallery's welcoming, family-friendly approach.
All sorts of trails and artist-led activity sessions
help children relate to its priceless collections
of paintings, porcelain and furniture, as well as
weaponry, and small visitors often go home
clutching their own masks, collages, hats and
watercolours. Award-winning artists are often
in charge of the Little Draw sessions, held on
the first Sunday of the month from 1.30pm.

In the glass-roofed courtyard, which is also a
sculpture garden, is an Oliver Peyton-run
French brasserie; children's mains feature
organic meat and fish, and there's a two-course
deal for kids for just £9.50. *See also p152*
Neighbourhood Watch.

Buggy access. Disabled access: lift, toilet.
Nappy-changing facilities. Nearest picnic
place: courtyard benches. Restaurant. Shop.

Whitechapel Gallery

77-82 Whitechapel High Street, E1 7QX
(7522 7888, www.whitechapelgallery.org).
Aldgate East tube. **Open** 11am-6pm Tue,
Wed, Fri-Sun; 11am-9pm Thur. **Admission**
free. **Credit** MC, V. **5+**

This East End favourite looks comfortable
inside its expanded space, having appropriated
the old Whitechapel Library next door.
Whatever you think about the library having
being relocated and renamed the Idea Store, the
gallery has certainly benefited. The light and
airy spaces created by the expansion are
beautiful, and host a number of temporary
exhibitions. Especially lovely is the Clore

Creative Studio right at the top. This is where
children's drawing workshops for ages ten to
16 are held on Saturdays, 11.30am-1pm (£50
for five sessions). Family art workshops, trails
and activity packs are also available; see
website for details.

Buggy access. Café. Disabled access: lift,
toilet. Nappy-changing facilities. Nearest
picnic place: Christ Church Spitalfields.
Restaurant. Shop.

CHILDHOOD

Foundling Museum

40 Brunswick Square, WC1N 1AZ (7841
3600, www.foundlingmuseum.org.uk).
Russell Square tube. **Open** 10am-5pm
Tue-Sat; 11am-5pm Sun. *Tours* by
arrangement. **Admission** £7.50; £5
reductions; free under-16s. **Credit** MC, V.
Map p333 L4. **3+**

'Foundlings' was the affectionate name for the
residents of London's Hospital for the
Maintenance and Education of Exposed and
Deserted Children. Founded in 1739 by retired
sea captain Thomas Coram, it was largely
funded by donations from the painter William
Hogarth and the composer George Frideric
Handel. Over the next 215 years, the hospital
provided education for 27,000 children who had
been abandoned by their mothers.

As well as paintings by Hogarth and other
artists, the museum has a second-floor room
dedicated to Handel. Kids love the 'musical
chairs', with hidden speakers playing excerpts
from the composer's works. The best time to
visit the museum is on the first Saturday of
every month, when activities are laid on for
children: dressing up, listening to stories,
becoming a curator for the day or designing
cards might feature on the agenda. Extra
family fun days and storytelling sessions take
place on Thursdays during the school
holidays. Brilliant backpacks for three to fives
and five to eights can be borrowed for free at
any time; they're stuffed to the hilt with games,
puzzles, dressing-up gear, finger puppets and
more; themes include the sea, transport and
time with the foundlings. There is also a range
of trails to follow.

The bright, spacious café is worth visiting
too. An antique tavern clock counts the hours
and classical music hangs in the air. It's a
peaceful place to lunch thanks to its relatively
reclusive location, and the menu features
innovative sandwiches, pies and salads.

Sightseeing

There's also a good range of cakes and a cream tea. *See also p80* **Neighbourhood Watch**. *Buggy access. Café. Disabled access: lift; toilet. Nappy-changing facilities. Nearest picnic place: Brunswick Square, Coram's Fields. Shop.*

London International Gallery of Children's Art

Waterlow Park Centre, Dartmouth Park Hill, N19 5JF (7281 1111, www.ligca.org). Archway tube. **Open** 10am-4pm Fri-Sun. **Admission** free; donations appreciated. **No credit cards. 5+**

LIGCA has moved from the O2 Centre to this much more pleasant location in Highgate's Waterlow Park (*see p142*). The gallery celebrates the creativity of children all over the world with temporary exhibitions that change every few months. Art materials are left out for any young visitor who might want to get creative; staff also offer children's birthday parties. The gallery is manned by volunteers, so phone before setting out.
Buggy access. Disabled access: lift, toilet. Nappy-changing facilities. Nearest picnic place: Waterlow Park.

Pollock's Toy Museum

1 Scala Street (entrance on Whitfield Street), W1T 2HL (7636 3452, www.pollockstoy museum.com). Goode Street tube. **Open** 10am-5pm Mon-Sat. **Admission** £5; £4 reductions; £2 3-16s; free under-3s. **Credit** AmEx, MC, V. **5+**

In a quiet corner of Fitzrovia, occupying two townhouses, this museum is a warren of wonderfully atmospheric rooms and creaky, narrow staircases. It's named after Benjamin Pollock, the last of the Victorian toy theatre printers: to see examples of his tiny tableaux, visit room six. Elsewhere, there are treasures gathered from nurseries across the world, from delicate china dolls to mechanical tin toys and dapper lead soldiers. Adults are more likely to appreciate the nostalgia value of the old board games and playthings, but the museum shop has child appeal, with its reproduction cardboard theatres, wind-up music boxes, animal masks and tin robots.
Nearest picnic place: Crabtree Fields, Colville Place. Shop.

Ragged School Museum

46-50 Copperfield Road, E3 4RR (8980 6405, www.raggedschoolmuseum.org.uk). Mile End tube. **Open** 10am-5pm Wed,

Thur; 2-5pm 1st Sun of mth. **Admission** free; donations appreciated. **No credit cards. 6+ (during term time), 2+ (school holidays)**

Thomas Barnardo arrived in London to train as a doctor in 1866. But when he came face to face with the poverty, overcrowding, disease and lack of provision for poor children to get an education, he jettisoned his plans and set up his first Ragged School. The largest of these was established here, just by Regent's Canal, ten years later. The buildings have now been converted into a fascinating museum, with gallery areas revealing what life was like in the Victorian East End. There's also a mock-up of a classroom where mock lessons – complete with slates, dunce hats and a costume-clad teacher – are staged for today's children; they're open to people of all ages on the first Sunday of the month. The 45-minute lessons start at 2.15pm and 3.30pm; book on arrival at the museum, as places are limited. In the holidays, special events run on Wednesdays and Thursdays (check the website for details). There's also a Victorian kitchen and displays on local history and industry.
Buggy access. Café. Disabled access: toilet. Nappy-changing facilities. Nearest picnic place: Mile End Park. Shop.

V&A Museum of Childhood

Cambridge Heath Road, E2 9PA (8983 5200, 8980 2415 recorded information, www.vam.ac.uk/moc). Bethnal Green tube/rail or bus 8. **Open** 10am-5.45pm daily. **Admission** free. Under-12s must be accompanied by an adult.
Credit MC, V. **1+**

When this iron building was first erected here in 1872 its purpose as a museum was pretty vague. Exhibits were mainly those left over from the Food and Animal Products collections of the Great Exhibition. Its development into the Museum of Childhood was almost an accident; when post-World War I curator Arthur Sabin noticed that many of the museum's visitors were bored-looking children, he decided to pepper the galleries with child-friendly objects and toys. These days, it's a real treasure trove. The well-stocked shop and Benugo café are on the ground floor; note the 19th-century black and white mosaic floor tiles, made by female prisoners in Woking jail. The mezzanine and upper floors are configured to house the permanent collections, alongside temporary and touring exhibitions. From The Tiger Who Came to Tea to Mog and Pink

My Sport Kung Fu
Ethan, 8

What inspired you to take up kung fu?
My brother goes to capoeira and I thought I'd like to try something else. Dad took me to watch a karate class and a kung fu class and I liked the kung fu best. I thought the karate teacher was a bit shouty.

What do you like about your sport?
I like the rolls best – my favourite is a diagonal front shoulder roll. I've made new friends there too. There's a boy called Sebastian who I really like.

What level are you at?
I just started recently. My teacher always encourages us to try our best. He shows us new moves in slow motion.

What's next for you in your sport?
I'd like to get better at the rolls I know already and learn some more.

Which events would you like to see at the London 2012 Olympic Games and Paralympic Games?
The Pole Vault.

Sightseeing

Rabbit (until 4 Sept 2011) is a retrospective of children's author and illustrator Judith Kerr, featuring original illustrations from *The Tiger Who Came to Tea*, *Mog* and *Pink Rabbit*. Kerr's first picture book, *The Tiger Who Came to Tea*, was written as a bedtime story for her own children and was published in 1968. It soon became a classic and by the time it celebrated its 40th anniversary in 2008, it had been translated into 11 languages and sold over five million copies. Alongside original artwork, notes and sketches from the book, children can enjoy stepping into Sophie's kitchen to have tea with a life-size tiger.

A lot of thought has gone into making this museum child-friendly; after all, it's a tease to see so many toys and not be able to play with them. To compensate, there are activity stations in each area with Lego, stickle bricks, a sandpit, board games, rocking horses, a book corner and many other treats. In the high-ceilinged, open gallery space, the encouragement to play means the din inside is redolent of an indoor playcentre. It's not conducive to studying what's inside the cases, which is a shame for adults; some of the exhibits – like the 1780s models of a Chinese rock garden and the 1825 Viennese model theatre – merit a bit of contemplation.

Buggy access. Café. Disabled access: lift, toilet. Nappy-changing facilities. Nearest picnic place: basement, museum grounds. Shop.

ETHNOGRAPHY

British Museum

Great Russell Street, WC1B 3DG (7323 8000, 7323 8299, www.britishmuseum.org). Holborn, Russell Square or Tottenham Court Road tube. **Open** *Galleries* 10am-5.30pm Mon-Thur, Sat, Sun; 10am-8.30pm Fri. *Great Court* 9am-6pm Mon-Thur, Sun; 9am-11pm Fri, Sat. *Tours* Highlights 10.30am, 1pm, 3pm daily; phone for details. Eye Opener tours, phone for details. **Admission** free; donations appreciated. *Temporary exhibitions* prices vary. *Highlights tours* £8; £5 under-11s, reductions. *Eye Opener tours* free. **Credit** AmEx, DC, MC, V. **Map** p333 K5. **5+**

The British Museum opened its doors to the public in 1759 and was free even then to 'all studious and curious persons' who wanted to take advantage of its collections. Visitors have now reached six million per year and for good reason: there's an incredible array of treasures from across the globe. Other museums would give their eye teeth for a fraction of its priceless relics, which include the Rosetta Stone, the Lewis Chessmen, the Anglo-Saxon helmet from Sutton Hoo and the Parthenon (Elgin) Marbles. Rooms 62 and 63 of the Roxie Walker galleries are top of most children's agendas; it's here that the mummies reside, exerting an eerie spell over visitors. The Africa galleries, full of vivid

Petrie Museum of Egyptian Archaeology.

colours and spooky masks, and Living & Dying – a surreal collection of tribal objects relating to death and mortality from the collection of the Wellcome Trust – are also atmospheric.

Norman Foster's two-acre covered Great Court was an inspired idea, and equals Tate Modern's Turbine Hall (*see p85*) for vast indoor spaces that children love to feel tiny in. The café at the far end is overpriced, but it's a lovely light place to sit, and no one seems to mind if you bring a picnic.

Plans were passed in December 2009 for a large expansion of the building on its north side. A new conservation wing (much of it underground) will allow the museum's staff more opportunity to save ancient treasures, while above ground, a large new exhibition space will take the pressure off audience crushes for temporary exhibitions. Meanwhile, children can enjoy the walk-through Australian Landscape curated by Kew Gardens on the west lawn of the museum forecourt until 16 October 2011. Saints, Relics and Devotion in Medieval Europe (until 9 Oct 2011), a major exhibition looking at some of the finest sacred treasures of the medieval age, might also interest budding historians.

Inventive and free family events run on Saturdays, ranging from Islamic tile-painting workshops to creating a manga comic, while digital photography-based sessions are held on selected Sundays at the Samsung Digital Photography Centre. Handling sessions take place daily in various galleries and there are some fantastic trail booklets available in the Paul Hamlyn Library that help children of different ages get the best out of the museum. *See also p80* **Neighbourhood Watch**.

Buggy access. Cafés. Disabled access: lift, toilet. Nappy-changing facilities. Nearest picnic place: Russell Square. Restaurant. Shops.

Horniman Museum

100 London Road, SE23 3PQ (8699 1872, www.horniman.ac.uk). Forest Hill rail or bus 122, 176, 185, 312, 356, 363, P4, P13. **Open** 10.30am-5.30pm daily. **Admission** free; donations appreciated. **Credit** MC, V. **3+**

This has to be one of the most child-friendly museums in all London. The Horniman Museum was founded by Victorian tea trader Frederick John Horniman, an inveterate collector of all sorts of curios. As his worldwide travels continued, his collection grew far too large for the family home in Forest Hill; undaunted, he commissioned a new museum to

contain it, which opened to the public in 1901. It's not so much what's here as how it's presented. Head straight to the Hands On Base, where there are boxes of puppets and masks to try out and all sorts of other objects to handle. The Natural History Gallery has skeletons, fossils, pickled animals, stuffed birds and insects in glass cases, presided over by an overstuffed walrus (never having seen such a beast before, the taxidermist didn't realise it ought to have thick folds of skin).

There's an aquarium, and the Nature Base, which has lots of enticing interactive exhibits about the natural world. But whatever you do, save time for the wonderful Music Gallery, where 1,600 instruments are displayed in floor-to-ceiling glass cases. What excites children are the two large, white touch-screen 'tables' in the middle of the room that enable them to choose and listen to pieces of music featuring the different instruments. Adjoining the gallery is a Hands On room, this time giving young visitors carte blanche to bash away at world instruments – including little hollow wooden frogs from South-east Asia, Tibetan singing bowls and a 'flip-flop-o-fone'. Outside, the 16-acre gardens have an animal enclosure with rabbits, goats and chickens, an elegant conservatory and a picnic spot with superb views. Bali – Dancing for the Gods (until 8 Jan 2012) is a blockbuster exhibition looking at Balinese culture and dance.

Buggy access. Café. Disabled access: lift, toilet. Nappy-changing facilities. Nearest picnic place: museum gardens. Shop.

Petrie Museum of Egyptian Archaeology

University College London, entrance through DMS Watson Library, Malet Place, WC1E 6BT (7679 2884, www.petrie.ucl.ac.uk). Goodge Street or Warren Street tube, or bus 29, 73, 134. **Open** 1-5pm Tue-Sat. Closed Easter hols. **Admission** free; donations appreciated. **No credit cards**. **Map** p333 K4. **7+**

This museum was originally set up as a teaching resource for the lecturers and students of UCL. William Flinders Petrie was a professor at the University and this collection was amassed partly from his own excavations at sites around the world and partly from a large bequest from 19th-century collector Amelia Edwards. In this age of touch-screen technology and interactive bells and whistles, the museum's old-fashioned glass cabinets are practically a museum piece in their own right.

Its eccentricity imbues the museum with an inimitable charm: some corners are so dimly lit, staff lend out torches. They're also endearingly keen, and happy to talk about the collection. As one chap charmingly explained to us, Amelia Edwards was 'more interested in how ordinary Egyptians lived from day to day than in bling' – which means the collections are focused on everyday minutiae such as beads, tools, amulets and clothes. Children can write their name in hieroglyphs, make a pot, or dress like an Ancient Egyptian; it's simple stuff, but great fun. The skeleton in a pot, dating from around the third millenium BC, also enthralls saucer-eyed small fry, along with a mummified head and various fragmentary remains. There are also family activity days; see the website. *See also p80* **Neighbourhood Watch**.
Buggy access. Disabled access: lift, toilet. Nearest picnic place: Gordon Square. Shop.

EMERGENCY SERVICES

London Fire Brigade Museum
Winchester House, 94A Southwark Bridge Road, SE1 0EG (8555 1200, www.london-fire.gov.uk). Borough tube or Southwark tube/rail or bus 344. **Open** by appointment 10.30am, 2pm Mon-Fri. **Admission** £3; £2 7-14s, reductions; £1 under-7s. **Credit** MC, V. **Map** p334 O9. **5+**
Winchester House was where London's chief fire officers worked until 1937. Now it's a museum dedicated to the history and ongoing work of the capital's mighty Fire Brigade. Any child with a fire engine fixation will relish the chance to come here. Visits are by appointment only, which means an expert guide will take you round the collection, comprising memorabilia, photos, uniforms, paintings and equipment, showing how firefighting has changed since the Great Fire of 1666. Small children are most smitten with the shiny fire engines, ranging from an 1830s model to red and brass beauties. Although they're not allowed to touch the fire engines, kids are given fireman uniforms to try on, as well as colouring materials. Booking is essential.
Buggy access. Disabled access: toilet. Nearest picnic place: Mint Street Park. Shop.

Museum & Library of the Order of St John
St John's Gate, St John's Lane, EC1M 4DA (7324 4005, www.sja.org.uk/museum). Farringdon tube/rail, or bus 55, 63, 243.

Open 10am-5pm Mon-Sat. Closed bank hol weekends. *Tours* 11am, 2.30pm Tue, Fri, Sat. **Admission** free; suggested donations for tours £5; £4 reductions. **Credit** MC, V. **Map** p334 O4. **5+**
The St John Ambulance organisation has a long history of training older children in the skills of first aid. The museum devoted to the Order of St John's history has been undergoing a major Heritage Lottery-funded redevelopment and reopened in November 2010. A double-height Link Gallery with an interactive timeline now compliments existing exhibits: bandages printed with first aid instructions, first-aid kits and archaic-looking ambulances, along with archaeological finds, armour, coins and seals dating back to the Order's earliest years. The redevelopment also includes a children's trail and a learning space, along with a new entrance through the 16th-century gatehouse. Family activities include trails, gallery actor sessions, family tours and activity packs. Keep an eye on the website for more details.
Buggy access (ground floor). Disabled access: lift (limited access), toilet (ground floor). Nearest picnic place: Clerkenwell Close. Shop.

GREAT LIVES

Apsley House
149 Piccadilly, W1J 7NT (7499 5676, www.english-heritage.org.uk). Hyde Park Corner tube. **Open** *Apr-Oct* 11am-5pm Wed-Sun & bank hols. *Nov-Mar* 11am-4pm Wed-Sun. Last admission 30 mins before closing. *Tours* by arrangement. **Admission** £6 (includes audio guide if available); £5.10 reductions; £3 5-16s; free under-5s. *Joint ticket with admission to Wellington Arch* £7.40; £6.30 reductions; £3.70 5-16s; free under-5s; £18.50 family (2+3). *Tours* phone for details. **Credit** MC, V. **Map** p332 G8. **5+**
This imposing mansion was once known as Number 1 London, because it was the first house visitors passed after going through the toll gates. It's still one of London's most impressive addresses, lording it over Hyde Park Corner. It was the family home of Arthur Wellesley, the first Duke of Wellington, who defeated Napoleon at Waterloo. His descendants still live in the building, but some of it has been given over to a museum about the duke, his campaigns and the fine art and precious antiques he brought back from his travels. Pieces include Canova's enormous marble statue of Napoleon in his birthday suit,

as well as paintings by Rubens and Van Dyck. The anniversary of the battle of Waterloo, in June, brings a weekend of soldierly activities, and there's an action sheet families can pick up anytime.

Buggy access. Nearest picnic place: Hyde Park. Shop.

Benjamin Franklin House

36 Craven Street, WC2N 5NF (7930 9121, 7925 1405 bookings, www.benjamin franklinhouse.org). Embankment tube or Charing Cross tube/rail. **Open** 10.30am-5pm Mon, Wed-Sun. **Admission** £7; £5 reductions; free under-16s. *Tours* noon, 1pm, 2pm, 3.15pm, 4.15pm Mon, Wed-Sun. Booking advisable. **Credit** MC, V. **Map** p333 L7. **6+**

The founding father of the United States lived just around the corner from Trafalgar Square in this 18th-century house for 16 years before the American Revolution. Here, he performed the fraught diplomatic job of 'mediating unrest' between his homeland and its colonial rulers. The house opened to the public in 2006 on Franklin's 300th birthday. It's not a museum exactly, but more of a historical experience enjoyed during guided tours led by actors who bring the history of the place to life. Projections and recorded sound recreate Franklin's London years and recount his many achievements, which include conceiving the ideas of lightning conductors, bifocal specs and fire insurance, identifying the Gulf Stream and coining enduring aphorisms such as 'early to bed and early to rise, makes a man healthy, wealthy and wise'.

Buggy access (ground floor). Nearest picnic place: Victoria Gardens, Embankment. Shop.

Charles Dickens Museum

48 Doughty Street, WC1N 2LX (7405 2127, www.dickensmuseum.com). Russell Square tube. **Open** 10am-5pm daily. **Admission** £7; £5 reductions; £3 5-15s; free under-5s. **Credit** AmEx, DC, MC, V. **Map** p333 M4. **8+**

Dickens wrote *Oliver Twist* and *A Christmas Carol* in this house, his home for three years. The writer has given us a vivid picture of Victorian London through his work and the building is crammed with memorabilia and artefacts; in the basement, visitors can see a 25-minute film on Dickens's life in London. Weekly children's 'handling sessions' let young visitors write with Dickens's pen and hold various other possessions. These take place most Wednesdays, but call ahead as they are run by volunteers. There are two mini-trails for children, based on Dickens's stories, plus walking tours of Dickensian London. Great Expectations is a new £3.1m project to restore, redevelop and improve the museum, timed to coincide with the bicentenary of Dickens's birth

Benjamin Franklin House.

Sightseeing

in 2012. At the heart of the project is the museum's expansion and the redisplay of rooms at 48 Doughty Street, returning them to their traditional Victorian-era appearance. *Buggy access (ground floor). Café. Nearest picnic place: Coram's Fields, Russell Square. Shop.*

Dr Johnson's House

17 Gough Square, off Fleet Street, EC4A 3DE (7353 3745, www.drjohnsons house.org). Chancery Lane or Temple tube, or Blackfriars rail. **Open** *May-Sept* 11am-5.30pm Mon-Sat. *Oct-Apr* 11am-5pm Mon-Sat. *Tours* by arrangement (groups of 10 or more). **Admission** £4.50; £3.50 reductions; £1.50 under-16s; £10 family (2+ unlimited children). *Tours* free, booking essential. *Evening tours* by arrangement; phone for details. **No credit cards.** **Map** p334 N6. **6+**

Preserved in an atmospheric little square off Fleet Street is this four-storey Georgian house, which was home to Dr Samuel Johnson, author of the *Dictionary of the English Language*. He lived here with his cat, Hodge – described by his master as 'a very fine cat indeed'. Johnson fed his beloved moggie on oysters; hence the oyster shells at the foot of the bronze statue of Hodge outside the house. It's one of the few items that will really interest children, although they might enjoy trying on replica Georgian costumes in the garret or watching the ancient film playing on a loop of actors embodying the doctor and friends. There is also a children's mini guide and trail available from the front desk.
Buggy access. Nearest picnic place: Lincoln's Inn Fields. Shop.

Florence Nightingale Museum

St Thomas's Hospital, 2 Lambeth Palace Road, SE1 7EW (7620 0374, www.florence-nightingale.co.uk). Westminster tube or Waterloo tube/rail. **Open** 10am-5pm daily. **Admission** £5.80; £4.80 5-15s, reductions; free under-5s; £16 family (2+5). **Credit** AmEx, MC, V. **Map** p333 M9. **5+**

This museum reopened in 2010, after a £1.4 million refurbishment for the centenary of Florence Nightingale's death. The story of the Lady with the Lamp is told afresh in three pavilions located in the grounds of St Thomas's Hospital on the South Bank. The new exhibits are eye-catching, with imaginative interactive features, including an audio tour listened to on stethoscopes. Florence Nightingale's important

status in Key Stage One and Two of the National Curriculum means school holidays are always busy at the museum dedicated to her life. Among the objects on display are her beloved, hand-reared pet owl, Athena (stuffed, and looking slightly wild of eye) and the medicine chest she took to Turkey. Trails for children are available, and art and history activities run during school holidays.
Buggy access. Disabled access: toilet. Nappy-changing facilities. Nearest picnic place: benches by hospital entrance, Archbishop's Park. Shop.

Sherlock Holmes Museum

221B Baker Street, NW1 6XE (7935 4430, www.sherlock-holmes.co.uk). Baker Street tube or bus 74, 139, 189. **Open** 9.30am-6pm daily. **Admission** £6; £4 6-16s; free under-6s. **Credit** AmEx, MC, V. **Map** p327 F4. **6+**

Rarely has a fictional address had more resonance. The house is set up as if the fictional master detective and his amiable sidekick are in situ. So, too, is their long-suffering landlady, Mrs Hudson, who can tell you all you need to know about the great man. Nose about Holmes's study, take a seat in his armchair by the fireplace and investigate his personal effects: the deerstalker cap, pipe, violin and magnifying glass are all present and correct. Upstairs is the room belonging to his associate, Dr Watson, while the third-floor exhibit rooms contain wax models of scenes from the stories; Holmes and his dastardly arch-enemy, Professor Moriarty, can be seen in the same room.
Nearest picnic place: Regent's Park. Shop.

Sir John Soane's Museum

13 Lincoln's Inn Fields, WC2A 3BP (7405 2107, www.soane.org). Holborn tube. **Open** 10am-5pm Tue-Sat; 10am-5pm, 6-9pm 1st Tue of mth. *Tours* 11am Sat. **Admission** free; donations appreciated. *Tours* £5; free under-16s. **Credit** MC, V. **Map** p331 M5. **7+**

When Sir John Soane was Professor of Architecture at the Royal Academy, he was already opening his house and collections to students on a weekly basis. After his death in 1837, the house was turned into a museum – kept, as Soane had asked, as near to how he had left it as possible. The collections reflect his passion for an eclectic mix of artefacts and paintings, but the joy is not just in what is here, but also how Soane chose to present it; there are all sorts of ingenious nooks and crannies. It's particularly atmospheric if you visit on the first

Night at the Museum

During daylight hours, London is awash with brilliantly child-friendly museums. From the murky re-creation of 19th-century Wapping at the Museum of London Docklands' Sailortown to the quaking, shaking Kobe supermarket at the Natural History Museum in South Kensington, kids can be entertained and educated in one fell swoop. And since 2009, the opportunities for edutainment have continued after dark during the annual three-day Museums at Night festival.

An offspring of Nuit des Musées, the festival has quickly established itself as a cultural calendar favourite, and in the last few years the nationwide campaign has seen everything from film nights and children's sleepovers to discos at numerous venerable institutions. In May 2011, major events in the capital included a Renaissance Night at the National Gallery featuring drawing from a life model, Renaissance music by candlelight and a spooky storytelling session for kids; a chance to sneak an after-hours peek behind the palace gates at the Enchanted Evening at Kensington Palace; and a chilling but child-friendly demonstration of the 19th-century anaesthetic-free amputations performed in Victorian times during Surgery by Gaslight & Other Medical Tales at the Old Operating Theatre Museum. Meanwhile, Apsley After Dark provided a rare opportunity to wander the more civilised surroundings of Apsley House, also known as No.1 London, with curtains drawn and chandeliers lit.

With almost 300 museums and galleries taking part in the festival, and some 345 events to choose from, there's plenty on offer around the city for night birds of all ages, but perhaps the star of the show for youngsters is the Royal Observatory, Greenwich, which hosted a Cosmic Family Fun Night in 2011 with a whole galaxy of activities, family workshops and special planetarium shows, along with Q&A sessions with resident astronomers during which visitors could quiz the experts on space exploration and the stars – enough to fire the imagination of even the most reluctant mini museum-goer. For more details on events for Museums at Night 2012, go to www.culture24.org.uk/museumsatnight.

Tuesday of the month, when it stays open late and is lit by candlelight; there can be lengthy queues for admission.

The old kitchen is used for holiday workshops for children of seven and above (£18 whole day/£10 half day, book in advance): youngsters learn how to make a mosaic, create a relief sculpture, paint a self-portrait and frame it, or get stuck into plaster moulding. There are also free drop-in family sessions on the third Saturday of the month (1.30-4.40pm). Children aged seven to 13 can sign up to the Young Architects Club, which meets on the first Saturday of the month. Note that buggies cannot be accommodated.

Opening up the Soane is a new, £7 million project to restore, refurbish and improve the museum, opening up Soane's top-floor 'private apartments'. Phase I of the project is due to be completed by 2012.

Nearest picnic place: Lincoln's Inn Fields. Shop.

LONDON & LOCAL

Bruce Castle Museum

Lordship Lane, N17 8NU (8808 8772, www.haringey.gov.uk). Wood Green tube then bus 123 or 243, or Seven Sisters tube/rail then bus 123 or 243, or Bruce Grove rail. **Open** 1-5pm Wed-Sun. **Admission** free; donations appreciated. **No credit cards. 4+**

This splendid, Grade I-listed 16th-century mansion is a delightfully unexpected find in an otherwise unremarkable-looking suburban street. When the mansion's gardens were opened as a park, it was the first public one of its kind in Tottenham. Inside the house, displays are devoted to the history and achievements of Haringey and its residents – more interesting than you might think, as the borough was home to both madcap illustrator William Heath Robinson and Rowland Hill, the inventor of the Penny Post.

The museum's Inventor Centre has numerous buttons to press and levers to pull. There are black-and-white photos dating back to the days when the area was open countryside and White Hart Lane a sleepy country track. Football fans should keep an eye out for the displays on Tottenham Hotspur and read the surprising history of Walter Tull, one of the first black football players in Britain. There are free activity sheets for kids, including a nature trail that rambles around the pleasant park outside,

Florence Nightingale Museum. *See p94.*

plus free art and craft sessions for families from 2pm to 4pm on Sundays year-round, with extra school holiday sessions.

Buggy access. Disabled access: lift, toilet. Nappy-changing facilities. Nearest picnic place: museum grounds. Shop.

Brunel Museum

Brunel Engine House, Railway Avenue, SE16 4LF (7231 3840, www.brunel-museum.org.uk). Rotherhithe rail. **Open** 10am-5pm daily. **Admission** £2; £1 reductions; free under-16s. **No credit cards. 5+**

The Thames Tunnel, created by the Brunel father and son team Sir Marc and Isambard Kingdom, was the first underwater tunnel in the world. The Brunels worked from 1825 until 1843 to create the underwater passageway running from Rotherhithe to Wapping; young Isambard nearly drowned in the process. The story of what the Victorians hailed as 'the eighth wonder of the world' is told in this museum in the original engine house, while the tunnel itself is now used by the East London overland rail line. A major new refurbishment was completed in late 2009, giving the museum a tea room with views over the river, an activity centre and also access to the Grand Entrance Hall for special events once a month. There's plenty for children to do, with a special wipe-clean drawing table in the award-winning sculpture garden and craft activities at weekends. There's also a popular summer play-scheme; in 2011 a blacksmith will again be working with children to create a permenant piece of sculpture to sit in the grounds. The giant figure of Brunel that is owned by the museum is always a big player in the Bermondsey and Rotherhithe carnivals.

Buggy access. Café. Disabled access: toilet. Nappy-changing facilities. Nearest picnic place: museum gardens & riverbank. Shop.

Crystal Palace Museum

Anerley Hill, SE19 2BA (8676 0700, www.crystalpalacemuseum.org.uk). Crystal Palace rail. **Open** *Summer* 11am-4.30pm Sat, Sun, bank hols. *Winter* 11am-3.30pm Sat, Sun, bank hols. **Admission** free. **7+**

Housed in the old engineering school where John Logie Baird invented television, this 'exhibition of an exhibition' tells the story of the majestic, glittering glass hall that moved from Hyde Park to give this area its name. It's a friendly, if rather old-fashioned museum, with artefacts and photos in glass cases, although there are some video and audio presentations about the great glass building, which burned to the ground in November 1936. A small Logie Baird display marks the birth of home entertainment; from June 1934 the Baird Television Company occupied four studios at Crystal Palace. Note that opening hours are limited, as the museum is run by volunteers.

Buggy access. Nearest picnic place: Crystal Palace Park. Shop.

Hackney Museum

Technology & Learning Centre, 1 Reading Lane, off Mare Street, E8 1GQ (8356 3500, www.hackney.gov.uk/cm-museum.htm). *Hackney Central rail.* **Open** 9.30am-5.30pm Tue, Wed, Fri; 9.30am-8pm Thur; 10am-5pm Sat. **Admission** free. **No credit cards. 3+**

This lively museum is a community-focused affair, with plenty to keep kids busy. Displays include exhibits on immigration in the area and a re-creation of Cooke's pie and eel shop, plus activity stations and touch-screen interactive exhibits that tie into the history of the borough. Other highlights include a re-created Saxon boat that kids can pile up with goods (the original is displayed under glass in the floor) and a section on the Matchbox car factory, founded in Hackney in 1952. Toddlers can settle into the reading corner while older kids dress up in Victorian clobber and try making matchboxes – an industry that employed countless children in Victorian times.

Sightseeing

London Canal Museum. *See p98.*

Interactive art and role-playing workshops take place on Wednesday and Thursday afternoons, while the temporary exhibition changes every four months.

Buggy access. Disabled access: toilet. Nappy-changing facilities. Nearest picnic place: benches in square, London Fields. Shop.

Islington Museum

Finsbury Library, 245 St John Street, EC1V 4NB (7527 3235, www.islington.gov.uk/ museum). Angel tube or Farringdon tube/rail, or bus 153. **Open** 10am-5pm Mon, Tue, Thur-Sat. **Admission** free. **No credit cards. 5+**

Islington Museum's collection sits under the Finsbury Library, where it was rehoused in purpose-built galleries in 2008, after a funding injection from the Heritage Lottery Fund. Exhibits are organised into nine themes including Wartime, Childhood and Leisure, and the displays span centuries of local history, from the days when Islington dairies provided the milk for medieval London (check out the centuries-old cow's skull) to the rise of the mighty Arsenal football club. Children will enjoy the sections on Edwardian school life, and the special activity desks and quiz screens. Call or check online for half-term and summer holiday events.

Buggy access. Disabled access: lift, toilet. Nearest picnic place: Northampton Square. Shop.

Kew Bridge Steam Museum

Green Dragon Lane, Brentford, Middx TW8 0EN (8568 4757, www.kbsm.org). Gunnersbury tube, then bus 237 or 267, or Kew Bridge rail, or bus 65, 391. **Open** 11am-4pm Tue-Sun, bank hols. **Admission** (annual ticket, allows for multiple visits) £9.50; £8.50 reductions; £3.50 5-15s; free under-5s. Under-16s must be accompanied by an adult. **Credit** MC, V. **5+**

The museum inside this Victorian riverside pumping station celebrates the golden age of steam. At weekends, selected steam engines – the pumping variety, as well as the locomotive sort – burst into life, powered by a 1920s Lancashire boiler. The fascinating Water for Life gallery saturates you with facts about the history of water supply and usage in London, including information on the spread of cholera, while Down Below takes you down the sewers to learn about the work of their creator, Joseph Bazalgette, and the whiffy world of toshers (sewer scavengers). *Thomas Wicksteed*, a

narrow-gauge steam locomotive, gives rides on Sundays between April and October; family activities are also held during the holidays.

Buggy access. Café (Sat, Sun). Disabled access: lift, toilet. Nappy-changing facilities. Nearest picnic place: Kew Green. Shop.

London Canal Museum

12-13 New Wharf Road, N1 9RT (7713 0836, www.canalmuseum.org.uk). King's Cross tube/rail. **Open** 10am-4.30pm Tue-Sun, bank hols. Last entry 4pm. **Admission** £3; £2 reductions; £1.50 5-15s; free under-5s. **Credit** MC, V. **Map** p331 M2. **5+**

This charming museum is housed in what was once the ice warehouse of Italian-Swiss ice-cream entrepreneur Carlo Gatti. It chronicles the history of everything canal-related, as well as exploring the once highly lucrative ice trade. Kids can clamber aboard the narrowboat, *Coronis*, and get a taste of life on the waterways; an activity corner has books and building blocks to create your own tunnel; and there's the chance to learn how to tie a sheepshank and clove hitch. Most atmospheric is the ice well, once used to store imported ice from Norway; it could be kept here for months before being delivered around London. Visitors have taken to tossing coins into the cool, dark space; extra points if you can hit the bucket. Upstairs, a life-size model horse makes convincing horsey noises in his stable, while there are four videos on canal life to watch and regular temporary exhibitions. The back of the museum leads on to Battlebridge Basin, once a grimy industrial wharf, now lined with pretty residential canal boats and converted warehouses. For those with the energy, the shopping hubs of Camden and Islington are within walking distance along Regent's Canal. *See also p140* **Neighbourhood Watch**.

Buggy access. Disabled access: lift, toilet. Nappy-changing facilities. Nearest picnic place: museum terrace, canal towpath. Shop.

London Transport Museum

The Piazza, WC2E 7BB (7379 6344, www.ltmuseum.co.uk). Covent Garden tube. **Open** 10am-6pm Mon-Thur, Sat, Sun; 11am-6pm Fri. **Admission** £13.50; £10 reductions; free under-16s. **Credit** AmEx, MC, V. **Map** p333 L7. **2+**

Londoners are reminded every time there's a tube strike that the capital would grind to a halt without its essential travel system. This much-loved museum does a sterling job of presenting a fascinating and entertaining

My London 2012
Barbara, 24

How will you be participating in the London 2012 Olympic Games and Paralympic Games?
I don't know yet. Obviously, I'd like to be part of the Torch Relay! I helped to decide what music will be played during the ceremonies.

How did you come to be involved?
I heard about the Inspire Programme through the British Council – I was there doing some work as a Global Changemaker for Diversity and Inclusion. I'm not particularly sporty but I'm really passionate about youth projects.

Tell us about what you have been working on as part of the Inspire Programme?
I'm one of the co-ordinators of the Young Leaders Programme. I have championed youth participation in the Games at board meetings and I organise local events that promote the Olympic Values of inclusion, diversity and inspiration.

What do you hope your involvement in London 2012 will inspire you to achieve after the Games have finished?
I'd like to build on some of the skills I've learned in marketing and communications.

Which events would you like to see during London 2012?
Athletics would be the one for me. I'd also like to see any dance-related Cultural Olympiad events.

Sightseeing

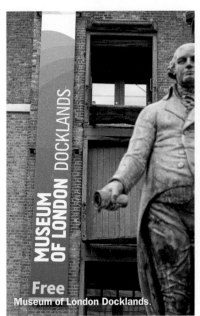

Free
Museum of London Docklands.

Sightseeing

history of transport in the capital, with 20 vehicles to explore along the way. The posters are glorious too – particularly the stylised, often wonderfully avant-garde designs of the 1920s and '30s. The museum's temporary exhibitions are usually worth making a special visit for. Sense and the City (until March 2012) explores how people in the past imagined the London of the future and how new technology will influence city living over the next ten years. The exhibition has been developed in partnership with the Royal College of Arts and will be accompanied by a lively talks and events programme. *See also p64* **Neighbourhood Watch**.
Buggy access. Café. Disabled access: lift, toilet. Nappy-changing facilities. Nearest picnic place: museum picnic room, Piazza. Shop.

Museum of London

150 London Wall, EC2Y 5HN (7001 9844, www.museumoflondon.org.uk). Barbican or St Paul's tube, or Moorgate tube/rail.
Open 10am-6pm daily. Last entry 5.30pm.
Admission free. **Credit** MC, V. **Map** p334 P5. **6+**
The £20 million redevelopment of the lower galleries of this excellent museum opened in May 2010. Anyone who calls themselves a

Londoner should make a visit one of their top priorities. It's all massively appealing to children thanks to some highly imaginative exhibits that put interactivity and discovery at the forefront of their design. Visitors enter the new galleries through the Sackler Hall, where a specially commissioned LED art installation by the Light Surgeons, LDN24, an ever-changing picture of London over 24 hours that stretches right around the walls, has pride of place.

Once inside the galleries, the first thing you notice is the sleek design of the new interiors. Glass panels in the floors reveal collections underfoot. Cubby holes in the walls are stuffed with interesting objects. Interactivity features strongly, and touchscreens allow visitors to ask questions about life expectancy during Hogarth's time, say, or to explore Charles Booth's poverty maps or find out what's in the water of a London well. Memorable exhibits include the original (and magnificent) Selfridges lifts, and the wall panels from an 18th-century debtor's prison featuring some interesting graffiti.

By comparison, the upstairs galleries now look a bit old-fashioned, but children will still enjoy the attempts made to get them involved in the history of London, from dressing-up clothes, to a stylish video presentation about the Black Death to a walk-in reconstruction of a Saxon hut.

Buggy access. Café. Disabled access: lift, toilet. Nappy-changing facilities. Nearest picnic place: Barber Surgeon's Garden. Shop.

Museum of London Docklands

West India Quay, Hertsmere Road, E14 4AL (7001 9844, www.museumoflondon.org.uk/ docklands). Canary Wharf tube or West India Quay DLR. **Open** 10am-6pm daily. Last entry 5.30pm. **Admission** free. **Credit** MC, V. **4+**

The Museum of London's Docklands sister is just as fascinating as its older sibling, and since April 2010 is free for anyone to get in. It lies in a beautiful converted warehouse overlooking a large wharf and has a wealth of absorbing exhibits. Displays devoted to migration and river trade explore the history of how 'the world came to the East End', with plenty of nautical relics and atmospheric recreations. Must-sees for kids include Sailortown, a murky, full-size recreation of 18th-century Wapping (look out for the wild animal emporium), the gibbet cage (where captured pirates met their end) and the Mudlarks Gallery, crammed with interactive exhibits and with a soft play area for under-fives. The galleries on the modern history of the docks are more interesting for adults than children, but everyone can learn something from the London, Sugar & Slavery and Docklands at War exhibitions. Many of the displays come with an entertaining audio commentary, voiced by *Time Team*'s Tony Robinson.

Temporary exhibition Pirates: The Captain Kidd Story (until 30 Oct 2011) traces the story of the real pirates who ruled our seas over 300 years ago. Original artefacts, archaeological finds and interactive displays reveal London's links with piracy, including the capital's gruesome history as a place of execution for pirates. Follow the true story of the infamous Captain Kidd, who met his end at Wapping's Execution Dock.

Costumed storytelling sessions and craft workshops take place at the museum on some Saturdays (check website for dates), with extra sessions held during the school holidays. The line-up has plenty to interest younger children, including storytimes and Monday play sessions for under-fives. *See also p106* **Neighbourhood Watch**.

Buggy access. Café. Disabled access: lift, toilet. Nappy-changing facilities. Nearest picnic place: quayside benches, refectory. Restaurant. Shop.

Museum of Richmond

Old Town Hall, Whittaker Avenue, Richmond, Surrey TW9 1TP (8332 1141, www.museumofrichmond.com). Richmond tube/rail. **Open** 11am-5pm Tue-Sat. **Admission** free. **No credit cards.** **4+**

Leafy Richmond is an area with abundant royal connections, from the 12th-century Henry I to Elizabeth I, 400 years later; fittingly, the town's museum was opened by Queen Elizabeth II. There are permanent and temporary displays on its illustrious residents of days gone by, plus a gallery of work by local artists. Engaging family workshops run during the school holidays – discovering one of the beautiful painted tiles in the museum, say, before creating your own.

Buggy access. Disabled access: lift, toilet. Nearest picnic place: Richmond Green, riverside. Shop.

Old Royal Naval College & Discover Greenwich

King William Walk, SE10 9LW (8269 4747, 8269 4799 tours, www.oldroyalnavalcollege. org). Cutty Sark DLR or Greenwich DLR/rail. **Open** 10am-5pm daily. *Tours* 2pm daily. **Admission** free. *Tours* £5; free under-16s. **Credit** MC, V. **5+**

A new £6 million development opened in March 2010 at the Old Royal Naval College. Discover Greenwich is a brand new visitor centre designed to introduce visitors to the Greenwich story before they go on and visit its individual world-famous attractions. The central exhibition space in the centre tells 500 years of fascinating history using interactive models and some previously unseen artefacts. There's also a space for temporary exhibitions, the Clore Learning Centre, a shop, a Tourist Information Centre, plus a new restaurant with micro brewery. In short, it's the place to come if you're planning a family day out in Greenwich and don't know quite where to start.

Sir Christopher Wren drew up the plans for the Old Royal Naval College, a show-stopping Baroque masterpiece all the lovelier for its riverside location. Originally it was a shelter for retired seamen, who were given bed and board, plus a shilling a week. In the late 19th century, the buildings were occupied by the Royal Naval College, before passing into the hands of the Greenwich Foundation. The University of Greenwich and Trinity College of Music are now in residence, but the exquisite neo-classical chapel and Painted Hall are open to the public. The hall is an outstanding feat of trompe l'oeil,

Sightseeing

and it took 19 years to paint; see if the kids can spot the Pocahontas-like figure who represents the Americas on the Upper Hall's central ceiling panel. Check the website for seasonal events such as the Big Draw or the May Fair. *See also p132* **Neighbourhood Watch**.
Buggy access. Café. Disabled access: toilet. Nappy-changing facilities. Nearest picnic place: Naval College grounds. Restaurant. Shop.

Wimbledon Windmill Museum

Windmill Road, Wimbledon Common, SW19 5NR (8947 2825, www.wimbledonwindmill. org.uk). Wimbledon tube/rail. **Open** *Apr-Oct 2-5pm Sat; 11am-5pm Sun, bank hols. School groups by appointment only.* **Admission** *£2; £1 under-16s, reductions; £5 family (2+4).* **No credit cards. 5+**
Wimbledon Common's windmill was built in 1817 by carpenter Charles March, at the request of locals who wanted to grind their own wheat. Having been a private residence for some years, these days it's a small museum, run by volunteers and open weekends only. On the ground floor, there's a film about how windmills work, a display showing how the windmill was built, and a collection of woodworking tools used in its restoration. The first floor is more hands-on, with a working model of the windmill in action, the chance for children to have a go at grinding wheat with a saddle-stone or hand quern, and commentaries at the push of a button. Climbing the ladder takes you up to the tower, where you can see the sails' operating machinery turning on blusterous days.
Buggy access (ground floor). Nearest picnic place: Wimbledon Common. Café. Shop.

MUSIC

British Music Experience

O2 Bubble, Millennium Way, Greenwich, SE10 0BB (8463 2000, www.britishmusic experience.com). North Greenwich tube. **Open** 11am-7.30pm daily. **Admission** £11.50; £9.25 reductions; £6.75 6-17s; free under-6s. **Credit** MC, V. **Map** p332 H6. **5+**
Memorabilia from pop and rock stars from 1945 to the present day is only the start of things at this most modern of museums. Interactivity is key, and kids of all ages will have a ball as they learn how to throw some shapes from the last 60 years in the Dance the Decades booth. Hey DJ is a virtual record box where you can listen to a catalogue of singles, learning about their significance in the annals of rock history along the way. Where It's At is an interactive map of the country revealing where British talent emerged from. There's also a chance to have a go at singing, playing guitar, keyboards and drums and using a mixing desk in the Gibson Interactive Studio.
Buggy access. Disabled access: lift; toilet. Nappy-changing facilities. Nearest picnic place: riverside. Shop.

Discover Greenwich. *See p101.*

Sightseeing

My Sport Diving
Daniel, 14

Who inspired you to take up diving?
My older brother.

What do you like about your sport?
The achievement of getting a new dive right and performing in competitions. My favourite dives are the Front Forward 2.5 Somersault Pike or the Back 1.5 Somersault 1.5 Twist off a 3m springboard.

What level are you at?
I started when I was seven and was performing by the time I was nine, then I was competing at a national level by the time I was ten. I train four times a week for a total of 17 hours.

What's next for you in your sport?
I want to get to Elite level by the time I'm 16 or 17, then British Championship level as soon as I can.

Which events would you like to see at the London 2012 Olympic Games and Paralympic Games?
I'd like to see the Men's 3m and 10m Diving Finals. Also, I was talking to my dad and we'd like to see the Basketball and 100m Final for the atmosphere.

Sightseeing

Sightseeing

Handel House Museum

25 Brook Street (entrance at rear), W1K 4HB (7495 1685, www.handelhouse.org). Bond Street tube. **Open** 10am-6pm Tue, Wed, Fri, Sat; 10am-8pm Thur; noon-6pm Sun. **Admission** £6; £5 reductions; £2 6-16s (free Sat); free under-6s. **Credit** MC, V. **Map** p332 H6. **5+**

This Georgian townhouse was Handel's home from 1723 until his death in 1759. The permanent collection at the Handel Museum includes paintings, letters, scores and a reproduction of his harpsichord. The house interiors have been painstakingly restored but children are encouraged to visit, with free entry on Saturdays, plus the odd family-friendly musical event (the Thursday evening recitals are aimed more at adults). The child-friendly ethos extends to trails, quizzes and activities to go with the displays.

Buggy access. Disabled access: lift, toilet. Nappy-changing facilities. Nearest picnic place: Hanover Square. Shop.

Musical Museum

399 High Street, Brentford, Middx TW8 0DU (8560 8108, www.musicalmuseum. co.uk). Kew Bridge rail. **Open** 11am-5.30pm Tue-Sun, bank hols. Last entry 4.30pm. **Admission** £8; £6.50 reductions; free under-16s. **Credit** MC, V. **5+**

Children who find themselves all thumbs when it comes to music lessons will be deeply impressed by the ingenious self-playing pianos and violins on display at this museum of automatic instruments. Other exhibits include clockwork musical boxes, orchestrions (a mechanical instrument that sounds like a large ensemble), musical toys and barrel organs. Most are in working order and are demonstrated by the staff, with their functions fully explained. Upstairs is a concert hall with an orchestra pit from which a Wurlitzer console slowly rises, as it did in cinemas in the 1930s; check the online events diary for performances and films.

Buggy access. Café. Disabled access: lift, toilet. Nappy-changing facilities. Nearest picnic place: riverside. Shop.

NATURAL WORLD

Garden Museum

Lambeth Palace Road, SE1 7LB (7401 8865, www.gardenmuseum.org.uk). Lambeth North tube or Waterloo tube/rail, then bus 507, or bus C10, 77. **Open** 10.30am-5pm Mon-Fri, Sun; 10.30am-4pm Sat (closed 1st Mon of mth). **Admission** £6; free-£5 reductions; free under-16s. **Credit AmEx, MC, V. Map** p333 L10. **6+**

At first glance, a museum about gardening perhaps wouldn't have obvious appeal for most children, but step into this tranquil setting – a deconsecrated church by the Thames – and it's surprising how enticing it can be. Inside, the collection of tools and gardening paraphernalia has some unexpected oddities, including a weird-looking 'vegetable lamb' (believed for centuries to be half lamb, half plant), a set of pony boots (worn by lawnmower-pulling horses to prevent their hooves from marking the grass) and a cunning, cat-shaped bird scarer.

Outside, the old graveyard has some distinguished residents: the Tradescants, a pioneering family of gardeners and botanists; Captain William Bligh, of *Bounty* fame; and half a dozen archbishops of Canterbury. The wild garden is awash with valerian, poppies, harebells and cow parsley, while the 17th century-style knot garden is a riot of colour in summer, enclosed in neat box-hedge borders.

Buggy access. Café. Disabled access: toilet. Nappy-changing facilities. Nearest picnic place: Archbishop's Park. Shop.

Natural History Museum

Cromwell Road, SW7 5BD (7942 5000, www.nhm.ac.uk). South Kensington tube. **Open** 10am-5.50pm daily. **Admission** free; charges apply for special exhibitions. **Credit** MC, V. **Map** p329 D10. **4+**

What kids always remember about the Natural History Museum isn't the grace of the museum's stately façade but the moving dinosaurs inside. In 2011, new exhibition Age of the Dinosaur (until 4 September) will reinterpret the museum's popular dinosaur specimens and animatronic beasties.

The museum splits its exhibits into four colour-coded zones, each with its own marvels. In Blue Zone, inside the mammals gallery, the sabre-toothed tiger skeleton elicits a delicious shudder, while a life-size model of a blue whale quietens all but the loudest of children. The Green Zone encompasses the child-friendly and fiendishly popular Creepy Crawlies exhibit: watching leaf-cutter ants at work, exploring a termite mound and gawping at the world's longest stick insect (a twiggy, leggy 56.7cm beast) are among its attractions. Geology takes centre stage in the Red Zone, which you can

Culture Shop

In days gone by, it was almost impossible to take the kids round a museum without going away with a bag of overpriced and nigh-on useless gadgets to remember the day by. But even these were better than the alternative onslaught of tears if you dragged them straight through the shop towards the exit instead. So, what's changed? Well, museum shops are still annoyingly located within eyeshot of children as they leave, but the difference now is that the pocket money dross and dodgy reproductions have been replaced with stuff you might actually want to buy for your little darlings.

The best options in South Kensington's museum cluster are at the V&A and the Science Museum. The V&A offers gifts themed around current exhibitions. So, to tie in with Peter Rabbit: the Tale of the Tale, you could pick up anything from a set of mounted prints (£6) to a flatpack birdhouse (£7). Over at the Science Museum, meanwhile, the shop is almost as impressive as the museum itself, with a vast floor space stacked with all manner of buzzing, whirring, glowing treats, from potato-powered clocks to full-scale chemistry laboratories, plus plenty of wallet-friendly pocket puzzles and torches.

The Museum of London is sparkling after a £20 million refurbishment. Its thrilling lower ground floor gallery is the perfect place to take the kids, and the shop's not bad either with a kitsch selection of capital treats, from build a London taxi kits to a solar-powered waving Queen. Along similar lines, the London Transport Museum stocks all manner of

souvenirs based around the capital's iconic tube logo and map. Transport of a different kind fills the shelves of the National Maritime Museum's excellent shop in Greenwich, with a vast fleet of naval knick-knacks to float your kids' imagination.

If you're pressed for time, all these museums have online shops, but a personal expedition is much more fun – and you can even take in an exhibition while you're at it.

Sightseeing

Neighbourhood Watch
Docklands

Cesar Pelli's dramatic **One Canada Square**, set at the centre of a veritable mini-Manhattan of commercial skyscrapers at the northern tip of the Isle of Dogs, was built in 1991. It held the title of the UK's tallest habitable building until it was overtaken in late 2010 by the Shard, over at London Bridge, which is set to top it by several hundred feet when finished. With its distinctive pyramid roof, flashing aircraft warning beacon and wispy plume of steam at its apex, One Canada Square remains an iconic symbol, although unfortunately you have to work in the building to enjoy the views from within.

Docklands is the semi-official name given to the massive redevelopment of this eastern stretch of the Thames. And here on the Isle of Dogs (more of a peninsula, actually), where great ships once lined up in impressive docks, there are now shiny office blocks, luxury flats and the biggest cluster of high-rise buildings in Europe. That said, a day out here makes a surprisingly pleasant family excursion – the land around the buildings is essentially a very large and well-tended garden with no traffic to worry about.

These days, the area is easily accessible from the centre of town. The **Docklands Light Railway** (7363 9700, www.tfl.gov.uk/dlr) zips along raised tracks and gives great views over the area. Children will be fascinated by the driverless trains and can even pretend they're in control of the train if you travel outside peak time and manage to nab seats in the glass-fronted lead carriage.

The area is now also served by the Jubilee line. Visitors disembark in the sleek, cavernous Canary Wharf underground station, which was designed by Norman Foster; the area around the curved entrances has been made into a pretty Japanese garden.

But perhaps the most scenic way to travel here is by boat, aboard one of the scheduled Thames Clippers services

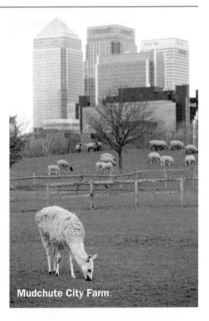

Mudchute City Farm.

(0870 781 5049, www.thamesclippers.com), which ferry commuters up and down the Thames between Embankment and Canary Wharf. If you want to combine Canary Wharf with some more traditional sightseeing, then consider buying a Rail & River Rover ticket (£13.50, £6.75 children, free under-5s, £33 family), which allows a day's travel on the DLR with unlimited trips on the City Cruises sightseeing boats that run between Greenwich Pier, Tower, Waterloo and Westminster. But don't be too quick to leave. This centre of commerce has its tourist attractions too.

Trails and sails

With its clean lines and neat landscaping, Docklands is a bit like a model town, and children will enjoy exploring the bridges, pathways and open stretches of water. To give some purpose to your roaming, tackle one of the three excellent walking trails (entitled Transitions, Open Spaces and Architecture & Design) downloadable at www.canarywharf.com (click on the 'arts and events' link). The first tackles the rich history of Docklands, while the second leads you around the area's various gardens. The third has all sorts of facts about the buildings (existing and planned) and leads visitors past various artworks and sculptures that are dotted around. Our favourites are Ron Arad's red spike Windwand and his Big Blue at Westferry Circus, and Lynn Chadwick's Couple on Seat in Cabot Square.

Emma Biggs's wonderfully intricate mosaics, embedded into the floor of Jubilee Place shopping centre, evoke the area's past ('London used to be a city of ships. A thousand vessels a week passed through the docks').

For some idea of what this city of ships once looked like, head for the thoroughly enjoyable **Museum of London Docklands** (*see p101*). Follow the bouncing bridge (it's supported on floats) from Cabot Square; the museum is in a row of converted 19th-century warehouses on the edge of West India Quay. Inside, there are some fantastically evocative photographs, paintings, prints and models of the bustling docks as they would have been when this area was London's industrial heart. The museum's three jam-packed floors tell the story of the Thames, the port of London and its people, from Roman times up to the Docklands redevelopment, including the chance to walk through a full-scale mock-up of a dingy riverfront alley during the mid 1800s (Sailortown).

Children will be rewarded for their learning when they get to the Mudlarks Gallery, with all its hands-on discovery games. It's so popular that entry is by timed ticket. There's also a great café where for every adult meal bought a child eats for free.

Great escape

If all this talk of industry and business is making the children feel old before their time, it might be the moment to grab some fresh air and a spot of country life in the heart of east London. A short south-bound DLR ride from Canary Wharf takes you to Mudchute. Here, in the shadow of Docklands' high rises, lies **Mudchute City Farm** (*see p155*).

From Mudchute station, take the raised path past the parkland and allotments, where you can play spot-the-llama as you make your way towards the farm entrance. The closer you get, the more audible the resident ducks, chickens, pigs, goats, donkeys and horses become. Inside sprawl acres of fields and pastures; this is one of the largest city farms in Europe. If helping to feed the animals makes you a bit peckish, head for the farm's acclaimed café, Mudchute Kitchen, for a scrumptious farmhouse breakfast or slab of cake.

If animals aren't the order of the day, there's always Island Gardens (cross the main road from the eponymous station), with its beautiful view of Greenwich on the other side of the Thames. Cross via the spookily drippy Victorian foot tunnel that runs below the river; the attendant-operated lifts (7am-7pm Mon-Sat, 10am-5.30pm Sun) are big enough for a fleet of buggies. You're not allowed to cycle through the tunnel, though, so any bike-riders will have to dismount and push their trusty steeds.

Also in the area: Nando's, Wagamama, Pizza Express.
1802 Museum In Docklands *No.1 Warehouse, Hertsmere Road, West India Key, E14 4AL (7538 2702, www.museumindocklands.org.uk).* Great food and plenty of atmosphere.
Carluccio's Caffè *Reuters Plaza, E14 5AJ (7719 1749, www.carluccios.com).* Child-friendly and reasonably priced.
Gun *27 Coldharbour, E14 9NS (7515 5222, www.thegundocklands.com).* A smart gastropub that does great chips and welcomes nippers.
Mudchute Kitchen *Mudchute Farm, Pier Street, E14 3HP (7515 5901, www.mudchutekitchen.org).* Fresh, flavoursome farm grub.
Smollensky's *1 Reuters Plaza, E14 5AJ (7719 0101, www.smollenskys.com).* Great steaks and very popular with kids. *See p269.*

Sightseeing

Jewish Museum.

access directly from the museum's Exhibition Road entrance. It's a dramatic, dark escalator ascent through the centre of the earth. At the top you'll find the ground-shaking earthquake simulator – a reliable source of giggles (and a few shrieks of alarm). Finally, the Orange Zone comprises the wildlife garden and the new Darwin Centre buildings, where children can spy on scientists as they go about their work. They'll also enjoy the giant touch screens exploring the specimens inside the glass display cases.

If seeing the scientists at work inspires the kids to get hands-on, take them down to the Investigate Centre in the main museum's basement (open weekday afternoons and weekends; call ahead to check times). Here, seven to 14s can study specimens (some living) through a microscope, and note their findings. Temporary exhibitions are also worth keeping an eye on; 2010's Butterfly Explorers was so popular, it's back for summer 2011 as Sensational Butterflies and runs until 25 September 2011. It allows visitors to walk among hundreds of butterflies and witness the extraordinary stages of their metamorphosis from caterpillar to butterfly.

The museum has a restaurant, a café and a sandwich bar, and there are also indoor and outdoor picnic areas if you'd rather bring your own grub. Since January 2010, the museum has run a monthly sleepover. Children taking

part must be aged eight to 11 and accompanied by a parent (groups must be a minimum of five children and one adult, £45 per person). Night activities include a torchlit adventure around the museum, plus a live show about beasties and the creation of an enormous paper and clay dinosaur. *See also p120* **Neighbourhood Watch**.

Buggy Access. Cafés. Disabled access: lift, toilet. Nappy-changing facilities. Nearest picnic place: basement picnic room, museum grounds. Restaurant.

RELIGION

Jewish Museum

129-131 Albert Street, NW1 7NB (7284 7384, www.jewishmuseum.org.uk). Camden Town tube. **Open** 10am-5pm Mon-Thur, Sun; 10am-9pm Thur; 10am-2pm Fri. **Admission** £7; free-£6 reductions; £17 family (2+4). **Credit** MC, V. **4+**
The Jewish Museum has been in Camden since 1992, in a Victorian house on Albert Street, just off Parkway. In 2010, it reopened its doors to reveal a £10 million expansion, into the building behind – a former piano workshop. The first impression is of light and space in the area that leads out from the original house, now home to the ticket and information desk and shop. The Welcome Gallery hosts a permanent

exhibition designed to shoot down any pre-existing stereotypes visitors may have of the Jewish community in London today. Videos play on screen strips hanging from the ceiling and introduce us to an Indian-born grandmother, a taxi driver, an ex-army engineer and a smoked salmon manufacturer. Then it's straight to the medieval mikveh – a ritual bath found in the City of London and rehoused here – before going up the stairs.

Exhibitions have been designed with imagination and a keen desire to appeal to all ages. There is lots for children to enjoy while they learn (including various trails). In the permanent exhibition History: A British Story, they can play the Great Migration boardgame, try on some traditional wedding clothes, smell chicken soup, plait some challah bread, play Yiddish karaoke, and listen to first-hand stories of those who lived in the crowded East End. The Judaism: A Living Faith gallery exhibits beautiful ceremonial objects alongside videos of families celebrating the important annual festivals like Purim, Hanukkah and Passover. The gallery documenting the Holocaust is small and very moving, but can be avoided if parents think their children are too young to be introduced to the subject. Back downstairs is the inviting café with its bleached-wood tables and high ceilings; try a rougalach (like a dense croissant with chocolate between the folds), or some classic chicken soup with dumplings.
Buggy access. Café. Disabled access: toilets. Nappy-changing facilities. Nearest picnic place: Regent's Park. Shop.

Museum of Methodism & John Wesley's House

Wesley's Chapel, 49 City Road, EC1Y 1AU (7253 2262, www.wesleyschapel.org.uk). Moorgate or Old Street tube/rail. **Open** 10am-4pm Mon-Sat; 12.30-2pm Sun.
Admission free, donations appreciated.
Credit MC, V. **Map** p335 Q4. **8+**
This lovely chapel was built by John Wesley in 1778, and is known as the cathedral of world Methodism. The chapel and surrounding buildings form a surprisingly quiet corner for contemplation just behind the busy City Road. Wesley called it 'perfectly neat but not fine', although there are many more adornments now than in his day. Down in the crypt, the museum has a permanent display charting the history of Methodism, while Hogarthian prints depict poverty, alcoholism and moral degradation in 18th-century England. Look out for lunchtime recitals making use of the chapel's organ.

Wesley's neighbouring house has been restored to 18th-century simplicity; much of the furniture is of the period, although the tiny four-poster in the bedroom is reproduction, as is the curious 'chamber horse' in the study – an early form of home-gym equipment.
Buggy access. Disabled access: lift, toilet. Nappy-changing facilities. Nearest picnic place: enclosed courtyard at entrance, Bunhill Fields. Shop.

SCIENCE & MEDICINE

Alexander Fleming Laboratory Museum

St Mary's Hospital, Praed Street, W2 1NY (7886 6528, www.imperial.nhs.uk/stmarys). Paddington tube/rail or bus 7, 15, 27, 36. **Open** 10am-1pm Mon-Thur; also by appointment. Closed bank hols. **Admission** £4; £2 5-16s, reductions; free under-5s.
No credit cards. Map p329 D5. **8+**
In the era of the superbug, this shrine to antibiotics is both increasingly relevant and a relic from a simpler time. Visitors explore a re-creation of the laboratory where Alexander Fleming discovered penicillin back on 3 September 1928. Exhibits and a video celebrate Fleming's life and the role of penicillin in fighting disease. Staff run tours for family and school groups; note that the museum is not accessible to the disabled.
Nearest picnic place: canalside, Hyde Park. Shop.

Hunterian Museum

Royal College of Surgeons of England, 35-43 Lincoln's Inn Fields, WC2A 3PE (7869 6560, www.rcseng.ac.uk/museums). Holborn tube. **Open** 10am-5pm Tue-Sat.
Admission free; donations appreciated.
Credit MC, V. **Map** p334 M6. **4+**
The museum's namesake, John Hunter (1728-93) was a pioneering surgeon and anatomist, appointed physician to King George III. He amassed thousands of medical specimens; after he died, the collection was enhanced and expanded by others. The Hunterian is quite possibly the weirdest museum in all of London – and the most wonderful, some would say. Its gleaming glass cabinets are filled with row upon row of specimen jars, containing human and animal remains of every description in various states of disease and dissection: brains, hearts, hernias, big toes, paws and jaws, all spookily suspended in formaldehyde. Children

Sightseeing

My Sport Sailing
Berry, 10

What inspired you to take up sailing?
Me and my friend did a course one summer holiday. My friend gave up because she didn't like getting wet, but I really liked it. Then I heard there was a youth club so I started going every Saturday, and I've made new friends there.

What do you like about your sport?
I just love going out on the reservoir in the open space and controlling the boat. Mostly you can do anything you want, except on days when there's lots of algae.

What level are you at?
I've got up to level three, which is rigging the boat.

What's next for you in your sport?
Mostly I go out on a Fun Boat or a Topaz, but I'd like to try taking out one of the bigger boats like the Zephyr.

Which events would you like to see at the London 2012 Olympic Games and Paralympic Games?
I would love to see the Swimming and Athletics.

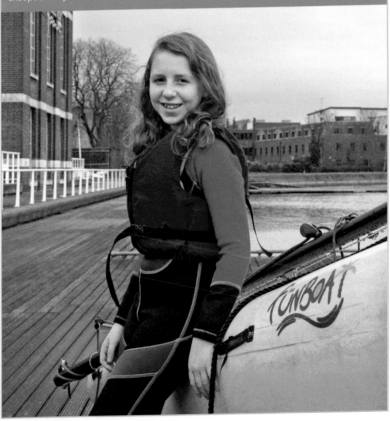

(and grown-ups) of a grisly bent will be gripped by the exhibits, but more sensitive souls and younger kids should probably steer clear.

The most famous pieces in the collection are the brain of mathematician Charles Babbage and the towering skeleton of 'Irish Giant' Charles Byrne, who stood a towering 2.2m (7ft 7in) tall in his socks. There are trails for children to complete, along with a skeleton suit to try for size and a fabric body part game; medically themed events for fives to 12s take place during school holidays, led by costumed actors (booking is essential). Free tours take place at 1pm on Wednesdays.

Buggy access. Disabled access: lift, toilet. Nearest picnic place: Lincoln's Inn Fields. Shop.

Old Operating Theatre, Museum & Herb Garret

9A St Thomas's Street, SE1 9RY (7188 2679, www.thegarret.org.uk). London Bridge tube/rail. **Open** 10.30am-5pm daily. Closed 15 Dec-5 Jan. **Admission** £5.90; £4.90 reductions; £3.40 6-15s; free under-6s; £13.80 family (2+4). **No credit cards. Map** p335 Q8. **7+**

This museum is a real one-off. Each step up the narrow, rickety, wooden spiral staircase leads you further from present-day London, and towards the quiet ghosts of the past. The Herb Garret smells pungently of fennel and other herbs and contains a jumble of ghoulish exhibits packed under its dark eaves. Nineteenth-century amputation kits and terrifying obstetric implements jostle with bits of Victorians preserved in jars and early anatomical charts.

Go through a narrow antechamber to find Europe's oldest operating theatre, perched rather incongruously and incredibly inside the roof of St Thomas's Church (St Thomas's Hospital was on this site until it moved to Lambeth in 1862), where re-enactment demonstrations at 2pm every Saturday bring the traumas of pre-anaesthesia surgery gorily to life. On Saturday mornings at 11.30am there are children's workshops exploring 18th- and 19th-century medicine, while at 2pm on Sundays there are lectures about how herbs were used as drugs.

Nearest picnic place: Southwark Cathedral Gardens. Shop.

Royal London Hospital Museum

St Philip's Church, Newark Street, E1 2AA (7377 7608, www.bartsandthelondon.nhs.uk/ museums). Whitechapel tube. **Open** 10am-

4.30pm Tue-Fri. **Admission** free, donations welcome. **Credit** MC, V. **7+**

The Royal London Museum lies in the former crypt of St Philip's Church; its entrance is down an unprepossessing side street, at the bottom of an unlikely set of steps. Inside, exhibits chronicle the history of what was once the biggest general hospital in the UK: the Royal London opened in 1740, so there's a lot of history to explore.

The museum devotes a section to each century, with special displays relating to the hospital's most famous patients and staff, including Thomas Barnardo, Florence Nightingale, John Merrick (the Elephant Man) and Edith Cavell. The development of nursing and childcare is traced through displays of starchy uniforms, and there's a forensics case with a copy of Jack the Ripper's notorious 'From Hell' letter. Most entertaining, however (and a welcome respite if you've been dragging children about all day), is the 1934 X-ray control unit that could have been created by a mad inventor from a sci-fi B-movie, and the plummily narrated documentaries, dating from the 1930s to the '60s. These show, for example, children wearing pilot's goggles receiving doses of ultraviolet light at a time when London smog prevented the natural synthesis of vitamin D.

Buggy access. Café (in hospital). Disabled access: lift, toilet. Nappy-changing facilities (in hospital). Nearest picnic place: hospital garden. Shop.

St Bartholomew's Hospital Museum

West Smithfield, EC1A 7BE (7601 8152, www.bartsandthelondon.nhs.uk/aboutus/ st_bartholomews_hospital.asp). Barbican or St Paul's tube. **Open** 10am-4pm Tue-Fri. *Tours* (Church & Great Hall) 2pm Fri. **Admission** free. *Tours* £5; £4 reductions; free under-16s accompanied by adult. **No credit cards. Map** p334 O6. **12+**

The museum is located in the North Wing of this famous London hospital, an institution that's been part of the city's landscape since the 12th century. A video relates the story of the hospital's origins as a refuge for chronically sick people hoping for a miraculous cure. Audio loops give a flavour of what it was like to work here as a 13th-century sister, say, or a 15th-century apprentice surgeon. The exhibits include 19th-century watercolours and sketches of various diseases, leather lunatic restraints, a wooden head used by medical students to practise their drilling techniques on and

Sightseeing

Sightseeing

photographs documenting the slow progress of nurses from drudges to career women. Don't miss the two huge paintings by local lad William Hogarth.

Café (in hospital). Nearest picnic place: hospital grounds.

Science Museum

Exhibition Road, SW7 2DD (7942 4000, www.sciencemuseum.org.uk). South Kensington tube. **Open** 10am-6pm daily. **Admission** free; charges apply for special exhibitions. **Credit** MC, V. **Map** p329 D9. **4+**

This venerable museum celebrated its centenary in 2009 and kicked off a period of extensive development. By 2015, there will be a new façade, a massive rooftop extension devoted to cosmology and astronomy, and two new permanent galleries. The brand new atmosphere gallery exploring climate change is now open (*see p8* **Air Today, Gone Tomorrow**). Meanwhile, the existing attractions remain just as much fun as they've always been. No one's too young or old to get a kick out of a visit here: the Science Musuem is a temple to scientific knowledge and discovery that welcomes inquisitive visitors of all ages. Icons of science (Stephenson's Rocket locomotive, Crick and Watson's DNA model) are treated with due respect, but this place couldn't be less stuffy with its games, simulators and interactive exhibits.

The jewel in its crown is the Launchpad, where 50 hands-on exhibits and experiments keep kids agog; here, they can make a rainbow, check out their chilly noses on the thermal imaging screen, attempt to run a radio on pedal-power or take a dizzying turn on the rotation station. It's aimed at eight to 14s, but appeals to all ages. Other areas cater to younger children: five to eights can explore the Pattern Pod, while under-sixes race around the magical, multi-sensory Garden play areas, whose marvels include computerised flowers and giant building blocks. Extra charges apply for the IMAX cinema and the third-floor motionride simulator – though both are free for members. If you're planning to eat here, the Deep Blue Café is a reliable bet (*see p248*). It's in the Wellcome Wing, which reopened in 2010 after an extensive refurbishment.

As you'd expect, the museum attracts hordes of visitors during the school holidays. Book ahead if you want to catch a film, and try to arrive at Launchpad at 10am to avoid lengthy queues. Free half-hour tours on different themes are held throughout the year, while Science Night sleepovers (eight to 11s) are another big draw. It's £45 well spent, as kids get the chance to take part in hands-on science activities and explore the galleries before hunkering down for the night: you need to book well in advance, and the minimum group size is five children and one adult. During school holidays workshops and storytelling sessions are also on offer. *See also p120* **Neighbourhood Watch**.

Buggy access. Cafés. Disabled access: lift, toilet. Nappy-changing facilities. Nearest picnic place: Hyde Park, museum basement and 1st floor picnic areas. Restaurant. Shop.

Wellcome Collection

183 Euston Road, NW1 2BE (7611 2222, www.wellcomecollection.org). Euston Square tube or Euston tube/rail. **Open** 10am-6pm Tue, Wed, Fri, Sat; 10am-10pm Thur; 11am-6pm Sun. **Admission** free. **Credit** MC, V. **14+ (parental advisory)**

The man behind this collection was Sir Henry Wellcome, a pioneering 19th-century pharmacist, philanthropist and entrepreneur, who amassed an idiosyncratic selection of artefacts relating to the medical profession, a tiny proportion of which is displayed in the permanent Medicine Man section of the museum. Unlike many of London's medical museums, the Wellcome Collection displays its exhibits in modern, airy galleries that are well laid out and stuffed to the brim with eye-opening curios. Sensitive children might find some of the items too grisly (the vicious, bladed torture chair; the slips of real human skin) or too saucy (Japanese sex aids, phallic amulets), but older children will get a kick out of seeing a religious mendicant's nail sole sandals, a mummified body from Peru, Napoleon's toothbrush and a lock of George III's hair.

Medicine Now presents exhibits on the themes of genomes, malaria, obesity and the body. The permanent sections are bolstered by a programme of excellent temporary exhibitions that examine various aspects of life and death. Dirt (until 31 Aug 2011) examines the filthy reality of everyday life, from a Victorian London street to a New York landfill site in 2030. The events programme, suitable for teenagers, includes talks and microscopy workshops. There's also a good bookshop, and a superb Peyton & Byrne café, serving meals, fabulous cakes and a good selection of teas.

Buggy access. Café. Disabled access: lift, toilet. Nappy-changing facilities. Nearest picnic place: Gordon Square. Shop.

Science Museum.

SPECIALIST

Bank of England Museum

*Entrance on Bartholomew Lane, off
Threadneedle Street, EC2R 8AH (7601
5491, 7601 5545 cinema bookings, www.
bankofengland.co.uk/education/museum).
Bank tube/DLR.* **Open** 10am-5pm Mon-
Fri. Closed bank hols. **Admission** free.
Credit MC, V. **Map** p335 Q6. **5+**

Visitors walk first into Sir John Soane's
beautiful 18th-century banking hall (restored
to its original mahogany splendour) where
the bewigged and bestockinged mannequins
instantly appeal to younger visitors'
imaginations. Permanent displays of notes,
coins and early handwritten cheques illustrate
a chronological history of banking, which is
summed up in an educational film. There are
lots of terribly impressive paintings, cartoons
and pieces of furniture on display, but children
will be much more excited by the everyday
tools of the banking trade like calculators,
weights, inkwells and the interactive foreign
exchange desk.

One consistently popular exhibit is the gold
bar: put a hand into a perspex case and try to
lift the bar encased within. Its weight – 12.7kg
(28lb) – will come as a shock to anyone who has
ever fantasised about scarpering with a sack
full of bullion. Activity sheets and quizzes for
different age groups can be downloaded from
the website before setting off, or picked up from
the museum on arrival.

*Buggy access. Disabled access: toilet. Nappy-
changing facilities. Nearest picnic place:
St Paul's Cathedral Garden. Shop.*

Clink Prison Museum

*1 Clink Street, SE1 9DG (7403 0900,
www.clink.co.uk). London Bridge tube/rail.*
Open *June-Sept* 10am-9pm daily. *Oct-May*
10am-6pm Mon-Fri; 10am-9pm Sat, Sun.
Admission £6; £5.50 3-15s, reductions;
free under-3s; £14 family (2+2). **No
credit cards. Map** p334 P8. **6+
(parental advisory)**

Borough Market and Bankside look neater and
sleeker every year, but for a reminder of the
area's murky past, look no further than this
museum. The clinking of inmates' manacles,
fetters and chains is what gave this former
prison its name. In operation from 1247 until
1780, it was the place where thieves, prostitutes,
debtors and – after the Reformation – priests
were incarcerated. The list of allowed
punishments included scourging with rods, the
rack, breaking on the wheel and being crushed
under heavy weights. Jailers were not paid well,
so provided small creature comforts to rich

inmates, at a price, and allowed whorehouse madams to carry on the trade for which they were imprisoned in return for a cut of the takings. The museum tries to recreate the atmosphere of the prison with candlelight, sawdust on the floor and moans and groans coming from the waxwork prisoners. Brave visitors can 'try on' some of the torture devices, such as a scold's bridle. Children of a sensitive disposition may be scared – particularly at the entrance, where a waxwork man in a cage whimpers as you descend the stairs. *See also p48* **Neighbourhood Watch.**

Buggy access. Nearest picnic place: Southwark Cathedral Gardens. Shop.

SPORT

London's big four – Arsenal, Chelsea, Tottenham and West Ham – all offer stadium tours that take fans behind the scenes. So does Wembley Stadium (*see p172*), home of the England team and host of cup finals in several sports and major pop concerts. Arsenal and Chelsea have also made space for club museums. Largely speaking, these appeal to partisan supporters, but London's football scene has a fascinating history and the museums have plenty to interest fans of rival teams as well.

Arsenal Museum

Northern Triangle Building, Drayton Park, N5 1BU (7619 5000, www.arsenal.com). Arsenal or Holloway Road tube, or Drayton Park rail. **Open** 10am-6pm Mon-Sat; 10am-5pm Sun. *Match days* 10am until 30mins before kick-off. **Admission** £6; £3 under-16s, reductions; free under-5s. *Tour & museum* £15; £8 under-16s, reductions; free under-5s. *Legends tour* £35; £18 under-16s, reductions; free under-5s. No tours match days. **Credit** MC, V. **7+**

There is plenty of room for a museum in the vast Emirates Stadium. Fans will find it housed in the North Triangle building, directly opposite the north entrances. It offers a lavish celebration of all things Arsenal. Fans of the team will be thrilled by all the exhibits, but there's also plenty to appeal to the visitor with a more general interest, particularly in the sections that deal with how the club developed. Visitors can pick up a phone to hear an account of the club's early days, initially as Dial Square FC, after its formation by workers at the Woolwich Arsenal munitions factory. The club's more recent triumphs are marked with audio-visual displays, signed shirts, medals and other memorabilia. There are also sections on the Gunners' all-conquering women's team and on the club's FA Cup and European adventures.

Buggy access. Disabled access: lift, toilet. Nearest picnic place: Finsbury Park. Shop.

Guards Museum. *See p117.*

Sightseeing

Chelsea Museum

*Stamford Bridge, Fulham Road, SW6
1HS (0871 984 1955, www.chelseafc.com/
tours). Fulham Broadway tube.* **Open**
10.30am-4.30pm daily. *Tours* every 30mins
11am-3pm daily. Closed match days
& day before Champions League game.
Admission £6; £4 under-16s. *Tour
& museum* £15; £9 under-16s. **Credit**
AmEx, MC, V. **7+**
Chelsea are often mocked by other clubs for
having no history, but they've still managed to
put together a cracking museum. Appropriately
enough, it's located in the stand that occupies
what was once the club's most notorious asset,
the Shed, a crumbling terrace of matchless
notoriety. These days, fans have more to shout
about and the museum gives pride of place to
recent acquisitions, such as José Mourinho's
moody overcoat. There's also plenty on the
club's history of glorious inconsistency, terrible
away kits and affinity with celebrity – this is
probably the only museum in the country that
features a photograph of Raquel Welch (in a
Chelsea kit and gun holster, no less). Kids
will love the two huge scale models of the
ground, and the chance to see the kits belonging
to icons like Frank Lampard and Didier
Drogba. They can also star in their own
Chelsea-themed newspaper headline. Entry
comes with an excellent tour that takes in the
dressing room and dugouts.
*Buggy access. Café. Disabled access (call
ahead): lift, toilets. Nappy-changing
facilities. Nearest picnic place: Brompton
Cemetery. Shop.*

Lord's Cricket Ground & MCC Museum

*St John's Wood Road, NW8 8QN (7616
8595, www.lords.org). St John's Wood
tube or bus 13, 46, 82, 113, 274.* **Open**
Tours Apr-Oct 10am, noon, 2pm daily.
Nov-Mar noon, 2pm Mon-Fri; 10am,
noon, 2pm Sat, Sun. Closed some match
& preparation days; phone for details.
Admission £15; £9 5-15s, reductions;
free under-5s; £40 family (2+2). **Credit**
AmEx, MC, V. **8+**
The museum at Lord's Cricket Ground is the
oldest sporting museum in the world and
probably best enjoyed as part of one of the
tours, which take place twice daily Monday to
Friday, and three times a day at weekends.
Though relatively small, the museum is a
treasure trove of artefacts, from early bats,
balls, paintings and scorecards – some going

back more than 200 years – to mementoes of
modern times; there is also footage of some of
the best moments in cricket's history.
The must-see exhibit, of course, is the original
Ashes urn. This was first presented following
what a *Sporting Times* reporter called the
'death of English cricket', when the Australian
tourists condemned the England side to their
first ever defeat at the Oval in 1882. When
England went 2-0 up in the four-match series in
Australia, a group of Melbourne society women
burned a bail from the top of some cricket
stumps, placed the ashes inside the urn and
presented them to the visiting captain.
The ground tour also offers visitors a look
around the famous pavilion, its Long Room
and committee rooms and, of course, the home
and away dressing rooms and their balconies,
as well as the media centre, the grandstand and
cricket centre. Tours do not take place on
match days.
*Buggy access. Disabled access: toilet, lift.
Nearest picnic place: St John's churchyard
playground. Shop.*

Wimbledon Lawn Tennis Museum

*All England Lawn Tennis Club,
Church Road, SW19 5AE (8946 6131,
www.wimbledon.org/museum). Southfields
or South Wimbledon tube, then bus 493.*
Open 10am-5pm daily. Spectators only
during championships. *Tours* phone for
details. **Admission** *Museum* £11; £9.50
reductions; £6.75 5-16s; free under-5s.
Museum & tour £20; £17 reductions; £12.50
5-16s; free under-5s. **Credit** MC, V. **8+**
A visit to the museum is included in a tour of
the grounds. It's a high-tech shrine to all things
tennis and worth a visit for anyone with even
so much as a passing interest in the game. In
the cinema (with 200° screens), a film of a game
between Maria Sharapova and Nuria
Llagostera Vives allows visitors to see each
move from five different camera angles,
illustrating the body science of the game.
Meanwhile, in a mock-up of a 1980s changing
room, three-time Wimbledon champ John
McEnroe (well, in hologram form at least) is
waiting to take you on a tour behind the scenes
and share his reminiscences.
Visitors are guided through Wimbledon's
history, decade by decade, as it developed into
a British sporting institution. You can also try
on tennis outfits from different ages (and feel
the weight difference between court outfits for
men and women from 1884), test your reflexes
on interactive consoles such as Reaction Station

Sightseeing

and You Are the Umpire, and listen to broadcast snippets and interviews from significant final matches. Audio and visual guides are also available. Recommended.
Buggy access. Café. Disabled access: lift, toilet. Nappy-changing facilities. Nearest picnic place: venue grounds. Shop.

World Rugby Museum, Twickenham & Twickenham Stadium

Twickenham Stadium, Rugby Road, Twickenham, Middx TW1 1DZ (8892 8877, www.rfu.com/museum). Hounslow East tube, then bus 281, or Twickenham rail. **Open** *Museum* 10am-5pm Tue-Sat; 11am-5pm Sun. Last entry 4.30pm, ticket holders only match days. *Tours* 10.30am, noon, 1.30pm, 3pm Tue-Sat; 1pm, 3pm Sun (no tours match days). **Admission** *Combined ticket* £14; £8 under-16s, reductions; free under-5s; £40 family (2+3). Advance booking advisable.
Credit AmEx, MC, V. **7+**

Fascinating for anyone interested in rugby, this museum boasts the largest collection of memorabilia in the world. With elegant presentation, it charts the history of the game from – and indeed before – William Webb Ellis famously picked up the ball and ran with it during a football game at Rugby School in 1821. Visitors learn how a proper set of rules was developed, about the split with northern clubs that led to the emergence of rugby league, and about the spread of the game throughout the country and overseas. Displays include strange-shaped early rugby balls, a jersey from the first-ever rugby international between Scotland and England in 1871, signed shirts from down the decades and a timeline of the history of the game, alongside major world developments. The upper floor has a library and temporary exhibition room. The museum can sometimes be closed after match days; phone to check.
Buggy access. Disabled access: toilet. Nearest picnic place: benches around stadium. Shop.

WAR & THE ARMED FORCES

Churchill War Rooms

Clive Steps, King Charles Street, SW1A 2AQ (7930 6961, www.iwm.org.uk). St James's Park or Westminster tube, or bus 3, 12, 24, 53, 159. **Open** 9.30am-6pm daily. Last entry 5pm. **Admission** £15.95; £12.80 reductions; free under-16s (incl audio guide). **Credit** MC, V. **Map** p333 K9. **7+**

Just beneath Whitehall sits a time capsule of World War II that is part of the impressive Imperial War Museum group. The nine cramped rooms of the Churchill Suite were where Britain's leaders conducted wartime business, while bombs exploded in the streets overhead. With its low ceilings and concrete bomb protection, it's an atmospheric (if slightly stifling) installation that brings the wartime period vividly to life. The map room is particularly evocative. Another, larger space in the warren of tunnels houses the multimedia Churchill Museum. Its centrepiece is a large timeline; an award-winning digital archive that chronicles every major incident of Churchill's life, from the Boer War to his twilight as an after-dinner speaker and recipient of awards. There's also a kind of virtual peepshow of Churchill's home in Chartwell, Kent. The great man's voice, face and words come at you from all sides, and in every possible format. It's far from stiff and stuffy, and will appeal to most children – even if they end up simply playing around with all the technology. Staying here too long, though, would drive you mad: it's like being inside Winston's mind.

The temporary exhibition Undercover: Life in Churchill's Bunker opened in 2009 and has been so successful it is being extended until 2013. Family workshops linked to the exhibition will continue to take place in the school holidays; check the website for more details.
Buggy access. Café. Disabled access: lift, toilet. Nappy-changing facilities. Nearest picnic place: St James's Park. Shop.

Firepower Royal Artillery Museum

Royal Arsenal, SE18 6ST (8855 7755, www.firepower.org.uk). Woolwich Arsenal DLR/rail. **Open** 10.30am-5pm Wed-Sun & daily during school hols. Last entry 4pm. **Admission** £5; £4.50 reductions; £2.50 5-16s; free under-5s; £12 family (2+2 or 1+3). **Credit** MC, V. **7+**

Lots of children remain fascinated by warfare, artillery and soldiers despite parents and teachers discouraging too much active celebration. Occupying a series of converted Woolwich Arsenal buildings close to the river, the Gunners Museum is dedicated to the soldiers of the Royal Artillery (not the north London Premier League team). There is a footballing connection, though, which is remembered in the touching introductory film in the Breech Cinema: Arsenal FC started out as Woolwich Arsenal, when a group of armaments workers had a kickabout. After the

Imperial War Museum. *See p119.*

film, brace yourselves for the Field of Fire audio-visual display, where four massive screens relay archive film footage of very loud warfare (dry ice included).

Even more appealing to youngsters is the Camo Zone, where they can get their fingers on a trigger at the firing range, using sponge balls. There's also a bungee run and the chance to drive some radio-controlled tanks (activities cost £1.50 each and are supervised by friendly soldiers in fatigues). There are war game events recreating major battles with model soldiers on many weekends, so check the website for dates.

The on-site Gun Pit café is a reasonably priced place for rations, although if the weather's good, bring a picnic and enjoy the Thameside vista.
Buggy access. Café. Disabled access: lift, toilet. Nappy-changing facilities. Nearest picnic place: riverside. Shop.

Guards Museum
Birdcage Walk, SW1E 6HQ (7414 3271, www.theguardsmuseum.com). Victoria tube/rail. **Open** 10am-4pm daily. Last entry 3.30pm. **Admission** £4; £2 reductions; £1 ex-military; free under-16s. **Credit** (shop) AmEx, MC, V. **Map** p332 J9. **7+**
This small museum is dedicated to the history of Her Majesty's five foot regiments – the Scots, Irish, Welsh, Grenadier and Coldstream Guards. It houses military relics – flags, medals,

uniforms, drums and weapons – covering every campaign in the regiments' histories. Children will probably get the most out of it as a follow-up to seeing the Changing of the Guard at nearby Buckingham Palace (*see p57*). Highlights include the Grand Old Duke of York's bearskin (he commanded in peacetime, hence the nursery rhyme), plus assorted military medals, uniforms and personal effects. Worksheets for eight- to 14-year-olds add an extra dimension to a visit, and staff let kids try on bearskin hats and regimental tunics: they can have their photo taken for £5. The museum shop has an impressive collection of toy soldiers. *See also p54* **Neighbourhood Watch**.
Buggy access. Disabled access: lift. Nearest picnic place: St James's Park. Shop.

HMS Belfast
Morgan's Lane, Tooley Street, SE1 2JH (7940 6300, www.iwm.org.uk). Tower Hill tube or London Bridge tube/rail. **Open** *Mar-Oct* 10am-6pm daily. *Nov-Feb* 10am-5pm daily. Last entry 1hr before closing. **Admission** £13.50; £10.80 reductions; free under-16s. **Credit** MC, V. **Map** p335 R8. **4+**
HMS *Belfast* is another member of the impressive Imperial War Museum family. The vessel itself is the only surviving large light cruiser to have served in World War II. She went on to active service in Korea, before taking on peace-keeping duties in the 1950s and '60s.

Sightseeing

Belfast has been preserved to reflect the different decades of her service and the various campaigns she served in.

With her nine decks, the ship is a vast playground of narrow ladders, stairs, cabins and walkways. There are guided tours, but it's just as much fun to scramble around the ship at random, from bridge to boiler room, galley, sick bay, dentist's, NAAFI canteen and mess deck; there's even an operating theatre on board. Models of sailors chatting, eating, cooking and having their teeth drilled add to the entertainment.

Drop-in family activities take place during the holidays (check the website for details), which might involve crafts, music or dance.

Buggy access. Café. Disabled access: toilet. Nearest picnic place: Potters Fields Park. Shop.

Household Cavalry Museum

Horse Guards, Whitehall, SW1A 2AX (7930 3070, www.householdcavalrymuseum. org.uk). Embankment or Westminster tube, or Charing Cross tube/rail. **Open** *Mar-Sept* 10am-6pm daily. *Oct-Feb* 10am-5pm daily. **Admission** £6; £4 5-17s, reductions; free under-5s; £15 family (2+3). **Credit** MC, V. **5+**
There are all sorts of curios in this museum, including a cork leg, some silver kettledrums and a deadly pistol ball. There are also, as you'd expect, lots of regimental uniforms, medals and tack. The Household Cavalry comprises the oldest and most senior regiments in the British Army and, as well as enjoying a display of their ceremonial role (detailed below) visitors can watch video diaries of serving soldiers. The museum is separated from the stables by a glass wall, so you can sometimes see the magnificent horses being rubbed down after their official duties.

The Cavalry mounts the guard on Horse Guards Parade every day at 11am (10am on Sunday): this is actually a better place to see them in action than Buckingham Palace (*see p57*), since the crowds are thinner here, and you're not held far back from the action by railings. After the old and new guards have stared each other out in the centre of the parade ground for a quarter of an hour, if you nip through to the Whitehall side, you'll catch the departing guard's hilarious dismount choreography, which involves a synchronised, firm slap of approbation on each horse's neck before the gloved troopers all swing off. During school holidays, children can settle down to listen to a story in the museum, follow detective trails or join craft workshops. *See also p54* **Neighbourhood Watch**.

Buggy access. Disabled access: toilet. Nearest picnic place: St James's Park. Shop.

National Maritime Museum.

Imperial War Museum

Lambeth Road, SE1 6HZ (7416 5000, www.iwm.org.uk). Lambeth North tube or Elephant & Castle tube/rail. **Open** 10am-6pm daily. **Admission** free; charges may apply for special exhibitions. **Credit** MC, V. **5+**

Military exploits couldn't be less fashionable, but the Imperial War Museum still has an important role to play. Expecting a child to engage with the concept of a moral war might be too much to ask, but they can certainly begin to understand the effects of conflict on civilian life. Of course, there will be some guilty voyeurism too. There are guns, planes (some hanging from the ceiling), submarines, cannons, tanks and paintings of war in the main galleries. But there's far more to the museum. The collection covers conflicts, especially those involving Britain and the Commonwealth, from World War I to the present day. A clock (which was set running at midnight on 1 January 2000, when the number of lives lost during the wars of the 20th century stood at 100 million) continues to count those dying in conflicts – calculated to be two per minute.

Family-friendly temporary exhibitions include the Children's War (until Feb 2012), which looks at rationing, evacuation, air raids and blackouts from a child's perspective; and Once Upon a Wartime: Classic War Stories for Children (until 30 Oct 2011), a major new exhibition that delves into the pages of well-loved books, bringing five stories of war – *War Horse, Carrie's War, The Machine Gunners, The Silver Sword* and *Little Soldier* – to life. Wander through life-size sets, peer into intricate scale models and explore themes of loyalty, separation, excitement, survival and identity.

The unflinching Holocaust Exhibition, which traces the history of anti-semitism and its shameful nadir in the death camps, is not recommended for under-14s. Upstairs, Crimes Against Humanity is a minimalist space in which a film exploring genocide and ethnic violence rolls relentlessly; it's also unsuitable for under-16s.

The museum is housed in what was once the Bethlehem Royal Hospital (better known as Bedlam) on Lambeth Road, and really needs a whole day to explore. Luckily, the café is good and the grounds are perfect for a picnic, so pace yourselves. Check for one-off family-friendly events on the museum's website.

Buggy access. Café. Disabled access: lift, toilet. Nappy-changing facilities. Nearest picnic place: museum grounds. Shop.

National Army Museum

Royal Hospital Road, SW3 4HT (7730 0717, 7881 2455 recorded information, www.national-army-museum.ac.uk). Sloane Square tube or bus 11, 137, 239. **Open** 10am-5.30pm daily. **Admission** free. **Credit** (shop) AmEx, MC, V. **Map** p329 F12. **3+**

The history of the British Army as told by this museum will satisfy a child's love of all things gruesome (notices alert parents if there's anything unsuitable for younger children coming up). There are lots of permanent galleries as well as temporary exhibition hall the White Space, so don't try and see everything in one go. Most appealing to children will be the English Civil War helmet that they can try on; the chainmail armour they can gasp at the weight of; the immense model of the Battle of Waterloo, with 75,000 toy soldiers; and the skeleton of Napoleon's horse. The Redcoats Gallery shows how Brits conquered the world, while Nation in Arms covers both World Wars, with a reconstruction of a World War I trench and a particularly good jungle area. We also liked the way we were exhorted to join the 1914 army by a virtual recruiting sergeant as soon as we stepped through the door.

The Kids' Zone and regular themed weekend events have gone a long way to broadening the museum's appeal. The Kids' Zone is a free, interactive learning and play space for under-tens, with a castle and a cavalry charge of rocking horses, and opportunities to join in art activities, play board games or read; it can be booked by the hour for birthday parties. There's also a soft play area for babies. *See also p126* **Neighbourhood Watch**.

Buggy access. Café. Disabled access: lift, toilet. Nappy-changing facilities. Nearest picnic place: museum benches, Chelsea Hospital grounds. Shop.

National Maritime Museum

Romney Road, SE10 9NF (8858 4422, 8312 6565 information, www.nmm.ac.uk). Cutty Sark DLR or Greenwich DLR/rail. **Open** 10am-5pm daily. **Admission** free; donations appreciated. **Credit** MC, V. **4+**

As a World Heritage site, it's no wonder the attractions at Greenwich are being targeted for inclusion in the Olympic hoo-ha of 2012. The new Sammy Ofer Wing at the National Maritime Museum is due to open in summer 2011 and will include a new interactive gallery for younger visitors, among other things. Expect some upheaval in the meantime, with

Sightseeing

Neighbourhood Watch
South Kensington

Bringing up children in traffic-clogged London can be difficult at times, but when you visit South Kensington, you realise that the pros vastly outweigh the cons – where else in the world could you wander between three world-class museums, a cutting-edge art gallery and probably the capital's best playground, all without opening your purse?

With the culture come the crowds, of course, and the Science Museum, Natural History Museum and Victoria & Albert Museum attract millions of visitors each year to gawp at rockets, blue whales and ancient carpets. Most arrive via Exhibition Road, which until recently was an unpleasantly traffic-clogged artery. But now it is changing for the better, with an innovative shared use redesign, with a kerb-free single surface and a minimum of street furniture and barriers.

Weather permitting, it's traditional to make for the green swathes of **Hyde Park** after a morning's museum-strolling for a picnic. At one and a half miles long and about a mile wide, you should be able to find somewhere to lay out the cucmber sandwiches.

Dem bones

The **Natural History Museum** (*see p104*) is a big place, so start by picking up a free map from one of the information desks. Upon production of a parental credit card (a £25 refundable deposit is required), under-sevens can be kitted out with an Explorer backpack, with a pith helmet and binoculars. Themed Discovery Guides for five to 12s cost a pound. Now you're all set to go.

Generations of children have stood in the lofty central hall and gazed up at the mighty diplodocus cast, which has stood here for over a century. He was a vegetarian – unlike the animatronic T-Rex. Bravado runs high in the long, snaking queue that leads to his lair, though his swishing tail, baleful eyes and low growl strike fear into the stoutest of hearts – and can be too much for smaller children.

Solace can be found in the creepy crawlies gallery, where even toddlers can tower over the mini-beasts; watching the leaf-cutting ants toiling away is strangely therapeutic. If your offspring are more in the mood for destruction, head for the Power Within gallery, devoted to volcanoes and earthquakes. Step inside the 'quake simulator, which recreates the effects of the 1995 Kobe earthquake, and prepare to be all shook up in a mocked-up supermarket.

Not tired yet? Good, because there's plenty more to see – the gleaming new Darwin Centre for starters. Make sure you check out the programme of Nature Live talks, too; many are aimed at families, with topics ranging from carnivorous plants to bats or jungle beetles. And if a day isn't long enough here for the kids, book them a place on one of the monthly sleepovers (8-11s), including a torchlit dino discovery tour and a kip beneath the diplodocus.

Super science

For an all-round top day out, it's hard to beat the **Science Museum** (*see p112*), with its boy's own galleries chock full of cars, rockets, trains and ships. And it's not all 'look, don't touch' – the gloriously interactive Launchpad gallery is bursting with levers to pull, bridges to build and bubbles to blow. For proper explanations of why and how, children are advised to collar one of the museum's Explainers: walking, talking mines of information, clad in bright orange T-shirts.

Under-eights may have some trouble reaching and operating some of the exhibits in Launchpad; they can get hands-on in the Pattern Pod (suitable for over-fives). Younger ones can explore the Garden play zone down in the basement, donning orange waterproofs to mess about with boats and floats and constructing wobbly edifices from huge building blocks.

A right royal collection

It might seem like a less than obvious place to take the children, but that's precisely the appeal of the august **Victoria & Albert Museum** (see p86). The galleries are dotted with oddities that hold an unexpected appeal for children: Tippoo's Tiger, a bizarre, life-size 18th-century automaton depicting a man-eating tiger in the middle of his dinner, is always a hit. Then there are the impossibly tiny miniature portraits, towering platform shoes, impassive golden deities and swashbuckling samurai swords.

Though most of the priceless pieces are safely stowed behind glass, you can poke and prod certain exhibits: pick up a map and look for the hands-on symbols. A range of themed backpacks are also available to borrow, full of hands-on activities, including jigsaws, stories, puzzles, construction games and things to handle. If you're visiting on a Sunday, the new Drop-in Design events send children off around the V&A to hunt for design clues and ideas, before heading back to the Sackler Centre to create imaginative new designs using a range of materials. Themes might include choosing your favourite outfit from the V&A collection and designing a fancy accessory to complete the costume.

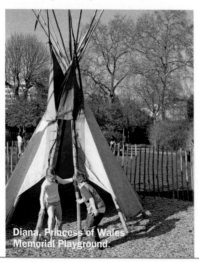

Diana, Princess of Wales
Memorial Playground.

Pirate ships & pedalos

After a morning in your museum of choice, an afternoon in Hyde Park and **Kensington Gardens** (see p143) is just the job. A ten-minute walk away, over 300 acres stretch before you. Horse-riders trot briskly along Rotten Row, in-line skaters speed past, and picnic-toting families hike across the grass in search of a scenic spot. Stroll up to the Serpentine, London's biggest boating lake, and take to the water in a pedalo; cheats can catch the eco-friendly solarshuttle across.

Head over to the southern side of the Serpentine for the Diana, Princess of Wales memorial fountain; sit on the edge and cool your toes; proper dips are best taken in the park's **lido and paddling pool**.

North of here, in Kensington Gardens, is a tribute to the princess that children will enjoy even more: the vast and vastly entertaining **Diana, Princess of Wales Memorial Playground** (see p143), although queues can build up on warm summer days. Another draw is the famous statue of Peter Pan, on the west bank of the Long Water. It appeared on May Day morning, 1912, accompanied by a brief announcement in the Times: 'There is a surprise in store for the children who go to Kensington Gardens to feed the ducks in the Serpentine this morning.' Pay your respects to Peter, then head off to search for fairies in the flowerbeds.

Also in the area: Carluccio's Caffè, Gourmet Burger Kitchen, Paul.
Café Crêperie 2 Exhibition Road, SW7 2HF (7589 8947, www.kensington creperie.com). Bustling joint that serves up sweet and savoury crêpes.
Le Pain Quotidien 15-17 Exhibition Road, SW7 2HE (7486 6154, www.lepainquotidien.co.uk). Pricey but tasty tartines, salads and cakes.
Lido Café on the Serpentine Hyde Park, W2 2UH (7706 7098). Down-to-earth, delicious grub in a splendid spot.
Orangery Kensington Palace Kensington Gardens, W8 2UH (7376 0239, www.hrp.org.uk). Afternoon tea and light lunches served in stunning surrounds.

Sightseeing

the outdoor play area and several galleries closed at the time of writing. Britain's seafaring heritage takes centre stage at this vibrant, appealing museum. Themed galleries address everything from the perils faced by early explorers to the slave trade. In the Ships of War gallery, doll's house owners will dream of getting their hands on the impossibly intricate model ships that were built for the Royal Navy in the 17th and 18th centuries; the Royal George is a beauty. In the All Hands gallery, kids can have a go at loading up a cargo ship or sending a semaphore signal, while the Bridge Gallery has a simulator where they can attempt to steer a ferry into port.

The Museum Highlights trail takes children through the galleries in search of golden mermaids, the fatal bullet hole in Nelson's blood-stained jacket and, best of all, a real-life pirate's sword, while weekends and school holidays bring a good assortment of activities to get stuck into. Up the hill, the Royal Observatory and Planetarium (*see p46*) are also part of the NMM complex. *See also p132* **Neighbourhood Watch**.

Buggy access. Café. Disabled access; lift, toilet. Nappy-changing facilities. Nearest picnic place: Greenwich Park, museum grounds. Shop.

Royal Air Force Museum Hendon

Grahame Park Way, NW9 5LL (8205 2266, www.rafmuseum.org). Colindale tube or Mill Hill Broadway rail, or bus 303. **Open** 10am-6pm daily. *Tours* daily; phone for details. **Admission** free. *Tours* free. **Credit** MC, V. **3+**

Hendon Airfield has existed here since 1910, hence its claim to be the birthplace of aviation in Britain. Hangers full of over 100 aircraft form the main attraction of this museum. They include a Camel, Tempest, Tiger Moth, Mosquito and Harrier – all parked at ground level or hung in dogfight poses from the rafters of the ultra-modern Milestones of Flight building. Excitingly, helicopters jut above your head as you sit in the café. Don't miss the miniature parachutists going up and down in a tube or dropping off a wire into the hands of kids eager to learn about the laws of gravity.

Plenty of other interactive games are available in the Aeronauts gallery, many in the guise of pilot aptitude tests. Only the flight simulator (over-eights only) carries an extra charge: everything else is gloriously free, so don't exhaust the kids with a full tour; you can come back as often as you like. More low-key

than the Milestones of Flight gallery are the atmospheric, dimly lit Battle of Britain building and the restored Grahame-White Factory.

There is plenty of lethal hardware on display, from World War II doodlebugs to modern cluster bombs and cruise missiles, so be ready to field questions about man's inhumanity to man as you walk around the galleries. Special activity days take place throughout the year, particularly on military holidays; older kids can learn the principles of rocket science, while youngsters build their own cardboard flying machines. See the website for upcoming events.

Activities for children and adults take place all year, with a cluster in the summer holidays. The ever-popular workshops (book ahead) can include activities like hot-air balloon making, rocket science, and Search and Rescue role-play. Quizzes, Pulsar Battlezone interactive laser games, face-painting, aircraft displays and giant garden games might also be on the cards. *Buggy access. Café. Disabled access: lift, toilet. Nappy-changing facilities. Nearest picnic place: on-site picnic area. Restaurant. Shop.*

Winston Churchill's Britain at War Experience

64-66 Tooley Street, SE1 2TF (7403 3171, www.britainatwar.co.uk). London Bridge tube/rail. **Open** *Apr-Oct* 10am-5pm daily. *Nov-Mar* 10am-4.30pm daily. **Admission** £12.95; £6.50 reductions; £5.50 5-15s; free under-5s; £29 family (2+2). **Credit** AmEx, MC, V. **Map** p335 Q8. **8+**

This museum is small and cramped, but that's part of the point. The first excitement is the descent from the street into the museum, via an original London Underground lift. Once below, visitors are delivered straight into a mocked-up Blitz-era Underground shelter, with sounds of an air raid rumbling overhead. The convincing set includes bunks, a temporary kitchen and library, original posters and newsreel clips from the time. Other displays explore the roles of women at war, the life of evacuated children and rationing. An ex-evacuee is on hand to show you his childhood photos, there's a BBC broadcasting room and a pub, and children will enjoy trying on tin helmets and gas masks in a dressing-up corner. The visit ends in a full-size street, where a bomb has just exploded – all chillingly staged to make you think the action occurred moments before. An hour or so probably suffices for the whole place. *Buggy access. Disabled access: toilet. Nearest picnic place: Southwark Cathedral gardens. Shop.*

Parks & Gardens

Head for the open air.

Londoners owe a great debt to royalty and philanthropists over the centuries. Both parties may have been a lot more privileged and wealthy than the average Joe, but they have been responsible for creating and preserving some of London's best open spaces. And as any Londoner knows, the sheer variety is thrilling. As well as ancient trees, well-stocked borders and beds, and landscaping to rival any rural stately home, there are often plenty of other attractions.

On top of finding somewhere for the children to run wild and explore, you'll discover great cafés and restaurants – **Holland Park** (*see p137*), **St James's Park** (*see p144*), **Coram's Fields** (*see p134*); galleries – **Dulwich Park** (*see p134*), **Hyde Park** (*see p143*); zoos – **Regent's Park** (*see p143*), **Battersea Park** (*see p129*); city farms – **Crystal Palace Park** (*see p134*), **Lee Valley Park** (*see p146*); open-air theatres – **Regent's Park** (*see p143*); and open-air swimming pools – **Hampstead Heath** (*see p136*), **Brockwell Park** (*see p130*). What's more, most of them are free to get into.

In these pages, we've listed Royal Parks, wild urban spaces, local parks, adventure playgrounds and the surprising large open spaces reserved for Londoners by forward-thinking planners over the centuries.

BOTANIC GARDENS

More botanic beauties can be found in **Chumleigh Gardens** (Burgess Park; *see p130*), the herb garden at the **Geffrye Museum** (*see p77*), **Ham House** (*see p62*), **Hampton Court Palace** (*see p59*) and **Syon House Gardens** (*see p66*).

Chelsea Physic Garden

66 Royal Hospital Road (entrance on Swan Walk), SW3 4HS (7352 5646, www.chelsea physicgarden.co.uk). Sloane Square tube or bus 170. **Open** *Apr-Oct* noon-5pm Wed-Fri; noon-6pm Sun, bank hol Mon. *Tours* times vary, phone to check. **Admission** £8; £5 5-15s, reductions; free under-5s. *Tours* free. **Credit** MC, V. **Map** p329 F12.

A working garden since 1673, the Chelsea Physic has long been at the vanguard of botanical research. The Pharmaceutical Garden is planted out according to medical specialisms including oncology, cardiology, dermatology and psychiatry; the Garden of World Medicine is planted by geographical area. Perfumery and Aromatherapy borders are full of plants which yield scents and oils, while the vegetable and fruit garden specialises in rare varieties. Bees in the Mediterranean Garden provide honey for the shop and there's also a café that serves light snacks and lunches (plus some evening meals in high summer). Come during school holidays for the Family Activity Days, including in 2011 Lotions and Potions – an Introduction to Herbal Medicine for over-sixes, a Forensic Biology Workshop for over-eights, and Paper Making for beginners for over-sixes.

Buggy access. Café. Disabled access: toilet. Nappy-changing facilities. Shop.

Royal Botanic Gardens (Kew Gardens)

Richmond, Surrey, TW9 3AB (8332 5655, 8940 1171 information, www.kew.org). Kew Gardens tube/rail, Kew Bridge rail, or riverboat to Kew Pier. **Open** *Apr-Aug* 9.30am-6.30pm Mon-Fri; 9.30am-7.30pm Sat, Sun. *Sept-Oct* 9.30am-6pm daily. *Late Oct-early Feb* 9.30am-4.15pm daily. *Early Feb-late Mar* 9.30am-5.30pm daily. Last entry 30mins before closing. *Tours* 11am, 2pm daily. **Admission** £13.90; £11.90 reductions, late entry (after 4.45pm); free under-17s. **Credit** AmEx, MC, V.

Kew Gardens may be famous for its rich botanical heritage, but it has countless other attractions more suitable for exciting younger visitors. First stop for the little ones is the Climbers & Creepers adventure playground. Here, kids can clamber into a flower and dig for 'fossilised plants', while real insects buzz amid see-through habitats. This is also the base where eight- to 11-year-olds and their guardians can come for a Midnight Rambler sleepover, which offers the chance to track local wildlife and earn prizes (£40 per person, April to October; book well in advance). Right next door is new outdoor play area Treehouse Towers, which is full of scramble nets, slides, giant swings, zip wires and towers.

Second favourite, particularly on a freezing winter's day, is the lush, tropical Palm House, where children love climbing the spiral staircases to the upper walkways, and are delighted by the discovery of the Marine Display tanks in the basement. Don't forget the outdoor Treetop Walkway, 60ft up in the air. The rest of Kew's 300 acres has an amazing array of monuments, gardens and landscapes. The famous Pagoda is one of 40 Grade II-listed structures within Kew's walls (although you can no longer climb to the top and enjoy the views), while the Minka House was originally a farmhouse outside Okazaki City in Japan. The scaled-up badger sett is also brilliant fun.

If you're walking around the gardens on foot, pick up a free map at the ticket office. Smaller children might prefer to ride the Kew Explorer people-mover, which plies a circular route around the gardens (£4; £1 reductions). There are cafés and restaurants dotted here and there, but on a fine day you can't beat a picnic. Summer art shows, live music and a winter ice rink in front of the Temperate House (check website for dates) make Kew a year-round treat. *Buggy access. Cafés. Disabled access: toilet. Nappy-changing facilities. Restaurants. Shop.*

CEMETERIES

Abney Park Cemetery & Nature Reserve

Stoke Newington High Street, N16 0LN (7275 7557, www.abney-park.org.uk). Stoke Newington rail or bus 73, 106, 149, 243, 276, 349. **Open** *Cemetery dawn-dusk daily. Visitors centre 10am-2pm Mon-Fri.* **Admission** free.
Abney Park is one of London's 'Magnificent Seven' garden cemeteries. Laid out in 1840, it was a model of non denominational tolerance whose chapel welcomed allcomers. The chapel is currently in a tumbledown state, but funds have been raised to reroof and repoint before the whole thing collapses. There's also money for a fence around the children's garden and to repair the old iron gates at the main entrance. Abney Park is just as winsomely decayed as Highgate Cemetery but without the entry fee or Marx pilgrims. It's a chaotic jumble of Victorian graves, trees, and blind corners. The slowly decaying monuments – urns, angels, Celtic crosses, saints and shepherds – add romantic interest to what's now a local nature reserve (it was Hackney's first), where birds, butterflies and bats make their home.

There's an environmental outdoor classroom at the Stoke Newington High Street entrance, which hosts free workshops for children and adults: go on a mini beast hunt, examine beetles and bugs at close quarters, or take a tree tour and learn about the hundreds of different varieties on site. The visitors' centre doubles as a shop for guides to green London and other environmentally aware literature. From the Church Street entrance path, avoid turning left if you want to steer clear of men seeking men. *Buggy access. Disabled access: toilet (visitors centre). Shop.*

Brompton Cemetery

Fulham Road, SW10 9UG (7352 1201, www.royalparks.org.uk). West Brompton tube/rail. **Open** *Summer 8am-8pm daily. Winter 8am-4pm daily.* **Admission** free.
This is one of the finest Victorian cemeteries, and with its formal layout, grand central avenue, and chapel based on St Peter's Basilica in Rome, one of the most distinctive. It has more than 35,000 monuments to the dead, commemorating the famous and infamous, including suffragette Emmeline Pankhurst, shipping magnate Sir Samuel Cunard and boxer 'Gentleman' John Jackson, who taught Byron to box; his grave is marked by a lion. The peace is regularly disturbed by Chelsea FC's home games at neighbouring Stamford Bridge. Bond fans might also like to know that the cemetery was used as a set in *GoldenEye*. *Buggy access. Disabled access.*

Highgate Cemetery

Swain's Lane, N6 6PJ (8340 1834, www.highgate-cemetery.org). Highgate tube. **Open** *East cemetery Apr-Oct 10am-5pm Mon-Fri; 11am-5pm Sat, Sun. Nov-Mar 10am-4pm Mon-Fri; 11am-4pm Sat, Sun. West cemetery by tour only; phone for*

Sightseeing

details. **Admission** *East cemetery* £3; £2 reductions. *West cemetery tours* £7; £5 reductions; £3 8-16s. **No credit cards.**

In 2009, Highgate Cemetery was upgraded to a Grade I-listed park. Not bad for somewhere that, as recently as 1981, was thoroughly neglected, with a tangle of brambles, overgrown self-sown trees and crumbling exterior walls and buildings. The cemetery is most famous for housing the grave of Karl Marx (East cemetery), and you'll often see pilgrims making their way to it through neighbouring Waterlow Park (*see p142*).

Children love the wild wood feel of the place; thanks to its angels, shrouded urns and broken columns, this beautiful boneyard has a romantic atmosphere of ivy-covered neglect. Officially, youngsters are discouraged from visiting, unless they're coming to see the grave of a relative – but if you long to pay your respects to Marx, Mary Ann Evans (aka George Eliot), Christina Rossetti, scientist Michael Faraday, or any of the other eminent figures who now repose in the East cemetery, you can bring children along, as long as they behave well. The atmospheric West cemetery, with its Lebanon Circle Vaults, Egyptian Avenue and Terrace Catacombs, is out of bounds to casual visitors; adults and children aged eight and over can take a guided tour. Both sites close for funerals, so phone before you visit.

Buggy & disabled access (East cemetery only).

Kensal Green Cemetery

Harrow Road, W10 4RA (8969 0152, www.kensalgreencemetery.com). Kensal Green tube/rail or bus 18, 52. **Open** *Apr-Sept* 9am-6pm Mon-Sat; 10am-6pm Sun. *Oct-Mar* 9am-6pm Mon-Sat; 10am-5pm Sun. *All year* 10am-1pm bank hols. *Tours* 2pm Sun. **Admission** free. *Tours* £5; £4 reductions.

This was the first commercial cemetery in London when, during Victorian times, the population grew too fast to be served by the city's existing churchyards. Behind an impressive neoclassical gate lie 72 acres of trees, shrubs, graves and monuments between the Grand Union Canal and Harrow Road – there's a contemporary art gallery on site too. Kensal Green is one of London's 'Magnificent Seven' garden cemeteries and was divided into a consecrated section for Anglicans and an unconsecrated alternative for dissenters. Various 19th-century greats repose here, including Isambard Kingdom Brunel, William Thackeray, Anthony Trollope and Wilkie Collins, but the most impressive monuments are the ornate mausoleums of lesser names. There's also a Greek Revivalist chapel and mysterious catacombs, which you can visit on the two-hour guided cemetery tours that take place on Sunday afternoons (over-12s only). The annual Open Day is usually held on the first Saturday in July (check the website for details), and has a village fête atmosphere with face painting, stalls, dressing-up and a motorcade of hearses.

Buggy access. Disabled access: toilet.

West Norwood Cemetery

Norwood Road, SE27 9JU (7926 7999, www.westnorwoodcemetery.com). West Norwood rail or bus 2, 68, 196, 315, 322, 432, 468. **Open** *Summer* 8am-6pm Mon-Fri; 10am-6pm Sat, Sun. *Winter* 8am-4pm Mon-Fri; 10am-4pm Sat, Sun.

Admission free.

Another of London's 'Magnificent Seven' Victorian garden cemeteries, West Norwood has more listed monuments than any other English cemetery – look out for Mrs Beeton and Sir Henry Tate (the man behind the creation of Tate Britain after his proposed donation of British art to the National Gallery was refused in the late 19th century). For a place associated with death, there's a lot of life going on. The cemetery is a green haven where a great variety of wildlife chirps, slithers and scampers amongst the gothic grandeur. Look out for kestrels and tawny owl, who use the place as a hunting ground, and enjoy the bluebells, wild primroses and daffodils in spring. Managed by Lambeth Council, this sloping 40-acre site includes habitats such as planted flower beds and shrubbery, scrub, vegetated walls and tombstones. In the highest part of the cemetery, there's also an area of ancient trees, possibly a fragment of the original Great North Wood from which Norwood gets its name.

Buggy access.

CITY SPACES

The Greenway

0870 240 6094, www.walklondon.org.uk.

Who would have thought a sewage pipe could make such an interesting day out? The Greenway is a three-mile walking trail and cycleway that has been fashioned along the embankment of a large pipe that carries you-know-what from north London to the works at Beckton. It's part of the Capital Ring circular

Neighbourhood Watch
Chelsea

Saatchi Gallery.

Originally a fishing village, Chelsea was a 'village of palaces' by the 16th century as large mansions sprang up along the picturesque riverfront to house the likes of Sir Thomas More. Artists and poets (Whistler, Carlyle, Wilde) followed from the 1880s, before the Swinging Sixties and punk made the area synonymous with new culture revolutions.

Nowadays, though, the mohicans and revolutionary culture are long gone, replaced by mochachinos and rarefied couture. That said, it's an attractive area for a stroll with the kids in tow, from the Bugaboo-filled aisles of department store Peter Jones to the mercilessly modern art of the new **Saatchi Gallery** (see p82) You may not be able to afford to move to SW3, but there's no reason not to sample the high life for a bit.

Shopping vs culture
At Sloane Square, named after Sir Hans Sloane who provided the foundation collections for the British Museum, you could pop into the **Royal Court**, the stylish home of cutting-edge theatre. Check out the website for occasional backstage tours (www.royalcourttheatre .com). Alternatively, browse the stylish home of middle class retail, aka Peter Jones, set in a refurbished 1930s building with excellent views from its top-floor café. More smart shopping prospects loom at the pedestrianised

Duke of York Square, which also makes a relaxing post for an al fresco lunch stop for hungry kids. Also here is the **Saatchi Gallery** (see p82). It holds envelope-pushing temporary exhibitions, many of which appeal to children.

Continue the upscale shopping opportunities on the King's Road. The western end – known as World's End – was once the home of Vivienne Westwood's shop at no.430, with its backwards-spinning clock. If you've walked all the way here, you deserve to rest your tired legs in Cremorne Gardens, a riverside park with uplifting views east to Old Ferry Wharf and west to exclusive Chelsea Harbour.

War – what is it good for?
The 500-year history of the British Army is told at the **National Army Museum** (see p119). Don't be put off by the rather severe modern exterior of the museum; some eccentric exhibits and displays, together with an exciting programme of family events, make this friendly museum far more entertaining than you might think.

Sure, there are a number of dry displays of regimental items – old uniforms (including the kit of ex-army athlete and Olympic medallist Dame Kelly Holmes), kit bags and the like – but there are also fascinating highlights: a model of the Battle of Waterloo, starring 75,000 toy soldiers; the skeleton of Napoleon's beloved mount, Marengo; and Florence Nightingale's lamp. Children love the more bizarre exhibits, such as the frostbitten fingers of Major 'Bronco' Lane, conqueror of Mount Everest. The Redcoats Gallery starts at Agincourt in 1415 and ends with the redcoats in the American War of Independence; Nation in Arms covers both World Wars, with reconstructions of a trench in the World at War (1914-1946) exhibition, and a D-Day landing craft. There's more military hardware, including a hands-on Challenger tank simulator, up in the Modern Army exhibition. (Note that certain exhibitions are not suitable for younger children. Faces of Battle includes previously unseen photographs and footage of Britain's faceless war wounded, displayed alongside contemporary uniform sculptures tracing their surgery, rehabilitation and recovery.)

WAACS at War looks at the role of the women who 'did their bit' for the WWII war effort. Their roles included cooking and waiting on officers, serving as clerks, telephone operators, store-women, drivers, printers, bakers and cemetery gardeners. There is also information on the women who disguised themselves as men to go and fight.

Themed weekend events (check the website for details), which usually involve costumed interpreters and craft activities, have gone a long way to broadening the museum's appeal, as has the Kids' Zone – a free interactive learning and play space. It's the sort of place you can bring all your troops to, as its attractions include construction, reading and art activity and board-game areas tailored for under-tens, including a soft-play area for babies.

Gardeners' world

This area is famous for its annual Flower Show held towards the end of May, and the Chelsea Royal Hospital, just around the corner from the Army Museum, is where it's held. The show is an awesome sight and the intricate, colourful displays and show gardens will enthrall children, although it's over-fives only – toddlers are, understandably, deemed too much of a risk. Tickets need to be booked way in advance for the three public days. Also in the neighbourhood are the year-round delights of the **Chelsea Physic Garden** (*see p123*). London's oldest botanic garden can be reached via Flood Street, one of the many attractive side roads branching off King's Road. The garden was set up in 1673, but the key phase of development was under Sir Hans Sloane in the 18th century. Its beds contain healing herbs and rare trees, dye plants and medicinal vegetables; plants

are also sold. Public opening hours are restricted because this is primarily a centre for research and education. There are two deep ponds and poisonous plants, so it's not suitable for very small children, and there must be two adults for every two children under 18.

That said, the education department organises activity days for older children on themes such as Gardening for Beginners or Gardening Photography over the Easter and summer holidays. Activity days should generally be pre-booked, and are suitable for seven- to 11-year-olds (although there are some for four- to six-year-olds and nine-to 13-year-olds). For a full list of dates, visit the website (www.chelsea physicgarden.co.uk). Educational visits and teacher-training days can also be arranged.

Refreshments

Also in the area: Pizza Express.
Benihana *77 King's Road, SW3 4NX (7376 7799, www.benihana.co.uk).* Japanese teppanyaki, with highly entertaining chefs.
Big Easy *332-334 King's Road, SW3 5UR (7352 4071, www.bigeasy.uk.com).* Cajun fare for sharing: steaks, sticky ribs, crab and the like.
Gelateria Valerie *Duke of York Square, King's Road, SW3 4LY (7730 7978).* Enticing Italian-style *gelato* in 24 scrumptious flavours.
Itsu *118 Draycott Avenue, SW3 3AE (7590 2400, www.itsu.com).* Polished Japanese fare.
Left Wing Café *9 Duke of York Square, SW3 4LY (7730 7094, www.patisserie-valerie.co.uk).* Part of the Patisserie Valerie cake-and-café chain.
Manicomio *85 Duke of York Square, King's Road, SW3 4LY (7730 3366, www.manicomio.co.uk).* Pasta, pizza and a shaded terrace.
National Army Museum Café *National Army Museum, Royal Hospital Road, SW3 4HT (7730 0717, www.national-army-museum.ac.uk).* Think solid, sturdy grub: meatballs, fish, chips.
Paul *134 King's Road, SW3 4X8 (7581 9611, www.paul-uk.com).* An outpost of the ever-reliable French bakery chain.

Sightseeing

My Sport Judo
Duncan, 14

What inspired you to take up judo?
I went to watch my dad and the man who is now my coach fight in a competition. My dad passed away a few years ago, but he started judo at school, so he'd been doing it for 40 years.

What do you like about your sport?
I like the competing best. I wouldn't want to participate in a sport that didn't have a competitive element.

What level are you at?
Just below British Squad standard.

There's not really a term for it, but I'm above County level. I'm a blue belt, so I've got the brown and black belts to go.

What's next for you in your sport?
I'd like to get to British Squad standard and then compete at Olympic level. I think the 2016 Olympics might be too close, but I'm hoping for 2020 if not.

Which events would you like to see at the London 2012 Olympic Games and Paralympic Games?
Athletics and Judo.

walk around London's suburbs, and the wide, bonded gravel track lifts intrepid urban explorers above the surrounding cityscape.

Great views of Canary Wharf and the Millennium Dome were already a draw, along with architectural curiosities such as the Byzantine-style Victorian Abbey Mills Pumping Station (known as the Cathedral of Sewage). But every month, the views from this raised walkway get more exciting. The Greenway skirts the Olympic Park, so walkers and cyclists can see the mass of cranes and builders at work as they construct venues for the London 2012 Olympic and Paralympic Games.

There's also a community art and education centre called the View Tube to visit, and the lovely Container Café (*see p245*) is a pleasant place to sit and watch the progress down below. Two distinctive new gates at the Wick Lane and Canning Town entrances have been commissioned by the Olympic Delivery Authority by artist group the Klassnik Corporation. Bikeworks (8980 7998, www.bikeworks.org.uk) hires bikes out at £6 per hour, and also offers guided bike rides of the nearby developments. For further details of the Capital Ring route, visit www.walklondon.org.uk.

Postman's Park

Between King Edward Street & Aldersgate Street, EC1R 4JR (7374 4127). St Paul's tube. **Open** *Summer* 8am-7pm daily. *Winter* 8am-4pm daily. **Admission** free. **Map** p334 O6.

This park was opened in 1880, and is made up of bits of several former churchyards. It acquired its name after becoming the lunchtime favourite of postal workers from a nearby sorting office (long since demolished). The park is a lovely curio, especially for children of reading age, as it is best known for the Watts Memorial to Heroic Sacrifice. The memorial is a canopy-covered expanse of ceramic plaques, inscribed in florid Victorian style, that pay tribute to ordinary people who died trying to save others. 'Frederick Alfred Croft, Inspector, aged 31', begins one typical thumbnail drama. 'Saved a Lunatic Woman from Suicide at Woolwich Arsenal Station, But was Himself Run Over by the Train, Jan 11, 1878'. Many of the dead heroes were children, who tried to rescue drowning companions; their fates make gruesome lessons for their latter-day counterparts. In late spring, the handkerchief tree is also spectacular.

Buggy access.

LOCAL PARKS

Alexandra Park & Palace

Alexandra Palace Way, N22 7AY (8444 7696 park, 8365 2121 information, www.alexandrapalace.com). Wood Green tube or Alexandra Palace rail, or bus W3, 144. **Open** *Park* 24hrs daily. *Palace* times vary, depending on exhibitions. **Admission** free.

It's not the prettiest of London's palaces, and there's something soulless about a building that has never been lived in, but Alexandra Palace continues to serve the purpose for which it was built… Pleasure. It was constructed as 'The People's Palace' in 1873, with the intent of providing affordable entertainment for all, although the original building burned down just 16 days after its opening. (It was speedily rebuilt, and re-opened two years later.) Inside, Ally Pally is mainly used for exhibitions, fairs and gigs, but there's also an ice-skating rink that reopened in January 2011 after a £2.3 million refurbishment. Outside, the views over London are spectacular and almost worth the trip on their own. But there's plenty more to do than just gawp at the city below. The children's playground behind the palace is a well-equipped and wholesome place in which to take the air, with a café next to the boating lake and a skateboard park for older kids. The pitch-and-putt course is down the hill towards Alexandra Palace station and popular with older children, and there's a farmers' market at the Hornsey Gate Entrance on Sundays (10am-3pm). The Grove is the more sheltered area of the park (between the Palace and Muswell Hill) and is very popular for family picnics; a lovely new indoor play centre called Little Dinosaurs (*see p178*) opened here in late 2009. Annual visits from the funfair and circus are popular, as is Bonfire Night in November, which brings stunning pyrotechnics that can be seen for miles around (although it had to be cancelled in 2010 due to lack of funds).

Buggy access. Café. Disabled access: lift, toilet. Nappy-changing facilities (ice rink).

Battersea Park

SW11 4NJ (8871 7530, 8871 7539 adventure playground, www.wandsworth. gov.uk). Sloane Square tube, then bus 19, 137, or Battersea Park or Queenstown Road rail. **Open** 8am-dusk daily. **Map** p329 F13.

Many of London's parks are very well established, but that doesn't mean they never change. Battersea Park opened a new Winter

Sightseeing

Garden in March 2011 which has transformed a neglected area next to the Sun Gate into a haven of sights and smells designed by Dan Pearson to be full of colour and interest from autumn to spring. This is a continuation of the splendid restoration projects that began in 2004. Battersea Park was originally laid out in 1858 on land which was once a popular spot for duelling (the Duke of Wellington fought an abortive duel here in 1829, deliberately aiming wide of his opponent, the Earl of Winchilsea, who for his part shot his pistol into the air). Facilities range from fun water features (a boating lake, elegant fountains and a riverside promenade) to state-of-the-art sporting facilities and play areas, including a toddlers' playground and a challenging adventure playground for five to 16s. Bikes can be hired out from London Recumbents next to the Millennium Arena (7498 6543, www.london recumbents.com; open at weekends, bank holidays and during school holidays Easter to August); there are rowing boats and a land train in July and August, and open fishing is available from mid June to mid March; for permits, call 8871 7530. Battersea Park is also home to a rich array of wildlife, and the London Wildlife Trust has nature reserves here.

The Gondola al Parco café (7978 1655) serves Italian food, with tables overlooking the boating lake and live music on summer evenings. The prettiest landmark, though, is the Peace Pagoda, donated in 1985 by Japanese monks and nuns to commemorate Hiroshima Day. It stands serenely opposite the Children's Zoo (*see p158*) on the park's northern edge. *Buggy access. Café. Disabled access: toilet. Nappy-changing facilities.*

Brent Lodge Park

Church Road, W7 3BL (07940 021183, www.ealing.gov.uk). Hanwell rail or bus E1, E2. Open 7.30am-dusk daily. **Open** *Maze & animals* times vary, phone for details. *Indoor centre* 1.30-3pm Sat, Sun. **Admission** free. **No credit cards.**
This delightful local park is known as the Bunny Park, thanks to the rabbits that inhabit the Animal Centre, alongside sheep, goats, monkeys, mongooses, birds and reptiles. There's a café and a good playground, plus a maze with a look-out tower in its centre that was planted to mark the Millennium. The centre organises children's activity days in summer; phone the number above for details. *Buggy access. Café. Disabled access: toilet. Nappy-changing facilities.*

Brockwell Park

Dulwich Road, SE24 0PA (www.brockwell park.com). Herne Hill rail. **Open** 7.30am-dusk daily. **Admission** free.
When Lord Roseberry declared this park open in 1892 he said, 'whatever happens, this is preserved for you and your descendents forever as an open space'. He hadn't reckoned on Lambeth Council, who recently shaved off a corner of the park to make way for a new road junction. Luckily, it would take more than that to spoil this lovely park. Tucked away behind the grassy slopes on the Tulse Hill side is one of south London's best playgrounds, which has recently had a refurbishment. There's an aerial slide, a massive sandpit and sections for different age groups; nearby are the duck ponds and the huge new paddling pool.

There's lots to do besides, with the community greenhouses offering digging pits and planting workshops, plus a long-established BMX track and all-weather tennis courts. The beautiful walled garden is also worth seeking out, especially in summer, when you can try a mulberry from the tree inside. On the Herne Hill side, the 1930s lido has been restored to its former pomp and is open from May to September; it's packed on sunny days. Whippersnappers (7738 6633, www.whipper snappers.org) runs kids' music classes at the lido complex year-round. The new Lido Café (*see p251*) is proving popular with locals.

It's a steep walk to the top of the hill, but worth it for the view north over the city. Take a breather at the late Georgian Brockwell Hall country house, now a café serving great wedges of lasagne and other pasta dishes, plus own-made cakes. The park also hosts lots of events throughout the year, including the popular country show every July (*see p18*). *Buggy access. Café. Disabled access: toilet. Nappy-changing facilities.*

Burgess Park

Albany Road, SE5 0RJ (7703 4275, www.southwark.gov.uk). Elephant & Castle tube/rail, then bus 12, 42, 63, 68, 171, 343. **Open** 24hrs daily. *Lake area* 8am-dusk daily. **Admission** free.
Burgess Park is one of the largest in south London, but it's not one of the best known. It was formed during the 1950s clear-up of World War II Blitz damage by demolishing 30 streets, filling in a canal and clearing several derelict factory buildings. Since then the park has grown in stages, but never with an overall plan; luckily, in an area that sorely needs community

Queen Elizabeth Olympic Park

A new green space for London.

Following the 2012 Games, the Olympic Park will officially be reopened as the Queen Elizabeth Olympic Park in 2013. Visible for miles around will be the Orbit, Anish Kapoor's towering art sculpture. It will remain part of the London skyline indefinitely, as will the sporting venues within the park: Zaha Hadid's Aquatics Centre (with its two 50m pools and diving pool) plans to have a family-friendly café and crèche, and the Velodrome and BMX Track will be developed into a VeloPark suitable for all ages and abilities, with the addition of a road cycle circuit and mountain bike course.

If you and the children want to see some of these as they go up, head along to the Container Café (*see p245*) or take a bike ride along the fringes of the park on the three-mile Greenway trail (*see p125*).

The Queen Elizabeth Park will also retain the artworks commissioned by the Olympic Delivery Authority. These include decorative bridges by Martin Richman and Jason Bruges Studio, and wildflower meadows designed by the Klassnik Corporation.

Sightseeing

spaces, it's about to get a £6 million overhaul. Locals have asked for a cultural hub, cycle tracks, a café with outdoor seating, more benches along the old towpath and a complete renovation of the existing playground, games room and kart and bicycle track (7525 1101). The work is due to be finished in March 2012.

At present, most community activities are based in the Chumleigh Gardens section of the park, which is home to the Southwark Rangers Football team, a great little café with fry-ups, quiches, salads and jazz on sunny Sundays, and a thriving Peckham Sure Start scheme. Various garden styles are employed in the series of interconnecting plots; English country garden, fragrant Mediterranean, meditative Islamic and a splendid Caribbean garden. The Heart Garden is a fruit and vegetable patch planted, tended and harvested by people with long-term illnesses. There are also lots of community allotments. *Buggy access. Café. Disabled access: toilet.*

Clissold Park

Stoke Newington Church Street, N16 5HJ (7923 3660 park ranger, www. clissoldpark.com). Stoke Newington rail or bus 73, 149, 476. **Open** 7.30am-dusk daily. **Admission** free.

The landscaping of this park has never been its strong point – Clissold Park is almost totally flat and you can see traffic from most sightlines – but it's mightily popular with Stoke Newington families. An £8.9 million Lottery-funded refurbishment was finished off in spring 2011 which has improved on an already successful formula. The popular animal enclosures have a new butterfly dome and an aviary; the lakes have been drained and replanted; there's a new multi-use Games Area and Wheels Park, and Clissold House has had some much needed TLC – let's hope the new café is more exciting than the old one.

There's a paddling pool in summer, while the large playground has a good choice of activities for all ages. Younger children love scaring themselves on the wobbly bridge, while older kids favour the aerial four-way see-saw. Next to the playground, the tennis courts are home to the Hackney wing of the City Tennis Centre (7254 4235), offering family tennis evenings, coaching, junior clubs and tournaments. The One O'Clock club is near the duck ponds.

Neighbourhood Watch
Greenwich

Greenwich is an irresistible mixture of maritime, royal and horological history, a combination that's earned it recognition as a UNESCO World Heritage Site. Isolated from the capital's main attractions in the deepest reaches of south-east London, Greenwich's historical significance belies its backwater location, not least because it's where the Prime Meridian lies (every map reference point in the world is measured from here).

When the Thames was the beating heart of London, Greenwich became a place of world renown, with a Royal Palace built on its slopes in the 15th century (Henry VIII and Elizabeth I were both born here). It is also famed for its maritime links and the National Maritime Museum, the world's largest, showcases all sorts of nautical knick-knacks in a wonderfully accessible display.

Behind the riverside attractions, the green expanse of Greenwich Park rises up steeply to the domed Royal Observatory, perched on its lofty hilltop. This capacious former royal hunting ground will fittingly host the Equestrian events during the London 2012 Games.

Greenwich may be a trek, but with so much fresh air, beautiful architecture and educationally improving sights packed into a small suburban enclave, it's no wonder that weekending families flock here for an action-packed day out.

A life on the ocean wave

The Thames has always been the lifeblood of Greenwich, and there is no more fitting way to arrive in SE10 than aboard a smart Thames Clipper (www.thamesclippers.com), which you can catch from Waterloo, Embankment or Blackfriars piers. You'll come ashore right by the **Cutty Sark** (www.cuttysark. org.uk). This plucky little tea clipper embarked on her maiden voyage in 1869, and sailed all over the world; in 1954 she retired to Greenwich's dry docks. She's currently in the midst of

Royal Observatory & Planetarium.

a huge renovation project (which faced a severe setback when a fire broke out in May 2007, apparently caused by a vacuum cleaner overheating), and is due to reopen in 2012 (see p67).

Begin the day at the new visitor centre, **Discover Greenwich** (see p101), which opened in 2010 and combines a permanent exhibition on the history of Greenwich with a Tourist Information Centre and other amenities. It's a short stroll upriver, on the site of Sir Christopher Wren's **Old Royal Naval College** (see p101). The Baroque College is an imposing affair, set in splendid gardens. It's free to peek at the chapel and magnificent Painted Hall – though the latter's lofty depictions of allegorical scenes may not appeal to children. Weekend and school holiday 'Tactile Tales' sessions bring the stories to life, though, with the help of a special storytelling rug. Costume-clad historical figures also pop by at weekends, so you might meet a loquacious Samuel Pepys or a 19th-century Greenwich pensioner.

Just across Romney Road, the **National Maritime Museum** (see p119) is a tribute to the nation's rich seafaring history, with vast collections of maritime art, maps, instruments and naval attire. Loading cargo, firing cannons and steering a ferry safely into port in the All Hands and Bridge galleries sorts out the salty sea dogs from the cack-handed landlubbers (check opening hours before you turn up). After a quick foray to see the highlights of the collection (the blood-stained jacket complete with bullet-hole in which Nelson met his end, for instance, or Prince Frederick's gorgeously gilded State Barge), it's time to press on.

Toe the line

North from here, past rusting piers and boarded-up factories, lies Greenwich Peninsula, dominated by the **O2 Arena**. The fortunes of this once-maligned structure have improved considerably since a change of name and use, and it is set to be a key London 2012 venue, when it will be known as the North Greenwich Arena. As a sign of its success, planning permission has been granted for a cable car that would link the O2 with the Royal Victoria Dock across the Thames (*see p71*).

There's no cable car to tackle the steep ascent across Greenwich Park to the **Royal Observatory & Planetarium** (*see p46*), but it's well worth the effort. The Observatory is topped by an onion-shaped dome that houses the world's seventh largest telescope, and the mysterious-looking Time Ball – a red bobble, on top of a pole – that was first erected in 1833. Every day it rises to the top of its mast then falls at precisely 1pm; in the days before clocks and watches were common, the ships that plied the river relied on it.

After admiring the view, head for the courtyard. The Meridian Line that marks the place where the eastern and western hemispheres meet is set in the flagstones; posing for a picture with one foot on each side is de rigueur (although will now cost you £10, since they began charging in March 2011). At night, a dramatic green laser beam is projected into the sky to mark the line.

Inside, the star turns are the Weller Astronomy interactive galleries (where you can touch a four-and-a-half-million-year-old meteorite) and the spectacular Planetarium. Be engulfed in dust storms on Mars or swoop over earth's polar ice caps before re-emerging, blinking, into the daylight.

The green, green grass of Greenwich

Sprawling across 183 acres, **Greenwich Park** (*see p143*) is the area's crowning glory. It's big enough to accommodate all sorts, from entwined lovers to frisbee- and ball-chasing kids and families.

The boating lake is at the Greenwich end of the Park, to the left from Park Row; there's also a decent playground by the Maze Hill entrance, with storytelling sessions, puppeteers, dance and crafts in the summer holidays. Summer Sundays also bring trumpet trios and brass bands to the bandstand, which is towards the Blackheath end of the park.

The park's teeming with wildlife, too – not least the herd of red and fallow deer that roams the enclosed Wilderness area, which has hides for nosy humans dotted around its perimeter (it's in the south-eastern corner of the park). You can also take a gander at the Secret Garden Wildlife Centre, which runs wildlife-related activities and tours of the nature trail on its once-monthly drop-in days. If you're lucky (and very quiet) you might hear a woodpecker at work in the trees. Bring a picnic, or try one of our suggestions below.

Refreshments

Also in the area: Pizza Express.
Gourmet Burger Kitchen *45 Greenwich Church Street, SE10 9LB (8858 3920, www.gbkinfo.com).* Towering burgers, cooked to order, with scaled-down versions for smaller appetites.
Greenwich Union *56 Royal Hill, SE10 8RT (8692 6258, www.greenwich union.com).* Superior pub grub; there are child-sized portions of fish and chips and roasts on Sundays.
Observatory Café *Royal Observatory, Blackheath Avenue, SE10 8XJ (8312 8639).* A scenic sun terrace and decent food.
Pavilion Tea House *Greenwich Park, Blackheath Gate, SE10 8QY (8858 9695, www.pavilionteahouse.co.uk).* Quality café fare in gracious park surroundings. *See p253.*
S&M Café *Peninsula Square, SE10 0PE (8305 1940, www.sandmcafe.co.uk).* Everyone loves bangers and mash in a retro British caff.

Sightseeing

The first Lollibop festival took place in 2010, and other events, like a visit from Carter's Steam Fair, take place in the summer. *Buggy access. Café. Disabled access (not café): toilet. Nappy-changing facilities (on request).*

Coram's Fields

93 Guilford Street, WC1N 1DN (7837 6138, www.coramsfields.org). Russell Square tube. **Open** *Summer* 9am-7pm daily. *Winter* 9am-dusk daily **Admission** free. **Map** p333 L4.
Thomas Coram established the Foundling Hospital for abandoned children on this spot in 1747. Part of the old estate now houses the Foundling Museum (*see p87*), a thoughtful retelling of the story of Thomas Coram and his charity's vast achievements. The Foundling Hospital itself was demolished in the 1920s, when its operations moved out to the countryside. Newspaper proprietor Lord Rothermere donated funds to create a children's park on the site, which is simply the best for miles around with an adventure playground, small animal enclosure and café. *See also p80* **Neighbourhood Watch**.
Buggy access. Café. Disabled access: toilet. Nappy-changing facilities.

Crystal Palace Park

Thicket Road, SE20 8DT (8778 9496 park ranger, www.bromley.gov.uk). Crystal Palace rail or bus 2, 3, 63, 122, 157, 227. **Open** 7.30am-dusk daily. **Admission** free.
Joseph Paxton's Crystal Palace, from which this park takes its name, is long gone. The glittering glass structure, originally created to house Hyde Park's Great Exhibition of 1851, was moved here after the exhibition; in 1936, it burned down in a devastating fire. The park, though, remains – and recently changed hands. The London Development Agency has taken over from the local council, and has big plans for its future, including five new gateways and improvements to the National Sports Centre, café and community facilities. Proposals also include a treetop walk, a maze and a boating lake. But there's a trade-off which isn't delighting the locals – the LDA says the improvements must be funded by selling off part of the park for housing development.
Let's hope the campaigning groups win the fight – once it's gone, it's gone. As it is, Crystal Palace Park is an atmospheric place, enshrined in local folklore. A beautifully landscaped lake complex is home to Benjamin Waterhouse Hawkins' Victorian dinosaur sculptures, which

caused outrage by backing up the theory of evolution, yet continue to give pleasure to kids – especially the T-Rex, who recently got a new arm (the tree he was gripping grew, and snapped off the old one). This was also the site where the Girl Guide movement was born, when a group of determined girls faced down Baden Powell at a Scout rally and demanded to join. The park's city farm reopened in 2008, and is still expanding its opening hours and programme of activities (*see p130*).
Buggy access. Café. Disabled access: toilet. Nappy-changing facilities.

Dulwich Park

College Road, SE21 7BQ (7525 2000, www.southwark.gov.uk). North Dulwich rail or bus 12, 40, 176, 185, P4. **Open** 8am-dusk daily. **Admission** free.
Dulwich Park got a gold award in 2010's RHS London in Bloom awards. It's partly thanks to the concerted efforts of the monthly Dig the Park sessions during which volunteers, organised by the Friends Association, planted 500,000 bulbs and seeded the wildflower meadows. But Dulwich Park – landscaped on the 'Five Fields' meadows that lay here before – isn't just a pretty face. The locals adore it, and are even more proud after 2010's anniversary improvements. These include an outdoor gym for anyone aged 11 and above (situated near the playground); the return of boats and pedalos on the lake (and a new boating house); and a table tennis table in the playground (bats and balls will be available to borrow free of charge from the park manager's office). Being a fan of Dulwich Park is not a new thing though; Queen Mary was a regular visitor (one of the park's four gates is named after her), and was particularly fond of the spectacular American Garden, whose rhododendrons and azaleas bloom in May. Today's visitors can also enjoy the exceptionally child-friendly Pavilion Café (*see p252*), Whippersnappers toddler classes in College Lodge, a super playground, novelty bike hire (8299 6636, www.londonrecumbents. com) and a Barbara Hepworth sculpture, Divided Circle Two Forms.
The playground is one of the best in the area, with web-like climbing facilities, swings, slides and the Ability Whirl, a safe, robust roundabout that can be used by able-bodied and disabled children. A community officer runs a programme of children's activities from the Francis Peek Centre (phone for details).
Buggy access. Café. Disabled access: toilet. Nappy-changing facilities (café).

My London 2012
Sophie, 18

How will you be participating in the London 2012 Olympic Games and Paralympic Games?
I've registered to volunteer during the Games. I want to help out at the pool because I love the Aquatics Centre.

How did you come to be involved?
When I was in year ten, I was asked to be Young Ambassador for my school.

Tell us about what you have been working on as part of the Young Ambassadors Programme?
I've been helping to organise events in local primary and secondary schools which promote sport and healthy lifestyles. We also teach children about the Olympic and Paralympic values – determination, excellence, equality, respect, friendship and courage.

What do you hope your involvement in London 2012 will inspire you to achieve after the Games have finished?
I really enjoy volunteering. The more I do, the more I want to do. I hope I can also inspire others to do the same.

Which events would you like to see during London 2012?
The 100m and 200m Butterfly. I used to train competitively until I hurt my knee. I also want to see the Boccia at the Paralympic Games and watch my second cousin Jessica Hunter compete.

Sightseeing

Up the Creek

Wading in the Thames at Deptford.

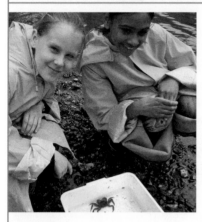

Set on an unremarkable south-east London street, the entrance to **Deptford Creekside Centre** (*see p145*) comes as something of a surprise. Inside and out, shelves are stacked with treasures from the creek's muddy depths: floral-sprigged tea cups, rusty tools, broken toys, a medley of bones from an old slaughterhouse and even a forlorn-looking old typewriter, with gravel and moss wedged between its keys. There's no time to dawdle if you're here for the centre's speciality, though: low-tide creek walks along the riverbed, led by Nick Bertrand – an affable chap with a biblical beard, and an expert raconteur. The centre has all the necessary gear: enormous thigh-high waders (wear old clothes), wooden poles and, for rainy days, a rail of ancient yellow oilskins. Once you're in the river, the pole comes into its own, both for balance and for testing the way ahead.

The riverscape changes all the time depending on the light, tide and season. 'The creek's mud is just donkey brown in winter,' says Nick, 'but in the spring it will start to green. By autumn it goes the colour of baked custard.'

It's perfectly easy to avoid getting stuck in the mudflats if you follow Nick's instructions, though he has had to fish the odd malefactor out over the years: 'It's a messy, wet experience,' he says.

Messy and wet is just how some of the creek's inhabitants like it. Take a closer look and it's teeming with life, from dragonflies, crabs and grey wagtails to the odd kingfisher. Nick comes armed with a net and tray, and turns up goby, flounders and translucent gammarus shrimp. Eagle eyes can spot all manner of flotsam and jetsam, too. Afterwards it's time for a thorough hosing down, and a fortifying mug of tea.

Hampstead Heath

NW5 1QR (8348 9908, www.cityoflondon. gov.uk/openspaces). Kentish Town tube or Gospel Oak or Hampstead Heath rail, or bus 214, C2, C11. **Open** dawn-dusk daily. **Admission** free.

Hampstead Heath is actually several parks rolled into one, and the variety of its landscaping keeps Londoners endlessly enthralled with its beauty. It's less than four miles from Trafalgar Square, but up here, it's possible to believe that you are in the deepest reaches of the countryside. At the north end there's the Hill Garden and Pergola (the listed pergola, which was built in the 1920s by Lord Leverhulme to join together two parts of his estate, is free to enter and fun to explore) and Golders Hill Park, which includes a small zoo. There's also the Hampstead Heath Extension which by itself is 125 acres. South of Hampstead Lane is the Kenwood Estate, run separately by English Heritage, which retains the feel of a country estate and houses an art gallery in the main house (*see p77*) and the fantastic Pavilion Café in the former outbuildings (*see p253*).

The wild heathland in the middle is full of magnificent trees and places to get lost in. It's about as far from the manicured flowerbeds of the Royal Parks as you could hope to find. Fishing is available in six of the ponds (though you need a rod licence and a free Heath fishing permit). There are also tennis courses, bat walks, nature trails, a 'secret garden' and a wildlife pond. Clowns, magicians, musicians, storytellers and puppeteers perform in various locations throughout the year, with more appearances in summer. The Rookie Rangers wildlife club is for eight- to 12-year-olds, and meets once a week in the spring and summer holidays and once a month during term time (for information call 7482 7073). Check the website and local press for news of the Hampstead Heath consultation and management plan, and for details of family events.

Down on Parliament Hill Fields to the south, facilities include an imaginative playground and paddling pool, still looking spanking new after its award-winning refurb, and packed with state-of-the-art equipment designed to challenge children rather than keep them boringly safe. There's a superb One O'Clock Club, a running track and a lido down here too, though families might want to try a more adventurous swimming experience in the open-air swimming ponds. Also look out for the Stone of Free Speech, which was here in the 17th century and marked the place where open discussion of all subjects was permitted. *Buggy access. Cafés. Disabled access: toilet. Nappy-changing facilities.*

Highbury Fields

Highbury Crescent, N5 1RR (7527 4953, www.islington.gov.uk). Highbury & Islington tube/rail or bus 19, 30, 43, 271. **Open** *Park* 24hrs. *Playground* dawn-dusk daily. **Admission** free.

The Borough of Islington has 127 parks and open spaces, but none of them are very large. In fact, this 29-acre park is as big as they get, and much needed by the families who live nearby. Get the children to imagine the scene when, in 1666, 200,000 Londoners fled here to escape the Great Fire. Hidden behind Highbury Pool and a series of high bushes is an unusual playground that combines old-fashioned thrills (such as a circular train requiring Flintstones-style propulsion, and an excitingly long, steep slide) with more recent additions, such as the flying fox and giant, web-like climbing frames. The outdoor tennis courts have been refurbished, and are used by the excellent Islington Tennis Centre. There's also a swimming pool, football and netball pitches and the Oasis café. A stroll across Highbury Fields takes you from busy Upper Street past imposing period terraces to Highbury Barn, a trendy enclave with several excellent food shops, restaurants and child-friendly cafés. *Buggy access. Café.*

Holland Park

Ilchester Place, W8 6LU (7938 8170, www.rbkc.gov.uk). Holland Park tube or bus 9, 27, 28, 49. **Open** 7.30am-30min before dusk daily. **Admission** free. **Map** p330 A9.

The largest of Kensington and Chelsea's parks takes in 55 classy acres. There are so many beautiful nooks and crannies to explore that it's worth a day trip in its own right. Children over five will want to start with the many and varied excitements on offer at the adventure playground (there's an alternative playground for under-fives too). After that, the paths take you past formal gardens and fountains, imperious peacocks and plenty of squirrels and rabbits. Visitors may even have see some pigs rooting around in the undergrowth in the early months of 2010 (used here instead of pesticides to clear scrub from the woodland areas). In 2011 a wildflower meadow will be planted on the area the pigs cleared.

Also of interest in Holland Park is its open-air theatre, peaceful Japanese Garden with a pond full of colourful koi carp, and Ecology Centre which provides information, site maps and nets for pond-dipping. Whippersnappers (7738 6633, www.whippersnappers.org) puts on weekly musical and puppet workshops in the Youth Hostel, and the Friends of Holland Park organise holiday activities for five- to ten-year-olds. Also in the park are tennis courts, sports fields and two art spaces, the Ice House and the Orangery. Take public transport unless it's a Sunday, as parking is expensive.

Come lunchtime, there's the smart but surprisingly child-friendly Belvedere (*see p258*) for special occasions, or an Italian café and ice-cream kiosk for everyday treats. On sunny days though, well-to-do families from the rather chichi surrounding neighbourhoods lay out their rugs and hampers for all-day picnics.

Leighton House Museum, on the edge of Holland Park, has just reopened after a major refurbishment, and although there are no children's activities planned at present, anyone with a passing interest in stunning Islamic tiles or in seeing the opulent Arab Hall should make a diversion. *Buggy access. Café. Disabled access: toilet. Nappy-changing facilities. Restaurant.*

Mile End Park

Locksley Street, E14 7EJ (7364 4147, 7093 2253 children's park, www.tower hamlets.gov.uk). Mile End tube. **Open** 24hrs daily. *Children's park* 10am-dusk daily. **Admission** free.

Sightseeing

Richard II met the angry peasant army led by Wat Tyler in 1381 just south of Mile End Road to promise an end to serfdom and feudalism. These days, people gather here for more recreational purposes. Mile End Park was a long time in the making, and it is still developing. The idea for it was first mooted in the 1940s, but it took 50 years for the various strips to emerge as parkland. It comprises 90 acres of reclaimed industrial land, which runs south of Victoria Park in a long strip alongside Regent's Canal. For many Londoners it is the quintessential modern urban park, divided into dramatically different sections. The south end of the park has a great playground, with a rope slide, scrambling wall, complicated climbing frame, swings and a see-saw, as well as a dedicated area for under-fives that includes a vast sandpit. New apparatus installed in the playground is designed to appeal to children with disabilities as well as to their able-bodied playmates, with a huge, bird's-nest-style swing and a ramped bridge. A new skateboard park arrived in 2009.

There's also the Ecology Park, with its large climbing wall; the site-specific works and pavilion of the Arts Park; the Terraced Garden; the Sports Park (including Mile End Stadium); the canalside Kirk's Place, which is good for picnics; and an electric go-kart track. Structured events for children expanded during 2009 (the year of the 'Playful Park') and now there are plenty of clubs and activities during term time and in the holidays. There's also a green-fingered club started up in the six new children's gardens. In the middle of the park, the café and Palm Tree Pub provide refreshments.
Buggy access. Café. Disabled access: toilet. Nappy-changing facilities.

Morden Hall Park

Morden Hall Road, Morden, Surrey SM4 5JD (8545 6850, www.nationaltrust.org.uk). Morden tube. **Open** 8am-6pm daily. **Admission** free.
The main attraction here is the 125 acres of uncommonly beautiful National Trust parkland, which is perfect for family picnics and cycle rides. The park sits on the floodplain of the River Wandle, creating marshy wetlands that shelter a whole host of birds (look out for leggy herons and the bright blue flash of a kingfisher), and the restored Rose Garden is a fragrant diversion in summer. In October 2010, the Heart of the Park project began the renovation of the 19th century stable block. Visitors will be able to view the progress from October 2011 – plans include an Archimedes screw (a modern waterwheel) that will generate electricity for the new café and exhibition space Morden Hall itself is run as a private restaurant, but there's the wonderful Snuff Mill watermills to enjoy and the existing Environmental Centre, which runs children's activities on the first and third Sundays of the month. Craftspeople, furniture restorers and artists occupy many of the old estate buildings, and the Riverside Café (inside the old walled Kitchen Garden) is a relaxing place to take stock of the lovely surrounds (there's a second hand bookshop too).
Buggy access. Café. Disabled access: toilet. Nappy-changing facilities. Shop.

Queen's Park

Kingswood Avenue, NW6 6SG (8969 5661, www.cityoflondon.gov.uk/openspaces). Queen's Park tube/rail. **Open** 7.30am-dusk daily. **Admission** free.
Oddly, this park is managed by the City of London, even though its borders are a long way from the Square Mile. It's been this way since the 1879 Royal Agricultural Exhibition. It's an appealing park, well used by locals, and another example of the way in which a great park can transform the urban area around it. Queen's Park's playground already has a giant sandpit, a paddling pool (resurfaced in 2010) and patrolling wardens, and plans are afoot to give it a naturalistic makeover. Four new pygmy goats have joined the rabbits, chickens, ducks and guinea pigs in the small animal enclosure. At the northern end is a wild, overgrown area, where a nature trail displays pictures of the small beasts you might encounter. The café serves own-made cakes and local Disotto's ice-cream. There's also a lovely ornamental garden, a pitch-and-putt area, a pétanque pitch and six all-weather tennis courts. Children's entertainment takes place at the bandstand during the summer holidays. Each September, the annual Queen's Park Day brings fancy dress competitions, face painting, a dog show and puppetry.
Buggy access. Café. Disabled access: toilet. Nappy-changing facilities.

Ravenscourt Park

Ravenscourt Road, W6 0UL (www.lbhf. gov.uk). Ravenscourt Park tube. **Open** 7.30am-dusk daily. **Admission** free.
This decent local park was a little scuffed around the edges until a Friends of Ravenscourt Park association was set up in 2008 and in 2009 the park was given a Green Flag Award for the

first time. Nestling between the messy bustle of Hammersmith and the quiet splendour of Chiswick, it's a hidden oasis of bucolic tranquility. The first mention of Ravenscourt Park was in the 14th century; documents record the existence of a manor house, surrounded by a moat that was fed by Stamford Brook. Disaster struck during World War II, when the house was devastated by an incendiary bomb. Only the stable block survived, and is now home to the park café. It's conveniently close to the adventure playground.

There are three other play areas which feature a paddling pool, a nature trail, passable tennis courts, a bowling lawn and a pitch-and-putt course. Bonfire night is the biggest date in the diary, as enormous crowds gather to 'ooh' and 'ahh' over spectacular rockets that bathe the park in an ethereal glow. In April, the ever-popular Carter's Steam Fair rolls into the park. *Buggy access. Café. Disabled access. Nappy-changing facilities.*

Southwark Park

Gomm Road, SE16 2UA (7237 1230 art gallery, www.southwark.gov.uk). Canada Water tube. **Open** *Park* 7.30am-1hr before dusk daily. *Gallery (during exhibitions)* Summer noon-6pm Wed-Sun. Winter 11am-4pm Wed-Sun. **Admission** free.

This was one of the first parks to be opened by the Metropolitan Board of Works in the 19th century. In 2001, a pretty new bandstand and a decent children's play area were added; over a decade later the whole place is still looking shipshape, thanks to the efforts of the energetic Friends of Southwark Park committee and the vandal-busting wardens. There is plenty to encourage older children to take up sports, with an athletics track (often used by Millwall Football Club, along with the astroturf pitches) and free tennis courts. There's also a Young Friends of Southwark Park group for eight- to 14-year-olds that has started a community allotment scheme and completed a colourful mural (call 7525 2000 for details). The park also has a thriving arty scene, the hub of which is the Café Gallery Project. It holds frequent exhibitions and workshops on Saturdays and during summer holidays, called the DIY Family Art Club; check online at www.cafegallery projects.com for details of the club, and the summer Children's Exhibition and winter Open Exhibition. Parkside Café & Bar, across from the gallery, serves hot meals and sandwiches. *Buggy access. Café. Disabled access: toilet. Nappy-changing facilities (in gallery).*

Thames Barrier Park

North Woolwich Road, E16 2HP (7476 3741, www.thamesbarrierpark.org.uk). Pontoon Dock DLR. **Open** 7am-dusk daily. **Admission** free.

After the London 2012 Olympics, the Queen Elizabeth Park will be the capital's newest major green space. Until then, the Thames Barrier Park holds the title, and was London's first new park in half a century when it opened in 2000. Its lush sunken gardens and undulating topiary, coupled with views over the fabulously sculptural silver fins of the Thames Barrier, means visitors don't forget the experience in a hurry.

The Barrier's visitors' centre is on the south side; the tea pavilion serves excellent coffee. A concrete and granite channel the width of a small motorway, called the Green Dock, is filled with fragrant honeysuckle and wavy yew hedges: it has superb hide-and-seek potential, with the two pedestrian bridges overhead adding an extra dimension to the game. The kids will also want to go wild at the fountain plaza, where 32 vertical jets beg to be played with. On the riverfront is the Pavilion of Remembrance, erected to remember local victims of the Blitz. The manicured, flat lawns are perfect for picnics and games; there's also a playground packed with apparatus, plus a basketball hoop and five-a-side court.

The park is fantastic for waterfowl-watching too: ducks, geese, swans and oyster catchers pick around on the gleaming mudflats, herons feed along the shore at low tide, and large numbers of teal, shelduck and cormorants enjoy the river's bounty. *Buggy access. Café. Disabled access: toilet. Nappy-changing facilities.*

Victoria Park

Old Ford Road, E3 5DS (8985 1957, www.towerhamlets.gov.uk). Mile End tube or Cambridge Heath or Hackney Wick rail, or bus 8, 26, 30, 55, 253, 277, S2. **Open** 8am-dusk daily. **Admission** free.

Victoria Park sits in the borough of Tower Hamlets, one of the five host boroughs to the London 2012 Olympics. So it's no surprise that the park has secured £12 million for improvements. These will include a new skate park, an improved model boating lake and better sports facilities.

Queen Victoria opened this park in 1845 when thousands of Eastenders signed a petition asking for a public park in the area (it's often referred to as 'The People's Park'). It was laid

Sightseeing

Neighbourhood Watch
Camden

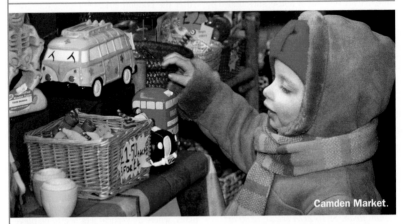

Camden Market.

Despite efforts at gentrification, much of Camden Town still has a grungy vibe. But the grime is part of the charm of an area that is seen by many as the cradle of British rock music, an image that reached its peak during the Oasis/Blur rivalry in the mid 1990s.

Apart from dragging the kids around on a nostalgia-fuelled tour of the area's rock 'n' roll drinking haunts, there's plenty to interest youngsters of all ages, including the newly expanded Jewish Museum, the iconic Roundhouse, gorgeous Regent's Canal and ever popular (and improving) London Zoo. Older children and teenagers, meanwhile, will love the famous market, with its colourful, chaotic mix of street food vendors, stalls touting vintage clobber, cheap accessories and incense sticks.

On the waterfront
Cutting through the market is Regent's Canal, which opened in 1820 to provide a link between east and west London for horse-drawn narrowboats loaded with coal. Join the canal at Camden Lock, where the manually operated twin lock is the first stopping point. It's particularly exciting if a boat happens to be coming through.

The towpath in either direction leads to some great finds; note that although it is a designated cycle route, the path is too narrow for all but the most proficient of cyclists (scooters should be fine). To the east, a decent stroll away, are the bucolic delights of **Camley Street Natural Park** (*see p144*), a small but thriving nature reserve run by the London Wildlife Trust. A little further along, just past the tunnel under York Way, in the Battlebridge basin, lies the **London Canal Museum** (*see p98*), an old-fashioned but homely shrine to life on Britain's canals; there's a children's corner and a real narrowboat to explore, along with the ice house used by enterprising ice-cream maker Carlo Gatti, who imported enormous blocks of ice from the frozen lakes of Norway.

From Camden Lock going west, families can stop off at the exclusive enclave of **Primrose Hill**, where kite flying and picnics in the park are popular pastimes and the cafés and shops have a chichi villagey feel. Carry on a little further, and you will begin to hear the strange grunts, squeals and squawks emanating from one of the capital's biggest attractions; **London Zoo** (*see p158*), a great day out in itself. The expanse of **Regent's Park** (*see p143*) is just beyond, with a very good playground at the Gloucester Gate entrance.

Of course, you don't have to content yourself with merely walking alongside the water. The London Waterbus Company (www.londonwaterbus.co.uk) runs canal boat trips to Little Venice, where families could stop and see a performance at the **Puppet Theatre Barge** (*see p207*). If you want to go through the lock on a boat, the Jenny Wren goes from Walker's Quay (7485 4433, www.walkersquay.com) and heads to Little Venice on a round trip.

Market value

Camden Market is absolutely heaving at weekends (it's one of the top five tourist attractions in London), so try to come on a weekday if you don't want to lose sight of small children; most shops and stalls are open all week long. Also be aware that Camden Town tube station is exit-only on Saturday and Sunday, which means a fairly long walk to Chalk Farm or Mornington Crescent for the tube if you don't want to catch the bus.

There are several different markets and hundreds of stalls to browse here, so pace yourself and be picky. Discerning shoppers tend to bypass the first market you reach after turning north from the tube station – the one at Buck Street bearing the legend 'Camden Market' – unless your party includes a teenager who is desperate for goth T-shirts, stripey tights and cheap tat.

North of the road bridge on Chalk Farm Road is the former Canal Market. Closed after a fire in February 2008, it reopened in May 2009 with a new name, the **Canal Lock Village**, and an eclectic assortment of stalls, plus some groovy seats that look like mopeds. Alternatively, head straight for **Camden Lock Market**. Launched in 1975, this is where the whole thing began. There is a lovely open-air square of stalls and shops selling good quality crafts, jewellery, textiles, alternative fashion and accessories.

The extensive **Stables Market**, just north of Camden Lock, is the latest and largest addition. Small children will enjoy the large bronze statues of horses and workers, although parents might be scared of losing their little darlings in this warren of blind corners. There are plenty of jumbled displays of ethnic doo-dads, vintage clothes and furniture, and lots of child-friendly novelties and stalls that will intrigue older kids.

Something for the grey matter

If all that shopping gets tiring, you could always incorporate some culture into your Camden experience. On the road north towards Chalk Farm is the hugely atmospheric **Roundhouse** (*see p203*), famed for its groundbreaking gigs in the 1960s and '70s (the Doors, Hendrix and Bowie all took to the stage here). Reopened in 2006, it offers an avant-garde programme of music and theatre, including a successful RSC season in 2010/11. The Roundhouse Studio also runs excellent radio, film and music workshops for teenagers in the school holidays. Courses (minimum age is 14) are dirt cheap and include the likes of Sound Engineering.

South of here, just off Parkway, is the **Jewish Museum** (*see p108*), which reopened in 2010 after a major refurbishment project, and explores Jewish life in Britain since 1066.

Refreshments

Also in the area: Belgo Noord, Fresh & Wild, Pizza Express, Strada, Wagamama.
Diner *2 Jamestown Road, NW1 7BY (7485 5223, www.goodlifediner.com).* Burgers, hotdogs, fries and milkshakes delight the kids.
InSpiral *250 Camden High Street, NW1 8QS (7428 5875, www.inspiralled.net).* Kids will love the seats overlooking the canal in this vegan and raw food café.
Marine Ices *8 Haverstock Hill, NW3 2BL (7482 9003, www.marineices.co.uk).* A classic Italian that hasn't changed in years. *See p260.*
Tupelo Honey *27 Parkway, NW1 7PN (7284 2989, www.tupelo-honey.co.uk).* A homely café, serving solid, healthy grub and cakes.
Yum Cha *27-28 Chalk Farm Road, NW1 8AG (7482 2228).* Flawless dim sum that appeal to all ages.

Sightseeing

out by Sir James Pennethorne – a pupil of John Nash, who designed Regent's Park – and has been much loved ever since. You can see the influence of the grand master in the landscaping of this gracious green space, and by 2012 it will look even better, thanks to a lottery grant of £4.5 million being awarded in early 2010. Restoration of the Burdett-Coutts Fountain, Chinese Pagoda, Old English Garden and the stone sculpture of the Dogs of Alcibiades are planned.

With its imposing, wide carriageways, ornate lampposts and wrought-iron gates, Victoria Park is the only place out east where you can pretend you're in the countryside. There are fish in the Western Lake (you can help deplete the stock by applying for a free fishing licence); Britain's oldest model boat club convenes around the other lake, near Crown Gate East, every second Sunday. The Pools Playground, with its landscaped paddling pools, is a real favourite with all ages, and there's a fallow deer enclosure on the east side, tennis courts and a bowling green, plus football, hockey and cricket pitches. The jolly Lakeside Pavilion Café is packed to the rafters by families enjoying great organic food, sausages from Marylebone's famous Ginger Pig butchers and memorable coffee.

Buggy access. Café. Disabled access: toilet. Nappy-changing facilities.

Waterlow Park

Highgate Hill, N6 5HG (8348 8716 Lauderdale House, 8341 4807 café, www.waterlowpark.co.uk). Archway tube or bus 143, 210, 271, W5. **Open** 7.30am-dusk daily. **Admission** free.

Waterlow Park isn't one of London's most famous, but it should be. The beautiful landscaping, and its position on a hillside overlooking Hampstead Heath to the west, makes it one of the prettiest parks in the capital. Once it was the garden of charming, 16th-century Lauderdale House, but it was donated to the public by low-cost housing pioneer Sydney Waterlow, who saw it as a 'garden for the gardenless'. With its majestic vistas, mature trees, formal gardens, tennis courts and beautiful seasonal planting, it's a delightful spot all year round.

Lauderdale House has a café on its west-facing terrace, and runs a year-round programme of kids' activities that includes music, dance and drama classes, and lively children's theatre events every Saturday morning. Until recently, a small toddlers' area

was the only formal playground, but a new adventure playground, built from natural materials, was opened in early 2009. Aimed at six to 13s, it can be found to the west of the lowest pond. In the old depot building, Waterlow Park Centre houses exhibitions and has an activities room available for hire. Of late, there has been talk of restoring the aviary, but a final decision has not yet been reached.

Buggy access. Café. Disabled access: toilet.

West Ham Park

Upton Lane, E7 9PU (8472 3584, www.cityoflondon.gov.uk/openspaces). Stratford tube/rail or bus 104, 238. **Open** 7.30am-30mins before dusk daily. **Admission** free.

Newham's largest park has been maintained by the City of London since locals persuaded the corporation to buy what was then a private botanic garden for the public in 1874. Its ornamental gardens and established trees are glorious; as one of the few London parks to have its own plant nursery, it also has spectacular border planting. The growing collection of Liquidambar trees are a blazing mass of reds, oranges and purples in the Autumn. Full time park attendants make it feel safe, while the playground has plenty of colourful climbing apparatus. Highlights include a wooden prairie locomotive to clamber on, a Wendy house corner and the pre-war paddling pool, open from late May to August, while in March 2011, a swing and roundabout for wheelchair users were installed. The Wildlife Education Garden that opened in early 2010 now has a pond-dipping platform and an insect hotel.

More unusually, some community vegetable plots have recently been established here to encourage locals to grow their own. There are 12 tennis courts (lucky locals have access to the annual tennis clinic, which is held in June), three cricket nets (Essex CCC runs free training for under-16s in July), two match-quality cricket tables, two football pitches (one all-weather), a running track and a rounders area. From late July to August, free children's events are held at the bandstand on Monday and Friday afternoons (3-4pm); a very popular bouncy castle (also free) appears on Wednesdays (noon to 5pm); and there are occasional Sunday concerts. The only thing missing is a café, though an ice-cream van takes up position near the playground from Easter to October.

Buggy access. Disabled access: toilet. Nappy-changing facilities.

Wimbledon Common

Windmill Road, SW19 5NR (8788 7655,
www.wpcc.org.uk). Putney rail, then bus 93
bus, or bus 85. **Open** 24hrs daily.
Admission free.

With more than 1,000 acres of woodland,
scrubland and heathland, the Common is a
haven for joggers, walkers and anyone who
loves the outdoors. There are cricket, football
and rugby pitches, a golf course, a bog, nine
ponds, and around 16 miles (over 25km) of
bridleways. There's also a windmill, which is
now a museum (*see p102*). The common is
patrolled by rangers, on horseback and on foot,
who are a mine of information about the
common and nearby Putney Heath, both of
which are designated SSSIs (Sites of Special
Scientific Interest). They're based in the
Information Centre, which also provides leaflets
on the plant and animal life on the common, as
well as the history of the area; it's open seven
days a week. Best of all is a video microscope
showing insects and other flora and fauna in
minute detail; specimens are changed regularly,
and you can insert your own for display. Every
Saturday at 9am, there's a free park run
organised by volunteers; the Wildlife Watch
Club for eight- to 14-year-olds takes place on
the first Sunday of the month (10am-noon, £2).
Buggy access. Café. Disabled access: toilet.
Nappy-changing facilities (café).

ROYAL PARKS

Bushy Park

Hampton Court Road, Hampton
Court, Surrey TW12 2EJ (8979 1586,
www.royalparks.org.uk). Hampton Wick,
Hampton Court or Teddington Rail, or bus
111, 216, 265, 411, R68. **Open** *Pedestrians*
Jan-Aug, Oct, Dec 24hrs daily. Sept, Nov
8am-10.30pm daily. *Vehicle access* 6.30am-
dusk daily. **Admission** free.

This is the second largest of the Royal Parks,
but perhaps one of the least familiar to
Londoners. It sits right next to its more famous
neighbour, Hampton Court Park; its central
attraction, the majestic, mile-long Chestnut
Avenue, was designed by Christopher Wren as
a grand driveway to Hampton Court Palace.
During World War I and II, much of the park's
open land was dug up to grow vegetables, and
Eisenhower (who didn't fancy being in the
centre of town), made his base here – hence the
memorial near the Warren Plantation. The last
few years have seen the park enhanced in

myriad small ways, including extra planting,
improved paths and the renovation of the Diana
fountain, thanks to an injection of lottery cash.
The Pheasantry Welcome Centre opened in
2009 and has a café with terrace, loos and an
education and community room.
Buggy access. Café. Disabled access: toilet.

Greenwich Park

Blackheath Gate, Charlton Way, SE10 8QY
(8858 2608, www.royalparks.org.uk). Cutty
Sark DLR or Greenwich DLR/rail, or Maze
Hill rail, or bus 1, 53, 177, 180, 188, 286,
or riverboat to Greenwich Pier. **Open** 6am-
dusk daily. **Admission** free.

The oldest of the Royal Parks is part of the
Greenwich World Heritage Site. It's a lovely,
hilly stretch of green affording wonderful views
over the Thames, to Docklands and the City.
There's a deer park, boating lake, playground,
community orchard and tennis courts. *See also*
p132 **Neighbourhood Watch**.
Buggy access. Cafés. Disabled access: toilet.
Nappy-changing facilities.

Hyde Park & Kensington Gardens

W2 2UH (7298 2100, www.royalparks.
org.uk). Hyde Park Corner, Knightsbridge,
Lancaster Gate or Marble Arch tube, or
bus 2, 8, 10, 12, 23, 73, 94. **Open** *Hyde*
Park 5am-midnight daily. *Kensington*
Gardens 6am-dusk daily. **Admission** free.
Map p327 E7.

London's largest central park makes for a
fantastic family excursion, but don't expect to
see all its attractions in one day. In Hyde Park,
there's the famous Serpentine, with its rowing
boats, pedal boats, and solarshuttle. There's
also an education centre where children can
learn about wildlife. In Kensington Gardens,
don't miss the fantastic Diana, Princess of
Wales Adventure Playground with its
imaginative pirate ship and treetop walkways.
A new allotment° opened in 2010. Check online
for up-and-coming events, which include some
brilliant guided walks: bats, autumn leaves and
tree identification are among the themes. *See*
also p120 **Neighbourhood Watch**.
Buggy access. Cafés. Disabled access: toilet.
Nappy-changing facilities. Restaurant.

Regent's Park

NW1 4NR (7486 7905, 7724 4069 boating
lake, www.royalparks.org.uk). Baker Street,
Camden Town, Great Portland Street or
Regent's Park tube. **Open** 5am-dusk daily.
Admission free. **Map** p330 G3.

Sightseeing

This grand circular park was designed by John Nash as the Prince Regent's garden for a summer house that was never built. With its sports fields, boating lake, several playgrounds, rose garden and the star attractions of London Zoo and the Open Air Theatre within its boundaries, this is a park with something for everyone. *See also p152* **Neighbourhood Watch**.

Buggy access. Cafés. Disabled access: toilet. Nappy-changing facilities. Restaurant.

Richmond Park

Richmond, Surrey TW10 5HS (8948 3209, www.royalparks.org.uk). Richmond tube/rail or Norbiton rail. **Open** *Summer* 7am-dusk. *Winter* 7.30am-dusk. **Admission** free.

The largest of London's Royal Parks is known for its herds of red and fallow deer that roam freely across the land, a source of endless fascination for children. The deer have been here since Charles I brought his court here in 1625 to avoid the plague. The park is also home to two shire horses called Billy and Massey and all sorts of birds and insects. Children who don't get out of town much should be taken straight to the Isabella Plantation, a tranquil 40 acre woodland garden that's dotted with streams and bridges. Planted with azaleas, magnolias and rhododendrons, it's best seen in all its glory in early summer or late September. The Isabella Plantation was granted a slab of Heritage Lottery Fund money in December 2010, and plans to use it to start a programme of community activities.

There are plenty of places to picnic, and the park's Petersham Gate has a playground. From the top of nearby King Henry VIII's mound (the hot-tempered king had a hunting lodge here), you get a spectacular view right across London (you can even spot the dome on St Paul's Cathedral on a clear day). Alternatively, you could stroll along Terrace Walk, a Victorian promenade that runs from philosopher Bertrand Russell's childhood home, Pembroke Lodge (now a licensed café, and a good lunch spot), and beyond the park to Richmond Hill. A well-kept cycle path follows the perimeter; hire kids' bikes and adult bikes with tag-alongs or kid's seats from Roehampton Gate (7581 1188). There are several good spots for kiting and lessons in power kiting are available (www.kitevibe.com). Like all the Royal Parks, Richmond hosts a summer events programme for families. For details, consult the notice at the gate lodge or check out the website.

Buggy access. Disabled access: toilet. Café. Restaurant.

St James's Park

SW1A 2JB (7930 1793, www.royalparks.org.uk). St James's Park tube or bus 3, 11, 12, 24, 53, 211. **Open** 5am-midnight daily. **Admission** free. **Map** p333 K8.

St James's is the park that keeps closest to its royal connections, with the Changing of the Guard and the Trooping of the Colour taking place on Horse Guards Parade. It's also surrounded by three palaces; Westminster (the Houses of Parliament), St James's and Buckingham. There's a rich array of birdlife to spot, from pelicans and black swans to ducks. Watch out for the grey squirrels who are tame enough to eat from your hand but can suddenly turn aggressive. There's a playground up near the Buckingham Palace end, and some allotments where demonstration gardeners offer advice from May to September. *See also p54* **Neighbourhood Watch**.

Buggy access. Café. Disabled access: toilet. Nappy-changing facilities. Restaurant.

WILDLIFE SANCTUARIES

Camley Street Natural Park

12 Camley Street, N1C 4PW (7833 2311, www.wildlondon.org.uk). King's Cross tube/rail. **Open** 10am-5pm daily. **Admission** free. **Map** p331 L2.

Incredibly, this small nature reserve, created from an old coal yard in 1984, has survived the massive redevelopment of King's Cross and St Pancras International. Its two acres sit on the banks of Regent's Canal, and are run by the London Wildlife Trust. Enter the wrought iron gates and you will soon notice that the air is filled with butterflies and bees as you explore the winding nature trails, ponds and lovingly-tended wildflower meadows. The creatures that rely on the park range from kestrels and kingfishers to bats and bloodworms. The reserve has lots to offer in terms of children's activities, particularly during summer, when the peaceful atmosphere is punctured by the clamour of kids tearing about during the weekday and weekend playschemes trying out pond-dipping and mini-beast hunting. Family volunteering schemes offer the chance to grow your own vegetables, and conservation skills training is available to young people. If it weren't for the St Pancras train announcements floating across the boundary fences, you could almost imagine you were anywhere.

Buggy access. Disabled access: toilet. Nappy-changing facilities.

Creekside Centre

14 Creekside, SE8 4SA (8692 9922,
www.creeksidecentre.org.uk). Deptford Bridge
or Greenwich DLR, or bus 53, 177, 188.
Open call for details. **Admission** free,
walks vary check for details.
Deptford Creek is a tributary of the Thames
and this centre allows visitors to explore its
diverse wildlife and rich heritage. Low tide
walks take place on selected weekend days for
accompanied nine-year-olds and above and
there's also a programme of puppet theatre.
See also p136.
Buggy access. Disabled access: toilet.

Greenwich Peninsula Ecology Park

Thames Path, John Harrison Way, SE10
0QZ (8293 1904, www.urbanecology.org.uk).
North Greenwich tube, bus 108, 161, 422,
472, 486. **Open** 10am-5pm Wed-Sun.
Admission free.
Once known as Greenwich Marsh, when this
area was mostly agricultural fields, it became
heavily industrialised in the 19th century. Now
this small corner of the peninsula has reversed
the process. The Ecology Park is a pond-
dipping, bird-watching paradise. The park is
reserved for school visits on Mondays and
Tuesdays; the rest of the week, you'll have this
wetland area, with its woodland, marsh,
meadowland, lakes and streams, all to yourself.
Buggy access. Disabled access: toilet.
Nappy-changing facilities.

Highgate Wood & Queen's Wood

Muswell Hill Road, N10 3JN (8444 6129,
www.cityoflondon.gov.uk/openspaces).
Highgate tube, bus 43, 134, 263. **Open**
7.30am-dusk daily. **Admission** free.
Best known of the two is popular Highgate
Woods on the north side of Muswell Hill Road,
where the wide paths suit buggies and budding
cyclists. For families, the centrepiece of
Highgate Woods is its large, well-equipped
playground, complete with sandpits, climbing
equipment of various levels of difficulty and a
flying fox ride that gets very busy at peak times.
Great thought has gone into providing fun and
challenges for the various age groups, and
there's a separate area for the under-fives to call
their own. The playground is pleasantly shady
in summer – cooler for all concerned, as well as
making hats and sun cream less of a repetitive
chore. Highgate's other great asset is its café (*see*
p253), reached by crossing the cricket pitch. The
food is the usual park fare – soups, pasta dishes
and cake predominate – but the quality is a cut

above what you'll find elsewhere. Throughout
the year, an imaginative set of activities is
offered in the woods, from outdoor storytelling
sessions to evening bat watches, beetle safaris
and treasure hunts. These should encourage
your youngsters to explore the less well-trodden
areas of the woods for a proper adventure.
Consult the website before setting out, as some
events require pre-booking.
   Queen's Wood is the quieter section of this
vast woodland area – originally part of the
ancient Forest of Middlesex – perhaps because
it offers some very steep climbs. Its dense oaks
and hornbeams drown out traffic noise, giving
the impression that you're rambling through a
wild wood miles from the city. Listen out for the
woodpeckers, whose pecking reverberates
around the sun-dappled glades. There's also a
deeply thrilling rope swing, if you can find it.
Buggy access. Café. Disabled access: toilet.
Nappy-changing facilities.

London Wildlife Trust Centre for Wildlife Gardening

28 Marsden Road, SE15 4EE (7252 9186,
www.wildlondon.org.uk). East Dulwich rail.
Open 10.30am-4.30pm Tue-Thur, Sun.
Admission free.
Nestling off an unassuming residential street in
Peckham, this was once a grubby council bus
depot, but the London Wildlife Trust took it on
in the late 1980s and now it's a demonstration
garden loved by local families. There's a herb
garden, pond area, summer meadow, bog
garden, chalk bank, stag beetle sanctuary and
mini-beast village, not to mention a nursery
where visitors can pick up plants for their own
gardens. For children, there's a play area,
sandpit and parent-and-toddler group, and the
visitors' centre has tanks of fish and stick
insects to peep at. The local community tend
the raised beds and the garden's beehives
produce the centre's 'Peckham Honey'.
Buggy access. Disabled access: toilet.
Nappy-changing facilities. Shop.

Parkland Walk

NE London (Finsbury Park, Stroud Green,
Crouch End, Highgate Muswell Hill) N4, N8,
N6, N10 (www.parkland-walk.org.uk).
Finsbury Park tube, Highgate Tube, Crouch
Hill BR. **Open** 24hrs daily. **Admission** free.
The longest nature reserve in London forms
part of the Capital Ring walking and cycling
route and runs the length of the disused
Northern Heights railway line that links
Finsbury Park with Highgate, and Highgate

Sightseeing

Sightseeing

with Alexandra Palace. It cuts through the terraced backs of Stroud Green, Crouch End and Muswell Hill on the way. The path was resurfaced in 2009, so it's less muddy than it used to be, but retains a hint of wilderness you won't find in most of London's parks.

Highgate to Finsbury Park is the longer and more interesting stretch, and a gentle downhill stroll all the way; it's also a popular cycle route that's a safe ride for kids. Just after the disused platforms of the old Crouch End Station, look out for the Spriggan climbing out of one of the arches – a disconcerting sculpture by Marilyn Collins that's said to have inspired Stephen King to write his short story 'Crouch End'.

The Parkland Walk heads into Finsbury Park at the Oxford Road Gate; straight ahead, weary walkers can seek refreshment in the café by the boating lake. Finsbury Park's fantastic playground, built with a £5 million Heritage Lottery Fund, is also close by. Local kids are disappointed that the playground halfway down the walk with its rope swings, wooden walkways and slides down the steep bank has been largely closed off and partially dismantled.

WIDE OPEN SPACES

Epping Forest

Information Centre, High Beech, Loughton, Essex IG10 4AF (8508 0028, www.cityof london.gov.uk/openspaces). Loughton or Theydon Bois tube, or Chingford rail. **Open** *Information Centre* Summer 11am-6pm daily. Winter 10am-3pm daily. *Forest* 24hrs daily. **Admission** free.
A day out in the country within easy access of the city. Epping Forest is 12 miles (19km) long and several miles across. Commoners still have grazing rights and, each summer, English Longhorn cattle can be seen chewing the cud. For most visitors, it's the walking, horse riding or cycling opportunities that are the biggest draw. The forest contains Iron Age earthworks and two listed buildings – the Temple in Wanstead Park and the 16th-century Queen Elizabeth's Hunting Lodge (Rangers Road, E4 7QH, 8529 6681; under-16s must be accompanied by an adult). The latter has a quiz trail, weekend craft activities and Tudor-themed dressing up; in the kitchen area, you can smell food made from 400-year-old recipes.

Work on the Branching Out Project began in 2009 and will take five years to complete. Using Heritage Lottery money, there are plans for a new Interpretation Centre next door to Queen Elizabeth's Hunting Lodge; an education programme; improved trails and a visitor hub to encourage visitors to go deeper into the forest.

If you're coming by public transport, be prepared for some exercise. Chingford railway station gives access to the Hunting Lodge and some lovely strolls at the south end. Loughton and Theydon Bois (Central line) are the forest's nearest tube stops, though it's a two-mile uphill walk from both. The best advice is to get a map and plan your route in advance – or take the car. At High Beech car park there's a small tea hut, as well as the Epping Forest Field Centre. *Buggy access. Disabled access: toilet. Nappy-changing facilities. Shop.*

Lee Valley Park

Hackney, Walthamstow, Waltham Abbey, Cheshunt, Broxbourne, Hoddesdon, E10-EN11 (01992 717711, www.leevalleypark. org.uk). **Open** 24hrs daily. **Admission** varies; phone or check website for details.
After London 2012, another two miles of open parkland will be added to what's already a 26 mile-long park straddling the river Lee. It has a network of lakes, waterways, parks and countryside areas, and there's plenty to do. A gentle guided walk is a good way to start; the well-signposted park is ideal for picnics, walking or fishing. It's also a nature lover's paradise. Some 32 species of mammals are said to make their home in the park. Waymarked walks, some providing easy buggy access, take you to see orchids, grasshoppers and waterlilies. The birdwatching is excellent too.

Other attractions include the Lee Valley Riding Centre and Lee Valley Ice Centre (for both, *see pp161-190*), which offers family sessions at the weekends and during school holidays. The erstwhile Eastway Cycle Circuit has been rebuilt into the Velodrome and BMX Track (*see p131* **Queen Elizabeth Olympic Park**). Lee Valley Boat Centre (Old Nazeing Road, Broxbourne, Herts EN10 7AX, 01992 462085, www.leevalleyboats.co.uk) hires boats by the hour and organises narrowboat holidays. There's also the brand new Lee Valley White Water Centre (www.leevalleypark.org.uk).

The town of Waltham Abbey, which borders the park, has plenty of cafés and shops and an Augustinian abbey. The Royal Gunpowder Mills (Beaulieu Drive, Waltham Abbey, Essex EN9 1JY, 01992 707370, www.royalgunpowder mills.com) and Epping Forest (*see left*) are also just a ten-minute drive from the town. *Buggy access. Disabled access: toilet. Kiosk. Nappy-changing facilities.*

Meet the Animals

Go wild with an urban safari.

Animals may be two a penny in the countryside, but they rarely come with added attractions. London's nature reserves, aquariums, zoos and city farms know that variety is key to a great day out and provide all sorts of extra entertainment, from playgrounds and carousels to giant snakes and ladders and horse rides. The sheer range of exotic animal species in the capital is enormous – where else can you see gorillas, lions, giraffes, locusts, Cuban crocodiles, giant turtles, Komodo dragons and white-faced whistling ducks all within a ten-mile radius of each other?

If simplicity is the order of the day, it's just as easy to feed a goat, stroke a sheep, hold a rabbit or watch a cow being milked. You just need to know where to look. Below we list the best places to see all these amazing creatures, but it's worth also worth having a look through the **Parks & Gardens** chapter (*see pp123-146*), as some of the capital's parks feature well-stocked animal enclosures.

AQUARIUMS

Horniman Museum

100 London Road, SE23 3PQ (8699 1872, www.horniman.ac.uk). Forest Hill rail or bus 176, 185, 197, 356, P4. **Open** 10.30am-5.30pm daily. **Admission** free; donations appreciated. **Credit** MC, V.

This wonderful museum (*see p91*) just got a little more accessible for east and north Londoners thanks to the new overground line from Dalston to Croydon. It has an amazing aquarium, which houses hundreds of species of aquatic animals and plants across seven distinct zones. Recent additions include some postman butterflies in the Iwokrama rainforest display, and a specialist jellyfish tank where these stunning critters can be viewed at close range. As visitors work their way around, they explore the diverse nature of ecosystems from across the globe and read about the threats such fragile environments face. Ecosystems covered include British pond life, Devonshire rockpools, Fijian coral reefs and mangrove swamps. Check the website for details of events and activities. *Buggy access. Café. Disabled access: lift, toilet. Nappy-changing facilities. Nearest picnic place: museum gardens. Shop.*

Sea Life London Aquarium

County Hall (riverfront entrance), Riverside Building, SE1 7PB (0871 663 1678, www.visitsealife.com). Westminster tube or Waterloo tube/rail. **Open** 10am-6pm Mon-Fri (last entry 5pm); 10am-7pm Sat, Sun (last entry 6pm). *Tours* (groups of 10 or more) phone for details. **Admission** £18; £12.50-£16.50 reductions; £12.50 3-15s; £55 family (2+2); free under-3s. **Credit** MC, V. **Map** p333 M9.

Not the cheapest family day out in London, but once inside the aquarium itself it's hard to remain peeved at the price. Last year's addition – the Rainforests of the World area – is deservedly popular; its collection of crocodiles, poison arrow frogs and piranhas (best seen at feeding time) keep children fascinated, and woodchip underfoot is a nice atmospheric touch. New to the area this year is a pair of Cuban crocodiles (which you won't see anywhere else in the UK). Only a few thousand of these intelligent crocs remain in the wild (these were bred in captivity). Another favourite attraction is the Shark Walk, where a floating glass platform allows visitors to walk just above the circling sharks. Around the aquarium, there are hundreds of varieties of fish and sea life from all over the world, including stingrays, Californian cownose rays and sea scorpions. We like the tunnel constructed from a 25-metre-long whale skeleton, beneath which visitors can view a tropical ocean of fish, coral and green turtles.

To get the best value, time your visit to coincide with feeding times (check the website for the day's schedule); the sharks are usually fed at 2.30pm. If you're pushing a buggy, enter and leave from the London Eye side; you'll avoid McDonald's and the tricky steps up to Westminster Bridge.

Buggy access. Disabled access: lift, toilet. Nappy-changing facilities. Nearest picnic place: Jubilee Gardens. Shop.

BUTTERFLY RESERVES

Butterfly World

Miriam Lane, Chiswell Green, Herts AL2 3NY (01727 869 203, www.butterflyworld project.com). **Open** *Apr-June, Sept* 10am-5pm daily. *July, Aug* 10am-6pm daily. **Admission** £8; £7 reductions; £5 3-16s, free under 3s; £23 family (2+2).

In an unlikely setting, just minutes from the M25, lies the largest hommage to the butterfly in the UK. The site is designed to look like an enormous butterfly head from the air and has been set up by property tycoon and butterfly obsessive Clive Farrell (he even has his own butterfly farm in Belize). Until Autumn 2011 when the 100m diameter walk-through biome opens, the butterfly tunnel here is a sneak preview of what's to come. Also already open is the butterfly breeding house, where kids can see first hand all the incredible stages of a butterfly's life cycle from egg to caterpillar to pupae to butterfly. The Insect Study Centre is often used by school groups during the week, but casual visitors are welcome to observe the specimens inside the transparent containers. The 20 acres of wildflower meadows (designed to attract and support native butterflies and insects) are a blaze of colour during summer, and the specialist gardens that stretch down one side of the site are also lots of fun. There's a playground under construction and the new café has a sheltered terrace that will prove popular with families on sunny days. What's more they don't make you walk through the well-stocked shop on your way out. It's an educational and fun day out.

Buggy access. Café. Disabled access: toilet. Nappy-changing facilities. Nearest picnic place: gardens. Shop.

FARMS

Belmont Children's Farm

The Ridgeway, Mill Hill, NW7 1QT (8959 3308, www.belmontfarm.co.uk). Mill Hill East tube, then bus 240. **Open** *Mar-Oct* 8am-6pm Mon-Fri; 9am-6pm Sat, Sun.

Nov-Feb 8am-5pm Mon-Fri; 9am-5pm Sat, Sun. **Admission** £4.50; free-£2 reductions; £12 family (2+2). **Credit** MC, V.

This new farm, set just beyond the North Circular, opened in 2009. It's green and leafy and looks very pretty. A walk down the slope from the car park brings you to the central buildings, which house small animals, rodents and birds – watch ferrets and chinchillas (like giant mice) race along tunnels. There are two small circular walks. The first takes you past the aviary, where rare breed poultry cluck and scrape, then past pigs and goats in pretty fenced enclosures. The second takes you past some owls and the farm's more exotic animals – the wallabies. The enclosures are clearly marked with information about individual species (factsheets can also be downloaded from the website in advance). Even parents might learn something: that goats have square pupils rather than round ones, for example, or that it takes three times as long to digest cow's milk as goat's milk. Children can join in at daily feeding sessions (11am-noon) or pet the smaller animals (11am-noon, 4-5pm). Tractor and trailer rides take place at noon, 2.30pm, 3.30pm and 4.30pm (adults £2; children £1). At the centre of the site, the spacious café specialises in waffles. There's a range of savoury and sweet options, with wholemeal and wheat-free waffles also available. All-day breakfasts are popular with everyone, and kids get their own menu, with a drink and a main course for £4.25. The farm also hosts children's parties.

Buggy access. Disabled access: toilet. Nappy-changing facilities. Nearest picnic place: farm picnic area.

Crystal Palace Park Farm

The Croft, Ledrington Road, SE19 2BS (8778 5572, www.crystalpalacepark farm.co.uk). Crystal Palace rail. **Open** noon-4pm Mon, Tue, Thur-Sun. **Admission** free.

Thanks to the opening of the new London Overground line from Dalston to Croydon (with Crystal Palace on a branch line that breaks off after Sydenham) it's now much easier to visit this farm. Crystal Palace Park Farm is very much a community-focused centre and well used by local schools, who get guided tours with an education officer. In the small yard and paddock, there are kune pigs, alpacas, goats and Shetland ponies, while the smaller animals are up a steep ramp. Children are always fascinated by the reptile room too. In the afternoons, casual visitors can often handle the smaller animals, if there's a free member of staff

Sightseeing

My Sport Tennis
Oskar, 9

What inspired you to take up tennis?
It was my mum's idea, but I thought it was a good one. Tom, my best friend from school and from my street, also goes.

What do you like about tennis?
I like the challenges of playing, and it's great to be outdoors on a court all year round. My favourite shot is the serve.

What level are you at?
I started three years ago. I'm in the top group for my age – it's a mixed group, but there are more boys than girls.

What's next for you in your sport?
I'd like to be able to slice the ball.

Which events would you like to see at the London 2012 Olympic Games and Paralympic Games?
I'd love to see the Tennis, the Long Jump and High Jump events in Athletics, and the Equestrian Jumping.

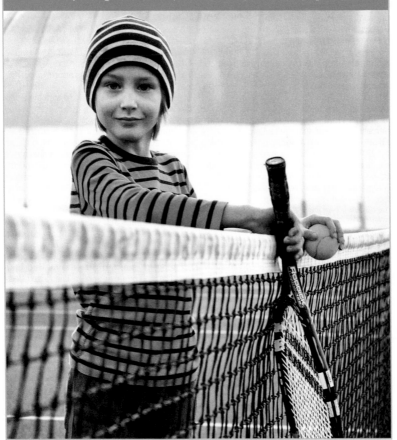

Sightseeing

handy. The neighbouring Capel Manor College (8778 5572, www.capel.ac.uk) runs full-time animal care courses for 16- to 18-year-olds. There's no café on site, but the surrounding park is perfect for leisurely family picnics. *Buggy access. Disabled access: ramp, toilet. Nappy-changing facilities. Nearest picnic place: Crystal Palace Park.*

Deen City Farm & Community Garden

39 Windsor Avenue, SW19 2RR (8543 5300, www.deencityfarm.co.uk). Colliers Wood tube, then bus 200. **Open** 10am-4.30pm Tue-Sun, bank hols. **Admission** free; donations appreciated. **No credit cards.**
Set on beautiful National Trust land within the Morden Hall Park Estate, Deen City Farm is noticeably more rural than London's other city farms. The farm is home to a wide range of unusual species – it's a member of the Rare Breeds Survival Trust. There are Shetland sheep, pigs, cows, ducks, chickens, geese, turkeys, peacocks, alpacas and a huddle of rabbits and guinea pigs that you can handle at certain times (check when you arrive). There's a generous area used for pony rides – it's £1 per ride for the under-eights on Wednesdays (noon), weekends (3pm) and school holidays – and the sandwiches and cakes in the cheerful café are refreshingly cheap (children's lunch packs are £3.50). There's also a pretty growing garden run by volunteers (children must be over 12 to secure a volunteer placement) and a grass maze. *Buggy access. Café. Disabled access: toilet. Nappy-changing facilities. Nearest picnic place: Morden Hall Park. Shop.*

Freightliners City Farm

Paradise Park, Sheringham Road, off Liverpool Road, N7 8PF (7609 0467, www.freightlinersfarm.org.uk). Caledonian Road or Holloway Road tube, or Highbury & Islington tube/rail. **Open** *Summer* 10am-4.45pm Tue-Sun, bank hols. *Winter* 10am-4pm Tue-Sun. **Admission** free; donations appreciated. **No credit cards.**
When this farm was set up behind King's Cross station in 1973, the animals were housed in old railway goods vans – hence the name. The farm moved to its current position behind the busy Holloway Road later in the decade. The half-hectare site is as much a community hub as a working farm with cookery lessons running in the café, volunteer bee-keeping activities, an Adopt an Animal scheme and a very busy timetable of events throughout the school holidays (check the website for details).

Freightliners is home to Olivia and Matilda the dexter cows, sheep, goats, Berkshire and British middle white pigs, as well as all kinds of poultry. The collection of animals, many of them rare breeds, is impressive. Giant Flemish rabbits are the biggest you'll see anywhere, while exotic cockerels with feathered feet squawk in your path. You can buy hen and duck eggs of all hues in the shop, plus seasonal, own-grown fruit, vegetables, plants and honey, all produced on the farm. The café, built by volunteers out of green oak and straw bales, is open on Friday, Saturday and Sunday and serves homemade soup, salads, sandwiches and cakes; it offers a healthy children's menu too. *Buggy access. Café. Disabled access: toilet. Nappy-changing facilities. Nearest picnic place: farm picnic area. Shop.*

Hackney City Farm

1A Goldsmiths Row, E2 8QA (7729 6381, www.hackneycityfarm.co.uk). Bethnal Green tube or Cambridge Heath Road rail. **Open** 10am-4.30pm Tue-Sun, bank hols. **Admission** free; donations appreciated. **Credit** MC, V.
Some people come for the award-winning onsite Frizzante café (*see p249*), others for the tiny patch of bucolic calm within a dense urban environment. Some come for the craft-based activities like pottery, upholstery, felt-making, mosaics and bee-keeping, others for the chance to get close to some live animals. Around the small courtyard, outbuildings house some very pretty golden Guernsey goats, sheep, pigs, Larry the donkey, chickens, geese and ducks, along with some smaller, fluffier animals, including rabbits and guinea pigs. The larger animals get to frolic in a small field out back during the day. The farm does a healthy trade in eggs, and has also started pig production by bringing in Tamworth pigs from Mudchute City Farm. The farm garden has raised beds full of seasonal vegetables, a plant nursery and a play area with a sandpit, wigwams and trails. Check the website for weekly activities aimed at children and parents; popular pottery drop-in sessions cost £5 for two hours. And there's always a lot going on in the school holidays. *Buggy access. Café. Disabled access: toilet. Nappy-changing facilities. Nearest picnic place: gardens. Shop.*

Hounslow Urban Farm

A312 at Faggs Road, Feltham, Middx TW14 0LZ (8831 9658, www.hounslow.info). Hatton Cross tube, then 15min walk, or bus 90, 285,

Sightseeing (sidebar)

490. **Open** *Summer* 10am-5.30pm daily (last entry 4.30pm). *Winter* 11am-4pm Sat, Sun (last entry 3pm). Times & days may vary, phone or check website for details. **Admission** £4.25-£5; £3.50-£4.25 reductions; £2.75-£3.50 2-16s; £12-£15 family (2+2); free under-2s. **No credit cards.**
Now here's something you don't see at many of London's city farms – pig racing. It's held every weekend, along with animal handling sessions. Bags of feed are on sale at the shop, which also sells cuddly toys, peacock feathers and all manner of animal-themed souvenirs, as well as giving shelter to the farm's parrot and its lounge of lizards. Hounslow Urban Farm is one of London's largest, with 29 acres to play with. The farm rears rare, endangered and historic breeds as part of a conservation programme, and houses British saddleback pigs, goats, ducks, Shetland ponies, alpacas, chipmunks and a donkey. Turn up at the right time of year and you could be lucky enough to feed the orphan lambs and peek at the piglets. You can even buy a small animal – such as a rabbit or a guinea pig – and get some helpful care advice. Activities are held during school holidays, with a children's entertainer promised on bank holiday Mondays and every Tuesday during the holidays. There is a picnic area and a shop, plus a brace of pedal tractors in the playground.
Buggy access. Disabled access: toilet. Nappy-changing facilities. Nearest picnic place: farm picnic area. Shop.

Kentish Town City Farm

1 Cressfield Close, off Grafton Road, NW5 4BN (7916 5421, www.ktcityfarm.org.uk). Chalk Farm tube or Kentish Town tube/rail or Gospel Oak rail. **Open** 9am-5pm daily. **Admission** free; donations appreciated. **No credit cards.**
London's oldest city farm may have changed its name since it was set up in 1972, but the ethos remains the same. This was the model for London's other community-led city farms, and provides much more than a chance to gawp at some livestock. The site is far larger than first appearances suggest, stretching way beyond the farmyard into fields and well-tended vegetable gardens. There's also a frog-filled pond with a dipping platform to investigate. Livestock includes farmyard ducks, goats, pigs, horses, cows, chickens and sheep, with some rare breeds. As well as petting the animals, children can get involved with their care by mucking out (arrive by 9am), feeding them (with supervision) and taking care of the site.

During the holidays, a host of activities are held in the farm centre and children's parties can be held here at weekends (hire includes use of the kitchen). Drop-in play sessions for under-fives take place on Tuesday and Wednesday mornings (10am-noon; £1) and there's a sing-song class on Mondays (9.30-10.30am; £3, concs £2). For older children, there are after-school clubs like practical city farming, pottery and cookery classes. There's a three-year waiting list to join the Camden Pony Club, which is based here, but the Riding School offers pony rides on Saturdays from March to September, weather permitting (1.30pm, £1). The farm welcomes school visits from all boroughs, and holds May Day celebrations, a summer horse show, an Easter egg hunt, Apple Day activities and a Christmas fair.
Buggy access. Disabled access: toilet. Nappy-changing facilities. Nearest picnic place: Hampstead Heath.

Lee Valley Park Farms

Stubbins Hall Lane, Crooked Mile, Waltham Abbey, Essex EN9 2EF (01992 892781, www.leevalleypark.org.uk). Broxbourne or Cheshunt rail. **Open** *Mid Feb-Oct* 10am-5pm daily. Closed Nov-mid Feb. **Admission** £7; £5.60 reductions, 2-16s; free under-2s; £28 family (2+3). **Credit** MC, V.
Not the cheapest of city farms, but you do get two farms for the price of one. Hayes Hill is a traditional farm and rare breeds centre, while Holyfield Hall is its commercial neighbour. At Hayes Hill, try persuading your children that the animals are more exciting than the pedal tractors, Bundle Barn soft play feature or new Hilltop Adventure Zone (featuring a giant jumping pillow and a 20ft climbing tower). They can also meet Tallulah the Tamworth and Barbara the Berkshire pig, as well as some Essex pigs (a seriously endangered species). Also in residence are Ella and Evie the goats, sheep, llamas, water buffalo and chickens. In the spring, visitors are encouraged to bottle-feed the new lambs. Stroking Rex the 'therapy' rabbit is another draw – but watch out for Newton the bearded dragon. If this all seems a bit cosy, then go and watch the cows being milked over at Holyfield Hall (from 2.30pm daily) and learn about large-scale dairy production. There are guided tours for school parties, tractor-trailer rides and pig races at various times in the year (weather permitting).
Buggy access. Café. Disabled access: toilet. Nappy-changing facilities. Nearest picnic place: farm picnic areas. Shop.

Sightseeing

Neighbourhood Watch
Marylebone

ZSL London Zoo.

Hemmed in by relentlessly busy Oxford Street to the south and relaxed Regent's Park to the north, Marylebone is a fashionable district that has become a magnet for moneyed Londoners. Its leafy squares, terraces of Georgian townhouses and boutique-lined high street – home to a slew of fancy family favourites such as Little White Company, Cath Kidston and chic French label Bonpoint – are perfect for a leisurely stroll, particularly on Sundays when one of London's largest farmer's markets sets up shop here.

Once the children's tolerance for shopping has worn off, Regent's Park is a hop, skip and a jump away, while for rainy days, the Wallace Collection is a little-known treasure. Kids may be unmoved by the promise of Old Masters and 18th-century porcelain, but the magnificent armoury is another matter entirely. And if you really want

them to wax lyrical about their day out in Marylebone, then cough up for a celebrity-filled photo frenzy at legendary Madame Tussauds.

Up in arms

Entrance to the **Wallace Collection** (*see p87*), a grand, 18th-century townhouse-turned-museum, is absolutely free; inside, all sorts of treasures await. Anyone with a penchant for chivalry, derring-do and gory battles will be enraptured by the array of armour and weaponry, ranging from gold-inlaid scimitars and creepy, beak-fronted helmets to mighty cannons and gleaming suits. Elsewhere, you can gawp at Frans Hals' *Laughing Cavalier* (neither laughing nor a cavalier, but sporting a magnificent moustache), marvel at Louis XV's commode and admire Catherine the Great's lovely Sèvres porcelain ice-cream cooler.

Kids can try the weighty suits of armour on for size in the Conservation Gallery, or pick up a free Warrior Kings trail – which takes you round all manner of jewel-encrusted weaponry. Visiting on the first Sunday of the month? Then prepare to get sketching at one of the Little Draw drop-in workshops. There are also armour-handling, hat-designing and watercolour-painting sessions on the busy events calendar; most of them cost a mere £4.

Wax lyrical

If all that sounds terribly serious and you've got cash to burn, you could head down to the gaudy attractions of **Madame Tussauds** (*see p70*). Where else could you have your picture taken next to Amy Winehouse, Johnny Depp and the Queen in one afternoon? Yes, when it comes down to it they're just waxwork models, but Madame Tussauds isn't world famous by accident; a lot of effort has been put in to contextualising the figures and providing interactive excitement. The Spirit of London ride in a small version of a London taxi is our personal favourite.

Head upmarket

Marylebone is a mecca for foodies, thanks to fine food emporiums such as La Fromagerie and the Ginger Pig (both on Moxon Street), and a host of swish restaurants. More exciting to children is the vibrant **Marylebone Farmer's Market** (www.lfm.org.uk), where grown-ups can sample slivers of whiffy cheese and compare olive oils while kids eye up the slabs of home-made cake. It's held on Sunday mornings in the Cramer Street car park, which is just off the high street. If you're around on Saturday, head for the chichi **Cabbages & Frocks** (www.cabbagesandfrocks.co.uk) market, in the grounds of St Mary's Parish Church. Friendly stallholders sell jewellery and clothes alongside salamis, artisan breads and all sorts of on-the-spot little somethings to keep you going until lunch. Topped with pastel swirls of icing and covered with pretty handmade sugar flowers, Peggy's Cupcakes are irresistible.

Coming up roses

To work off your foodie excesses in the fresh air, head for **Regent's Park** (*see p143*), one of London's most genteel patches of green. In early summer, the breeze is particularly fragrant, as the Inner Circle's magnificent rose gardens come into bloom. There's plenty of resident wildlife, too, particularly around the lakes (where you can take a boat out for half an hour or more). In summer, families might want to plan ahead and see a puppet show or family-friendly Shakespeare at the **Open Air Theatre** (*see p212*), but there's always plenty of sport to watch as well, on the many pitches up on the north side.

Also at the north end of the park, the famous **ZSL London Zoo** (*see p158*) awaits. Though entrance charges are substantial, the zoo does offer 36 acres to explore filled with more than 600 species. There are far too many attractions to list – though we've got a soft spot for the gorillas, the tireless ants in B.U.G.S., the Komodo dragon in the reptile house, and the incredible tigers. Loads of special events run throughout the day, too, from storytelling sessions in the brilliant Animal Adventure children's zoo and play area or meet-the-spider events, to Animals in Action and the classic penguins' feeding time.

Refreshments

Also in the area: Ask, Carluccio's Caffè, Paul, Ping Pong, Pizza Express, Giraffe, Wagamama.
Boathouse Café *The Boating Lake, Hanover Gate, Regent's Park NW1 4NU (7724 4069)*. Survey the boating lake from the terrace at this family-friendly joint, serving pizza, pasta and snacks.
Fishworks *89 Marylebone High Street, W1U 4QW (7935 9796, www.fishworks. co.uk)*. The £5 kids' menu includes fishfingers, fishcakes and mussels, with ice-cream to follow.
Golden Hind *73 Marylebone Lane, W1U 2PN (7486 3644)*. Proper fish and chips, and a warm welcome for families.
Honest Sausage *Inner Circle, off Chester Road, Regent's Park NW1 4NU (7224 3872, www.honestsausage.com)*. Bacon butties or free-range bangers.

Sightseeing

Interactive Fun

Education and entertainment combined at the Wetland Centre.

Birdwatching is just the start of a day out at the **WWT Wetland Centre** in Barnes (*see p156*). In the latter half of 2010, a series of new interactive exhibits opened that explore different environmental concerns. The beautiful Rain Garden encourages visitors to make the most of rainwater supplies in their own gardens and the emphasis on recycling is also revealed by the pavilion, which is made out of an old shipping container adorned with a grass roof (you can observe the flowers on top through a periscope). Children love the paths between the ponds (leather shoes beware), and using the foot pumps to channel water along the mini viaducts.

Also launched in summer 2010 beside the Discovery Centre was Pond Safari, an exhibit allowing kids to look at what's in the ponds, courtesy of an underwater camera. The picture quality isn't great, but kids love the fact that they can control the camera with a joystick and zoom buttons. They'll also enjoy the new digital pond inside the Discovery Centre, which offers several games, the best of which is 'Feed the Dragonfly'. And to top it all off, the new Down the Plughole exhibit, mounted inside an actual sewage pipe (never used for the purpose), does the simple job of reminding us what not to put down the plughole.

Sightseeing

Mudchute City Farm

Pier Street, Isle of Dogs, E14 3HP (7515 5901, www.mudchute.org). Crossharbour, Mudchute or Island Gardens DLR. **Open** 9am-5pm Tue-Sun, bank hols. **Admission** free; donations appreciated. **No credit cards**.

Views of Canary Wharf's towers reminds visitors to this 27-acre farm that they are not far from civilisation, but clever landscaping creates a touch of bucolic peace in the middle of the urban Isle of Dogs. The Pet Corner has been revamped, with cute, brightly painted wooden houses built for the smaller animals (petting sessions are available 9.30am to 4pm on request). Once the kids have seen the smaller animals, there are lots of paths through well-established woods and hedgerows to explore, past fields of donkeys, goats, pigs, sheep, cows and llamas. Families can join a duck walk at 9am and 3pm (4pm in summer) and also help to feed the larger animals, which adds to the excitement. A new farm shop started trading in August 2010, stocking toys, plants, edible treats and local produce. Mudchute Kitchen (the farm's respected café) was taken over by new management in 2010, but the catering has lost none of its appeal. The facilities are available for hire for private parties. There's an after-school club for five- to 12-year-olds.

Buggy access. Café. Disabled access: toilet. Nappy-changing facilities. Nearest picnic place: farm picnic area. Shop.

Newham City Farm

Stansfeld Road, E6 5LT (7474 4960). Royal Albert DLR or bus 262, 300, 376. **Open** *Summer* 10am-5pm Tue-Sun. *Winter* 10am-4pm Tue-Sun, bank hols. **Admission** free; donations appreciated. **No credit cards**.

Newham has been here for over 30 years now. Alongside the usual farmyard poultry, sheep, pigs and goats is the largest animal on the farm: Blaze, a shire horse, who pulls a dray cart that visitors can ride in. There are also some smaller, furrier chaps (rabbits, guinea pigs and two ferrets), a twittering house of finches and Sarah the barn owl (named after one of the siblings in the Owl Babies children's book). The visitors' centre runs plenty of holiday activities, such as the ever-popular 'Be a Farmer for a Day' sessions (you will need to book these in advance) and various other drop-in activities. Fun Days offer the likes of sheep-shearing demonstrations and felt-making, and visitors can also taste the honey produced by bees from the farm's own hives. There's a new play area for toddlers with ride-on toys and a recently

built covered outdoor learning space that doubles up as a picnic area. As we went to press, the café was relocating to a larger space. *Buggy access. Café. Disabled access: toilet. Nappy-changing facilities. Nearest picnic place: farm picnic area. Shop.*

Spitalfields City Farm

Buxton Street, off Brick Lane, E1 5AR (7247 8762, www.spitalfieldscityfarm.org). Whitechapel tube. **Open** *Summer* 10am-4.30pm Tue-Sun. *Winter* 10am-4pm Tue-Sun. **Admission** free; donations appreciated. **No credit cards**.

This compact community farm is a world away from the encroaching towers of the Square Mile. There's a full complement of pigs, sheep and poultry, plus donkeys and a pony. Outside the farmyard, there is much to see in the gardens, including unusual vegetables in the growing plot. Children will love the large treehouse, which is as good as anything in London's more formal adventure playgrounds. In spring, the Wildlife Garden is gorgeous, as bluebells, snowdrops and foxgloves nod in the pungent breeze, scented by wild garlic. Keen eight- to 12-year-olds can join the Young Farmers' Club, which runs a play scheme on Saturdays from 10.30am to 3.30pm. Activities include looking after the animals and cooking over an outdoor fire. There's also an after-school club on Thursdays. Vegetables, fruit and plants are on sale and annual events include the Sheep and Wool Fayre in May, Spitalfields Show and Green Fair in September, Apple Day in October and Christmas Fair.

Buggy access. Disabled access: toilet. Nappy-changing facilities. Nearest picnic place: farm picnic area.

Surrey Docks Farm

South Wharf, 309.5 Rotherhithe Street, SE16 5ET (7231 1010, www.surreydocks farm.org.uk). Surrey Quays or Rotherhithe rail. **Open** 10am-5pm Tue-Sun. **Admission** free; donations appreciated. **No credit cards**.

When this community farm was dreamt up in 1975, the surrounding area looked very different. These days, the site is bordered by the gated developments and luxury flats of Docklands, but inside the farm gates the ethos remains much the same. Sheep, goats and chickens mooch around a central farmyard, while out in the pens there are organically reared cows, pigs, horses and a donkey, fenced in by delightful wrought-metal railings – handiwork of resident blacksmith Kevin Boys

Sightseeing

(a working forge on the premises offers classes to local schoolchildren). Kids can also learn about food production from the dairy, milking barn, bee room, orchard, herb garden and vegetable plots. If the kids seem inspired, they can return on the third Saturday of every month for Young Farmers' Club (eight- to 13-year-olds).

A new manager arrived on site in 2010 and improvements are already in evidence. The farm café is now run by Frizzante (which also runs the highly successful café at Hackney City Farm); there's a monthly market on the first Saturday of the month selling local produce, arts, crafts and more; and there's also a raft of new yoga classes available in the refurbished Riverside Room.

Buggy access. Café. Disabled access: toilet. Nearest picnic place: riverside. Shop.

Vauxhall City Farm

165 Tyers Street, SE11 5HS (7582 4204, www.vauxhallcityfarm.info). Vauxhall tube/rail or bus 2, 36, 44, 77. **Open** 10.30am-4pm Wed-Sun. **Admission** free; donations appreciated. **No credit cards.**
Vauxhall's answer to the countryside is this tiny spot of mud, muck and enthusiasm. Many of the animals – the rare breed pigs and cows, alpacas, goats and sheep – inhabit a specially constructed straw-bale animal house, built by Barbara Jones in 2001, with sedums on the roof to attract bees. Start here and then wander through to the duck pond and community garden. There's no café, but you can picnic undercover near the rabbit and chicken enclosures. The farm runs pony-riding lessons in nearby Spring Gardens for children and riders with disabilities, hosts a weekly Ruby Rhymes under-fives singing group, and holds classes in art, spinning, dyeing and weaving (plants for natural dyes are grown in a special garden, along with vegetables). The ecology garden was refurbished in 2010 and now hosts pond-dipping sessions and mini-beast hunts.
Buggy access. Disabled access: toilet. Nappy-changing facilities. Nearest picnic place: Spring Gardens.

WETLAND RESERVES

Greenwich Peninsula Ecology Park

Thames Path, John Harrison Way, SE10 0QZ (8293 1904, www.urbanecology.org.uk). North Greenwich tube or bus 108, 161, 422, 472, 486. **Open** 10am-5pm Wed-Sun. **Admission** free; donations appreciated.

This site was a former gasworks, but is now the only significant patch of green on the peninsula. It underwent a huge regeneration project in 1997 to become a freshwater habitat for frogs, toads, newts and many species of bird. Take to the hides to watch the birds without disturbing them, or borrow the necessary equipment to get up close and personal with the wildlife (the visitors' centre provides pond-dipping nets, trays, magnifiers, bug jars and binoculars). There are themed quiz trails and word searches, and children can collect the materials to make paintings, collages or sketches. Look at the website for details of drop-in activities during the school holidays.
Buggy access. Disabled access: toilet. Nappy-changing facilities. Nearest picnic place: Southern Park.

WWT Wetland Centre

Queen Elizabeth's Walk, SW13 9WT (8409 4400, www.wwt.org.uk/london). Hammersmith tube then bus 33, 72, 209 (alight at Red Lion pub) or 283 (Duck Bus direct to Centre). **Open** *Summer* 9.30am-6pm daily. *Winter* 9.30am-5pm daily (last entry 1hr before closing). *Tours* 11am, 2pm daily. *Feeding tours* 3pm daily. **Admission** £9.95; £7.40 reductions; £5.50 4-16s; free under-4s; £27.75 family (2+2). *Tours* free. **Credit** MC, V.
This wetland reserve is one of London's best-kept secrets, probably because it's just outside the centre. If you can get children past the giant snakes and ladders game (with giant dice), there are 104 acres for them to stretch their legs in, along paths that take them past the main lake, reed beds, ponds and wetland meadows. The big draw here is the birdlife. Every season brings new migratory visitors such as New Zealand's beautiful black swans. Our favourites were the white-faced whistling ducks, who break into a chorus if you whistle to them in the right tone. There's a bat house, plus six observation hides; the largest is the three-storey Peacock Tower. A series of new exhibits exploring the environment was added in 2010 (see *p154* **Interactive fun**). Visitors can take free guided tours with well-informed, friendly bird-watchers every day at 11am and 2pm, or feed the birds with a warden at 3pm. At weekends there's also a noon walk around the World Wetlands section. Children aged three to 11 will happily ignore the birds and play for hours in the adventure playground, shooting through the water vole tunnels, tackling the climbing walls and flying through

My Sport Boxing
Viddal, 13

What inspired you to take up boxing?
I watched it on TV with my dad, and I loved seeing boxers like Roy Jones fight in competitions. Dad first took me down to the club when I was six.

What do you like about boxing?
It teaches you discipline and how to handle yourself in and out of the ring. I also like it when you win and everyone praises you.

What level are you at?
I won the National Final last year, and I'm in it again this year. I know I can beat my opponent. I train two hours a day, every day. It's school. Come home. Change.

Go boxing. Come home. Eat. Sleep. And I run on Saturdays and Sundays.

What's next for you in your sport?
I'd like to get to Rio in 2016, but unfortunately I'm going to be too young to compete at London 2012. By the time I'm 18, I'd like to turn professional.

Which events would you like to see at the London 2012 Olympic Games and Paralympic Games?
I'd like to watch the people I've sparred with before, like Charlie Edwards and Andrew Selby, compete at Boxing. Also, I'd love to see some of the Football and the Athletics events.

Sightseeing

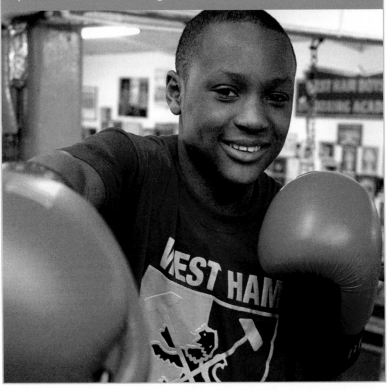

the air on the zip wire. There's a self-service restaurant with views over the main lake, serving hot meals and snacks.
Buggy access. Café. Disabled access: lift, toilet. Nappy-changing facilities. Nearest picnic place: centre picnic areas. Shop.

ZOOS

Battersea Park Children's Zoo
Queenstown Road, Battersea Park, SW11 4NJ (7924 5826, www.batterseazoo.co.uk). Sloane Square tube then bus 137, or Battersea Park or Queenstown Road rail, or bus 156, 345. **Open** *Summer* 10am-5.30pm daily (last entry 4.30pm). *Winter* 10am-4.30pm daily. **Admission** £7.50; £6 reductions, 2-15s; free under-2s; £25 family (2+2). **Credit** MC, V. **Map** p329 F13.
Battersea Children's Zoo is a much smaller outfit than London Zoo and the entry price reflects this. Here they can watch a coati snuffling in the undergrowth, squirrel monkeys and brown capuchins prancing about, mice running around in their own doll's house and tortoises munching through salad. The more adventurous can crawl down a pair of tunnels, popping up in a bubble in the meerkats' den. Toddlers love the New Zealand kune pigs, who provide top vocal entertainment with their snorting and snuffling. At weekends and holidays, visitors can watch the animals being fed (feeding time for meerkats and otters is 11am and 2.30pm; for monkeys it's 11am and 3pm) and get friendly with the farm animals at Barley Mo Farm at noon and 3.30pm. Look at the website for one-off themed events during the school holidays. The Lemon Tree café provides basic lunch fare, and there's a pretty good playground for all ages.
Buggy access. Café. Disabled access: toilet. Nappy-changing facilities. Nearest picnic place: zoo picnic area. Shop.

ZSL London Zoo
Outer Circle, Regent's Park, NW1 4RY (7722 3333, www.zsl.org). Baker Street or Camden Town tube, then bus 274. **Open** *Mar-June, Sept, Oct* 10am-5.30pm daily. *July, Aug* 10am-6pm daily. *Nov-Feb* 10am-4pm daily. Last entry 1hr before closing. **Admission** (including £1.80 voluntary contribution) £20.50; £19 reductions; £16.40 3-15s; free under-3s; £65 family (2+2 or 1+3). **Credit** AmEx, MC, V. **Map** p330 G2.

Quite simply, a brilliant family day out. London Zoo continues its transformation year on year, with its animals rehoused in imaginative enclosures and interactive elements introduced successfully across the site. The most exciting addition in recent years is Gorilla Kingdom, where visitors can get within a foot of three adult gorillas – albeit separated by a sheet of reinforced glass. A baby gorilla was born to one of the females in October 2010 and he's become a star attraction. In line with the 'natural habitat' philosophy of zookeeping, the lovely beasts also have a large area of landscaped greenery to explore. There's so much to do and see at the zoo that the best way to enjoy it is with an annual pass (which also gains a discount on rides and in the cafés, and offers members free parking on weekdays in termtime). Otherwise get here early if you want to see everything. By the canal, Into Africa has giraffes displaying their magnificently long tongues, and the strange Okapi looking on stoically as the zebras prance around in the next enclosure. Try and spot a cheeky monkey in the Meet the Monkeys walkthrough and marvel at the extraordinary natural world inside the B.U.G.S insect extravaganza. The Butterfly Paradise tunnel is always a favourite, as are the aquarium and penguin pool (which was undergoing major refurbishment as we went to press). Between these attractions lurk lions, tigers, hippos, camels and flamingos: all impossible to walk past quickly.

Daily events include the entertaining Animals In Action display at noon, which has the audience ducking as hawks, vultures, owls and parrots soar millimetres above their heads for strategically placed titbits while a keeper relays amusing anecdotes. Better than a science lesson any day. One of our favourite attractions is Tim Hunkin's charming clock, just outside the Blackburn Pavilion bird house, which grinds into mechanical action every half hour. The Children's Zoo was designed for children by children. Here, kids can groom goats and sheep, meet the llamas, climb with coatis, explore the tunnels in the Roots Zone or listen to a story in the tipi. The Splash Zone is a great diversion on warm days, but take spare clothing. There's also a playground, bouncy castles and two carousels. For those who want to get really close to the animals, the zoo holds Junior Keeper for the Day events for 11- to 15-year-olds. *See also p152* **Neighbourhood Watch**.
Buggy access. Café. Disabled access: toilet. Nappy-changing facilities. Nearest picnic place: zoo picnic areas. Restaurant. Shop.

Activities

Sport & Activities

Faster, higher, stronger.

When London was awarded the right to host the 2012 Olympic and Paralympic Games, the bid's success owed much to the emphasis placed on the importance of youth participation in the future of sport. And the post-2012 future looks bright for east Londoners, as venues such as the Aquatics Centre, the Handball Arena and the Velodrome gear up to serve the local community with world-class facilities after the record breakers have all gone home.

Luckily, the capital wasn't in bad shape, sports-wise, before London 2012. There's a wider choice of sports facilities than elsewhere in the country, with plenty of pools, tennis courts, cricket pitches and climbing walls to go round. And that's not to mention all those gorgeous free green spaces listed in **Parks & Gardens** (*see pp123-146*) for an ad hoc kickabout.

There are also plenty of professionals to help make exercise fun. Organisations running activity clubs for toddlers include **Tumbletots** (www.tumbletots.com) and **Crechendo** (www.crechendo.com), while local councils run affordable (often free) sports camps in the school holidays. On top of that, many independent schools host a variety of private youth sports organisations that put on intensive rugby, football, tennis and cricket coaching when term ends. So there really is no excuse – get out there!

ACTIVE PLAY

Indoor play centres

Bramley's Big Adventure
136 Bramley Road, W10 6TJ (8960 1515, www.bramleysbig.co.uk). Latimer Road tube. **Open** *Term-time* 10am-6pm Mon-Fri; 10am-6.30pm Sat, Sun. *Holidays* 10am-6.30pm daily. **Membership** £20/yr. **Admission** *Members* £2.95 under-4s; £4.75 over-4s; free adults. *Non-members* £3.95 under-4s; £5.75 over-4s; 60p adults. **Credit** AmEx, MC, V.
Organised chaos reigns at Bramley's, tucked beneath the Westway flyover. The centrepiece is a giant three-level play frame, incorporating slides, ball pools, swings and dens, with separate areas for less rambunctious under-fives and babies. There's no time limit on play sessions during the week, so children can play all day; free Wi-Fi lets parents catch up on work while their offspring tear about. Commendably, the café offers organic and fair trade grub. Children's parties include meals and party bags. *Buggy access (must be locked up outside). Café. Disabled access: toilet. Nappy-changing facilities.*

Eddie Catz
68-70 High Street, SW15 1SF (0845 201 1268, www.eddiecatz.com). Putney Bridge tube. **Open** 9.30am-6pm Mon-Sat; 10am-6pm Sun. **Admission** £4.50 under 90cm; £5.50 90cm-1.55m; £1 over 1.55m; free babies under 8mths. **Credit** MC, V.
For tinies, Eddie Catz offers a soft play area and movement and music classes (for which an extra charge applies). Toddlers and older children, meanwhile, can enjoy a modestly sized adventure play frame, as well as a dressing-up area, video games and air hockey. Membership deals are available (from £65 for six months), as are birthday parties; the Wimbledon branch also offers laser tag parties for six to 12s. *Buggy access. Café. Disabled access: lift, toilet. Nappy-changing facilities. Shop.*
Branch 42 Station Road, SW19 2LP (8288 8178).

Gambado
7 Station Court, Townmead Road, SW6 2PY (7384 1635, www.gambado.com). Fulham Broadway tube or bus 391. **Open** 9.30am-6.30pm daily. **Admission** £7.75 1-2s; £9.75 3-12s; £2.50 adults; free under-1s. **Credit** MC, V.

Cheery staff and masses of things to do mean Gambado is eternally popular, despite the hefty entry fee. Kids soon vanish into the depths of the thrilling multi-level climbing frame, which incorporates ball ponds, slides (enclosed twirly tunnels plus bumpy ones large enough for parents to join in), trampolines, assault courses and mini dodgems. Tinies get a soft-play section with big Lego bricks and face painting. You can refuel on healthy fare at the café, and there's free internet access for the adults. At weekends, it's usually full of birthday parties. *Buggy access. Café. Disabled: toilet. Nappy-changing facilities.*

Little Dinosaurs

The Actual Workshop, The Grove, Alexandra Park, N22 7AY (8444 1338, 07957 457771 mobile, www.littledinosaurs.co.uk). Alexandra Palace rail. **Open** 9.30am-5.30pm Mon-Fri; 10am-5.30pm Sat; 10am-5pm Sun. **Admission** £3.50-£4.50; adults & under-1s free. **Credit** AmEx, MC, V.

Indoor adventure play centres are loved by kids and tolerated through gritted teeth by adults in a fix on a cold or rainy day. Little Dinosaurs is a thoroughly pleasant venue for all the family, whatever the weather. Inside is the usual playframe with slides, tunnels, mats and padded obstacles, but Little Dinosaurs has plenty of windows and it's also in the middle of a lovely park. On warmer days, the doors are thrown open to the air and guests can venture out into the grassy outdoor area (fenced off securely from the park), where there's a terrace with tables and chairs and toys to amuse smaller children, plus a bouncy castle. The café serves good coffee, children's and adults' meals and snacks. *Buggy access. Café. Children's menu. Disabled: toilet. High chairs. Nappy-changing facilities.*

Tumble in the Jungle

245 Wood Street, E17 3NT (0870 626 0710, www.tumbleinthejungle.co.uk). Walthamstow Central tube or Wood Street rail. **Open** 9.30am-6pm Mon, Wed-Fri; 10am-6pm Tue, Sat, Sun. **Admission** £3.50 (£2.50 before 11am); £1 adults; free under-1s. **No credit cards.**

Walthamstow's indoor play centre is designed on a jungle theme, with separate areas divided by age group. There's a soft play area for babies, a small playframe for toddlers to test their muscles on, and a larger frame for older kids to run riot around. Staff provide extra entertainment and activities from time to time; look out, too, for the water sensory room, the interactive dance mats and the sports arena. As these things go, Tumble in the Jungle's prices are pretty reasonable, and there's a café for the adults to escape to for a bit of peace and quiet. *Buggy access. Café. Children's menu. Disabled access: toilet. High chairs. Nappy-changing facilities.*

ARCHERY

Archery first developed as a sport during medieval times, but today bowmen fire arrows at the boss (target) at more than 150mph. The London 2012 competition will take place at Lord's cricket ground, but budding Robin Hoods can fire off a few arrows at the venues listed below.

2020 Archery

7515 4944, www.2020archery.co.uk.
2020 Archery is based at the T47 sports centre near London Bridge and runs a junior Young Archers club every Saturday morning for over-sevens (10-11.30am). Sessions cost £10 each. For more information, contact Aisha (youngarchers@live.co.uk).

Experience Archery

07961 870 170, www.experiencearchery.com.
This mobile, London-based outfit organises 90-minute 'have-a-go' sessions for complete beginners over eight (£25), along with birthday parties for over-sevens (max 10 children).

BADMINTON

Kids always love whacking a shuttlecock on the beach, and there are plenty of courts to carry on the fun in London.

David Lloyd Leisure

0844 543 9783, www.davidlloydleisure.co.uk.
There are several David Lloyd centres doted around the capital, and they are designed to be very family-friendly. The courts and equipment are generally excellent. Check out the website or phone for your nearest venue.

Michael Sobell Leisure Centre

Hornsey Road, N7 7NY (7609 2166, www.aquaterra.org). Finsbury Park tube/rail.
This leisure centre near the Holloway Road has up to 12 badminton courts to hire on a pay-and-play basis (£8-£12.50/55mins). There's also a

Activities

Saturday badminton clinic for youngsters (10am-noon, £4.50), featuring coaching and games. Players of all standards are welcome.

BOXING

Boxing London
Left Hook, Unit 1, 1 Martha Street, E1 2PX (07956 293768, www.boxinglondon.co.uk). Shadwell DLR.
The bags may be well punched, but the tuition with former super-middleweight contender Enzo Giordano is excellent and the atmosphere good-humoured. Kids are welcome from seven upwards with their parents, or from ten on their own. Classes (noon-1.30pm daily, 7-8.30pm Mon-Fri) cost £5 each plus £30 annual membership. A new space in north London is opening in 2011.

Islington Boxing Club
20 Hazellville Road, N19 3LP (07920 280230, www.islingtonboxingclub.org). Archway tube.
This friendly, down-to-earth boxing gym runs both recreational and academy sessions for under-16s. Membership fees are £20 per year and classes cost £3 per session.

CIRCUS SKILLS

Not perhaps a traditional sport, but you have to develop fitness, flexibility and physical skill to be any good at it.

Albert & Friends Instant Circus
8237 1170, www.albertandfriends instantcircus.co.uk.
Held at two west London venues, Albert's marvellous after-school and holiday circus workshops teach three to 16s skills such as juggling, diabolo, unicycling and stilt-walking – and how to assemble a human pyramid. Over-eights can attend aerial sessions and learn corde lisse, static trapeze and other daredevil feats.

Circolombia
Roundhouse, Chalk Farm Road, NW1 8EH (0844 482 8008, www.roundhouse.org.uk). Chalk Farm tube. **Admission** £2.
This youth circus troupe from Colombia holds drop-in Circus Skills classes for 14- to 19-year-olds. The programme is a mix of street dance, acrobatics and circus tricks, and the team will teach flips, jumps and tumbles as well as juggling, stilt walking and diabolo.

Circus Space
Coronet Street, N1 6HD (7729 9522, www. thecircusspace.co.uk). Old Street tube/rail.
Accompanied by their intrepid parents, under-eights can enrol for a term of Tiny Tops circus skills and games. The Sunday morning 'Circus Fusion and Circus Focus classes introduce eight-to 11-year-olds to acrobatics, juggling, static trapeze and more; once tutors think kids are ready, they can join the Big Tops. Gifted over-11s can try out for the London Youth Circus.

CLIMBING

Castle Climbing Centre
Green Lanes, N4 2HA (8211 7000, www.castle-climbing.co.uk). Manor House tube, bus 141 341.
This climbing centre is splendidly housed in an old Victorian pumping station. Classes for nine-to 14-year-olds are held on Monday and Tuesday, and during the holidays; over-14s may climb unsupervised, with parental permission, once they have passed an assessment. For private tuition, the Gecko Club (www.geckos. co.uk) is based here (£40/hr plus £12.50 admission). Call for details of the party service.

Mile End Climbing Wall
Haverfield Road, E3 5BE (8980 0289, www.mileendwall.org.uk). Mile End tube.
Eight- to 16-year-olds can attend beginner sessions on weekday evenings and Saturday and Sunday mornings at this popular east London wall. Action-packed birthday parties for over-sevens can be held here, and there's a busy summer holiday programme.

Swiss Cottage Climbing Wall
Swiss Cottage Leisure Centre, Adelaide Road, NW3 3NF (7974 2012, www.climb london.co.uk). Swiss Cottage tube.
This impressive leisure centre is home to a 14-metre wall and bouldering area, and offers a Junior Rock Club (7-16s) on weekday evenings and Sunday mornings, and Pebbles (4-7s) on Monday and Friday afternoons and Saturday mornings. Birthday parties can also be booked.

Westway Climbing Centre
1 Crowthorne Road, W10 6RP (8969 0992, www.westwaysportscentre.org.uk). Latimer Road tube.
There are 120 lines and 350 routes to explore at Westway's impressive climbing centre. The cheapest way to get on the wall is to queue up

for one of the drop-in sessions on Monday and Wednesday afternoons for five- to six-year-olds (4-5pm; £5.50), and seven- to 14-year-olds (4.30-6pm; £4.50), or the family session for over-fours on Sunday mornings (10-11.30am; £5.50 juniors, £10 parents). There are also bookable classes throughout the week, and birthday parties for over-fours can be held here too.

CRICKET

Kia Oval
Kennington, SE11 5SS (7820 5700, www. surreycricket.com). Oval tube. **Admission** *Surrey matches* £15-£96; £7.50-£48 under-16s. **Credit** MC, V.
Surrey's homely – but still Test-class – cricket ground in Kennington offers an admirable youth programme.

Lord's Cricket Ground
St John's Wood Road, NW8 8QN (7289 1300 Middlesex, www.middlesexccc.com/ 7432 1000 MCC, www.lords.org). St John's Wood tube, or bus 13, 46, 82, 113, 274. **Admission** *Middlesex matches* £15-£20; £5-£8.50 under-16s, reductions. **Credit** MC, V.
Even the youngest of fans will have heard of Lord's, the home ground of Middlesex and main ground for England. Tours allow visitors a glimpse behind the scenes and access to the Long Room, where a gallery depicts the great and good of the sport. Fans can also peek at the players' dressing rooms and the MCC Museum, where the Ashes urn is stored. For more details, *see p115*. Lord's is hosting the Olympic Games Archery competition during London 2012.

Playing cricket

Cricket is still associated with toffs – an image not helped by a sharp decline in cricket-playing in state schools. Various initiatives have been launched to raise the profile of the national summer sport.

In 1990, a group of volunteers formed Capital Kids Cricket (www.capitalkids cricket.co.uk) to promote cricket for children in the inner city; the website has a 'where to play' section.

Ken Barrington Cricket Centre
Brit Oval, Kennington, SE11 5SS (7820 5739, www.surreycricket.com). Oval tube.

MCC Indoor School
Lord's Cricket Ground, St John's Wood Road, NW8 8QN (7616 8612, www.lords. org/kids). St John's Wood tube or bus 13, 46, 82, 113, 274.

Middlesex County Cricket Club
East End Road, N3 2TA (8346 8020, www. middlesexccc.com). Finchley Central tube.

Cricket Coaching Excellence
www.coachingcricketexcellence.co.uk.
Based in Ealing, west London, Coaching Cricket Excellence is run by ex-Middlesex all-rounder Peter Wellings and offers a vast range of holiday courses, weekend nets, children's parties and academies for both softball and hardball practice. Winter courses take place at indoor sports centres in Ealing/Acton, while the summer courses take place outdoors in the handsome surroundings of Ealing Cricket Club.

CYCLING

British children still fall behind their continental peers when it comes to taking the bike to school. In Britain, 90 per cent own bikes, but fewer than three per cent cycle to school.

In 2008, the government pledged £55 million to train pupils to ride safely. Safe Routes to Schools supports projects that encourage cycling and walking to school, by improving street design, calming traffic and linking with the National Cycle Network. Most local authorities include Safe Routes to Schools schemes in their local transport plans. Sustrans (www.sustrans.org.uk) is the pressure group that is working to create a safer environment for cycling.

Check out Bike to School Week (www.bikeforall.net) and the London Cycling Campaign (www.lcc.org.uk).

Bikeability
www.bikeability.org.uk.
A nationwide scheme, designed to give young cyclists the skills and confidence to ride their bikes on the roads. Kids are encouraged to achieve three levels of cycling proficiency, and can begin learning the skills as soon as they start riding a bike.

Activities

A celebration of great sporting moments

My Sport Wheelchair Rugby
Matthew, 11

What inspired you to take up wheelchair rugby?
The fact that it's the best sport ever and I might get the opportunity to travel the world.

What do you like about your sport?
It's fun and exciting.

What level are you at?
I started about a year ago and I now do training practice twice a week.

What do you think is next for you in your sport?
I'll see how it goes.

Which events would you like to see at the London 2012 Olympic Games and Paralympic Games?
I don't know a lot about the Olympics. Perhaps I'll go along and see what happens. I'd like to see some of the Rugby events and also some of the Basketball matches.

Activities

Capital Sport – Gentle Cycling

01296 631671, www.capital-sport.co.uk.
Gentle cycling holidays and bike tours through London and along the River Thames. The Thames and Royalty Tour and day tours from London Bridge are ideal for families and take in palaces, royal parks and riverside cycling.

Cycle Training UK

7231 6005, www.cycletraining.co.uk.
Instructors offer individual tuition and accompanied journeys to school anywhere in Greater London. Of its participants, 81 per cent have said they cycle more often and more confidently. The website has details of London boroughs offering free or subsidised training.

Herne Hill Velodrome

Burbage Road, SE24 9HE (www.hernehill velodrome.com). Herne Hill rail.
Many south London children begin their cycling careers here at the venerable home of track cycling, founded in 1892 and still going strong. The VC Londres club was set up to encourage children on to bikes, and holds weekly Friday evening sessions.

London Recumbents

7498 6543 Battersea Park, 8299 6636 Dulwich Park, www.londonrecumbents.co.uk.
London Recumbents offers an enormous range of bikes for hire and sale at Dulwich and Battersea Parks. There are various trailer attachments, tandems and child seats to accommodate children, plus high-quality kids' bikes (including the low-lying, head-turning recumbent trikes, which kids adore).

London School of Cycling

7249 3779, www.londonschool ofcycling.co.uk.
The London School of Cycling offers private tuition for all ages and abilities, as well as cycle maintenance workshops for beginners with small class sizes.

DANCE

Dance is a great way to keep fit, and with the popularity of TV shows like *Strictly Come Dancing* and *Got to Dance*, it's a sport that is cloaked in glamour. London is a great place to get the best out of dance classes as it's full of talented teachers from an eclectic range of disciplines.

Discos & clubs

Start them early with toddler dance classes that are as fun for the adults as the kids. The following events take place at various venues across town; check online to find out where the next disco will be.

Baby Loves Disco

www.babylovesdisco.co.uk.
An import from the US, BLD is thriving on these shores. Sunday afternoon discos take place in a handful of venues, accompanied by choice 1970s and '80s tunes.

Planet Angel

www.planetangel.net.
Planet Angel's Sunday afternoon 'Chilled' gatherings have been running in north London since 2001. They aim to create a positive, safe, social environment for children of all ages.

Whirl-Y-Gig

www.whirl-y-gig.org.uk.
This long-established collective welcomes families to its events – they're a joyous mix of carnival and alternative clubbing, with some eclectic tunes. A favourite venue for events is Jacks (7-9 Crucifix Lane, SE1 3JW). Under-18s must be accompanied by a parent, and you have to call ahead.

Tuition

For all things dance-related in the capital, including children's classes for all abilities, visit www.londondance.com.

Amici Dance Theatre

Various venues around London (8964 5060, www.amicidance.org).
This organisation runs weekly dance and creative movement classes for all abilities and ages 7+ to adults on Wednesday evenings (7-9pm) at the Lyric Hammersmith. The sessions result in a touring show every two years and aim to integrate performers with and without disabilities. There's a long waiting list, but Amici also run occasional open workshops.

Barking and Dagenham Youth Dance

Abbey Sports Centre, Axe Street, Barking, Essex IG11 7NX (8270 8373, www.barking anddagenhamyouthdance.co.uk). Barking tube/ rail. Fees £3 per session. **No credit cards.**

Swimming Tips Rebecca Adlington

Where did you learn to swim and at what age?
I started learning to swim when I was four at Sherwood swimming pool in Mansfield, Nottingham. When I was 12, I joined the Nova Centurion swimming club in Nottingham.

Who was the biggest influence on you becoming an Olympic champion?
Bill Furniss, who has been my coach since I was 12. Bill recognised my potential and encouraged me through my teenage years up to Olympic gold. When I was younger, I didn't really have any heroes. Today, I respect and admire people like Chris Hoy.

What is the best way to learn to swim – with parents or at lessons?
Both have their benefits. It's great for parents to introduce their babies to the water at an early age and build their confidence in the water. However, lessons can help improve technique.

What is a good age to start?
As soon as possible. Introduce your baby to the water at an early age. Babies and children who have taken to swimming classes have been shown to do better in gripping, reaching and balance tests than those who haven't. Making water fun is really important, so splash and play with toys in the bath to help build up water confidence.

How would you encourage a child who is scared of water to learn to swim?
It's important to encourage your child to be adventurous in the water and the best way to do this is by making it fun! There is a wide range of games and toys, including dive rings and water balls, to get them excited about swimming.

What equipment is helpful to children learning to swim?
Kickboards are great for helping to develop breathing and kicking technique. There's a lot for kids to concentrate on when they first start learning. By using a kickboard, they have one less thing to worry about.

Rebecca Adlington is Ambassador of Speedo's Learn to Swim Initiative. For more details, visit the website at www.speedo.co.uk.

Activities

Weekly open street dance classes take place during term time. One-hour classes for six- to 11-year-olds are at noon, while 12- to 19-year-olds get a two-hour class from 1pm to 3pm. The current teacher is Claudimar Neto, finalist on *So You Think You Can Dance.*

Chisenhale Dance Space
64-84 Chisenhale Road, E3 5QZ (8981 6617, www.chisenhaledancespace.co.uk). Mile End tube. **Fees** £36 2-8s, £24 reductions; free 12-17s youth group. **Credit** MC, V.
This Bow-based dance studio offers creative dance courses for two to eights, plus a Saturday

youth group where 11 to 17s are taught a blend of street, contemporary, jazz and creative dance. Guest choreographers from other disciplines, from ballet to Bollywood, have been known to drop in to share their wisdom.

Coconut Grove
336 Ladbroke Grove, W10 5AH (8969 8371, www.coconutgrovestudios.com). Ladbroke Grove tube. **Fees** £180-£900/yr. **No credit cards.**
These sleek, light-filled studios are busy all day and evening with a varied timetable of classes. Babies and toddlers can try out Maestro Music,

where they're introduced to musical instruments and singing, or Jumping Jacks, which combines singing with movement. Classes for older children are divided by age (four to sevens; eight to 11s; 12 to 17s) and range from ballet and street dance to musical theatre dance.

Buggy access. Café. Children's menu. Nappy-changing facilities. Play area.

Dance Attic

368 North End Road, SW6 1LY (7610 2055, www.danceattic.com). Fulham Broadway tube. **Fees** £2/day; £40/6mths; £70/yr; £15/6 mths, £25/yr 13-16s. **Classes** £5-£7. *Children's ballet* £50-£62/11wk term. **Credit** MC, V.
Ballet classes for over-threes go up to intermediate level, with RAD exams at each grade. There's also a shop stocking leotards, ballet shoes and other dance essentials.
Shop.

Danceworks

16 Balderton Street, W1K 6TN (7629 6183, www.danceworks.net). Bond Street or Marble Arch tube. **Classes** times vary; phone for details. **Fees** *Membership* £2-£5/day; £80-£180/year. *Classes* £4-£11/class. **Credit** AmEx, MC, V.
Six studios occupy Danceworks' stately Victorian premises, offering a vast array of adults' classes. For kids (two to 18s), there's ballet, jazz and tap, plus drop-in street dance for 11 to 16s with the Impact Youth Academy.
Nappy-changing facilities.

Diddi Dance

07973 982790, www.diddidance.com.
Exuberant dance and movement classes for two to fours. Try a free taster sessions before committing to a four- or eight-week block. Themed birthday parties can also be arranged.

East London Dance

Various venues around east London (8279 1050, www.eastlondondance.org). **Classes** times vary; phone for details. **Fees** free-£1. **No credit cards**.
Brazilian samba, street dance and creative, contemporary styles are favoured by this creative community. Check out the upcoming programme of free On the Move dance classes for young people. Brink Open Company Dance is for 11 to 16s.

Funky Chicks Academy

Various venues around south London (8302 6992, www.funkychicksacademy.com).

Classes times vary; phone for details.
Fees £7-£10. **Credit** MC, V.
This all-female group of performers is taking the junior dance scene (over-threes) by storm. There are now six Funky Chicks Academies dotted around south London and Kent with classes ranging from street dance to funky ballet. Pupils begin by learning the steps to the tracks from the Funky Chicks' new album (www.funkychicks.co.uk), and every year there's a big stage production which gives everyone a chance to show off their moves.

Greenwich Dance Agency

Borough Hall, Royal Hill, SE10 8RE (8293 9741, www.greenwichdance.org.uk). *Greenwich rail.* **Classes** times vary; phone for details. **Fees** *Drop-in* £4 0-2s; £3 13-20s. *Courses* £40-£48/term 6-12s. **Credit** MC, V.
A packed programme has something for children of all ages, starting with relaxed drop-in classes for under-threes. At the other end of the spectrum, 13 to 20s can work with professional choreographers, fusing multiple styles and techniques. In all age groups, the focus is on creativity and having fun.
Buggy access. Disabled access: toilet. Nappy-changing facilities.

Impact Dance

Lime Door, Unit 9, 11 Plough Yard, EC2A 3LP (07500 115206, www.impact dance.co.uk). **Classes** 12.15-1.30pm Sat (12-19s); 2.30am-3.30pm Sat (7-11s); 1.30-2.30pm Sat (Creative training; 7-19s). **Fees** £5 per class; £4 creative training. **No credit cards.**
Impact Dance aims to teach street dance moves, while encouraging self-confidence, self-esteem and teamwork. Open training sessions take place on Saturday mornings and are split into two age groups – seven to 11s and 12 to 19s. Those that show flair and dedication might be picked by the teachers to join the Impact Dance Youth Company on Saturday afternoons, which leads to performance opportunities as well as more focused tuition.
Buggy access.

Laban

Creekside, SE8 3DZ (8691 8600, www.laban. org). Cutty Sark DLR or Deptford rail. **Classes & fees** vary; phone for details. **Credit** AmEx, MC, V.
Deptford is the slightly unlikely home to this stunning contemporary dance conservatoire, designed by Herzog & de Meuron. Children's movement, contemporary dance and ballet

Activities

lessons run throughout the week, though many have a sizeable waiting list. Once your child is in a class, however, the experience is fantastic; the annual Children's Show, presenting work by students aged four-14, showcases the kids' talents – and is packed with proud parents. *Buggy access. Disabled access: toilet. Café. Nappy-changing facilities.*

Pineapple Performing Arts School
7 Langley Street, WC2H 9JA (8351 8839, www.pineapplearts.com). Covent Garden tube. **Classes** *Drop-in* 1-2pm (under-13s), 2-3pm (12-16s) Sat; 1-2pm (12-16s), 2-3pm (under-13s) Sun. *Term classes* 11am-noon (3-4s), 11am-1pm (4-5s); 11am-2pm (5-12s), 2-5pm (13-17s) Sun. **Fees** £90/12wk term 3-4s; £295/12wk term over-4s; £6 drop-in session; £195 holiday course. *Trial class* £25. *Registration fee* £30-£35. **Credit** MC, V. **Map** p331 L6.
Drop-in musical, theatre, dance, ballet and street dance classes are held at these legendary Covent Garden studios every weekend; just turn up, hand over your £6 and dance. Those prepared to commit to 12-week terms can sign up for the lively Sunday School, comprising 'Pineapple Chunks' sessions for tinies, junior classes for kids and early teens, and senior classes for 13- to 17-year-olds. Intensive musical theatre and street dance courses are offered during the Easter and summer holidays. *Café.*

The Place
17 Duke's Road, WC1H 9PY (7121 1100 box office, 7121 1090 classes, www.theplace.org.uk). Euston tube/rail. **Classes** times vary; phone for details. **Fees** £90-£99/11wk term; £5 discount for 2nd or subsequent class taken by same student or a sibling. **Credit** MC, V. **Map** p331 K3.
The ethos at this contemporary dance hub is that anyone can learn to dance; the centre is accessible to all ages, as well as to the disabled. There is, however, a waiting list. A steady stream of parents and kids head here on Saturdays, when classes for five- to 18-year-olds range from playful, free-form First Moves sessions to contemporary dance. More unusually, there are choreography classes for children, and all-boys 'Energiser' sessions. Shift, a company for talented 13- to 19-year-old dancers, meets twice weekly during term time to perform work by a range of choreographers; hotly contested auditions are held in September. *Bar. Buggy access. Café. Disabled access: toilet.*

Royal Academy of Dance
36 Battersea Square, SW11 3RA (7326 8000, www.rad.org.uk). Clapham Junction rail or bus 170. **Classes** times vary; phone for details. **Fees** £6.50-£12.50/class; £65-£150/term. **Credit** AmEx, MC, V.
The Academy's studios are a hotbed for all sorts of dance styles. Popular classes include West End jazz, tap and contemporary, with various offerings for different age groups and abilities. The ballet department accepts pupils of three and above, and there are all-boys' ballet lessons for six to nines and eight to 11s. Summer schools and workshops keep dance-mad children busy during school holidays. *Buggy access.*

PARALYMPIC SPORT

The London 2012 Paralympic Games will see the largest ever team of British Paralympians take on the world's best in front of a home crowd. The 11 days of competition will see almost 4,200 athletes battling it out across 20 sports in 15 different venues. Such exposure is great news for Paralympic sport in general, and many mainstream sports clubs are now offering classes specifically tailored towards disabled people in everything from tennis to sailing. The Parasport website (www.parasport.org.uk), a joint initiative between the British Paralympic Association (BPA) and Deloitte, allows users to search a comprehensive database of clubs.

FENCING

Central London Fencing Club
Ground Floor Gym, Greycoat Hospital School, St Michael's Building, 98 Regency Street, SW1P 4GH (07765 181659, www.centrallondonfencingclub.com). Pimlico tube.
This club welcomes over-fives to learn fencing at its weekly children's sessions, held on Wednesdays (6.30-7.30pm). Children learn how to hold a weapon, footwork, bladework, how to attack, how to defend, fencing tactics and international rules. All fencing equipment is provided initially. The monthly fee for the classes is £38 per child.

Activities

Little Kickers.

Activities

Fencing Academy

Seymour Leisure Centre, Seymour Place, W1H 5TJ (07779 123715, www.musketeers club.co.uk). Edgware Road tube.

The Musketeers' Club, the Fencing Academy's club for young Zorros, runs weekly Friday evening sessions for 6-7s (Mini Musketeers), 8-9s and 10-12s. Fees are approx £55 per month for over-eights, but there is an introductory four-session beginner course (£45) too.

FOOTBALL

Playing football

Boys and girls over six can learn football skills on coaching courses, fun days and clinics at all of London's professional clubs, staffed by FA-qualified coaches. For venues and dates, check the club websites (details are generally listed on the 'Community' pages).

Football Academy

Langston Road, Loughton, Essex IG10 3TQ (8502 8950, www.footballacademyuk.com). Debden tube.

This centre has ten all-weather, floodlit, five-a-side pitches for hire. Holiday and weekend sessions are led by FA-qualified coaches under the guidance of former West Ham player Kenny Brown and other ex-professionals.

Goals Soccer Centres

www.goalsfootball.co.uk.

There are 12 of these centres in London. Each has all-weather, floodlit pitches with junior leagues, birthday parties and coaching at weekends and school holidays.

Lambeth Dribblers

8835 9570.

Part-funded by Chelsea, this project provides free coaching for young children on the astroturf at Brixton Recreation Centre, while enabling enthusiastic dads (it's specifically aimed at fathers, not mothers) to have an enjoyable kickaround with their kids.

Little Foxes

7376 0006, www.thelittlefoxesclub.com.

These very popular training sessions take place at a number of west London parks and indoor centres, and usually feature some skills training followed by a 'proper' game. Coaches are enthusiastic and engaging, and kids can enrol at 18 months to 12 years, with groups divided into petite, tiny, cheeky and super.

Little Kickers

01235 859250, www.littlekickers.co.uk.

Hugely popular classes developed by a group of FA-qualified coaches and nursery-school teachers for pre-schoolers (18 months and up) as a gentle introduction to football. The programme operates all over London.

London Football Academy

8882 9100, www.londonfootball academy.co.uk.

Holiday courses, skill schools, birthday parties and inexpensive Saturday morning soccer school sessions in Alexandra Park.

Peter Hucker Soccer

8536 4141, www.peterhucker-soccer.com.

Former Queens Park Rangers goalkeeper Peter Hucker runs this highly rated scheme. Based in Barking and Wanstead, this organisation offers weekly pay-and-play coaching sessions, and matchplay. It can also arrange footballing parties for five- to 16-year-olds. Hucker was also responsible for founding the East London & Essex Small-Sided Soccer League (07961 867501, 01375 650833, www.eleleague.com).

Powerleague

www.powerleague.co.uk.

There are 13 Powerleague centres dotted around the capital, each providing all-weather, floodlit pitches. Most centres offer coaching, mini matches at weekends and during the school holidays, as well as junior leagues. You can also book a pitch for a birthday party.

Sharpshooters Football

07873 583366, www.sharpshooters football.co.uk.

Tooting Bec Common and other venues in south-west London host Sunday pay-and-play sessions for four- to 11-year-olds, plus holiday courses and footie-themed birthday parties. Talented youngsters can join 'Sharp Shooter Select' sessions.

South East London & Kent Youth Football League

www.selkent.org.uk.

Leagues for young players, from mini soccer for under-sevens to 11-a-sides for under-16s. The website includes a useful 'players wanted' page, including a section on girls' football teams.

Activities

South London Special League
8319 8111, www.sl-sl.co.uk.
This league helps players with special needs to participate in football. The London FA website (www.londonfa.com) has an extensive section devoted to opportunities for children with physical and learning disabilities, and many of the community programmes run by London's professional clubs cater for special needs.

Watching football

The football season runs from August to May, and club websites include regularly updated ticket information. Ticket prices and membership packages are far too numerous to list for each club; as a rule, Premier League match seats are £30-£60 for an adult, but are reduced by up to half for kids and members (if discounts are offered) for some cup fixtures. Coca-Cola Championship and Coca-Cola League prices are around £15-£40, with reductions for children and members.

Wembley Stadium
Wembley, HA9 0WS (0844 980 8801, www.wembleystadium.com). Wembley Park tube or Wembley Central tube/rail, or Wembley Stadium rail.
Wembley Stadium is a cracking ground that's built on an epic scale; the top tier is up in the clouds and the overhead arch is a suitably iconic replacement for the famous twin towers. You can also take excellent tours of the stadium that explore everything from the press box to the tunnel. The tours end in the royal box, where fans get to brandish a battered FA Cup to the piped cheers of the crowd. Wembley may be grand, but it can be surprisingly easy to procure a ticket for less distinguished fixtures.

Barclays Premier League

Arsenal
Emirates Stadium, Ashburton Grove, N7 7AF (7619 5000, www.arsenal.com). Arsenal or Holloway Road tube.
For the club's museum, *see p114.*

Chelsea
Stamford Bridge, Fulham Road, SW6 1HS (0871 984 1955, www.chelseafc.com). Fulham Broadway tube.
For the club's museum, *see p115.*

Fulham
Craven Cottage, Stevenage Road, SW6 6HH (0870 442 1222, www.fulhamfc.com). Putney Bridge tube.
Stadium tours are available.

Tottenham Hotspur
White Hart Lane, Bill Nicholson Way, 748 High Road, N17 0AP (0844 844 0102, www.spurs.co.uk). White Hart Lane rail.
Tours 11.30am, 2pm Mon-Fri; 10am, noon, 2pm non-match Sats. **Admission** *Tours* £15; £8 under-16s, reductions. **Credit** MC, V.
Book in advance for tours of pitchside, tunnel, changing rooms, boardroom and press room. Don't turn up on spec, as they don't always run.

West Ham United
Boleyn Ground, Green Street, E13 9AZ (0871 222 2700, www.whufc.com). Upton Park tube.
Tours take place during school holidays, for which you must book in advance.

Coca-Cola Championship

Crystal Palace
Selhurst Park, Whitehorse Lane, SE25 6PU (8768 6000, www.cpfc.co.uk). Selhurst rail.

Queens Park Rangers
Loftus Road, South Africa Road, W12 7PA (08444 777 0777, www.qpr.co.uk). White City tube.

Watford
Vicarage Road, Watford, Herts WD18 0ER (0844 856 1881, www.watfordfc.com). Watford High Street rail.

Coca-Cola League

Barnet
Underhill Stadium, Barnet Lane, Herts, EN5 2DN (8441 6932, www.barnetfc.com). High Barnet tube.

Brentford
Griffin Park, Braemar Road, Brentford, Middx TW8 0NT (0845 345 6442, www.brentfordfc.premiumtv.co.uk). Brentford rail.

Charlton Athletic
The Valley, Floyd Road, SE7 8BL (0871 226 1905, www.charlton-athletic.co.uk). Charlton rail.

My London 2012
Bonnita, 19

How will you be participating in the London 2012 Olympic Games and Paralympic Games?
I hope to be working in catering onsite during the Games.

How did you come to be involved?
I was studying at my community college and I was recommended because I work hard.

Tell us about what you have been working on as part of the Young Ambassadors Programme?
I went over to the Vancouver Winter Olympics with two others from my college to volunteer – we cooked for local celebrities and others at Games-related shows and events, and we won a teamwork award.

What do you hope your involvement in London 2012 will inspire you to achieve after the Games have finished?
I want to set up my own catering business and bring more young people into catering. I'm working in a children's play centre at the moment, but I'm looking at business plans.

Which events would you like to see during London 2012?
During London 2012 I'd like to see the Opening Ceremony and some of the Swimming events.

Activities

Central London Junior Golf Academy.

Leyton Orient
Matchroom Stadium, Brisbane Road,
E10 5NE (0871 310 1881, www.leyton
orient.com). Leyton tube.

Millwall
The Den, Zampa Road, SE16 3LN (7232
1222, www.millwallfc.co.uk). South
Bermondsey rail or Surrey Quays tube.

GOLF

Golf isn't the easiest sport for kids to pick
up, so the English Golf Union (*see p175*)
has developed Tri-Golf for six- to 12-
year-olds, and is introducing the game

in primary schools. Discover the basics
at one of London's driving ranges. The
TopGolf system (www.topgolf.co.uk) is
a point-scoring game using balls with a
microchip inside. TopGolf is played at
its centres in Addlestone (01932 858551),
Chigwell (8500 2644) and Watford
(01923 222045).

Central London Junior Golf Academy
Burntwood Lane, SW17 0AT (8871 2468,
www.clgc.co.uk). Tooting Bec tube or
Earlsfield rail, or bus G1.
Junior membership of the academy (£35 annual
fee) gets children priority booking and a
discount on after-school sessions (£85 with
discount for an eight-week course) and Easter
and Summer camps (£175 per week with
discount for six- to eight-year-olds; £225 per
week with discount for nine to 16s). Individual
lessons are £20/30min and £40/hr.

Duke's Meadows
Dan Mason Drive, W4 2SH (8994 3314,
www.dukesmeadows.com). Hammermith
tube, then 190 bus.
This nine-hole pay-and-play course on the
banks of the Thames at Chiswick operates one-
hour after-school and weekend coaching
sessions (Wed, Sat, Sun) for over-fours (£80 for
a six-week course), along with full-day holiday
camps, with all equipment supplied. Individual
lessons are £22/30mins. It costs £13.50 to play
a round at weekends, £10 on weekdays.

Urban Golf
Kensington Shopping Mall, 125 Kensington
High Street, W8 5SF (7248 8600,
www.urbangolf.co.uk). High Street
Kensington tube.
If you fancy a round of golf without having to
leave the city, then Urban Golf operates three
indoor golf venues kitted out with state-of-
the-art simulators loaded with 52 of the world's
most famous courses. At the Kensington
branch, six- to 12-year-olds can join a four-week
course (£80, 10-11am, 11am-noon Sun) to grasp
the fundamentals of the game, with all
equipment supplied.

GYMNASTICS

BackFlip Performers
Venues throughout London (8940 7998,
www.backflipperformers.com).

BackFlip Performers was launched by five-time British aerobics gymnastics champion Katie Cannon in 2008. Groups are divided into Little Flippers (2-4s), Flippers (4-6s) and BackFlippers (7-12s), and as they move up, kids will master everything from handstands to backflips. There are also loads of week-long camps on offer that end in a performance for parents.

Governing Bodies

Amateur Boxing Association of England
0114 223 5654, www.abae.co.uk

British Rowing
8237 6700, www.britishrowing.org

British Swimming
01509 618700, www.swimming.org

Badminton England
01908 268400,
www.badmintonengland.co.uk

BaseballSoftballUK
7453 7055, www.baseballsoftballuk.com

British Canoe Union
0845 370 9500, www.bcu.org.uk

British Dragon Boat Racing Association
www.dragonboat.org.uk

British Fencing Association
8742 3032, www.britishfencing.com

British Gymnastics
0845 129 7129, www.british-gymnastics.org

British Mountaineering Council
0161 445 6111, www.thebmc.co.uk

British Orienteering Federation
01629 734042,
www.britishorienteering.org.uk

British Tenpin Bowling Association
8478 1745, www.btba.org.uk

British Waterski
01932 560007, www.britishwaterski.org.uk

England Squash & Racketball
0161 231 4499,
www.englandsquash.com

England & Wales Cricket Board
www.ecb.co.uk

England Basketball
0114 284 1060,
www.englandbasketball.co.uk

English Golf Union
01526 354500,
www.englishgolfunion.org

English Table Tennis Association
01424 722525,
www.englishtabletennis.org.uk

Football Association
7745 4545, www.thefa.com

Interactive
7717 1699, www.interactive.uk.net

Lawn Tennis Association
8487 7000, www.lta.org.uk

London Baseball
www.londonsports.com/baseball

London Windsurfing Association
01895 846707,
www.lwawindsurfing.co.uk

National Ice Skating Association
0115 988 8060, www.iceskating.org.uk

Royal Yachting Association
0845 345 0400, www.rya.org.uk

Rugby Football Union
0871 222 2120, www.rfu.com

Ski Club of Great Britain
8410 2000, www.skiclub.co.uk

Wheelpower
01296 395995, www.wheelpower.org.uk
The umbrella body for 17 wheelchair sports, from archery to rugby.

Activities

Activities

The Little Gym

Venues throughout London,
www.thelittlegym.co.uk.
The first Little Gym opened in 1976, and since then it has expanded into a global enterprise. All ages are covered, from parent/child classes at four months up to primary gymnastics (6-12s), when the mat, vault, bar and beam all start to make an appearance. Birthday parties can be arranged at the weekends, while themed holiday camps cover any remaining spare time.

KARTING & MOTOR SPORTS

Karts exceed speeds of 30mph (50kph) and are suitable for over-eights: there are two pedals (stop and go) and no gearbox. These venues welcome children and can be booked for parties.

Brands Hatch

Fawkham, Longfield, Kent DA3 8NG
(01474 872331, www.motorsport
vision.co.uk). Swanley rail, then taxi.
The biggest motor racing venue in the area, Brands Hatch has loads of things to do on two and four wheels, including YoungDrive!, which puts over-13s in control of a BMW 1 series.

Playscape Racing

390 Streatham High Road, SW16 6HX
(8677 8677, www.playscape.co.uk).
Streatham rail.
Bookable for children's parties (over-eights only) or half-hour taster sessions. Enthusiasts can join the Kids' Racing Academy, on the first Saturday of each month (8.30am-1pm, £40).

MARTIAL ARTS

Training in martial arts imparts body awareness, assertiveness and resilience. Most local sports centres will be home to at least one martial arts club; many more are based in church halls and community centres. Try to find a club with a lively but disciplined atmosphere, and well-organised and age-appropriate teaching. Ask instructors about their qualifications: the grading systems in judo and karate, for example, help ensure teachers are of a suitable standard. Note, however, that a black belt is not a teaching qualification. Ask for proof of insurance cover: martial arts usually involve physical contact, and accidents can happen.

Budokwai

4 Gilston Road, SW10 9SL (7370 1000,
www.budokwai.co.uk). South Kensington tube.
The Budokwai was founded in 1918 and is one of the oldest martial arts clubs in Europe. Based in South Kensington, the club offers judo classes for five-year-olds and upwards, with karate starting from the age of six.

Hwarang Academy

Swiss Cottage Community Centre, 19
Winchester Road, NW3 3NR (0845 094
3978, www.taekwondo-london-2012.com).
Swiss Cottage tube.
Tae kwon do, a Korean martial art, is now an Olympic sport. These classes are for four-year-olds and upwards.

London School of Capoeira

Units 1 & 2, Leeds Place, Tollington Park,
N4 3RF (7281 2020, www.londonschool
ofcapoeira.co.uk). Finsbury Park tube/rail.
Capoeira is a Brazilian martial art, combining acrobatics, music and dance, in which creative play is a strong element. Classes at the London School of Capoeira are for six- to 16-year-olds, and are suitable for complete beginners.

Moving East

St Matthias Church Hall, Wordsworth Road,
N16 8DD (7503 3101, www.movingeast.
co.uk). Dalston Kingsland rail.
Judo and aikido (as well as dance and capoeira) classes for children are held at this friendly centre devoted to Japanese martial arts.

Shaolin Temple UK

207A Junction Road, N19 5QA (7687 8333,
www.shaolintempleuk.org). Tufnell Park tube.
Shi Yanzi, a 34th generation fighting monk, and other Shaolin masters teach traditional kung fu, Chinese kick-boxing, meditation and t'ai chi at this temple. Weekly classes for children (fives and above) are also offered.

PARKOUR

Also known as free-running, the sport is best seen as a sort of urban ballet in which practitioners use the furniture of

My Sport Swimming
Flora, 6

What inspired you to take up swimming?
I wanted to learn how to swim so that I could go underwater.

What do you like about your sport?
I like my teacher a lot and I like being able to swim from one side of a pool to the other without touching the floor.

What level are you at?
I'm at level 2B – I've just moved up a class.

What's next for you in your sport?
I want to learn how to jump into the pool without getting water up my nose and how to swim underwater with my eyes open.

Which events would you like to see at the London 2012 Olympic Games and Paralympic Games?
I'd really love to see any of the Equestrian, Gymnastics and Swimming events.

Activities

the street – bollards, rooftops, railings etc – to get themselves from place to place as gracefully and athletically as possible.

Parkour Generations

07825 410134, www.parkour generations.com.
Information on classes, coaching and events.

RIDING

Riding is one of the most rewarding sports going (as well as one of the most expensive). Greater London is full of riding stables, some in unexpected places: the Isle of Dogs and Catford both boast their very own riding schools. The back of a horse is a great vantage point from which to view London's stunning greenery, from **Richmond Park** (*see p144*) to **Epping Forest** (*see p146*). If you ring in advance, some places will happily let you watch a lesson; ask the stables if they run taster sessions.

Riders must wear a BSI-approved hard hat (establishments usually lend or rent) and boots with a small heel rather than trainers or wellies. Lessons must be booked in advance. **Decathlon** (*see p280*) is a great place for buying inexpensive equipment and clothes. Some centres run 'Own a Pony' days and weeks, and offer birthday party packages. Many stables can cater easily for riders with disabilities, though not all have equipment to winch riders on to horses or ponies. All the establishments listed below are British Horse Society-approved (www.bhs.org.uk); it is not advisable to ride at non BHS-approved centres.

Deen City Farm & Riding School

39 Windsor Avenue, SW19 2RR (8543 5858, www.deencityfarm.co.uk). Colliers Wood tube, then 20min walk, or Phipps Bridge tramlink, or bus 200. **Lessons** *Group £20-£22/45min. Individual £21/30min.*
Lessons for children aged eight and over in flatwork and jumping (there's no hacking), from beginner to advanced. Over-12s can volunteer

at the yard at weekends and in school holidays. 'Own a Pony' days for eight- to 16s cost a mere £20 per day (without ride) or £30 (with ride), and competitions are held throughout the year. The school is a Pony Club Centre, and approved by the Riding for the Disabled Association.

Ealing Riding School

17-19 Gunnersbury Avenue, W5 3XD (8992 3808, www.ealingridingschool.biz). Ealing Common tube. **Lessons** *Group £27/hr. Individual £36/hr.*
Under-fives can learn beginner's or improver's skills in flatwork or jumping; lessons take place in an outdoor manège. Pony days (£60), held in the school holidays, include two hours of lessons and four hours learning stable management and essential skills such as mucking out and grooming.

Hyde Park & Kensington Stables

63 Bathurst Mews, W2 2SB (7723 2813, www.hydeparkstables.com). Lancaster Gate tube. **Lessons** *Group £59/hr. Individual £89-£99/hr.*
Hour-long lessons for children aged five and up with patient, streetwise ponies; prices reflect the glamorous location. The stables is a Pony Club Centre (£22 annual fee) with a membership of around 50 children.

Kingston Riding Centre

38 Crescent Road, Kingston-upon-Thames, Surrey KT2 7RG (8546 6361, www.kingstonridingcentre.com). Richmond tube/rail, then bus 371, or Norbiton rail then 10min walk. **Lessons** *Group £39-£41/hr. Individual £60-£78/hr.*
There are 25 horses at this well-equipped yard, which caters to all levels of riders. Richmond Park is used for hacks, and the owners organise regular events, competitions and popular courses for children aged eight and up (£168 for four days). The centre's facilities include a floodlit indoor school, an outdoor arena and, in summer months, a cross-country course. Closed on Mondays.

Lee Valley Riding Centre

71 Lea Bridge Road, E10 7QL (8556 2629, www.leevalleypark.org.uk). Clapton rail or bus 48, 55, 56. **Lessons** *Group £19/hr. Individual £35-£40/30min, £48-£53/45min. Taster session £10-£13/30min.*
The friendly Lee Valley Riding Centre offers placid ponies on which to enjoy the wide open spaces of Walthamstow Marshes. The superb

facilities include one indoor and two floodlit outdoor arenas; experienced riders can tackle the cross-country course. Children aged from three-and-a-half can book in for private lessons, while over-fours can participate in group lessons. Over-tens with some riding and pony-handling experience can become stable helpers, and there are also 'Own a Pony' sessions in the school holidays.

London Equestrian Centre

Lullington Garth, N12 7BP (8349 1345, www.londonridingschool.com). Mill Hill East tube. **Lessons** *Group £28/hr. Individual £26-£32/30min.*

There are 30 horses and ponies at this yard, which caters for riders of all abilities; there's even a Tiny Tots session for three-year-olds. The centre is affiliated to the Pony Club, and runs pony days and weeks in school holidays. Birthday parties are held here, and young people aged from 13 can help out at the yard in return for free rides.

Mount Mascal Stables

Vicarage Road, Bexley, Kent DA5 2AW (8300 3947, www.mountmascalstables.com). Bexley rail. **Lessons** *Group £18/50min. Individual £26/50min.*

Down in south London, this busy centre is home to 40 horses and ponies, and gives lessons to over-fives. Children's fun days (£35; for riders six years and above with some experience) allow kids to practise riding, experience stable management and play a variety of games. The centre features two indoor schools, two outdoor grass arenas and two outdoor all-weather manèges. More experienced riders can hack out in the stunning Joyden's Wood. Birthday parties for six to 12 kids can be arranged during weekends or school holidays.

Mudchute Equestrian Centre

Mudchute Park & Farm, Pier Street, E14 3HP (7515 0749, www.mudchute.org). Mudchute, Crossharbour or Island Gardens DLR, or bus D3, D6, D7, D8. **Lessons** *Group £16-£19/hr. Individual £30-£40/45min.*

This hugely popular riding school at the Mudchute City Farm *(see p155)* on the Isle of Dogs is friendly, down-to-earth and very welcoming to new riders. Lessons are some of the most reasonably priced in London, and are open to children over seven. It's a Pony Club Centre, enabling local kids who don't own a pony to study for badges and certificates, and to participate in related activities during the school holidays (gymkhanas, dressage competitions and so on).

Ross Nye's Riding Stables

8 Bathurst Mews, W2 2SB (7262 3791, www.rossnyestables.co.uk). Lancaster Gate tube. **Lessons** *Group £50/hr. Individual £60/hr.*

At the posher end of the spectrum, this stables forms the Hyde Park branch of the Pony Club; membership gives reduced prices for lessons, which take place in the park. Clients aged from six can learn to ride here.

Stag Lodge Stables

Robin Hood Gate, Richmond Park, SW15 3RS (8974 6066, www.ridinginlondon. com). East Putney tube or Putney rail, then bus 85, or Kingston rail then bus 85. **Lessons** *Group £35/hr. Individual £30/30min, £45-£60/hr.*

There are 40 or so horses and ponies (ranging from Shetlands to Irish hunters) at this stables in historic Richmond Park. Three to sevens can enjoy half-hour leading rein rides through the park (£20-£25); jumping or flatwork lessons for all abilities take place in one of two outdoor manèges. There are pony weeks for the over-sixes in school holidays and half term (£275 for four days) – book well ahead.

Trent Park Equestrian Centre

Bramley Road, N14 4UW (8363 8630, www.trentpark.com). Oakwood tube. **Lessons** *Group £25-£33/hr. Individual £38-£42/hr.*

A caring attitude towards young riders (fours and over) and this equestrian centre's location make it a popular place to ride. Hacking is £30 per hour, Pony Days are £65 and four-day riding weeks (£240) are held in the school holidays.

Willowtree Riding Establishment

The Stables, Ronver Road, SE12 0NL (8857 6438, www.willowtreeridinglondon.co.uk). Grove Park or Lee rail. **Lessons** *Group from £10/30min, £20/hr. Individual from £35/45min, £40/hr.*

The Welsh ponies are particularly popular at this friendly yard, where children over four can learn to ride. Young and nervous riders are welcome. Lessons (flatwork only) take place in a covered, full-size indoor arena. Most teaching is at weekends and in the holidays.

Activities

Capital Growth

The legacy of London 2012 will be felt across many of London's 32 boroughs. Here are just some of the exciting planned and completed sporting projects.

Barking & Dagenham

The £9 million Mayesbrook Park Handball Centre will be completed in January 2012 and will become the home of British Handball after the Olympic and Paralympic Games. It will be a Games Time Training Venue for Handball, Wheelchair Rugby and Paralympic Judo. The brand new Becontree Heath Leisure Centre opened in May 2011.

Enfield

Enfield is spending £8.9 million upgrading its leisure centres. This will provide better gym facilities and swimming, more all-purpose games pitches and programmes to suit all ages and abilities. The Queen Elizabeth Athletics Stadium is being brought back into use with a relaid track and a refurbished stadium building.

Greenwich

Greenwich Council's £4.8 million Olympic Legacy project is called 'Playground to Podium' and the improvements so far include 15 new outdoor gym sites at parks across the borough, 23 new or completely refurbished playgrounds in parks and open spaces, and many new pitches, courts and training areas for a variety of sports. The borough is also bidding for funding to create a BMX racing track at Hornfair Park, refurbish Charlton Lido and create a 50-metre heated pool, as well as develop an equestrian training centre to provide a riding facility for the local community.

Hillingdon

Boris Johnson recently opened the new £31 million Hillingdon Sports & Leisure Complex (the 1930s lido on site was restored into the bargain). Hillingdon Borough also opened the brand new Botwell Green Sports & Leisure Centre in Hayes in 2010.

Islington

Work is underway to refurbish the Ironmonger Row Baths in EC1 by 2012. Islington is also investing £1.5 million in refurbishing the Sobell Sports Centre.

Lewisham

Lewisham is currently building a brand new leisure facility at Loampit Vale that will house a state-of-the-art 25-metre swimming pool, fitness suite and indoor climbing wall. In 2008, a new 25-metre swimming pool was installed at the Wavelengths centre in Deptford. Works also included a refurbished gym, health suite and fitness centre. The Victorian Forest Hill Pools is set to reopen in September 2012 after a five-year closure. The new leisure centre will include a 25-metre pool, a 16.7-metre learner pool, gym, studios, community room and café. The Ladywell Arena running and athletics track was also recently refurbished.

Sutton

Westcroft Leisure Centre in Carshalton is set to receive a £10.8 million refurbishment that will create a new eight-lane 25-metre competition-standard swimming pool, a bigger teaching pool, a new sports hall, six massage and treatment rooms, two dance studios and a gym with 170 workout stations. The building will also house a crèche, café, IT facilities and new library.

Wimbledon Village Stables

24A-B High Street, SW19 5DX (8946 8579, www.wvstables.com). Wimbledon tube/rail.
Lessons £55-£80/hr.
Although it caters mainly for adults, children are welcome at this centre, which has a small selection of quiet, safe ponies and a holiday scheme for five- to ten-year-olds (£170 for three afternoons). Riding takes place on Wimbledon Common, where the centre has two outdoor arenas for flatwork and jumping lessons. Riders must become members to ride regularly.

RUGBY UNION

A bargain compared to football. All the London clubs feature top players, and there's never any problem getting hold of tickets. The rugby season runs from September to May. Several of these clubs also have mini rugby leagues; contact the individual clubs for more information.

Guinness Premiership

Harlequins
Twickenham Stoop Stadium, Langhorn Drive, Twickenham, Middx TW2 7SX (8410 6000, www.quins.co.uk). Twickenham rail. **Admission** £20-£40; £10-£40 2-16s.

Saracens
Vicarage Road, Watford, Herts WD18 0EP (01727 792800, www.saracens.com). Watford High Street rail. **Admission** £13.50-£60; £4.50-£15 2-16s.

National League

London Welsh
Old Deer Park, Kew Road, Richmond, Surrey TW9 2AZ (8940 2368, www.london-welsh. co.uk). Richmond tube/rail. **Admission** £15; £10 reductions; free under-16s.

Playing rugby

Little Foxes
7376 0006, www.thelittlefoxesclub.com. Although centred on football coaching, this well-managed company also runs weekend tag rugby sessions for over-fours (12-1pm Sat) in Hyde Park. There are two groups available – Cheeky Foxes (5-6yrs) and Super Foxes (7+).

Rugbytots
0845 313 3242, www.rugbytots.co.uk. Rugbytots uses skills such as running with the ball, finding space, kicking, catching and scoring a try to encourage youngsters to develop core skills like balance, agility and co-ordination. The age range for the sessions is two to seven.

SKATEBOARDING & BMX

Just as popular now as they were in the 1970s, skateboarding and BMX mean getting fit and making friends. For details of festivals and special events look at the Skateboarders Association website (www.ukskate.org.uk). BMX became an Olympic sport in 2003 – check the website of the governing body of British cycling (www.britishcycling. org.uk) for news.

BaySixty6 Skate Park
Bay 65-66, Acklam Road, W10 5YU (8969 4669, www.baysixty6.com). Ladbroke Grove tube. **Membership** free. **Prices** £6/5hrs Mon-Fri; £6/4hrs Sat, Sun; £3 beginners 10am-noon Sat, Sun.
This famous park sprawls beneath the Westway and includes a vert ramp, medium half-pipe, mini ramp and funboxes, grind boxes, ledges and rails aplenty. Some skaters complain about the £6 entry fee, but the high quality of the ramps goes some way to making up for it.

Cantelowes Skatepark
Cantelowes Gardens, Camden Road, NW1 (www.cantelowesskatepark.co.uk). Kentish Town tube/rail or Camden Road rail. **Open** 11am-9pm daily.
After a £1.5m makeover, this free skatepark on Camden Road reopened in 2007 and draws a devoted crowd of regulars. It has hosted qualifying rounds for Quiksilver's Bowlriders championship for the last two years.

Harrow Skatepark
Christchurch Avenue, Wealdstone, Middx HA3 5BD. Harrow & Wealdstone tube/rail. This skatepark has a clover leaf, kidney bowls and a challenging concrete half-pipe.

Meanwhile
Meanwhile Gardens, off Great Western Road, W10 (www.mgca.f2s.com). Westbourne Park tube. Close to the Grand Union Canal, this community garden's skatepark features three concrete bowls of varying steepness and size, but no flatland – not for wobbly beginners.

SKATING

On ice

Temporary rinks pop up all over town in winter time inside museums, galleries, parks and shopping centres.

Activities

Alexandra Palace Ice Rink

Alexandra Palace Way, N22 7AY (8365 4386, www.alexandrapalace.com). Wood Green tube or Alexandra Palace rail, or bus W3.

This lofty recently refurbished arena runs courses for children aged five to 15 on Saturday mornings and early on weekday evenings.

Broadgate Ice Arena

Broadgate Circle, EC2A 2BQ (7505 4000 Summer, 7505 4068 Winter, www.broadgateice.co.uk). Liverpool Street tube/rail.

A compact, City-based rink open from mid November until late January, which is very child-friendly. It's often less crowded than the capital's other outdoor rinks.

Lee Valley Ice Centre

Lea Bridge Road, E10 7QL (8533 3154, www.leevalleypark.org.uk). Clapton rail.

Disco nights are a big hit at this modern, well-maintained and comparatively warm rink. It's never too busy, and the ice rink is a good size. Lessons are also offered.

Michael Sobell Leisure Centre

Hornsey Road, N7 7NY (7609 2166, www.aquaterra.org). Finsbury Park tube/rail.

This small ice rink was closed as we went to press, as contractors tried to solve a major fault with the rink. Check with the centre for details of its reopening date. The rink usually hosts well-attended after-school sessions and six-week courses for children. Anyone over four is welcome; children can have ice-skating birthday parties here too, with all the necessary equipment provided. The leisure centre also offers ice hockey sessions for the over-sixes.

Queens

17 Queensway, W2 4QP (7229 0172, www.queensiceandbowl.co.uk). Bayswater or Queensway tube.

Beginners and families are well looked after at this ice rink, which holds legendary disco nights on Fridays and Saturdays. Children's lessons cost £65 for a six-week course. Hot Belgian waffles in the café are a big hit with kids. There's also a 12-lane tenpin bowling centre *(see p189)*.

Somerset House

Strand, WC2R 1LA (7845 4600, www.somersethouse.org.uk). Holborn or Temple tube.

The magnificent courtyard at Somerset House is probably London's most iconic temporary rink when it is iced over from late November to late January. Enjoy a skating session before embarking on an improving interlude in the art galleries *(see p84)*.

Streatham Ice Arena

386 Streatham High Road, SW16 6HT (8769 7771, www.streathamicearena.com). Streatham rail.

A hugely popular venue that offers the combined attractions of an ice rink and karting track (Playscape, *see p176*). Locals have campaigned for improvements, with particular concern for the future of the rink (Streatham has had one since 1931); see Streatham Ice Skating Action Group's website at www.sisag.org.uk. The rink offers reasonably priced six-week courses for all ages, including classes for toddlers.

On tarmac

Citiskate (www.citiskate.co.uk) teaches hundreds of Londoners of all ages how to skate in parks, leisure centres and schools. The instructors hold qualifications from UKISA (United Kingdom Inline Skating Association); lessons are available daily.

Citiskate's weekly Sunday Rollerstroll (www.rollerstroll.com) and Battersea Park's Easy Peasy skate on Saturday (www.easypeasyskate.com) are popular, family-friendly group skates.

SKIING & SNOWBOARDING

There are a number of dry ski slopes in the London area. Bear in mind that the minimum requirement for use is to be able to perform a controlled snowplough turn and use the ski lift.

Bromley Ski Centre

Sandy Lane, St Paul's Cray, Orpington, Kent BR5 3HY (01689 876812, www.c-v-s.co.uk/ bromleyski). St Mary Cray rail or bus 321.

There are two lifts to serve the 120m (394ft) main slope, and there's also a mogul field and nursery slope. Skiing and snowboarding taster sessions cost £42.50 for 4 hours for children aged 7-15. Booking is essential.

Activities

Sandown Sports Club

More Lane, Esher, Surrey KT10 8AN
(01372 467132, www.sandownsports.co.uk).
Esher rail.
A big but friendly ski centre with four nursery
slopes and a curving, 120m (394ft) main slope.
The open practice sessions are strictly for
competent skiers and snowboarders; otherwise,
there are lessons for under-sevens (£27/30mins)
and seven-and-overs (£49/hr). Call for details of
parties, during which kids can speed down the
slopes on sledges and circular 'ringos'.

Snow Centre

St Albans Hill, Hemel Hempstead, Herts,
HP3 9NH (0845 258 9000, www.thesnow
centre.com) Hemel Hempstead rail then taxi.
This indoor snow centre in Hemel Hempstead
opened in 2009 and claims to be the best and
biggest in the UK. The main slope is 160m
(525ft) and has two lifts, and there's also a 100m
(328ft) lesson slope equipped with rope tows.
There are lessons for over-threes and a snow
school in half-term and school holidays.

Snozone

Xscape, 602 Marlborough Gate, Milton
Keynes, Bucks MK9 3XS (0871 222 5670,
www.snozoneuk.com). Milton Keynes
Central rail.
One of the UK's largest indoor snow domes,
with three slopes (in reality they're joined, so
they resemble one wide slope): two of 170m
(558ft) and one of 135m (443ft), with button lifts
running all the way to the top. The place can
feel a bit like a big fridge as it is below freezing
on the slopes, but it's a good (if pricey) place to
find your ski legs. Three-and-overs can also try
a spot of tobogganing (under-sevens must be
accompanied by a grown-up).

SWIMMING

As part of the drive towards increasing
fitness for 2012, many London boroughs
provide free swimming at designated
times for under-17s (under-19s in
Hackney) under the Swim4Life scheme.
Children must pre-register to take part
in the scheme; visit www.gll.org for a
list of participating authorities.

Most local authority pools run lessons
for children, plus parent-and-baby
sessions to develop water confidence

in those as young as three months. These
are very popular, so they may have long
waiting lists; ask at your local pool for
details. Also look out for mobile pools.

Most of the pools recommended below
are open daily; phone for session times,
prices and further information.

Barnet Copthall Pools

Champions Way, NW4 1PS (8457 9900,
www.gll.org). Mill Hill East tube.
There are three pools and a diving area here,
with coaching and clubs to join if you fancy
taking the plunge.

Brentford Fountain Leisure Centre

658 Chiswick High Road, Brentford, Middx
TW8 0HJ (0845 456 6675, www.fusion-
*lifestyle.com/centres/Brentford_Fountain_*
Leisure_Centre). Gunnersbury tube or
Kew Bridge rail.
A very pleasant leisure facility which has a
warm, shallow teaching pool, an exciting 40m
(130ft) aquaslide, underwater lighting, a flume
and a wave machine.

Crystal Palace National Sports Centre

Ledrington Road, SE19 2BB (8778 0131,
www.gll.org). Crystal Palace rail.
The National Sports Centre in the middle of
Crystal Palace Park houses one of the capital's
two 50m (160ft) Olympic-size pools; this
venerable pool also has fine diving facilities.

Goresbrook Leisure Centre

Ripple Road, Dagenham, Essex RM9 6XW
(8227 3976, www.barking-dagenham.
gov.uk). Becontree tube.
The fun pool in this Dagenham leisure centre
has fountains, as well as cascades; Saturday
afternoons bring pool parties. There's also a
small area for proper length swimming.

Ironmonger Row Baths

1-11 Ironmonger Row, EC1V 3QF (7253
4011, www.aquaterra.org). Old Street
tube/rail.
Currently being refurbished and closed
until May 2012, the Ironmonger Row Baths
are one of only three remaining Turkish baths
in London.

Kingfisher Leisure Centre

Fairfield Road, Kingston, Surrey, KT1 2PY
(8541 4576, www.dcleisurecentres.co.uk).
Kingston rail.

Activities

Horse Play

Horseball may sound like some medieval equine tournament, but the truth is this high-octane knockabout only came into being some 40 years ago. Think of a game that mixes basketball with the rough and tumble of rugby and the adrenaline rush of abseiling, all played on horseback, and you'll start to get a picture of this brilliantly fast-paced game, which is open to competent riders of any age. Devised in the 1970s by two brothers from Bordeaux, who were asked by the French authorities to invent a sport that could be played by anyone, it's now got some 4,000 fans in France, and competitors young and old are saddling up in countries as far afield as Argentina. Unlike elitist polo, players don't need a string of pricey ponies to join in either, because you ride the same horse for the duration of the game. You don't even need your own steed at the Lee Valley Riding Centre in east London – it's one of the only establishments in the country that will let you ride a borrowed horse for your session. The game is played on an arena measuring 20 metres by 60 metres, with a goal at either end that looks like a vertical basketball hoop, and the ball is a football encased in a leather harness – six looped straps enable you to pick it up, hold it, catch it and tug it from the hands of other players. To get the kids involved, you need to trot them down to the Lee Valley Riding Centre (*see p178*), where junior riders who can walk, trot and canter can try out horseball for £18.20 per session. If they're hooked after that, they can join the Lee Valley Horseball Club Cadets (8-12s) or Juniors (12-16s). With an annual fee of £50, plus £15 for each weekly session, it's good value – and it sure makes a change from mucking out.

This family-friendly centre has a teaching pool, plus a main pool with a beach area and wave machine. In other words, there's a little something for everyone.

Latchmere Leisure Centre
Burns Road, SW11 5AD (7207 8004, www.dcleisurecentres.co.uk). Clapham Junction rail.
The Latchmere Leisure Centre has a decent swimming pool for those who want to swim lanes. There's also a teaching pool and a beach area, with a wave machine and slide that will appeal to children.

Leyton Leisure Lagoon
763 High Road, E10 5AB (8558 8858, www.gll.org). Leyton tube or bus 69, 97.

This east London pool has various flumes, slides, fountains, rapids and cascades to liven up swimming sessions.

Pavilion Leisure Centre
Kentish Way, Bromley, Kent BR1 3EF (8313 9911, www.bromleymytime.org.uk). Bromley South rail.
Large leisure pool with shallows, flumes and a wave machine and a separate toddlers' pool.

Queen Mother Sports Centre
223 Vauxhall Bridge Road, SW1V 1EL (7630 5522, www.courtneys.co.uk). Victoria tube/rail.
The three terrific pools in this centre mean it's popular with schoolkids; it's also possible to take diving lessons here. Birthday parties can also be celebrated in the pool or sports hall.

Spa at Beckenham

24 Beckenham Road, Beckenham, Kent BR3 4PF (8650 0233, www.bromleymytime. org.uk). Clock House rail.
An award-winning leisure centre with loads of sports facilities, two swimming pools, the Buzz Zone soft-play area for children and a crèche for younger ones.

Tottenham Green Leisure Centre

1 Philip Lane, N15 4JA (8489 5322, www. haringey.gov.uk). Seven Sisters tube/rail.
This perennially popular leisure centre has lane swimming and diving in the main pool, and slides in the 'beach pool'.

Waterfront Leisure Centre

Woolwich High Street, SE18 6DL (8317 5000, www.gll.org). Woolwich Arsenal rail or bus 96, 177.
Greenwich borough's flagship centre. Four pools, six slides, waves, rapids and a water 'volcano' keep the crowds happy.

Open-air swimming

London's outdoor pools (lidos) are in a mixed state. Some are in terminal decline, while others have been reopened after expensive refurbs. For full details of London's outdoor pools (and to join the campaign to reopen those that have closed), visit www.lidos.org.uk.

Brockwell Lido

Brockwell Park, Dulwich Road, SE24 0PA (7274 3088, www.brockwell-lido.co.uk). Herne Hill rail. **Open** Apr-Sept; check website for times. **Admission** check website for details.
Rescued from the dead, this wonderful 1930s lido has been transformed by a Heritage Lottery Fund grant. Whippersnappers runs a brilliant range of classes at the pool, from babies' and toddlers' drop-in sessions to kathak dance classes for five to sevens and circus skills, acrobatics and street dance for older kids. The café was reopened in 2009, and has proved a hit with local families.

Finchley Lido

Great North Leisure Park, Chaplin Square, High Road, North Finchley, N12 0GL (8343 9830, www.gll.org). East Finchley tube. **Open** check website. **Admission** check website.

There are two indoor pools here, but it's the outdoor pool and sun terrace that make it such a draw for locals in the summer.

Hampstead Heath Swimming Ponds & Parliament Hill Lido

7332 3505, www.cityoflondon.gov.uk. Lido: Parliament Hill Fields, Gordon House Road, NW5 1LP. Gospel Oak rail. Men & women's ponds: Millfield Lane, N6. Gospel Oak rail. Mixed pond: East Heath Road, NW3. Hampstead Heath rail. **Open** check website for times. **Admission** Lido £2-£4.50; £2.90 reductions; £13.40 family (2+2). Ponds £2; £1 reductions. Season tickets and early/late entry discounts available.
Hampstead's wonderfully atmospheric pools are reserved for children of eight and above; under-15s must be supervised. The unheated, Grade II-listed lido is thronged with families on sunny afternoons, and also has a paddling pool.

Hampton Heated Open Air Pool

High Street, Hampton, Middx TW12 2ST (8255 1116, www.hamptonpool.co.uk). Hampton rail. **Open** times vary according to season so check website **Admission** £5.60 weekends; £4.60 weekdays; £3.70 reductions; £2.90-£3.20 children (4-15); £15.50 family (2+3).
The water is heated to 28° at this pool, and when the sun's shining it's hard to beat. There's a shallow learner pool for babies and toddlers, and group and private swimming lessons are offered. The complex is open all year round.

London Fields Lido

London Fields Westside, E8 3EU (7254 9038, www.gll.org). London Fields rail or bus 26, 48, 55, 106, 236. **Open** call for details. **Admission** £4.15; £2.50 under-16s.
Another recently resurrected lido. Hackney Council reopened this 50m (164ft) pool in autumn 2006. The water's heated to 25°, and there are two on-site cafés at which to refuel.

Oasis Sports Centre

32 Endell Street, WC2H 9AG (7831 1804, www.gll.org). Tottenham Court Road tube. **Open** 7.30am-9pm Mon-Wed, Fri; 7.30am-8.30pm Thur; 9.30am-5.30pm Sat, Sun. **Admission** £4.05; £1 5-16s; free under-5s.
This excellent 28m (90ft) outdoor pool is open all year round, and is particularly appealing on winter days, when steam rises from the surface (if you can persuade the kids to brave the chilly

Activities

dash from the changing rooms). Families should avoid lunchtimes or after work, when stressed media types descend in force.

Park Road Pools

Park Road, N8 8JN (8341 3567, www. haringey.gov.uk/leisure). Finsbury Park tube, then W7 bus. **Open** call for details. **Admission** £4.50; £2 children.

Crouch End's lido dates from 1929 and stretches out to 50 metres. The centre includes diving areas, a children's pool, exercise studios, a steam and sauna room and strips of lawn that lend themselves to lounging about on when the sun's shining. A range of watery classes is on offer, including antenatal exercise and children's swimming lessons.

Pools on the Park

Old Deer Park, Twickenham Road, Richmond, Surrey TW9 2SF (8940 0561, www.springhealth.net). Richmond rail. **Open** 6.30am-7.45pm Mon; 6.30am-10pm Tue; 6.30am-9pm Wed, Thur; 6.30am-8.30pm Fri; 8am-5.45pm Sat; 7am-5.45pm Sun. **Admission** £4.30; £1.70-£3.25 reductions; free under-5s. Prices may vary during peak season.

This well-maintained sports complex inside the picturesque Old Deer Park features a 33m (110ft) heated outdoor pool, and one the same size and temperature inside.

Serpentine Lido

Hyde Park, W2 2UH (7706 3422, www. serpentinelido.com). Knightsbridge or South Kensington tube. **Open** *May* 10am-6pm Sat, Sun. *June-mid Sept* 10am-6pm daily. **Admission** £4; £1-£3 reductions, free under-3s.

Right in the centre of town, this picturesque freshwater pool and its paddling pool are a London institution, exerting a siren song to parents and their offspring on summer's days.

Tooting Bec Lido

Tooting Bec Road, SW16 1RU (8871 7198, www.wandsworth.gov.uk). Streatham rail. **Open** *late May-Aug* 6am-7.30pm daily. *Sept* 6am-4.30pm daily. *Oct-late May* 7am-2pm daily (club members only). **Admission** £5; £3.20 reductions, under-16s; free under-5s.

At 94m (308ft) by 25m (82ft), this art deco beauty is the second largest open-air pool in Europe. Understandably, it's very popular with locals, and has a paddling pool for splash-happy toddlers.

TABLE TENNIS

Finsbury Leisure Centre

Norman Street, EC1V 3PU (7253 2346, www.aquaterra.org). Old Street tube.

This leisure centre in east London runs a couple of weekly table tennis coaching sessions for seven- to 16-year-olds (6-9pm Fri; 5-9pm Sun). There is no need to book and all equipment is provided. Sessions cost £3.70 and all levels are welcome.

TENNIS

Tennis for Free (TFF) is a campaign to give free access to Britain's 33,000 public courts to increase participation in tennis nationwide. It's aimed to help all ages, regardless of ability, background, race and financial circumstance. To learn more about the scheme, visit www.tennisforfree.com, type in your borough and check availability.

Holiday tennis courses at Easter and in the summer can be found in most London boroughs, but need booking well ahead: keep an eye on council websites and contact your local sports development team for details. British Tennis publishes free guides giving contacts for private clubs and public courts listed by borough or county, along with contact details for local development officers; it also holds details of tennis holidays available.

David Lloyd Leisure

0844 543 9783, www.davidlloydleisure.co.uk. All David Lloyd centres are family-friendly, if not exactly cheap, and the courts and equipment are excellent.

Hackney City Tennis Clubs

Clissold Park Mansion House, Stoke Newington Church Street, N16 9HJ (7254 4235, www.hackneycitytennisclubs.co.uk). Stoke Newington rail or bus 73. **Open** *Mar* 10am-5.30pm Mon-Fri; 9am-5.30pm Sat, Sun. *Apr-Sept* 10am-7.30pm Mon-Fri; 9am-7.30pm Sat, Sun. *Oct, Nov* 10am-4.30pm Mon-Fri; 9am-4.30pm Sat, Sun. *Dec-Feb* 10am-3.30pm Mon-Fri; 9am-3.30pm Sat, Sun. **Court hire**

Activities

My Sport Football
Joe, 13

What inspired you to take up football?
I always really liked sport so wanted to join a team. I first started playing at school, then joined a junior Sunday league team when I was eight.

What do you like about your sport?
I just find it fun. I like being in a team with my friends and I like scoring goals.

What level are you at?
I was training at Fulham FC, but it took ages to get there and back so I've gone back to playing football just for fun.

What's next for you in your sport?
I'd like to carry on playing in a Sunday league team and enjoy it.

Which events would you like to see at the London 2012 Olympic Games and Paralympic Games?
Athletics, especially the jumping events and the short sprints. I'd also like to watch the Football.

Activities

£5.50/hr; £2.50 under-16s (10am-5pm Mon-Fri). Phone to check availability.

Part of a nationwide LTA programme to make inner-city tennis facilities cheaper to use and easier to find, this is Britain's first City Tennis Club (with courts in Clissold Park, London Fields and Millfields). Sessions for three- to 16-year-olds are offered during term time (one hour per week costs from £25 for five weeks of lessons), with free racquets and balls; holiday courses are also available. There are additional CTCs in Highbury Fields (Islington) and Eltham Park South (Greenwich).

Islington Tennis Centre

Market Road, N7 9PL (7700 1370, www. aquaterra.org). Caledonian Road tube. 7am-11pm Mon-Thur; 7am-10pm Fri; 8am-10pm Sat, Sun. **Court hire** *Non-members* Indoor £24/hr; £10/hr 5-16s. Outdoor £10/hr; £4.50/hr 5-16s.

Developed under the LTA's Indoor Tennis Initiative, the centre offers subsidised coaching. It also runs half-hour coaching sessions for three- to five-year-olds.

Redbridge Sports & Leisure Centre

Forest Road, Barkingside, Essex IG6 3HD (8498 1000, www.rslonline.co.uk). Fairlop tube. **Open** 6.30am-11pm Mon-Fri; 8am-9pm Sat; 8am-10pm Sun. **Court hire** prices vary; phone for details.

An independent charitable trust runs this outstanding sports centre. There are eight indoor and six outdoor courts to use as a member or 'pay as you play'. There are holiday activities for six- to 14-year-olds, 'fun play' sessions and a short tennis club for under-eights.

Rocks Lane Multisports Centres

Barnes Centre *Opposite Ranelagh Avenue, SW13 0DG (8876 8330, www.rockslane.co.uk).* **Open** 10am-10pm Mon-Fri; 9am-6pm Sat, Sun. **Court hire** *Daytime* £9/hr. *Floodlit* £13.50/hr.

Chiswick Centre *60 Chiswick Common Road, W4 1RZ (8994 1313, www.rockslane. co.uk).* **Open** 10am-10pm Mon-Fri; 10am-6pm Sat, Sun. **Court hire** *Daytime* £9/hr. *Floodlit* £13.50/hr.

Between its two centres in Barnes and Chiswick, there are an impressive 13 floodlit artificial grass courts and four hard courts available to book in advance or on a pay-and-play basis. There are holiday courses for three- to 12-year-olds (£8/hr), and they can also organise tennis parties.

Sutton Tennis Academy

Rose Hill Recreation Ground, Rose Hill, Sutton, Surrey SM1 3HH (8641 6611, www.sjtc.org). Morden tube or Sutton Common rail. **Open** 6am-10pm Mon-Fri; 7am-9pm Sat, Sun. **Court hire** *Indoor* £20; £15 under-18s. *Outdoor* £8; £6 under-18s. *Clay* £13; £11 under-18s.

Frenchman Erich Dochterman, who has taught various ATP- and WTA-ranked players, is head coach at this acclaimed tennis school. There are residential courses for players seeking professional status and a scholarship scheme linked to Cheam High School. Children can be steeped in tennis culture from the age of three with Tiny Tots classes, mini tennis and holiday programmes. Facilities include six red clay, ten acrylic and 11 indoor courts.

Westway Tennis Centre

1 Crowthorne Road, W10 6RP (8969 0992, www.westway.org). Latimer Road tube. **Open** 8am-10pm Mon-Fri, Sun; 8am-8pm. **Court hire** *Indoor* £16-£22.50; £10-£16 4-18s. *Outdoor* £8-£9; £5-£7 4-18s.

The Westway, another product of the LTA's Indoor Tennis Initiative, follows a similar model to Islington (*see left*): it's excellent for subsidised coaching and courses, short tennis and transitional tennis. There are eight indoor and four outdoor clay courts for kids to play on.

Will to Win

www.willtowin.co.uk.

Will to Win works in partnership with the Royal Parks to deliver community tennis in Hyde Park, Regent's Park and Greenwich Park, as well as running centres in Ealing and Chiswick. The website lists all the available courses and holiday camps for youngsters.

TENPIN BOWLING

Many centres have ramps, bumpers and lightweight balls to make things easier for small children. Admission to the following centres averages around £6 per game, including shoe hire.

Acton Tenpin

Royale Leisure Park, Western Avenue, W3 0PA (0871 873 3150, www.tenpin.co.uk). Park Royal tube. **Open** noon-1am Mon-Thur; noon-2am Fri; 10am-2am Sat; 10am-12.30am Sun. **Credit** MC, V.

Activities

1st Bowling Lewisham
11-29 Belmont Hill, SE13 5AU (8852 6688). Lewisham rail/DLR. **Open** 10am-11pm Mon-Sat; 10am-10.30pm Sun. **Credit** MC, V.

Funland
Trocadero Centre, 1 Piccadilly Circus, W1D 7DH (7292 3642, www.funland.co.uk). Piccadilly Circus tube. **Open** 10am-1am daily. **Credit** MC, V.

Hollywood Bowl Finchley
Great North Leisure Park, Chaplin Square, off Finchley High Road, N12 0GL (8446 6667, www.hollywoodbowl.co.uk). East Finchley tube, then bus 263. **Open** 10am-midnight Mon-Thur, Sun; 10am-1am Fri, Sat. **Credit** MC, V.

Hollywood Bowl Surrey Quays
Mast Leisure Park, Teredo Street, SE16 7LW (7237 3773, www.hollywoodbowl. co.uk). Canada Water DLR. **Open** 10am-11.30pm Mon-Thur, Sun; 10am-midnight Fri, Sat. **Credit** MC, V.

London Palace Superbowl
Elephant & Castle Shopping Centre, 2 Elephant & Castle, SE1 6TE (7252 6677, www.palacesuperbowl.com). Elephant & Castle tube. **Open** 11am-11pm daily. **Credit** MC, V.

Queens
17 Queensway, W2 4QP (7229 0172, www.queensiceandbowl.co.uk). Bayswater or Queensway tube. **Open** 10am-11.30pm daily. **Credit** AmEx, MC, V.

Rowans Tenpin Bowl
10 Stroud Green Road, N4 2DF (8800 1950, www.rowans.co.uk). Finsbury Park tube/rail. **Open** 10.30am-12.30am Mon-Thur, Sun; 10.30am-2.30am Fri, Sat. **Credit** MC, V.

TRAMPOLINING

Harrow Trampoline Club
Canons Sports Centre, North London Collegiate School, Edgware HA8 7RJ (8905 6895, www.harrowtrampolineclub.co.uk). Classes on Wednesday evenings and Sunday mornings cater for two levels. The class for five- to nine-year-olds is designed specifically for young children with little or no trampolining experience, while classes for over-nines are recreational and suitable for anyone.

Michael Sobell Leisure Centre
Hornsey Road, N7 7NY (7609 2166, www.aquaterra.org). Finsbury Park tube/rail. The Sobell Centre has a strong trampolining tradition and runs drop-in sessions for children from four to 16 years every weekday after school, and on Saturday and Sunday mornings. Sessions cost £4. There is no need to book, you can just turn up. Tickets go on sale half an hour before the sessions start.

WATERSPORTS

London is a river city, so there are plenty of opportunities to take to the water in canoes, dinghies or rowing boats and meander down the Thames. It's also worth checking out the city's many reservoirs.

Ahoy Centre
Borthwick Street, SE8 3JY (8691 7606, www.ahoy.org.uk). Deptford rail or Cutty Sark DLR.
This is the place to come for sailing, rowing and (for older children and teens) powerboating on the Thames, and in Surrey and Victoria Docks. Members help run the centre, which keeps prices down and fosters a community spirit.

BTYC Sailsports
Birchen Grove, NW9 8SA (8205 0017, www.btycsailsports.org.uk). Neasden or Wembley Park tube/rail.
Dinghy sailing, windsurfing, basic training and RYA courses on the Welsh Harp reservoir.

Canalside Activity Centre
Canal Close, W10 5AY (8968 4500, www.rbkc.gov.uk). Ladbroke Grove tube or Kensal Rise rail, or bus 52, 70, 295.
Utilising the Grand Union canal, this centre offers various canoeing lessons and water safety classes.

Docklands Sailing & Watersports Centre
Millwall Dock, 235A Westferry Road, E14 3QS (7537 2626, www.dswc.org). Crossharbour DLR. **Membership** £110/yr adult; £20/yr under-16s; £220/yr family (2+3).

Activities

My Sport Gymnastics
Lily, 6

What inspired you to take up gymnastics?
My mum took me to baby gym when I was really little and I liked all the things that we did there. When I was three, I started proper gym classes.

What do you like about your sport?
I like swinging on the bars and bouncing on the trampoline. I also like doing forward rolls and cartwheels.

What level are you at?
I'm in the advanced recreational class. There are 16 girls in my class and we have three coaches teaching us. The older gymnasts train at the same time as us and they are very, very good.

What's next for you in your sport?
I am going to learn a routine for the summer exam and I will get a badge with a number on it.

Which events would you like to see at the London 2012 Olympic Games and Paralympic Games?
I would like to see the Gymnastics, Swimming and Cycling, because these are all the things I like to do.

This watersports centre offers canoeing, dragon-boat racing, windsurfing and dinghy sailing for over-eights. Non-members can also take part in open sessions; phone for details.

Globe Rowing Club

Trafalgar Rowing Centre, 11-13 Crane Street, SE10 9NP (www.globerowingclub. co.uk). Cutty Sark DLR or Maze Hill rail.
A friendly, Greenwich-based rowing club that offers competitive as well as recreational rowing and sculling on a stretch of river from Tower Bridge to the Thames Barrier.

John Battleday Waterski

Thorpe Road, Chertsey, Surrey KT16 8PH (01932 579 750, www.jbski.com). Chertsey rail.
With three world-class lakes to choose from, plus a comprehensive training programme, this is the ideal place to give youngsters a taste of waterskiing with one of the club's kids' beginner courses (2x15mins, £45).

Lea Rowing Club

Spring Hill, E5 9BL (Club house 8806 8282, www.learc.org.uk). Clapton rail.
Rowing and sculling classes, and holiday courses for children aged ten or above who can swim at least 50 metres.

Lee Valley White Water Centre

Station Road, Waltham Cross, Herts EN9 1AB (08456 770 606, www.leevalleypark. org.uk). Waltham Cross station.
The White Water Centre was the first new London 2012 venue to open to the public. The centre will be open until autumn 2011, when it will close for the main event in 2012. The centre will then reopen to the public a few months after the Games. Activities include canoeing and kayaking, but for a real thrill book your kids in (over-13s) on a half-day Ride the Rapids session (£49), with at least four rafting runs down the new white-water course.

Stoke Newington West Reservoir Centre

Green Lanes, N4 2HA (8442 8116, www. gll.org). Manor House tube or bus 141, 341.
Environmental education and watersports centre for dinghy sailing.

Surrey Docks Watersports Centre

Greenland Dock, Rope Street, SE16 7SX (7237 4009, www.fusion-lifestyle.com). Canada Water tube.
Eights and over can learn sailing, windsurfing and canoeing in this sheltered dock during the holidays. RYA courses are also available.

Westminster Boating Base

136 Grosvenor Road, SW1V 3JY (7821 7389, www.westminsterboatingbase.co.uk). Pimlico tube or Vauxhall tube/rail.
This canoeing and sailing club for over-tens asks for donations rather than fees.

YOGA

Yoga is a fantastic way to maintain children's co-ordination, flexibility and concentration, but pick an approved and registered course. The biggest name in yoga for kids is **YogaBugs** (www.yoga bugs.com). The company teaches three-to seven-year-olds at a variety of venues, using a mix of storytelling and songs to capture children's attention. Yoga'd Up is the next step, offering classes for eight-to 12-year-olds. The **Special Yoga Centre** (*see below*) is a registered charity that offers one-to-one sessions for infants with disabilities.

The following centres run classes for children; check websites for details.

Holistic Health

64 Broadway Market, E8 4QJ (7275 8434, http://holistichealthhackney.co.uk). London Fields rail or bus 26, 48, 55, 106, 236.

Iyengar Institute

223A Randolph Avenue, W9 1NL (7624 3080, www.iyi.org.uk). Maida Vale tube.

Sivananda Yoga

Vedanta Centre, 51 Felsham Road, SW15 1AZ (8780 0160, www.sivananda.co.uk). Putney Bridge tube or Putney rail.

Special Yoga Centre

The Tay Building, 2A Wrentham Avenue, NW10 3HA (8968 1900, www.special yoga.org.uk). Kensal Rise rail.

Yoga Junction

The Old Flower Shop, 93A Weston Park, N8 9PR (8347 0000, www.yogajunction.co.uk). Harringay rail or bus W5.

Activities

Arts & Entertainment

Capital culture, from preschool puppetry to big-name ballet.

One of the biggest joys about bringing up children in London is the sheer mass of cut-price, top-drawer culture on offer to them across the city. From fun-sized Philharmonic concerts at the **Southbank Centre** (*see p193*) to open-air Shakespeare at the **Regent's Park Open Air Theatre** (*see p212*), youngsters are able to enjoy the arts on a grand scale – but, and here's the clever part, without bankrupting parents in the process.

Many museums and galleries (*see pp74-122*) and attractions (*see pp46-73*) run special events and family days year-round, with a particularly busy programme at weekends and during the school holidays. There are myriad delights on offer, with not a hint of starch and ceremony: child-friendly concerts, story sessions, meet-the-orchestra events and drop-in arts and crafts activities among them. When it comes to theatre (*see pp204-215*), meanwhile, the line-up runs from endlessly innovative children's theatre companies and venues such as **Oily Cart** (*see p207*) and the **Unicorn Theatre** (*see p213*) to big-budget Christmas pantos, or crowd-pleasing touring shows based on Fifi, Angelina, Lola and co.

Children can also try their hand at all sorts of creative activities. Whether your offspring are into drama, music, cookery, art or film-making, drop-in classes, after-school clubs and longer courses abound; kids can try out circus skills one day, sculpture the next. They might just uncover a hidden talent for stilt-walking or a penchant for percussion – and have a whale of a time in the process.

ARTS CENTRES

Barbican Centre

Silk Street, EC2Y 8DS (box office 7638 8891,cinema 7382 7000, www.barbican. org.uk). Barbican tube or Moorgate tube/ rail. **Open** *Box office* (by phone) 9am-8pm Mon-Sat; 11am-8pm Sun; (in person) 9am-9pm Mon-Sat; noon-9pm Sun. **Admission** *Library* free. *Exhibitions, films, shows, workshops* phone for details. **Membership** £20-£105/yr. **Credit** AmEx, MC, V. **Map** p334 P5.

This angular, concrete art complex may look slightly foreboding, but venture inside and you'll be pleasantly surprised. Maps and painted yellow lines lead confused visitors through the residential blocks that surround the centre – an intricate maze of walkways, stairs, identikit towers and split level ramps. There are some pockets of unexpected calm for everyone to enjoy: the fountains in the inner courtyard, the Waterside Café and the library, with its extensive children's section. Best of all is the conservatory, open to the public on Sunday afternoons (unless hired for a private event), where exotic palms, ferns and flowers soar towards the sky and stately koi carp patrol the ponds.

The Barbican's busy programme of cultural offerings also has plenty to appeal to small fry. For starters, there's the excellent Saturday morning Family Film Club, with a lively mix of movies, themed activities and monthly workshops. Screenings (£3-£5) are aimed at kids aged five to 11 and their parents; book ahead. One-off mini-seasons and special events for families also dot the Barbican's calendar, including the Animate the World! animation-fest in May and the London Children's Film Festival in November. The complex is home to the London Symphony Orchestra (www.lso.co.uk), whose Discovery Family Concerts combine music and storytelling to great effect, with pre-concert workshops in the foyer. *Buggy access. Cafés. Disabled access: lift, toilet. Nappy-changing facilities. Restaurants. Shops.*

Rich Mix

35-47 Bethnal Green Road, E1 6LA (7613 7498, www.richmix.org.uk). Shoreditch High Street rail. **Open** *Box office* 9.30am-9.30pm daily. **Admission** prices vary; phone for details. **Credit** MC, V.

This vast former textiles factory now houses a cross-cultural arts and media centre – with an edgy, East End flavour all of its own. There are monthly storytelling and performance poetry sessions, plus inexpensive film-making workshops for five to 12s on selected Sundays and school holiday dates, with a maximum of ten youngsters per session. Meanwhile, Saturday and Sunday mornings bring Kids' Cine Time, with tickets at a mere £1.50 for adults or children; major Hollywood releases and animations dominate the programme. Family tickets, available before 5pm on weekdays and all day on Saturdays and Sundays, are also brilliant value, while friendly parent and baby screenings take place on Monday evenings. Check online for details of

the youth programme, which could encompass anything from graffiti projects to krumping and Bollywood dance classes. *Buggy access. Cafés. Disabled access: lift, toilet. Nappy-changing facilities.*

Southbank Centre

Belvedere Road, SE1 8XX (0844 847 9910, www.southbankcentre.co.uk). Embankment tube or Waterloo tube/rail. **Open** *Box office & foyer* 10am-8pm daily. *Hayward Gallery* 10am-6pm Mon-Thur, Sat, Sun; 10am-10pm Fri. **Admission** prices vary; phone for details. **Credit** AmEx, MC, V. **Map** p333 M8.

Set by the Thames, with the London Eye looming overhead, the Southbank Centre is a cultural behemoth of many parts – namely the Royal Festival Hall, the Queen Elizabeth Hall, the Hayward Gallery and the Saison Poetry Library. It offers a heady mix of theatre, puppet shows, contemporary and classical music, circus performances, dance and art, including plenty of free events; the website has a comprehensive rundown of upcoming child-friendly offerings – which might run the gamut from Funharmonics classical concerts, with pieces chosen for their child appeal, to free beatboxing workshops.

Simply wandering about can be richly rewarding, though – you might stumble across a weird sound sculpture, find dancers waltzing across the terrace, encounter some science buskers or catch a gospel choir in full throttle.

Activities

Barbican Centre. *See p192.*

The school holidays also mean more family activities, with treasure trails, performances, storytelling and large-scale drawing escapades, usually all free. Meanwhile, the Royal Festival Hall's music learning space, Spirit Level, includes a great technology area where young people can experiment with composition and sound-making (make sure you book the workshops well in advance). *See also p48* **Neighbourhood Watch**.
Buggy access. Cafés. Disabled access: lift, toilet. Nappy-changing facilities. Restaurants.

Tricycle Theatre & Cinema

269 Kilburn High Road, NW6 7JR (box office 7328 1000, www.tricycle.co.uk). Kilburn tube or Brondesbury rail. **Open** *Box office* 10am-9pm Mon-Sat; 2-8pm Sun. *Children's shows* 11.30am, 2pm Sat. *Children's films* 1pm Sat. **Tickets** *Theatre* (Sat) £5-£6; £4 reductions. *Films* (Sat) £5; £4 reductions, under-16s. **Credit** MC, V.
An art gallery, cinema and theatre in one, with its own buzzy café and bar, the Tricycle has deep local roots and a real community feel. There's a brilliant line-up of children's theatre, events and groups, from preschooler activity sessions and performances of *Goldilocks and the Three Bears* (teddies are welcome too),

Old Mother Hubbard and the like to drama workshops and youth theatre groups for older children and teens. Half-term and holiday workshops focus on magic, theatre, circus skills and even fuzzy felt, while term-time after-school classes currently include guitar and street dance. Kids' cinema matinée screenings are at 1pm on Saturdays.
Buggy access. Disabled access: lift, toilet. Nappy-changing facilities. Restaurant.

CINEMAS

The capital is superb for cinema, catering to film buffs of all ages. As well as a wealth of kids' cinema clubs and weekend matinée screenings to choose from, children even have their own festival. The London Children's Film Festival generally takes place in November; its headquarters are the Barbican (*see p192*), but independent cinemas city-wide also get involved in the family fun.

If you don't mind blowing the budget on the latest blockbuster screening and a bucket of absurdly priced popcorn,

Southbank Centre. *See p193.*

On the Waterfront

Most of the Aquatics events for the London 2012 Olympic Games will be taking place beneath the stunning wave-shaped roof of the Zaha Hadid-designed Aquatics Centre, as some 17,500 spectators crowd in to cheer on home-grown heroes such as Rebecca Adlington and Tom Daley in their hunt for medals. But in the run-up to the main event, there's plenty of other watery action for east Londoners to dip their toes into.

One of the most appealing options is the Floating Cinema, which will be meandering along the waterways of the five Olympic host boroughs during June and July 2011 as part of CREATE (www.createlondon.org), an annual festival which features more than 200 events and brings together the very best in home-grown, world-class artistic talent from across east and south-east London. Developed by artists Nina Pope and Karen Guthrie (known collectively as Somewhere) and designed by Hackney-based architect Studio Weave, the Floating Cinema will host on-board screenings and larger outdoor film events and provide a base for cultural participation galore.

This cultural cavalcade is setting sail under the flag of the Portavilion project (www.portavilion.com), a mobile public art commission which last year saw an inflatable pavilion doing the rounds of 13 London parks and public spaces. The Floating Cinema won't break any world records as it chugs sedately through Greenwich, Hackney, Newham, Tower Hamlets and Waltham Forest before finally pulling into the Olympic Park itself, but CREATE is more of a marathon than a sprint as the organisers look to establish a legacy for this area of east London that stretches way beyond the sporting summer of 2012.

Activities

BFI Southbank.

go to Leicester Square. It's home to the glitzy, glossy flagships of **Vue** (0871 224 0240, www.myvue.com), the **Odeon** (0871 224 4007, www.odeon. co.uk) and the **Empire** (0871 4714 714, www.empirecinemas.co.uk). Some of the big chains also do their own version of Watch with Baby screenings, as first pioneered at the **Clapham Picturehouse** (*see p197*) and now a regular feature in all Picturehouses. In addition to the cinemas below, don't forget the **Tricycle** (*see p194*).

BFI IMAX

1 Charlie Chaplin Walk, SE1 8XR (7199 6000, www.bfi.org.uk/imax). Waterloo tube/rail. **Open** *Box office* (by phone) 10.30am-7.30pm daily; (in person) from 30mins before screening. **Admission** £14; £9.75-£10.75 reductions; £9.25 3-14s; free under-3s. *IMAX short films* £8.50; £6.25

reductions; £5.25 4-14s; free under-4s. **Credit** MC, V.
A distinctive circular structure set in a sunken traffic island by Waterloo station houses the UK's biggest cinema screen – over 20m (65ft) high and 26m (85ft) wide. Children love donning 3D glasses to watch special effects-heavy films such as *Tron: Legacy*; it's an intense, larger-than-life experience, so avoid anything too alarming for younger children. Non-IMAX mainstream films are also shown. *See also p48* **Neighbourhood Watch**.
Bar. Buggy access. Café. Disabled access: lift, toilet. Nappy-changing facilities.

BFI Southbank

Belvedere Road, SE1 8XT (box office 7928 3232, www.bfi.org.uk). Embankment tube or Waterloo tube/rail. **Open** *Box office* (by phone) 11.30am-8.30pm daily; (in person) 11am-8.30pm daily. **Tickets** £5-£9.50 non-members; £5-£8 members; phone for children's prices. **Membership** £40/yr. **Credit** AmEx, MC, V. **Map** p333 M8.

Following a 2007 revamp, the four-screen British Film Institute (better known as the BFI) has gone from strength to strength. Check the schedule for parent and toddler showings and kids' screenings, both of which combine classic and current hits. At the weekly Fundays, activities accompany the film and the Benugo café-bar serves a special menu. Another brilliant feature is being able to watch film and television clips in the Mediatheque. *See also p48* **Neighbourhood Watch**.
Buggy access. Café. Disabled access: lift, toilet. Nappy-changing facilities. Restaurant.

Clapham Picturehouse

76 Venn Street, SW4 0AT (0871 902 5727, www.picturehouses.co.uk). Clapham Common tube or bus 35, 37. **Open** *Box office (by phone) 9.30am-8.30pm daily; (in person) noon-8.30pm daily. Kids' club activities 11.15am, screening 11.45am Sat.* **Tickets** £7-£11; £6-£9 reductions. Kids' club £3. **Membership** Kids' club £4/yr. **Credit** MC, V.

This much-loved local cinema was the first in London to offer parent-and-baby screenings. Big Scream! sessions for parents and under-ones still run every Thursday at 10.30am, and innovative autism-friendly screenings have also been introduced. There are Kids' Club Saturday matinées for three- to ten-year-olds, with craft workshops before the film; young members can go into the projection room and start the film as a birthday treat.
Buggy access. Café. Disabled access: toilet. Nappy-changing facilities.

Electric Cinema

191 Portobello Road, W11 2ED (7908 9696, www.the-electric.co.uk). Ladbroke Grove or Notting Hill Gate tube or bus 52. **Open** *Box office 9am-8.30pm Mon-Sat; 10am-7.30pm Sun.* **Tickets** *Kids' club* £5-£6.50. *Workshops* (1st Sat of month) £3. **Credit** AmEx, MC, V. **Map** p326 A7.

A far cry from your average multiplex, Notting Hill's Electric Cinema brings a touch of glamour to a trip to the flicks. Plush leather seating, footstools and tables make for a truly luxurious cinematic experience, with superior snacks to munch on; adults can quaff a glass of chilled pinot grigio or even a cocktail. There's a Saturday morning Kids' Club (10.30am), while friendly Electric Scream! shows for parents and under-ones are held at 11am on Mondays (except bank holidays).
Buggy access. Disabled access: lift, toilet.

Greenwich Picturehouse

180 Greenwich High Road, SE10 8NN (0871 704 2059, www.picturehouses.co.uk). Cutty Sark DLR or Greenwich rail/DLR. **Open** *Box office (by phone) 9.30am-8.30pm daily; (in person) 11am-10pm daily. Kids' Club activities 11am Sat, screening 11.30am.* **Tickets** £6-£10; £5.50-£6.50 under-14s, reductions. *Kids' club* £4.50. **Membership** Kids' club £4.50/yr. **Credit** AmEx, MC, V.

Opened in 2005, the four-screen Greenwich outpost of the acclaimed Picturehouse chain has its own tapas bar. There's a children's film club on Saturday morning, suitable for fives to 15s, plus Big Scream! events at 11.30am on Wednesday and Friday.
Buggy access. Café. Disabled access: lift, toilet. Nappy-changing facilities. Restaurant.

Phoenix

52 High Road, N2 9PJ (8444 6789, www.phoenixcinema.co.uk). East Finchley tube. **Open** *Box office 15mins before first screening. Kids' club noon Sat, £2.* **Tickets** £6-£9; £6 under-16s, reductions. **Credit** MC, V.

East Finchley's single-screen art deco treasure offers Bringing Up Baby screenings (normally held on Wednesdays) and Saturday afternoon Kids' Club movies, kicking off with a hands-on activity workshop, games or a quiz and aimed at five- to eight-year-olds. The cinema can also be hired out for birthday parties; phone for details.
Buggy access. Nappy-changing facilities. Disabled access: lift, toilet.

Rio Cinema

103-107 Kingsland High Street, E8 2PB (7241 9410, www.riocinema.co.uk). Dalston Kingsland or Dalston Junction rail. **Open** *Box office (by phone) 2-8pm daily; (in person) from 15 mins before screening. Children's screening 4pm Tue; 11am Sat.* **Tickets** £7-£9; £5.50 2-16s; *Children's screening* £2.50; £1.50 under-16s. **Credit** MC, V.

Expect an engaging mix of films at this Dalston favourite, which isn't afraid to eschew predictable Hollywood fodder in favour of more interesting smaller films and classics. Youthful members of the Saturday Morning Picture Club are given a special card to be stamped, with a free visit after ten stamps and a poster after 25 – a generous offer, considering how

Activities

inexpensive tickets are. A parent-and-baby club operates on selected Tuesday and Thursday lunchtimes, with a secure place to park pushchairs, and the school holidays bring daily matinées for five- to 15-year-olds.
Buggy access. Café. Disabled access: toilet.

Ritzy Picturehouse

Brixton Oval, Coldharbour Lane, SW2 1JG (0871 704 2065, www.picturehouses. co.uk). Brixton tube/rail. **Open** *Box office* (by phone) 9.30am-8.30pm daily. *Kids' club* 10.30am Sat. **Tickets** *£6.50-£10; £5-£9 under-14s. Kids' club £2 3-15s.* **Membership** *Kids' club £3/yr.* **Credit** MC, V.
Opened in 1911, this landmark has survived numerous owners and name changes, not to mention near-demolition and redevelopment plans. Now part of the Picturehouse family, it hosts Big Scream! sessions on Fridays at 11am, open to parents with under-ones. Children as young as three can join the inexpensive Saturday Kids' Club, and there are regular autism-friendly screenings; call the box office or check online for details. There's also a laid-back café bar, with a kids' menu.
Buggy access. Café. Disabled access: lift, toilet. Nappy-changing facilities.

Stratford East Picturehouse

Theatre Square, Salway Road, E15 1BX (0871 704 2066, www.picturehouses.co.uk). Stratford tube/rail/DLR. **Open** *Box office* (by phone) 9.30am-8.30pm daily. *Kids' club* 10.50am Sat. **Tickets** *£4-£9; £4 under-15s. Kids' club £6; £3 3-10s.* **Membership** *Kids' club £4/yr.* **Credit** MC, V.
Attractions for families and children at this east London Picturehouse branch include a children's film club where creative activities, fun and games take place before a screening. The club is suitable for three- to ten-year-olds, and membership entitles you to attend the first film for free.
Bar. Buggy access. Disabled access: lift, toilet. Nappy-changing facilities.

COMEDY

Comedy Club 4 Kids

Soho Theatre, 21 Dean Street, W1D 3NE (7478 0100, www.sohotheatre.com). Tottenham Court Road, Leicester Square or Oxford Circus tube. **Open** *Box office* 10am-7pm Mon-Sat. **Credit** MC, V.
Map p331 K6.

The Soho Theatre's monthly Comedy Club 4 Kids is a winning combination of top-flight adult comedic talent and gags, without the rude bits. Well, not all the rude bits. This is aimed at children, after all, so there is a fair amount of scatologically inclined material, but nothing that would make parents blanch. It's staged along the same lines as a late-night comedy club, with the compère whipping the audience into a heckle-inducing frenzy, before the first (often palpably nervous) comedian takes to the stage.
Bar. Buggy access. Café. Disabled access: lift, toilets. Nappy-changing facilities. Restaurant.

DANCE

See also **Chisenhale Dance Space**, **Laban** and **The Place** (for all, *see pp166-169*).

Royal Opera House

Bow Street, WC2E 9DD (7304 4000 box office, www.royaloperahouse.org). Covent Garden tube. **Open** *Box office* 10am-8pm Mon-Sat. *Tours* daily (times vary, book in advance). **Tours** £10; £9 reductions; £7 9-16s. **Credit** AmEx, MC, V. **Map** p333 L6.
Don't be daunted at the prospect of visiting one of the world's great opera houses with kids in tow: families are warmly welcomed. Inside it's bright and airy, with sumptuous costumes on display and splendid views over Covent Garden's crowds and street entertainers from the upstairs café. An engaging line-up of special events runs from puppet-making in the light-flooded Paul Hamlyn Hall to musical, magical afternoons with players from the orchestra, choreographers and composers, where everyone gets involved. *See also p64* **Neighbourhood Watch**.
Buggy access. Café. Disabled access: lift, toilet. Nappy-changing facilities. Restaurant. Shop.

Sadler's Wells

Rosebery Avenue, EC1R 4TN (0844 412 4300, www.sadlerswells.com). Angel tube. **Open** *Box office* 10am-8pm Mon-Sat. **Credit** AmEx, MC, V.
As the epicentre of dance in London, Sadler's Wells attracts all sorts of dance superstars – including some child-friendly companies, such as the London Children's Ballet. Elsewhere in the programme, there's lots to interest older

My Sport Ballet
Polly, 3

What inspired you to take up ballet?
My big sister goes to ballet and I always wanted to join in and dress up in her clothes. Now I go to my own class.

What do you like about your sport?
I like running around on tiptoes and I like skipping. My teacher says I'm very good at skipping.

What level are you at?
I started going to ballet when I was two years old and I've just been moved up to the next class now I'm three years old.

What's next for you in your sport?
I want to learn how to do a pirouette like my sister. Sometimes she helps me do an arabesque.

Which events would you like to see at the London 2012 Olympic Games and Paralympic Games?
I don't know what that means. Tell me about it.

Activities

Laban. *See p168.*

children, including Breakin' Convention – a high-octane annual hip hop jamboree. In the adjacent Lilian Bayliss Theatre, the two-week Connect Festival is another good bet for families, mixing lively workshops with performances from dancers of all ages. The Peacock Theatre (Portugal Street, WC2A 2HT, 0844 412 4322) is a satellite venue for Sadler's Wells, with family shows every Christmas.
Bar. Buggy access. Cafés. Disabled access: lift, toilet. Nappy-changing facilities. Restaurant.

LITERATURE
Libraries

British Library
96 Euston Road, NW1 2DB (7412 7676, 7412 7797 learning, www.bl.uk). Euston or King's Cross tube/rail. **Open** 9.30am-6pm Mon, Wed-Fri; 9.30am-8pm Tue; 9.30am-5pm Sat; 11am-5pm Sun, bank hols. **Credit** MC, V. **Map** p333 K3.
Even cynical small fry can't fail to be impressed by the sheer scale of the British Library – a red brick behemoth that's home to over 150 million pieces of writing. What's more, its collection is growing at a fearsome rate: every year, the library receives a copy of everything published in the UK and Ireland, including books, newspapers, maps, magazines, prints and

drawings. Its most prized treasures are on display in the dimly lit Sir John Ritblat Gallery, including the Magna Carta, Lewis Carroll's *Alice's Adventure Under Ground* and some scribbled Beatles lyrics. Temporary exhibitions in the PACCAR Gallery are often accompanied by hands-on workshops and special events, while a smaller gallery in the entrance hall contains interactive displays on music and culture linked to the National Sound Archives.

The education department arranges regular storytelling sessions and hands-on arty workshops (carnival mask-making, perhaps, or drawing your own magnificent map) during the school holidays – see www.bl.uk/learning for details. Finally, the café is a Peyton and Byrne establishment, which means delectable treacle tarts, extravagantly topped cupcakes and a nice line in quiches, proper sausage rolls and hot meals – at a price, mind.
Buggy access. Café. Disabled access: lift, toilet. Nappy-changing facilities. Restaurant. Shop.

Charlton House
Charlton Road, SE7 8RE (8856 3951, www.greenwich.gov.uk). Charlton rail or bus 53, 54, 380, 422. **Open** *Library* 2-7pm Mon, Thur; 9.30am-12.30pm, 1.30-5.30pm Tue, Fri; 9.30am-12.30pm, 1.30-5pm Sat. *Toy Library* (term-time only) 9.30am-12.30pm Tue, Thur, Fri. **Admission** free. **No credit cards.**

This handsome, early 17th-century red brick mansion now houses a community centre and library. Traces of its past grandeur remain – not least the creaky oak staircase, marble fireplaces and ornate plaster ceilings. The library has a good children's section, and runs preschooler play and story sessions. Charlton Toy Library (8319 0055, www.charltontoy library.co.uk) is also based here, and has music and story sessions on Thursday mornings. The mulberry tree outside, dating from 1608, still bears fruit that sometimes finds its way into the crumbles, cakes and chutneys sold in the Mulberry Café. Visit at 1pm on a Friday and you'll be treated to a free concert by musicians from the Trinity College of Music, who also put on a soaring Christmas concert.

Buggy access. Café. Disabled access: lift, toilet. Nappy-changing facilities.

Idea Store

321 Whitechapel Road, E1 1BU (7364 4332, www.ideastore.co.uk). Whitechapel tube. **Open** 9am-9pm Mon-Thur; 9am-6pm Fri; 9am-5pm Sat; 11am-5pm Sun. **Credit** MC, V.

You can't miss Whitechapel's gleaming, glass-fronted Idea Store – a bold, 21st-century take on the library, built by Adjaye Associates. In addition to its book collections, it offers state-of-the-art learning and information services and an airy fourth-floor café. All sorts of groups meet here, from toddler and parent get-togethers to drop-in homework clubs – there's even a gathering for comic book and manga fans (nine to 16s). For 16 and overs, the borough's network of Idea Stores offer over 900 courses. A handful of courses are aimed at families – among them, creative dance, art and design and cookery classes for parents and children. Call or check online for dates, prices and age restrictions.

Buggy access. Café. Crèche. Disabled access: lift, toilet. Nappy-changing facilities.
Branches 1 Gladstone Place, Roman Road, E3 5ES (7364 4332); 1 Vesey Path, East India Dock Road, E14 6BT (7364 4332); Churchill Place, E14 5RB (7364 4332).

Peckham Library

122 Peckham Hill Street, SE15 5JR (7525 2000, www.southwark.gov.uk). Peckham Rye or Queen's Road rail, or bus 12, 36, 63, 171. **Open** 9am-8pm Mon, Tue, Thur, Fri; 10am-8pm Wed; 10am-5pm Sat; noon-4pm Sun. **No credit cards.**

Will Alsop's unusual-looking, inverted L-shaped library plays host to a rich array of children's activities, including creative baby and toddler sessions and family reading groups. Mondays and Fridays bring in the Homework Club (4-7pm), while the teenage reading group's activities range far beyond literary discussions: open mic nights, creative writing workshops, debates and manga nights were on the schedule the last time we dropped by. An extended programme of holiday workshops is also offered.

Buggy access. Disabled access: lift, toilet. Nappy-changing facilities.

Storytelling

Discover

383-387 High Street, E15 4QZ (8536 5555, www.discover.org.uk). Stratford tube/rail/ DLR. **Open** *Term-time* 10am-5pm Tue-Fri; 11am-5pm Sat, Sun. *Holidays* 10am-5pm Mon-Fri; 11am-5pm Sat, Sun. **Admission** £4.50; £4 reductions; free under-2s; £14 family (2+2). **Credit** MC, V.

This Stratford-based storymaking centre is a hotbed of creativity, with an imaginative story garden. Kids can stand in 'Hootah' cones and have their stories recorded for a visiting space monster, or just enjoy themselves on the themed playground equipment. Indoors, the story den features interactive exhibitions about tales from around the world, and children can go on a trail across an indoor river via a wooden footbridge that talks, take a trip on the Lollipopter or explore the secret cave. It's a brilliant place to hold a birthday party; call for details.

Buggy access. Café. Disabled access: lift, toilet. Nappy-changing facilities.

MUSIC

Tuition

artsdepot Signing Choir

5 Nether Street, N12 0GA (8369 5454, www.artsdepot.co.uk). West Finchley or Woodside Park tube. **Classes** 12.30-2.30pm Sat during term-time. **Fees** free.

Sing and sign classic pop songs, current chart hits and musical show tunes at this weekly choir session which takes place on Saturday afternoons during term time. Anyone aged between 13 and 19 is welcome to this inclusive

Activities

course, although places must be booked in advance. *See also p208.*

Blackheath Conservatoire

19-21 Lee Road, SE3 9RQ (8852 0234, www.conservatoire.org.uk). Blackheath rail. **Classes** times vary; phone or check website for details. **Fees** from £79/term. **Credit** MC, V.

Musical children can enrol in all sorts of classes and courses here, covering everything from percussion playing to jazz singing. If one-on-one tuition is too expensive, kids can learn different instruments in small groups, divided into three different age ranges. There are various choirs and instrumental ensembles, meeting mainly on Saturdays, plus vibrant music, drama and art courses all year round. *Buggy access.*

Blueberry

Various venues (8677 6871, www.blueberry playsongs.co.uk). **Fees** from £70/10wk term. **Credit** AmEx, MC, V.

Operating in south-west and west London, these jolly little groups are aimed at parents and tinies (six months to threes). Sessions involve a good sing-song, with grown-ups guiding their offspring through the accompanying actions, and cheery group games. For Blueberry birthday parties, *see p223.*

Centre for Young Musicians

Morley College, 61 Westminster Bridge Road, SE1 7HT (7928 3844, www.cym. org.uk). Lambeth North tube. **Classes** 9am-5pm Sat term-time only. **Fees** vary. **No credit cards.**

Children must audition for a place on the Saturday classes that run at the Centre for Young Musicians and its two satellite annexes – Notre Dame High School and Johanna Primary School. Auditions are held for all levels and staff have a keen eye for musical potential, although absolute beginners shouldn't apply. Open access courses for six to 18s run in the school holidays, alongside GCSE revision sessions; check online for details. *Buggy access. Café. Disabled access: toilet. Nappy-changing facilities.*

Guildhall School of Music & Drama

Silk Street, EC2Y 8DT (7382 7160, www.gsmd.ac.uk/juniors). Barbican tube or Moorgate tube/rail. **Classes** 8am-6pm Sat. **Fees** basic course from £2,310/term. **Credit** MC, V.

Only the most talented young musicians are singled out to undertake this world-class conservatoire's Junior Guildhall instrumental training, with classes on Saturday mornings. Entry is by audition, and standards are extremely high. There are kindergarten classes for children aged four to six and music classes for 10- to 18-year-olds. The school also runs a String Training Programme for beginners aged four to 11, with instrumental training and music appreciation. Talented musicians who can't afford the fee can apply for local authority grants or Guildhall scholarship funding. The Guildhall's Drama Course (for 13- to 18-year-olds) involves a more informal audition process.

Musical Express

Southfields Methodist Church, 423 Durnsford Road, SW19 8EE; Wimbledon Rugby Club, Barham Road, Copse Hill, SW20 0ET (8946 6043, www.musical express.co.uk). **Classes** times vary; phone for details. **Fees** 1st session free, then from £6/class. **No credit cards.**

Set up by a music therapist, Musical Express groups cater for babies and under-sixes, giving young children the means to express themselves and develop core social skills with instruments and 'action songs'. Parents and carers must accompany under-threes, though older children attend alone. Hour-long sessions for over-threes include some time spent mastering Jolly Phonics, in which children learn each letter's sound with the help of an accompanying action.

Music House for Children

Bush Hall, 310 Uxbridge Road, W12 7LJ (8932 2652, www.musichouseforchildren. co.uk). Shepherd's Bush Market tube. **Classes** times vary; phone for details. **Fees** £7/drop-in class. **Credit** MC, V.

Headquartered in Bush Hall, a beautifully restored former dance hall in Shepherd's Bush, this well-established operation provides tuition for all ages. Puppets and bubbles keep tinies spellbound at baby music sessions, while toddlers are inspired to throw all sorts of weird and wonderful shapes at the story-led creative dance classes. Older children can learn keyboard, singing, percussion and drums, guitar, ukulele and violin, with a maximum of five pupils per class; two-to-one lessons offer an even wider choice of instruments, and cost £15 per child for a half-hour class (nine to 15s). There's home tuition for fives and overs, too,

Activities

starting at £20 for half an hour, plus various holiday shows and workshops.
Buggy access. Disabled access: toilet. Nappy-changing facilities.

Royal College of Music
Prince Consort Road, SW7 2BS (7589 3643, www.rcm.ac.uk). South Kensington tube or bus 9, 10, 52, 452. **Classes** 9am-5pm Sat. **Fees** vary; phone for details. **Map** p329 D9.
Children (aged eight to 18) who pass the stringent auditions can attend individually tailored lessons at this august establishment. Lessons run from 9am to 5pm on Saturdays, in conjunction with the school term, and focus almost exclusively on classical instruments. As you'd expect, it's heavily oversubscribed. For inspiration, check online for details of (usually free) performances staged by pupils throughout the year.
Buggy access. Disabled access: lift, toilets.

Trinity College of Music
King Charles Court, Old Royal Naval College, SE10 9JF (8305 4444, www.tcm.ac.uk). Cutty Sark DLR. **Classes** 9am-6pm Sat. **Fees** £715/term. **No credit cards.**
This superb conservatoire was the first in the UK to open its doors to schoolchildren on Saturdays, back in 1906. 'Intensive but fun' all-day sessions at Junior Trinity (three to 19s) nurture musical creativity with improvisation and composition work; students are also encouraged to play in ensembles. String Time, a special programme for young players aged from three to 11, also takes place on Friday afternoons and Saturday mornings. Auditions are held in March and May, and you can hear the current students in action at the college's tuneful Open Days.
Buggy access. Café. Disabled access: lift, toilets.

Venues

Cadogan Hall
5 Sloane Terrace, SW1X 9DQ (7730 4500, www.cadoganhall.com). Sloane Square tube. **Open** *Box office* 10am-8pm Mon-Sat. **Tickets** £10-£35. **Credit** MC, V. **Map** p332 G10.
Concerts in this fine former church-turned-concert hall near Sloane Square are delightfully varied, running from dignified quartets and orchestral performances to big band shows. Of

most interest to children are the Southbank Sinfonia Orchestra's Saturday Spectaculars, when children can dabble in various craft activities, meet the musicians, and then listen to a suitably lively 45-minute concert.
Bar. Buggy access. Disabled access: lift, toilet. Nappy-changing facilities.

English National Opera
The Coliseum, St Martin's Lane, WC2N 4ES (7632 8484 education, 7632 8300 box office, www.eno.org). Leicester Square tube. **Open** *Box office* 10am-6pm Mon-Sat. **Tickets** £10-£90. **Credit** AmEx, MC, V. **Map** p331 L7.
Family Days at the ENO involve hands-on activities and theatre tours, linked to the current production; join the mailing list for updates on forthcoming events. Preschoolers can be dropped off at Opera Tots while their parents attend the opera, while seven to 12s can attend Opera Stars sessions, which promise operatic adventures and activities.
Bar. Buggy access. Disabled access: lift, toilet. Nappy-changing facilities. Restaurant.

Roundhouse
Chalk Farm Road, NW1 8EH (7424 9991, 0844 482 8008 box office, www.roundhouse.org.uk). Chalk Farm or Camden Town tube. **Open** *Box office* 11am-6pm Mon-Sat. **Tickets** £5-£50. **Credit** MC, V.
The iconic former railway engine shed is Camden's pride and joy, hosting arty gigs, theatre and visually stunning multimedia events, as well as quirky contemporary circus and performance acts. While not all the shows are suitable for families with children, creative opportunities for young people lie at the heart of the Roundhouse Studios, tucked below the circular hall. The eclectic workshops for 11-25s held here often focus on multimedia skills: filming as part of a camera crew, producing a radio show and costume design have all featured in the past, at a mere £2 a day. *See also p140* **Neighbourhood Watch.**
Bars. Buggy access. Disabled access: toilet. Nappy-changing facilities. Restaurant.

Royal Albert Hall
Kensington Gore, SW7 2AP (7589 8212, www.royalalberthall.com). South Kensington or Knightsbridge tube. **Open** *Box office* 9am-9pm daily. **Tickets** £5-£150. **Credit** AmEx, MC, V. **Map** p329 D9.

Activities

The 5,200-capacity rotunda hosts special Family Proms during the annual BBC Proms, from July to September. The Proms Plus series, meanwhile, comprises free family events at the nearby Royal College of Music, involving musical activities and workshops that provide a bit of background on the stories behind the music. In the daytime, guided tours let you peep at the auditorium; one child can go free with every paying adult (£8). Note that the tour isn't suitable for under-sevens.

Bars. Buggy access. Café. Disabled access: lift, toilet. Nappy-changing facilities. Restaurants. Shop.

Wigmore Hall

36 Wigmore Street, W1U 2BP (7935 2141, 7258 8227 education, www.wigmore-hall. org.uk). Bond Street or Oxford Circus tube. **Open** *Box office* 10am-7pm daily (8.30pm on performance nights). **Tickets** £10-£30. **Credit** AmEx, MC, V. **Map** p330 H5.

This art deco hall oozes grandeur. Happily, small fry are made very welcome, thanks to a busy programme of family, community and outreach projects. The star attraction is Chamber Tots: these music and movement classes for two- to five-year-olds are immensely popular. Once-monthly family concerts are also great fun, and suitable for five-and-overs. Regular Family Days bring opportunities to try a spot of composing, join a junk jam or meet the musicians.

Bar. Buggy access. Disabled access: toilet. Nappy-changing facilities. Restaurant.

THEATRE

Tuition

Allsorts

34 Crediton Road, NW10 3DU (8969 3249, www.allsortsdrama.com). Kensal Green tube/rail or Kensal Rise rail. **Classes** phone for details. **Fees** £100-£180/10wk term; from £80 4-day workshop; 20% sibling discount. **Credit** MC, V.

Alumni from Allsorts have won starring roles in big-budget flicks: Anna Popplewell (Susan in the *Chronicles of Narnia*) enrolled here at the age of six. Children (four to 18) don't need any previous experience to sign up for the Saturday school and holiday workshops; working in small groups, they are encouraged to take a creative approach, with role-playing and improvisation. Teachers can also arrange bespoke at-home acting tuition and drama parties.

Dramarama

8446 0891, www.dramarama.co.uk. Holiday courses: South Hampstead High School, Maresfield Gardens, NW3 5SS. Term-time classes: South Hampstead Junior School, Netherhall Gardens, NW3 5RN. Finchley Road & Frognal rail. **Fees** phone for details. **No credit cards**.

Kids of all ages and abilities can get involved in acting with Dramarama's after-school clubs, Saturday workshops and holiday courses. Three- to four-year-old thespians can become Dramatots, while older children work towards Trinity Guildhall Performance Art exams; these are recognised qualifications, and the more advanced grades can be converted into university entrance UCAS points. There's also a birthday party service for six to 14s, with possible themes ranging from mermaids to murder mysteries.

Helen O'Grady's Children's Drama Academy

01481 200250, www.helenogrady.co.uk. **Classes** times vary; phone for details. **Fees** £98/14wk term. **Credit** MC, V.

The academy's weekly one-hour workshops aim to build kids' self-esteem, confidence and social skills. The lower and upper primary groups (five to eights and nine to 11s, respectively) work on clear speech and fluent delivery, while the Youth Theatre (13-17s) develops more advanced dramatic techniques. They have also recently introduced a preschool group (three to fives). A production is held at the end of the summer term. Check the website to find your nearest group.

Hoxton Hall

130 Hoxton Street, N1 6SH (7684 0060, www.hoxtonhall.co.uk). Hoxton rail. **Classes** times vary; phone for details. **Fees** £20/8wk term. **No credit cards**.

This refurbished Victorian music hall runs a vibrant after-school Youth Arts programme for seven to 19s, incorporating dance, drama and music. Children's abilities and ideas are taken seriously here, and they're given plenty of access to the hall's extensive facilities: seven- to ten-year-old musicians can compose and record their own songs in the recording studio, while the street dance group (11-17s) devises performances for the main stage with the help of professional choreographers and dancers.

Buggy access. Café.

Activities

Music House for Children. *See p202.*

The Bubble's exemplary arts programme includes term-time theatre groups for six to eights, nine to 12s and 13-17s. There are no nail-biting auditions; all you need to take part are enthusiasm and commitment (though there may be a waiting list, as places are much in demand). Check online for details of the summer Open Performance Theatre Project, open to all ages, and the Bubble's groups in Forest Hill and Rotherhithe.

Millfield Theatre School

Silver Street, N18 1PJ (box office 8807 6680, www.millfieldartscentre.co.uk). Silver Street rail/34, 102, 144, 217, 231, W6 bus. **Open** *Box office* 10am-6pm Mon-Sat. **Classes** (4-5s) 10.30am-noon, (6-7s) 12.30-2pm, (8-14s) 11am-2pm Sun. **Fees** (4-5s, 6-7s) £100/10wk term; (8-14s) £185/10wk term. **Credit** MC, V.

Millfield House, where the Millfield Theatre School is based, reopened in late spring 2011 after a major refurbishment. Details of the programme for the Millfield Theatre School, which will run Sunday afternoon drama sessions for 14- to 21-year-olds, were still being finalised as we went to press, but the venue will also offer Saturday and Sunday morning dance classes (ballet, tap, etc) for ages three and up. There is also a programme of after-school clubs in the week. The theatre itself (refurbished in 2009) presents a regular calendar of musicals, comedies and drama, as well as some perky touring shows and the time-honoured Christmas panto.
Buggy access. Disabled access: toilets.

Lewisham Youth Theatre

Broadway Theatre, Catford Broadway, SE6 4RU (8690 3428, box office 8690 0002, www.lewishamyouththeatre.com). Catford or Catford Bridge rail or bus 75, 181, 185, 202, 660. **Classes** *Junior Youth Theatre* (8-11s) 75 mins Wed, Sat. *Senior Youth Theatre* (15-21s) 6-8pm Mon, Thur. **Credit** (Box office) MC, V.

Lewisham Youth Theatre has forged a reputation for innovation, variety and high standards. It has also stuck firmly to its aim of making theatre accessible to all: there are no auditions, and classes and workshops are free. Most recruitment takes place in schools, but some places are allocated on a first come, first served basis. All classes work towards full productions, and there is some crossover between junior and senior groups. For details of children's theatre performances at the Broadway Theatre, *see p208.*
Buggy access. Disabled access: toilets.

London Bubble Theatre Company

5 Elephant Lane, SE16 4JD (7237 4434, www.londonbubble.org.uk). Bermondsey, Canada Water or Rotherhithe tube. **Open** *Box office* June-Sept 10am-6pm Mon-Fri. **Classes** phone for details. **Fees** phone for details. **Credit** MC, V.

National Youth Music Theatre

Head office: 2-4 Great Eastern Street, EC2A 3NW (7422 8290, www.nymt.org.uk). Old Street tube/rail. **Classes** phone or check website for details. **Fees** prices vary; phone for details. **No credit cards.**

The National Youth Music Theatre's glittering list of alumni speaks for itself, featuring the likes of Jamie Bell, Matt Lucas, Sheridan Smith and Jude Law. The company continues to audition young hopefuls for its amazing shows; check online for details of upcoming auditions and regional workshops. Stage-management opportunities appeal to those keen to work behind the scenes, while accomplished young musicians can nab orchestral roles.

Perform

Office: 49 Chalton Street, NW1 1LT (0845 400 4000, www.perform.org.uk). **Classes**

Activities

Activities

Royal Albert Hall. See p203.

phone for details. **Fees** £143.10/10wk term (weekday); £200.80/10wk term (weekends); free trials. **Credit** MC, V.

The four Cs (confidence, communication, concentration and co-ordination) are the focus at Perform – and you're never too young to start learning the basics. Story- and song-packed Mini Ps classes are aimed at three month- to three-year-olds, while sessions for four to eights and eight to 12s blend acting, singing and dancing. The website has details of venues, information on the party service, and the latest on holiday workshops such as the all-singing, all-dancing Popstar Superstar.

Stagecoach Theatre Arts

Head office: Courthouse, Elm Grove, Walton-on-Thames, Surrey KT12 1LZ (01932 254333, www.stagecoach.co.uk). **Fees** £318/12-13wk term (6-16s); £159/ 12-13wk term (4-7s). **Credit** MC, V.

From humble beginnings in Surrey, this performing arts school has become a global concern, with an attendant performers' agency

for young people that's the largest in the UK. The school itself has 60 branches in London alone, offering its starry-eyed young pupils a solid grounding in dance, drama and singing. Four to sixes start with half an hour's tuition in each discipline per week, which climbs to an hour for older children. Some students work towards exams in their second or subsequent year, while third-year pupils can also audition for the Stagecoach National Showcase Production, staged in London. Holiday workshops are organised too.

Sylvia Young Theatre School

1 Nutford Place, W1H 5YZ (7258 2330, www.sylviayoungtheatreschool.co.uk). Edgware Road or Marble Arch tube. **Classes** phone for details. **Fees** *Classes* £70-£92/11wk term. *Summer school* (10-18s) £300/wk. **Credit** MC, V.

Thanks to the surfeit of soap stalwarts and pop stars who have honed their talents here over the years (Billie Piper, Amy Winehouse, Leona Lewis and Keeley Hawes among them), Sylvia

Young's has become a household name. The full-time stage school (with around 160 pupils aged from ten to 16) and Saturday school (fours to 18s) are famously oversubscribed; there are also evening classes on Thursdays. The Easter and summer holidays bring assorted theatre and musical theatre workshops for fame-hungry eights and overs.

Puppet theatres

Little Angel Theatre

14 Dagmar Passage, off Cross Street, N1 2DN (7226 1787, www.littleangel theatre.com). Angel tube or Highbury & Islington tube/rail, then bus 4, 19, 30, 43. **Open** *Box office* 10am-6pm Mon-Fri; 9am-4pm Sat, Sun. **Tickets** £6-£13. **Credit** MC, V.

Tucked away off Cross Street, this little puppet theatre has been up and running since 1961. The setting, an old Victorian temperance hall, is charming, while the shows' themes, styles and stories are drawn from an array of cultural traditions. Productions are often aimed at fives and above, with occasional shows for the very young and special baby-friendly performances, plus the odd adults-only show. The Saturday Puppet Club offers weekly sessions for various age groups; for a one-off puppet-making workshop, book a place on a family fun day. *Buggy access. Disabled access: toilet. Nappy-changing facilities. Shop.*

Puppet Theatre Barge

Opposite 35 Blomfield Road, W9 2PF (7249 6876, www.puppetbarge.com). Warwick Avenue tube. **Open** *Box office* 10am-6pm daily. **Tickets** £10; £8.50 under-16s, reductions. **Credit** AmEx, MC, V.

The fact that this diminutive theatre is afloat enchants younger visitors almost as much as the prospect of a performance. The 55-seater barge is moored on the towpath in Little Venice between November and mid July, with marionette shows at 3pm on Saturdays and Sundays and more frequent performances in the holidays. Come July, the barge floats merrily off down the Thames to perform at Richmond, with a show every day except Sunday during August, and weekend performances during September and early October. Pay attention to the age recommendations, as longer shows can be pretty tiring for little ones, and book ahead to secure seats near the front. *Buggy access.*

Touring companies

Kazzum

7749 1123, www.kazzum.org.
The Kazzum children's theatre collective has toured schools, theatres, libraries, parks and festivals with its productions, which range from playful interactive pieces to specially commissioned plays that tackle hard-hitting contemporary issues. A desire to celebrate difference and diversity lies at the heart of Kazzum's body of work.

Oily Cart

8672 6329, www.oilycart.org.uk.
Oily Cart's performances are aimed at two groups who might otherwise miss out on the magic of theatre: very young children and children with special needs. At its brilliant, multi-sensory productions, children in the audience become part of the performance, invited to explore the set and interact with the delightfully quirky performers. One previous show involved on-stage baking, making for a wonderfully fragrant auditorium (every member of the audience left with a freshly baked Christmas bun); in another, toddlers tugged on ropes to start the music and lights, and pedalled away to set a Heath Robinson-esque machine whirring into motion. Shows tour the country, but most start in London with a three- to six-week run: audience sizes are tiny, so tickets are snapped up by those in the know.

Quicksilver Theatre

www.quicksilvertheatre.org.
Led by its dynamic joint artistic directors, Guy Holland and Carey English, this Hackney-based children's theatre collective tours the UK with its innovative productions. The company has a firm grasp of what preschoolers enjoy ('small shows for small people in small places'), but are equally adept when it comes to producing visually striking, thought-provoking plays for older children. Creative collaborations with other companies reap rich rewards.

Theatre Centre

7729 3066, www.theatre-centre.co.uk.
Founded in 1953 by the late Brian Way (a pioneering director, educator and writer), the Theatre Centre takes its productions to schools, theatres and festivals across the country. The company has a reputation for excellence and technical invention, and also champions up-and-coming new writers. Lisa

Activities

Evans' *The Day the Waters Came*, which looks at the devastation wreaked by Hurricane Katrina, is touring during 2011 and suitable for 13 and overs.

Theatre-Rites
7928 4875, www.theatre-rites.co.uk.
Theatre-Rites first made its name with daring, site-specific works, starting with 1996's astounding *Houseworks*, which took over an entire house in Brixton. Staging shows in the unlikeliest of venues (a hospital ward, say, or a disused salts factory) is still a major strand of its work, but the company isn't afraid to branch out. Its shows might involve puppets, percussionists, trapeze artists and jugglers; whatever the theme, the visuals are invariably stunning. Mischief, an award-winning, inventive collaboration with choreographer Arthur Pita, adds dance into the mix – along with giant, bendy foam shapes and an onstage keyboard- and guitar-playing beatboxer. There are generally two to three touring productions a year, which always stop down in London for a night or two.

Venues

Albany
Douglas Way, SE8 4AG (8692 4446, www.thealbany.org.uk). Deptford rail or bus 21, 36, 47, 136, 171, 177, 188, 225, 453. **Open** *Box office* 9am-9pm Mon-Fri; 10am-5pm Sat; 2hrs before performance Sun. **Tickets** *Family Sunday* £5. **Credit** MC, V.
Deptford's sparky multimedia and performing arts centre retains a lively neighbourhood focus. Family Sunday events (September to April) range from specially written pieces and musical stories with sing-along songs to the jumping Baby Grooves disco; tickets cost a fiver. There's a programme of free activities for teenagers too; check the website or sign up to the Facebook group. The venue can also be hired out for parties.
Buggy access. Café. Disabled access: lift, toilet. Nappy-changing facilities.

artsdepot
5 Nether Street, N12 0GA (8369 5454, www.artsdepot.co.uk). West Finchley or Woodside Park tube. **Open** *Box office* 9am-5.30pm Mon-Fri; 10am-5.30pm Sat; noon-5.30pm Sun (later during performances). **Tickets** free-£20. **Credit** AmEx, MC, V.

This dynamic north London arts centre throws open its doors to children and families, offering a richly varied line-up of performances, classes and courses. Children's theatre shows take place in the 150-seat studio on Saturdays and Sundays, with a different company in residence each week.

For those that would rather take to the stage, Bright Sparks Theatre Company (eight to 12s) meets on Thursday, and there are Saturday drama and story making sessions for younger children; meanwhile, artsdepot members aged from 13 to 19 can attend free playwriting and drama groups. Other offerings on the busy learning programme run the gamut from terrific messy play mornings to street dance and art classes. Innovative summer holiday activities might involve anything from turning recycled materials into artistic masterpieces to learning fast-paced dance routines to accompany the latest chart hits.

As we went to press, artsdepot's future was under threat after nearly £200,000 of council funding was cut completely for 2011.
Buggy access. Café. Disabled access: lift, toilet. Nappy-changing facilities.

BAC (Battersea Arts Centre)
Lavender Hill, SW11 5TN (7223 2223, www.bac.org.uk). Clapham Common tube, then bus 345, or Clapham Junction rail, or bus 77, 77A, 156. **Open** *Box office* 10am-6pm Mon-Fri; 3-6pm Sat. **Tickets** free-£15. **Credit** MC, V.
Its Victorian premises may look eminently traditional, but inside the BAC is a hotbed of ground-breaking theatre. In the past, shows have tended to be for adults, but ambitious plans are afoot to produce more work that's both for and by young people. In the meantime, 12 to 25s can join the in-house young people's theatre group, YPT. Its members often get the chance to work with the BAC's prestigious guest companies and artists (the likes of Punchdrunk and Forced Entertainment), which has resulted in some brilliantly experimental pieces. There's also an inexpensive little café, which serves simple, child-friendly grub (macaroni cheese, sausage and onion sarnies and chocolate brownie for afters).
Bar. Buggy access. Café. Disabled access: lift, toilet. Nappy-changing facilities.

Broadway Theatre
Catford Broadway, SE6 4RU (8690 0002, www.broadwaytheatre.org.uk). Catford or Catford Bridge rail, or bus 75, 181, 185,

202, 660. **Open** *Box office* 10am-6pm Mon-Sat. **Tickets** £3.50-£22. **Credit** MC, V.

Sadly, this art deco theatre's Saturday morning ROAR! matinées are no more, but the main auditorium still hosts the rollicking Christmas pantomime and other large-scale shows. Note that there are no performances from the end of July to the beginning of September, as the entire theatre shuts down for the summer. The acclaimed Lewisham Youth Theatre (*see p205*) is also based at the theatre, with drama groups for various ages.

Buggy access. Café. Disabled access: lift, toilet. Nappy-changing facilities.

Chickenshed

Chase Side, N14 4PE (8292 9222, www.chickenshed.org.uk). Cockfosters or Oakwood tube. **Open** *Box office* 10am-6pm Mon-Fri; 10am-5pm Sat. **Tickets** *Shows* £4.50-£20. *Workshops* phone for details. **Credit** AmEx, MC, V.

Since its inception in 1974, Chickenshed has firmly upheld its ethos that 'everyone is welcome, and everyone is valued'. Over-fives can join the Children's Theatre group, while the Youth Theatre is open to over-13s: the waiting list is enormous, but we're assured that everyone eventually gets in. On Friday and Saturday, colourful Tales from the Shed performances bring all sorts of stories to life for under-sevens.

Bar. Buggy access. Café. Disabled access: lift, toilet. Nappy-changing facilities. Shop.

Colour House Children's Theatre

Merton Abbey Mills, Watermill Way, SW19 2RD (8542 5511, www.colourhouse theatre.co.uk). Colliers Wood tube. **Open** *Box office* 10am-5pm daily; 1hr before show. **Shows** 2pm, 4pm Sat, Sun. **Tickets** £3.50-£9. **Credit** MC, V.

Witty, often musical renditions of classics such as *Sleeping Beauty* and *Robinson Crusoe* are the forte at this sweet little riverside venue, which has also started staging puppet shows. After-show birthday parties with a mini disco can be arranged, with front row seats for the

Lion King. *See p215.*

Activities

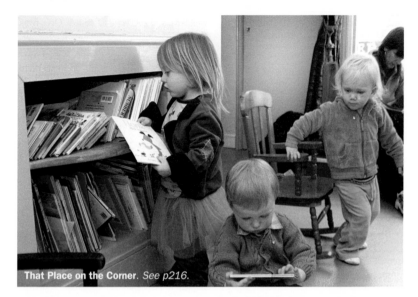

That Place on the Corner. *See p216.*

guests and a tuneful rendition of *Happy Birthday* from the cast at the end of the performance. Call for details of children's theatre workshops and groups.
Buggy access. Disabled access: toilet. Nappy-changing facilities (in Merton Abbey Mills). Shop.

Hackney Empire

291 Mare Street, E8 1EJ (8985 2424 box office, www.hackneyempire.co.uk). Hackney Central rail or bus 38, 106, 253, 277, D6. **Open** *Box office* 10am-6pm Mon-Sat. **Tickets** prices vary; phone for details. **Credit** MC, V.
This Hackney institution is up and running again after some major problems with funding: have a gander at the website for details of forthcoming performances. The star of the show is the annual Christmas pantomime, and 2010 saw a great production of *Jack and the Beanstalk*, with a captivating performance from resident dame Clive Rowe and brilliantly imaginative sets.
Buggy access. Disabled access: toilet. Nappy-changing facilities.

Half Moon Young People's Theatre

43 White Horse Road, E1 0ND (7709 8900, www.halfmoon.org.uk). Limehouse DLR/rail. **Open** *Box office* Apr-Sept 10am-6pm Mon-Fri. Oct-Mar 10am-6pm Mon-Fri; 9.30am-4.30pm Sat.* **Tickets** £6. **Credit** MC, V.
As well as staging children's theatre shows from September to April, this place also nurtures creative talent. Seven youth theatre groups give kids aged between five and 17 the chance to express themselves: there are no auditions to get in, and young people are encouraged to join in regardless of race, sex, ability or financial situation. In the holidays, there are various hands-on workshops and courses, often culminating with a performance for friends and families on the final day.
Buggy access. Disabled access: lift, toilet. Nappy-changing facilities.

HMV Hammersmith Apollo

46 Queen Caroline Street, W6 9QH (8563 3800, tickets 08448 444748, http://venues.meanfiddler.com/apollo/ home). Hammersith tube. **Open** *Box office* (in person) from 4pm on show days; (by phone, Ticketmaster) 24hrs daily. **Tickets** prices vary, call for details; child discount for children's show tickets. **Credit** MC, V.
Hammersmith's spacious Apollo mostly houses comedians off the telly and international music acts, but it's worth checking the listings for more family-friendly fare. The line-up for 2011 includes appearances from Australia's ever-popular kids' act the Wiggles, who are touring

the UK with their Greatest Hits show, and Michael Flatley's foot-tapping extravaganza *Lord of the Dance.*
Bars. Buggy access. Disabled: toilet. Nappy-changing facilities.

Jackson's Lane

269A Archway Road, N6 5AA (8341 4421, www.jacksonslane.org.uk). Highgate tube.
Open *Box office* 10am-10pm Tue-Sat; 10am-5pm Sun. **Tickets** £5.95-£12.50.
Credit MC, V.
This handsome red brick Gothic church conversion is home to a 170-capacity theatre, a wonderfully atmospheric dance studio and four additional rehearsal and workshop spaces. Touring children's theatre companies take to the stage on Sundays at 2pm, while a splendid programme of children's courses includes unusual offerings such as film-making or fencing, along with tap, drama and dance for tinies with energy to burn.
Bar. Buggy access. Café. Disabled access: toilet. Nappy-changing facilities.

Lauderdale House

Highgate Hill, Waterlow Park, N6 5HG (8348 8716, www.lauderdalehouse.co.uk). Archway tube, then bus 143, 210, 271, W5.
Open *Box office* 30mins before performance.
Tickets £4.50; £3 reductions. **Credit** MC, V (£2 charge).
Set amid ornamental gardens on the edge of peaceful Waterlow Park, this grand 16th-century mansion was once home to Nell Gwynne, the mistress of Charles II. Art and photography exhibitions now occupy its stately lobby (occasionally expanding into the upper and lower galleries), but the big lure for parents is the jam-packed kids' activities programme. In term-time, most of the action takes place at weekends: Saturdays bring energetic panto-style children's shows and sing-along sessions at 10am and 11.30am, while Sunday mornings are set aside for family-friendly classical music concerts (recommended from five or six years and up). Weekday drop-in classes for pre-schoolers focus on music, art and movement; the programme expands in the school holidays to incorporate workshops in art, dance and drama for kids of all ages.
Buggy access. Café. Disabled access: toilet.

Lyric Hammersmith Theatre

Lyric Square, King Street, W6 0QL (0871 221 1722, www.lyric.co.uk). Hammersmith tube. **Open** *Box office* 9.30am-5.30pm

Mon-Sat (until 8pm on performance days).
Tickets children's shows £8; £6 reductions; £25 family (2+2). **Credit** MC, V.
The Lyric remains one of London's most forward-looking theatres for children's programming, largely thanks to its pioneering Creative Learning schedule. It gives 11- to 19-year-old west Londoners access to high-quality arts facilities and teaching, with an after-school club, courses and workshops. Fourteen-to 21-year-olds can also join the Lyric Young Company (£7), which yields rich returns in the shape of weekly drama classes, one-off masterclasses and the chance to audition for the company's shows.
The studio is the venue for most kids' events: top-notch weekend theatricals, school holiday workshops and preschooler specials in the week. Look out for rambunctious Messy Play workshops (£3), held after selected Saturday and Sunday shows; there are only 25 places on each, so book as early as you can. Parents can join in, or slope off to the café for brunch and a rest.
Buggy access. Café. Disabled access: lift, toilet. Nappy-changing facilities.

National Theatre

South Bank, SE1 9PX (7452 3000 box office, 7452 3400 information, www.nationaltheatre.org.uk). Waterloo tube/rail. **Open** *Box office* 9.30am-8pm Mon-Sat. **Credit** AmEx, MC, V. **Map** p333 M8.
The National's trio of world-class theatres (the Olivier, the Lyttleton and the Cottesloe) cater mainly to grown-ups, but in the last few years there have been familiy-friendly productions of Shakespeare's *Twelfth Night* and Terry Pratchett's *Nation,* as well as stage adaptations of more obvious children's stories such as *Beauty and the Beast.* But you don't need to shell out for a ticket to have fun here. For a start, there are the free early evening concerts held in the foyer from Monday to Saturday (and on Saturday lunchtimes), which could include anything from swirling, foot-stamping flamenco to boogie woogie piano. Another spot with plenty going on is the outdoor Theatre Square – home to the terrific Watch This Space season, which generally runs from July to mid September. Wacky street theatre performers, art installations, intrepid tightrope-walkers and puppeteers run riot on the astroturf lawn; for a full run-down of what's going on, check online.
Nurturing new talent is part of the agenda. New Connections commissions renowned playwrights and authors (William Boyd, David

Activities

Mamet and Anthony Horowitz have contibuted in the past) to write a new play for young performers, which schools and youth theatres nationwide can then produce.

If you'd rather peek behind the scenes, backstage tours (£7, £6 under-18s; £13 family; not suitable for under-sevens) lead visitors into the rehearsal rooms, costume and prop workshops, dressing rooms and stages. *See also p48* **Neighbourhood Watch**.

Bars. Buggy access. Café. Disabled access: lift, toilet. Nappy-changing facilities. Restaurants. Shop.

Nettlefold Theatre

West Norwood Library Centre, 1 Norwood High Street, SE27 9JX (7926 8070, www.lambeth.gov.uk). West Norwood rail or bus 2, 68, 196, 468. **Open** *Box office* 9am-10pm Mon-Sat. **Tickets** £5. **Credit** MC, V.
This 200-seat theatre is built into West Norwood Library and runs four child-oriented shows a year (usually on a Saturday at 2pm). Check the blog at http://nettlefoldhall.blogspot. com for details, and listings of other performances and events: a magic show was among the offerings last time we looked.
Buggy access. Disabled access: lift, toilet. Nappy-changing facilities.

New Wimbledon Theatre

The Broadway, SW19 1QG (0870 060 6646, www.theambassadors.com/new wimbledon). Wimbledon tube/rail. **Open** *Box office* 10am-start of performance Mon-Sat. **Tickets** phone for details. **Credit** AmEx, MC, V.
A steady stream of touring hits swap the bright lights of the West End for the suburban surrounds of Wimbledon to be staged at this popular theatre. Among the highlights for 2011 are *The Sound of Music* and *The Jungle Book*. The end-of-year pantomime is always a spectacular, no-expense-spared affair.
Bars. Buggy access. Disabled access: lift, toilet. Shop.

Open Air Theatre

Inner Circle, Regent's Park, NW1 4NU (0844 826 4242 box office, www.openair theatre.org). Baker Street tube. **Open** *Box office* (by phone) 24hrs daily; (in person) 10am-6pm Mon-Sat Mar-Sept. **Tickets** £10-£50. **Credit** AmEx, MC, V. **Map** p330 G3.
If forecasters predict a hot summer, be sure to book ahead for the charming Open Air Theatre

in Regent's Park. However old you are, there's something magical about seeing Shakespeare performed amid a leafy, rustling semi-circle of trees. The season always includes a musical and a children's play; in 2010 it was *Macbeth*, 're-imagined for everyone aged six and over', in 2011 *Pericles*, in the same style. If rainy weather stops play, tickets will be exchanged for a later performance – subject to availability – but umbrellas, thick jumpers and blankets are always highly advisable.
Buggy access. Café. Disabled access: toilet.

Pleasance

Carpenters Mews, North Road, N7 9EF (7609 1800, www.pleasance.co.uk). Caledonian Road tube or bus 91, 390. **Open** *Box office* 10am-8pm Mon-Sat; noon-6pm Sun. **Tickets** free-£11. **Credit** MC, V.
The London arm of the famous Edinburgh Fringe venue isn't at an address that you'd stumble across by accident, but it's worth making the effort to get here. The building was once used for storing timber by the London Omnibus Company, and makes for a spacious venue. Youth theatre company Young Pleasance is based here and offers regular term-time drama classes for children. Check the website for family-friendly productions.
Bar. Cafe. Disabled: toilet, lift. Nappy-changing facilities.

Polka Theatre

240 Broadway, SW19 1SB (8543 4888, www.polkatheatre.com). South Wimbledon tube or Wimbledon tube/rail, then bus 57, 93, 219, 493. **Open** *Box office* (by phone) 9.30am-4.30pm Mon; 9.30am-5.30pm Tue-Fri; 10am-4.30pm Sat; (in person) 9.30am-4.30pm Tue-Fri; 10am-4.30pm Sat. **Tickets** £7.50-£16. **Credit** MC, V.
This children's theatre pioneer has been up and running since 1979. Daily shows are staged by touring companies in the main auditorium, while shorter works for babies and toddlers take over the Adventure Theatre once a week. There are in-house productions, workshops and storytelling sessions for families and schools. Productions for summer 2011 include *All Join In!*, which celebrates the work of Quentin Blake with a mix of songs, stories and dance, and *Archaeology – A Worm's Story*, created for one- to three-year-olds. Dramatic offerings aside, there's an appealing little playground and wendy house, a reading corner and a cheerful café – a top place for lunch. The

Polka Youth Theatre runs a number of theatre groups for different ages (three to 17s), with fees of £65 to £95 per term, while day-long workshops are a treat for children in the school holidays. There are after-school groups for three to 13s, with end-of-term performances for friends and family.
Buggy access. Café. Disabled access: lift, toilet. Nappy-changing facilities.

Shakespeare's Globe

21 New Globe Walk, SE1 9DT (7401 9919, 7902 1500 tours, www.shakespeares-globe.org). Southwark or Mansion House tube, or London Bridge tube/rail. **Open** *Box office* 10am-6pm daily. *Tours* May-Sept 9am-12.30pm daily. Oct-Apr 10am-5pm daily. **Tickets** £5-£35. *Tours* £10; £8.50 reductions; £6.50 5-15s; free under-5s; £25 family (2+3). **Credit** AmEx, MC, V. **Map** p334 O7.

Fidgety younger kids won't be inclined to sit – or stand – through shows at this meticulously reconstructed Elizabethan theatre, but older children will appreciate the atmospheric setting. Eight to 11s can also attend Childplay sessions on selected Saturdays, watching part of the play as groundlings and taking part in themed workshops. A huge range of talks, tours and activities – many conducted by staff wearing full period costume – takes place with schools during term time, while holiday workshops and excellent seasonal events open the floor to families. *See also p48* **Neighbourhood Watch**.
Bar. Buggy access. Café. Disabled access: lift, toilet. Nappy-changing facilities. Restaurant.

Stratford Circus

Theatre Square, Stratford, E15 1BX (8279 1001, box office 0844 357 2625, www.stratford-circus.com). Stratford tube/rail/DLR. **Tickets** £5-£6. **Classes** phone for details. **Credit** MC, V.

Stratford Circus is a vibrant contemporary performing arts venue, situated close to the 2012 Olympic site and Stratford City. Along with a host of child-friendly productions, there are also plenty of classes for kids of all ages – parent and baby dance classes, drawing sessions with guest teachers such as Simon Bartram (creator of the *Man on the Moon* series), and a Saturday morning Creative Club. There is also a decent café, Circus Eats, on site.
Bar. Café. Disabled access: lift, toilet. Nappy-changing facilities.

Unicorn Theatre for Children

147 Tooley Street, SE1 2HZ (7645 0560 box office, www.unicorntheatre.com). London Bridge tube/rail. **Open** *Box office* 9.30am-6pm Mon-Fri; 10am-6pm Sat; noon-5pm Sun. **Tickets** £9.50-£16.50. **Credit** MC, V. **Map** p335 R9.

London Brass Rubbing Centre. *See p217.*

Activities

Set on the South Bank, this airy, modern theatre was designed in collaboration with local schoolchildren. A giant sculpture of a white unicorn rears above theatre-goers in the foyer, while performance spaces include the 300-seater Weston Theatre and more intimate Clore Theatre. Staging is often inventive: the set for a production of *Twelfth Night* was a living, growing garden, which happily sprouted away during the month-long run. In-house productions are accompanied by special Family Days, where everyone's encouraged to muck in with the activities and workshops; prices include tickets to the show, and the chance to meet the actors afterwards. Visiting theatre companies also drop in for shorter runs, presenting all sorts of brilliant plays and puppet shows for nought to 19s.
Buggy access. Café. Disabled access: lift, toilet. Nappy-changing facilities.

Warehouse Theatre
Dingwall Road, Croydon CR0 2NF (8680 4060, www.warehousetheatre.co.uk). East Croydon rail. **Open** *Box office* 10am-5pm Mon; 10am-8.30pm Tue; 10am-10pm Wed-Fri; 2-10pm Sat; 3-7pm Sun. **Tickets** £5-£6.50. **Credit** AmEx, MC, V.
Housed in a converted Victorian cement warehouse, hidden away behind East Croydon station, the Warehouse is an unassuming gem. Theatre4Kidz shows take place on selected Saturdays, while a variety of touring shows entertain those as young as two. Croydon Young People's Theatre (CRYPT) offers a creative base for 13- to 16-year-olds; it meets 2-5pm every Saturday during term time, and puts on an annual summer show. The fee per term is a mere £12, and application forms are available online.
Bar. Buggy access. Café. Disabled access: toilet.

West End shows

As well as calling the box office to find out what ages shows are suitable for, it's a good idea to check the running length. With many musicals clocking in at two hours, the outing can turn into a frenzy of wriggling and plaintive needing-the-loo requests. If you've got young children in your party, it's probably best to avoid the West End altogether and go to a more intimate, child-specific venue in another part of town, where the plays are shorter, the house lights brighter and the bangs less likely to scare.

For two weeks in August, families can take advantage of **Kids Week** (www.kidsweek.co.uk). Run by the **Society of London Theatres** (SOLT, 7557 6700, www.officiallondontheatre.co.uk), it offers five to 16s free admission to West End shows, provided they are accompanied by a paying adult; up to two additional children can get in at half-price. Children can also go backstage, meet the stars and take part in workshops. For more on Kids Week, and information on the capital's best family-friendly shows, subscribe to the free family bulletin on the SOLT website.

Also keep a lookout for Sam Mendes's new West End musical version of *Charlie and the Chocolate Factory*, which is expected to open in late 2011.

Billy Elliot the Musical
Victoria Palace Theatre, Victoria Street, SW1E 5EA (0844 811 0055, www.billyelliot themusical.com). Victoria tube/rail. **Times** 7.30pm Mon-Sat. *Matinée* 2.30pm Thur, Sat. **Tickets** £19.50-£65. **Credit** AmEx, MC, V. **Map** p332 H10.
It would take a pretty cynical heart not to be warmed by this tale of a motherless miner's son with a passion for ballet, set to music by none other than Sir Elton John. The production (adapted from the film) contains strong language, and isn't suitable for under-eights.
Bars. Disabled access: toilet.

Grease
Piccadilly Theatre, 16 Denman Street, W1D 7DY (0844 412 6666, www.grease themusical.co.uk). Piccadilly Circus tube. **Times** 7.30pm Mon-Thur, Sat; 8.30pm Fri. *Matinée* 3pm Sat; 5.30pm Fri. **Tickets** £15-£57.50. **Credit** AmEx, MC, V. **Map** p332 J6.
Carina Gillespie joined the cast of Grease as Sandy in January 2011. Die-hard fans can't get enough of this musical. The soundtrack delivers hit after hit: 'Summer Nights', 'Greased Lightnin'', 'You're The One That I Want'… Just try to stop yourself singing along.
Bars. Disabled access: toilet.

Activities (vertical side text)

Legally Blonde

*Savoy Theatre, Strand, WC2R 0ET
(0870 164 8787, www.legallyblonde
themusical.co.uk). Charing Cross tube/rail.*
Times 7.30pm Mon-Sat. *Matineé* 2.30pm
Thur, Sat. **Tickets** £28.50-£66. **Credit**
AmEx, MC, V. **Map** p333 L7.
An award-winning, highly enjoyable if
somewhat daft story about the exploits of its
indomitably girly, pink-loving heroine (played
by Susan McFadden) and her equally chic
chihuahua, Bruiser, as the pair hit Harvard Law
School in pursuit of Simon Thomas's Warner.
It's a Broadway transfer that keeps tongue
firmly in cheek.
Bars. Disabled access: toilet.

Lion King

*Lyceum Theatre, Wellington Street,
WC2E 7RQ (0844 844 0005, www.disney.
co.uk/musicaltheatre). Covent Garden tube
or Charing Cross tube/rail.* **Times** 7.30pm
Tue-Sat. *Matinée* 2pm Wed, Sat, Sun.
Tickets £21-£64. **Credit** AmEx, MC, V.
Map p333 L7.
Most kids are familiar with Simba the lion,
thanks to Disney's classic film; the stage
production ups the ante with stunning sets, a
combination of puppetry and live actors and a
heady cocktail of West End choruses and
African rhythms.
Bars. Disabled access: toilet.

Mamma Mia!

*Prince of Wales Theatre, Coventry Street,
W1V 8AS (0844 482 5165, www.mamma-
mia.com). Piccadilly Circus tube.* **Times**
7.30pm Mon-Thur, Sat; 8.30pm Fri. *Matinée*
5pm Fri; 3pm Sat. **Tickets** £20-£67.50.
Credit AmEx, MC, V. **Map** p333 K7.
Despite a somewhat sketchy plot, *Mamma Mia!*
is awash with feel-good, singalong Abba hits.
Bars. Disabled access: toilet.

Les Misérables

*Queen's Theatre, Shaftesbury Avenue,
W1D 6BA (0844 482 5160, www.lesmis.
com). Leicester Square or Piccadilly
Circus tube.* **Times** 7.30pm Mon-Sat.
Matinée 2.30pm Wed, Sat. **Tickets**
£15-£62.50. **Credit** AmEx, MC, V.
Map p331 K6.
This musical version of Victor Hugo's tale of
revolution in 19th-century France has been
running for 25 years – longer than the young
visitors to its Kids' Club have been alive. The
two-and-a-half hour experience gives eights to

15s the chance to tour backstage, meet a cast
member and re-enact a scene from the show.
Bars. Disabled access: toilet.

Shrek the Musical

*Theatre Royal Drury Lane, Catherine
Street, WC2B 5JF (0844 871 8810,
www.shrekthemusical.co.uk). Covent Garden
tube.* **Times** 7.30pm Mon, Wed-Sat. *Matineé*
3pm Thur, Sat, Sun. **Tickets** £15-£65.
Credit AmEx, MC, V. **Map** p333 L/M6.
Classic fairytale fun as Shrek (Nigel Lindsay)
and loyal steed Donkey (Richard Blackwood)
set off on their quest to rescue Princess Fiona
(Amanda Holden) from a tower guarded by a
lovesick dragon.
Bars. Disabled access: toilet.

Stomp

*Ambassadors Theatre, West Street,
WC2H 9ND (0844 811 2334, www.stomp
london.com). Leicester Square tube.* **Times**
8pm Mon, Thur-Sat; 6pm Sun. *Matinée*
3pm Thur, Sat, Sun. **Tickets** £20-£49.50.
Credit AmEx, MC, V. **Map** p331 K6.
An international smash hit, Stomp finds music
in all kinds of everyday objects – including the
kitchen sink. The show's a blast, and the lack
of dialogue means that it's accessible to
everyone, young and old.
Bars.

Wicked

*Apollo Victoria, Wilton Road, SW1V 1LG
(0844 826 8000, www.wickedthemusical.
co.uk). Victoria tube/rail.* **Times** 7.30pm
Mon-Sat. *Matinée* 2.30pm Wed, Sat.
Tickets £15-£65. **Credit** AmEx, MC, V.
Map p332 H10.
Mark Evans joined the cast of this smart, pacy
rejoinder to the *Wizard of Oz* in February 2011,
in the role of Fiyero. For eights and above.
Bars. Disabled access: toilet.

Wizard of Oz

*London Palladium, Argyll Street, W1F
7TF (0844 412 2957, www.wizardofoz
themusical.com). Oxford Circus tube.* **Times**
7pm Tue; 7.30pm Wed-Sat. *Matinée* 2.30pm
Wed, Sat; 3pm Sun. **Tickets** £25-£62.50.
Credit AmEx, MC, V. **Map** p330 J6.
Follow the yellow brick road to the Palladium
for Andrew Lloyd Webber's new production of
the children's movie classic, with Danielle Hope,
winner of TV's *Over the Rainbow*, as Dorothy,
and Michael Crawford playing the Wizard.
Bars. Disabled access: toilet.

Activities

Activities

WORKSHOPS & ACTIVITIES

Harringay Club

50 Tottenham Lane, Crouch End, N8 7EE (8348 2124, www.ymcahornsey.org/harringayclub). Hornsey rail. **Open** 9am-10pm Mon-Thur; 9am-8pm Fri; 9am-2pm Sat, Sun. **Fees** £4 drop-in classes; course prices vary, call for details. **Credit** MC, V.

A fantastic council-run resource that has all sorts going on throughout the week and at weekends. There's a mixture of drop-in classes and workshops and bookable courses for all ages. Activities range from cookery and music to gymnastics, ballet, yoga and karate, and some classes cater for children as young as two. *Buggy access. Cafe. Children's menu. Disabled: toilet. High chairs. Nappy-changing facilities.*

huggle

8-10 Winchester Road, NW3 3NT (7483 2826, www.huggle.co.uk). Swiss Cottage tube. **Open** 9am-6pm Mon-Fri; 9am-5pm Sat; 11am-4pm Sun. **Classes** £6-£15. **Credit** AmEx, MC, V.

This brilliant new shop opened at the end of 2010 and is a very welcome addition to the area. Its huggle lounge offers a comprehensive programme of activities throughout the week, including old fave Amanda's Action Kids, Little Supernovas' drama workshops, Diddi Dance's funky preschool dance classes and even Russian for Kids. *Buggy access. Café. Delivery service. Disabled access: toilet. Nappy-changing facilities.*

Maggie & Rose

58 Pembroke Road, W8 6NX (7371 2200, www.maggieandrose.co.uk). Earl's Court or West Kensington tube. **Classes** times vary; phone for details. **Fees** £500/yr membership; from £180/12wk course. **Credit** MC, V.

This 'private members' club' for families is aimed squarely at upwardly mobile mummies and daddies. Membership brings discounts on its imaginative range of activities, but prices are still on the steep side. A half-term afternoon cookery workshop might cost £50 for members and £70 for guests, for example. Birthday parties can also be arranged. *Buggy access.*

That Place on the Corner

1-3 Green Lanes, N16 9BS (7704 0079, www.thatplaceonthecorner.co.uk). Highbury & Islington tube/rail or Canonbury rail, or bus 21, 73, 141, 276, 341, 476. **Open** 9.30am-6pm Mon-Thur; 9.30am-8pm Fri; 10am-8pm Sat; 10am-3.30pm Sun. **Classes** £4-£5. **Credit** MC, V.

Alongside its splendid, family-friendly café (*see p254*), That Place offers a whole host of children's activities. Preschoolers can get stuck into Rucksack Music, Gymboree Gym arts, Music with Mummy and Tip Toes Dance, to name but a few of the classes, while kids of all ages are welcome to join the face-painting and pizza-baking sessions. *Buggy access. Café. Disabled access: toilet. Nappy-changing facilities.*

Archaeology

Museum of London Archaeology

7410 2228, www.museumoflondon archaeology.org.uk.

Keen beans can sign up for the Museum of London's Young Archaeologists Club (YAC), which is aimed at eight to 16s. It has two branches in central London, with once-monthly meet-ups in Hackney and Rotherhithe. Activities include walking the Thames foreshore to collect objects washed up at low tide, identifying animal bones and making mosaics Roman-style.

Young Archaeologists Club @ UCL

Institute of Archaeology, 31-34 Gordon Square, WC1H 0PY (7679 7495, www.ucl.ac.uk/archaeology).

The Institute of Archaeology supports a children's club for eight- to 16-year-olds which meets on the third Saturday of each month, from 11am till 1pm; call first to enquire about becoming a member.

Art & crafts

All Fired Up

34 East Dulwich Road, SE22 9AX (7732 6688, www.allfiredupceramics.co.uk). East Dulwich or Peckham Rye rail. **Open** 9.30am-6pm Mon-Sat; 11am-5pm Sun. **Fees** *Studio* £3/day. *Workshops & courses* phone for details. **Credit** AmEx, MC, V.

The shelves of plain white ceramics (from crockery cartoon characters to sensible plates, bowls and mugs) are crying out for colour – which kids happily apply, with varying levels of accuracy. Tables are equipped with palettes,

sponges, water and brushes, while friendly staff offer tactful advice. Painted objects are glazed, fired, gift-wrapped and ready for collection in ten days. Birthday parties are run for groups of ten or more children, aged five to 15 (from £12 per head).
Buggy access.

Art 4 Fun
172 West End Lane, NW6 1SD (7794 0800, www.art4fun.com). West Hampstead tube/rail. **Open** 10am-6pm Mon, Wed, Thur, Sat, Sun; 10am-8pm Tue; 10am-10pm Fri. **Fees** *Studio* £5.95/day. *Workshops & courses* phone for details. **Credit** AmEx, MC, V.
Children can give full rein to their artistic talents, daubing designs on to ceramics, T-shirts, tiles and flower pots. Tie-dye, mosaic-making, pottery and glass-painting are among the other options. Arty parties are a speciality, with no minimum numbers required, and there are half- and full-day school-holiday workshops for six to tens.
Buggy access. Café.

Art Yard
318 Upper Richmond Road West, SW14 7JN (8878 1336, www.artyard.co.uk). Mortlake rail or bus 33. **Classes** *Term-time* 4-5.30pm Mon, Tue, Wed, Thur. *School hols* 10am-3.30pm Mon-Fri. **Fees** £145/term. **Credit** MC, V.
This appealingly chaotic, colourful studio hosts all sorts of after-school art clubs and school holiday courses and workshops. They might involve creating paintings, prints, collages and papier-mâché masterpieces – or even a spot of cookery.
Buggy access.

Colour Makes People Happy
53 Grove Vale, SE22 8EQ (7207 1120, www.sieclecolours.com). East Dulwich rail. **Classes** *phone for details.* **Fees** phone for details. **Credit** MC, V.
Ostensibly, this new shop is here to sell eco-friendly paint, but Colour Makes People Happy also has a workshop space where children can paint clogs with all sorts of imaginative designs. There's no formal workshop timetable as yet, so phone ahead to book.
Buggy access.

London Brass Rubbing Centre
St Martin-in-the-Fields, Trafalgar Square, WC2N 4JJ (7766 1122, www2.stmartin-in-the-fields.org). Leicester Square tube or Charing Cross tube/rail. **Open** 10am-6pm Mon-Wed; 10am-8pm Thur-Sat; noon-5pm Sun. **Fees** from £4.50. **Credit** MC, V. **Map** p333 L7.
The revamped London Brass Rubbing Centre is far more fun than it sounds. Enter the futuristic lift and sink beneath the pavement to the large, bright open space below that was once a series of murky vaults. Sure, there could be a few more tables for actual brass rubbing, given the vast area available, but it's a very pleasant atmosphere in which to create an artwork for the wall at home. Children can choose from the smaller replica brasses: a dragon, a decorative elephant, a unicorn, or various historical figures, including William Shakespeare. The nice people at the counter will tape the paper to the block, lend out crayons and give instruction in the gentle art of brass rubbing.

Shirley Stewart's Pottery Courses
Lewisham Arthouse, 140 Lewisham Way, SE14 6PD (8694 9011, www.shirley stewart.co.uk). Deptford Bridge DLR or New Cross rail. **Fees** £70/10 sessions, plus £15 for materials and firings (payable in advance). **Credit** phone for details.
Lewisham Arthouse is a co-operative based in a Grade II-listed building. Artists rent studio space here, and Shirley Stewart is among them. Her throwing and studio pottery workshops for ages five and over are held during term time, though extra sessions can be arranged for the holidays. Parties are available for £12 per child, which includes materials and firings.
Buggy access. Disabled access (ground floor): toilet.

Smarty Paints
85 Nightingale Lane, SW12 8NX (8772 8702, www.smartypaints.co.uk). Clapham South tube or Wandsworth Common rail. **Open** 10am-6pm Mon-Sat; 11am-6pm Sun. **Fees** *Studio* £6. **Credit** AmEx, MC, V.
Everyone can get involved at this bright ceramic painting studio in south London: printing small children's paint-covered hands and feet is a popular option, though there are all manner of stencils and brushes for more complex designs. Children's classes include T-shirt painting.
Buggy access.

Activities

My Sport Capoeira
Adaora, 7

What inspired you to take up capoeira?
My school friend Tom said to try it out because he liked it, and the class is right opposite my house so it's easy to get to.

What do you like about your sport?
I like the combination of movement and music. Our teacher is funny but he makes you work at the same time.

What level are you at?
I'm at level two, so I've got a different belt now. The first one is just plain. I've been going for over a year now.

What's next for you in your sport?
I'd like to get to the top level.

Which events would you like to see at the London 2012 Olympic Games and Paralympic Games?
My granny had a letter through the door about it – she lives in Leytonstone. I'd like to go and see the running races and the Long Jump.

Activities

Cooking

Billingsgate Seafood Training School

Office 30, Billingsgate Market, Trafalgar Way, E14 5ST (7517 3548, www.seafood training.org). Canary Wharf tube. **Open** phone or see website. **Fees** see website for details. **Credit** MC, V.

Planning a coastal staycation this year? The parent and child courses at Billingsgate's superb seafood school will prepare you for making the most of all the delicious fresh fish you'll find while you're there. The lessons teach some seriously useful skills: cleaning squid, skinning fish, preparing sardines and gutting mackerel. Participants consume one of the three fishy dishes they've made for lunch, taking the other two home to impress the rest of the family – along with all sorts of gory stories with which to impress squeamish younger siblings. Children must be eight or over to participate.

La Cucina Caldesi

118 Marylebone Lane, W1U 2QF (7487 0750, www.caldesi.com). Baker Street or Regent's Park tube. **Open** 10.30am-12.30pm Sat. **Fees** £40. **Credit** AmEx, MC, V.

Not content with having a great restaurant in Marylebone, the Caldesi family also built a small cookery school around the corner. It offers children's classes on Saturdays and in the school holidays, with sessions aimed at different age groups (six to 12s and teenagers). The courses aim to teach kids how to prepare a menu based on healthy seasonal ingredients, while the teenagers' courses are targeted at budding chefs who already have some experience but would like to know more, and feature short demonstrations, hands-on cooking and plenty of tasting.

Divertimenti

33-34 Marylebone High Street, W1U 4PT (7486 8020, www.divertimenti.co.uk).

This specialist cookery shop runs a full programme of classes on everything from macaroons to Chinese dumplings. Children's classes are listed under 'Growing Gourmets' and are divided up by age group (5-9s and 10-14s). There's a maximum of 12 children in each Growing Gourmet class and previous themes have included Mexican food, Italian food and, of course, Cupcakes.

Kiddy Cook

07976 619648, www.kiddycook.co.uk.

Veronika Wyper runs the Twickenham franchise of Kiddy Cook, an organisation that encourages kids to get interested in food at a really young age. Cookie Tots is aimed at two-to four-year-olds, and introduces ingredients and cookery skills alongside storytelling, music and games. There aren't many places that a two-year-old can go in this town and be encouraged to get busy with raw eggs, real saucepans, metal graters and hob tops. The sessions take place on weekdays at the Methodist Church in Teddington and Winchester Hall in St Margarets.

Kids' Cookery School

107 Gunnersbury Lane, W3 8HQ (8992 8882, www.thekidscookeryschool.co.uk). Acton Town tube. **Open** *Office* 9am-5.30pm Mon-Fri. **Fees** *School hols* £15/75mins; £30/2.5hrs; £50/5hrs. **No credit cards.**

Over in Acton, registered charity the Kids' Cookery School has purpose-built kitchens that exist primarily to teach the principles of healthy cooking and eating to children. During term time, the centre concentrates on local schoolkids, but throughout the holidays cookery sessions for children of three and above are offered on a bookable basis. Sessions vary in length according to what's on the menu; 'classes' run for one-and-a-quarter hours, 'workshops' for two-and-a-half hours and 'study days' for five hours. Fees are low, considering all ingredients are included in the price, and assisted places are available for those on low incomes. What do parents do while their offspring are whipping up dinner for all the family? They can either wait in the reception area or come back and collect their little chefs at the end of the session.

Buggy access. Disabled access.

Munchkins

8269 1331, www.munchkinskids cooking.co.uk.

Munchkins runs hands-on, jolly sessions that work wonders with fussy eaters. The team, which was set up by a friendly former primary school teacher, runs children's cooking courses and private classes in term time, as well as during the school holidays. It can also arrange baking or make-your-own-meal parties, with optional extras such as games and face-painting; prices for the parties start from £110 for six kids.

Activities

Activities

Recipease

*48-50 St John's Road, SW11 1PR (3006
0001, www.jamieoliver.com/recipease).
Clapham Junction tube/rail.*

Jamie Oliver just won't let the matter of
children's food rest. As if his highly publicised
campaign of squeezing junk food out of schools
wasn't enough, he also wants them to learn to
cook from scratch at a young age. To this
end, his cookery school-cum-cookshop-cum-
deli-cum-advice centre for foodies in Battersea,
Recipease, offers sessions for local schools
and privately bookable classes for children
aged eight and above (who must be
accompanied by an adult). They can start with
fairly simple skills like decorating biscuits and
making pancakes, but can soon graduate to
first lessons in 'Champion knife skills'.
Children of 12 and above can join any of the
Easy to Learn classes, but must also be
accompanied by an adult.

*Buggy access. Cafe. Disabled: toilet.
High chairs. Nappy-changing facilities.*

You Make a Cake

*10 Bellevue Road, SW17 7EG (8767 3395,
www.youmakeacake.com). Balham tube/rail
or Wandsworth Common rail.*

This lovely new venue was opened in 2010
by Emma Hollands, who wanted to create
somewhere that offered all the ingredients,
equipment and recipes in one place to
encourage some fabulous home baking. Fees
include the ingredients and cake decorations
and someone to clear up all the mess, which
has to be worth double when baking with
children. It's a fantastic venue for children's
birthday parties, where they can make the cake
the main event.

*Buggy access. Disabled access: toilet.
Nappy-changing facilities.*

Film & new media

For a cinema-mad child's dream
birthday treat, check out **Movie
Parties** (*see p223*).

Film Club

www.filmclub.org.

Film Club aims to put movies on the (extra)
curriculum by loaning films to participating
after-school film clubs, free of charge, and
running specially devised film seasons. The
website also contains a useful list of films,
categorised by age group.

Film London

www.filmlondon.org.uk.

From shorts to features, London's film and
media agency supports emerging and
established talent across the capital.

Filmsteps

0844 324 5414, www.filmsteps.com.

Fast-paced five-day summer holiday film
schools (£275) teach seven- to 16-year-olds the
essentials of making a feature film, from
planning the storyboards to operating the
cameras. Thrillingly, their handiwork is
premièred at a red-carpet screening, which
guests are able to attend. Meanwhile, term-time
Film Schools meet in Maida Vale, Belsize Park
and Teddington once a week, producing
everything from pop videos to film trailers; they
cost £235 per term, but there are sibling
discounts and scholarships.

First Light

www.firstlightmovies.com.

Funded by the UK Film Council, First Light
funds film projects for five- to 18-year-olds,
offering courses across the country via schools
and educational groups. Its subsidiary website,
www.filmstreet.co.uk, provides a bright and
breezy starting point for under-12s to explore
and discover filmmaking, while www.media-
box.co.uk offers funding for projects involving
13- to 19-year-olds.

Mouth That Roars

*23 Charlotte Road, EC2A 3PB (7729
2323, www.mouththatroars.com). Old
Street tube/rail.* **Open** 5-8pm Wed, Thur;
noon-5pm Sat.

This east London charity offers training in
video production for young people. Thirteen-
to 19-year-olds who live in Hackney can
make a film in a day at its MTR Studio 23
studio and editing suite (sessions are free and
are run on a drop-in basis), which also hosts
weekly film screenings.

Young Film Academy

7387 4341, www.youngfilmacademy.co.uk.
Fees from £95/day; £390/4 day course.
No credit cards.

'Passion starts early' is the Young Film
Academy's ethos, and its courses, workshops
and movie parties aim to inspire fledgling
filmmakers (seven to 18s). It's all fast-paced,
hands-on stuff, whether the youngsters are
making a film in a day or taking part in the
Four Day Film School.

Parties

Pump up the volume.

Whether it's a no-expense spared extravaganza or an afternoon of pass-the-parcel and pin the tail on the donkey, good parties are all about the planning. Those aiming to impress can hire a fire engine, employ a science boffin to ensure proceedings go with a bang, or arrange an arty afternoon of jewellery-making; the options are endless. Then again, you may decide that the most memorable sort of knees-up needs nothing more than games, balloons and bunting, with a candle-topped cake at the end.

Whatever sort of party you've got in mind, and whatever your budget, there are places and people that can help. Entertainers of every stripe can hold small guests enthralled, while specialist enterprises run from eco-friendly party bag companies to a gluten-free baker's. Alternatively, professional party planners will organise the whole thing – at a price.

If the thought of rampaging, sugar-fuelled kids and accidental spillages sends a chill down your spine, there are plenty of reasonably priced halls; that extra £50 could be worth it to save your carpet. Most play centres also offer party deals, although it's often cheaper to ignore the package and just turn up; check if their insurance allows cakes with candles.

We've focused on birthdays, but the teen-friendly companies are all great for bah and bat mitzvahs, and many entertainers also specialise in keeping tiny wedding guests amused.

ACTIVITY PARTIES

Arts & crafts

For more artistic options, *see p217*. East Dulwich's **All Fired Up** (*see p217*) offers arts and crafts parties.

Arty Party
8675 7055, www.artyparty.co.uk.
A team of professional artists arrive with all the materials to make jewelled mirrors, jaunty wooden boats, towering giraffes and other crafty items in their two- to three-hour party packages. Staff are pretty undaunted by rowdy kids, having held workshops for crowds of 400 at park fun days. They charge £230 for up to 20 kids aged over four.

Jewel Party
3176 0546, www.jewelparty.co.uk.
Children as young as four return home from a Jewel Party bedecked in necklaces, rings and bracelets of their own making. Parties are themed according to the materials used, with beads and sweetie jewellery the big favourites. Boys enjoy the Fimo clay workshops, bashing out Gothic signet rings and pirate-style necklets. Prices start with the 40-minute bracelet workshop at £75. Otherwise, standard packages start at £150 for one-and-a-half hours. All are for up to ten kids with invites included.

Pottery Café
735 Fulham Road, SW6 5UL (7736 2157, www.pottery-cafe.com). Parsons Green tube or bus 14, 414. **Open** 11am-6pm Mon; 10am-6pm Tue-Sat; 11am-5pm Sun.
Credit MC, V.
This café and paint-your-own studio offers children's parties for £19.95 a head. In a separate party room, kids aged seven and over can make a joyful mess painting their very own piece of pottery. It's not just mugs and plates; most popular with the kids are the beautiful money-boxes, shaped like dragons and fire-engines. The package includes invites, balloons,

Activities

Cookie Crumbles

0845 601 4173, www.cookiecrumbles.net.
Kids from four to 15 prepare their own three-course meals during these absorbing parties. Even non-foodie children enjoy bashing out dough and getting covered in flour while preparing such goodies as pizza snakes and ricotta ravioli. Two-hour parties start at £165 for six kids, with CC providing all ingredients and equipment; you won't have to lift a spoon. The company also produces birthday gift boxes, containing everything small chefs need to bake various sweet treats. Over the years, Cookie Crumbles' workshop programmes have taught over 10,000 children how to cook, so you can rest assured they really know their onions… and sausages, and tiramisu.

You Make a Cake

10 Bellevue Road, SW17 7EG (8767 3395, www.youmakeacake.com). Balham tube/rail or Wandsworth Common rail.
The most exciting thing for children at any birthday party is usually the birthday cake. So why not make it the main event? At this colourful and well-stocked new cookery venue, children's parties involve baking and decorating cup-cakes. It's fantastic fun, and best of all, someone else tidies up.

Pretty Pollies

(07944 821 391, www.prettypollies.com).
Pretty Pollies organise chocolate-making parties which have children of five and above taking home a selection of chocolates and a lollipop they have made themselves. They also design the packaging in which to take the goodies home (no need for party bags!). Pretty Pollies can come to you or host the party in their own workshop space. Prices start at £160 for a two-hour party.

Firemen

Hot Hire

07947 028899, www.hot-hire.co.uk.
Imagine the thrill as a real fire engine turns up at your party, complete with qualified fireman on board. Kids get to ride in the fire engine and try out the hose, followed by an optional disco and games (you can sound the siren if your party is on private land). Hold your party on a school night and the fire engine can even meet your guests at the school gate and drive them to the venue. Party packages for three- to 16-year-olds start at £99.

a party leader, sandwiches and a drink – as well as the glazed and fired results of the children's artistic endeavours. (You return a week later to collect the pieces.) You're welcome to bring your own food and cake.
Buggy access. Café. Disabled access. Nappy-changing facilities.
Branch 322 Richmond Road, Twickenham, Middx TW1 2DU (8744 3000).

Soap & Bubble Company

8402 7565, www.soapandbubble.com.
Soap & Bubble arrive equipped with all the ingredients to make soaps, chocolate lip balm, body glitter, bubble bath and even floating ducks. All they ask you to provide is some space and a large table. The team will even tidy up afterwards, leaving you with a spotless house and a child eager to jump in the bath to test their home-made concoctions. Parties last for an hour-and-a-half and cost £195 for up to eight kids aged eight and above.

Cookery

For cookery lessons and workshops, *see also pp219-220* **Kids' Cookery School**, **Munchkins** and **La Cucina Caldesi**.

Pamper parties

Mini Makeovers

8398 0107, www.minimakeovers.com.

Girlies aged five to 15 are treated to a makeover and manicure, before rounding things off with a celebratory disco. The little ones adore being prettied up as fairies and princesses, while tweens tend to favour the Hannah Montana and *High School Musical* parties. The basic package costs £160 for eight kids, with dance classes, photoshoots and limousine hire all available as optional extras.

Performance

For more clubs and companies that run term-time music and drama courses, as well as staging parties, *see pp191-220* **Arts & Entertainment**.

Blueberry Playsongs Parties

8677 6871, www.blueberryplaysongs.co.uk.

These fun, guitar-led musical parties for one- to six-year-olds involve dancing, bubbles, party games and puppets. Packages start from £95, including 20 balloons and a gift for the birthday child. *See also p201.*

Drama Parties

0151 336 4302, www.dramaparties.com.

Parties organised by the Little Actors Theatre Company give four- to 14-year-olds the chance to experience a full drama workshop with a party atmosphere. Themes include murder mystery, pirates and Halloween; if the birthday boy or girl has a particular passion, then you can suggest your own theme. Prices start at £130 for an hour, with invites and thankyou cards thrown in.

Funky Chicks

8302 6992, www.funky-chicks.co.uk.

Dayglo Lycra-clad dancers host these disco parties that are aimed at five- to 12-year-olds. Competitions, dressing up and party games accompany a dance class, with the birthday child taking a starring role in the final performance. You'll probably need to hire a hall to accommodate the team's acrobatic moves and body popping, and make sure you book well in advance as they are becoming very popular. Spectacular parties start at £550 for two hours. The Funky Chicks also now run a Funky Chicks Academy (see the website for more details).

Jigsaw

8447 4530, www.jigsaw-arts.co.uk.

This long-running stage school also offers imaginative singing, dancing (everything from ballet to cheerleading moves and hip hop) and drama parties. Jigsaw's experienced tutors will put three- to 12-year-old partygoers through their performing paces and the parties cost from £120 for an hour.

Kate Gielgud Acting Parties

8964 5490, www.tiddleywinks.co.uk.

Custom-written dramas that centre on the birthday child are Kate's speciality. Born with an infectious passion for drama (she's Sir John's great-niece), her parties are absorbing affairs with themes such as James/Jane Bond and classy murder mysteries. Prices start at £300 for two hours, and Kate arrives with scripts and costumes. Plays can be adapted for four- to 13-year-olds.

Movie Parties

7387 4341, www.movie-parties.co.uk.

Movie-mad eight- to 16-year-olds get eight hours to plan, rehearse, shoot, edit and screen their own film with a team of professionals. Each child is given a DVD of the finished result to take home with them. Themes include *Charlie's Angels*, *Harry Potter* and *Pirates of the Caribbean*, using your house and local

You Make a Cake.

Activities

Activities

Sport Parties

Campaign Paintball.

Campaign Paintball
01932 865999,
www.campaignpaintball.com.
Take the short jaunt out to Cobham, where Campaign's site is divided into action-packed play zones. The eerily authentic Dodge City is a big hit, along with the Jungle Zone and spooky Dark Tower. Packages for ten- to 15-year-olds cost £24.95 per child including 300 paintballs, seven games, tuition and a barbecue lunch. The day ends with a trophy presentation. They also do mini paintball sessions for eight- to ten-year-olds. Sessions last for three hours and cost £23 per child.

League One Sports Academy
8446 0891, www.leagueone.co.uk.
Children's football parties (three to 12s) with a bit of basketball and cricket thrown in for good measure. The coaches keep up the party atmosphere, taking into account any varying skill levels, with the birthday child receiving a trophy to take home. Parties start at £190 for 90 minutes, and all the equipment is provided. The company's headquarters are in north London, but staff will consider coming to you if you have enough space.

Little Dinosaurs
8444 1338, www.littledinosaurs.co.uk.
Play centres are terrific for active parties, especially for toddlers too young to grasp the rules of sporting games. Little Dinosaurs has something different to offer – beautiful outside space in the middle of a park, where kids can get a breather from the playframe and parents can escape the noise. Charging from £12 per child, Little Dinosaurs offers unlimited drinks, your own host and a buffet tea.

Mallinson Sports Centre
8342 7272, www.highgateschool.org.
This sports centre is within Highgate School, so you get exclusive use of the pool and sports centre for the birthday packages. Choose from Mini Sports and Bouncy Castle Parties for 5-7s and Sports and Swimming Parties for 6-15s (with raft races, dodge ball, mini hockey and basketball). The party finishes with 45 minutes for a party tea (bring your own food) in the social room which can be decorated by you or the staff. Parties last for two hours and cost £255-£285 for 25 children.

Talacre Sports Centre
7974 8765, www.camden.gov.uk/talacre.
This fantastic sports centre in Kentish Town has a fully equipped gymnasium with sprung floor and crash mats, a large and airy sports hall, and Treetops Play Centre all under the same roof. Choose

League One Sports Academy.

from a Gymnastics Party (£172.30 for ten children, £210.25 for 20), a Multisports Party (£112.15 for 12 children, £137.35 for 24) or a Trampolene Party (£112.15 for 12 children, £137.35 for 24). All parties are supervised by the friendly and charismatic staff, who are passionate about sports and soon manage to get all the children involved and enjoying themselves. Bring your own food to set out in one of the party spaces upstairs.

Experience Archery
07824 507 260,
www.experiencearchery.com.
Archery parties are for ages 8+. Children love the sense of satisfaction when they learn a new skill. Experience Archery can bring the archery equipment to your garden or a park, or suggest a suitable venue. The organisers build in lots of games as well as tuition and safety instructions, and you can choose to add the element of competition too, with medals given out for the top three archers of the day.

All Star Lanes
7313 8363, www.allstarlanes.co.uk.
Choose from the main hall or private rooms at any of the three All Star Lanes venues in Holborn, Brick Lane or Bayswater. Indoor bowling is an all-weather sport, so there's no need to worry about potential rain. There are lighter balls and ramps for small children to get the best out of the bowling, but there's also karaoke to distract them in between games. The private room usually costs £300 per hour (which includes shoe hire), but there's a discount for children's parties. Prices in the main hall are £5.75 per person, per game (under 12s).

Little Sports Stars
07722 334 864,
www.little-sports-stars.co.uk.
Catering for children aged two and up, Little Sports Stars can tailor your child's party to individual specifications. If your child hates sport, they can disguise the main event as activity games; if they are nuts about one particular discipline,

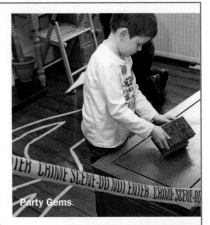

Party Gems.

they can devote the whole party to one sport. They cover London and the Home Counties and prices start at £45 for a sports party for 10 children.

Party Gems
8582 4460, www.party-gems.co.uk/ sport-party.
Party Gems can suggest the perfect venue or turn up at a home or prebooked hall. Their sports party package lasts for two hours with an hour of activity, followed by a half-hour tea, then half an hour's further activity to round things off. Races and games are formed using skills from different sports, and there's always a tournament at the end with medals going to every child for their performance. You can also have a specialist party based around one sport.

Archway Leisure Pool
7281 4105, www.aquaterra.org/ archway-leisure-centre.
Swimming parties are fantastic fun at Archway leisure pool, with its sloping 'beach' to one side, wave sessions, water jets, river run, flume and spa pools. You get exclusive use of the pool for one hour for £250. Bear in mind that children under eight must be accompanied by adults at a ratio of 2:1. You can book an area adjacent to the pool for a self-catering party. It's not the most glamorous spot, but the kids won't care.

Activities

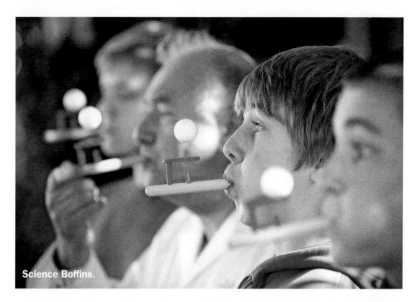

Science Boffins.

parks as the backdrop to all sorts of scenes of derring-do; finally the kids get the chance to leap over your garden fence brandishing a sword with total impunity. It costs £1,300 for a maximum of 12 guests.

Puzzles

Puzzle Party
0844 848 2822, www.happypuzzle.co.uk.
Children are divided into teams at a puzzle party, and each team works on the same challenges – although the emphasis is on completion rather than winning. Pick from giant road maps, marble runs, code-breakers, optical illusion puzzles and more. The parties work equally well at home or in a hired hall, are hosted by an entertainer, and are best for ages six and above. Call for prices.

Science & nature

Animal Magic
01323 482211, www.animal-magic.co.uk.
Lindsey Parker and her team bring a host of furry, scaly and feathered friends to parties for one- to 16-year-olds. The little ones will love holding and stroking rabbits and guinea pigs, while teens are likely to be fascinated by the geckos and snakes. Particularly popular is 'Mouse Town', a wooden construction put together by the kids, for a colony of mice to explore. Parties, starting from £140 for one hour, can be themed – *Harry Potter*, for example, might involve meeting a crew of owls, snakes and a bearded dragon. The team bring their own disinfectant to wipe up any little animal accidents.

Science Boffins
0800 019 2636, www.scienceboffins.com.
Kids' excitement levels reach a peak as mini volcanoes erupt, balloons self-inflate, light goes round corners and bottles become rockets. For parents, it's pretty exciting that all experiments are guaranteed safe and mess-free. Parties start at £195 for one hour, which buys you a qualified boffin who'll hold five- to 11-year-olds entranced with competitions and experiments of an educational bent.

Steve the Snakeman
07966 766 284,
www.stevesreptileparties.com.
Steve Ludwin is a musician by trade, but in his spare time he breeds reptiles, and he loves to bring them out to meet people. Steve's sessions last 75 minutes, during which he will teach kids fascinating facts while they get to hold snakes, chameleons, iguanas, amphibians and spiders. The sessions are suitable for ages three and above.

CAKES

Cake Store
111 Sydenham Road, SE26 5EZ (8778 4705, www.thecakestore.co.uk). Sydenham rail. **Open** 8am-5.30pm Mon-Sat. **Credit** MC, V.
This Sydenham-based cake specialist can deliver its creations to the whole of London. Colourful cakes include pirate galleons, ballet shoes, toadstools and dalmatian puppies – there's nothing this bakery cannot construct from a humble vanilla sponge, it seems. Prices start at around £75 for the themed designs (generally serving 35); smaller, more traditional cakes, inscribed with a birthday message, cost considerably less.
Buggy access. Delivery service. Disabled access.

Chorak
122 High Road, N2 9ED (8365 3330). East Finchley tube or bus 263. **Open** 8am-6pm daily. **No credit cards.**
Novelty handmade birthday cakes start at £68 for a 25- to 35-portion job, going up to £105 for a 65-portion extravaganza. Cartoon favourites are a speciality, whether it's a picture iced on to a cake or a 3D creation leaping out at your guests. Eggless cakes are available.
Branch 229-231 Muswell Hill Broadway, N10 1DE (8815 5998).

Crumbs and Doilies
8874 8885, www.crumbsanddoilies.co.uk.
These days, cupcakes are de rigueur on the kids' party circuit. Gone are the squabbles over slice sizes and wilting paper plates; instead, each child can clutch their very own cake in a sticky fist. Crumbs and Doilies are a leader in this revolution, offering no less than nine flavours and over 200 different decorations. Organic eggs, flour, lemons and vanilla are used, along with Valrhona chocolate. A dozen cupcakes will set you back £24; pastel stands on which to display them (from £10) are an optional extra. Tasting can be done at the Saturday stall at the King's Road farmer's market and at new sweet shop Chocodeli (24 Upper Tachbrook Street, SW1V 1SW).

Dunn's
6 The Broadway, N8 9SN (8340 1614, www.dunns-bakery.co.uk). Finsbury Park tube/rail, then bus W7, or Crouch Hill rail, or bus 41, 91. **Open** 7am-6pm Mon-Sat; 8am-6pm Sun. **Credit** MC, V.

Fruit- or sponge-based party cakes are adorned with stars like Upsy Daisy and Ben 10, or the birthday child's photograph (prices start at £46). Older kids may enjoy the glamour of seeing themselves on the magazine cover cake (£75). A standard sponge cake (14 servings) costs £28.
Buggy access. Delivery service. Disabled access.

Euphorium Bakery
202 Upper Street, N1 1RQ (7704 6905, www.euphoriumbakery.com). Highbury & Islington tube/rail. **Open** 7am-9.30pm Mon-Fri; 8am-9.30pm Sat, Sun. **Credit** MC, V.
Starting from £13 for an eight-inch cake, even the basic numbers here are banana- or apple-flavoured, filled with berries or covered in crisp chocolate. Prices include your choice of message, which can be iced on to the cake or inscribed on a choccie plaque. A gluten-free Chocolate Lovers Cake is available (£30 for ten servings).
Buggy access.
Branches 79 Upper Street, N1 0NU (7288 8788); 26A Chapel Market, N1 9EN (7837 7010); 211 Haverstock Hill, NW3 4QN (7431 8944); 45 South End Road, NW3 2QB (7794 2344).

Konditor & Cook
22 Cornwall Road, SE1 8TW (7261 0456, www.konditorandcook.com). Waterloo tube/rail. **Open** 7.30am-6.30pm Mon-Fri; 8.30am-3pm Sat. **Credit** AmEx, MC, V.
Chocolate curly whirly, lemon chiffon and frosted carrot cakes are among the specialities of this famed London bakery. Dinky 'magic cakes' are perfect for parties; mini lemon fondant fancies iced with pictures or letters that can be lined up to spell out a name or birthday message. An eight-inch cake starts at £21, while Magic Cakes cost £35 per dozen.
Buggy access. Delivery service. Disabled access.
Branches throughout the city.

Lola's Kitchen
16 Lansdowne Road, Berkeley Square, W1J 8QF (7495 6166). **Open** 8am-7pm Mon-Fri; 10am-6pm Sat. **Credit** MC, V.
Lola's lovely cupcakes come in a dizzying array of flavours (chocolate, coconut, peanut butter, rocky road and red velvet, to name but a few), with a seemingly endless array of decorations. The online ordering system is easy to use and purchases can be delivered or picked up. Traditionalists who like one big cake to slice

My Sport Hockey
Isabel, 15

What inspired you to take up hockey?
I followed my sister, I wanted to be in the same team as her. I first started when I was 11, but new people are coming in age nine and above.

What do you like about your sport?
It keeps you fit and it's fun. I play at the front and I love scoring goals. It's also good for meeting new people.

What level are you at?
I've got into the Essex Junior Academy. I have Sunday training for Essex, then I play every Tuesday evening and Saturday morning for Waltham Forest.

What's next for you in your sport?
I'd like to go as far as I possibly can. If you do well, they put you through to summer camp and then, ultimately, the England trials.

Which events would you like to see at the London 2012 Olympic Games and Paralympic Games?
I would love to see the Athletics, Swimming and Cycling.

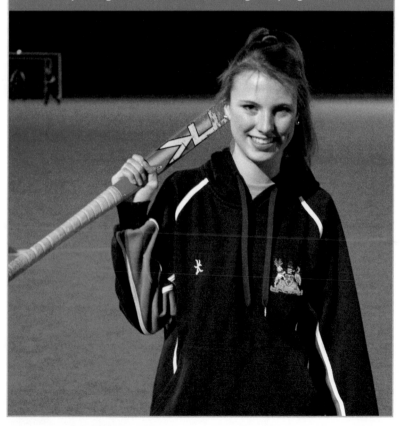

Activities

can go for proper birthday cakes, adorned with mini cupcakes, or the 'showgirl' – a giant cupcake that feeds 15 people (£45). Mini cupcakes start at £1.10 apiece, with a minimum order of 24. If you want to taste before you buy, Lola's wares are stocked in Harrods, Selfridges, Topshop Oxford Street and various high-end delis.
Delivery service.

Margaret's Cakes of Distinction
224 Camberwell Road, SE5 0ED (7701 1940). Elephant & Castle tube/rail, then bus 12, 45, 68, 176. **Open** 9am-5pm Mon-Sat. **No credit cards.**
Margaret takes considerable care over her pretty sponge- or madeira-based cakes, all of which can be personalised with individual marzipan figures. A basic birthday number starts at £25.
Buggy access. Disabled access.

Marnie Searchwell
7735 1444, www.marniesearchwell.co.uk. **No credit cards.**
Gluten-free cakes in a variety of enticing flavours are Marnie's speciality, and they really are delectable. She tries to use organic ingredients as much as possible, from the eggs to the buttercream, and is also happy to alter recipes for those sensitive to dairy, eggs and corn. A simple, iced seven-inch cake starts at £45, with more elaborate creations starting at £70. Every cake is delivered by Marnie and her son, so do give her at least two weeks' notice. She also offers a near-impossible to resist cake of the month club.
Delivery service.

Primrose Bakery
69 Gloucester Avenue, NW1 8LD (7483 4222, www.primrosebakery.org.uk). Chalk Farm tube. **Open** 8.30am-6pm Mon-Sat; 10am-5.30pm Sun. **Credit** MC, V.
Primrose Bakery sells gorgeous cupcakes and swirly layer cakes that come in a flurry of unusual flavours, such as lime and coconut or rose (decorated with petals), as well as the more classic vanilla and chocolate offerings (which are made using 70 per cent cocoa). Mini alphabet cupcakes forming the birthday child's name are particularly popular. Mini cupcakes start from £1.25 each, and celebration cakes are around £30.
Buggy access. Delivery service.
Branch 42 Tavistock Street, WC2E 7PB (7836 3638).

COSTUMES

If you are looking for inexpensive TV character or classic costumes (princesses, pirates and the like), it's worth checking out Asda, Mothercare, Argos and TK Maxx. For more toyshops and boutiques with dressing-up gear, *see pp296-298.*

Online

J&M Toys
0113 288 7716, www.jandmtoys.co.uk.
Over 150 costumes for children aged between three and eight are stocked by this fancy dress specialist: soldiers, brides, snowmen, firemen, pilots and many more. The fabulous astronaut all-in-one, for example, costs around £20, while the nifty nurse's uniform is a steal at just £12.95. There are also nativity costumes – a boon for parents not gifted in the art of sewing.

Natural Nursery
01392 499394, www.naturalnursery.co.uk.
Natural Nursery sells a dinky range of ethically traded dressing-up outfits for toddlers (18 months to five years old). The range includes pretty bumble bee, ladybird, ballerina and fairy dresses, along with adorable dinosaur and dog costumes (£15.99-£23.99).

Shops

Angels
119 Shaftesbury Avenue, WC2H 8AE (7836 5678, www.fancydress.com). Leicester Square or Tottenham Court Road tube. **Open** 9.30am-5.30pm Mon, Tue, Thur, Fri; 10.30am-7pm Wed. **Credit** AmEx, MC, V.
This Oscar-winning costumiers stocks some 10,000 outfits in myriad themes, catering for kids, adults and even dogs. Anakin Skywalker, Jack Sparrow, sword-waving warrior kings and sugary-hued princess dresses are among the offerings. Order online or pop into the shop to try before you buy. Prices start at around £20.
Buggy access. Disabled access. Mail order (0845 054 8854).

Escapade
45-46 Chalk Farm Road, NW1 8AJ (7485 7384, www.escapade.co.uk). Camden Town tube. **Open** 10am-7pm Mon-Fri; 10am-6pm Sat; noon-5pm Sun. **Credit** AmEx, MC, V.

Activities

A host of TV hero dress-ups include Ben 10, the *High School Musical* cast, Lewis Hamilton, Spongebob and the Teletubbies. The full range is available online, with a selection in Camden to try for size. Fairies, cowboys and authentic-looking astronauts are also stocked, along with nativity costumes; prices start at £10.99. Giant cardboard characters (from £26.99) can be bought to enhance your party, Winnie the Pooh, Daleks and a talking C-3PO among them.
Buggy access. Delivery service.
Disabled access.

Harlequin
254 Lee High Road, SE13 5PL (8852 0193). Hither Green or Lewisham rail/DLR, or bus 21, 261. **Open** 10.30am-5pm Mon; 10am-5.30pm Tue, Thur, Fri; 10am-1pm Wed; 10am-5pm Sat. **Credit** MC, V.
Ever-popular princess, knight and bandit outfits start at £9.95, with Spider-Man, Scooby Doo and Batgirl from £24.95. Harlequin also specialises in accessories, so the shop is lined with hats, boas, wigs and pompoms.
Buggy access.

Party Superstores
268 Lavender Hill, SW11 1LJ (7924 3210, www.partysuperstores.co.uk). Clapham Junction rail or bus 39, 77, 345. **Open** 9am-6pm Mon-Wed, Fri, Sat; 9am-7pm Thur; 10.30am-4.30pm Sun. **Credit** AmEx, MC, V.
All manner of fancy dress kits are supplemented by shelf upon shelf of accessories, wigs and hats (from £1.99). Superheroes are big with the boys, with full Batman regalia costing from £24.99;

girls like to browse the drawers of glittery wands, tiaras and fairy wings. Over 50 different sorts of themed tableware are also stocked, while the full balloon service includes inflation and delivery.
Buggy access. Delivery service.
Disabled access.

Preposterous Presents
262 Upper Street, N1 2UQ (7226 4166, www.preposterouspresents.co.uk). Highbury & Islington tube/rail. **Open** 10am-6pm Mon-Sat; 12.30-4.30pm Sun. **Credit** MC, V.
PP specialises in putting an outfit together completely from scratch – you just have to tell them who you want to be transformed into, and they will then flit around gathering the necessary accessories and wigs until you look the part. Ready-assembled costume sets are also available, including knights, fairies and various animals (from £15); accessory kits start at £4.99. Whoopee cushions, itching powder and fake blood abound.
Buggy access. Disabled access.

ENTERTAINERS

Action Station
0870 770 2705, www.theactionstation.co.uk.
Entertainers of all shapes and specialities are represented by this agency, from storytelling spacemen, spies, mermaids, cheerleaders and cowgirls to drama teachers, make-up artists, fire-eaters, jugglers and DJs. Children of all ages are catered for, while prices start at £150 for an hour.

Ali Do Lali
07789 720294, www.dralidolali.co.uk.
Do Lali arrives on a magic carpet, then proceeds to thrill the assembled youngsters with fire eating, sword swallowing and magic. Toddlers particularly like his puppets and special drawing board – an illustration of the birthday child which magically comes alive. A one-hour show starts at £160. If you've booked him before, Do Lali pledges to deliver a different act whenever he returns.

Amanda
07855 376837, www.amandasactionkids.co.uk.
Bringing new meaning to the words 'high energy', Amanda whirls one- to six-year-olds through two giddy hours of dancing, music and parachute games, like some sugar-coated

Primrose Bakery. See p229.

Angels. *See p229.*

Su Pollard. Prices start at £150 for a party led by one of her team, but it's worth shelling out an extra £50 for Amanda herself.

Christopher Howell

7993 4544, www.childrens-magician.co.uk.
A respected close-up magician, Howell puts on absorbing shows for children. An hour-long party (from £200) features magic, storytelling, balloon modelling and the chance for kids to perform various illusions. Shows are suitable for children aged four to seven.

Jenty the Gentle Clown

07957 121764,
www.jentythegentleclown.com.
Specialising in parties for under-threes, Jenty can also hype it up with a disco and limbo dancing for kids up to 11. Traditional games, face-painting, magic and singalongs with the banjo are all part of the fun. Jenty charges £145 for one hour, £195 for two.

Juggling John

0845 644 6659, www.jugglingjohn.com.
John has four party packages to suit different age ranges, from babies to ten-year-olds, with ball juggling to amuse the tinies and fire juggling for those with older kids (and high ceilings). Magic, clowning and escapology also feature. Prices start at £185 for an hour.

Magic Mikey

0844 335 6646, www.magicmikey.co.uk.
A one-man powerhouse who thrills four- to 12-year-olds with a mixture of puppetry, balloon modelling, games, magic and, above all, humour. Mikey also comes with a belting disco. His two-hour shows cost around £295.

Mel's Magic

01992 552026, www.mels-magic.co.uk.
Used to intimate gatherings as well as large crowds, Mel is adept at both mingling and performing close-up tricks, as well as presenting her full show (ages three to ten) complete with a magically appearing live rabbit. You can also book her circus skills workshop, where kids of six and above can learn to unicycle, juggle and stilt-walk. Her fees start at £165 for one hour.

Merlin Entertainments

01494 479027, www.merlinents.co.uk.
Merlin is sure to represent a party host of your liking: clowns, magicians, puppeteers and DJs can be hired here, and circus skills workshops, craft parties, musical workshops and animal encounter shows can all be arranged. Staff are adept at mixing and matching performers for larger events: you could have an animal show with a break for magic in the middle. Prices start at £140 for an hour-long performance.

Mr Happy Magic

01245 426016, www.mrhappymagic.com.
Parties are packed with magic, games, puppets and an optional disco. Happy (his real name since he changed it by deed poll) is ably assisted by Charlie the Dog – beloved by his audience of three- to seven-year-olds. Two hours of silliness start at £170.

Silly Millie the Clown

7823 8329, 07939 239397,
www.sillymillietheclown.co.uk.
Expect happy, giggly parties with Silly Millie's cheeky take on party games, karaoke, plate spinning and magic. Three- to nine-year-olds adore her shows, and the older children get taught a card trick or two. From £100 per hour.

HALLS FOR HIRE

Dragon Hall

17 Stukeley Street, WC2B 5LT (7404 7274, www.dragonhall.org.uk). Holborn tube.
Open 9am-10pm daily. **No credit cards.**

Activities

This centrally located community centre has three rooms, with kitchen facilities, for hire. The airy, 200-seater main hall is £55 per hour with a PA system as an optional extra. The main hall comes with tables and chairs and has a dancefloor.

East Dulwich Community Centre

46 Darrell Road, SE22 9NL (8693 4411, www.eastdulwichcommunitycentre.org.uk). East Dulwich rail. **Open** 8am-10pm Mon-Sat; 8am-8.30pm Sun. **No credit cards.**
A sturdy hall with a kitchen, with room for 90 kids, costs from £35 an hour. There's a stage, toilets and a large playground.

Highbury Fields One & Two O'Clock Club

Bandstand, Highbury Fields, Baalbec Road, N5 1UP (7704 9337, www.islington.gov.uk). Highbury & Islington tube/rail. **Open** *Summer* noon-6pm Sat, Sun. *Winter* 10am-4pm Sat, Sun. **No credit cards.**
At weekends, you can hire this children's centre – complete with all the play equipment, a kitchen and also a private outdoor space – from £90 in the winter, and £100 in the summer.

Old Cholmeley Boy's Club

68 Boleyn Road, N16 8JG (07963 778636). Dalston Kingsland rail. **Open** 9am-6pm daily. **No credit cards.**
A quirky venue with a large main room, scattered with sofas, where 150 kids can party (£50-£70 for an afternoon). Kitchen and music facilities are available, as is a terrace.

EQUIPMENT HIRE
Play equipment

Cool Parties

0844 450 0045, www.cool-parties.co.uk.
After ten minutes on this website, you could fill your garden with bouncy castles, slides, trampolines, inflatable sumo wrestlers, a rodeo bull and a quad bike circuit. A package of soft play equipment, perfect for toddlers, starts at £95 per day, while a full inflatable obstacle course costs from £175. Cool can also provide you with more sensible gear such as marquees, staff, child-sized tables and hall hire in north and west London. Entertainment packages, including electric car parties and teddy bear-making sessions start at around £15 per child.

PK Entertainments

07771 546676, www.fairandfete.co.uk.
An entire old-fashioned funfair can be hired through PK; that includes swingboats, hoopla, roundabouts and chair-o-planes. If money's no object you can hire everything, or pick a favourite stall or two. Prices start at £100 for the coconut shy (complete with 50 nuts), with slippery poles going for £120 and swingboats for £160. The company can also provide Punch & Judy, stilt-walkers and assorted entertainers.

Marquee hire

Sunset Marquees

Unit 5, Glenville Mews, Kimber Road, SW18 4NJ (8874 4897, www.sunsetmarquees.com). Southfields tube. **Open** 8am-6pm daily. **No credit cards.**
Sunset offers marquees in all sizes, with no pegs or hammering required (some models simply pop up). That means you can erect your marquee on hard surfaces as well as grass, and the process is blissfully fuss-free. A small marquee for 15 children starts at £190 for a weekend's hire. Chairs, lighting and stages can also be provided.
Delivery & set-up service.

Sound equipment

Capital Hire

Unit 9, Acorn Production Centre, 105 Blundell Street, N7 9BN (7249 6000, www.capitalhire.com). Caledonian Road & Barnsbury rail. **Open** 9am-6pm Mon-Sat. **Credit** MC, V.
Rob and his friendly team can loan you a two-speaker sound system with iPod mixer from £70 for a three-day hire. Units with whizzy LED lighting are £40 and, if the church hall is a bit scuffed, they even hire out dancefloors from 50p per square foot. A twinkling star cloth backdrop (from £40) will transform even the dowdiest of venues into the best disco in town.
Delivery & set-up service.

Young's Disco Centre

2 Malden Road, NW5 3HR (7485 1115, www.justadisco.co.uk). Chalk Farm tube. **Open** by appointment 9am-7pm Mon-Sat. **Credit** MC, V.
The special children's party package (including sound system and disco lights) costs from £95 for 24 hours' hire. On top of that, Young's

My London 2012
Masuma, 17 & Kushnoor, 18

How will you be participating in the London 2012 Olympic Games and Paralympic Games?
Masuma: I'm in communication with some of the Jamaican athletes in a shared knowledge programme.
Kushnoor: I've applied to volunteer to show people around.

How did you come to be involved?
Masuma: I heard about it in secondary school.
Kushnoor: One of my teachers at college told me about the Young Ambassadors Programme.

Tell us about what you have been working on as part of the Young Ambassadors Programme?
Masuma: I teach basketball, netball, cricket and football to younger children in Tower Hamlets.

Kushnoor: I'm teaching children from years four to six badminton, cricket, basketball and netball. It's nice teaching young kids, and showing them there are better things to do with their time than sitting indoors.

What do you hope your involvement in London 2012 will inspire you to go on and achieve after the Games have finished?
Masuma: I hope to be able to bring out some big sporting talents in the children around my local area.
Kushnoor: I'd like to keep promoting participation in and enjoyment of sport to younger kids.

Which events would you like to see during London 2012?
Masuma: Athletics and Swimming.
Kushnoor: Javelin Throw.

Activities

can provide DJs, bubbles, dancefloors and candyfloss machines, and prides itself on its set-up service, delivery and collection. *Delivery & set-up service.*

ORGANISERS

See also p298 **Mystical Fairies**.

Adam Ants
8959 1045, www.adamantsparties.com.
Ants can sort out all kinds of party-related tasks, from providing paper plates to arranging the entertainment for the big day. Girls can arrive in style in a Cinderella coach drawn by two white shetland ponies, while boys might just want to give the bouncy castles a good bashing. Traditional sports days can also be organised. Call for prices.

Birthday Dreams
7700 2525, www.birthdaydreams.co.uk.
Kinloch Castle in Islington, Birthday Dreams' spectacular venue, can be transformed into a jungle, princess palace or knight's fort for your child's party. Captivating entertainers include Safari Pete, with his animal encounters party. Castle packages start at £475, which includes full catering; there are even canapés for the parents. Party bags and waiting staff are also provided, so entertainers can stay in character while the serious business of sandwich serving is going on. BD can also organise parties in your home, with a clean-up service as extra.

Boo! Productions
7287 9090, www.booparties.com.
Offering breathtaking bespoke parties, Boo! can transform your venue, with every inch decorated to create a magical underwater world, a pirate ship or even the set of The *Wizard of Oz.* The cast of actors restage your favourite tales, with themed arts and crafts, games and audience participation; check out the video on the website. For those with less room (and cash), there are 'Entertainer in a Suitcase' packages from £170. Full venue transformation starts at £2,000, but staff can also snazz up a lounge with a backdrop and props.

Jasmine's Magic Parties
7249 9118, www.jasminesmagic parties.co.uk.
Choose your party to suit any age group from the large range on offer. Choices include singalong parties for toddlers, Wizards and

Escapade. *See p229.*

Witches for three to sevens, and Circus Skills or Disco Divas parties for five to nines. Jasmine and her team can also arrange to bring tables, chairs, tablewear, party bags and food, balloons, birthday cakes and more.

Nellie Shepherd Events
01625 533247, www.childrensartparties. co.uk, www.nelliespartyshop.co.uk.
The expert Shepherd and her team organise themed parties, transforming your chosen venue into a winter wonderland, fairy glade or circus then adding entertainment, face-painting and catering. Packages start at £2,000. You can also hire each element separately: a decorations box, say, or a themed crafts party.

Pro-Active 4 Parties & Entertainment
0845 257 5005, www.childrensentertainers hertfordshire.com.
These high-octane parties focus on sports, circus skills and discos. A long list of themes includes *Gladiators*, Boot Camp, *X Factor*, Mini Olympics, *High School Musical* and the ever popular Active Mayhem, which features an array of team sports. Staff are happy to come to your home, but most of the activities require plenty of space, and walls impervious to footballs. Parties are for children aged four and above, and prices start at £200.

Activities

Twizzle Parties

8392 0860, www.twizzle.co.uk.
Put your party into Twizzle's safe hands and you won't have to arrange a thing. From decorations, entertainment and play equipment to catering, sound equipment and venue hire, Twizzle offers a bespoke party service for one-to 16-year-olds (from £165). Pick and mix from its incredibly extensive recommendations; a toddler party could feature a nursery rhyme sing-along, supervised soft play and face painting, while teens might opt for quad bikes or a session in a recording studio.

PARTYWARE & PARAPHERNALIA

Baker Ross

0844 576 8922, www.bakerross.co.uk.
This online store has hundreds of ideas for craft parties and gifts, be they beady, sparkly or foamy. It also offers fun novelty balloons, no end of budget party bag toys and all manner of DIY decorations.

Balloonland

12 Hale Lane, NW7 3NX (8906 3302, www.the-party-shop.co.uk). Edgware tube or Mill Hill Broadway rail, or bus 221, 240. **Open** 9am-5.30pm Mon-Fri; 9.30am-5.30pm Sat. **Credit** AmEx, MC, V.
Balloons come any way you want them at Balloonland. Flat or inflated, plain or shaped, latex or foil… they can even arrive singing or as part of a bouquet. Balloonland also stocks general party goods, including party bags, paper plates and tablecloths covering pretty much every TV and film theme imaginable. The balloons are available to order online, but you need to call the shop if you want them pre-inflated or delivered.
Buggy access. Delivery service.
Disabled access.

Circus Circus

176 Wandsworth Bridge Road, SW6 2UQ (7731 4128, www.circuscircus.co.uk). Fulham Broadway tube. **Open** 10am-6pm daily. **Credit** MC, V.
Friendly staff are happy to talk you through the enormous range of partyware, and can also help to source caterers, venues and bouncy castle hire. Plates and decorations abound, adorned with Barbie, Peppa Pig and other heroes of the small screen. Balloon arches, party games, fancy dress and piñatas complete the stock.
Buggy access. Delivery service.
Disabled access.

CYP

01279 444707, www.cyp.co.uk.
CYP offers a dizzying array of CDs, downloads and musical games. Kids can sing along with the Fimbles, listen to CDs of fairytales or groove with the party DVDs. Many of the CDs come with free activity sheets. Prices start at £5.

Happy Green Earth

0845 388 0931, www.happygreenearth.com.
This online independent specialises in eco-friendly party bags in designs ranging from pirates to polka dots. Prices start at 10p for pink or blue candy-striped paper bags. Fillers include chocolate lollies and appealing wooden trinkets, such as balsa wood gliders and heart-shaped mirrors. Beeswax candles, cotton bunting and biodegradable balloons also feature.

Kidzcraft

01793 327022, www.kidzcraft.co.uk.
Click on the theme of your choice and Kidzcraft will present you with a range of crafty ideas for your very own art party. All manner of craft kits are available here, including pottery to paint and treasure chests to adorn (from £2.50). T-shirt decorating kits are another hot seller. Proud hosts can submit photos of the kids' efforts to the online gallery.

Activities

Party Party. See p236.

Little Cherry

01784 470570, www.littlecherry.co.uk.
Want to avoid the post-party guilt of sending bags full of plastic waste to the landfill? Little Cherry stocks biodegradable, compostable and recycled partyware. The recycled paper plates come in vivid colours – or your guests can eat off sialli- or palm-leaf plates. The cotton and recycled paper party bags can be bought ready-filled or empty.

Mexicolore

7622 9577, www.mexicolore.co.uk.
Mexicolore makes and imports authentic Mexican piñatas (made of papier maché, not cardboard). Prices start at £30, and staff will make up custom designs to order. Fill it up (the traditional stuffing is sweeties) and let the kids expend all that excess energy bashing it to bits.

Non-Stop Party Shop

214-216 Kensington High Street, W8 7RG (7937 7200, www.nonstopparty.co.uk). High Street Kensington tube or bus 10, 27, 391.
Open 9.30am-6pm Mon-Sat; 11am-5pm Sun.
Credit AmEx, MC, V.
A great shop to browse, whether you're after cards, fancy dress and wigs or tableware and decorations. Non-Stop specialises in bespoke balloon decorations to personalise your venue; for those that just want some balloons to kick about, you can buy a pump or hire a helium cylinder. This is also one of the few London shops where you can buy fireworks year round.
Buggy access. Delivery service.

Party Ark

01572 748609, www.partyark.co.uk.
This user-friendly website sells partyware in TV, classic and age-specific themes. The one-click party packs have everything you need in your chosen theme in one package, so you don't have to browse. Another nice touch is the ideas panels for bewildered parents – a description of who each TV character is and what your child will expect from, say, an *Angelina Ballerina* or a *Lazy Town* party (the latter involves Daddy donning a purple catsuit).

Party Party

3 & 11 Southampton Road, NW5 4JS (7267 9084, www.partypartyuk.com). Chalk Farm tube or Gospel Oak rail, or bus 24. **Open** 9.30am-5.30pm Mon-Sat.
Credit MC, V.
No.3 stocks decorations and a large range of bargain balloons, while No.11 is the shop to go to for tableware and costumes. If you'd rather not leave the sofa, you can browse the entire stock online. Knowledgeable staff can talk you through the numerous balloon options; you can even bring in last year's foil numbers to be reinflated. A lovely range of piñatas are also stocked. If you don't fancy excitable children wielding a big stick in your house, go for a 'pull' piñata, which showers the kids with sweeties once they locate the lucky ribbon.
Buggy access. Delivery service. Disabled access.

Party Party

9-13 Ridley Road, E8 2NP (7254 5168, www.ppshop.co.uk). Dalston Kingsland rail or bus 30, 38, 56, 67, 76, 149, 236, 242, 243, 277. **Open** 9am-5.30pm Mon-Thur; 9am-6.30pm Fri, Sat.
Credit MC, V.
A stalwart of the east London party scene, Party Party has opened a second branch in Kilburn, stocking the same dizzying array of banners, fancy dress, piñatas and partyware. A massive selection of cake decorations and novelty bakeware takes centre stage, from ready-made icing (£4.29) for nervous chefs to 3D train-shaped baking pans (£14.49) for the more ambitious. Even the candles are special, with footballs, jungle characters and dinosaurs ready to grant your birthday wishes.
Buggy access. Mail order.
Branch 206 Kilburn High Road, NW6 4JH (7624 4295).

Party Pieces

01635 201844, www.partypieces.co.uk.
Lovely tableware, party bags, decorations and CDs galore. Of particular note are the cake kits (with everything you need to create a 3D masterpiece in your kitchen) and the 'scene setters'; giant backdrops that turn your walls into Dora's jungle or a princess's ballroom. Other stock includes party game kits, candy floss and popcorn machines, and some splendid invitations and thank-you cards. Filled party bags start at £1.50, and there are loads of brilliant bits and bobs for under a pound if you'd rather assemble your own.

Planet Party

8346 5432, www.planetparty.co.uk.
Beautiful partyware in classic or unusual themes, including spaceman, ballerina, bowling or sleepovers. Planet Party can also arrange your entire shindig in their Finchley venue or your home and supply party bags.

Consumer

Make it a great day out in London

With fun toys, gifts, books and accessories from The London 2012 Shop, located conveniently at St Pancras International, Paddington Station, Heathrow Terminal 5 and John Lewis Oxford Street.

london2012.com/shop

Eating

Masses of choice for mini mouths.

If you want your children to diversify from the staple fishfinger/pasta diet, there's nowhere better than London to tease young palates. Nowadays even the chains (see p246) have to make things interesting to compete with fantastic family-run favourites and exciting newcomers across town. Parents can make freezer food at home; when they go out, they expect something created from good, fresh ingredients, containing vitamins and lots of flavour.

So, where to go for something a little different? Try dim sum in Chinatown at **Joy King Lau** (see p256), take in a tasting menu of Indian cuisine at **Tamarind** (see p263), sample some Mexican tamales and quesadillas at **Taqueria** (see p264) or experiment with what's hot off the teppanyaki grill at **Matsuri** (see p264).

At the other end of the scale, British comfort food has made a forceful return to hip menus everywhere, a development that means children are just as happy dining at the latest Modern European restaurants like **Hix** (see p266) and **Dean Street Townhouse** (see p265), as at the new cafés springing up across town like **Hackney Pearl** and **Hurwendeki** (for both, see p250). To celebrate this trend, we've picked out the best places to go out for breakfast (see p242) and afternoon tea (see p255).

BRASSERIES

Banners
*21 Park Road, N8 8TE (8348 2930).
Finsbury Park tube/rail then bus W7.*
Meals served 9am-11.30pm Mon-Thur;
9am-midnight Fri; 10am-4pm, 5pm-midnight
Sat; 10am-4pm, 5-11pm Sun. **Main courses**
£9.25-£15.75. **Set lunch** £7.75 2 courses.
Credit MC, V.
If it ain't fixed… Banners has been serving up its 'global home cooking' to Crouch End for nearly two decades now, and is showing no signs of waning in popularity. The menu ranges from Sri Lankan to Caribbean via good old Blighty, and is complemented by a list of specials. Smoothies and floats are popular with children, and there's a long list of cocktails plus decent Argentinian chardonnay by the glass for parental pick-me-ups. Children get a long menu all to themselves, featuring grilled chicken, rice and peas, egg and chips, hamburger and chips or a 'tiny meal', which consists of mashed potato, baked beans and grated cheese for £1.95. Local mums and dads return time and time again, drawn by the all-day service and laid-back vibe. The decor is funky but lived-in, and the large, well-used noticeboard adds a sense of community spirit.
Buggy access. Children's menu (£2.95-£4.75). Crayons. High chairs. Toys.

Chapters
*43-45 Montpeller Vale, SE3 0TJ (8333 2666, www.chaptersrestaurants.com).
Blackheath rail.* **Breakfast served** 8-11.30am Mon-Fri; 8am-noon Sat; 9am-noon Sun. **Lunch served** noon-3pm Mon-Sat; noon-4pm Sun. **Tea served** 3-6pm Mon-Sat; 4-6pm Sun. **Dinner served** 6-11pm Mon-Sat; 6-9pm Sun. **Main courses** £8.95-£24.95. **Credit** AmEx, MC, V.
Families with children are welcomed by the friendly staff at this all-day restaurant. On bright days they can sit outside overlooking Blackheath itself. Back inside, they are usually led subtly up to the first floor, leaving couples and adult groups in peace downstairs. Exposed brickwork, wooden floorboards, banquette seating and scatter cushions create a relaxed, informal setting. The all-day dining strapline translates into a menu that spans eggs benedict and cream teas to delicately flavoured fish dishes and hearty traditional roasts. Children

Banners. *See p239.*

can choose between macaroni cheese, sausage and mash or fish and chips, and there's vanilla ice-cream with chocolate sauce for pudding. *Buggy access. Children's menu (£3.95-£4.50). Disabled access: toilet. High chairs. Nappy-changing facilities.*

Depot

Tideway Yard, 125 Mortlake High Street, SW14 8SN (8878 9462, www.depot brasserie.co.uk). Barnes Bridge or Mortlake rail, or bus 209. **Brunch served** 9.30-11.30am Sat. **Lunch served** noon-3pm Mon-Fri; 12.30-3.30pm Sat; noon-5pm Sun. **Dinner served** 6-11pm Mon-Sat; 6-10pm Sun. **Main courses** £10.50-£19.50. **Set lunch** £12.50 2 courses, £15.50 3 courses. **Credit** AmEx, DC, MC, V.
The setting of this smart Barnes institution – a courtyard by the Thames – is a big part of

its appeal, but the food is also a draw. At lunchtime, choose from salads including crispy duck and watercress or watermelon, feta and toasted pumpkin seed. Then there's a selection of fish and shellfish dishes, meats and grills, many of which you can choose as a smaller plate. The kids' menu includes pasta, fishcakes and roasts on Sundays; for pud, there's ice-cream. A monthly colouring-in competition awards the winner and two guests a free meal. *Buggy access. Children's set meal (£5.50). Crayons. High chairs. Nappy-changing facilities. Tables outdoors (12, courtyard).*

Electric Brasserie

191 Portobello Road, W11 2ED (7908 9696, www.the-electric.co.uk). Ladbroke Grove tube. **Meals served** 8am-11pm Mon-Fri; 8am-5pm, 6-11pm Sat; 8am-5pm, 6-10pm Sun. **Main courses** £10-£28. **Set lunch** (noon-7pm Mon-Fri) £13.50 2 courses, £16.50 3 courses. **Credit** AmEx, MC, V.
This sparkling Portobello Road stalwart has a flair for making even long-suffering mums feel like A-listers, with its flash clientele and sleek internal decor. In fair weather, the front terrace fills with media types cutting deals over ice buckets; grab a table if you can, but it's a bit cramped for buggies. Tables in the front room are subject to the clatter of the open kitchen, but it sure soaks up any noisy toddler tantrums. At the rear is the dining room proper, an intimate wooden space lined with red leather banquette seating and chunky wooden tables, and lent an art deco feel by the central chandelier. Kids will love anything from the mid-price all-day brunch menu (served noon-5pm) which features crumpets with Nutella, yoghurt and honey, French toast, egg and bacon baps, croque monsieurs and more. Service is exemplary. *Buggy access. Children's menu (£6.50). Crayons. Disabled access: toilet. High chairs. Nappy-changing facilities. Tables outdoors (6, terrace).*

Gallery Mess

Saatchi Gallery, Duke of York's HQ, King's Road, SW3 4LY (7730 8135, www.saatchi-gallery.co.uk). Sloane Square tube. **Breakfast served** 10-11.30am daily. **Meals served** 11.30am-9.30pm Mon-Sat; 11.30am-7pm Sun. **Main courses** £9.50-£17. **Set tea** (2.30-6pm) £12. **Credit** AmEx, MC, V. **Map** p329 F11.
In fine weather, the most covetable tables for families are outside overlooking the traffic-free Duke of York Square; you don't get forgotten

out there as staff are an attentive bunch. Inside, the brasserie has a sense of space thanks to vaulted ceilings and lots of light, and is full of modern art (all for sale), which offers a point of interest for children of all ages. Visuals aside, the food makes a visit worthwhile in itself. The menu runs from breakfast to late supper and includes an afternoon tea, with sandwiches, scones and cakes. From 11.30am onwards, you can order dishes such as English asparagus with poached egg, hollandaise and prosciutto; a sharing plate of Spanish charcuterie served with honey, olives and bread; tortellini with goat's cheese, red pepper and a smoked tomato sauce; or a burger with all the trimmings. This last dish is hard to resist – the chips are good and the burger tastes as close to homemade as you'll find in London. Children of 12 and under can have two courses from their own short menu for £9.95. Go on a Saturday and you can browse the farmers' market while you're there.
Buggy access. Children's menu (£9.95). Disabled access: toilet. High chairs. Nappy-changing facilities. Tables outdoors (30, terrace).

Joanna's

56 Westow Hill, SE19 1RX (8670 4052, www.joannas.uk.com). Crystal Palace or Gipsy Hill rail. **Breakfast served** 10am-noon daily. **Meals served** noon-11pm Mon-Sat; noon-10.30pm Sun. **Main courses** £10.95-£29.95. **Set menu** (lunch Mon-Sat, dinner Mon-Thur) £12.95 2 courses, £16.95 3 courses. **Credit** AmEx, MC, V.
Happy, chattering south Londoners create a bustling atmosphere here, and the friendly staff welcome children. There's a children's menu available until 6pm featuring chicken breast and vegetables, sausage and mash, hamburgers, roast beef, and fish and chips. Joanna's opened in 1978 as a burger bar and piano joint but has matured into a relaxed, colonial-style dining room with comfortable leather chairs, linen-clad tables and whirring ceiling fans. Food leans towards the traditional – roast beef and yorkshire pud, lobster, crispy haddock goujons with minted pea purée, fluffy cottage pie, caesar salad – and there's a fine selection of steaks and proper burgers. Desserts are old-school: squidgy chocolate brownie sundae or subtly spiced caramelised apple pancake with vanilla ice-cream. The best tables are by the windows, with views reaching as far as the City.
Buggy access. High chairs. Tables outdoors (4, pavement).

National Café

East Wing, National Gallery, Trafalgar Square, WC2N 5DN (7747 5942, www.the nationalcafe.com). Charing Cross tube/rail. **Breakfast served** 8-11.30am Mon-Fri; 10am-11.30pm Sat, Sun. **Lunch served** noon-5pm daily. **Dinner served** 5.30-11pm Mon-Sat. **Tea served** 3-5.30pm daily. **Meals served** 10am-5pm Sun. **Main courses** £12.50-£16.50. **Set lunch** £21.50 2 courses, £25 3 courses. **Set dinner** £28 2 courses, £32 3 courses. **Credit** MC, V. **Map** p333 K7.
The soaring ceilings, large windows, beautiful woodwork and red leather banquette seating create a spacious and welcoming room for families. This Peyton and Byrne operation charges high prices, but the surroundings almost make up for it. Children get their own menu, which includes grilled chicken and beans, burger and chips, and a dish of the day, but they would probably be far happier with one of the speciality ice-creams (including strawberry cheesecake and apple crumble). For adults, the set lunch offers a small saving, or there's a cheaper bakery area at the back that does sandwiches. It's a great place to get away from the tourist throngs for a while, although on our last visit service was nonchalant at best.
Buggy access. Disabled access: toilet. High chairs. Children's menu (£4.50-£6.50). Nappy-changing facilities.

Tate Modern Café: Level 2

2nd Floor, Tate Modern, Sumner Street, SE1 9TG (7401 5014, www.tate.org.uk). Southwark tube/London Bridge tube/rail/ Blackfriars rail. **Meals served** 10am-6pm Mon-Thur, Sun; 10am-10pm Fri, Sat. **Main courses** £6.95-£10.50. **Credit** AmEx, MC, V. **Map** p334 O7.
On our last visit, service was brusque and hard to come by once we were seated, but the Tate Modern Café remains an understandable favourite with families on a Bankside day out. With a morning of artistic appreciation behind you, it's a large and accommodating spot to settle for a good meal. Kids can choose pasta with tomato sauce, ham and cheese melt on foccacia or own-made fishfingers with chips, then settle down to brownie with chocolate sauce or banana split with ice-cream and fruit salad. What's more, for every adult main course ordered, a child's main course is free. Floor-to-ceiling windows framing the Thames provide passing entertainment, but there are also art and literacy activities on the kids' menus to keep idle hands busy. It's top-quality food,

Consumer

The Big Breakfast

There's nothing like getting out and seizing the day. And because you have kids, you'll be up earlier than most other London thrill-seekers, especially at weekends. Make the most of this and get to your destination at breakfast time – before the brunch set turn up.

Caravan

11-13 Exmouth Market, EC1R 4QD (7833 8115, www.caravanonexmouth. co.uk). Farringdon tube/rail. **Meals served** 8am-10.30pm Mon-Fri; 10am-10.30pm Sat; 10am-4pm Sun. **Main courses** £4.50-£16. **Credit** AmEx, MC, V. This new Exmouth Market favourite was runner-up in Time Out's Best New Local Restaurant 2010. Get here at 8am midweek or 10am at weekends to sample the breakfast menu in relative peace. Most children will love the 'crumpets with too much butter' for £2.50, the banana caramel porridge and cream for £4.80 or one of the muffins (cheese and ham/rhubarb) for £2. Expect touches of fusion – the head chef is New Zealander Miles Kirby, late of the Providores. The casual vibe and industrial-funky design – rough wooden tables, white pipework, an enamel jug filled with daisies, light fittings made from old-fashioned cow-milking bottles – are part of the appeal, but it's the food that is the main draw. That said, parents shouldn't miss the coffee. Caravan has quickly developed an excellent reputation for its onsite roasts.
Buggy access. Disabled access. High chairs. Tables outdoors (2, pavement).

Fifteen

15 Westland Place, N1 7LP (3375 1515, www.fifteen.net). Old Street tube/rail. Trattoria **Breakfast served** 7.30-10.45am Mon-Sat; 8-10.45am Sun. **Lunch served** noon-3pm daily. **Dinner served** 6-10pm daily. **Main courses** £14-£21. *Restaurant* **Lunch served** noon-3pm daily. **Dinner served** 6.30-10pm daily. **Main courses** £17.50-£23. **Set lunch** (Mon-Fri) £24 2 courses, £28 3 courses, £34 4 courses. *Both* **Credit** AmEx, MC, V.

The London flagship of Jamie Oliver's charity operation has undergone a facelift. A lick of paint and signature hot pink carpet in the basement dining room brighten the venue, but tinny aluminium chairs in the ground-floor trattoria feel less welcoming than the former studied rustic look. Not so great for an evening meal then, but the airy, buzzy space provides the perfect place to linger over a feel-good weekend breakfast. Fifteen's cuisine is broadly Italian, but at breakfast time it's a different story. Cooked breakfasts, pastries and healthier fruit- and cereal-based options will all appeal to children. There's an emphasis on careful sourcing from quality producers and it's all of a reliable standard. Arrive here at 7.30am on a Saturday or 8am on a Sunday to beat the crowds.
Booking essential (restaurant). Disabled access: toilet (trattoria). High chairs. Nappy-changing facilities.

The Luxe

109 Commercial Street, E1 6BG (7101 1751, www.theluxe.co.uk). Liverpool Street tube/rail or Shoreditch High Street rail. Café-bar **Open** 8.30am-11.30pm Mon-Sat; 9.30am-10pm Sun. **Meals served** 8.30am-4.30pm Mon-Sat; 9.30am-4.45pm Sun. **Main courses** £7.50-£11.50. *Restaurant* **Lunch served** noon-3pm Mon-Fri; noon-4pm Sun. **Dinner served** 6-10.45pm Mon-Sat. **Main courses** £13-£15. *Both* **Credit** AmEx, MC, V.
Masterchef judge John Torode's new venture is set in Spitalfields' Grade II-listed Old Flower Market building. It's reminiscent of his other venture, Smiths of Smithfield, in that a different experience is offered on each floor. The basement bar (a music venue) is dark and moody. Centrepiece of the premium-priced first-floor dining room is a show kitchen – with white marble bar cut out and filled with logs – and the cooking. Best for families is the ground-floor café-bar with its charming terrace at the back. It's a great spot for breakfast (waffles, sausage butties, mushrooms on toast with poached eggs and hollandaise).

Ottolenghi.

the odd coloured Pantone chair at the communal Corian table) is the epitome of sleek, all the better to put the focus on the colourful dishes. Try to steer children past the incredible window cake displays or you'll never escape without a box of sweet treats to take home. *Buggy access. Disabled access: toilet. High chairs. Tables outdoors (2, pavement). Takeaway service.* **Branches** 63 Ledbury Road, W11 2AD (7727 1121); 1 Holland Street, W8 4NA (7937 0003); 13 Motcomb Street, SW1X 8LB (7823 2707).

Tom's Kitchen

Somerset House, Strand, WC2R 1LA (7845 4646, www.tomskitchen.co.uk). Embankment or Temple tube, or Charing Cross tube/rail. **Breakfast served** 8-11am Mon-Fri. **Brunch served** 10am-4pm Sat, Sun. **Lunch served** noon-3pm Mon-Fri. **Dinner served** 6-10pm Mon-Sat. **Main courses** £25-£30. **Credit** AmEx, MC, V. **Map** p333 M7.
Tom Aikens' new venture at Somerset House is an extension of what he's been doing at his Chelsea Green original, but on a much grander scale. In the gracious riverside rooms, diners can choose between semi-circular red leather banquettes, blond wood chairs or bar-side tables. From April until autumn, the stately terrace overlooking the Thames becomes another wing of the restaurant, and is the best bet for families with fidgety toddlers. Breakfast is our favourite time to visit. The croissants, pancakes and waffles with caramelised apples are superb, the ingredients for the full English sourced carefully, the coffee just so. Service is friendly and unobtrusive, and no one seemed to mind a toddler wandering around from room to room. If the prices are a bit steep (£3 for a latte; £6.50 for two eggs on toast), you can always visit Tom's Deli across the stone-flagged corridor, which serves the same great coffee more cheaply, as well as sandwiches, cakes and salads. Take it with you into the courtyard outside or sit inside at one of the Deli's own tables. *Buggy access. Disabled access: toilet. High chairs. Tables outdoors (30, terrace). Takeaway service.*

Juices, smoothies and milkshakes also feature strongly on the menu. *Buggy access. Disabled access: lift, toilet. High chairs. Nappy-changing facilities. Disabled: lift; toilet. Tables outdoors (3, pavement). Takeaway service.*

Ottolenghi

287 Upper Street, N1 2TZ (7288 1454, www.ottolenghi.co.uk). Angel tube or Highbury & Islington tube/rail. **Meals served** 8am-10pm Mon-Wed; 8am-10.30pm Thur-Sat; 9am-7pm Sun. **Main courses** £8-£10. **Credit** AmEx, MC, V.
The Islington branch of Ottolenghi is the biggest, with tables to seat around 50 and a kitchen producing food from breakfast until late. Ottolenghi's cooked breakfasts are some of the best in town, but what children remember is not just the food, but also being able to operate the toaster themselves (there's one on each table at breakfast time to toast the cornucopia of breads on offer). There are also muffins and pastries out front, and hot delights such as cinnamon French toast made with brioche and served with yoghurt and compote or buffalo mozzarella tortilla with red pepper salsa. The cool, mostly white interior (there's

Consumer

with an emphasis on quality over quantity; ingredients are carefully sourced and seasonal wherever possible. Get here by 12.15pm at the latest if you want to be led straight to a table. *Buggy access. Children's set menu (£5.10 11am-3pm daily). Disabled access: lift, toilet. High chairs. Nappy-changing facilities.*

CAFES

Blue Mountain Café

18 Northcross Road, SE22 9EU (8299 6953, www.bluemo.co.uk). East Dulwich rail. **Meals served** 9am-10pm Mon-Sat; 10am-6pm Sun. **Main courses** £4.50-£8. **Credit** AmEx, MC, V.

Blue Mountain was already an East Dulwich institution long before the arrival of Bugaboos and loft conversions, and it continues to draw the crowds with its quality all-day breakfasts and calorific cake selection. The perennial bestseller is the Full Monty: herby butcher's sausage, bacon, beans, portobello mushroom, grilled tomato, chunky toast, a choice of eggs and a cup of tea. Interesting lunchtime specials include the likes of jerk chicken (£7.95), herby salmon and haddock fishcakes (£6.85), and burgers. The funky mosaic patio, made by local artists, is a sunny spot to observe the bustle of Northcross Road (particularly its Saturday market), and is packed with families and freelancers during the week. Long the envy of neighbouring up-and-coming enclaves such as Honor Oak, Blue Mountain now has a branch in Sydenham.

Buggy access. Children's menu (£3-£5). High chairs. Nappy-changing facilities.
Branch 260 Kirkdale, SE26 4RS (8659 6016).

Boathouse Café

Hanover Gate, Regent's Park, NW1 4NU (7724 4069, www.companyofcooks.com). Baker Street or Regent's Park tube. **Meals served** 10am-4pm daily. **Main courses** £3.70-£5.75. **Credit** MC, V.

Company of Cooks runs this small outlet in Regent's Park, along with the Honest Sausage and the more upmarket Garden Café. The big draw of the Boathouse Café is its proximity to the recently renovated Hanover Gate Playground, which now has two separate play areas – traditional equipment for younger children and timber treehouse climbing structures for the older kids. And as the name suggests, it's also right next to the boating lakes. There are only seven tables inside, but on bright days families can make the most of the 15 large outdoor tables. The menu is very simple – two types of pasta, flatbread pizza with a choice of toppings, sandwiches and salads – but the café does what it does in typically satisfying Company of Cooks style. It also sells great ice-creams and cakes.

Buggy access. Children's menu (£3.75). High chairs. Tables outdoors (15, terrace). Takeaway service.

Brew House

Kenwood, Hampstead Lane, NW3 7JR (8341 5384, www.companyofcooks.com). Bus 210, 214. **Meals served** Oct-Mar 9am-dusk daily. Apr-Sept 9am-6pm daily (7pm on concert nights). **Main courses** £6.95-£11.95. **Credit** MC, V.

A weekend institution for families pretending that they live in the countryside for a morning. Donning wellies and arriving with bikes, dogs and off-road buggies, the wealthy and famous are regular visitors to the Brew House. It's a self-service café run by Company of Cooks in a spectacular setting next to Kenwood House (*see p77*). The large walled, tiered terrace is a favourite spot on sunny days. Breakfasts are hearty, with huge sausages, scrambled eggs, good bacon, field mushrooms and tomatoes; on bright weekend mornings, be here by 10am to stake out a table. For lunch, there's a choice of quiche and salad, a generous meat dish or soup with various accompaniments. Children can have smaller portions of the day's dishes, or a bowl of macaroni cheese that's enough to fill an adult. The complicated queuing system takes a while to get used to, and at busy times the hot food service can seem interminably slow. But somehow, none of this matters once the food is on the table. If you want a quick sandwich, ice-cream or coffee, there's a serving hatch around the corner (with plenty of extra seating).

Buggy access. Children's menu (£2.75-£4). Disabled access: toilet. High chairs. Nappy-changing facilities. Tables outdoors (70, garden). Takeaway service.

Café on the Rye

Strakers Road, SE15 3UA (8693 9431, www.cafeontherye.co.uk). Peckham Rye rail. **Meals served** 9am-5.30pm daily. **Main courses** £3.50-£7. **No credit cards.**

Like a lot of park cafés in London, this is a very pleasant surprise. It opened in 2007 and hasn't had a quiet day since. Location is key and it helps that the café is right next to the One O'Clock Club, but people also come back for the

wholesome and delicious food, ranging from full breakfasts to toasted ciabattas, classic English sandwiches and appealing regular specials – and don't overlook the moist and tasty cakes. The Just 4 Kids menu offers simple sandwiches – Marmite, cream cheese, ham and tuna mayo – or pasta with tomato or bolognese sauce; sausage and beans, and scrambled eggs and beans on toast. The café also serves Jude's ice-cream – once tasted, never forgotten. The architecture is pretty tasty too: the circular wooden frontage faces the vast green expanse of Peckham Rye, and there are chairs to sit on outside and enjoy the scenery on fine days.
Buggy access. Children's menu (£2.50-£3.75). Crayons. Disabled access: toilet. High chairs. Nappy-changing facilities. Tables outdoors (7, park; 16, garden). Takeaway service. Toys.

Café Rex

172-174 Muswell Hill Broadway, N10 3SA (8444 3463, www.caferex.co.uk). East Finchley tube, then bus 102, 234 or 603. **Meals served** 9am-9.30pm Mon-Wed; 9am-10pm Thur, Fri; 8am-10pm Sat; 9am-6.30pm Sun. **Main courses** £6.95-£10.95. **Set lunch** £4.95 1 course. **Set dinner** £10 2 courses, £13 3 courses. **Credit** MC, V.
Families didn't take long to find this new café in Muswell Hill, a monied suburb surprisingly short of good, independently run places to eat. The atmosphere is part coffee bar, part gastropub and part greasy spoon, with matching chairs, bare bricks, sofas and bright

Café Rex.

ceiling lights. We like the place, with its all-day breakfasts, Fairtrade coffee and hearty British dishes (steak and kidney pie, fish and chips and other classics, with a nod to the nation's adopted favourites like chicken tikka masala and lasagne). Just in case you forget the theme, there is a massive Union Jack on the wall. Kids get their own choice of mains for £3.50 a pop (with baked beans on toast providing a cheaper option), but most would be happy with the main menu. Puddings are a continuation of the nursery food ideal, featuring treacle tart, apple pie and Eton mess or scones and toasted tea-cakes for afternoon treats. We can see Café Rex rolling out as a mini chain across north London.
Buggy access. Children's menu (£2.95-£4.50). Disabled acceess: toilet. High chairs. Nappy-changing facilities. Tables outdoors (2, pavement).

Common Ground

Wandsworth Common, off Dorlcote Road, SW18 3RT (8874 9386). Wandsworth Common rail. **Meals served** 9am-5.15pm Mon-Fri; 9am-5.30pm Sat, Sun. **Main courses** £3.50-£9. **Credit** MC, V.
Service might lack smiles, but the floor might need scrubbing more often, but this remains a local institution, mainly because of its pole position in the middle of Wandsworth Common. With cricket pitches on one side and a pristine bowling green on the other, this former lodge building keeps things simple. There are wooden floors and wooden tables in the conservatory, a generous patio with tables outside, and a cosier room with sofas and buckets of toys where parent and toddler groups meet on weekdays. The food is tasty, if a little on the expensive side, and there's a children's menu that includes home-made chicken goujons or locally made sausages served with mash or chips and broccoli or peas. There are also simple sandwiches and a range of cakes.
Buggy access. Children's menu (£3.95-£4.50). High chairs. Nappy-changing facilities. Play area. Takeaway service.

Container Café

The View Tube, The Greenway, Marshgate Lane, E15 2PJ (07702 125081, www. theviewtube.co.uk). Pudding Mill Lane DLR. **Meals served** 9am-5pm Mon-Fri; 10am-6pm Sat, Sun. **Main courses** £3.50-£8. **Credit** AmEX, MC, V.
This café isn't in the position to attract casual passers-by. It's located within the View Tube, a community centre opposite the Olympic Park

Chain Reaction

Even those who sniff at chains before having children must eventually concede that they have their place. On a family day out in London, sometimes cheap and recognisable is just what's required. Here are some of our favourites.

Byron

222 Kensington High Street, W8 7RG (7361 1717, www.byronhamburgers. com). High Street Kensington tube. **Meals served** noon-11pm Mon-Thur; noon-11.30pm Fri, Sat; noon-10.30pm Sun. **Main courses** £6.25-£8.50. **Credit** AmEx, MC, V. **Map** p328 A9.
Rapid expansion means there are now 11 branches of this hamburger specialist across London. The menu is short and simple, the 6oz plain burger costs just £6.25, and Byron delivers on its promise to create moist pink hamburgers in very good buns. Children get two courses for £6.25 and can choose between mini hamburgers, chicken burgers, veggie burgers or macaroni cheese. Pudding is vanilla ice-cream or chocolate brownie. *Buggy access. Children's menu (£6.25). Crayons. Disabled access: toilet. High chairs. Nappy-changing facilities. Tables outdoors (3, pavement). Takeaway service. Toys.* **Branches** throughout the city.

Carluccio's Caffè

Reuters Plaza, E14 5AJ (7719 1749, www.carluccios.com). Canary Wharf tube/DLR. **Meals served** 7am-11.30pm Mon-Fri; 9am-11.30pm Sat; 10am-10.30pm Sun. **Main courses** £6.95-£13.95. **Credit** AmEx, MC, V.
Carluccio's understands that children want something to happen as soon as they sit down. And lo and behold; grissini, a soft drink and some paper and crayons appear at the table. The clattering acoustics common to most branches isn't exactly soothing, but the warmth of the service, tasty grub and shelves of aspirational deli items keep enticing the customers back. Children can choose from a selection of pasta shapes and sauces, or there's chicken and potatoes, ravioli and lasagne. To

finish, the little darlings get an individual tub of Carluccio's Italian ice-cream. *Buggy access. Children's set meal (£5.95). Crayons. Disabled access: toilet. High chairs. Nappy-changing facilities. Tables outdoors (25, piazza). Takeaway service.* **Branches** throughout the city.

Giraffe

Units 1&2, Riverside Level 1, Royal Festival Hall, SE1 8XX (7928 2004, www.giraffe.net). Waterloo tube/rail. **Meals served** 8am-11pm Mon-Fri; 9am-10.30pm Sat, Sun. **Main courses** £7.25-£14.95. **Set dinner** (5-7pm Mon-Fri) £8.45 2 courses. **Credit** AmEx, MC, V. **Map** p333 M8.
There is a reason why this Giraffe is heaving with families. The kids' menu is lengthy and reasonable, and the setting on the Thames is fabulous. Kids can choose a cooked breakfast (sausage, eggs, beans and toast, or a veggie version) until 4pm, or opt for something from the lunch/dinner menu, which includes grilled chicken, pasta pomodoro or cottage pie (£3.75-£4.25). Ice-cream is £1.35 per scoop. For the adults, substantial salads offer a healthy alternative to the burgers and noodle dishes. Desserts are on the small side, though the warm chocolate brownie with hot chocolate sauce is always a treat. *Buggy access. Children's menu (£4.75 noon-5pm Mon-Fri). Crayons. Disabled access: toilet. High chairs. Nappy-changing facilities. Tables outdoors (40, terrace). Takeaway service.* **Branches** throughout the city.

Haché

24 Inverness Street, NW1 7HJ (7485 9100, www.hacheburgers.com). Camden Town tube. **Meals served** noon-10.30pm Mon-Fri; noon-11pm Sat; noon-10pm Sun. **Main courses** £5.95-£12.95. **Credit** AmEx, MC, V.
Any gourmet burger bar should be able to shine on basic burgers, and Haché still excels. The portions are large and the meat first-rate, with good-quality extra toppings. There's a wide range of

burgers to choose between, from beef, duck, lamb and venison to a welcome vegetarian selection; chips, meanwhile, can be frites-style, skinny or fat. Decent crêpes have been added to the desserts, but brownies are the thing to have. *Buggy access. High chairs. Takeaway service. Tables outdoors (2, pavement).* **Branch** 329-331 Fulham Road, SW10 9QL (7823 3515).

Nando's

57-59 Goodge Street, W1T 1TH (7637 0708, www.nandos.com). Goodge Street tube. **Meals served** 11.30am-11pm Mon-Thur; 11.30am-11.30pm Fri, Sat; 11.30am-10.30pm Sun. **Main courses** £5.80-£10.60. **Credit** AmEx, MC, V. **Map** p330 J5.

The appeal of Nando's lies in its simplicity, lack of ceremony and keen prices. With wooden tables and chairs and a menu that centres around freshly grilled chicken, it's not quite a fast food restaurant – but it's not a million miles away (meal deals, bottomless refills on drinks and a super-casual vibe). Chicken served with spicy peri peri sauce of varying degrees of fierceness is the mainstay, while sides dishes (corn on the cob, thick-cut chips) make for a filling, decent value meal. Kids get their own menu featuring chicken in various guises and a choice of veggie burger or bean burger. It's a steal at £4.10 for a main course, side dish and dessert. *Buggy access. Children's set meal (£4.15). Disabled access: toilet. Crayons. High chairs. Nappy-changing facilities. Tables outdoors (1, pavement).* **Branches** throughout the city.

Pizza Express

Lion House, Richmond, TW9 1RE (8948 7460, www.pizzaexpress.com). Richmond tube/rail. **Meals served** 8.45am-11pm Mon-Thur, Sun; 8.45am-midnight. **Main courses** £8.50-£12. **Credit** AmEx, MC, V.

The latest London branch of Pizza Express is a test run for a new generation of the old pizza chain favourite. It has been designed with consultation from a theatre director, artists, sound technicians and one of the founders of Mumsnet. Booths and sound-reflective lighting cut down the noisy clatter of the modern restaurant experience. You can even plug an iPod in to create your own soundtrack, and press a button that lights up when you need service. Children can entertain themselves at a central drawing table between courses, or make their own pizza. The children's menu understands that you have to keep the treats coming for children to sit still for any length of time. It's £6.25 for dough balls and crudités, pizza or pasta, a sundae and a bambinoccino. Waiters are trained to deal with families, so greet children with a smile rather than a grimace. *Buggy access. Children's menu (£6.25). Disabled access: toilet. High chairs. Nappy-changing facilities. Play area. Takeaway service.* **Branches** throughout the city.

Wagamama

11 Jamestown Road, NW1 7BW (7428 0800, www.wagamama.com). Camden Town tube. **Meals served** noon-11pm Mon-Sat; noon-10pm Sun. **Main courses** £6.65-£12.75. **Credit** AmEx, DC, MC, V.

Wagamama was the first – and is still one of the best – canteen-style pan-Asian diners. Children get their own menu featuring a couple of choices of noodle and rice dishes, but most would enjoy plenty of the dishes from the main menu too. To drink, there's saké, juices and free green tea. *Buggy access. Children's menu (£2.85-£4.35). Crayons. Disabled access: toilet. High chairs. Nappy-changing facilities. Takeaway service.* **Branches** throughout the city.

Consumer

Pizza Express.

on the Greenway walking and cycling route. Once through the unlikely looking paths of the greatest building site in London, you can't miss the View Tube – it's made out of old shipping containers and painted bright yellow. Inside the café, a blackboard has a short list of hot eats like bacon baguettes, tomato and basil scrambled egg on toast, pies and soup of the day, and further temptations rest on the counter: moist chocolate brownies, cookies and appealingly overstuffed savoury croissants. The coffee is excellent and the mismatched furniture, funky decor and changing art makes for a relaxed atmosphere. What children will enjoy most, though, are the views of the cranes and buildings across the Olympic Park below. *Buggy access. Disabled access: lift, toilet. Tables outdoors (12, terrace). Takeaway service.*

Daylesford Organic

208-212 Westbourne Grove, W11 2RH (7313 8050, www.daylesfordorganic.com). Ladbroke Grove or Notting Hill Gate tube. **Open** 8.30am-7pm Mon-Sat; 10am-4pm Sun. **Main courses** £9.95-£13.95. **Credit** AmEx, MC, V. **Map** p326 A6.
This, the newest Daylesford branch, is spread over three floors, with a raw food bar in the basement, a bustling café on the ground floor, and a larder of fabulous produce from the home farm in Gloucestershire upstairs. Hip and sophisticated Notting Hill families turn up in droves to this farm shop-cum-brasserie and pretend they're living the simple life. Their carefully coordinated weekend outfits sit perfectly against the understated decor: whitewashed boarding, stripped wood, and woven baskets overflowing with expensive organic produce. Wandering around Daylesford, you can't help thinking of Harry Enfield and Paul Whitehouse's 'I Saw You Coming' sketch and sniggering. The café's menu is limited, but has enough to tempt: buttery pastries, a nursery food staple such as shepherd's pie, eggs royale with perfect, oozing yolks, and salads for the health-conscious. Service can be terrible, especially when it's busy, but the ingredients are the finest. If you lived nearby, you'd be here often too. *Buggy access. Crayons. Disabled access: lift, toilet. High chairs. Nappy-changing facilities. Tables outdoors (6, pavement). Takeaway service.* **Branches** 44B Pimlico Road, W11 2RH (7881 8060); Selfridges, 400 Oxford Street, W1A 1AB (0800 123 400).

Deep Blue Café

Science Museum, Exhibition Road, SW7 2DD (7942 4488, www.sciencemuseum. org.uk). South Kensington tube. **Meals served** 11am-4pm daily. **Credit** MC, V. **Map** p329 D9.
The Deep Blue Café had a refurbishment last year but it's back, serving families taking a break from the Science Museum's many attractions (for which, *see p112*). Getting to the café is an adventure in itself; you pass an Apollo lunar module, a Model T Ford and Stephenson's Rocket, among other things. Once there, the café has views over the Wellcome Wing that inspire further exploration. Deep Blue serves pizza and pasta dishes, and a small range of grills and salads. Children's mains come in at a reasonable £3.95-£4.25, although puddings can rack up the bill with fruit salad starting at £3.95. *Buggy access. Children's menu (£3.95-£4.25). Disabled access: toilet. High chairs. Nappy-changing facilities.*

Fait Maison

Ravenscourt Park, Paddenswick Road, W6 0UG (8563 9291, www.fait-maison.co.uk). Ravenscourt Park tube. **Meals served** *Summer* 8am-6pm daily. *Winter* 8am-4.30pm daily. **Main courses** £3.95-£7.50. **No credit cards.**
Fait Maison has several outlets in west London, but our favourite, simply for location alone, is this one in Ravenscourt Park. Collapse into an

Franco Manca.

Consumer

inviting sofa and tuck into supersized croissants and mega-meringues, or order lunch. There are various enticing salads and hot dishes on the board, all at reasonable prices and served in decent portions. There are also freshly cooked pizzas on the menu, and the atmosphere is cheerful and chilled: park your pram by your table and grab a high chair or head for the outdoor seating. If you've been on the swings, racing round the park or tackling the shops in nearby Hammersmith, this is the ideal place to recover. Amanda's Action Kids holds classes here on Thursday afternoons and Friday mornings. At the nearby Goldhawk Road branch, there's a more varied programme of activities, from yoga on Wednesday mornings to cookery classes on Mondays (at 10am and 2pm) and art classes on Thursdays (10am).
Buggy access. Children's menu (£3.90). Disabled access: toilets. Tables outdoors (6, park). Takeaway service.
Branches 3 Stratford Road, W8 6RQ (7937 2777); 245 Goldhawk Road, W12 8EU (8222 8755).

Franco Manca

144 Chiswick High Road, W4 1PU (8747 4822, www.francomanca.co.uk). Turnham Green tube. **Meals served** noon-11pm Mon-Thur, Sun; noon-11.30pm Fri, Sat. **Main courses** £4.50-£6.95. **Credit** MC, V.
Franco Manca's original incarnation in Brixton market is small, but legendary among pizza purists. This new branch is much more spacious, but still serves the same great food. The sourdough is left to rise for 20 hours before baking, and its ingredients are largely organic. Pizzas (some with simple toppings like tomato, basil and mozzarella, some with more unusual combinations such as ricotta and pork) are disarmingly good. There are around eight pizzas on the menu at any one time and a few starters. Most children adore pizza, so get them used to the good things in life early on.
Buggy access. Disabled access: toilet. High chairs. Nappy-changing facilities. Tables outdoors (6, pavement). Takeaway service.
Branch 4 Market Row, Electric Lane, SW9 8LD (7738 3021).

Frizzante at City Farm

1A Goldsmith's Row, E2 8QA (7739 2266, www.frizzanteltd.co.uk). Hoxton rail or bus 26, 48, 55. **Meals served** *Summer* 10am-4pm Tue, Wed, Fri-Sun; 10am-4pm, 7-10pm Thur. *Winter* 10am-4pm Tue-Sun. **Main courses** £5-£13. **Credit** MC, V.

Frizzante has long been the envy of other London City Farms, and it's now got a second home at a riverside location within Surrey Docks Farm (*see p155*). The original, here at Hackney City Farm, is a surprisingly rural corner in a densely urban spot. Frizzante manages to look like an outsized farmhouse kitchen with colourful oilcloth-covered tables and a make-do-and-mend style. Work up an appetite for the hearty portions by meeting the pigs, chickens, geese, sheep and goats in the farmyard outside. Visitors tend to opt for the blackboard specials if they're not tucking into one of the legendary breakfasts, so it's worth arriving early before dishes sell out. Children can choose from simple beans on toast (£2.50), pasta with tomato sauce and cheese (£4) and other dishes on the same theme. For pudding, there are incredibly good home-made ice-creams and cakes. Babies are catered for with Ella's Kitchen purée from the shelves. The welcome is warm and the atmosphere delightfully laid-back, and there's outside seating for warm days.
Buggy access. Children's menu (£2.25-£4.25). Disabled access: toilet. High chairs. Nappy-changing facilities. Tables outdoors (12, garden). Takeaway service.
Branch Surrey Docks Farm, South Wharf, Rotherhithe Street, SE16 5ET (7231 1010).

Gracelands

118 College Road, NW10 5HD (8964 9161, www.gracelandscafe.com). Kensal Green tube. **Meals served** 8.30am-5pm Mon-Fri; 9am-5pm Sat; 9.30am-3pm Sun. **Main courses** £4.50-£12.95. **Credit** AmEx, MC, V.
With its wooden floors, rustic tables and light and airy interior, this is a popular spot for local families. The large pavement terrace is a bonus too. The all-day breakfast menu, lunchtime specials, cakes and pastries are made with great attention to detail and there's a fantastic salad bar that deserves exploration (a mixed plate with quiche is £7.50). Portions are large, so canny parents can easily share with their offspring. A play area inside the café with toys and books, as well as the fantasic resource of Gracelands Yard next door (which offers workshops for children like sewing clubs, yoga classes, baby music sessions and Mini Picasso art classes), means this family-focused café is always packed. All in all, a great local treasure, but one that knows it's got a captive market.

Consumer

Buggy access. Children's set meal (£3.50).
Disabled access. High chairs. Nappy-changing
facilities. Play area. Tables outdoors
(4, pavement; 12, garden). Takeaway
service. Toys.

Haberdashery

*22 Middle Lane, N8 8PL (8342 8098,
www.the-haberdashery.com). Archway tube
or Hornsey rail, then bus 41.* **Meals served**
8am-6pm Mon-Fri; 9am-6pm Sat, Sun. Main
courses £6-£9. **Credit** AmEx, MC, V.
There aren't many cafés with outdoor space in
Crouch End. Spiazzo, the Italian café on the
Broadway, has the best pitch, with tables lined
up along the square by the town hall. But it's
expensive, service is often brusque bordering
on rude, and it feels ungenerous (last time we
were there, we asked for honey to sweeten our
mint tea; a tiny saucer arrived and £1 was
added to the bill). Haberdashery, which arrived
at the tail end of 2009, has a lovely sheltered
garden out the back and, with its higgledy-
piggledy combo of textiles, threads and
buttons, myriad porcelain cups and saucers
hanging from the wall and the gentle burble of
old vinyl in the background, is a friendly place
to come. The place – and the service – is
charming. It serves classic breakfasts in the
morning, light lunches afterwards and a
fantastic array of muffins, cakes and biscuits.
The kids' menu has its own range of breakfasts,
mains and drinks. Adult lattes are served in
mammoth bowls and have good coffee bean
flavour. Haberdashery clearly cares about the
food it serves, which manifests itself in the
quality of the ingredients and a careful menu.
It has already become a Crouch End institution,
with photo exhibitions, barboot sales and more.
Children also love the trays and jars of unusual
sweets at the counter.
*Buggy access. Children's menu (£3.50-
£4.75). High chairs. Nappy-changing
facilities. Tables outdoors (12, garden/
pavement). Takeaway service.*

Hackney Pearl

*11 Prince Edward Road, E9 5LX (8510
3605, www.thehackneypearl.com). Hackney
Wick rail.* **Lunch served** 10am-4pm,
dinner served 6-10pm daily. **Main
courses** £9.50-£14.50. **Credit** MC, V.
The owners of Hackney Pearl have made
something special out of not very much. That's
why we awarded them Best New Café 2010.
Hackney Pearl is a café-bar that's very sure of
itself and perfectly fits the brief for a friendly

neighbourhood hangout for families in the
daytime and the local arty crowd in the evening.
With its community-focused informality, the
place feels like a reaction to 'regeneration
projects' promised by developers. Two former
shop units are enlivened by Formica tables,
colourful rugs and old dressers, with shelves on
the walls full of books to browse through. The
compact menu lists simple but imaginative
food: a bright Turkish-style meze plate with
superb bread or sweetcorn fritters with chilli
jam and crème fraîche. You're also treated to
well-sourced drinks (Square Mile coffee,
Meantime beer, bloody marys, an extensive
wine list) and an atmosphere so relaxed it's
almost horizontal. The venue has become at one
with the Wick through involvement with
artists' studios and events such as the Hackney
Wicked festival. It may be out of the way for
most, but a visit here is a heartening experience.
*Buggy access. Disabled access: toilet. High
chairs. Nappy-changing facilities. Tables
outdoors (5, terrace). Takeaway service.*

Hurwundeki Café

*299 Railway Arches, Cambridge
Heath Road, E2 9HA (7749 0638,
www.hurwundeki.com). Bethnal Green tube
or Cambridge Heath rail.* **Meals served**
7am-7pm Mon-Fri; 9am-7pm Sat, Sun.
Main courses £4.20-£8. **No credit cards**.
The Hurwundeki empire began in Shoreditch
with a boutique and salon. Now, there's also a
café in Bethnal Green in one of the railway
arches by Cambridge Heath station. The words
emblazoned on the outside are 'Café, Antique,
Play', and that pretty much sums up the ethos.
Many bits of the mismatched furniture are for
sale and there's great coffee and sandwiches,
cakes and breakfast goods on the service
counter. The kids will love the sense of
discovery about the place, and the large closed-
in, sand-filled terrace out front; see if they can
spot gnomes in the undergrowth, a rocking
horse, the table football table and a Cinderella-
style pumpkin carriage they can climb into.
*Buggy access. Tables outdoors (10, garden).
Takeaway service. Toys.*

Inn the Park

*St James's Park, SW1A 2BJ (7451 9999,
www.innthepark.com). St James's Park or
Westminster tube.* **Meals served** *Summer*
8am-10pm Mon-Fri; 9am-9.30pm Sat; 9am-
6pm Sun. *Winter* 8am-5pm Mon-Fri; 9am-
5pm Sat, Sun. **Main courses** £14.50-£20.50.
Credit MC, V. **Map** p333 K8.

Consumer

Haberdashery.

Oliver Peyton's venture in St James's Park keeps to a seasonal British menu, but families don't so much come for the food as the fantastic setting. The timber-clad, glass-fronted park café couldn't be more idyllic. The tables on the terrace overlook St James's Park and the picturesque Duck Island; even the indoor tables have lovely views, thanks to floor-to-ceiling windows. The restaurant is pricey (there is a children's menu, but it'll set you back £7.50 for a main course), but families can head to the more modestly priced self-service area where offerings include soups, sandwiches, pies and cakes. If it's a special occasion, you can book a summer barbecue for a party (minimum 25 people).

Buggy access. Children's menu (£7.50).
Disabled access: toilet. High chairs. Nappy-
changing facilities. Tables outdoors
(40, patio). Takeaway service.

Lido

Serpentine Lido, Hyde Park, W2 2UH (7706 7098, www.companyofcooks.com). Hyde Park or Knightsbridge tube. **Meals served** *Jan, Feb, Nov, Dec* 8am-4pm daily. *Mar, Oct* 8am-5pm daily. *Apr* 8am-6pm daily. *May* 8am-7.30pm daily. *June* 8am-8pm daily. *July, Aug* 8am-9pm daily. *Sept* 8am-7pm daily. **Main courses** £7.50-£12.50. **Credit** MC, V. **Map** p327 E8.
Company of Cooks took over the running of this lakeside café, which occupies a prime spot near Hyde Park's famous Serpentine, in 2010. The building itself was constructed in 1931 and originally used as the changing rooms for the

neighbouring Lido, built under the instruction of George Lansbury for the 'recreation of working class people'. Families flock here for the relaxed atmosphere, huge terrace (seats 300) and views over the Serpentine. There are high chairs and a decent baby change area, along with newspapers should the grown-ups get any snatched moments of peace. The menu veers from simple retro (knickerbocker glory, calamares) to hot dishes with a bit more ambition (steak with béarnaise sauce and salad, lobster rolls), and there's a short but functional kids' menu featuring burgers, pizza and fishfingers, accompanied by chips. Lido is licensed, so parents can go continental with lunch, or even brazen it out with a breakfast cocktail. For those in the mood for a dip before or after refreshments, the Lido and paddling pool – open from May to September – are just next door.

Buggy access. Children's menu (from £4).
Disabled access: toilet. High chairs. Nappy-
changing facilities. Tables outdoors (70,
park). Takeaway service.

Lido Café

Brockwell Lido, Dulwich Road, SE24 0PA (7737 8183, www.thelidocafe.co.uk). Herne Hill rail or Brixton tube/rail then bus 37. **Meals served** 9am-4pm Mon, Sun; 9am-10pm Tue-Sun. **Main courses** £8.50-£13. **Credit** MC, V.
This locally run café has become a Herne Hill favourite since it opened in 2009. The well-executed comfort food is reason enough to make the journey, but the café has also become

Consumer

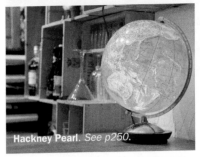

Hackney Pearl. *See p250.*

a cultural hub for the community, putting on regular theme nights – Portuguese wine tasting evening, Colombian night. The simple decor makes the most of the stylish 1930s interior, with large windows overlooking the pool area. Outside, from spring to autumn, there's a large seating area on the terrace – fenced off from the pool itself – with a hut selling barbecued food and salads, fresh juices and real fruit lollies. Inside, the children's menu features favourites like own-made fishfingers with chips or salad, tomato pasta, and burger and chips; there are also toys to keep little hands amused. Whippersnappers runs music sessions for the under-fives daily at 9.45am (pre-booking required) and drop-in classes on Tuesdays at 1.45pm, Fridays at 11.15am and Saturdays at 9.45am.

Buggy access. Children's menu (£4). Disabled access: toilet. High chairs. Nappy-changing facilities. Tables outdoors (15, terrace). Takeaway service.

Parlour
167 Stoke Newington Church Street, N16 0UL (7923 0654). Stoke Newington rail or bus 73. **Meals served** *8am-6.30pm daily.* **Main courses** *£2.25-£4.40.* **Credit** *AmEx, MC, V.*

This relative newcomer on the Stokey scene is still packing them in. It specialises in gluten-, wheat- and dairy-free grub for hungry people of all ages. A wide selection of fillings are available on various different breads, or inside jacket potatoes. Freshly squeezed juices and fruit smoothies are a healthy and delicious option, and the own-made waffles a real treat – especially when they come slathered with banana, toffee and whipped cream. Relaxed, friendly staff and shabby-but-almost-chic decor complement the rustic food. There is a shady courtyard and a playroom stacked full of toys, books and games.

Buggy access. Disabled access. High chairs. Nappy-changing facilities. Play area. Tables outdoors (3, garden). Takeaway service. Toys.

Pavilion Café, Dulwich
Dulwich Park, off College Road, SE21 7BQ (8299 1383, www.pavilioncafedulwich.co.uk). North Dulwich or West Dulwich rail. **Meals served** *Summer 8.30am-6pm daily. Winter 8.30am-4pm daily.* **Main courses** *£3.50-£8.* **Credit** *AmEx, MC, V.*

As the name suggests, this café was a former cricket pavilion, and very pretty it is too. Inside, the great home-cooked food and cheap Wi-Fi service make it popular with families and home-workers alike, all looking to escape the confines of their own four walls. It's busy on weekdays and crammed to the rafters at weekends. Local suppliers include Moxon's Fish, William Rose Butcher and Monmouth Coffee, and the café promises to use organic ingredients wherever possible. The well-balanced menu has serious child appeal, offering grilled chicken, penne pasta, Scotch beefburgers, chunky chips and sandwiches. There's also organic baby food, Innocent smoothies and garishly coloured ice drinks, plus raisins, crisps, fruit and crayons (obviously not for eating). There are always vegetarian, vegan and wheat-free options on the menu too. For afters, there's Beechdean ice-cream – also sold through a side hatch in summer. Daily specials for grown-ups are overshadowed by the all-day breakfasts of top-quality sausages and bacon, free-range eggs and chunky toast (white or wholemeal). As well as serving great food, the café has also become a social hub, providing information on local events, a colourful play corner, baby changing facilities and clean toilets, and bird food for feeding the ducks; it can also cater for birthday parties. Outdoor tables offer verdant views in summer; in winter, it's a cosy spot to warm up

over a hot chocolate (with a shot of rum for the grown-ups). If you don't like children, you may want to give this place a wide berth; if you have some of your own, it's a lifesaver.
Buggy access. Children's menu (£1.50-£4.50). Disabled access: toilet. High chairs. Nappy-changing facilities. Play area. Tables outdoors (12, terrace). Takeaway service.

Pavilion Café, Victoria Park

Victoria Park, Crown Gate West, E9 7DE (8980 0030, www.the-pavilion-cafe.com). Bus 277 or 425. **Meals served** *Summer* 8.30am-5pm daily. *Winter* 8.30am-4pm daily. **Main courses** £4-£8. **No credit cards.**
This lovely glass-roofed pavilion is a cosy spot any time of the year, although on sunny days tables overlooking the beautiful lake and fountain are at a premium. Kids can feed the ducks while their parents try to snatch a bit of conversation, and the coffee is great. Cakes and breakfasts are legendary, but there is more serious fare on the menu like roast beef with potato salad. Everything is written up on blackboard walls and ingredients are all well sourced (Ginger Pig meats, Monmouth coffees) and, wherever possible, organic. Service is friendly and informed, but you can also opt for takeaway and find a park bench.
Buggy access. Children's menu (£2-£4). Disabled access: toilet. High chairs. Nappy-changing facilities. Tables outdoors (15, park). Takeaway service.

Pavilion Café, Highgate

Highgate Woods, Muswell Hill Road, N10 3JN (8444 4777). Highgate tube. **Meals served** 9am-1hr before park closing daily. **Main courses** £6-£10. **Credit** AmEx, MC, V.
Serving the good families of Highgate and Muswell Hill, this café is always packed. It's set in a clearing amid the ancient trees of Highgate Woods, and has a large fenced-in terrace which keeps toddlers penned within parental sightlines. Indoor space is limited to seven tables, but a covered area provides shade in summer and shelter in winter. While the main menu is Mediterranean-influenced, the children's dishes are more straightforward: burger and chips and pasta are the favourites. Save room for pudding: the ice-cream is very good indeed, as are the warm, densely moist brownies. Service is presided over by the ever-attentive head waiter, whose charm puts a twinkle in local mums' eyes.

Buggy access. Children's set meal (£3.75-£3.95). Crayons. Disabled access: toilet. High chairs. Nappy-changing facilities. Tables outdoors (30, garden). Takeaway service.

Pavilion Tea House

Greenwich Park, Blackheath Gate, SE10 8QY (8858 9695, www.companyofcooks. com). Blackheath rail or Greenwich rail/DLR. **Meals served** *Summer* 9am-5.30pm Mon-Fri; 9am-6pm Sat, Sun. *Winter* 9am-4pm daily. **Main courses** £5.50-£7.95. **Credit** MC, V.
You are best off visiting this hexagonal park café during the week; at weekends, the painfully slow service means the queue is always enormous. The menu is full of appealingly hearty fare, with meaty specials, generously filled sandwiches and a good value all-day breakfast menu. It's licensed, so you can wash your lunch down with a glass of wine. Options for children include pasta dishes and baked beans on toast, but limited indoor space means parents are requested to leave pushchairs outside. If you're not too full after the large main courses, the own-made cakes are very good.
Buggy access. Children's menu (£3-£4). Disabled access: toilet. High chairs. Nappy-changing facilities. Tables outdoors (15, patio).

S&M Café

4-6 Essex Road, N1 8LN (7359 5361, www.sandmcafe.co.uk). Angel tube or bus 19, 38. **Meals served** 7.30am-11pm Mon-Fri; 8.30am-11pm Sat, Sun. **Main courses** £6.95-£11.95. **Credit** AmEx, MC, V.
'Eat yourself happy' exhort the mosaic tiles on the floor, and it's difficult not to comply when people all around you are tucking into comfort food of this magnitude. Original Italian caff trappings have been preserved, from the steel-edged laminated tables to the magnificent art deco façade. The retro look may appeal to adults, but there's plenty here for children to enjoy too, and the ambience is welcoming and relaxed. As well as the eponymous sausage and mash – available in various varieties – there are sides such as Heinz baked beans and cauliflower cheese, and a down-to-earth breakfast menu featuring the likes of beans on toast and boiled eggs with soldiers (there's an all-day breakfast, too, including just about everything). Other mains such as fishcakes and meat pies round out the choices, and there's even toad in the hole.

Consumer

Consumer

*Buggy access. Children's set meal (£3.95).
Crayons. High chairs. Nappy-changing
facilities. Takeaway service.*
Branches 48 Brushfield Street, E1
6AG (7247 2252); 268 Portobello Road
W10 5TY (8968 8898).

That Place on the Corner

*1-3 Green Lanes, N16 9BS (7704 0079,
www.thatplaceonthecorner.co.uk). Highbury
& Islington tube/rail or Canonbury rail, or
bus 21, 73, 141, 276, 341, 476.* **Meals
served** 9.30am-6.30pm Mon-Thur; 9.30am-
8pm Fri; times vary, check website for
details Sat, Sun. **Main courses** £4.85-
£9.50. **Credit** MC, V.
The yummy mummies of Stoke Newington
keep coming back to this airy café on the corner
of Newington Green. And why wouldn't they?
TPOTC is run by two local mums who
understand the desires of their regulars, which
include home-cooked food, entertainment for
under-sixes and the knowledge that they're not
alone in their parental endeavours (adults
aren't allowed in unless they're with a child).
There's a buggy park by the door, an inviting
play corner with brightly coloured cushions, a
well-stocked book shelf and a large dressing-
up cupboard. Daily music, ballet, dance and
arts and crafts sessions are held in the main
café (check the website for timetable). The
children's menu is a collection of old favourites
like sausage and mash, pasta, pizza (kids can
put the toppings on themselves), burgers and
cottage pie, all own-made and served with a
portion of veg. Babies are also catered for with
a daily organic vegetable purée, available in
different textures for those with and without
teeth. Adults get similar comfort food to the
children, albeit in larger portions.
*Buggy access. Children's menu (£2.90-
£5.50). Crayons. Disabled access: toilet. High
chairs. Nappy-changing facilities. Play area.*

Tide Tables

*2 The Archways, Riverside, Richmond,
Surrey TW9 1TH (8948 8285, www.tide
tablescafe.com). Richmond tube/rail.* **Meals
served** 9am-6pm daily. **Main courses**
£2.70-£6.50. **Credit** MC, V.
Nestled inside the last archway under
Richmond Bridge before it spans the Thames,
this café's biggest draw is its location. On fine
weather days (it's a seasonal café open from
Easter to November), customers sip organic
coffee out on the gravelled terrace while looking
at the river. It is patronised by pumped-up

joggers stopping by for an energy drink as well
as more laid-back dog-walkers; parents,
meanwhile, praise its toddler-friendly garden
and welcoming attitude to children. New
mothers also flock here in droves, attracted by
the comfy sofas and wholehearted support of
breastfeeding. Offering toothsome vegetarian
fare with a North African influence, as well as
the usual pastries and muffins, the menu rates
highly in terms of nutrition and variety.
Regulars are treated like old friends, while
newcomers are charmed by the affable owners.
It's also just past the embarkation point for
boats to Hampton Court (*see p59*).
*Buggy access. Children's menu (£2.70).
High chairs. Takeaway service.*

Upper Deck

*London Transport Museum, The Piazza,
WC2E 7BB (7598 1356, www.ltmuseum.
co.uk). Covent Garden tube.* **Meals served**
10am-6.30pm Mon, Tue, Sun; 10am-7pm
Wed, Thur, Sat; 11am-7pm Fri. **Main
courses** £4-£8.50. **Credit** AmEx, MC, V.
Map p333 L7.
Kids will be mesmerised by the huge set
of traffic lights suspended from the ceiling at
the mezzanine café within the brilliantly
conceived London Transport Museum (*see
p98*), although you don't have to visit the
museum to eat here. Staff are incredibly helpful,
parking buggies out of site and appearing with
high chairs and menus as soon as you arrive.
Children can have a half-price, half-portion
version of most of the adult meals, which
include burger and chips, beans on toast, pasta,
panini and soup (adults will also appreciate the
good-looking cocktail menu). Then it's off to the
Piazza for some street entertainment.
*Buggy access. Children's menu (£2-£4.25).
Disabled access: lift, toilet. High chairs.
Nappy-changing facilities.*

V&A Café

*Victoria & Albert Museum, Cromwell Road,
SW7 2RL (7942 2000, www.vam.ac.uk).
South Kensington tube.* **Meals served**
10am-5.15pm Mon-Thur, Sat, Sun; 10am-
9.30pm Fri. **Main courses** £6-£10.
Credit MC, V. **Map** p329 E10.
The main corridor of the café is white, spare
and a little antiseptic; for a more atmospheric
experience, head to the fabled trio of tearooms
off to the side which remain much as they
looked in the mid 19th century. The Morris
room is in dark green and gold, the Gamble
room is lofty and light with ceramic pillars, and

Anyone for Tea?

Children love joining in with anything that smacks of adult sophistication – tiered plates with tiny cakes and teapots with strainers invariably delight. Here's our pick of child-friendly afternoon tea spots.

The Orangery

Kensington Palace, Kensington Gardens, W8 4PX (0844 482 7777, www1.hrp.org.uk). High Street Kensington or Notting Hill Gate tube. **Meals served** *Summer* 10am-6pm daily. *Winter* 10am-5pm daily. **Main courses** £9-£14. **Credit** AmEx, MC, V. **Map** p326 C8.

OK, so it's not one of the cheapest dining options in London, but it is in a lovely spot. The picturesque Orangery is within the palace grounds, but you don't have to pay the entrance fee to dine here. At weekends, prepare to queue among tourists and locals seeking regal refuge and refuelling. Children will be drawn to the central table piled high with plump scones, huge meringues and a wide assortment of traditional cakes, and be delightedly flummoxed by the choice. In the afternoons, tables are filled with people enjoying finger sandwiches and a selection of cakes on tiered plates; young ones get their own version of the various afternoon tea selections. The interior features of the Orangery give the proceedings a sense of occasion, but on warm days the best views are from tables outside on the vast veranda overlooking the gardens, where kids can run around while their parents indulge in a glass of prosecco. *Buggy access. Crayons. Disabled access. High chairs. Tables outdoors (15, terrace). Toys.*

Orange Pekoe

3 White Hart Lane, SW13 0PX (8876 6070, www.orangepekoeteas.com). Barnes Bridge rail or bus 209. **Meals served** 7.30am-5.30pm Mon-Fri; 9am-5.30pm Sat, Sun. **Main courses** £4.50-£8. **Credit** AmEx, MC, V.

Wooden tables, white brick walls, flamboyant wallpaper and pretty tea cups on cherub plinths provide a charming

Orange Pekoe.

setting in one of our favourite tea rooms. Orange Pekoe won our Best Tea Room award in 2008 and has barely put a foot wrong since. It's right on the river at Barnes, and friendly young staff cope well with the stream of customers. Traditional Afternoon Tea costs £16.95 and includes finger sandwiches, cakes and scones. Shelves of black canisters bear witness to the seriousness with which tea is taken here; around 50 loose leaf teas and 20 herbal infusions are available, from the café's own breakfast blend to high-grade Japanese green tea *gyokuro asahi*, costing £26 for 100g. You can try any tea for £3.60 a pot and the coffees are good too. If you're coming for lunch, arrive early to get a table and choose from cheese or pâté platters, sandwiches, and hot snacky dishes (soup, cheese on toast, eggs florentine). While you're in Barnes, visit the fantastic Wetland Centre (*see p156*). *High chairs. Nappy-changing facilities. Tables outdoors (7, pavement). Takeaway service.*

the Poynter room is cosy despite its stained glass fox. Even kids who aren't impressed by the baroque tiling will probably like the huge ball chandeliers – especially if they're also given a little something from the luscious cake selection. And there's a good selection of savouries too, with a hot food counter serving crispy roasts (from pork and apple to pesto-drizzled aubergine) and an adventurous sandwich bar. Kids' portions (for the under-tens) are available from both counters for £4.95, the place is buggy-friendly and high chairs are provided. As a good-weather option, there are tables outside in the courtyard; fountains bubble in the shallow lake at the centre.
Buggy access. Disabled access: toilet. High chairs. Nappy-changing facilities.

CHINESE

Dragon Castle
100 Walworth Road, SE17 1JL (7277 3388, www.dragoncastle.eu). Elephant & Castle tube/rail. **Meals served** noon-11.30pm Mon-Sat; 11.30am-10.30pm Sun. **Main courses** £9-£25. **Set meals** £16.80-£34.80 per person (min two) 2-3 courses. **Credit** AmEx. MC, V.
Set among the tower blocks of Elephant & Castle, this vast, gaudy banqueting hall has an abundance of gilded accents and friendly service. Dragon Castle is a commendable attempt to re-create an authentic Hong Kong dining experience, complete with carp ponds and a menu that runs to duck tongues and poached eels. Unadventurous children can choose instead from the first-rate dim sum menu, as these savoury morsels will really appeal to children. We loved the simple steamed corn-fed chicken in a lightly spicy root ginger stock, deep fried soft shell crabs, and tiny spare ribs. It's best to stick to the Cantonese dishes on the menu as the Sichuan- and Beijing-style dishes can lack flavour.
Buggy access. Disabled access: toilet. High chairs. Takeaway service.

Joy King Lau
3 Leicester Street, WC2H 7BL (7437 1132, www.joykinglau.com). Leicester Square or Piccadilly Circus tube. **Dim sum served** noon-5pm Mon-Sat; 11am-5pm Sun. **Meals served** noon-11.30pm Mon-Sat; 11.30am-10.30pm Sun. **Main courses** £4.60-£20. Set meal £10-£35 per person (minimum 2). **Credit** AmEx, MC, V. **Map** p333 K7.

A divergent bunch of dim sum devotees flock to this Chinatown restaurant. The atmosphere is always family-friendly, although it's a little cramped for buggies over its four floors. Its menu is comprehensive, but Joy King Lau is best known for dim sum, which draws a high proportion of Chinese punters. There is much to appeal to children, from yam croquettes to crispy spring rolls and dumplings (although come early for these as they lose their delicacy as the afternoon progresses). The sweet dim sum is just as good: egg custard tart, mango pudding, and crisp deep-fried custard buns.
Buggy access. Disabled access: lift. High chairs. Takeaway service.

Royal China
30 Westferry Circus, E14 8RR (7719 0888, www.royalchinagroup.co.uk). Canary Wharf tube/DLR or Westferry DLR. **Dim sum served** noon-4.45pm daily. **Meals served** noon-11pm Mon-Thur; noon-11.30pm Fri, Sat; 11am-10pm Sun. **Dim sum** £2.65-£4.20. **Main courses** £8.50-£25. **Set meal** £30-£38 per person (min two). **Credit** AmEx, DC, MC, V.
Royal China was one of the first to introduce Londoners to the delights of proper dim sum, raising the standard of this popular lunchtime choice. The chain remains consistently dependable for its good-quality cooking, and the fact that this branch overlooks the Thames makes it a good choice for families visiting Docklands for the day. Staff glide discreetly among guests, providing recommendations and ensuring smooth service. We were delighted by unctuous braised pork belly with preserved cabbage, silky steamed cod with dried yellow bean sauce, and a perfect dish of Chinese broccoli in ginger juice. A vast menu means there's something to appeal to all tastes.
Booster seats. Buggy access. Disabled access: toilet. Nappy-changing facilities. Tables outdoors (23, terrace). Takeaway service.
Branches 24-26 Baker Street, W1U 7AB (7487 4688); 13 Queensway, W2 4QJ (7221 2535); 805 Fulham Road, SW6 5HE (7731 0081).

FISH

Ark Fish Restaurant
142 Hermon Hill, E18 1QH (8989 5345, www.arkfishrestaurant.com). South Woodford tube. **Lunch served** noon-2.15pm Tue-Sat. **Dinner served** 5.30-

9.45pm Tue-Thur; 5.30-10.15pm Fri, Sat.
Meals served noon-8.45pm Sun. **Main courses** £7.50-£24.50. **Credit** MC, V.
You can't get more East End than this spacious family-run restaurant. Fish is sourced from Billingsgate and the appetiser menu runs like the start of a nursery rhyme: whelks, winkles, cockles and fresh peeled prawns. For the main course, adults can choose their fish and dictate whether they want it deep-fried, poached or grilled, while children under 12 are offered cod, scampi or chicken with chips plus a soft drink and ice-cream for £6.50. Waiting staff and fellow diners are straight-talking cockneys with a great line in comic self-expression. Ark sticks to traditional fish dishes with no twists. When your raw ingredients are this good, why bother?
Buggy access. Children's menu (£6.65). High chairs. Nappy-changing facilities.

Belgo Noord

72 Chalk Farm Road, NW1 8AN (7267 0718, www.belgo-restaurants.com). Chalk Farm tube. **Lunch served** noon-5pm daily. **Dinner served** 5-11pm Mon-Sat; 5-10.30pm Sun. **Main courses** £9.95-£16.95. **Set lunch** £6.95 1 course. **Credit** AmEx, MC, V.
Beer, mussels and chips made this chain famous, but if it seems a strange choice of venue for children, read on. The menu also includes a decent array of alternatives. The sausage with *stoemp* mash, beer-basted rotisserie chicken or Hoegaarden beer-battered haddock and frites reflect the prominent Belgian theme – as do the staff, who are quirkily dressed in traditional Trappist monks' habits. Food is served in cool, industrial surroundings with an open kitchen; noisy but cheerful. The other great reason to bring children here is that they qualify for a free two-course menu when an adult orders a main from the à la carte menu. Helpful, speedy service means you can be in and out of the door in under an hour, but the kids' menu has plenty of puzzles and colouring if parents prefer to linger.
Crayons. Children's menu (free with paying adult). High chairs. Nappy-changing facilities. Tables outside (4, pavement).
Branches throughout the city.

Olley's

65-69 Norwood Road, SE24 9AA (8671 8259, www.olleys.info). Herne Hill rail or bus 3, 68. **Lunch served** noon-3pm Tue-Sat.

Pavilion Café, Victoria Park.
See p253.

Consumer

Consumer

Dinner served 5-10.30pm Tue-Sat;
5-9.30pm Sun. Main courses £12.45-
£18.45. Set lunch £5.50 1 course.
Credit AmEx, MC, V.

Situated right by Brockwell Park on the Herne
Hill side – you can't miss its colourful exterior
– Olley's is a great place to come after an
exhausting session in the playground. The fish
and chips are first rate (choose from 20 species)
and there's a series of celebrity specials. The
Cilla Black Experience involves haddock and
chips with interesting sides. The Guy Dimond
Experience (named after *Time Out* magazine's
food critic) is battered lemon sole fillet with
chips and a lemon wedge. High chairs are
clingfilm-wrapped for each use so your child
won't be picking up the last kid's peas. The
children's menu consists mainly of the usual
'nuggets and chips' options, but there are also
calamares and prawns available. The staff
will also bring small portions of the steamed
dishes on request. The creamy mushy peas
are among the best in London, and the chips
also deserve a special mention, being blanched
before frying.

*Buggy access. Children's menu (£4-£4.50).
Crayons. Disabled access: toilet. High chairs.
Nappy-changing facilities. Tables outdoors
(12, pavement). Takeaway service.*

Toff's

*38 Muswell Hill Broadway, N10 3RT (8883
8656, www.toffsfish.co.uk). Highgate tube,
then bus 43, 134.* Meals served 11.30am-
10pm Mon-Sat. Main courses £8.95-
£22. Set lunch £9.25 1 course. Credit
AmEx, DC, MC, V.

Toff's has been a Muswell Hill institution since
1968, and it's got the awards to prove it. At
frying time, there's always a long queue of
customers stretching out of the door. Behind
the bustling takeaway counter at the front, a
pair of saloon-style swing doors (which
children love) lead to a more serene restaurant.
Toff's large choice of fish can be ordered in
plain or matzo-meal batter, or grilled for a
healthier alternative – a rarity in most chippies.
There's also a well-executed children's menu
featuring proper fish and own-made chips. If
you can squeeze anything else in, there are
salads (tomato and red onion, olive-topped
coleslaw, Greek), soups, deep-fried camembert
and traditional British puds, served in veritable
ponds of custard.

*Buggy access. Children's menu (£3.95-
£4.95). Crayons. Disabled access: toilets.
High chairs. Takeaway service.*

FRENCH

Belvedere

*Holland House, off Abbotsbury Road,
in Holland Park, W8 6LU (7602 1238,
www.whitestarline.org.uk). Holland Park
tube.* Lunch served noon-2.15pm Mon-
Sat; noon-2.30pm, 2.30-5pm Sun. Dinner
served 6-10.30pm Mon-Sat. Main
courses £12-£25. Set meal (Sat, Sun)
£24.95 3 courses. Credit AmEx, MC, V.

Once the ballroom of Holland House, this art
deco gem set right in the middle of Holland
Park is a lofty haven of mannered calm. A
piano tinkles away in the background, black-
aproned waiters glide between the tables and
french doors open on to the manicured lawns
beyond. It certainly doesn't look very child-
friendly at first glance. But looks can be
deceptive; staff couldn't be more welcoming,
and this is a superb place to have a special
family lunch with the grandparents, especially
on a Sunday when the three-course set menu
attracts lots of families with young children in
tow. There's no designated children's menu,
but the chef will happily whip up a range of
child-friendly classics (pasta, sausage and
mash, meat and vegetables without the rich
sauces) at a reduced price on request. With the
park and impressive adventure playground
just outside, this makes a family day out that
everyone will remember.

*Buggy access. Disabled access (ground floor,
call ahead). High chairs. Tables outdoors
(5, terrace).*

Galvin Café a Vin

*35 Spital Square, entrance on Bishops
Square E1 6DY (7299 0404, www.galvin
restaurants.com). Liverpool Street tube/rail
or Shoreditch High Street rail.* Breakfast
served 8-11.30am Mon-Fri; 9-11.30am
Sat, Sun. Lunch served noon-3pm daily.
Dinner served 6-10pm Mon-Sat; 6-9.30pm
Sun. Main courses £11-£14. Set meal
(lunch, 6-7pm) £14.95 2 courses. Credit
AmEx, MC, V.

Galvin Café a Vin forms part of the Galvin
brothers' expanding empire, and in the latter
half of 2010 (along with sister restaurant
Galvin La Chapelle) it started hosting family-
friendly sunday lunches. Galvin Café a Vin is
the cheaper of the two options, with the adult
menu coming in at a reasonable £14.95 and the
children's menu at £9.50, both for two courses.
The restaurant has terraces at the front and
back, while inside the room is dominated by a

magnificent six-metre-long pewter bar. It's a handsome spot, and pleasantly quiet most weekends after the Friday exodus of City financiers. Roasts are cooked in the wood-fired oven and you can expect a choice of dishes like roast shoulder of new season lamb with red cabbage, roast pork belly with celeriac and apples or roast salmon with caponata and rocket. Children always get roast chicken with posh mashed potato and green beans, and ice-cream with chocolate sauce to follow. As the name suggests (it opened as Café de Luxe, but has since been renamed Café a Vin) there's an emphasis on wine, with plenty by the glass and 'pot' as well as by the bottle. On Sundays, there are newspapers to entertain the parents, while children can choose between the toys and board games on offer.

Buggy access. Children's menu (£6.50-£8.50). Disabled access: toilet. High chairs. Nappy-changing facilities. Tables outdoors (6, terrace).

Almeida

30 Almeida Street N1 1AD. (7354 4777, www.danddlondon.com). Angel tube or Highbury & Islington tube/rail. **Lunch served** noon-2.30pm Tue-Sat; noon-3.30pm Sun. **Dinner served** 5.30-10.30pm Mon-Sat. **Main courses** £19.50. **Credit** AmEx, MC, V.

Almeida is unusual in the D&D London group (formerly Conran Restaurants) for being an establishment with a local feel to it. Keenly priced set menus are the bedrock of any establishment opposite a theatre, and the *menu du jour* doesn't disappoint at £15.95 for two courses. Start, maybe, with spiced butternut squash velouté or terrine of ham hock and foie gras with piccalilli; follow with braised suckling pig or sea bream with creamed leeks and a shellfish foam. The dessert list is a highlight too. The children's menu is priced at £10 for two courses and offers a choice of shepherd's pie, steamed fish or herb gnocchi for main courses, chocolate pudding, chocolate mousse or own-made ice-cream to follow. Children with more savoury palates can choose a starter instead. Almeida trundles along like the trolleys of *fermier* cheese and own-made charcuterie that made the restaurant so refreshing when it first opened back in 2001. Head chef Alan Jones uses British ingredients (Scottish langoustines, Maldon rock oysters, Severn & Wye smoked salmon, Denham Estate lamb) to produce refined French cuisine with modern accents, including

a stated emphasis on steaming and poaching to create lighter dishes.

Buggy access. Children's menu (£6.50-£8.50). Disabled access: toilet. High chairs. Nappy-changing facilities. Tables outdoors (6, terrace).

GASTROPUBS

Old Dairy

1-3 Crouch Hill, N4 4AP (7263 3337, www.theolddairyn4.co.uk). Finsbury Park tube or Crouch Hill rail. **Open** noon-11pm Mon-Wed; noon-midnight Thur; noon-1am Fri, Sat; noon-9.30pm Sun. **Lunch served** noon-3.30pm, **dinner served** 6.30-10.30pm Mon-Fri. **Meals served** noon-10pm Sat, Sun. **Main courses** £10-£14. **Credit** MC, V.

Since this Victorian former dairy was taken over by Realpubs, its reputation has improved dramatically, and with its ornate friezes of life in a Victorian dairy along the outside walls, it's a local landmark too. Menus mix classic pub favourites (beer-battered haddock and chips with mushy peas; ribeye steak and chips) with modern dishes featuring a strong European influence (pork, cheese and chianti sausage with mushroom tagliatelle; pan-fried Scottish salmon with curried aubergine, mint yoghurt and an onion bhajia). Sunday roasts are popular too, so it's best to book. This delightful building is so big that there are plenty of spaces to choose from, whether you want a quiet corner or something busier. Staff are friendly and clued-up, and children get their own menu featuring sausage and mash, fish and chips or pasta with tomato sauce (they can also have any main dish on the menu at a reduced size for half the price). On Tuesdays, Wednesdays and Thursdays (noon-5pm), there are drop-in parent and toddler sessions (under-fours) with soft mats, toys and books to keep the little ones amused. On Tuesday afternoons an entertainer hosts creative sessions.

Buggy access. Children's menu (£6.50). Crayons. Disabled accesss: toilet. High chairs. Nappy-changing facilities. Toys.

Orange Public House & Hotel

37-39 Pimlico Road, SW1W 8NE (7881 9844, www.theorange.co.uk). Sloane Square tube. **Open** 8am-11.30pm Mon-Thur; 8am-midnight Fri, Sat; 8am-10.30pm Sun. **Breakfast served** 8-11am daily. **Meals served** noon-10.30pm Mon-

Sat; noon-9.30pm Sun. **Main courses** £12.50-£16.50. **Credit** AmEx, MC, V. **Map** p332 G11.

This newcomer was runner up in the Best New Gastropub category in 2010's Time Out Eating and Drinking Awards. The stripped wood, textured paint and potted orange trees – a glossy urban interpretation of rusticity –

provide a perfect fit for the posh locale. It's an elegant, airy conversion of a former brewery where the 'pub' part of the equation is a single ground-floor room, the 'gastro' aspect a dining room beside the bar (no bookings taken) and the first-floor restaurant a little plusher. Kids get their own meal deal with a wood-fired margherita pizza followed by own-made ice-

Bouled Over

Gelateria Danieli

16 Brewers Lane, Richmond, Surrey, TW9 1HH (8439 9807, www.gelateria danieli.com). Richmond tube/rail. **Open** Summer 10am-10pm daily. *Winter* 10am-6pm daily. **Ice-cream** £2/scoop. **Credit** MC, V.

Squeezed into a narrow shopping arcade, marked at one end by two jolly guardsmen standing to attention outside a chocolate shop, this small gelateria dishes out superior sorbets and ice-creams to be savoured around Richmond Green. Wooden floorboards and a couple of chairs inside make it cosy in winter but rather cramped in summer, when queues stretch out of the door. When they're not rushed off their feet, the friendly staff might invite you to try before you buy.

Buggy access. Takeaway service. **Branches** Bentalls Centre, Wood Street, Kingston-upon-Thames, Surrey KT1 1TX (8141 5098); 47 Queenstown Road, SW8 3RG (7720 5784, open summer only).

Gelato Mio

138 Holland Park Avenue, W11 4UE (7727 4117, www.gelatomio.co.uk). Holland Park tube. **Open** 7.30am-10pm Mon-Wed, Sun; 8.30am-11pm Fri, Sat; 9am-10pm Sun. **Ice-cream** £2.90/scoop. **Credit** MC, V.

Still only in its third summer, this stylish, orange-hued parlour already has three branches. The welcome is enthusiastic and typically Italian. Customers may be invited to have a taste before choosing; last time we were here we plumped for a gorgeous strawberry sorbet with sharp fruity flavours. There's seating inside; alternatively, take your ice to nearby Holland Park. The ever-changing menu

may include *nocciola* (hazelnut), *stracciatella* (chocolate chip) and *arrancia* (orange sorbet). *Buggy access. Tables outdoors (2, pavement). Takeaway service.* **Branches** 37 Pembridge Road, W11 3HG (7727 0194); 138 St John's Wood High Street, NW8 7SE (0011 3889); 495 Fulham Palace Road, SW6 6SU (0011 3907).

Gelateria Valerie

9 Duke of York Square, SW3 4LY (7730 7978, www.patisserie-valerie.co.uk). Sloane Square tube. **Open** 8am-7pm Mon-Sat; 10am-7pm Sun. **Ice-cream** £1.85/scoop. **Credit** AmEx, MC, V.

A cone's throw away from the Saatchi Gallery, this glass-walled branch of the ever-expanding Patisserie Valerie chain is a shining island in the heart of Chelsea's prime retail site. There's plenty of outside seating looking over the fountains in summer, while stools lining the glass shopfront are perfect for a spot of people watching. Ferrero Rocher, amarena cherry, rum baba and mascarpone are among the yummy flavours on offer.

Buggy access. Disabled access. Tables outdoors (20, Duke of York Square). Takeaway service. **Branches** throughout the city.

Marine Ices

8 Haverstock Hill, NW3 2BL (7482 9003, www.marineices.co.uk) Chalk Farm tube. **Open** 10.30am-11pm Tue-Sat; 11am-10pm Sun. **Ice-cream** £2.10/scoop. **Credit** MC, V.

It's hard to resist the ice-cream at this family-run London stalwart when you see the line of people queuing outside for a scoop of their favourite. Yield to cream for £7.50 (they can also choose a half-size, half-price portion of some of the main courses). Adults can enjoy some well-judged plates of food, from creamily rich chicken liver parfait for starters (which arrived in a little French kilner jar, open but with the pâté sealed off by a layer of port jelly, served with pickled walnuts and toast) to perfectly juicy scallops in a gentle lemon and garlic butter. Main courses include dishes like crispy, salt-crusted sea bream, which came with a minty pea sauce, squeaky beans and peas, and little herb dumplings. Tempting puds include sticky toffee pudding with butterscotch ice-cream or pecan nut pie with clotted cream. Daring or desperate parents might also resort to the

temptation: they're worth every calorie. There's a great selection, from toffee crunch to maple walnut, along with a choice of divine fruit sorbets such as mango or melon.
Buggy access. Disabled access. Takeaway service.

Morelli's Gelato Counter
Harrods Food Hall, 87-135 Brompton Road, SW1X 7XL (7893 8959, www.morellisgelato.com). Knightsbridge tube. **Open** 9am-9pm Mon-Sat; noon-6pm Sun. **Ice-cream** £3.95/scoop. **Credit** AmEx, MC, V.
From its beginnings in a 1930s seaside art deco premises (the original branch in Broadstairs is still trading), Morelli's has expanded into Harrods and Selfridges. Done out in Italian marble, the Harrods concession is a smart affair. But it's the ice-cream that counts. Twenty flavours of freshly made gelato are served daily from an almost endless repertoire. Sundaes range from the classic to the exotic; try a Chairman's Delight, with vanilla, banana, mango, lemon, mango sauce, whipped cream, fig compote and coconut sauce.
Takeaway service.

Oddono's
14 Bute Street, SW7 3EX (7052 0732, www.oddonos.com). South Kensington tube. **Open** 11am-11pm Mon-Thur, Sun; 11am-midnight Fri, Sat. **Ice-cream** £2/scoop. **Credit** AmEx, MC, V.
With its minimalist interior and retro seating, this place is all about quality; the focus is on premium ingredients and classic flavours. Even on a grey day, regulars troop in for their fix of vaniglia, made from Madagascan vanilla pods. The pistachio was brilliant, with generous sprinkles of the namesake nut.

Buggy access. Disabled access. Takeaway service. Tables outdoors (3, pavement).
Branches Selfridges, 400 Oxford Street, W1A 1AB (7318 3344); Whiteleys, 151 Queensway, W2 4YN (7792 6023).

Parlour
1st floor, Fortnum & Mason, 181 Piccadilly, W1J 9FA (7734 8040, www.fortnumandmason.com). Piccadilly Circus tube. **Open** 10am-7.30pm Mon-Sat; noon-5pm Sun. **Ice-cream** £3/scoop. **Credit** AmEx, MC, V.
Decorated in ice-cream pastels, there's a definite sense of occasion about the Parlour. Pricey but gorgeous adult sundaes (£12) are matched by children's versions for £8: Tots Knickerbocker Glory features vanilla, strawberry and shortbread ice-creams with raspberries, pineapple, raspberry coulis and whipped cream. Children's cornets come adorned with two kinds of ice-cream.
Buggy access. Disabled access: toilet. Takeaway service.

Scoop
40 Shorts Gardens, WC2H 9AB (7240 7086, www.scoopgelato.com). Covent Garden tube. **Open** noon-9.30pm daily. Times vary, phone to check. **Ice-cream** £2.80/scoop. **Credit** MC, V.
A required stop if you're out and about in Covent Garden. One very generous dollop of intensely dark chocolate ice-cream spilled over the sides of the cone, and required some hastily executed licking. Sugar-, gluten- and milk-free varieties are avaliable for the diet-conscious. Flavours include Madagascan vanilla, Ethiopian coffee and São Tomé chocolate. Look out for summer events promoting unusual ingredients.
Takeaway service.

Consumer

Consumer

cocktail menu, which runs from the safe (bloody mary) to the outlandish (basil martini). Staff are smiley, helpful and relaxed, which is always a bonus when you've got children in tow.
Buggy access. Children's menu (£7.50). Crayons. Disabled access: toilet. Tables outdoors (5, pavement).

Wells

30 Well Walk, NW3 1BX (7794 3785, www.thewellshampstead.co.uk). Hampstead tube. **Open** noon-11pm Mon-Sat; noon-10.30pm Sun. **Lunch served** noon-3pm Mon-Fri; noon-4pm Sat, Sun. **Dinner served** 6-10pm Mon-Fri; 7-10pm Sat, Sun. **Main courses** £9.95-£18.95. **Credit** AmEx, MC, V.

The tables on the small terrace outside this pretty Georgian pub are usually crowded with Bugaboos, as parents stop off on their way to and from Hampstead Heath (a very short walk away). Inside, the ground-floor bar with charcoal coloured walls and black tiling is smartly relaxed and offers the same menu as the more formal upstairs dining rooms (a good choice for a romantic evening *sans enfants*). Menu combinations tend to be classic British and European, with a strong seasonal slant. Silky smooth, tangy gazpacho *castellano*, made with apple and cumin in addition to the usual tomatoes and peppers, comes well matched with a slab of brown olive bread and croûtons. King scallops were exceptionally succulent alongside pea purée, crunchy bacon and rich meat jus. Children get their own menu of sausages and mash, pasta or chicken goujons, although you could also order from the side dishes (cauliflower cheese, mashed potato or chips at £3 each). Many gastropubs provide a friendly welcome, but what impressed here was the warmth of the farewell. We'll be back.
Buggy access. Children's menu (£4-£7). Colouring books. Disabled access: toilet. High chairs. Nappy-changing facilities. Tables outdoors (8, patio).

INDIAN

Imli

167-169 Wardour Street, W1F 8WR. (7287 4243, www.imli.co.uk). Oxford Circus or Tottenham Court Road tube. **Meals served** noon-11pm Mon-Sat; noon-10pm Sun. **Main courses** £6-£15. **Set lunch** £10 platter. **Set dinner** £20 3 courses. **Credit** AmEx, MC, V. **Map** p331 K6.

Tsunami. *See p264.*

The owners of Tamarind in Mayfair (*see p263*) are on to the family dining market. Imli is Tamarind's cheaper sister and very much the diffusion range of a creative genius's work. It's a down-to-earth canteen that tries to be stylish yet keep prices moderate, and offers an interesting selection of dishes that avoid the obvious. Children get their own menu (£8.50 for three courses), with dishes designed to appeal to the greatest range of palates. Starters include gram flour and coriander wedges or mashed vegetables with hot toasted bread; main courses feature fried tilapia fish or minced lamb cooked with peas and coriander; puddings are own-made ice-cream or mango sorbet. Sometimes the service can be a bit perfunctory but it's a good place to encourage children to try something that stretches their repertoire. Imli very often has special offers and participates in online deals, and these can be worth checking out if you're particularly price-conscious.
Buggy access. Children's menu (£8.50). Disabled access: toilet. High chairs. Nappy-changing facilities. Takeaway service (noon-10pm daily).

Tamarind

20-22 Queen Street, W1J 5PR (7629 3561, www.tamarindrestaurant.com). Green Park tube. **Lunch served** noon-2.45pm Mon-Fri, Sun. **Dinner served** 5.30-10.45pm Mon-Sat; 6-10.30pm Sun. **Main courses** £14.50-£28. **Set lunch** £16.95 2 courses, £18.95 3 courses. **Set dinner** (5.30-6.45pm, 10.30-11pm) £25 3 courses. **Credit** AmEx, DC, MC, V. **Map** p332 H7.

Tamarind has been a Mayfair staple since it opened in 1995. The glamorous basement is showing some signs of wear, but the cooking is still excellent. Tamarind offers an attractive Sunday lunch deal: under-tens can eat from a three-course tasting menu for free, if they're with two or more adults eating from the main menu. Starters include spiced potato cakes and Indian-style fishfingers; for mains, there's grilled chicken, monkfish or paneer in masala sauce, served with veg and rice. Pudding is ice-cream with fruit. The open kitchen means kids can watch the chefs working with the tandoor oven. Note that children must be out by 7pm. *Children's set meal (£12.50, free under-10s, Sun lunch). High chairs. Takeaway service.*

INTERNATIONAL

Rainforest Café

20 Shaftesbury Avenue, W1D 7EU (7434 3111, www.therainforestcafe.co.uk). Piccadilly Circus tube. **Meals served** noon-10pm Mon-Fri; 11.30am-8pm Sat; 11.30am-10pm Sun. **Main courses** £13.10-£19.95. **Credit** AmEx, MC, V. **Map** p333 K7.

This West End institution puts passing families squarely in its crosshairs. It's expensive, but children love the whole experience and the café at least donates some of its profits to David Attenborough's charity, World Land Trust, which saves tropical forest habitats. The Rainforest Café aims to re-create a little bit of the rainforest right here on Shaftesbury Avenue with a soundtrack, animatronic animals, tropical fish tanks and other water features. The unchallenging global menu of meze, pasta, seafood, ribs, steaks and burgers is nothing out of the ordinary, although it does offer organic sausages, organic salmon and pasta for children alongside the more predictable burgers, goujons and pizza. Children's set meals comprise two courses; puddings are a range of extremely sweet and sticky bowlfuls. It's worth paying an extra £3 for the Adventure Meal, as it comes with a fantastic gift pack with mask, purse, stationery and sticker book. Score a table upstairs to sit amid the fish, elephants and gorillas; downstairs has far fewer animals and is much less thrilling for the children. Take a camera with a flash as it's incredibly dark inside. Bookings are not accepted.

Buggy access. Children's set meal (£11.95). Crayons. Entertainment: face painting, weekends & hols. High chairs. Nappy-changing facilities.

ITALIAN

Caponata

3-7 Delancey Street, NW1 7NL (7387 5959, www.caponatacamden.co.uk). Camden Town tube. **Lunch served** 9am-3pm Mon-Sat. **Dinner served** 6-11pm Mon-Sat. **Meals served** 10am-10pm Sun. **Main courses** £10-£18. **Set lunch** (noon-3pm daily) £10 2 courses. **Credit** AmEx, MC, V.

This surprisingly smart addition to the centre of Camden is next to the Forge music venue. It's versatile too; choose between the informal *osteria* at the front of the ground floor, the spectacular skylit central courtyard or the more intimate, formal dining room upstairs. There's no children's menu as such, but the chefs are more than happy to cook a smaller version of any dish from the menu or create a simple pasta dish (with arrabiata sauce or butter, say) for £4. Express lunch specials and the two-course set menu are keenly priced, but the carte isn't expensive. Dishes range from the familiar to inventive concoctions such as tea-smoked duck breast with caramelised gooseberries and raspberry dressing. Own-made bread is accompanied by Nocellara olive oil. The dessert list also offers several twists on classics (crunchy-topped bitter almond brûlée with apricot ice-cream, balsamic strawberries with saffron granita and vanilla cream). The all-Italian wine list contains 17 varieties by the glass; there are also many cocktails. Tight-trousered service is as smooth and sexy as a purring Lamborghini: not the Camden norm, that's for sure.

Buggy access. Disabled access: lift, toilet. High chairs. Nappy-changing facilities. Tables outdoors (4, pavement).

River Café

Thames Wharf, Rainville Road, W6 9HA (7386 4200, www.rivercafe.co.uk). Hammersmith tube. **Lunch served** 12.30-2.15pm Mon-Fri; 12.30-2.30pm Sat; noon,

Consumer

3pm Sun. **Dinner served** 7-9pm Mon-Thur; 7-9.15pm Fri, Sat. **Main courses** £12.50-£40. **Credit** AmEx, DC, MC, V.
London's most open of open kitchens fascinates children, who can watch chefs manning the wood-fired oven and the futuristic preparation hub. In summertime, another huge bonus is the spacious terrace surrounded by lawns and a 'roly poly' grass bank that toddlers and young children can enjoy in full view of their parents. There's also a herb and vegetable garden. Standards here continue to be just so, despite the death last year of co-founder Rose Gray. At Sunday lunch, exceptionally juicy middle white pork loin chop featured a subtle fennel rub and sat on plump, bead-like cannellini tossed with new season girolles. Swiss chard with crème fraîche was the accompaniment for wood-roast wild sea bass, but another service might see it partnered with peas *sott'olio* (preserved in oil) and spinach, or baked in a bag and served with *castelluccio* lentils and samphire. Children can choose a half-size pasta dish, which can be as plain or adventurous as they like. Desserts – almond and strawberry tart, Valpolicella summer pudding, the infamous chocolate nemesis – are lined up along a counter. Staff are young, friendly and dressed just a little more fashionably than the core Fulham and Kensington customer base, and the wine list is far more kindly priced than the menu, with the basic white wine a good grecanico from Sicily at £17.50 a bottle.
Buggy access. Crayons. Disabled access: toilet. High chairs. Nappy-changing facilities. Tables outdoors (35, terrace).

JAPANESE

Matsuri

15 Bury Street SW1Y 6AL (7839 1101, www.matsuri-restaurant.com). Green Park tube. **Lunch served** noon-2.30pm Mon-Sat; noon-3pm Sun. **Dinner served** 6-10pm daily. **Main courses** £19-£56. **Set meals** £48-£165. **Credit** AmEx, MC, V. **Map** p332 H7.
Benihana's star is on the wane after the closure of its Swiss Cottage branch, but the teppanyaki grill experience is still a favourite with families. After a devastating fire in 2009, Matsuri's Holborn outpost remains a ghostly shell, so fans of the restaurant should make their way to this larger St James's branch, where a dramatic basement space (filled with trinkets such as antique kimonos) is dedicated entirely to the craft. Diners are seated at islands around

double steel grills, manned by two teppanyaki chefs at peak times. The theatrics should get both adults and children squeaking with joy – a signature dessert, 'fireball' ice-cream, is produced by flambéeing a large block of vanilla ice-cream (the chefs turn down the lighting for this spectacle). *Okonomiyaki*, a Japanese street-food favourite, comes as a massive omelette full of bacon, shredded cabbage and soba noodles, topped with bonito fish flakes. There's also a sushi bar which offers a range of sashimi, sushi and sushi rolls, though the table-top food certainly steals the show. It's not a cheap dining option, but viewed as a piece of theatre, the price suddenly doesn't seem so steep.
Buggy access. Disabled access: toilet. High chairs. Takeaway service.

Tsunami

5-7 Voltaire Road, SW4 6DQ (7978 1610, www.tsunamirestaurant.co.uk). Clapham North tube. **Lunch served** 12.30-4pm Sat, Sun. **Dinner served** 6-10.30pm Mon-Thur; 6pm-midnight Fri-Sun. **Main courses** £7.70-£19.50. **Credit** MC, V.
This sultry Clapham restaurant might look more suitable for sophisticated adults than for children, with its grey, black and gold hues and subdued lighting, but local families (prams and all) have also claimed it as their own. So expect to see dressed-up trendies nibbling on edamame, but also children being spoon-fed creamy *nasu goma* (aubergine grilled with sesame paste). The dishes are elegantly presented, from a menu that gathers culinary influences from across the globe; orthodox, Tsunami is not. Over the years we've learnt to stick to the sushi and sashimi, which are generally faultless, or to order dishes that are restrained in their flavour combinations, like razor clams with fresh coriander, chilli, chives and vermicelli noodles. Children will find much to enjoy in the appetiser, tempura and sides menus, and the slick, glowing bar offers oriental-inspired cocktails if parents are in need of a pick-me-up.
Buggy access. Disabled access. High chairs. Takeaway service.
Branch 93 Charlotte Street, W1T 4PY (7637 0050).

MEXICAN

Taqueria

139-143 Westbourne Grove, W11 2RS (7229 4734, www.taqueria.co.uk). Notting Hill Gate tube. **Meals served** noon-11pm

Mon-Thur, Sun; noon-11.30pm Fri; noon-10.30pm Sat. **Main courses** £5.50-£8.50. **Set lunch** (noon-4.30pm Mon-Fri) £6 1 course. **Credit** MC, V.

Taqueria remains one of London's best venues for authentic Mexican food. This bright, disarming eaterie is intentionally more café/cantina than restaurant and kids get their own menu that consciously panders to a palate favouring blander flavours. Daytimes are family-friendly; under-fives can enjoy cheese or chicken quesadillas, or a combo plate that includes rice, plantain and avocado, and *licuados* (milkshakes) of mango, guava or chocolate. Tuesday is tamale day. High-quality ingredients feature strongly – the eggs, chicken and pork are free-range, the milk and cream organic, the scallops Marine Stewardship Council-certified – but prices are keen for the area. In the evening, tacos such as *cochinita pibil* (slow-cooked *achiote-* and citrus-marinated pork) with

Taqueria.

habanero-pickled onions, or *alambres* (char-grilled skirt steak with peppers and melted cheese), are great for nights of serious tequila sipping; the drinks list runs to 23 types of the Mexican spirit, plus beers, margaritas and wine. Owned by the Cool Chile Company (a familiar sight at markets, including Borough), Taqueria has a small selection of Mexican groceries for sale near the entrance.

Buggy access. Children's menu (£2.50). Disabled access: toilet. High chairs. Nappy-changing facilities.

MODERN EUROPEAN

Dean Street Townhouse

69-71 Dean Street, W1D 4QJ (7434 1775, www.deanstreettownhouse.com). Piccadilly Circus or Tottenham Court Road tube. **Breakfast served** 7.30-11.30am daily. **Tea served** 3-6pm daily. **Meals served** 11.30am-11.30pm Mon-Sat; 11.30am-10.30pm Sun. **Main courses** £15-£24. **Set meal** (5-7.30pm Mon-Fri) £16.50 2 courses, £19.50 3 courses. **Credit** AmEx, MC, V. **Map** p331 K6.

The food at this boutique Soho hotel is old-fashioned British and includes a superb mince and tatties – piquant, properly browned, full-flavoured, wonderful in texture, and tasting of… childhood. Yes, the Soho House group, still one of the coolest hospitality outfits in our city, has decided that the future is sherry trifle or treacle sponge with custard. Despite dishes such as grilled squid with spiced chickpeas or Cornish brill with ceps, much of the menu is deeply retro. It's also unusually well done, with such precision in the cooking and marvellous flavours that it would make any 1970s dinner-party host proud. Salt beef was near gelatinous in texture, yet an explosion of flavour; the brussels sprouts were young, tender, lightly cooked and nutty in taste. Families should avoid the busy bar and head to the quieter dining room, especially for high tea, when the Townhouse serves welsh or buck rarebit, macaroni cheese, sardines on toast, fishfingers and chips, and other nursery fare.

Buggy access. Disabled access: toilet. High chairs. Nappy-changing facilities. Tables outdoors (7, terrace).

My Dining Room

18 Farm Lane, SW6 1PP (7381 3331, www.mydiningroom.net). Fulham Broadway tube or bus 11, 14, 211. Bar **Open** 11am-

Consumer

midnight Mon-Sat; 11am-11.30pm Sun.
Meals served 11am-10.30pm Mon-Sat;
11am-10pm Sun. *Restaurant* **Meals served**
noon-10.30pm daily. *Both* **Main courses**
£9.95-£20. **Set lunch** (Sun) £19.50
3 courses. **Set meal** £15 2 courses.
Credit AmEx, MC, V.
Opened in 2010 around the corner from Fulham
Broadway, this has quickly become a word-of-
mouth favourite. Families love the fact that
children under six can eat for free from their
own menu when they come with a paying adult.
The menu includes fish and chips, spaghetti
bolognese, own-made chicken nuggets and
green peas. If groups pre-book, children can
have their own mini table and pint-sized chairs
set up next to the adults' table. At weekends,
there's also an entertainment corner with DVDs
and a Wii so that adults can enjoy the long
lunches they crave. The rear dining room is
adorned with metallic swirling wallpaper and
velvet panels. In similar vein to the decor, the
chef has ramped up the food from pub grub
(crisp fried goat's cheese) to something more
distinctive (it came with a beetroot purée and
designer leaves). There is certainly a generosity
of spirit here: staff brought us a foot-long
terrine (for one person) with the bidding to eat
as much as we liked. Many dishes are designed
to share, such as whole roast chicken or deeply
savoury veal and chorizo meatballs served in
one dish for the table. Killer puddings include
a rose crème brûlée, and perfect chocolate
fondant with molten centre.
*Buggy access. Children's menu (£6). Disabled
access: toilet. High chairs. Tables outdoors
(5, pavement; 4, terrace).*

Manson

*676 Fulham Road, SW6 5SA (7384 9559,
www.mansonrestaurant.co.uk). Parson's
Green tube.* **Lunch served** noon-3pm
daily. **Dinner served** 6-10.30pm Mon-Sat;
6-9pm Sun. **Meals served** 10am-10.30pm
Sat, Sun. **Main courses** £13.50-£22.50.
Set lunch £12.50 2 courses. **Credit**
AmEx, MC, V.
The sophistication of Gemma Tuley's cooking
easily outstrips Manson's casual, bistro-style
setting. Rump of lamb arrived perfectly pink,
yet tender, served on a modish black slate with
garnishes evocative of Morocco – some
chickpeas, plus a samosa-like pastry with a
lamb confit filling. Braised ox cheeks were
surrounded by herby green risotto and jus.
Many dishes are imaginative, yet firmly
grounded in European haute cuisine traditions.

Children can have anything from the main
menu at half price for a half portion. It might
help if they tend towards the gastronomically
adventurous, but few of them will be able to
resist such tempting treats as jerusalem
artichoke cheesecake with peanut butter. The
wine list is also pretty decent; locals were
quaffing bottles like they were ginger beer.
Criticisms? The fraught young waiters ran
around with desperate urgency, and the sound
of Fulham folk shouting at each other can be
rather off-putting.
High chairs. Tables outdoors (3, pavement).

Hix

*66-70 Brewer Street, W1F 9UP (7292
3518, www.hixsoho.co.uk). Piccadilly Circus
tube.* **Lunch served** noon-5.30pm daily.
Dinner served 5.30-11.30pm Mon-Sat;
5.30-10.30pm Sun. **Main courses** £14.75-
£35.50. **Set meal** (4.30-6.30pm, 10.30-
11.30pm Mon-Sat; noon-10.30pm Sun)
£15.50 2 courses, £19.50 3 courses.
Credit AmEx, MC, V. **Map** p332 J7.
Hix won the Time Out Eating and Drinking
Awards' Best New Restaurant 2010. The
ground floor dining room is more modern and
pared down than some of its stablemates, but
boasts crazy mobiles by Damien Hirst and
Sarah Lucas. Unlike the new Hix restaurant and
champagne bar in Selfridges, kids don't get
their own menu here. That's because the main
menu is more extensive in the first place, and
includes dishes like fishfingers, chips and
mushy peas, which can be scaled down for
younger customers, who also get colouring
books on arrival. Children will also like many
of the options on the 'Bar Snax' menu (including
pork crackling, parsnip croquettes and
sausages with mash). Prices are centre-of-town
high: a starter of whipped broad beans with
goat's curd and broad bean flowers fried in
scrumpy costs £10.25. However, as with all the
starters we tried – 'heaven and earth' (a mousse-
like black pudding), prawn cocktail, and salt
beef salad – it was delightful. Main courses
(including hangar steak with beets, watercress
and horseradish) didn't disappoint either.
Puddings range from traditional (ice-creams
and summer pudding) to unusual (sea
buckthorn berry posset). All were top-notch.
The wine list is similarly assured. Service
throughout is friendly yet professional. All in
all, much though we like the more meat-
obsessed, male-heavy Hix Oyster & Chop
House, this Soho operation has snatched pole
position. The dimly lit basement bar, Mark's, is

a homage to New York – albeit with a bar billiards table – from the tin ceiling tiles to the professionally mixed cocktails (come without the children one evening and try a lovely, lip-pursing Forbidden Sour).

Buggy access. Crayons. Disabled access: toilet. High chairs. Nappy-changing facilities.

Branches Hix Oyster & Chop House, 36-37 Greenhill Rents, Cowcross Street, EC1M 6BN (7017 1930); Hix at Selfridges, 400 Oxford Street, W1A 1AB (7499 5400).

Old Brewery

Pepys Building, Old Royal Naval College, SE10 9LW (3327 1280, www.oldbrewery greenwich.com). Cutty Sark DLR. Café **Meals served** 10am-5pm daily. **Main courses** £6-£16.50. *Bar* **Open** 11am-11pm daily. **Lunch served** noon-5pm, dinner served 6-10.30pm daily. **Main courses** £6-£16.50. *Restaurant* **Dinner served** 6-10.30pm daily. **Main courses** £10.50-£17.50. All **Credit** MC, V.

This new venture won Best New Design in the 2010 Time Out Eating and Drinking Awards. Set back from the street in the handsome, historic Pepys building, just behind the Cutty Sark, the Old Brewery has ambition. By day it's a café for the Discover Greenwich tourist attraction next door (*see p101*); by night it's a restaurant. There's a small bar, with tables outside in a large walled courtyard – a lovely spot for parents to test the 50-strong beer list that includes the artisan ales of the Meantime Brewery (the company behind this operation) plus a global array of bottled varieties. Inside, there is no danger of disturbing other diners in such a vast, high-ceilinged space. Maroon and dark orange walls are decorated with an abstract bottle pattern and a history of British brewing, with oversized aluminium light shades and a wave-like artwork of bottles. Meantime's gleaming copper brewing barrels dominate one end. The personable young staff are friendly, and red-clothed booths along one side offer privacy. The short lunchtime menu includes sandwiches and wraps, as well as dishes like fish and chips or Galloway beef burger (children's sandwiches are reasonably priced at £1.80). Clued-up locals should head here pronto; it's too good to leave to the tourists.

Buggy access. Children's option (£6). Disabled access: toilet. High chairs. Nappy-changing facilities. Tables outdoors (20, garden). Takeaway service.

NORTH AMERICAN

Bodean's

10 Poland Street, W1F 8PZ (7287 7575, www.bodeansbbq.com). Oxford Circus or Piccadilly Circus tube. **Lunch served** noon-3pm, **dinner served** 5.30-11pm Mon-Fri. **Meals served** noon-11pm Sat; noon-10.30pm Sun. **Main courses** £8-£16. **Credit** AmEx, MC, V. **Map** p330 J6.

Bodean's was set up seven years ago by a man from Kansas, where they take their barbecues very seriously. Five branches on, we can still say this is the best barbecue in the city. The Soho branch is our favourite for its street-level 'deli': a more casual arrangement where you walk in, order at the counter and tuck into a pared-down menu that omits some of the more superfluous choices – you don't go to Bodean's for enchiladas. It's all about the ribs, the pulled pork, the half chickens and the 'burnt ends' of beef brisket, smoked and slow-grilled to uncommon tenderness and served with the (inevitably) secret sweet and piquant sauce. Children eat free between noon and 5pm at the weekend when accompanied by an adult; options include barbecue chicken breast or slices of smoked beef, turkey or ham with fries or mash, with ice-cream to follow. At other times, the children's menu costs £5. Vegetarians should keep walking – there's nothing to see here. A bonus is that the formerly dreary choice of beer has been updated; you can now find the likes of Sierra Nevada ales, although they're not available in all branches.

Buggy access. Children's menu (£5, free noon-5pm Sat, Sun). High chairs. Nappy-changing facilities. Takeaway service.

Branches throughout the city.

The Diner

2 Jamestown Road, NW1 7BY (7485 5223, www.goodlifediner.com). Camden Town tube. **Meals served** 10am-11pm Mon-Thur; 10am-11.30pm Fri; 9am-11.30pm Sat; 9am-11pm Sun. **Main courses** £5-£10. **Credit** AmEx, MC, V.

The Diner determinedly checks most of the Americana boxes, from the lettering on the windows to the free filter coffee refills. It's a popular choice for families who enjoy sitting in the red leather booths inside, or out on the roof terrace on warm days. Kids get their own menu, but there are no meal deals here. Children's mains are £4.50, desserts are £3.80-£5 and milkshakes £4.20. The cooking could be better – even taking into account that this is what

Consumer

Consumer

Old Brewery. See p267.

raised right hand side. All the flavours of American diner cuisine are here – maple syrup, blueberries, key lime, monterey jack, bacon, beef and barbecue – and it's a great place to grab a reasonably priced meal in an upbeat setting. Beefburgers and shakes are the strongest suit, but the menu also takes in the likes of duck and grapefruit salad, and a meze plate. Kids have plenty of choice on their own menu (4oz burger, hot dog, pasta, or herb-coated chicken with barbecue sauce), but breakfast is served all day if that seems a more appealing option. Avoid coming here with children at night as the place morphs into a noisy West End drinking hole and party venue, with DJs and a stupendous choice of cocktails. *Buggy access. Children's menu (£2.95-£4.25). Crayons. Disabled access: toilet. High chairs. Takeaway service.*

Hard Rock Café

150 Old Park Lane, W1K 1QR (7629 0382, www.hardrock.com). Hyde Park Corner tube. **Meals served** 11.30am-12.30am Mon-Thur, Sun; 11am-1am Fri, Sat. **Main courses** £9.95-£15.95. **Credit** AmEx, MC, V. **Map** p332 H8.

The Hard Rock Café celebrates its 40th anniversary in 2011; it was one of the original American diners in London. But is it still worth visiting? Youngsters might be utterly bemused by the gold records on the walls – they won't recognise the format, never mind the names on the discs. Videos by A Flock of Seagulls and Billy Joel play without irony on myriad TV screens; and glass-fronted cabinets proudly display such consecrated treasures as a bass guitar once cradled by Felix Pappalardi of Mountain. Only the prices bring you back to the future: £13.25 for a burger and chips might not seem too bad if you're on holiday and unfamiliar with the value of sterling, but the relative absence of British accents tells its own story. The burgers are actually pretty darn good, and the children's menu is more fairly priced at £7.95 for a main course and drink. Further attractions on offer include occasional themed activities. *Buggy access. Children's set meal (£7.95). Crayons. Disabled access: toilet. High chairs. Nappy-changing facilities. Tables outdoors (10, terrace).*

many consider to be junk food – and you have to wonder why the Diner puts its name to the signature fries, which are simply sprinkled with coarse Cajun spice mix. Still, the corn dogs are devilishly moist, the burgers good-looking, and the adult drinks list fun (Sleeman's Honey Brown is on draught and served authentically chilled). For dessert, be sure to share the blueberry and peanut butter sundae – so wrong, yet so right. By contrast, the New York cheesecake wasn't even as good as the vanilla ice-cream accompanying it. Nonetheless, the sizeable queue of international customers waiting for tables keeps this joint jumping. *Buggy access. Children's menu (£4.50). Crayons. Disabled access: toilet. High chairs. Nappy-changing facilities. Tables outdoors (13, terrace; 8, pavement). Takeaway service.* **Branches** throughout the city.

Eagle Bar Diner

3-5 Rathbone Place W1T 1HJ (7637 1418, www.eaglebardiner.com) Tottenham Court Road tube. **Meals served** noon-11pm Mon-Wed; noon-midnight Thur, Fri; 10.30am-midnight Sat. **Main courses** £6.95-£15.50. **Credit** AmEx, MC, V. **Map** p331 K5.

It's best to arrive here before 12.30pm to secure a table before the local office workers start pouring in. Eagle Bar Diner never feels crowded once you're seated, though, particularly if you get one of the cosy brown leather booths on the

Lucky 7

127 Westbourne Park Road, W2 5QL (7727 6771, www.lucky7london.co.uk). Royal Oak or Westbourne Park tube. **Meals served**

noon-10pm Mon; 10am-10pm Tue-Thur; 9am-11pm Fri, Sat; 9am-10pm Sun. **Main courses** £4.75-£12.95. **Credit** MC, V.

At Tom Conran's teeny diner – just six green booths in front of an open kitchen – the day starts with 'cwoffee', bowls of Lucky Charms and Captain Crunch, breakfast burritos, pancakes, and fry-ups featuring hash browns. Later there are burgers, plus a choice of 'chiles', cobb and caesar salads, beer-battered onion rings, BLTs, crab cake sandwiches and the turkey dee lite (ground turkey white meat with bacon, cheese and avocado). Sweet-toothed diners will enjoy the chance to try a root-beer float, a cream soda or even an extra-thick shake with Oreos and peanut butter. Prices reflect the challenging rents in this corner of town, so look elsewhere to find London's best-value fast food, although the introduction of a children's menu helps a little. Nevertheless, Lucky 7 is a welcome alternative to the burger chains. *Children's menu (£6.45-£7.45).*
Takeaway service.

Smollensky's on the Strand

105 Strand, WC2R 0AA (7497 2101, www.smollenskys.com). Embankment tube or Charing Cross tube/rail. **Meals served** noon-11pm Mon-Thur; noon-1am Fri, Sat; noon-10pm Sun. **Main courses** £9.95-£29.95. **Credit** AmEx, MC, V. **Map** p333 L7.
During the week this basement steakhouse is full of suits and meetings, but between noon and 5pm every Saturday and Sunday it basically becomes a modern, food-based playgroup. Balloons and cartoons are handed out, there's a magician on hand until 4pm, plus PlayStations to amuse older children. The menu is full of simple, sturdy ribstickers, with an emphasis on steaks – which arrive with good chips and a choice of sauces. The children's menu features fish and chicken goujons, ribs, burgers and other filling staples. Mains are decent, but it's the puds which stick in the memory: moreish chocolate mousse and densely moist Mississippi mud pie are sublime.
Children's menu (£3.95-£7). Crayons.
Disabled access: toilet. Entertainment: clown, magician 1-4pm Sat, Sun. High chairs. Nappy-changing facilities.
Branch 1 Reuters Plaza, E14 5AG (7719 0101).

TGI Friday's

6 Bedford Street, WC2E 9HZ (7379 0585, www.tgifridays.co.uk). Covent Garden or Embankment tube, or Charing Cross
tube/rail. **Meals served** 11am-11.30pm Mon-Thur; 11am-midnight Fri, Sat; noon-11pm Sun. **Main courses** £8.29-£17.99. **Credit** AmEx, MC, V. **Map** p333 L7.
Londoners may think of TGI Fridays as a tourist trap, but prices are keen for this part of town. Children can get a mini burger or chicken pieces with sides for £2.99 and an ice-cream sundae for 99p. We recommend lunchtime visits at this busy Covent Garden branch, as the bar gets crowded after 5pm. The immensely cheery, overwhelmingly child-friendly staff here hand out balloons and activity packs to children, who are chatted to sweetly and even entertained on certain days (see the website for details). The food is varied, with an emphasis on sticky barbecues and tasty Tex-Mex dishes as well as the inevitable burgers and fries. Health-conscious kids can swap regular side dishes for healthier options – crudités, corn on the cob or vegetables. All that good will be undone at the pudding stage, when dirt and worm pie (for chocolate and fudge fiends), cheesecakes and the aforementioned sundaes are the order of the day. Free Heinz baby food is provided for babes of four to ten months accompanying a dining adult.
Buggy access. Children's set meal (£2.99-£4.99). Crayons. Disabled access: lift, toilet. Entertainment: face painting Sat, Sun lunch. High chairs. Nappy-changing facilities.
Branches throughout the city.

THAI

Blue Elephant

4-6 Fulham Broadway, SW6 1AA (7385 6595, www.blueelephant.com). Fulham Broadway tube. **Lunch served** noon-2.30pm daily. **Dinner served** 7-11.30pm Mon-Thur; 6.30-11.30pm Fri; 6-11.30pm Sat; 6.30-10.30pm Sun. **Main courses** £11.90-£28. **Set buffet** (Sun lunch) £30; £15 4-11s; free under-4s. **Credit** AmEx, DC, MC, V.
Diners who come here expecting a memorable experience generally get one – and that includes children, who are welcomed with crayons and, at the popular Sunday brunch, face painting. The Blue Elephant may be an international chain (with branches throughout Europe and as far afield as Jakarta), but for many it offers a fun introduction to Thai food and culture. A meal here starts with welcomes from traditionally costumed staff, who lead diners into a room festooned with tropical gardens, walkways and waterfalls. The menu attempts to cater for all,

Consumer

with dishes ranging from the predictable (chicken satay) to the slightly more esoteric (*larb gai*, a minced chicken salad more typical of north-eastern Thailand and Laos), and even includes an extensive vegetarian list. Presentation has echoes of royal Thai cuisine (all carved vegetables and impeccable plating), but sometimes style rules over substance as flavours tend towards the bowdlerised, with timid spicing. Still, that might go down well with conservative junior tastebuds.

Booking advisable (Sun lunch). Buggy access. Delivery service. Disabled access: toilet. Entertainment: face painting Sun lunch. High chairs. Nappy-changing facilities. Takeaway service.

TURKISH

Mangal II

4 Stoke Newington Road, N16 8BH (7254 7888, www.mangal2.com). Dalston Kingsland rail or bus 76, 149, 243. **Meals served** noon-1am Mon-Thur, Sun; noon-2am Fri, Sat. **Main courses** £8.45-£15.99. **Credit** MC, V.

Yes, this fine Turkish *ocakbasi* is popular with families of all nationalities. You can see why. Sweet-natured, efficient waiters in smart black shirts, matching black trousers and bright red ties serve uncomplicated grills to the strains of 'Ain't No Sunshine', and flavours are punchy. Of the few vegetarian options, *zeytin yagli pirasa* was an almost fizzily pickled salad that belied its bland description of 'leek and carrot in olive oil', while simple, light feta and parsley pastries (*musga böregi*) were fried to crisp perfection. The main focus is on what's produced under the metal extractor hood at the back. Star turn on this visit was *pirzola*: three tender salty lamb chops with their fat cooked perfectly to the point of almost melting away. Children in particular will relish the grilled chicken and *pide* and *saç* bread.

Buggy access. High chairs. Takeaway service.

Zara

11 South End Road, NW3 2PT (7794 5498) Belsize Park tube or Hampstead Heath rail. **Meals served** noon-11pm daily. **Main courses** £9.50-£15. **Set lunch** (noon-4pm) £8.50 2 courses. **Credit** AmEx, MC, V.

Families are drawn to Zara's homely vibe. At the back, where a skylight brightens the dining area and a fireplace keeps customers warm in winter, is a pile of board games, books and some bongos. Were it not for the red London buses idling nearby, you could imagine yourself ensconced in a village restaurant in Turkey, with rustic wooden chairs, coloured glass lanterns and terracotta floor tiles. The menu reads like a greatest hits of Anatolian cuisine, with plenty of grills. We love the *mücver* (courgette fritters with a molten centre of creamy cheese), offered as a vegetarian main course or hot meze with *kısır*. There's more cheesy succulence to be enjoyed in the moussaká, its rich layers of aubergine, lamb mince and béchamel contrasting with a virtuous side salad of crisp leaves and grated carrot. The yoghurt dip with spinach and garlic is nicely balanced if modestly sized – still, there's the kind offer of another basket of bread to accompany, and a simple, keenly priced wine list with some great Turkish bottles to try.

Buggy access. Crayons. High chairs. Tables outdoors (4, pavement). Takeaway service. Toys.

VIETNAMESE

Song Que Café

134 Kingsland Road, E2 8DY (7613 3222). Hoxton rail. **Lunch served** noon-3pm, **dinner served** 5-11pm Mon-Sat. **Meals served** 11am-11pm Sun. **Main courses** £4.50-£6.20. **Credit** MC, V.

Song Que doesn't look like much from the outside (or the inside, for that matter – the sparse, canteen-like decor is relieved only by a few jumble sale prints), but it remains one of the best Vietnamese restaurants in the capital, despite fierce local competition. The menu is regulation length for a London Vietnamese: a numbered please-all trawl through the cuisines of the north, the south and Hue. Although we have our favourites, almost every dish we've tried over the years has been brilliant. The Song Que beef pho – something every Vietnamese restaurant has to get right – is exemplary, with a deep, complex broth, quality meat and vibrant herbs. Other essential dishes include barbecued quail with an almost effervescent citrus dipping sauce, fresh and fried spring rolls, and ground spiced beef in betel leaf. Children are generally happy with steaming bowls of pho (noodle soup) or the delicately fashioned rice paper rolls stuffed with prawns, vegetables or chicken; orders are scrawled on the paper tablecloth, and appear with astonishing alacrity.

Buggy access. Disabled access: toilet. High chairs. Takeaway service.

Shopping

Where to go for prams, toys, clothes and everything in between.

London has so much choice to offer, with shopping opportunities changing and expanding all the time. Our new favourite this year is **huggle** (*see p272*), a large and stylishly presented shop that opened in Swiss Cottage in late 2010. Not only does it stock everything a London parent could ever need, it also offers all sorts of classes in the lounge area to make sure the kids have a good time too.

Many of London's more established shops also recognise the importance of enticing children inside as well as their parents, and you'll find play corners, toy boxes, train sets and colouring tables placed in strategic positions to amuse the little ones while you browse.

The city is well provided with independents selling wooden toys, hand-knitted bootees, sprigged cotton frocks and hip international childrenswear labels. It's hard to resist the nostalgic appeal of shops like **Their Nibs** (*see p288*), **Rachel Riley** (*see p286*) and **Bonpoint** (*see p284*). But if budget is an issue, why not head to fast expanding chain **Fara Kids** (*see p291*), specialist charity shops that take presentation seriously. The city's smaller bookshops also do a sterling job, with cosy chairs to curl up on, regular visits from children's authors, and good old-fashioned storytelling sessions.

Many parents tend to stay local for picking up their child-centric shopping needs. So at a party for a Crouch End child, say, most presents will have been bought from neighbourhood favourites such as **Soup Dragon** (*see p276*) or **Rub a Dub Dub** (*see p282*). However, our user-friendly area guides found throughout this chapter will encourage you to branch out and find something a little out of the ordinary.

ALL-ROUNDERS

Blue Daisy

13 South End Road, NW3 2PT (7681 4144, www.blue-daisy.com). Belsize Park tube or Hampstead Heath rail. **Open** 9.30am-6pm Mon-Fri; 10am-6pm Sat. **Credit** AmEx, MC, V.

When you first walk into this Hampstead baby boutique, it can seem as if there's not much here. But look a little closer and the minimalist presentation hides a wealth of great products to make parenting just that bit easier and more stylish. The shop stocks prams, toys, slings, organic lotions and changing accessories, clothes, potties, plastic crockery and a lot more besides. The layout has been thoughtfully designed with a play alcove for small children and a nappy-changing room,

while the generous floor space means it's also easy to bring buggies inside with you. *Buggy access. Nappy-changing facilities. Play area.* **Branch** 190 West End Lane, NW6 1SG (7435 3100).

Born

168 Stoke Newington Church Street, N16 0JL (7249 5069, www.borndirect.com). Bus 73, 393, 476. **Open** 9.30am-5pm Tue-Fri; 10am-6pm Sat; noon-5pm Sun. **Credit** MC, V.

Natural, organic and Fairtrade pregnancy products, baby equipment and clothes fill the shelves at Born, from Babygros and cotton nappies to sturdy scooters and brightly-painted toys. Practical gear includes Ergo's organic cotton baby carrier and sleek buggies from the

Kidsen. *See p274.*

likes of Phil & Teds and Bugaboo, alongside chemical-free toiletries and baby wipes and the shop's own brand of pregnancy massage oils. There's ample space to play and a sofa for breastfeeding mothers.
Buggy access. Delivery service. Disabled access: ramp. Nappy-changing facilities. Play area.

Harrods

87-135 Brompton Road, SW1X 7XL (7730 1234, www.harrods.com). Knightsbridge tube. **Open** 10am-8pm Mon-Sat; 11.30am-6pm Sun. **Credit** AmEx, DC, MC, V. **Map** p329 F9.
The fourth floor is the one to head for at Harrods, with room after room devoted to uniforms, party frocks, nursery gear, books and Babygros. Toy Kingdom (7225 6781) is a child's dream come true, with its jolly demonstrators and immense range of toys. Clothes begin with beautiful babywear, including ranges from Christian Dior and Roberto Cavalli, and go through ultra-smart tweedy garb from the Harrods label (think proper winter coats with velvet collars, and silk and tulle party dresses). Couture childrenswear includes mini togs by Burberry, Missoni, Miss Blumarine, Ralph Lauren and Armani. Footwear is by One Small Step One Giant Leap (*see p294*). There's face-painting, haircutting and lots of interactive fun in the holidays and at special events and launches. Children will also enjoy exploring the

rest of the store, including the food halls. The nursery department carries all the famous pram and buggy, cot, bed and high chair brands.
Buggy access. Café. Car park. Delivery service. Disabled access: lift, toilet. Hairdressing. Nappy-changing facilities.

huggle

8-10 Winchester Road, NW3 3NT (7483 2826, www.huggle.co.uk). Swiss Cottage tube. **Open** 9am-6pm Mon-Fri; 9am-5pm Sat; 11am-4pm Sun. **Credit** AmEx, MC, V.
This new shop opened at the end of 2010 and is a very welcome addition to Swiss Cottage. It's a spacious and stylish emporium stocking all the accessories of parenthood, from prams to highchairs, baby kit essentials, cool nursery furniture, unusual toys and design classics. It has a full programme of activities throughout the week in the huggle lounge. We particularly liked the P'kolino Little Reader armchairs, the Oeuf Sparrow cribs and the toy selection.
Buggy access. Café. Delivery service. Disabled access: toilet. Nappy-changing facilities.

Igloo

300 Upper Street, N1 2TU (7354 7300, www.iglookids.co.uk). Angel tube or Highbury & Islington tube/rail. **Open** 10am-6.30pm Mon-Wed; 10am-7pm Thur; 9.30am-6.30pm Fri, Sat; 11am-5.30pm Sun. **Credit** AmEx, MC, V.

Quirky toys, clothes and accessories, often from lesser-known labels, have made Igloo a mecca for chic north London parents. The premises are small but well stocked, with shelves of toys reaching to the ceiling – an enticing mix of sticker books, puppet-making kits, puzzles and skipping ropes, along with pedal cars, tipis and trikes. Racks of clothes cater for newborns to ten-year-olds, with a stellar selection of labels (fresh floral prints from Room Seven and hand-smocked frocks from I Love Gorgeous). The shoe corner has plenty of seating and some top-notch brands (Start-rite, Crocs, Camper, Angelus and Naturino, alongside some nifty dinosaur and bee wellies). All bases are covered: there's a mirrored parlour for children's haircuts, a drawing table and a gift-wrapping service. *Buggy access. Delivery service. Disabled access. Hairdressing.*
Branches 80 St John's Wood High Street, NW8 7SH (7483 2332); 227 King's Road, SW3 5EJ (7352 4572).

John Lewis
278-306 Oxford Street, W1A 1EX (7629 7711, www.johnlewis.co.uk). Bond Street or Oxford Circus tube. **Open** 9.30am-8pm Mon-Wed, Fri; 9.30am-9pm Thur; 9.30am-7pm Sat; noon-6pm Sun. **Credit** AmEx, DC, MC, V. **Map** p330 H6.
John Lewis is always a dependable port of call. Follow the stream of parents heading up to the fourth floor, dedicated to all things child-related, and take advantage of its knowledgeable staff and good service. As an all-rounder it's hard to beat, stocking everything from toys to school uniforms, clothes and sportswear, as well as nursery furniture and essentials; the down-to-earth buying-for-baby advice is a lifesaver for bemused first-time parents, and there's a free car seat-fitting advisory service. The toy department overflows with of-the-moment toys, educational games and old classics. But the real jewel in the store's crown is its shoe department

Consumer

Kids' Corner
Hampstead

Shopping in Hampstead is a wonderfully sophisticated experience. But although money practically oozes out of the brickwork up here, the area manages to retain something of a bohemian, creative vibe. Play spot the actor as you take a stroll down Flask Walk, with its old world charm, and let the shopping begin.

Mystical Fairies (*see p298*) is sheer heaven for those who like anything pink, sparkly and otherworldly. Pregnant women may miss the Hampstead branch of Formes, now closed – although the stylish and somewhat cheaper **Séraphine** (*see p291*), just north of the tube, affords some consolation.

For children needing to be shod, it would be hard to find a better shoe shop than the small but very well stocked **Cubs** (*see p293*) on Heath Street. Down Rosslyn Hill is toy shop **Happy Returns** (*see p297*) which caters for parties and presents for zero to fives. And at a lower gradient still, on South End Green near the Royal Free Hospital, there's the fantastic **Blue Daisy** (*see p271*), which stocks just about every accessory a baby

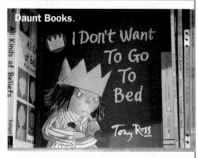

Daunt Books.

or parent could possibly want. The kids will love the special reading room at **Daunt Books** (*see p277*); once you've picked up a linen bag full of literary goodies, the whole family can head to neighbouring Hampstead Heath to let off some steam.

Not strictly in Hampstead, but well worth the short hop down the hill towards Swiss Cottage, **huggle** (*see p272*) is a supremely stylish new emporium offering everything from prams to street dance classes.

(Clarks, Start-rite, Kangaroo, Timberland), with its orderly ticket system, CBeebies on the telly and free face-painting sessions. On the fifth floor is a London 2012 store, which will occupy most of the floor from summer 2011.
Buggy access. Cafés. Delivery service. Disabled access: lift, toilet. Nappy-changing facilities.
Branches Brent Cross Shopping Centre, NW4 3FL (8202 6535); Wood Street, Kingston, Surrey KT1 1TE (8547 3000).

JoJo Maman Bébé

68 & 72 Northcote Road, SW11 6QL (7228 0322 maternity, 7223 8510 baby & children, www.jojomamanbebe.co.uk). Clapham Junction rail. **Open** 9.30am-5.30pm Mon-Sat; 11am-5pm Sun. **Credit** MC, V.
Launched in 1993 as an inexpensive maternity and babywear company, JoJo has expanded into a sizeable empire. While it's still primarily a catalogue-based retailer, a network of boutiques have sprung up across London, displaying some of its vast stock of clothes, equipment and furniture. Its own-label clothing lines are relaxed and affordable, with everything from maternity bras, yoga wraps and workwear for expectant mothers to swim nappies, stripy all-in-ones and dungarees for kids. The company adheres to a strong ethical code – a spirit exemplified by the organic cotton sleepsuits, and the Polartec fleeces made from recycled plastic bottles. JoJo also supports the Nema Foundation, which runs community projects in Mozambique.
Buggy access. Disabled access. Nappy-changing facilities.
Branches throughout the city.

Kidsen

111 Chamberlayne Road, NW10 3NS (8969 7565, www.kidsen.co.uk). Kensal Rise tube. **Open** 10am-5.30pm Mon-Fri; 10am-5pm Sat. **Credit** AmEx, MC, V.
Scandinavia comes to London with this bright and airy shop in Kensal Rise. Kidsen has a wide range of toys, from Brio train sets to Melissa and Doug dressing-up costumes and Lundby Stockholm doll's house furniture. Other favourites of ours include the 'rush hour' wallpaper, groovy wall stickers, space-age high chairs and sturdy but stylish shoes and outerwear. The shop has recently moved away from selling prams and car seats to concentrate on its children's furniture and interiors range. It's a good place to come for inspiration.
Buggy access. Delivery service. Disabled access. Play area.

Little White Company

90 Marylebone High Street, W1U 4QZ (7486 7550, www.thewhitecompany.com). Baker Street or Bond Street tube. **Open** 10am-6pm Mon-Sat; 11am-5pm Sun. **Credit** AmEx, MC, V. **Map** p330 G5.
All is calm, orderly and impossibly pretty at the Little White Company. Snowy cotton soft furnishings and crisp bedlinen are neatly arrayed alongside sweetly traditional nightwear and clothes (gingham pyjamas epitomise the look), and there's an attractive range of white-painted nursery furniture. Not everything's white, of course; striped towelling beach hoodies in fuchsia and navy, floral quilts and lengths of pastel-hued bunting add a splash of colour. Prices are reasonable considering the quality.
Buggy access. Delivery service.
Branch 261 Pavillion Road, SW1X 0BP (7881 0783).

Mamas & Papas

256-258 Regent Street, W1B 3AF (0845 268 2000, www.mamasandpapas.co.uk). Oxford Circus tube. **Open** 10am-8pm Mon-Wed, Fri; 10am-9pm Thur; 9am-8pm Sat; noon-6pm Sun. **Credit** AmEx, MC, V. **Map** p330 J6.
Amid the chaos of Regent Street, the flagship outpost for this buggy brand is a spacious, air-conditioned oasis. There are large changing rooms for bump and buggy manoeuvres, and assistants are at hand to advise on sartorial matters. As well as inexpensive baby clothes, maternity fashion and lingerie, there's a dizzying array of Mamas & Papas prams, pushchairs and car seats – the company's stock in trade. The first floor, meanwhile, is devoted to interiors, with a series of 'dream nursery' rooms displaying cots, changing tables, wardrobes and storage systems in all shapes and sizes. The first-floor Cibo café serves nutritious own-made fare for mothers-to-be and a straightforward children's menu.
Buggy access. Café. Delivery Service. Nappy-changing facilities.
Branches Brent Cross Shopping Centre, NW4 3FL (0845 268 2000); Level 1, Westfield Shopping Centre, W12 7GF (0845 268 2000); Tandem Shopping Centre, SW19 2NX (0845 268 2000).

Mini Kin

22 Broadway Parade, N8 9DE (8341 6898, www.minikin.co.uk). Finsbury Park tube/rail, then W7 bus. **Open** 9.30am-5.30pm Mon-Sat; 10.30am-4.30pm Sun. **Credit** MC, V.

London 2012 Souvenirs

London 2012 Shop
Unit 2A, St Pancras International, Pancras Road, King's Cross, NW1 2QP (7837 8558, *http://shop.london2012. com). King's Cross tube/rail.* **Open** 8am-9pm Mon-Fri; 8.30am-7.30pm Sat; 11am-6pm Sun. **Credit** V. **Map** p331 L3.

Browse for Games merchandise in person at the dedicated shop. You'll find everything from pin badges, mugs and die-cast models of double-decker buses to Stella McCartney-designed sportswear. There are also branches at Paddington (The Lawn, Paddington Station, W2 1H8, 7402 5616, http://shop.london2012.com) and Heathrow Terminal 5, along with a concession in John Lewis on Oxford Street (*see p273*).

Look out for additional shops opening at major transport hubs such as airports and stations as 2012 approaches.

Consumer

Small but perfectly formed, Mini Kin combines a modishly stocked children's clothing boutique with a hairdressing salon. An impeccably chic array of clothes includes frothy frocks from Noa Noa, plus No Added Sugar, Dandy Star, Bob & Blossom and Their Nibs, and there are fragrant salves, creams, oils and lotions courtesy of Burt's Bees, Green People and Earth Friendly Baby. Out back there is the hairdressing salon, decorated to look like a mythical forest with trailing ivy and branches; animal-painted chairs and charming staff conspire to coax recalcitrant tots into the hot seat. Haircuts start at £10.95.

Buggy access. Disabled access.
Hairdressing. Nappy-changing facilities.
Play area.

Mothercare

526-528 Oxford Street, W1C 1LW (0845 365 0515, www.mothercare.com). Marble Arch tube. **Open** 10am-8pm Mon-Sat; noon-6pm Sun. **Credit** AmEx, MC, V.
Map p330 G6.
Two floors house all manner of baby-related paraphernalia. It's great for bulk-buy basics such as muslins and plain rompers, and the maternity wear section often yields some good value, unexpected finds.
Buggy access. Delivery service. Disabled access: lift, toilet. Nappy-changing facilities.
Branches throughout the city.

Bobo Kids. *See p283.*

Pure Baby

208 Fulham Road, SW10 9PJ (7751 5544, www.purebaby.co.uk). Fulham Broadway or South Kensington tube, then bus 14, 414. **Open** 10am-6.30pm Mon-Wed, Fri, Sat; 10am-7pm Thur. **Credit** AmEx, MC, V.
Map p328 C12.
Located in a strategic spot near Chelsea & Westminster Hospital's Maternity Unit, Pure Baby is as smart and sleek as its well-heeled clientele. Cashmere playsuits and bootees, Bugaboo prams and organic cotton swaddling blankets are among the goodies on offer.
Buggy access. Delivery service.
Disabled access.

Soup Dragon

27 Topsfield Parade, Tottenham Lane, N8 8PT (8348 0224, www.soup-dragon.co.uk). Finsbury Park tube/rail, then bus W7. **Open** 9.30am-6pm Mon-Sat; 11am-5pm Sun. **Credit** AmEx, MC, V.
This cavernous grotto is piled high with colourful clothes and toys. It's an excellent spot to pick up imaginative, relatively inexpensive kids' clothes; the own-brand striped knits are great value. For lovers of bold prints, there are vibrant designs from Danish labels Katvig and Minymo, while the Kidorable in the Rain range is fun and practical. In addition to everyday clothes, there's a great selection of partywear and fancy dress. On the toy front, doll's houses, castles, farms and pirate ships fire up children's imaginations; there's also a dinky mini kitchen play area where kids can bang pots and pans about. Sign up to the mailing list for details of the regular warehouse sales.
Buggy access. Disabled access. Play area.
Branch 106 Lordship Lane, SE22 8HF (8693 5575).

EDUCATIONAL

Books

Several toy shops (*see p294*) also stock children's picture books.

Big Green Bookshop

Unit 1, Brampton Park Road, N22 6BG (8881 6767, www.biggreenbookshop.com). Turnpike Lane or Wood Green tube. **Open** 9am-6pm Mon, Tue, Thur-Sat; 10.30am-6pm Wed; noon-5pm Sun. **Credit** AmEx, MC, V.

Opened in 2008, this friendly local bookshop has developed a reputation for its excellent children's section. Young readers can relax here with their favourite tome and writers pop in to read and talk to the children.
Buggy access.

Bookseller Crow on the Hill

50 Westow Street, SE19 3AF (8771 8831, http://booksellercrow.moonfruit.com). Gypsy Hill rail. **Open** 10am-7pm Mon-Fri; 9.30am-6.30pm Sat; 11am-5pm Sun. **Credit** AmEx, MC, V.

A laid-back place to while away an afternoon, with a wealth of books for children and grown-ups. All the classics are present and correct, and there's a splendid selection of picture books.
Buggy access. Play area.

Bookworm

1177 Finchley Road, NW11 0AA (8201 9811, www.thebookworm.uk.com). Golders Green tube. **Open** 9.30am-5.30pm Mon-Sat; 10am-1.30pm Sun. **Credit** MC, V.

The shelves at this independent children's bookshop are piled high with treasures. Storytelling sessions for under-fives take place on Tuesdays (2pm), Thursdays (2pm) and Sundays (noon) when badges and stickers are handed out, while regular author visits give children the chance to meet their literary heroes and heroines.
Buggy access. Disabled access.

Children's Bookshop

29 Fortis Green Road, N10 3HP (8444 5500, www.childrensbookshoplondon.com). Highgate tube, then bus 43, 134. **Open** 9.15am-5.45pm Mon-Sat; 11am-4pm Sun. **Credit** AmEx, MC, V.

Clued-up staff and peaceful surrounds make this a relaxing place to pick up some new reading material. There's a children's corner with child-sized chairs and picture books at floor level, plus Thursday morning storytelling sessions for preschoolers, kicking off at 11am. Other book-related events, including regular author signings, are publicised in the shop's quarterly newsletter.
Buggy access.

Daunt Books

51 South End Road, NW3 2QB (7794 8206, www.dauntbooks.co.uk). Belsize Park tube or Hampstead Heath rail. **Open** 9am-6pm Mon-Sat; 11am-6pm Sun. **Credit** MC, V.

There's a cosy, welcoming reading room for children in the back of this branch of the well-loved independent, with seats where adults can read to children without fear of disturbing other customers. The room is cheerily decorated with fields and farm animals, and has a good shelf of books. Just outside is the children's book section, which offers a very good choice of titles for all ages.
Buggy access. Play area.
Branches throughout the city.

Golden Treasury

29 Replingham Road, SW18 5LT (8333 0167, www.thegoldentreasury.co.uk). Southfields tube. **Open** 9.30am-6pm Mon-Fri; 9.30am-5.30pm Sat; 10.30am-4.30pm Sun. **Credit** MC, V.

The sprawling premises of this brilliant children's bookshop house a host of titles, from books on pregnancy to teen fiction. In the unlikely event that you can't find what you're after, staff are happy to order it in. There's also an excellent programme of author events; past luminaries include Judith Kerr (*The Tiger Who Came to Tea*) and Emma Chichester Clarke (*Blue Kangaroo*).
Buggy access. Play area.

Lion & Unicorn

19 King Street, Richmond, Surrey TW9 1ND (8940 0483, www.lionunicornbooks. co.uk). Richmond tube/rail. **Open** 9.30am-5.30pm Mon-Fri; 9.30am-6pm Sat; 11am-5pm Sun. **Credit** MC, V.

Opened in 1977 (the late, great Roald Dahl was the guest of honour), this venerable bookshop has kept up with the times. 'The Roar', its quarterly online newsletter, is invaluable for book reviews and details of signings and special events. Staff are happy to advise on the diverse stock crammed into every nook and cranny.
Buggy access.

Owl Bookshop

209 Kentish Town Road, NW5 2JU (7485 7793). Kentish Town tube. **Open** 9am-6pm Mon-Sat; noon-5pm Sun. **Credit** MC, V.

A colourful collection of children's books take pride of place in the window at this tranquil independent bookshop; inside, titles are sorted by age and interest. The shop also hosts readings by local children's authors; for details, sign up to the mailing list.
Buggy access.

Consumer

Kids' Corner
Northcote Road

Northcote Music.

In stark contrast to the peaceful suburbia that surrounds it, Northcote Road is a buzz of activity. A steady stream of prams and pushchairs trundle along the pavements – so it comes as no surprise to find that the street is bursting with quality children's shops.

Located between Wandsworth and Clapham Commons, the area lays claim to a mix of upmarket clothes shops such as Jigsaw and Whistles, along with traditional butchers and bakers and small Italian cafés.

Upmarket children's brands such as **Petit Bateau** (*see p290*), **Fat Face Kids** (*see p290*), **Jigsaw Junior** (*see p290*), shoe-retailing mini-chain **One Small Step One Giant Leap** (*see p294*) and well-heeled one-stop shop **Trotters** (*see p288*) have all set up pitch here, alongside a host of imaginative independents.

One of the old-timers is the friendly **QT Toys** (*see p300*); along the road, **Northcote Music** (*see p279*) has long supplied local children with their first recorder. The rails at **Quackers** (*see p286*) offer gorgeous children's labels, while an outpost of handsome bed retailer **Aspace** (*see p282*) covers sleeping arrangements.

One new Northcote Road arrival in 2010 was **Letterbox** (*see p298*). The company's catalogue, stuffed full of well-sourced toys, games and storage solutions, has been dropping on to parents' front doormats for many years, but now Nappy Valley regulars can buy their fairy outifts without the need for added postage.

Tales on Moon Lane

25 Half Moon Lane, SE24 9JU (7274 5759, www.talesonmoonlane.co.uk). Herne Hill rail or bus 3, 37, 68. **Open** 9am-5.45pm Mon-Fri; 9.30am-6pm Sat; 10.30am-4.30pm Sun. **Credit** MC, V.

Beloved by local families, this award-winning children's bookshop is a delight. Bright, airy premises and enthusiastic staff encourage long visits, as does the wide range of books. The storytelling sessions are very popular (turn up early for a place on the sofa), and there's the odd puppet show. Check online for author events. *Buggy access.*

Victoria Park Books

174 Victoria Park Road, E9 7HD (8986 1124, www.victoriaparkbooks.co.uk). London Fields rail then bus 277. **Open** 10am-5.30pm daily. **Credit** MC, V.

With its book club, wall of book reviews from schoolchildren and popular patio area, this place oozes community spirit. Books are categorised by look and feel as well as content – there's a section for interactive titles, and children can get their hands on cloth, bath and buggy books. Other stock is divided into user-friendly sections: history, art, dinosaurs, reference, a Ladybird corner and more. Teenagers and adults are also catered for. Authors visit regularly and there are drop-in story sessions at 11am on Fridays. *Buggy access. Play area.*

Educational toys & games

Education Interactive

10 Staplehurst Road, SE13 5NB (8318 6380, www.education-interactive.co.uk). Hither Green rail. **Open** 9.30am-1.30pm Mon-Fri (by appointment weekday afternoons). **Credit** AmEx, MC, V.

As its name suggests, this place specialises in toys and games to expand the grey matter. Polydron building blocks and Times Table Lotto are among the educational offerings. *Buggy access.*

Fun Learning

Bentall Centre, Clarence Street, Kingston-upon-Thames, Surrey KT1 1TP (8974 8900, www.funlearning.co.uk). Kingston rail. **Open** 9.30am-6pm Mon-Wed, Fri; 9.30am-8pm Thur; 9am-6pm Sat; 11am-5pm Sun. **Credit** AmEx, MC, V.
You're encouraged to try before you buy at this independent retailer, which sells all manner of puzzles, computer games, art and craft activities and science experiment sets. It's a wonderful place for unusual presents (a paint-your-own chair, say), but there are affordable pocket money items too, ranging from balloon-making gunk kits to hatching dinosaur eggs. *Buggy access. Disabled access.*
Branch Brent Cross Shopping Centre, NW4 3FP (8203 1473).

Musical instruments

Chappell of Bond Street

152-160 Wardour Street, W1F 8YA (7432 4400, www.chappellofbondstreet.co.uk). Oxford Circus or Tottenham Court Road tube. **Open** 9.30am-6pm Mon-Fri; 10am-5.30pm Sat. **Credit** AmEx, MC, V.
Map p330 J6.
Chappell's three-storey premises showcase a gleaming array of instruments. It's a Yamaha piano and keyboard specialist. Some of the instruments (typically flutes, saxes, clarinets and trumpets) may be available on a rent-to-buy scheme, but quarter- and half-size instruments must be purchased. *Buggy access. Delivery service.*

Dot's

132 St Pancras Way, NW1 9NB (7482 5424, www.dotsonline.co.uk). Camden Town tube or Camden Road rail. **Open** 9am-5.30pm Mon-Sat. **Credit** AmEx, MC, V.
Run by an experienced music teacher, Dot's is a wonderfully friendly establishment. The shop sells new instruments – mostly stringed and wind, from recorders to violins – along with sheet music and books. There's a rent-to-buy scheme too. Check the website for tuition and second-hand instruments. *Repair service.*

Northcote Music

155C Northcote Road, SW11 6QB (7228 0074). Clapham Junction rail, then bus 319. **Open** 10.30am-6pm Mon-Fri; 10am-5pm Sat. **Credit** MC, V.
This friendly little music shop is tucked away next to QT Toys, somehow squeezing string, percussion and wind instruments (which you can rent or buy) into the tiny space, as well as brass and digital equipment. In the remaining space are the music books and sheet music, some of which are appropriate for younger children (including nursery rhymes for the piano and group sing-along pieces). It's popular, so try to avoid the after-school rush. *Buggy access. Delivery service. Repair service.*

Robert Morley

34 Engate Street, SE13 7HA (8318 5838, www.morleypianos.co.uk). Lewisham DLR/rail. **Open** 9.30am-5pm Mon-Sat. **Credit** MC, V.
To see if a child is serious about playing the piano, Morley's will hire one out, charging £250 for initial payment and delivery, then a monthly charge starting from £30. If, after a year, the child is still piano-friendly, you can buy it and get half the rental payments off the price, plus the delivery charge. Morley's also builds early keyboards such as clavichords, harpsichords and virginals. *Buggy access. Delivery service. Repair service.*

EQUIPMENT & ACCESSORIES

Gifts

Bob & Blossom

140 Columbia Road, E2 7RG (7739 4737, www.bobandblossom.co.uk). Hoxton rail or bus 55. **Open** 9am-3pm Sun. **Credit** MC, V.
Despite its restricted opening hours (coinciding with Sunday's famous flower market), B&B does a roaring trade in crochet-knit toys, retro spinning tops and wooden Noah's ark sets. The boutique also sells the brand's trademark T-shirts, hats and sleepsuits, boldly emblazoned with cheeky mottos. *Buggy access.*

Cachao

140 Regent's Park Road, NW1 8XL (7483 4422, www.cachaotoycafe.com). Chalk Farm tube. **Open** 8.30am-6pm daily. **Credit** AmEx, MC, V.

Consumer

Consumer

Get Fitted for London 2012

If your kids are joining in the big push to get active before London 2012, they're going to need some kit.

Ace Sports & Leisure
6 Fortress Road, NW5 2ES (7485 5367). Kentish Town tube. **Open** 9.30am-6pm Mon-Sat. **Credit** MC, V.
Ace, which has moved from its old setting opposite Kentish Town tube, has footwear for all sports, as well as junior rackets, bats and swimming equipment. There are also small baseball mitts and footballs in all sizes, first cricket bats and balls, and swimming accessories. *Buggy access. Disabled access.*

David J Thomas
8 Croxted Road, SE21 8SW (8766 7400). West Dulwich rail. **Open** 9.15am-5.15pm Mon-Sat. **Credit** AmEx, MC, V.
A school uniform and sports kit specialist with a great line in cheap equipment in junior sizes.
Buggy access.

Decathlon
Canada Water Retail Park, Surrey Quays Road, SE16 2XU (7394 2000, www.decathlon.co.uk). Canada Water tube. **Open** 9am-9pm Mon-Fri; 9am-7pm Sat; 11am-5pm Sun. **Credit** MC, V.
This huge store is crammed with gear for riding, snowsports, biking, fishing, walking and ballsports. The young staff are enthusiastic. Services include racket restringing and ski maintenance. *Buggy access. Disabled access. Repair service.*

Lillywhites
24-36 Lower Regent Street, SW1Y 4QF (0844 332 5602, www.sportsdirect. com). Piccadilly Circus tube. **Open** 10am-10pm Mon-Fri; 9.30am-10pm Sat; 11.45am-6pm Sun. **Credit** AmEx, MC, V. **Map** p333 K7.
A fixture since 1925, Lillywhites is still good for mainstream sports gear. It concentrates mainly on urban sporting activities, and especially football. *Buggy access. Disabled access. Mail order.*

Ocean Leisure
11-14 Northumberland Avenue, WC2N 5AQ (7930 5050, www.ocean leisure.co.uk). Embankment tube. **Open** 10am-7pm Mon-Fri; 10am-5pm Sat. **Credit** MC, V. **Map** p333 L8.

This shop-cum-café stocks Hello Kitty, Ravensburger, Toby Tiger, Crayola goods and more. It's a slightly odd set-up, with stock covering the walls of the café upstairs. This makes it a little tricky to browse. But there's also a downstairs room (albeit reached by a cramped staircase).
Buggy access.

Finnesse Lifestyle
453 Roman Road, E3 5LX (8983 9286, www.finnesselifestyle.com). Bethnal Green tube, then bus 8. **Open** 9.30am-6pm Mon-Sat. **Credit** AmEx, MC, V.
Alongside collections of organic and fair trade womenswear, accessories and home furnishings, Finnesse has a decent selection of children's clothes and toys from around the world. Marimekko, Hug and Organics for Kids are among the labels; Pia Wallen's snug little felted slippers would make a lovely gift for a newborn. *Buggy access.*

Maggie & Tom
345 Upper Street, N1 0PD (7359 7037, www.greenbaby.co.uk). Angel tube or Highbury & Islington tube/rail. **Open** 9.30am-5.30pm Mon-Fri; 10am-5pm Sat; 11am-5pm Sun. **Credit** MC, V.
This small chain of shops may have changed its identity from Green Baby to Maggie and Tom, but it still stocks the same line in Eco-friendly baby products and a range of children's clothes in organic cotton. The shop also stocks natural bedding and wooden toys. *Delivery service.*
Branches 5 Elgin Crescent, W11 2JA (7792 8140); 52 Greenwich Church Street, SE10 9BL (8858 6690).

O Baby
126 Fortis Green Road, N10 3DU (8444 8742). Highgate tube, then bus 43, 134. **Open** 9.30am-5.30pm Mon-Sat. **Credit** AmEx, MC, V.

Hidden away under the arches by Embankment, this watersports emporium sells all manner of sailing, scuba diving and surfing gear. Some of the stock – including the wetsuits, swimwear, Reef sandals and neoprene Aquashoes – comes in very small sizes. They also stock baby lifejackets, fins, masks and snorkels; and specialist children's scuba equipment can be ordered in.
Buggy access. Disabled access.

Slam City Skates

16 Neal's Yard, WC2H 9DP (7240 0928, www.slamcity.com). Covent Garden tube. **Open** 11am-7pm Mon-Sat; noon-5pm Sun. **Credit** AmEx, MC, V. **Map** p331 L6.
A well-stocked source of skateboards, sneakers, rucksacks and accessories, beloved of teen aficionados.
Branch 43 Carnaby Street, W1F 7EA (7240 2611).

Soccerscene

56-57 Carnaby Street, W1F 9QF (7439 0778, www.soccerscene.co.uk). Oxford Circus tube. **Open** 10am-7pm Mon-Wed, Fri, Sat; 10am-8pm Thur; noon-6pm Sun. **Credit** AmEx, MC, V. **Map** p330 J6.

Scaled-down replica kits, sturdy socks, goalie gloves and more, plus footie- and rugby-themed gifts and accessories.
Delivery service.
Branch 156 Oxford Street, W1D 1ND (7436 6499).

Speedo

41-43 Neal Street, WC2H 9PJ (7497 0950, www.speedo.com). Covent Garden tube. **Open** 10am-7pm Mon-Wed, Fri, Sat; 10am-8pm Thur; noon-6pm Sun. **Credit** AmEx, MC, V. **Map** p331 L6.
Swimming costumes, shorts and nappies, alongside all manner of aquatic accessories: armbands, snorkels, goggles and caps.
Buggy access. Disabled access.

Wigmore Sports

39 Wigmore Street, W1U 1QQ (7486 7761, www.wigmoresports.co.uk). Bond Street tube. **Open** 10am-6pm Mon-Wed, Fri, Sat; 10am-7pm Thur; 11am-5pm Sun. **Credit** AmEx, MC, V. **Map** p330 G6.
Junior stock at London's premier racket sports specialist (tennis, squash, badminton and more) includes footwear, shorter rackets and softer balls. There's a 'try before you buy' practice wall.
Buggy access. Delivery service. Disabled access.

Consumer

This shop sells fair trade and organic bedding, toys and clothes for babies and toddlers, as well as natural skincare products.
Buggy access.

Semmalina-Starbags

225 Ebury Street, SW1W 8UT (7730 9333, www.starbags.info). Sloane Square tube. **Open** 9.30am-5.30pm Mon-Sat. **Credit** MC, V. **Map** p332 G11.
Specialises in bespoke party bags. Wrapped in cellophane and garlanded with bright ribbons, the bags can be filled with all sorts of trinkets – from the neon-lit sweetie selection to bubbles, potty putty, hair bobbles, stationery and more.
Delivery service.

So Tiny London

64 Great Titchfield Street, W1W 7QH (7636 2501, www.showroom64.com). Oxford Circus tube. **Open** 10am-6.30pm Mon-Fri; noon-6pm Sat. **Credit** AmEx, MC, V.

There are beautiful presents for newborns to be unearthed at this compact shop, ranging from Bonnie Baby's sumptuous cashmere cardies to tongue-in-cheek Rolling Stones and Stone Roses Babygros. Tiny Mary Jane sock sets and knitted bonnets cater to more traditional tastes. The selection of new baby cards is excellent, with some lovely hand-printed designs. Clothes sizes go up to age eight; don't miss the sale rail, which offers generous reductions.
Buggy access. Nappy-changing facilities.

Bikes

Chamberlaine Cycles

75-77 Kentish Town Road, NW1 8NY (7485 4488, www.chamberlainecycles.co.uk). Camden Town tube. **Open** 8.30am-6pm Mon-Sat. **Credit** AmEx, MC, V.
Outside, ranks of gleaming, polished bicycles line the pavement; inside there are even more

to choose from, along with baby seats, trailer bikes, lights and the all-important locks.
Buggy access. Delivery service. Disabled access. Repair service.

D2 Leisure

143 Stoke Newington Road, N16 8BP (7254 3380, www.d2leisuregroup.co.uk). Rectory Road rail or bus 67, 76, 149, 243. **Open** 9am-5.30pm Mon-Fri; 9am-5pm Sat. **Credit** MC, V.
The bike shop formerly known as Daycock's has a great range of cycles in the kids' showroom, although most bikes can be ordered online via the website.
Buggy access. Disabled access. Repair service. **Branches** 201-203 Roman Road, E2 0QY (8980 4966); 70-72 Loampit Vale, SE13 7SN (8297 0225).

Edwardes

221-225 Camberwell Road, SE5 0HG (7703 3676). Elephant & Castle tube, then bus 12, 68, 176, P3. **Open** 8.30am-6pm Mon-Sat. **Credit** AmEx, MC, V.
A reliable general bike shop, Edwardes also stocks mounts for two to 12s (brands include Pro Bike, Bronx and Giant) along with accessories such as bike seats, helmets, trailers and tag-alongs.
Buggy access. Delivery service. Disabled access. Repair service.

Two Wheels Good

143 Crouch Hill, N8 9QH (8340 4284, www.twowheelsgood.co.uk). Finsbury Park tube/rail, then bus W7. **Open** 8.30am-6pm Mon-Fri; 9am-6pm Sat; 11am-5pm Sun. **Credit** AmEx, MC, V.
Although there isn't a wide range of children's bikes, the incredibly friendly and helpful staff are more than happy to offer recommendations on bikes you can order in from the Gary Fisher and Trek websites.
Buggy access. Disabled access. Repair service. **Branch** 165 Stoke Newington Church Street, N16 0UL (7249 2200).

Prams & accessories

See also pp271-276.

Babyworld

239 Munster Road, SW6 6BT (7386 1904). Fulham Broadway tube, then bus 211, 295. **Open** 10am-6pm Mon-Wed, Fri; 10am-5.30pm Sat. **Credit** AmEx, MC, V.

The premises may look small, but Babyworld certainly crams a lot in. Specialising in essential equipment for under-fives, its stock includes stairgates, prams, pushchairs, high chairs, breast pumps and toys from brands such as Medela, Tomy, Maclaren, Bugaboo and Mountain Buggy.
Buggy access.

Rub a Dub Dub

15 Park Road, N8 8TE (8342 9898). Finsbury Park tube/rail, then bus W7. **Open** 10am-6pm Mon-Sat; noon-4pm Sun. **Credit** MC, V.
All the biggest brands are present and correct at this well-stocked shop, from playfully hued Bugaboos to more rugged Mountain Buggy, Out 'N' About and Phil & Teds three-wheelers. Along with Tripp-Trapp high chairs, travel cots, muslins and UV-protecting pushchair covers, there are fun mouse-, tiger- and ladybird-shaped Wheelybugs for whizzing round the house, and plenty of toys. Eco-friendly nappy brands include Bambo and Nature Babycare, and there's a sweet-smelling array of chemical-free baby wipes.
Buggy access. Delivery service. Disabled access. Nappy-changing facilities. Play area.

The nursery

Aspace

140 Chiswick High Road, W4 1PU (8994 5814, www.aspaceuk.com). Turnham Green tube. **Open** 10am-6pm Mon-Sat; 11am-5pm Sun. **Credit** AmEx, MC, V.
The understated range at Aspace includes children's beds of every description, from white-painted four posters to solid oak bunks. Handsome wardrobes, sturdy chests of drawers and tasteful soft furnishings – mattresses, quilts, throws, curtains and cushions – round off the collection.
Buggy access. Delivery service. **Branches** 144 Northcote Road, SW11 6RD (7228 3074); 725 Fulham Road, SW6 5UL (0845 872 2611).

Blue Almonds

79 Walton Street, SW3 2HP (7584 8038, www.bluealmonds.co.uk). South Kensington tube. **Open** 10am-6pm Mon-Fri; 10.30am-5pm Sat. **Credit** MC, V. **Map** p329 E10.
The wooden nursery furniture in this shop – catering for a typical Kensington clientele – is prolifically painted with flowers, butterflies and

Consumer

sailing boats. Tartine et Chocolat blankets and cuddly toys are all soft and sweet, while the cool African print range makes a refreshing change if you're tired of conventional pastels.
Buggy access. Delivery service.

Bobo Kids
29 Elystan Street, SW3 3NT (7838 1020, www.bobokids.co.uk). South Kensington tube. **Open** 10am-6pm Mon-Sat. **Credit** AmEx, MC, V. **Map** p329 E11.
Not the cheapest shop you've ever set foot in, but as good for inspiration as for making actual purchases. Bobo Kids is a fine emporium showcasing the latest in funky furniture, lighting, bed linen, artwork and accessories for children's and teenagers' bedrooms. What's so refreshing about this place is the absence of straight pinks and blues, and princess and car motifs. It's junior minimalism with boho touches. We like the toddler bed – basically a padded silver box, the Mini China four poster bed, the fabrics and the Bunny night light.
Buggy access. Delivery service. Disabled access.

Chic Shack
77 Lower Richmond Road, SW15 1ET (8785 7777, www.chicshack.net). Putney Bridge tube, then bus 14, 22. **Open** 10.30am-5pm Mon-Sat. **Credit** MC, V.

Inspired by 18th-century French and Swedish antiques, Chic Shack's largely white-painted furniture and soft furnishings are delightfully elegant. The range includes cots, chests, toy boxes, wardrobes and pastel pink- or blue floral- and stripe-upholstered chairs.
Buggy access. Delivery service.

Dragons of Walton Street
23 Walton Street, SW3 2HX (7589 3795, www.dragonsofwaltonstreet.com). Knightsbridge or South Kensington tube. **Open** 9.30am-5.30pm Mon-Fri; 10am-5pm Sat. **Credit** AmEx, MC, V. **Map** p329 E10.
This Walton Street landmark has spawned a host of imitations. Its wooden furniture is hand-painted with bunnies and boats, soldiers and fairies; alternatively, you can come up with your own design. Beatrix Potter and Paddington Bear lampshades and bedspreads are in abundance.
Buggy access. Delivery service.

Natural Mat Company
99 Talbot Road, W11 2AT (7985 0474, www.naturalmat.com). Ladbroke Grove tube. **Open** 9am-6pm Mon-Fri; 11am-5pm Sat. **Credit** MC, V. **Map** p326 A5.
Behind a window hung with prints of children's illustrations is a range of solid nursery furniture, with a choice of organic mattresses and bedding.

Kids' Corner
Stoke Newington

Despite significant gentrification over the past decade or so, 'Stokey' still clings to its bohemian identity. Products with green credentials are easy to find round here; on Saturdays, there's a good farmers' market in the grounds of William Patten Primary School.

In an area that's famed for its high concentration of young families, shopping for children couldn't be easier. Most of the action is centred around the pleasant, café-dotted stretch of Church Street, making for a restful afternoon's lunching and browsing.

Toy shop **Route 73 Kids** (*see p300*) is a little less chichi now that Woolies on the High Street has closed, and has a great range of toys and games for under-tens. A few doors away, **Olive Loves Alfie** (*see p286*) is a showcase for the hottest childrenswear designers. One of the best children's shops in London is all-rounder **Born** (*see p271*), well stocked with clothes, prams, accessories, green nappies and more. Church Street is also home to a friendly branch of bike shop **Two Wheels Good** (*see p282*), although savvy parents will make for **D2 Leisure** (*see p282*) on the High Street for cheaper prices.

Down the road on Newington Green, **Three Potato Four** (*see p288*) – selling children's clothes, toys, books and offering haircuts – is a hop, skip and jump away from kids' café **That Place on the Corner** (*see p217*).

Knowledgeable staff can help you decide between the different materials; organic coir, latex straight from a rubber tree and mohair for mattresses, along with goose down and lambswool-stuffed cot bed covers and duvets. There are also baby jumpers in lambswool, cashmere blankets and cotton Babygros. *Buggy access. Delivery service.*

Nursery Window

83 Walton Street, SW3 2HP (7581 3358, www.nurserywindow.co.uk). Knightsbridge or South Kensington tube. **Open** 10am-6pm Mon-Sat. **Credit** AmEx, MC, V. **Map** p329 E10.

This supremely traditional nursery shop stocks beautifully made wooden cots and cribs, and all the blankets and quilts you could ever need. Prints are nostalgic and romantic, and despite the dry-clean only label, Sue Hill's cashmere knits are lovely. Waffle blankets with pink or blue satin trim are a fail-safe buy. *Buggy access. Delivery service.*

FASHION

Amaia

14 Cale Street, SW3 3QU (7590 0999, www.amaia-kids.com). Sloane Square or South Kensington tube. **Open** 10am-6pm Mon-Sat. **Credit** MC, V. **Map** p329 E11.

There's an appealingly nostalgic feel to the baby clothes and childrenswear at Amaia, from the knitted all-in-ones and T-bar shoes to the ruffled cotton sundresses. Boys' clothes are equally classic, with cotton shorts, cords and linen shirts. Expect to pay upwards of £50 for a little girl's day dress. *Buggy access.*

Aravore Babies

31 Park Road, N8 8TE (8347 5752, www.aravore.com). Highgate tube or Crouch Hill rail, or bus 41, 91, W5, W7. **Open** 10am-5.30pm Mon-Sat; noon-4pm Sun. **Credit** AmEx, MC, V.

This luxury brand for babies and under-fives has some covetable pieces, all made from fairly traded organic cotton and super-soft merino wool. At its small shop, gorgeous hand-knitted coats, dresses, bootees and dungarees nestle alongside delicate shawls and cot blankets. It also stocks a few other like-minded brands such as Bamboo Baby, Lille Barn, Tatty Bumpkin and the Erbaviva skincare range. *Buggy access.*

Biff

41-43 Dulwich Village, SE21 7BN (8299 0911, www.biffkids.co.uk). North Dulwich rail or bus P4. **Open** 9.30am-5.30pm Mon-Fri; 10am-6pm Sat. **Credit** AmEx, MC, V.

Occupying two shops, with a café next door, Biff has become a hub for local mums. At No.41 there's an enormous selection of shoes from the likes of Lelli Kelly, Converse, Crocs, Geox and Start-rite, and an equally broad range of clothing brands for boys and girls aged two to 16. Labels include Catamini, Pepe Jeans, Powell Craft, Bench, Roxy, Tartine et Chocolat, Quiksilver and Noa Noa. Next door caters to smaller fry, with baby gifts, Grobags, first shoes, swimwear and clothes for under-threes. *Buggy access. Disabled access. Play area.*

Bonpoint

15 Sloane Street, SW1X 9NB (7235 1441, www.bonpoint.com). Knightsbridge tube. **Open** 10am-6pm Mon-Sat. **Credit** AmEx, MC, V. **Map** p329 F9.

Describing itself as a 'French childrenswear couture house', Bonpoint brings Gallic panache and exquisite workmanship to the world of children's fashion. Charming bloomers, sundresses, linen shorts and jumpers are hard to resist, though the hefty price tags may make you think twice; the fragrant, well-heeled regulars don't bat an eyelid, *naturellement.* *Buggy access.*

Branches 256 Brompton Road, SW3 2AS (3263 5057); 197 Westbourne Grove, W11 2SE (7792 2515); 52-54 Marylebone High Street, W1U 5HR (7487 2512).

Burberry Children

199 Westbourne Grove, W11 2SB (7221 3688, www.burberry.com). Notting Hill Gate tube. **Open** 10am-6pm Mon-Sat; noon-6pm Sun. **Credit** AmEx, MC, V.

This glamorous flagship store on Westbourne Grove houses clothes with the same unusual twists on British classics offered by the adult Burberry line, only in miniature. The range goes from three months to 12 years, with a separate special occasion collection which features girls' skirts with gold mesh petticoats and smart blazers for boys. With their immaculate detailing and signature checked lining, the macs are hardest on parental credit cards, costing around £260 depending on age. T-shirts, bags and shoes are less expensive, but you'll struggle to find much for under £30. *Buggy access. Nappy-changing facilities. Play area.*

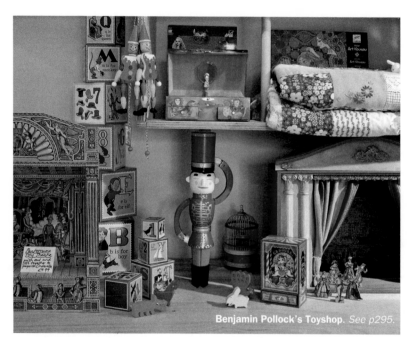
Benjamin Pollock's Toyshop. *See p295.*

Consumer

Caramel Baby & Child

77 Ledbury Road, W11 2AG (7727 0906,
www.caramel-shop.co.uk). Notting Hill Gate
or Westbourne Park tube. **Open** 10am-6pm
Mon-Sat; noon-5pm Sun. **Credit** AmEx,
MC, V. **Map** p326 A6.
Caramel's clothing range (0-12s) is effortlessly
chic. Ribbon-strap floral sundresses, crisp
smocks and beautifully cut woollen coats have
serious fashion appeal. As you might expect,
it's not cheap; check washing instructions, too,
as some pieces are made from silk or cashmere.
A small selection of vintage-inspired toys are
displayed downstairs, and there's a hair salon.
Buggy access. Hairdressing.
Branches 259 Pavilion Road, SW1X 0BP
(7730 2564); 291 Brompton Road, SW3 2DY
(7589 7001); Selfridges, 400 Oxford Street,
W1A 1AB (7318 3656).

Jakss

469 Roman Road, E3 5LX (8981 2233,
www.jakss.co.uk). Bethnal Green tube,
then bus 8. **Open** 10am-5.30pm Tue-Sat.
Credit AmEx, MC, V.
Founded in 1977, Jakss is a treasure trove
of children's designer togs, ranging from all-
in-ones for newborns to cutting-edge looks for
16-year-olds. The list of labels is vast: Ralph
Lauren, Armani, Jottum, Burberry, DKNY, CP
Company, Oilily and Stone Island fill the rails,
along with children's and adults' Birkenstocks.
Buggy access.

Jolie à Pied

82 Lordship Lane, SE22 8HF (8693 4509).
East Dulwich rail. **Open** 10am-6pm Mon-
Wed, Fri, Sat; 10am-7pm Thur; 11am-5pm
Sun. **Credit** MC, V.
Jolie à Pied has rebranded itself recently along
more utilitarian lines, with Hunter wellies and
hard-wearing Converse and Camper lines
taking prominence in the windows. Pretty
shoes are all very well, but children will jump
in puddles and climb trees in anything they
happen to have on, so footwear may as well be
up to the task.
Buggy access.

Little Bevan

53 Moreton Street, SW1V 2NY (7821 9499,
www.littlebevan.co.uk). Pimlico tube. **Open**
10am-5pm Mon-Sat. **Credit** AmEx, MC, V.
This charming shop in Pimlico stocks a range
of beautifully made and reasonably priced
everyday children's clothes. It also specialises

in bridesmaid and pageboy outfits and couture partywear. For the latter, make an appointment beforehand with the friendly staff.
Buggy access.

Notsobig

31A Highgate High Street, N6 5JT (8340 4455). Archway or Highgate tube. **Open** 10am-6pm Mon-Sat; 11am-5pm Sun.
Credit MC, V.
An eclectic blend of labels and designers makes Notsobig's shelves a pleasure to peruse. Swishy party dresses from I Love Gorgeous and Cacharel rub shoulders with cool casuals from American Outfitters and hip Parisian label Eva & Oli, Woolrich, No Added Sugar, Baby Issa and Love from Australia. Look out, too, for Little Linens' light, airy shirts and trousers. Dressing-up clothes from Bandicoot Lapin, tulle-skirted tutus sourced from Los Angeles, hand-made jewellery and a sterling selection of shoes round off the stock.
Buggy access. Delivery service.

Oh Baby London

162 Brick Lane, E1 6RU (7247 4949, www.ohbabylondon.com). Shoreditch High Street rail. **Open** 10am-6pm daily.
Credit MC, V.
Oh Baby's cute, colourful own brand baby and kids' clothes are all the rage in east London and beyond. Choose from body vests and bright T-shirts with slogans like 'The Future Is Mine' and 'I'm a Long Term Investment' to dresses and playsuits in bright prints.
Buggy access, Delivery service.

Olive Loves Alfie

84 Stoke Newington Church Street, N16 0AP (7241 4212, www.oliveovesalfie.co.uk). Finsbury Park tube/rail then bus 106, or bus 73, 393, 476. **Open** 10am-5.30pm Mon-Fri; 10am-5pm Sat, Sun. **Credit** AmEx, MC, V.
This design-led boutique stocks an inspired mix of clothing for children of all ages. Gorgeous and reasonably priced, its collection is full of nautical stripes, bright paisley patterns and bold graphic prints. Pieces by hugely popular Scandinavian designer Katvig fly out of the shop, as do Dandy Star's soft, 1970s-style T-shirts. New this year is a range of Marimekko's womenswear. Artfully arranged gifts and toys include painted wooden animals, hand-knitted cuddly toys and a washing line strung with hats; mothers-to-be will love the comfy cotton kimonos and organic bath products.
Buggy access.

Petit Aimé

34 Ledbury Road, W11 2AB (7221 3123, www.aimelondon.com). Notting Hill Gate tube. **Open** 10am-6.30pm Mon-Sat.
Credit AmEx, MC, V. **Map** p326 A6.
An offshoot of the acclaimed womenswear boutique next door, owned by French-Cambodian sisters Val and Vanda Heng-Vong, this white-painted boutique dresses newborns to 12-year-olds with the crème de la crème of Gallic labels, including Isabel Marant, Bonton and Antik Batik. Kitsch blankets, cushions and brightly coloured bedspreads from Petit Pan are a great way to liven up a nursery, and the hand-knitted rabbits will enchant younger children.

Quackers

155D Northcote Road, SW11 6QB (7978 4235). Clapham Junction rail, then bus 319. **Open** 9.30am-5.30pm Mon-Fri; 10am-5.30pm Sat. **Credit** MC, V.
Kids can root through the box of toys while their parents browse the rails. There's a healthy crop of Danish designers to choose from, including Minymo, Molo Kids, Phister & Philina and Louie Louis. Modish little cotton dresses and tiered skirts by Hilly Chrisp are superb summer buys, and there are playfully printed Hatley raincoats for autumn showers. Toys include floppy favourites by Moulin Roty and attractive wooden pull-alongs and trikes.
Buggy access.

Rachel Riley

82 Marylebone High Street, W1U 4QW (7935 8345, www.rachelriley.com). Baker Street or Bond Street tube. **Open** 10am-6.30pm Mon-Sat; 10.30am-5.30pm Sun.
Credit AmEx, MC, V. **Map** p330 G5.
There's a wonderfully wholesome, 1950s feel to Rachel Riley's designs, hand-made in her *atelier* in the Loire Valley. Cherry-print poplin frocks, beruffled bloomers and pleated pinafores are traditional without being stuffy; for the chaps, there are anchor- and aeroplane-print shirts and dapper striped pyjamas. Hand-made leather slippers are also available.
Buggy access. Delivery service.
Branch 14 Pont Street, SW1X 9EN (7259 5969).

Ralph Lauren Children's Store

143 New Bond Street, W1S 2TP (7535 4600, www.polo.com). Bond Street tube. **Open** 10am-6pm Mon-Wed, Fri, Sat; 10am-7pm Thur; noon-5pm Sun. **Credit** AmEx, MC, V. **Map** p330 H6.

Consumer

Consumer

Added Extras

When is a shop not just a shop? Why, when there's more to it than buying and selling, of course. Many of London's fabulous children's shops offer a timetable of events as well as shelves of great products. At **Davenports Magic** (*see p295*) in Charing Cross, regular beginners' magic courses for over-15s take place on Saturdays. Over in Hampstead, **Mystical Fairies** (*see p298*) runs fairy school sessions for three to eight-year-olds and offers fairy makeovers too. The recently opened **Ministry of Stories** in Hoxton (*see p298*) is a mysterious front for creative writing workshops for local kids that take place through the secret door. **Tales on Moon Lane** (*see p278*) and the **Children's Bookshop** (*see p277*) offer regular storytelling sessions either side of the north-south London divide, while new Swiss Cottage favourite **huggle** (*see p272*) has a whole roster of children's classes in the special lounge area, from music and dance to yoga.

huggle.

Ralph Lauren's beautifully made but eye-wateringly expensive outfits are displayed in suitably stately surrounds (mahogany panelling, sepia prints and strategically arranged rocking horses). There's more to the brand than polo shirts: the baby dresses and cashmere cable-knit cardigans, in particular, are gorgeously pretty.
Delivery service.
Branch 139-141 Fulham Road, SW3 6FD (7761 0310).

Sasti

8 Portobello Green Arcade, 281 Portobello Road, W10 5TZ (8960 1125, www.sasti. co.uk). Ladbroke Grove tube. **Open** 10am-6pm Mon-Sat. **Credit** MC, V.
Bold designs and colours ensure Sasti's clothes stand out from the crowd, whether you're buying cowboy-meets-Indian jeans with tan fringing down the side or a leopard print all-in-one. Everything is made in the UK, and prices are competitive, starting at around £12 for fleeces and long-sleeved T-shirts. The kitsch accessories also make great presents for cool kids.
Buggy access. Delivery service. Nappy-changing facilities. Play area.

Selfridges

400 Oxford Street, W1A 1AB (0800 123400, www.selfridges.com). Bond Street tube. **Open** 9.30am-8pm Mon-Wed, Sat; 9.30am-9pm Thur, Fri; noon-6pm Sun. **Credit** AmEx, DC, MC, V. **Map** p330 G6.
The sprawling third floor is chock full of well-known children's brands to browse through – predominantly clothes, although there are a few toy ranges (including Hello Kitty and VTech). All the major designers are represented, including Armani, Dior, Chloé and Tommy Hilfiger. Sonia Rykiel's range for girls features bright pink dresses with attached fabric flowers; for boys, John Galliano's jeans, khaki jackets and print T-shirts have lots of attitude. Slightly cheaper, and a favourite with fashionista parents, French brand Finger in the Nose's range includes rock 'n' roll essentials such as bootcut jeans and acid wash T-shirts. There's also a large shoe department, featuring Step2wo, and fancy dress costumes. Although there is no specific play space, there's plenty of room for children to run around; look out, too, for seasonal events such as Easter egg hunts.
Buggy access. Cafés. Delivery service. Disabled access: lift, toilet. Nappy-changing facilities.

Their Nibs

*214 Kensington Park Road, W11 1NR
(7221 4263, www.theirnibs.com). Ladbroke
Grove or Notting Hill Gate tube.* **Open**
10am-6pm Mon-Sat; noon-5pm Sun.
Credit AmEx, MC, V.

Their Nibs is known for its whimsical,
distinctive designs, featuring 1950s-style prints
and unusual colours. Signature prints include
a toadstool fairy pattern for girls' blouses and
dresses, and a pirate design for boys' shirts.
More elaborate party frocks cost up to £55, but
plenty of stock is a good deal cheaper; the
raincoats go for £20. The vintage emporium at
the back includes doll's houses, wooden toys,
clothes and prams, and there's a small range of
Stokke cribs and high chairs. Kids can play
with the blackboard, mini-kitchen and books or
have a haircut while you browse.
Buggy access. Hairdressing. Play area.
Branch 79 Chamberlayne Road, NW10 3ND
(8964 8444).

Three Potato Four

*Alliance House, Newington Green, N16 9QH
(7704 2228, www.threepotatofour.co.uk).
Canonbury rail or bus 73.* **Open** 10am-5pm
Mon-Fri; 9.30am-6pm Sat; 11am-5pm Sun.
Credit MC, V.

This colourful boutique's clothing collection
includes vibrant pieces by Dutch designer
Kik-Kid. There are gifts galore, too: shelves of
books, old-fashioned toys and Science Museum
games. A fairly reasonably priced children's
hair salon occupies a corner of the shop, and
there are a couple of train tracks to keep the
little ones occupied while you shop.
*Buggy access. Disabled access. Hairdressing.
Nappy-changing facilities. Play area.*

Trotters

*34 King's Road, SW3 4UD (7259 9620,
www.trotters.co.uk). Sloane Square tube.*
Open 9am-7pm Mon-Sat; 10am-6pm Sun.
Credit AmEx, MC, V. **Map** p329 F11.

With clothes, toys, accessories, toiletries, shoes
and books, Trotters is a one-stop shop for
beleagured parents. Exclusive designs from the
Chelsea Clothing Company include Liberty-
print dresses and nicely cut smocks, while boys
look shipshape in Petit Breton's stripy tops and
cotton shorts. There's a hairdressing station
with a big fish tank to distract the littl'uns
during their fringe trim; first-timers get a
certificate and a lock of hair for fond parents to
treasure. Stocked with Converse, Pom d'Api
and Start-rites, the shoe section also gives out

'first shoe' certificates. Other useful bits and
bobs on offer include organic sunscreens,
insulated lunchboxes and a range of Nitty
Gritty headlice treatments.
Buggy access. Delivery service. Hairdressing.
Branches 127 Kensington High Street, W8
5SF (7937 9373); 86 Northcote Road, SW11
6QN (7585 0572); 84 Turnham Green
Terrace, W4 1QN (8742 1195).

Others

Catimini

*52A South Molton Street, W1K 1SE (7629
8099, www.catimini.com). Bond Street tube.*
Open 10am-6.30pm Mon-Wed, Fri, Sat;
10am-7pm Thur; 11am-5pm Sun. **Credit**
AmEx, MC, V. **Map** p330 H6.

Startlingly bright colours and vibrant patterns
are Catimini's signature style, with crocheted
cardigans, patchwork cotton separates, sweet
baggy shorts and striped T-shirts.
Buggy access. Disabled access. Play area.
Branch 33C King's Road, SW3 4LX
(7824 8897).

Felix & Lilys

*3 Camden Passage, N1 8EA (7424 5423).
Angel tube.* **Open** 10am-6pm Mon-Sat;
11am-5pm Sun. **Credit** AmEx, MC, V.

Chelsea Toys.
See p295.

This boutique sells colourful designer togs for babies and children, including some chic Scandinavian brands (Ej Sikke Lej, IdaT and Katvig), Their Nibs and Nippaz With Attitude, plus old favourites like Bob & Blossom and Toby Tiger. Look out, too, for the quirky Ella & Otto sleeping bags. Toys include wooden food and pull-along pals.
Buggy access.

Frogs & Fairies

69A Highbury Park, N5 1UA (7424 5159). Highbury & Islington tube/rail. **Open** 10am-5.30pm Mon-Sat. **Credit** AmEx, MC, V.
Frogs and Fairies has streamlined its operation. It no longer sells shoes or clothing, concentrating instead on its range of toys and gifts. Goodies by Playmobil, Lego and Galt are favourites, as are the ubiquitous Micro-scooters. There's also a range of picture books and Jelly Cat soft toys.
Buggy access.

I Love Gorgeous

52 Ledbury Road, W11 2AJ (7229 5855, www.ilovegorgeous.co.uk). Notting Hill Gate or Westbourne Park tube. **Open** 10am-6pm Mon-Sat; noon-6pm Sun. **Credit** AmEx, MC, V.
Map p326 A6.
Stocking girls' clothes from newborn to 13 years, the rails of this small boutique are full of wonderfully tactile fabrics such as romantic georgette and soft cotton voile. Some of the designs are quite funky, like the hot pink star prints and lurex cardigans; others are much more innocent, with broderie anglaise trims and muted colours. There's a pretty collection of bridesmaid dresses downstairs.
Buggy access.

Love Me Again

37 Staplehurst Road, SE13 5ND (8244 0172, www.love-me-again.co.uk). **Open** 10am-5pm Tue-Sat. **Credit** AmEx, MC, V.
New and nearly new clothes and toys are the mainstays of this recently opened shop in Hither Green. Expect designer labels such as Kenzo and Burberry, middle range favourites like Gap and Mini Boden, and lots of cast-off toys. The shop runs occasional craft workshops for children (see the website for details).
Buggy access. Play area.

Marie Chantal

148 Walton Street, SW3 2JJ (7838 1111, www.mariechantal.com). Knightsbridge or South Kensington tube. **Open** 10am-6pm Mon-Sat. **Credit** AmEx, MC, V. **Map** p329 E10.

Immaculate detailing, smart cuts and expensive fabrics, as you'd expect from a range designed by the Crown Princess of Greece. The collection includes some very high-fashion items such as jumpsuits, though there's plenty to suit more staid tastes; tweed jackets and braces for the boys, for example.
Buggy access.
Branches 61A Ledbury Road, W11 2AA (7243 0220); 133A Sloane Street, SW1X 9AX (7730 8662).

Membery's

1 Church Road, SW13 9HE (8876 2910, www.memberys.com). Barnes Bridge rail. **Open** 10am-5pm Mon-Sat. **Credit** AmEx, MC, V.
Membery's stocks a good, solid range of baby gifts and quality clothing for small boys and girls up to eight years old. The range includes everything from nightwear to special occasion outfits; it's also particularly good for children's wedding wear.
Buggy access. Delivery service. Play area.

Oranges & Lemons/Pretty Pregnant

61 Northcross Road, SE22 9ET (8693 9010, www.prettypregnant.co.uk). East Dulwich rail. **Open** 9.30am-5.30pm Mon-Sat; 11am-5pm Sun. **Credit** MC, V.
This sister establishment to the Pretty Pregnant maternity brand stocks tiny outfits by Petit Bateau, Catimini and funky Dutch designer Kik-Kid, along with animal motif appliqué T-shirts by Lipfish and some sweet toys – Reggie the Big Eyed Dummy (£16) makes a change from the usual fluffy rabbits.
Buggy access.
Branches 102 Northcote Road, SW11 6QW (7924 4850); 13-15 Chiltern Street, W1U 7PG (7486 2531); 186 King's Road, SW3 5XP (7349 7450).

Tots Boutique

39 Turnham Green Terrace, W4 1RG (8995 0520, http://totschiswick.weebly.com). Turnham Green tube. **Open** 10am-6pm Mon-Sat; noon-5pm Sun. **Credit** AmEx, MC, V.
Across the road from Snap Dragon (*see p300*), Tots crams in a broad range of designer gear for babies and children. The frequently changing cache might include the likes of Mini A Ture, Lili Gaufrette, Gant and Kenzo. A drawing table and various toys keep the kids sweet as you shop.
Buggy access. Play area.

Consumer

Kids' Corner
Crouch End

This bohemian, middle-class and family-friendly neighbourhood has oddly been the home of a number of fantasy authors. Even Stephen King has visited; in his short story *Crouch End*, the area acts as an inter-dimensional portal. Meanwhile, a great range of independent toy and clothing shops encourage children to use their imagination and enter into their own fantasy worlds.

The original happy, hippy infant all-rounder **Soup Dragon** (*see p300*) continues to enchant children with its range of doll's houses, pirate ships and castles. And it no longer has competition from Goody Gumdrops on Crouch Hill, which closed down early in 2011. For gorgeous gifts, bohemian **Aravore Babies** (*see p284*) sells organic and handcrafted items such as sweet little linen dresses with crochet trims.

For the best pram and buggy advice in the area, head to **Rub a Dub Dub** (*see p282*) and pick up all the other child essentials you need at the same time. Meanwhile, feet can be properly fitted into comfy shoes at **Red Shoes** (*see p294*) and wayward hair groomed to perfection at **Mini Kin** (*see p274*). For a revolutionary adventure, Crouch End is also home to friendly bike boutique **Two Wheels Good** (*see p282*).

Chain stores

Adams
www.adams.co.uk
A good bet for inexpensive playwear, babywear and school uniforms.

Fat Face
www.fatface.com
Sporty, surf-inspired casualwear in muted colours for girls and boys.

Gap Kids
www.gap.eu
The pastel-hued babywear makes a safe and practical gift for new parents, while the childrenswear is hard-wearing.

H&M
www.hm.com
Cheap-as-chips and up-to-the-minute designs for babies, children and grown-ups.

Jigsaw Junior
www.jigsaw-online.com
Thrillingly, the branch at 190-192 Westbourne Grove, W11 2RH (7727 0322) has a silver slide instead of stairs to the basement.

Monsoon
www.monsoon.co.uk
Collections range from puff-sleeved T-shirts and turn-up jeans to lavish party frocks.

Petit Bateau
www.petit-bateau.com
Classic French cotton baby clothes, in floral, plain and trademark milleraies striped designs.

Zara
www.zara.com
The Spanish high-street giant offers unusual childrenswear, including beautiful dresses.

Maternity

Blossom Mother & Child
164 Walton Street, SW3 2JL (7589 7500, www.blossommotherandchild.com). South Kensington tube. **Open** 10am-6pm Mon-Sat; noon-5pm Sun. **Credit** AmEx, MC, V. **Map** p329 E10.
Only the most stylish maternity labels make it on to the hallowed shelves at this über-chic Walton Street boutique. The own-label range offers flattering, perfectly cut dresses, separates and lingerie, hanging alongside pieces by the likes of Missoni, Antik Batik and Clements Ribeiro; the denim bar offers bump-accommodating jeans from the hottest brands (True Religion, Citizens of Humanity, J Brand). Amazing bargains can sometimes be found in the website's sale section.
Buggy access.
Branch 69 Marylebone High Street, W1U 5JJ (7486 6089).

Elias & Grace

158 Regent's Park Road, NW1 8XN (7449 0574, www.eliasandgrace.com). Chalk Farm tube. **Open** 10am-6pm Mon-Sat; noon-6pm Sun. **Credit** MC, V.

Perfectly at home amid Primrose Hill's many chichi boutiques, Elias & Grace stocks a stylish combination of high fashion, luxury accessories and gifts. As well as hip labels for mothers-to-be (See by Chloé, Vivienne Westwood, J Brand), there's an international array of brands for babies and under-tens, among them Maan, Bonton, I Love Gorgeous, Marc Jacobs and Quincy. Toys and accessories include bags and dolls from Madame Mo, and Sparrowkids craft sets. A relaxed atmosphere, with plenty of room for pushchairs, a mini play area and friendly assistants, makes for hassle-free browsing.
Buggy access. Play area.

Séraphine

79B Hampstead High Street, NW3 1RE (7317 7030, www.seraphine.com). Hampstead tube. **Open** 10.30am-6pm Mon-Sat; noon-5pm Sun. **Credit** MC, V.

This boutique looks expensive but stocks surprisingly reasonably priced pregnancy wear from French designer Cécile Reinaud. The emphasis is on co-ordinated smart casual items for yummy mummies, in block colours. A small range of newborn baby clothes, nice Boo Boo smellies for baby and Mama Mio products for mothers means it's good for presents too.
Buggy access.
Branch 28 Kensington Church Street, W8 4EP (7937 3156).

HAIRDRESSING

Several shops listed elsewhere in this chapter incorporate a children's salon, with haircuts available on certain days of the week. See **Harrods** (*see p272*), **Caramel** (*see p285*), **Mini Kin** (*see p274*), **Trotters** (*see p288*), **Their Nibs** (*see p288*) and **Igloo** (*see p272*). For the ultimate in barnet styling, however, have a **Tantrum** (*see below*).

Tantrum

398 King's Road, SW10 0LJ (7376 3966, www.yourtantrum.com). Sloane Square tube, then bus 11, 19, 22, 319. **Open** 10am-6pm Tue-Fri; 9am-6pm Sat; 10am-5pm Sun. **Credit** AmEx, MC, V. **Map** p329 D12.

Billing itself as 'a revolutionary new concept in children's hairdressing', Tantrum spoils its young clients rotten with all sorts of bells and whistles. Aimed at an eight- to 14-year-old clientele, the basement area features a juice bar and games room, while the ground floor keeps the under-sevens amused with its buzzing locomotives and starry skies, as well as a general play area. In both areas, each styling chair is equipped with a swanky flatscreen TV and DVDs. The premises can also host children's parties; call for details.
Buggy access. Play area.

SAMPLE SALES

Junior Style

7689 3925, www.juniorstylesales.co.uk
Sharp-eyed shoppers can find discounts of up to 75% off designer labels at these regular sample sales. Sizes run from newborn to 12, while featured designers might include the likes of Replay, Cavalli, Evisu, Kenzo, Simonetta, Imps & Elfs and Ralph Lauren.

SECOND-HAND

Fara Kids

15 Hildreth Street, SW12 9RQ (8675 4137, www.faracharityshops.org) Balham tube. **Open** 9am-6pm Mon-Sat; 11am-5pm Sun. **Credit** MC, V.

This chain of nattily presented second-hand shops raises money for various children's charities. There are now ten Fara shops in London devoted entirely to the sale of kids' stuff after two new sites opened in 2010. This Balham outlet is one of the latest openings and sells toys, children's clothing and books, prams, nursery furniture and maternity wear. Fara is like the chic little sister of older, more established charity shops, and the way it's laid out makes the merchandise look as appealing as any high-street store.
Buggy access.
Branches throughout the city.

Merry-Go-Round

12 Clarence Road, E5 8HB (8985 6308). Hackney Central rail. **Open** 10am-5.30pm Mon-Sat. **Credit** MC, V.

This environmentally friendly agency trades on behalf of its clients in second-hand clothing, toys and baby equipment. Expect to find lots of high chairs, pushchairs, clothes, books and

Consumer

more, allowing budget- and eco-conscious families to be entirely kitted out with recycled goods. Go prepared for some serious browsing and buying; visitors generally leave with armfuls of purchases. Goods here are of a high quality. All the stock is clean and carefully checked; no missing puzzle pieces here. *Buggy access. Nappy-changing facilities.*

Merry Go Round
21 Half Moon Lane, SE24 9JU (7737 6452). Herne Hill rail. **Open** 9.30am-5pm Mon-Sat. **Credit** MC, V
This place is a rich hunting ground for second-hand children's clothes and school uniforms, along with maternity fashion.
Buggy access.

Clothes & Toys on the Web

Clothes

www.alexandalexa.com
If it's stylish, it's probably stocked here, from classics such as Cacharel to hip newcomers like Japanese brand Muchacha.

www.belleanddean.co.uk
Distinctive, etching-style animal drawings adorn the organic cotton sleepsuits, tank tops and T-shirts; prices are a steal.

www.dotanddaisy.co.uk
Dot and Daisy specialises in children's nightwear and bedlinen, stocking lines by Albetta, Frilly Lily, Powellcraft and more.

www.dandystar.com
Dandy eschews brash, lurid slogan Ts in favour of sweet, '70s-style designs with an appealingly worn-in, vintage look.

www.ellaandotto.com
The crisp colour prints on Ella & Otto products make the children's pyjamas, toddler sleeping bags, cot bedding and other accessories very appealing.

www.jakeandmaya.co.uk
A London-based mum started designing kids' clothes when her own two – Jake and Maya – were born. And lo, a range of super-cute coats, dresses, tunics and trousers was born.

www.jakesofsoho.co.uk
A percentage of the profits from Jakes goes towards the future of Jake, a boy with cerebral palsy. Kidswear consists of distinctive 'Lucky 7' slogan T-shirts (£12.50) and sweatshirts.

www.littlefashiongallery.com
Labels on this cult kids' fashion site range from Paul & Joe and Little Marc to lesser-known names: check out Swedish brand Mini Rodini's guitar-print Ts.

www.mashngravy.com
Scandinavian brands Katvig, Mini A Ture and Molo, British brands Let Them Eat Cake and Dandy Star, and more.

www.nippaz.com
One of the original purveyors of edgy, motto-print T-shirts.

www.noaddedsugar.co.uk
Once best known for its bold slogan prints, No Added Sugar now offers more subtle lines: the ruffled, floral dresses are lovely.

www.nordickids.co.uk
Some of the best childrenswear in the world hails from Scandinavia. Check out the cream of the crop, with Plastisock, Mini Rodini, Smafolk and more.

www.peaceandjam.co.uk
From daywear to partywear to footwear, this website stocks the lot. Labels include Converse, Elodie Details and Pepe Jeans.

www.snuglo.com
Lisa Quinn's range is typified by hip colours and bold type: 'I want chips, chocolate and cake' is a best-seller.

www.vincentshoestore.com
This Swedish company prides itself on its affordable, colourful kids' footwear. The range includes appealing gumboots, leather daisy-dotted baby shoes and patent Mary Janes.

Consumer

SHOES

Brian's Shoes
*2 Halleswelle Parade, Finchley Road, NW11
0DL (8455 7001, www.briansshoes.com).
Finchley Central or Golders Green tube.*
Open 9.15am-5.15pm Mon-Sat; 10.30am-
1.30pm Sun. **Credit** MC, V.

Brian's has kitted out generations of kids and
is known for its expert fittings.
Buggy access.

Cubs
*42 Heath Street, NW3 6TE (7431 0018).
Hampstead tube.* **Open** 10am-6pm Mon-Sat;
noon-6pm Sun. **Credit** AmEx, MC, V.

www.weeclothing.co.uk
Organic cotton T-shirts, sweatshirts
and sleepsuits with cute and colourful
felt animal designs on the front.

Toys

www.beasbeastlies.co.uk
Bea's Beastlies are a range of
handmade knitted critters with
personality.

www.believe-you-can.com
Fairy-themed dolls, mobiles, cushions
and hair accessories, plus gorgeous
animal bags. It's all fair trade too.

www.brightminds.co.uk
Sparky ideas that make learning fun,
from flowering magic gardens to
'explosive experiment' kits and slime
laboratories.

www.bumpto3.com
Traditional toys (baby walkers,
first bicycle, mini easels) and fun
newcomers – like the ingenious
build-your-own saxoflute.

www.gltc.co.uk
Everything from simple flower-pressing
kits and bubble-makers to spectacular
galleon-shaped climbing frames and
toy kitchens.

www.just-gorgeous.com
They stock the fabulous Miller Goodman
ShapeMaker wooden blocks, Brio toys
and Esthex musical animals, among
other things.

www.ladybirdprints.com
Choose an image from Ladybird Books'
archive and order it as a print or canvas;
Peter and Jane peering from a wigwam or

the cover of *Ned the Lonely Donkey* are
perfect for nostalgia-tinged nurseries.

www.lapinandme.co.uk
Lapin & Me sells the sweetest
toys we've ever seen: tin tea sets,
colouring-in sticker sets and reprinted
'40s storybooks.

www.larkmade.com
A small but sweet range of fair trade
gifts and soft toys, including quirky
cupcake- and doughnut-shaped
knitted rattles.

www.nigelsecostore.com
Everything in Nigel's online store
is eco-friendly. Choose between a
wooden puzzle map of Britain, wind-up
animal torches and animal-shaped
solar nightlights.

www.oregonscientific.co.uk
Oregon Scientific stocks a range
of children's toy laptops (featuring
educational games) that won't break
the bank.

www.ptolemytoys.co.uk
Ptolemy Toys sells fabulous toys,
baby products, dressing-up clothes
and educational goodies.

www.silverjungle.com
Beautiful paperback animal books
for small children and hardback
books for older children that relate
facts about endangered species.
A proportion of the cover price goes
towards protecting them.

www.sparrowkids.co.uk
Gorgeous felt kits for crafty children
aged five and up: available patterns
range from bird-shaped bags to rocket
pencil cases.

Consumer

This compact shoe shop has an impressive range of shoes for babies and children. Staff are friendly and patient, calmly measuring feet and fetching numerous pairs out of the store room until they are satisfied with the fit. Brands include Start-rite, Ricosta, Babybotte, Geox and Ralph Lauren, and there are plenty of wellies too. Children are enticed into being good with the promise of a free balloon.
Buggy access.

John Barnett
137-139 Lordship Lane, SE22 8HX (8693 5145). East Dulwich rail. **Open** 9.30am-5.30pm Mon-Sat; 11am-5pm Sun. **Credit** AmEx, MC, V.
This long-established Dulwich shoe shop has a great section for children. Brands include Clark's, Ecco, Skechers, Dr Martens and Kickers.
Buggy access. Disabled access.

Little Me
141 Hamilton Road, NW11 9EG (8209 0440). Brent Cross tube. **Open** 10.30am-6.15pm Mon-Thur; 10.30am-3pm Fri; 11am-4pm Sun. **Credit** MC, V.
A wide range of continental children's shoes, fitted with a precision shoe-measuring system.
Buggy access.

Merlin Shoes
44 Westow Street, SE19 3AH (8771 5194). Crystal Palace rail. **Open** 9.30am-5.30pm Mon-Sat. **Credit** MC, V.
Experienced, patient shoe fitters and a wide range of footwear make this place a firm favourite with local families.
Buggy access. Disabled access.

One Small Step One Giant Leap
3 Blenheim Crescent, W11 2EE (7243 0535, www.onesmallsteponegiantleap.com). Ladbroke Grove or Notting Hill Gate tube. **Open** 10am-6pm Mon-Fri; 9am-6pm Sat; 11am-5pm Sun. **Credit** MC, V.
Live near an outpost of this award-winning children's shoe shop and you'll never have to choose between comfort and style. Summer sandals, gumboots, Crocs, football boots, trainers and school sensibles are all present. The Bannock gauge is used for measuring, and staff take time to ensure a proper fit. A thoughtfully assembled range of labels runs the gamut from practical (Start-rite, Ecco, Ricosta) to playful (Lelli Kelly, Pom d'Api).
Buggy access.
Branches throughout the city.

Papillon
43 Elizabeth Street, SW1W 9PP (7730 6690, www.papillon4children.com). Sloane Square tube or Victoria tube/rail. **Open** 10am-6pm Mon-Fri; 10am-5pm Sat. **Credit** MC, V. **Map** p332 G10.
Ballet-style pumps in a rainbow of colours and prints feature largely here, but there are also school shoes and beach sandals for boys and girls, flip-flops, moccasins and bridesmaid shoes. Socks and tights are also sold, along with tiny, ribbon-tie baby shoes.
Buggy access.

Red Shoes
30 Topsfield Parade, N8 8PT (8341 9555). Finsbury Park tube/rail, then bus 41, W7. **Open** 10am-5.30pm Mon-Sat; noon-4.30pm Sun. **Credit** MC, V.
Fit and comfort are the key words at this child-friendly shoe shop, where children can match their parents with fashionable big brands such as Crocs, Birkenstock, Ecco and Camper.
Buggy access.

Shoe Station
3 Station Approach, Kew, Surrey TW9 3QB (8940 9905, www.theshoestation.co.uk). Kew Gardens tube. **Open** 9am-6pm Mon-Sat; 11am-5pm Sun. **Credit** MC, V.
Run by two mothers, the Station is a cheery little independent, staffed by trained Start-rite fitters. Children's shoes for every occasion are available, from child's size 2 to adult size 7. Brands include Start-rite (of course), Ricosta, Aster, Naturino, Babybotte, TTY, Mod8, Pom d'Api, Geox, Nike, Puma, Birkenstock, Primigi and Freed. Football boots, ballet shoes, slippers and wellies are also stocked.
Buggy access.

TOYS & GIFTS

Art Stationers/Green's Village Toy Shop
31 Dulwich Village, SE21 7BN (8693 5938). North Dulwich rail. **Open** 9am-5.30pm Mon-Sat. **Credit** MC, V.
The shop at the front is an Aladdin's cave of arts and crafts-related bits and pieces: pipe cleaners, beads, pompoms, stick-on jewels, sequins and beads, along with paints, pastels, stationery, clay and other materials. That's just half the story, though. A big sign bearing the legend TOYS has the children cantering down the passage for the booty: Sylvanian Families,

Petit Chou. *See p298.*

Playmobil, Crayola, Lego, Warhammer and other big brands. Lesser-spotted companies such as Tantrix and Wow are also represented. The enormous pocket money-priced range goes from a rubber goldfish to a magnetic car racer. *Buggy access.*

Benjamin Pollock's Toyshop

44 The Market, WC2E 8RF (7379 7866, www.pollocks-coventgarden.co.uk). Covent Garden tube. **Open** 10.30am-6pm Mon-Wed; Fri, Sat; 10.30am-7pm Thur; 11am-4pm Sun. **Credit** AmEx, MC, V. **Map** p333 L7.

In the South Piazza of the covered market in Covent Garden, this toy shop is crammed with traditional toys of all descriptions. There's something to appeal to everyone somewhere on the floor-to-ceiling shelves and hanging from the ceiling. It's like a toy shop from a film set. Look out for the beautiful marionettes, Russian dolls, spinning tops, glove puppets, jack-in-the-boxes and toy soldiers. They even stock praxinoscopes, which let children explore simple animation techniques. As you might imagine from a shop named after one of the greatest Victorian toy theatre makers, Benjamin Pollock's Toyshop is probably best known for its delightful selection of toy theatres. Choose between matchbox theatre sets, magnetic theatres or shadow puppet theatres (all for under £20), or go for something more lavish, like the Neptune wooden theatre with nine wooden characters, made by hand in Italy and priced at £195. *Buggy accesss. Mail order.*

Chelsea Toys

Chelsea Green, 53 Godfrey Street, SW3 3SX (7352 1718, www.chelseatoys.co.uk). South Kensington tube. **Open** 10am-5.30pm Mon-Thur; 10am-6pm Fri, Sat. **Credit** AmEx, MC, V. **Map** p329 E11.

This Chelsea favourite has changed its name and external look, but it's still full of fantastic toys, games and other child-friendly products. Chelsea Toys is a treasure trove of model cars, trains, planes and helicopters. There are ride-on toys, musical boxes, stationary sets, dressing-up clothes and building blocks, plus musical boxes, puzzles and board games; not forgetting unusual puppets and build-your-own wooden toys. Also, if you're looking to commission a top-of-the-range tree house for the garden, this is the place to come. They're not cheap, but some of them, particularly the designs created by Norfolk-based Flights of Fantasy, look like they've been lifted straight out of a fairytale book. *Buggy accesss. Delivery service.*

Davenports Magic Shop

7 Charing Cross Underground Shopping Arcade, WC2N 4HZ (7836 0408, www.davenportsmagic.co.uk). Charing Cross or Embankment tube. **Open** 9.30am-5.30pm Mon-Fri; 10.30am-4.30pm Sat. **Credit** AmEx, MC, V. **Map** p333 L7.

Kids love magic tricks. But even more than watching them, they like performing them. For magic and mystery, there's no better place in London than Davenports. It's lent an extra sense of enigma and otherworldliness by being at the end of one of the tunnels under Charing Cross station. When you walk in, it looks an unlikely source of joy, with its gloomy interior, frayed carpets and old-fashioned cabinets. But the staff in Davenports are enthusiasts and every customer gets their own magic display, as tricks are gleefully demonstrated until satisfaction has been reached. They'll help you get the right trick for any age group – stock goes from prank props to sophisticated card tricks and right up to complex illusions. Davenports has a range of items made exclusively for the shop, and also runs Magic Courses for beginners 16 years and over. *Delivery service.*

Consumer

Disney Store

360-366 Oxford Street, W1N 9HA (7491 9136, www.disneystore.co.uk). Bond Street tube. **Open** 9am-9pm Mon-Sat; noon-6pm Sun. **Credit** AmEx, MC, V. **Map** p330 H6.
Children make a beeline for this shrine to all things Disney, which sells figurines, stationery, toys, costumes and all manner of merchandise. Enduring favourites are the character dolls, lunchboxes, costumes and classic DVDs.
Buggy access. Disabled access.
Branches 10 The Piazza, WC2E 8HD (7836 5037); 1090-1091 Westfield Shopping Centre, W12 7GD (8811 1162).

Dotty Dot

67A St Helen's Gardens, W10 6LL (7460 3405, www.dotty-dot.com). Ladbroke Grove tube. **Open** 10.30am-5pm Tue-Sat. **Credit** MC, V.
This lovely shop stocks unusual products like the colourful modernist alphabet blocks by Alexander Girard, playful children's books designed by Katsumi Komogata, and knitted and felt animals and characters designed by Donna Wilson, who studied at the Royal College of Art. It also has a range of childhood favourites like spinning tops, craft kits, push-along toys and hobby horses. The shop has a self-confessed mission to move away from the culture of throwaway plastic rubbish. The toys are beautifully made and fashioned out of sustainable materials like wood and fabric.
Buggy access. Disabled access.

Early Learning Centre

36 King's Road, SW3 4UD (7581 5764, www.elc.co.uk). Sloane Square tube. **Open** 9.30am-6pm Mon-Sat; 11am-6pm Sun. **Credit** AmEx, MC, V. **Map** p329 F11.
A presence on British high streets since the 1970s, ELC has stuck to its ethos of encouraging imaginative play for babies and young children. Everything is sturdy, brightly coloured and reasonably priced. On Tuesday mornings (10am-noon), kids can get hands-on with the toys or try some craft activities at the drop-in play sessions.
Buggy access. Delivery service.
Branches throughout the city.

Fagin's Toys

84 Fortis Green Road, N10 3HN (8444 0282). East Finchley tube, then bus 102, 234. **Open** 9am-5.30pm Mon-Sat; 10am-3pm Sun. **Credit** MC, V.

Kids' Corner
East Dulwich

The buggies began rolling into this suburban patch of south London in the 1990s. Now the sprog scene centres around residential Northcross Road, home of original trendsetter the **Blue Mountain Café** (*see p244*), then spills out on to Lordship Lane. Although local favourite the Never Ending Story Bookshop has sadly now, er, ended, in its place sits jolly card shop **Postmark** (*see p299*), and there's plenty else to catch the eye and lighten the wallet.

Swish shoe boutique **Jolie à Pied** (*see p285*) stocks a small range of high-end footwear for toddlers and private-schooled princesses from the likes of Spanish label Maá. The more established **Oranges & Lemons** (*see p289*) has chic maternity clothes and babywear, while further down Northcross Road, the wonderful **Hope & Greenwood** (20 Northcross Road, SE22 9EU, 8613 1777, www.hopeandgreenwood.co.uk) lures you in with '40s dance tunes on the wireless and shelves stacked with jars of gobstoppers and lemon bonbons.

Back on Lordship Lane, the Dulwich branch of **Soup Dragon** (*see p276*) is an Aladdin's cave of groovy clothes, toys and micro scooters. The south London branch of the **JoJo Maman Bébé** (*see p274*) chain sits at one end of the high street; further down, the sensible **John Barnett** (*see p294*) makes sure little feet have something practical to put on.

For something altogether less sensible, a branch of toyshop **Just Williams** (*see p297*), will keep everyone happy. Also look out for newcomer **Colour Makes People Happy** (*see p218*), an eco-friendly paint shop offering clog painting sessions for children.

Consumer

Along with toys from the likes of Galt, Orchard, Brio, Lego, Playmobil, Meccano and Sylvanian Families, Fagin's has a central table of penny dreadfuls for party bags. Have fun choosing between little rubber fish and stretching aliens, powerballs, pots of slime, colouring sets and silk purses; prices run from 15p for a fortune-telling fish to £1.69 for magnetic marbles.
Buggy access. Disabled access. Play area.

Hamleys

188-196 Regent Street, W1B 5BT (0870 333 2455, www.hamleys.com). Oxford Circus tube. **Open** 10am-8pm Mon-Wed, Fri; 10am-9pm Thur; 9am-8pm Sat; noon-9pm Sun. **Credit** AmEx, DC, MC, V. **Map** p332 J7.

Arranged on seven noisy, bustling floors, with implausibly perky demonstrators, Hamleys has become a prime tourist draw. Most must-have toys are here – though Hamleys isn't immune to pre-Christmas panic when the cult toy of the moment becomes scarce. Down in the basement are the gadgets and construction toys, while the ground floor is devoted to soft toys and magic tricks. Floor one is games, science kits and sweets, two is for preschoolers, three is girls' stuff, four hobbies, models and remote control toys, and five is boys' toys and a nice little café. Though racing round the store is thrilling enough for most children, large-scale family events are held on site throughout the year. Check the schedule to find out who's planning to pop in; Scooby-Doo, perhaps, or SpongeBob SquarePants. In-store parties are also offered – although at £4,500 for ten kids, the Hamleys Sleepover is best left to young billionaires.
Buggy access. Café. Delivery service. Disabled access. Nappy-changing facilities. Play areas.

Happy Returns

36 Rosslyn Hill, NW3 1NH (7435 2431). Hampstead tube. **Open** 10am-5.30pm Mon-Fri; 10am-6pm Sat; noon-5.30pm Sun. **Credit** MC, V.

This fairly small toy shop doesn't have bags of choice, but the range is a clever mix of products with prices to suit everyone. Aimed at the zero to five age group, the shop is geared largely towards parties. Stock up on the celebration essentials then go hunting for presents. Look out for classics like glow stars or Etch-A-Sketch, or more modern toys by Jellycat; there's a big Sylvanian Families collection, plus toys by Galt, Schleich and Playmobil, doll's house accessories by Plan, and jolly chunky plastics by Wow Toys.
Buggy access.

Honeyjam

2 Blenheim Crescent, W11 1NN (7243 0449, www.honeyjam.co.uk). Ladbroke Grove tube. **Open** 10am-6pm Mon-Sat; 11am-4pm Sun. **Credit** MC, V.

Spinning tops, skipping ropes and traditional wooden toys from companies like Bigjigs and Le Toy Van delight nostalgia-hungry parents, while children deliberate over the pocket-money purchases. In the dressing-up section, boys can be transformed into knights and pirates, while little girls are enchanted by the reversible costumes: Snow White on one side and Sleeping Beauty on the other, or Cinderella in her ballgown and rags. There's a small collection of baby and infant clothes and an ever-expanding range of fair trade and eco-friendly products.
Buggy access. Disabled access.

Hoxton Street Monster Supplies

159 Hoxton Street, N1 6PJ (7729 4159, www.ministryofstories.org). Hoxton rail. **Open** 11am-5pm Sat, Sun. **Credit** MC, V.

This unusual shop sells monster supplies – freshly extricated nails, pickled eyeballs, farts in a jar and tins of unease. There are limited edition prints and stories, and the whole thing is a front for the creative writing workshops that go on behind the secret door. *See p10* **Den of Equity.**
Buggy access. Disabled access: toilet.

Just Williams

18 Half Moon Lane, SE24 9HU (7733 9995). Herne Hill rail. **Open** 9.30am-6pm Mon-Sat. **Credit** MC, V.

A blue-painted child's paradise, Just Williams has some top names in toys, with plenty of goodies from Brio, Sylvanians, Schleich and Playmobil. Traditionalists will approve of the wooden playthings from the likes of Bigjigs, Plan Toys, Pintoy and Santas, while Warhammer enthralls more bloodthirsty boys.
Buggy access.
Branches 106 Grove Vale, SE22 8DR (8299 3444).

Lapin and Me

14 Ezra Street, Columbia Road, E2 7RH (7739 4384, www.lapinandme.co.uk). Hoxton rail. **Open** 9.30am-3.30pm Sun. **Credit** AmEx, MC, V.

A treasure trove for lovers of unique items, Lapin and Me – set up by mother and daughter Madeleine and Delphine – had been a successful website for several years before

Consumer

opening a shop in 2009 just by Columbia Road market. The shop is beautifully laid out with colourful and enticing toys, many of them brought over from France and exclusive in the UK. Vibrant tea sets sit next to painted wooden guitars, knitted cuddle toys, unusual craft kits and stylish pull-along toys – there are also a few interior and accessory treats for adults. The shop's opening hours are limited to Sundays, but that means you can make a day of it and see one of London's most interesting street markets in full swing.
Buggy access. Delivery service.

Letterbox

99 Northcote Road, SW11 6PL (0844 573 4561, www.letterbox.co.uk). Clapham Junction tube/rail. **Open** 9am-6pm Mon-Sat; 11am-5pm Sun. **Credit** MC, V.
The popular catalogue for toys, games and bedroom accessories manifests itself in 3D form for the first time in London. This site on Northcote Road opened late in 2010 and its position along the main shopping thoroughfare in south London's nappy valley should ensure its success. Letterbox is great for traditional wooden toys, doll's houses, educational toddler toys, personalised gifts and dressing-up clothes for the 0-6 range.
Buggy access. Disabled access. Mail order.

Little Rascals

140 Merton Road, SW19 1EH (8542 9979). South Wimbledon tube. **Open** 9am-5.30pm Tue-Sat. **Credit** AmEx, MC, V.
Aimed at under-fives, this friendly, family-run local shop is full of appealing toys and gifts. Check out the handmade wooden book ends and money-boxes, and colourful greetings cards; for younger babies, there are Grobag sleeping bags and Taggies comforter blankets.
Buggy access.

Mystical Fairies

12 Flask Walk, NW3 1HE (7431 1888, www.mysticalfairies.co.uk). Hampstead tube. **Open** 10am-6pm Mon-Sat; 11am-6pm Sun. **Credit** MC, V.
There are several thousand small and pretty things in this shop, at least half of them hanging from silver branches overhead. Most of the merchandise is pink or sparkly and features princesses, ballerinas, flower fairies, pixies and elves. The back of the shop is an Aladdin's cave of costumes (mostly for girls, though there are some token wizard and pirate outfits). It's hard to leave empty-handed faced with this choice;

tea sets, trinkets, books, sticker sets, stationery, slippers, dressing gowns, pyjamas and duvet covers, wands, wings, craft sets and jewellery. Staff also run parties in the shop's fairy light-decked Enchanted Garden (the basement). Check the website for fairy school dates.
Buggy access.
Branch Bluewater Shopping Centre, Greenhithe, Kent DA9 9ST (01322 624997).

Never Never Land

3 Midhurst Parade, Fortis Green, N10 3EJ (8883 3997, www.never-never-land.co.uk). East Finchley tube. **Open** 10am-5pm Tue, Wed, Fri, Sat. **Credit** MC, V.
Much like the Sylvanian Families shop in Finsbury Park (*see p300*), this shop – around the corner from the main stretch of Muswell Hill's Fortis Green Road – is easily missed unless you know it's here. The main event is a fabulous selection of dolls' houses – many designs are unique to the shop. You can buy them flatpacked, pre-made or pre-made and painted, depending on your budget and your desire to participate in some DIY in miniature. The shop also stocks a delightfully detailed range of furniture and accessories for the doll's house interiors. Never Never Land may be a specialist shop, but it's not exclusive; service is friendly and there are plenty of other enticements for children of all interests, including castles, wooden kitchens, toys, puppets and appealing ride-on toys.

Patrick's Toys & Models

107-111 Lillie Road, SW6 7SX (7385 9864, www.patrickstoys.co.uk). Fulham Broadway tube. **Open** 9.30am-5.30pm Mon-Sat. **Credit** MC, V.
One of London's biggest toy and model shops, Patrick's is a major service agent for Hornby and Scalextric, attracting adult enthusiasts as well as kids. The model department specialises in rockets, planes, cars, military and sci-fi, while the general toy department has wooden toys, board games, soft toys and doll's houses.
Buggy access. Delivery service (local). Disabled access.

Petit Chou

15 St Christopher's Place, W1U 1NR (7486 3637, www.petitchou.co.uk). Bond Street tube. **Open** 10.30am-6.30pm Mon-Sat; noon-5pm Sun. **Credit** MC, V. **Map** p330 H6.
Artists Marty St James and Iveta Petrakova opened this shop just off exclusive Wigmore Street in 2005. The toys inside cater for the play

Consumer

Kids' Corner
Notting Hill

The leafy streets around Ladbroke Grove and Notting Hill are the original stamping ground of the yummy mummies and their offspring. Here, organic cotton-clad babies recline in expensive three-wheelers while their parents stroll around the shops; the streets leading off Portobello Road are sprinkled with brilliant boutiques and specialist shops, stocking all the smartest brands alongside trendsetting lesser-known labels.

For stylish children's clothing, there's no end of choice; start at the Ladbroke Grove (and cheaper) end of Portobello Road with **Sasti** (see p287) for hardwearing, 1970s-inspired designs. Girls will adore the romantic day dresses and party frocks at **I Love Gorgeous** (see p289), made from deliciously floaty fabrics; to ensure your child doesn't look out of place on the Riviera, **Petit Aimé** (see p286) stocks the best French childrenswear designers, while the clothes at **Marie Chantal** (see p289) are designed by no lesser figure than the Crown Princess of Greece. **Their Nibs** (see p288) also continues to enchant both parents and children with its vintage-inspired designs and

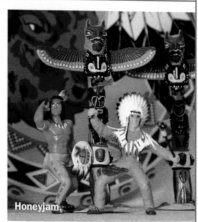

Honeyjam.

quirky prints; pirate-printed shirts and pyjamas for the chaps, and a sweet fairy design for girls. To complete the look, shoe store **One Small Step One Giant Leap** (see p294) has plenty of west London sole.

Old-fashioned toys and games can be found at the charming **Honeyjam** (see p297) on Portobello Road, run by two fabulously fashionable friends.

requirements of children from babies to ten-year-olds. The owners' artistic eye means that everything is impeccably stylish, and there's an emphasis on wooden and hand-crafted toys from all over the world. Unusual items include a London Routemaster with removable passengers, two vintage model pedal cars that come in green and red, floor puzzles in a suitcase and a pull-along construction train. Petit Chou also stocks puppet theatres, doll's houses, musical and role play toys.
Buggy access. Delivery service. Disabled access. Nappy-changing facilities. Play area.

Pollock's Toy Shop
1 Scala Street, W1T 2HL (7636 3452, www.pollockstoymuseum.com). Goodge Street tube. **Open** 10am-5pm Mon-Sat. **Credit** AmEx, MC, V. **Map** p330 J5.

These two adjacent townhouses in the heart of Fitzrovia are crammed with toys. Pollock's Toy Museum (see p88) inhabits most of the warren of rooms inside, but downstairs there's also a toy shop (the museum and shop are named after Benjamin Pollock, the last of the Victorian theatrical printers). It has plenty of pocket money items for sale, as well as larger toys; you'll find animal masks, wind-up music boxes, tin robots, games and cards, as well as reproduction cardboard theatres.
Buggy access.

Postmark
59 Northcross Road, SE22 9ET (8693 1133). East Dulwich rail. **Open** 10am-5.30pm Mon-Sat; 11am-5pm Sun. **Credit** MC, V.
Unable to live up to its name, the Never Ending Story Bookshop closed down a few years ago.

Its former premises are now occupied by this cheerful card shop, which also sells school stationery and toys for babies and toddlers. *Buggy access.*
Branch 123 Balham High Road, SW12 9AR (8675 7272).

Puppet Planet

787 Wandsworth Road, SW8 3JQ (07900 975276, www.puppetplanet.co.uk). Wandsworth Road rail. **Open** usually 9am-5pm Mon-Sat (call in advance). **Credit** AmEx, MC, V.
Children absolutely love browsing among the glove puppets and marionettes on the shelves of this puppet emporium, which also has a fabulous array of display puppets from around the world. Within seconds of entering the shop, youngsters will be creating full-blown productions in the hands-on corner, but be ready for some pressure to purloin a full blown puppet theatre (some of which are designed to hang from doorways) to take home.
Buggy access. Delivery service. Disabled access. Play area.

QT Toys

90 Northcote Road, SW11 6QN (7223 8637). Clapham Junction rail. **Open** 9.30am-5.30pm daily. **Credit** MC, V.
From Lego and Sylvanian Families sets to tubs of luridly hued Play-Doh, it's all here. There are also some educational games, craft and modelling kits and stationery for older kids.
Buggy access. Disabled access. Nappy-changing facilities.

Route 73 Kids

92 Stoke Newington Church Street, N16 0AP (7923 7873, www.route73kids.co.uk). Bus 73, 393, 476. **Open** 10am-5.30pm Mon-Sat; 11am-5pm Sun. **Credit** AmEx, MC, V.
Named after the bendy bus that chugs along Stoke Newington Church Street, this jolly toyshop caters to all budgets. A party bag-tastic table full of pocket money toys takes centre stage, and there's a great selection of traditional names such as Brio and Galt. It's geared towards parents looking for quality wooden toys rather than tacky plastic goods; PlanToys' eco-friendly rubberwood designs are particularly popular. Then there are books, puzzles, jigsaws, word games, craft packs, Jellycat animals and Starchild's soft leather baby shoes. The train and racing car tables are there to be played with.
Buggy access. Disabled access.

Snap Dragon

56 Turnham Green Terrace, W4 1QP (8995 6618). Turnham Green tube. **Open** 9.30am-6pm Mon-Sat; 11am-5pm Sun. **Credit** AmEx, MC, V.
A good general toy shop for big brands, Snap Dragon stocks a bit of everything: Lego, Playmobil, Brio and Sylvanian Families are among the biggest sellers, along with games and jigsaws from Orchard Toys and stacks of cuddly toys of all kinds. For rainy days, there's an abundance of classic board games, from Buckaroo to Boggle. There are generally a few sandpits and goalposts on the shop floor, while bulkier trampolines and wooden climbing frames by TP Toys can be ordered on request.
Buggy access. Delivery service.

Sylvanian Families

68 Mountgrove Road, N5 2LT (7226 1329, www.sylvanianfamilies.com). Finsbury Park tube/rail. **Open** 9.30am-5.30pm Mon-Fri; 9am-6pm Sat; 10am-4pm Sun. **Credit** AmEx, MC, V.
Scores of woodland critters line the shelves at this emporium of all things Sylvanian, along with every conceivable accessory. Here you can buy your favourite dressed-up animals from the numerous families, along with their homes, hospitals, schools, cars and furniture.
Buggy access.

Toy Station

6 Eton Street, Richmond, Surrey TW9 1EE (8940 4896, www.toy-station.co.uk). Richmond tube/rail. **Open** 10am-6pm Mon-Fri; 9.30am-6pm Sat; noon-5pm Sun. **Credit** (over £8) MC, V.
This bastion of good-quality playthings has two storeys filled with model animals, knights and soldiers, forts and castles, remote-controlled vehicles and more traditional wooden toys.
Buggy access. Disabled access.

Toys R Us

760 Old Kent Road, SE15 1NJ (7732 7322, www.toysrus.co.uk). Elephant & Castle tube/rail then bus 21, 56, 172. **Open** 9am-8pm Mon-Fri; 9am-7pm Sat; 11am-5pm Sun. **Credit** AmEx, MC, V.
The American retail giant generally has industrial quantities of the toy of the moment amid its mighty stockpile, though it can be hard to find an assistant.
Buggy access. Car park. Delivery service. Disabled access. Nappy-changing facilities.
Branches throughout the city.

Consumer

Directory

Directory

GETTING AROUND

PUBLIC TRANSPORT

The prices listed for transport and services were correct at the time of going to press, but do bear in mind that some prices (especially those of tube tickets) are subject to a hike each January.

Public transport information

Full details can be found online at www.thetube.com and www.tfl.gov.uk, or alternatively by phoning 0843 222 1234.

Transport for London (TfL) also runs Travel Information Centres that provide maps and information about the tube, buses, Tramlink, riverboats, Docklands Light Railway (DLR) and national rail services within the London area. You can find them in Heathrow Airport, as well as in Liverpool Street and Victoria stations.

London TravelWatch

6 Middle Street, EC1A 7JA (7505 9000, www.london travelwatch.org.uk). **Open** Phone enquiries 9am-5pm Mon-Fri.

This is the official campaigning watchdog, monitoring customer satisfaction with transport.

Fares, Oyster cards & Travelcards

Tube and DLR fares are based on a system of six zones stretching 12 miles (20 kilometres) out from the centre of London. A cash fare of £4-£4.50 per journey applies across the tube for zones 1-6 (£3.50 excluding zone 1); customers save up to £2.50 with Oyster pay-as-you-go (*see below*). Beware of £25 on-the-spot fines for anyone caught without a ticket.

Children aged under 11 travel free on buses, DLR and the tube. If you are using only the tube, DLR, buses and trams, Oyster pay-as-you-go will always be cheaper than a Day Travelcard (*see right*). If you are using National Rail services, however, the Day Travelcard may best meet your needs (children travelling with you can buy a Day Travelcard for £2). Under-16s get free travel on buses with an Oyster photocard.

Travelcards, valid for tubes, buses, DLR and rail services, can be the cheapest way of getting around. Travelcards can be bought at stations, as well as London Travel Information Centres or newsagents.

Day Travelcards

Peak Day Travelcards can be used all day Monday to Friday (except public holidays). They cost from £7.20 (£3.60 for under-16s) for zones 1-2, with prices rising to £14.80 (£7.40 for under-16s) for zones 1-6. Most people use the off-peak Day Travelcard, which allows you to travel from 9.30am Monday to Friday and all day Saturday, Sunday and public holidays. They cost from £5.60 (£2 for under-16s) for zones 1-2, rising to £7.50 (£2.60 for under 16s) for zones 1-6.

Oyster card

The Oyster card is a travel smartcard that can be charged with Pre-Pay and/or 7-day, monthly and longer-period (including annual) travelcards and bus passes. Oyster cards are currently available to adults and under-16 photocard holders when buying a ticket. Tickets can be bought from www.oystercard.com, at tube station ticket offices, London Travel Information Centres, some National Rail station ticket offices and newsagents. A single tube journey in zone 1 using Oyster to pay-as-you-go costs £1.80 at all times (65p for under-16s, children under 11 go free).

Children

Under-16s can travel free on buses and trams; under-11s travel free on the tube (those travelling without an adult, or who look over ten, will need to carry a 5-10 Oyster photocard; call 0845 330 9876 for information). Children aged 14 or 15 need a child – or 11-15 – photocard to travel at child rate on the tube and DLR, and get free travel on buses and trams.

An 11-15 Oyster photocard is required by children aged 11-15 years to get child-rate pay as you go on the Underground or DLR, or to buy 7-day, monthly or longer period travelcards.

London Underground

The tube in rush hour (8-9.30am and 4.30-7pm Monday-Friday) is not pleasant, so it is best to travel outside these hours with children, if possible.

Using the system

Tube tickets can be purchased or Oyster cards (see left) topped up from a ticket office or self-service machine. Ticket offices in some stations close early (around 7.30pm); it's wise to carry a charged-up Oyster card to avoid being stranded.

To enter and exit the tube using an Oyster card, touch it on the yellow reader that will open the gates. Make sure you touch the card when you exit the tube, otherwise you may be fined.

There are 12 Underground lines, colour-coded on the tube map; we've provided a full map of the London Underground on the back page of this book.

Timetable

Tube trains run daily from around 5.30am (except Sunday, when they start later). The only exception is Christmas Day, when there is no service. During peak times the service should run every two or three minutes.

Times of last trains vary, but they're usually around 11.30pm-1am daily, and 30 minutes to an hour earlier on Sunday. Debates continue as to whether to run the tube an hour later at weekends. The only all-night public transport is by night bus.

Fares

The single fare for adults within zone 1 is £4 (Oyster fare £1.60); for zones 1-2 it's £4 (Oyster fare £2.20 or £1.60). For zones 1-6 it's £4 (Oyster fare £3.80 or £2.20). The single fare for 11-15s in zones 1-6 is £2.20 (Oyster fare 65p with a valid 11-15 Oyster photocard), £1.70 for zones 2-6 (Oyster fare 65p). Children under 11 travel free at all times.

Docklands Light Railway (DLR)

The DLR (7363 9700, www.dlr.co.uk) runs driverless trains from Bank or Tower Gateway, close to Tower Hill tube (Circle and District lines), to Stratford, Beckton and the Isle of Dogs, then south of the river to Greenwich, Deptford and Lewisham. Trains run 5.30am to 12.30am Monday to Saturday and 7am to 11.30pm Sunday.

Fares

The single fare for adults within zone 1 is £4 (Oyster fare £1.80). For zones 1-2 it's £4 (Oyster fare £2.30 or £1.80). The zones 1-6 single fare is £4.50 (Oyster fare £4.20 or £2.40). In zones 2-3 it is £3.50 (£1.30 Oyster). Children under 11 travel free. Children aged 11-15 pay £2 (Oyster fare 65p) or £1.60 for zones 2-6 (Oyster fare 65p), while zones 2-3 for children is 80p (65p Oyster).

One-day 'Rail & River Rover' tickets combine unlimited DLR travel with hop-on, hop-off boat travel on City Cruises between Greenwich, Tower, Waterloo and Westminster piers. Tickets cost £14.50 for adults, £7.25 for kids and £37 (2 adults and up to 3 children under 16) for a family pass; under-5s go free.

Buses

New buses, with low floors for wheelchair and buggy users, and bendy buses with multiple-door entry and the 'pay before you board' schemes now make up much of the fleet. Buses in central London also require you to have an Oyster card or buy a ticket before boarding from pavement ticket machines. Be sure to have a ticket or swiped Oyster card on you while travelling: inspectors can slap a £25 fine on fare-dodgers. Of the famous open-platform Routemaster fleet, only Heritage routes 9 and 15 remain in central London.

Using an Oyster card (see p302) to pay as you go costs £1.20 at all times; the most you will pay a day is £3.90 on buses and trams. Paying by cash at the time of travel costs £2 per trip.

Children under 16 and students up to age 18 and resident in London travel free on buses. New Deal and 16+ Oyster fare is half-price (60p) for those in education outside London.

Night buses

Many night buses run 24 hours a day, seven days a week, and some special night buses with an 'N' prefix to the route number operate from about 11pm to 6am. Most services run every 15 to 30 minutes, but many busier routes have a bus around every ten minutes. Travelcards and Bus Passes can be used on night buses until 4.30am on the day after they expire. Oyster Pre-Pay and bus Saver tickets are also valid on night buses.

Green Line buses

Green Line buses (0844 801 7261, www.greenline.co.uk) serve the suburbs and towns within a 40-mile (64km) radius of London. Their main departure point is Ecclestone Bridge, SW1 (Colonnades Coach Station, behind Victoria).

Directory

Coaches

National Express (0871 781 8181, www.national express.com) runs routes to most parts of the country; coaches depart from **Victoria Coach Station**, a five-minute walk from Victoria rail and tube stations.

Victoria Coach Station

164 Buckingham Palace Road, SW1W 9TP (0871 781 8181, www.tfl.gov.uk/vcs). Victoria tube/rail. **Map** p332 H1. National Express, which travels to continental Europe as Eurolines, is based at Victoria Coach Station.

Rail services

Independently run services leave from the main rail stations. Travelcards are valid on services within the right zones. The very useful London Overground network, run by TFL (0845 601 4867, www.tfl.gov.uk/rail) extends across London, skirting the centre, and is currently being expanded.

If you've lost property at an overground station or on a train, call 0845 330 9882; an operator will then connect you to the appropriate station.

Family & Friends Railcard

www.family-railcard.co.uk. This is worth buying if you make even a couple of long rail journeys per year with the children, as the discounts it gives are substantial. The card costs £26 and lasts one year. Valid across Britain, it gives travellers with children one year of discounts from standard rail fares (a third off adult fares, 60 per cent off child fares, £1 minimum fare). Under-fives travel free. Up to two adults can be named as cardholders – they do not have to be related. The minimum group size is one cardholder and one child aged five to 15; maximum group size with one cardholder is four adults and four children. To pick up a form for the Family & Friends Railcard, visit your local staffed station.

London's mainline stations

Charing Cross *Strand, WC2N 5HS.* **Map** p333 L7.
For trains to and from south-east England (including Dover, Folkestone and Ramsgate).
Euston *Euston Road, NW1 1BN.* **Map** p331 K3.
For trains to and from north and north-west England and Scotland, and a line north to Watford.
King's Cross *Euston Road, N1 9AP.* **Map** p331 L2.
For trains to and from north and north-east England and Scotland, and suburban lines to north London.
Liverpool Street *Liverpool Street, EC2M 7PD.* **Map** p335 R5.
For trains to and from the east coast, Stansted Airport and East Anglia, and services to east and north-east London.
London Bridge *London Bridge Street, SE1 2SW.* **Map** p335 Q8.
For trains to Kent, Sussex, Surrey and south London suburbs.
Paddington *Praed Street, W2 1HB.* **Map** p327 D5.
For trains to and from west and south-west England, South Wales and the Midlands.
Victoria *115 Buckingham Palace Road, SW1W 9SJ.* **Map** p332 H10.
For fast trains to and from the channel ports (Folkestone, Dover, Newhaven); for trains to and from Gatwick Airport, and suburban services to south and south-east London.
Waterloo *York Road, SE1 7NZ.* **Map** p335 M9.
For fast trains to and from the south and south-west of England (Portsmouth, Southampton, Dorset, Devon), and suburban services to south London.

Tramlink

Trams run between Beckenham, Croydon, Addington and Wimbledon. Travelcards and bus passes taking in zones 3-6 can be used on trams; cash single fares cost £2 (Oyster fare £1.20 or 60p for 16- to 17-year-old photocard holders).

Water transport

The times of London's assortment of river services vary, but most operate every 20 minutes to hourly between 10.30am and 5pm, with more frequent services during the summer. Call the operators for schedules, or see www.tfl.gov.uk. Travelcard holders can expect one-third off scheduled riverboat fares.

Thames Clippers (0870 781 5049, www.thames clippers.com) runs a commuter boat service. Clippers stop at all London piers, including Embankment, Blackfriars, Bankside, London Bridge and Tower (near Tower Bridge). The names in bold below are the names of piers.

Royal Arsenal Woolwich – **Greenwich** (15mins) – **Masthouse Terrace** (4mins) – **Greenland Dock** (4mins) – **Canary Wharf** (5mins) – **Tower** (9mins) – **London Bridge** (4mins) – **Bankside**

Directory

(4mins) – **Blackfriars** (3mins) – **Embankment** (6mins); Thames Clippers (*see p304*).

Westminster – **Embankment** (5 mins) – **Festival** (5mins) – **London Bridge** (10mins) – **St Katharine's** (5mins); Crown River 7936 2033, www.crownriver.com.

Westminster – Greenwich (1hr); Thames River Services 7930 4097, www.westminsterpier.co.uk.

Westminster – Kew (1hr 30mins) – **Richmond** (30mins) – **Hampton Court** (1hr 30mins); Westminster Passenger Service Association 7930 2062, www.wpsa.co.uk.

Westminster – Tower (40mins); City Cruises 7740 0400, www.citycruises.com.

TAXIS

Black cabs

Licensed London taxis are known as black cabs – even though they now come in a wide variety of colours – and are a quintessential feature of London life. Drivers of black cabs must pass a test called the Knowledge to prove they know every street in central London and the shortest route to it. If a taxi's yellow 'For Hire' sign is switched on, it can be hailed. If a taxi stops, the cabbie must take you to your destination, provided it's within seven miles. Expect to pay slightly higher rates after 8pm on weekdays and all weekend.

You can book black cabs in advance. Both Radio

Taxis (7272 0272, www.radiotaxis.co.uk) and Dial-a-Cab (cash bookings 7253 5000, credit card bookings 7426 3420, www.dialacab.co.uk) run 24-hour services for black cabs (there's a booking fee in addition to the regular fare). Enquiries or complaints about black cabs should be made to the Public Carriage Office (www.tfl.gov.uk).

Minicabs

Be sure to use only licensed firms and avoid minicab drivers who tout for business on the street. There are plenty of trustworthy and licensed local minicab firms around in all areas, including Lady Cabs (7272 3300, www.ladyminicabs.co.uk), which employs only women drivers, and Addison Lee (0844 800 6677, www.addisonlee. com). Whoever you use, it's always a good idea to ask the price when you book and confirm it with the driver when the car arrives.

DRIVING

Congestion charge

Everyone driving into central London between 7am and 6pm Monday to Friday has to pay a £10 fee (£9 if you're

pre-registered with Autopay). Expect a fine of £60 if you fail to do so (rising to £120 if you delay payment).

Passes can be bought from newsagents, garages and NCP car parks; the scheme is enforced by CCTV cameras. You can pay by phone or online any time until midnight during the day of entry, or it's an extra £2 on the day following the day of travel. Payments are accepted until midnight on the next charging day after a vehicle has entered the zone. The Western extension of the Congestion Charge zone (which covered Chelsea, Kensington, Knightsbridge, Bayswater and Notting Hill) was scrapped at the beginning of 2011.

For information, phone 0845 900 1234 or go to www.cclondon.com. The Congestion Charge zone is marked on the Central London by Area map, *see p324.*

Parking

Central London is scattered with parking meters, but finding a vacant one can take ages. When you do, it'll cost you up to £1 for every 15 minutes to park there, and you'll be limited to two hours on the meter. Parking on a single or double yellow line, a red

Directory

line or in residents' parking areas during the day is illegal. In the evening (from 6pm or 7pm in much of central London) and at various times at weekends, parking on single yellow lines is legal and free. If you find a clear spot on a single yellow line during the evening, look for a sign giving the regulations. Meters are also free at certain times during the evenings and weekends.

NCP 24-hour car parks (0845 050 7080, www.ncp.co.uk) in and around central London are numerous but pricey. Fees vary, but expect to pay £10-£55 per day. NCP car parks can be found at Drury Lane, Parker Street, Parker Mews, and Upper St Martins Lane, WC2; and 2 Lexington Street, W1.

Driving out of town

Check your route for possible delays and roadworks. Try the route-planner service available from the RAC (www.rac.co.uk) or the AA (www.theaa.com).

CYCLING

Parents who want to find out more about cycle training can visit www.bikeforall.net for information, or log on to the websites below. Most local authorities include Safe Routes to Schools schemes in their local transport plans. Check the Sustrans website (www.sustrans.org.uk) for details. London Cycle Guide maps are available from some stations and bike shops, or the Travel Information Line (0843 222 1234).

London Cycling Campaign
7234 9310, www.lcc.org.uk.
Looks after the city's pedallers.

WALKING

The least stressful way to see London is on foot. A selection of street maps covering central London is on pp326-335 but you'll need a separate map of the city: both the standard Geographers' *A–Z* and Collins' *London Street Atlas* are very easy to use.

The Guy Fox *London Children's Map* is comprehensive and packed with colourful illustrations of city landmarks; buy it at www.guyfox.co.uk (£2.95), in bookshops or at tourist attractions.

RESOURCES

Councils

Barnet 8359 2000, www.barnet.gov.uk.
Brent 8937 1200, www.brent.gov.uk.
Camden 7974 4444, www.camden.gov.uk.
Corporation of London 7606 3030, www.cityoflondon.gov.uk.

Ealing 8825 5000, www.ealing.gov.uk.
Greenwich 8854 8888, www.greenwich.gov.uk.
Hackney 8356 3000, www.hackney.gov.uk.
Hammersmith & Fulham 8748 3020, www.lbhf.gov.uk.
Haringey 8489 0000, www.haringey.gov.uk.
Hounslow 8583 2000, www.hounslow.gov.uk.
Islington 7527 2000, www.islington.gov.uk.
Kensington & Chelsea 7361 3000, www.rbkc.gov.uk.
Lambeth 7926 1000, www.lambeth.gov.uk.
Lewisham 8314 6000, www.lewisham.gov.uk.
Merton 8274 4901, www.merton.gov.uk.
Newham 8430 2000, www.newham.gov.uk.
Richmond upon Thames 0845 612 2660, www.richmond.gov.uk.
Southwark 7525 5000, www.southwark.gov.uk.
Tower Hamlets 7364 5020, www.towerhamlets.gov.uk.
Waltham Forest 8496 3000, www.walthamforest.gov.uk.
Wandsworth 8871 6000, www.wandsworth.gov.uk.
Westminster 7641 6000, www.westminster.gov.uk.

Education

Advisory Centre for Education (ACE) 0808 800 5793, 7704 9822 exclusion advice line, www.ace-ed.org.uk. **Open** 10am-5pm Mon-Fri. Phone the centre for advice about your child's schooling; the advice line is for parents whose children have been excluded from school, have been bullied, or have special educational needs. School admission appeals advice is also available.
British Association for Early Childhood Education 136 Cavell Street, E1 2JA (7539 5400, www.early-education.org.uk). **Open** Phone enquiries 9am-5pm Mon-Fri. A charitable organisation that provides information on infant education from birth to eight years.
Gabbitas Educational Consultants Norfolk House, 30 Charles II Street, SW1Y

4AE (7734 0161,
www.gabbitas.co.uk). **Open**
9am-5.30pm Mon-Fri.
The consultants at Gabbitas
give advice to parents and
students on choosing an
independent school.
**Home Education Advisory
Service** PO Box 98, Welwyn
Garden City, Herts AL8
6AN (01707 371854,
www.heas.org.uk). **Open** Phone
enquiries 9am-5pm Mon-Fri.
Call for information if you
want to educate your child at
home. An introductory pack
costs £2.50, a year's
subscription £16.
**ISC Information Service
London & South-East** 7766
7070, www.iscis.uk.net. **Open**
Phone enquiries 9am-5pm
Mon-Fri.
The Independent Schools
Council Information Service
works to help parents find out
about independent schools.
Kidsmart www.kidsmart.org.uk.
Kidsmart is an internet safety
awareness programme run by
Childnet International, funded
by the DfES and Cable &
Wireless. Its guide is available
to all primary schools.
**National Association for
Gifted Children** Suite 1.2,
Challenge House, Sherwood
Drive, Bletchley, Milton Keynes,
Bucks MK3 6DP (0845 450
0295, www.nagcbritain.org.uk).
Open Phone enquiries 9am-
4pm Mon-Fri.
Support and advice on
education for gifted kids.
Parenting UK Unit 431,
Highgate Studios, 53-79
Highgate Road, NW5 1TL
(7284 8370, www.parenting
uk.org). **Open** Phone enquiries
9.30am-5pm Mon-Fri.
Information about parenting
classes and support for parents.
It was set up for people who
work with parents, but parents
can call as well.
**Pre-School Learning
Alliance** Fitzpatrick Building,
188 York Way, N7 9AD (7697
2500, www.pre-school.org.uk).
Open Phone enquiries 9am-
5pm Mon-Fri.
A leading educational charity
specialising in the early years.
It runs courses and workshops
in pre-schools around the
country for parents of children
under the age of five.

Fun & games

Activity camps

**Barracudas Young World
Leisure Group** Bridge
House, Bridge Street,
St Ives, Cambs PE27 5EH
(0845 123 5299, www.
barracudas.co.uk).
School holiday camps based in
schools in outlying countryside.
Children aged five to 16 are
welcome.
Cross Keys 48 Fitzalan
Road, N3 3PE (8371
9686, www.xkeys.co.uk,
www.miniminors.co.uk).
Day camps in Finchley for kids
aged 12 or under and rural
week-long camps in Norfolk,
for children aged up to 17.
EAC Activity Camps 45
Frederick Street, Edinburgh,
EH2 1EP (0131 477 7570,
www.eacworld.com).
Day and residential camps for
children aged five to 16 in
countryside sites.
PGL Alton Court, Penyard
Lane, Ross-on-Wye,
Herefordshire HR9 5GL (0844
371 0101, www.pgl.co.uk).
Sport and activity camps for
children aged seven to 16 in
the UK and Europe.
Wickedly Wonderful
Russett Cottage, Itchenor,
West Sussex PO20 7DD
(07941 231168, www.
wickedlywonderful.com).
A holiday company that runs
weekly buses from London
down to the beach during the
summer holidays.

Indoor play

Gymboree Play & Music
www.gymboree-uk.com.
A parent-and-child play
organisation for children
aged 16 months to four-and-
a-half years.
**National Association of
Toy & Leisure Libraries**
(NATLL) 1A Harwood
Street, NW1 8DN (7428 2286
helpline, www.natll.org.uk).
Open Helpline 9am-5pm
Mon, Tue, Thur.
For information on more
than 1,000 toy libraries
around the UK.
TumbleTots 0121 585 7003,
www.tumbletots.com. **Open**
Phone enquiries 9am-5.30pm
Mon-Fri.

Phone to find out about
TumbleTots play centres
in your area.

Health

Asthma UK 0800 121
6244, www.asthma.org.uk.
Open Helpline 9am-5pm
Mon-Fri.
Advice and help if you or your
child has asthma.
Contact-A-Family 0808 808
3555, www.cafamily.org.uk.
Open Helpline 9.30am-5pm
Mon-Fri.
Support for parents of children
with disabilities. This
organisation is a valuable
resource for those who feel
isolated while caring for their
disabled children.
Euro Pair Agency 8421
2100, www.euro-pair.co.uk.
An au pair agency that
specialises in French
candidates.
**Family Natural Health
Centre** 106 Lordship
Lane, SE22 8HF (www.
fnhc.co.uk, 8693 5515).
Open 9.30am-9.30pm Mon-
Thur; 9.30am-6pm Fri, Sat;
11am-5pm Sun.
A wide range of alternative
therapies, from acupuncture to
osteopathy, are practised here.
French classes, sing and sign
classes, children's yoga and art
therapy are also offered.
Family & Parenting Institute
430 Highgate Studios, 53-79
Highgate Road, NW5 1TL
(7424 3460, www.familyand
parenting.org). **Open** Phone
enquiries 9.30am-5.30pm
Mon-Fri; 24hr answerphone
other times.
A resource centre that produces
factsheets covering all aspects
of parenting.
**Food for the Brain
Foundation** 8788 3801,
www.foodforthebrain.org.
The Food for the Brain schools
project is designed to help
parents throughout the UK
make the right food choices to
help improve their children's
brain function, behaviour and
intelligence. A downloadable
leaflet, the 'Smart Food Smart
Kids Shopping Guide',
accompanies the scheme.
Greatcare www.greatcare.co.uk.
A useful resource for those
looking for childcare. Greatcare

Directory

Directory

has over 44,000 registered users, including nannies, au pairs, babysitters, mothers' helps and maternity nurses.
NHS Direct Helpline *0845 4647, www.nhsdirect.nhs.uk.* **Open** *Helpline* 24hrs daily. Confidential information and health advice; an invaluable resource.
WellChild Helpline *0845 458 8171, www.wellchild.org.uk.* This national charity offers practical and emotional support to sick children and their families.

Help & support

Bestbear *0870 720 1277, www.bestbear.co.uk.* **Open** 9am-6pm Mon-Fri; 24hr answerphone other times. Information about childcare agencies. now also provides a reference checking service
Childcare Link *0800 234 6346, www.childcarelink. gov.uk.* **Open** *Phone enquiries* 9am-5pm Mon-Fri. Provides a list of childcare organisations in your area.
ChildLine *0800 1111, www.childline.org.uk.* Confidential 24-hour helpline for young people in the UK. The counsellors are trained to listen and help with all kinds of issues, from bullying and abuse to drugs and STDs. Sometimes they put callers in touch with someone who can help further.
Daycare Trust *2nd Floor, Novas Contemporary Urban Centre, 73-81 Southwark Bridge Road, SE1 0NQ (7940 7510, 0845 872 6251 helpline, www.daycaretrust.org.uk).* **Open** 10am-1pm, 2-5pm Mon, Tue, Thur, Fri; 2-5pm Wed. A national charity that works to promote high-quality, affordable childcare. If you are a parent or carer paying for childcare, the www.paying forchildcare.org.uk site provides easy-to-read introductions to each of the main types of benefits, grants and subsidies that are available to help ease the financial burden of paying for childcare.
4Children *7512 2112, 7512 2100 information line, www.4children.org.uk.* **Open** *Phone enquiries* 9am-5pm Mon-Fri.

4Children is the national children's charity for children and young people aged up to 19. It works with government, local authorities, primary care trusts, children's service providers, and children and parents to ensure joined-up support for all children and young people in their local community.
Kids *6 Aztec Row, Berners Road, N1 0PW (7359 3635, www.kids.org.uk).* **Open** *Phone enquiries* 9.30am-5.30pm Mon-Fri.
An organisation that seeks to enhance the lives of disabled children, through play, leisure, education, family support, information, advice and training, with a view to empowering them in society.
Kidscape *2 Grosvenor Gardens, SW1W 0DH (7730 3300, 0845 120 5204 helpline, www.kidscape.org.uk).* **Open** *Helpline* 10am-8pm Mon, Tue; 10am-4pm Wed-Fri. Established by the indomitable child psychologist and mum Dr Michele Elliott, this was the first charity in the UK set up specifically to prevent bullying and child abuse in the family as well as at school. The helpline is for the use of parents, guardians or concerned relatives and friends of bullied children.
London Au Pair & Nanny Agency *www.londonnanny.co.uk.* Matches up families with child carers.
London Mums *www.londonmums.org.uk.* A group of new mums based in London who support each other by sharing views and tips online and organising activities for mums (and dads) and babies, such as trips to view exhibitions at the National Gallery, movies at the local cinema and nature walks.
Nannytax *PO Box 988, Brighton, East Sussex BN1 3NT (0845 226 2203, www.nannytax.co.uk).* **Open** *Phone enquiries* 9am-5pm Mon-Fri.
For £270 a year, Nannytax registers your nanny with the Inland Revenue, organises National Insurance payments and offers advice.

Night Nannies *7731 6168, www.nightnannies.com.* Night Nannies provides a list of qualified carers who may be able to offer respite from sleepless nights.
Parent Company *6 Jacob's Well Mews, W1U 3DY (0845 094 4220, www. theparentcompany.co.uk).* **Open** *Bookings* 9am-3pm Mon-Fri. The company runs first aid training courses for parents and carers of babies and children. The courses are delivered by paediatric nurses, either in the home or workplace.
Parent Courses *Holy Trinity Brompton, Brompton Road, SW7 1JA (7581 8255, www.htb.org.uk).* **Open** *Phone enquiries* 9.30am-5.30pm Mon, Wed-Fri; 10.30am-5.30pm Tue. Runs Parenting Course for parents with children under the age of 12, and Parenting Teenagers, for parents of children aged 13-18. Each course costs £30 and takes place over five weeks once a year.
Parentline Plus *0808 800 2222 helpline, www.parentlineplus.org.uk.* **Open** *Helpline* 24hrs daily. Organises nationwide courses on how to cope with being a parent. For more details, call the free helpline.
Parents for Inclusion *0800 652 3145 helpline, www.parentsforinclusion.org.* **Open** 10am-noon, 1-3pm Mon, Wed. Organises workshops for parents of disabled children as well as providing training for teachers who want to develop inclusion in their schools.
The Parent Practice *8673 3444 bookings, www.theparent practice.com.* A support and training group that promises to endow parents with the skills for transforming family life. It also produces CDs (£18.50; £33/pair) that provide harrassed mums and dads with practical strategies to make family life calmer, happier and more rewarding.
Parent Support Group *72 Blackheath Road, SE10 8DA (8469 0205 helpline, www.psg.org.uk).* **Open** *Helpline* 10am-8pm Mon-Thur; 24hr answerphone other times.

As well as the helpline, staff run one-to-one support sessions and offer courses on parenting skills to the parents and carers of adolescents who are acting in an antisocial or criminal manner.

Post-Adoption Centre
5 Torriano Mews, Torriano Avenue, NW5 2RZ (7284 0555, 7284 5879 advice line, www.postadoptioncentre.org.uk). **Open** *Advice Line* 10am-1pm Mon-Wed, Fri; 10am-1pm, 5.30-7.30pm Thur.
Registered charity providing advice, support and information for anyone affected by adoption, including adoptive/foster parents and their children, adopted adults, birth relatives and the professionals who work with them.

Simply Childcare
www.simplychildcare.com.
If you're seeking a nanny, check this website.

Sitters *0800 389 0038, www.sitters.co.uk.* **Open** *Phone enquiries* 9am-5pm Mon-Fri.
A babysitting agency with locally based nurses, teachers and nannies on its books.

FURTHER REFERENCE

Websites

BBC London
www.bbc.co.uk/london.
London-focused news, weather, travel and sport.

British Pathé
www.britishpathe.com
Newsreels, from spaghetti-eating contests to pre-war Soho scenes.

Children First
www.childrenfirst.nhs.uk.
Run by Great Ormond Street Hospital and the children's charity WellChild, this website has information on all aspects of healthy living, along with special sections about going into hospital.

Classic Cafés
www.classiccafes.co.uk.
A guide to the city's finest classic caffs.

Department for Education and Skills
www.parentscentre.gov.uk.

Advice on schools and other aspects of education.

Film London
www.filmlondon.org.uk.
London cinema, information about film in and around the capital, as well as London's film culture.

Get London Reading
www.getlondonreading.co.uk/books-in-london.
Map of London books by district. Also details reading events taking place around the city.

Greater London Authority
www.london.gov.uk.
The official website for the Mayor of London and the Greater London Authority.

Hidden London *www.hidden-london.com.*
The city's undiscovered gems.

Learning Partnership
www.thelearningpartnership.com.
The Learning Partnership's online guide to parenting, Top Tips for Tiny Tots (www.tt4tt.co.uk), provides new parents with essential information on pregnancy, birth and early development in one easy-to-use downloadable course.

London Footprints
www.london-footprints.co.uk.
Free walks around London, listed by area and theme.

London Parks & Gardens Trust *www.parkexplorer.org.uk.*
A website designed to help Key Stage 2 children learn more about the parks, gardens and open spaces of London.

London Randomness
http://london.randomness.org.uk.
Want to find Finnish food near a music shop? Great review site-cum-wiki for interesting places.

London Remembers
www.londonremembers.com.
A guide to the plaques and statues dotted around London.

London 2012
www.london2012.com.
The official website for the 2012 London Olympics. Details on what's happening, how to get involved and all things Olympics.

London Undergound Blog
http://london-underground.blogspot.com.
Daily tube blog.

Meteorological Office
www.metoffice.gov.uk.
The most accurate source of weather forecasts.

Nickel in the Machine
www.nickelinthemachine.com.
Blog on the history, culture and music of 20th-century London.

On a Bus *http://onabus.com.*
Enter a bus number and its route is mapped.

Parent Pages
www.parentpages.co.uk.
A useful listings site for families with children and professionals working with children.

The River Thames Guide
www.riverthames.co.uk.
Interesting places to stay, eat, drink and play, all along the riverbank.

Seety *www.seety.co.uk.*
Navigable photos of pretty much every London street.

Street Map
www.streetmap.co.uk.
Grid references and postcodes.

Time Out *www.timeout.com.*
Up-to-the-minute listings, features and reviews, plus critics' recommendations. The Kids section runs from info on city farms, workshops, museums and days out to new films, shows and festivals.

Transport for London
www.tfl.gov.uk.
The official website for travel information about tubes, buses, DLR and river services, as well as travel times and cycle routes. Use the journey planner to find the quickest routes to your destination, and check for any disruptions or delays. The planner can also find you cycling routes.

Visit London
www.visitlondon.com.
The official tourist board website, full of information and special offers.

Walkit *www.walkit.com/london.*
Type in your setting off point and destination, and find out how long it'll take to walk it. It'll even find you the route with the lowest pollution levels.

Wild Web
http://wildweb.london.gov.uk.
Wildlife in the city.

Yellow Pages Online
www.yell.com.
The best online resource for numbers and addresses.

Directory

A-Z Index

Directory

Directory

Directory

Directory

Area Index

Directory

Directory

Area Index

Directory

Legend	
Place of interest and/or entertainment . . .	
Hospital or college	
Railway station	
Park	
River	
Motorway	
Main road	
Main road tunnel	
Pedestrian road	
Airport	✈
Church	✚
Synagogue	✡
Congestion charge zone	Ⓒ
Underground station	⊖
Area name	SOHO

London Overview

Central London
by Area